Contents

S0-AVC-098

4   **Map of Principal Sights**

7   **Map of Touring Programmes**

10   **Places to Stay - Recreation**

13   **Introduction**

14   **Description of the Country**

18   **Historical Table and Notes**

20   **Rich history of the Loire Country**

29   **Famous names from the Loire Valley**

30   **Books to read**

31   **The Inhabitants of the Loire Valley**

32   **Art**

40   **Food and Wine**

43   **Sights**

209   **Practical Information**

210   **Travelling to France**

212   **General information**

218   **Calendar of Events**

220   **Admission Times and Charges**

236   **Index**

*The **Michelin maps** which accompany this guide are:*

PRINCIPAL SIGHTS

Worth a journey ★★★

Worth a detour ★★

Interesting ★

The names of towns or sights described in the guide appear in black on the maps throughout. See the index for page number.

72 Département number and boundaries

0 ——————— 30 km

TOURISM IN THE LOIRE VALLEY...

To know the region more thoroughly study your

MICHELIN MAP

The symbols indicate:

Picturesque routes

Panoramas, viewing points

Interesting sites and monuments

Footpaths,
State forests

Swimming pools, golf courses, etc.

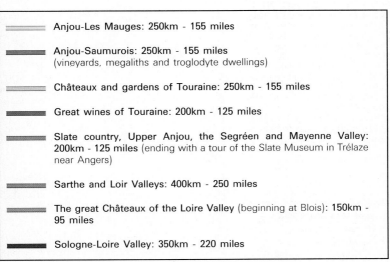

Anjou-Les Mauges: 250km - 155 miles

Anjou-Saumurois: 250km - 155 miles
(vineyards, megaliths and troglodyte dwellings)

Châteaux and gardens of Touraine: 250km - 155 miles

Great wines of Touraine: 200km - 125 miles

Slate country, Upper Anjou, the Segréen and Mayenne Valley:
200km - 125 miles (ending with a tour of the Slate Museum in Trélaze
near Angers)

Sarthe and Loir Valleys: 400km - 250 miles

The great Châteaux of the Loire Valley (beginning at Blois): 150km -
95 miles

Sologne-Loire Valley: 350km - 220 miles

PLACES TO STAY

For names and addresses see the chapter Practical Information at the end of the guide.

The mention Facilities under the individual headings or after place names in the body of the guide refers to the information given on these pages.
The map below indicates towns selected for the accommodation and leisure facilities which they offer to the holidaymaker. To help you plan your route and choose your accommodation consult the following Michelin publications.

Accommodation

The **Michelin Red Guide France** of hotels and restaurants and the **Michelin Guide Camping Caravaning France** are annual publications which present a selection of hotels, restaurants and camping sites. The final choice is based on regular on-the spot enquiries and visits. Both the hotels and camping sites are classified according to the standard of comfort of their amenities. Establishments which are notable for their setting, their décor, their quiet and secluded location and their warm welcome are distinguished by special symbols. The Michelin Red Guide France also gives the addresses and telephone numbers of the local Tourist Information Centres (Syndicat d'Initiative).

Youth hostels etc

Several organisations cater for children, school groups and adults and offer courses at moderate prices: the Youth Hostel in Tours (Auberge de Jeunesse), the Family Holiday Village (Village Vacances Familles) near Amboise, the Maison Rurale d'Education et d'Orientation at Neuvy-le-Roi.
A brochure on walking in the Loire region (Randonnées dans les Pays de la Loire) published by Loire Océan Gîtes et Itinéraires (LOGI) and available from the Departmental Tourist Committees of the Loire-Atlantique, Maine-et-Loire, Mayenne and Sarthe, provides information on overnight stops including youth hostels and other accommodation (Points d'Accueil Jeunes) all of which cater for walkers.

Paying guests

One of the charms of this region is the wealth of châteaux and manor houses, often in quiet and attractive settings. Certain of these privately-owned mansions open their doors to paying guests, who have the pleasure of enjoying the gracious surroundings for a moderate cost. For their addresses and terms apply to the **Regional Tourist Committees** or to the **Tourist Information Centres** in Tours, Saumur, Chinon or Blois.

An unusual form of accommodation

Until recently, troglodyte dwellings hollowed out of the tufa in some villages in Anjou, the Vendôme area and Touraine remained relics of the past. Today, many of them are being converted into weekend cottages, restaurants or hotel accommodation, thus reviving traditions of hospitality and promoting an unusual feature of the Loire Valley. In Rochecorbon near Tours, Rochemenier near Doué-la-Fontaine, St-Pierre-en-Vaux near Gennes and the area between Saumur and Montsoreau, an hotel, overnight stops known as **troglogites,** and restaurants serving local specialities, have been ingeniously and tastefully appointed. There are also a good many underground wine cellars that stock the best vintages.
For information on tours to troglodyte dwellings, or hotels and restaurants, apply in Saumur to the Carrefour Anjou-Touraine-Poitou or the Tourist Information Centre, and in Angers to the Departmental Tourist Committee.

Route planning, sports and recreation

The **Michelin 1:200 000 maps** in the series **51** to **90** and **230** to **246** cover the whole of France. Those which serve this guide are shown in the diagram on p 3. One glance will reveal the position of a place. In addition to information about the roads, the maps show beaches, bathing places on lakes and rivers, swimming pools, golf courses, race courses, gliding-grounds, aerodromes, forest roads, long-distance footpaths, etc.

Dont' leave anything to chance!
Consult 36 15 MICHELIN
to choose your route,
the sights to see,
and a hotel or restaurant.

Places to stay ●
0   30 km

RECREATION

For names and addresses see the Practical Information chapter at the end of the guide.

Walking

There is a network of footpaths covering the area described in the guide. Detailed topographical guides are available showing the routes of the long-distance footpaths (sentiers de grande randonnée – GR) and giving good advice to walkers.

The **GR 3** which follows the Loire Valley passes through the Orléans, Russy and Chinon Forests;
The **GR 3c** runs westwards across the Sologne from Gien to Mont-près-Chambord;
The **GR 3d** passes through the Layon vineyards;
The **GR 31** runs from Mont-près-Chambord, on the southeast edge of the Boulogne Forest, south to Souesmes passing through the Sologne woods;
The **GR 32** passes through the Orléans Forest from north to south;
The **GR 335**, "From the Loir to the Loire", runs north-south between Lavardin and Vouvray;
The **GR 35** follows the Loir Valley;
The **GR 36**, the English Channel to the Pyrenees route, crosses the region between Le Mans and Montreuil-Bellay;
The **GR 46** follows the Indre Valley.

Riding and pony trekking

Noted for its studs and the National Riding School at St-Hilaire-St-Florent near Saumur, the region has numerous riding centres which are open to visitors. Some serve as an overnight halt for those on trekking holidays.
Trekking guides indicating itineraries and overnight stops are published by regional and national associations.
Details of local equestrian centres are available from the Tourist Information Centres.

Cruising

In addition to the local sailing clubs centred on lakes, reservoirs and other stretches of water, the Loire basin offers opportunities for cruising enthusiasts to enjoy its waters. Pottering on the river is an original way to discover and appreciate to the full the beauty and calm of the riverside landscapes.
The **Maine** basin has good navigable stretches on the Oudon (downstream from Segré), on the Mayenne (downstream from Laval) and the Sarthe (downstream from Le Mans). Boats can be hired (no permit required) at Andouillé, Angers, Château-Gontier, Châteauneuf-sur-Sarthe, Chenillé-Changé, Grez-Neuville, Laval, Malicorne, Le Mans, Noyen-sur-Sarthe and Sablé.
The **Loire** offers similar opportunities, as do the various canals (Briare and Loire lateral canals) starting from Châtillon-sur-Loire (Loiret), Montargis (Loiret) and Rogny-les-Sept-Ecluses (Yonne).

Air trips

Throughout the year, weather permitting, it is possible to have a bird's eye view of the Loire Valley. Helicopters or small aircraft, such as the high-winged Cessna which has excellent visibility, fly over Chinon, Chambord, Chenonceau, Azay-le-Rideau and the Valley of the Kings, starting from the airport at Tours-St-Symphorien, and over Amboise, Cheverny, Beaugency and the Sologne from Blois-le-Breuil aerodrome. It is also possible to take a trip in a balloon.

Fishing

The swift or slow waters of the Loire Valley offer the fisherman various attractive possibilities.

Every type of authorised fishing is available: angling for gudgeon, roach and dace, or trying for pike or even the striped mullet which comes upstream as far as Amboise in summer, or catching the catfish, the tench and the carp in the holes in the Loire, the Indre and the Loir or in the pools in the Sologne which are also full of perch.

Trout can be found in the Creuse, the Sauldre, the streams of Anjou or the tributaries of the Loir while the Berry, Briare, or Orléans Canals contain eels and sometimes crayfish which can be caught with a dipping net.

Salmon and shad fishing require a flat-bottomed boat; the professionals have specialist equipment such as nets stretched across the river and held in place by poles fixed in the bed.

Regulations and open seasons – Both differ according to whether the water is classed in the first category (salmon-type fish) or in the second (non-salmon-type fish). Salmon fishing is forbidden from 17 June to 28 February and is confined to the Loire.

Useful tips – It is best to observe the local, departmental and national regulations and to join a fishing association approved by the Préfet. The membership card, duly stamped, allows three rods on second category water administered by a fishing association or one line on all public water.

Only one line is allowed on first category water and a supplementary stamp is required. Additional tax is payable on the right to cast, on fishing with nets and on fishing for salmon, etc.

On private property, where the fishing rights belong to the owner of the bank, this owner's permission must be obtained.

In the case of certain private lakes, which are excluded from the fishing legislation, the owner's permission (annual, monthly or daily permit) is the only formality required and can be granted at any time of the year.

Minimum size of catch – The national regulations state that the fisherman must return to the water any fish which does not attain the minimum permitted length (40cm for pike, 35cm for sauger, 23cm for trout, 50cm for salmon, 9cm for crayfish).

Hunting

The Loire country is very popular for hunting as its varied terrain provides a diversity of sport: stalking, beating, coursing or shooting.

The plains of the Beauce and the meadows of Touraine and Anjou provide good feeding grounds for partridge, quail, thrush and lark. Hares find cover in the copses and the fields of maize and sugarbeet. Wild rabbits breed in the sterile marshland as do partridges while pheasants favour the watering places, particulary in the Cisse Valley.

Red deer and roe deer are to be found in the thick woods around Baugé, in the forests of Château-la-Vallière and Loches and around Valençay.

Wild boar favours the deep forest of Orléans and Amboise and the neighbourhood of Chambord.

The islands and banks of the Loire provide nests for teal and mallard.

The Sologne is a favourite haunt of game: duck, teal and woodcock on the lakes and rivers, pheasants by the roadside, wild boar in the marshy brakes and deer in the woods.

It is necessary to be affiliated to a private association or to a communal hunting society.

Some bodies and private owners, however, issue permits for a single day only.

Cycling

The Fédération Française de Cyclotourisme and its departmental committees publish a number of cycling tours of varying lengths.

Although the country is fairly level, the Indre Valley, the Sologne, the forest tracks and, above all, the banks of the Loire, particularly away from the main roads, are very attractive. The ever-changing scene and the rich heritage of the Loire Valley greatly add to the pleasure of a cycling tour.

French Heritage Trails

The Historic Buildings Association (Caisse Nationale des Monuments Historiques et des Sites, 62 rue St-Antoine, 75004 Paris ☎ 44 61 21 50) has organised a wide selection of historic roads covering all of France. These follow in the footsteps of kings, courtiers, statesmen or writers; trace the development of an architectural style or art movement; or are planned round a particular theme. The heritage trails for Châteaux of the Loire include: the Plantagenets, Good King René, Queens, Consorts, Wives and Mistresses of Touraine, Prince of the Renaissance — François I, Jacques Cœur, The Loire Valley in the Footsteps of Kings, Parks and Gardens in Beauce, Val-de-Loire and Berry and the Marchlands of Brittany.

*The current edition of the annual **Michelin Red Guide France***
offers a selection of pleasant and quiet hotels in convenient locations.
Their amenities are included (swimming pools, tennis courts,
private beaches and gardens...)
as well as their dates of annual closure.

The selection also includes establishments which offer excellent cuisine : carefully
prepared meals at reasonable prices, Michelin stars for good cooking.

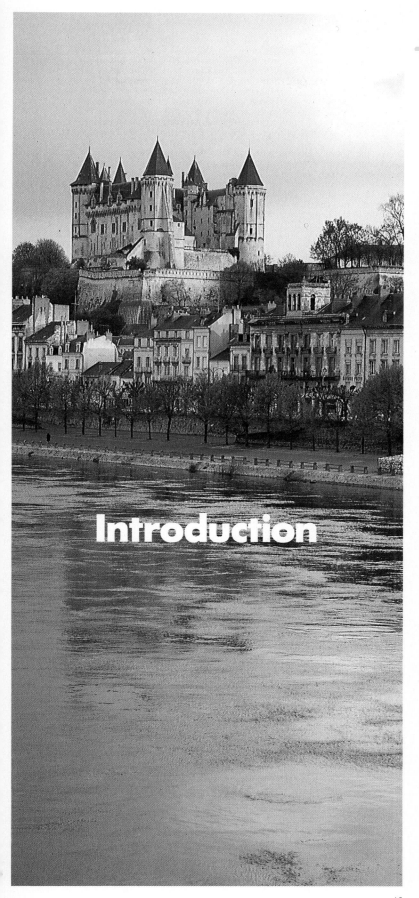

Introduction

DESCRIPTION OF THE COUNTRY

GEOLOGICAL FORMATION

The Loire region is enclosed by the ancient crystalline masses of the Morvan, Armorican Massif and Massif Central and forms part of the Paris Basin.

In the Secondary Era the area invaded by the sea was covered by a soft, chalky deposit known as **tufa,** which is now exposed along the valley sides of the Loir, Cher, Indre and Vienne. A later deposit is the limestone of the sterile marshlands **(gâtines)** interspersed with tracts of sands and clays supporting forests and heathlands. Once the sea had retreated, great freshwater lakes deposited more limestone, the surface of which is often broken down into loess or silt. These areas are known as **champagnes** or *champeignes*.

During the Tertiary Era the folding of the Alpine mountain zone created the Massif Central, and rivers descending from this new watershed were often laden with sandy clays which when deposited gave areas such as the Sologne and the Forest of Orléans. Later subsidence in the west permitted the ingress of the **Faluns Sea** as far as Blois, Thouars and Preuilly-sur-Claise. This marine incursion created a series of shell marl beds *(falunières)* to be found on the borders of the Ste-Maure Plateau and the hills edging the Loire to the north. Rivers originally flowing northwards were attracted in a westerly direction by the sea, thus explaining the great change in the direction of the Loire at Orléans. The sea finally retreated for good, leaving an undulating countryside with the river network the most important geographical feature. The alluvial silts **(varennes)** deposited by the Loire and its tributaries were to add an extremely light soil composed of coarse sand.

The limestone terraces which provided shelter and the naturally fertile soil attracted early human habitation, of which there are traces from the prehistoric era through the Gallo-Roman period (site of Cherré *qv*) to the Middle Ages (Brain-sur-Allonnes *qv*). This substratum is immediately reflected in the landscape; troglodyte dwellings in the limestone layers, vineyards on the slopes, cereals on the silt plateaus, vegetables in the alluvial silt; the marshy tracts of the Sologne were for many centuries untilled since they were unhealthy and unsuitable for any sort of culture.

THE LANDSCAPE

The landscaps described by Du Bellay, Balzac, Alain-Fournier or Genevoix have not lost their essential characteristics but have been modified by post-war urbanisation and the growth of industrial and commercial estates on the outskirts of towns.

The garden of France – From whatever direction one approaches the Loire region – across the immense plains of the Beauce, over the harsher Berry countryside or through the green wooded farmland *(bocage)* of the Gâtine Mancelle – one is always welcomed by the sight of vineyards, white houses and flowers.

For many foreigners this is perhaps one of the most typically French landscapes of all – a peaceful moderate and gentle countryside. But make no mistake, the "Garden of France" is not a sort of Eden full of fruit and flowers. The historian Michelet once described it as a "homespun cloak with golden fringes", meaning that the valleys – the golden fringes – in all their wonderful fertility bordered plateaux whose harshness was only tempered by occasional fine forests.

Northern Berry – This region lying between the Massif Central and the Loire country includes the **Pays Fort,** an area of clay soil sloping down towards the Sologne *(see Luçay-le-Mâle, qv)*. The melancholy atmosphere of the landscape is described by Alain Fournier in his novel *Le Grand Meaulnes*. Between the Cher and the Indre is the **Champagne,** an area of limestone silt pockmarked with holes *(mardelles)*.

Orléanais and Blésois – Below Gien the valley opens out, the hills are lower and a refreshing breeze makes the leaves tremble on the long lines of poplars and willows. This is the gateway to the Orléanais which covers the Beauce, the Loir Valley (ie the Dunois and Vendômois), the Sologne and Blésois (Blois region). In the vicinity of St-Benoît the valley, commonly known as the **Val,** is a series of meadows; beyond, horticulture predominates with the growing of seedlings and rosebushes on the alluvial deposits known locally as *layes*. There is a proliferation of greenhouses, some with artificial heating. Orchards and vineyards flourish on the south-facing slopes.

Touraine Landscape

From Orléans to Chaumont along its northern bank, the Loire eats into the **Beauce** limestone and then into the flinty chalkland and tufa. On the south the river laps the alluvial sands brought down by its own waters, and which, besides growing asparagus and early vegetables, are also covered in dense brushwood, where the kings of France once used to hunt. The great châteaux then begin: Blois, Chambord, Cheverny, Chaumont...

The **Beauce**, the granary of France, a treeless plain covered with a thin layer (2m - 6ft maximum) of fertile silt or loess, extends into the area between the Loire and Loir known as the Petite Beauce where silt gives way to clay in Marchenoir Forest. In the **Sologne** *(qv)* and the **Forest of Orléans** meagre crops alternate with pools and woodland.

Touraine – The comfortable opulence of the **Loire Valley** delights the visitor already attracted by the luminous beauty of the light. The blue waters of the Loire, which flow slowly between golden sandbanks, have worn a course through the soft tufa chalk. Channels abandoned by the main river are divided into back-waters *(boires)* or occupied by tributary streams such as the Cher, Indre, Vienne *(qv)* and Cisse.

From Amboise to Tours the flinty chalk soil of the valley slopes is clad with vineyards producing the well-known Vouvray and Montlouis wines. **Troglodyte** houses have been carved out of the white tufa.

The **Véron** *(qv)*, lying between the Loire and the Vienne, is a patchwork of small fields and gardens bordered by rows of poplars.

The **Gâtine** of Touraine, between the Loir and Loire, was once a great forest; the area is now under cultivation, although large tracts of heath and woodland still exist: Chandelais and Bercé Forests.

The main features of the Touraine **Champeigne,** where the fields are studded with walnut trees, are the Forests of Brouard and Loches and the Montrésor Gâtine. The plateaux of Montrichard and Ste-Maure *(qv)* are similar in many ways to the Champeigne.

Anjou – Anjou, like the Touraine, has little physical unity but is typified more easily by the gentleness of its countryside, so lovingly described by the poet Du Bellay.

The north bank of the Loire consists of a fertile alluvial plain **(varenne de Bourgueil)** where spring vegetables flourish surrounded by the famous vineyards planted on the warm, dry gravels lying at the foot of the pine-covered hills. Between the Loire and the Authion, which is lined with willows, green pastures alternate with rich market gardens growing vegetables, flowers and fruit trees. The land below Angers is covered with vineyards especially the famous Coulée de Serrant vineyard.

The pleasant **Saumurois**, which lies south of the Loire and extends from Fontevraud and Montsoreau to Doué-la-Fontaine and the Layon Valley *(qv)*, has three differing aspects: woods, plains and hillsides; the slopes are often clad with vineyards, which produce excellent wine including the white wine to which the town of Saumur has given its name. The many caves in the steep, tufa valley sides of the Loire around Chênehutte-les-Tuffeaux are now used for mushroom growing.

North of the river lies the sandy **Baugeois** *(qv)*, an area of woods (oak, pine and chestnut) and arable land.

Angers marks the border between the schist countryside of Black Anjou and the sharply contrasting limestone of White Anjou. The countryside is greener, heralding an area of wooded farmland – le Bocage Segréen and the **Mauges** *(qv)* – which is characterised by a patchwork of small fields surrounded by hedge-topped banks crisscrossed by deep lanes leading to small farmsteads. Around Angers, nursery and market gardens specialise in flowers and seedlings.

Maine – Only the southern part of this region is included in the guide.

The Lower Maine **(Bas-Maine)** otherwise known as Black Maine, is a region of sandstones, granites and schists and wooded farmland. Geographically this area is part of the Breton Armorican Massif. The Upper Maine **(Haut-Maine)**, covering the Sarthe and Huisne basins, is known as the White Maine because of its limestone soils.

THE ECONOMY

The bountiful Loire Valley assures a comfortable livelihood.

Activities of the past – Many of the traditional local activities have disappeared: namely the growing of saffron in the Gâtinais; of anise, coriander and liquorice in Bourgueil; of madder; and the silk industry based on the mulberries and silkworms introduced to Touraine by Louis XI. The once-familiar fields of hemp around Bréhémont and Béhuard have dwindled in number as have the dependent rope-workers.

Cottage industries have disappeared too, although Villaines is still a centre for wickerwork, but coopers, cartwrights and sabot makers are now few and far between. The flints of Meusnes and Villentrois are no longer used for the firearms industry.

Gone also are the blacksmiths' forges which were once so numerous on the forest outskirts. The coal of the Layon Basin is no longer mined.

The drastic decline in river traffic on the Loire has resulted in the closure of the boatyards at Angers and the sail-making factories at Ancenis. There is however still a demand for slates from Trélazé against fierce competition but the very fine white tufa stone from Bourré and Pontlevoy, which distinguishes the houses of Touraine, is no longer quarried. The only quarries still being worked are St-Cyr-en-Bourg and Louerre which supply workshops with stone for restoration.

Nowadays it is only in the museums that the old trades can be observed (flintstone museum at Meung-sur-Loire and Luçay-le-Mâle; slate museums at Trélazé and Renazé, the Blue Mine at Noyant-la-Gravoyère, and the local museum at Montjean-sur-Loire).

Agriculture

Vines *(p 42)*, cereals and fodder crops are to be found nearly everywhere but it is the great variety of fruit and vegetables which most astonishes the visitor.

Fruit – Ripening well in the local climate the succulent fruits of the region are renowned throughout France. Many have a noble pedigree: the *Reine-Claude* plums are named after Claude de France, the wife of François I, the *Bon-chrétien* pears originated from a cutting planted by St Francis of Paola *(qv)* in Louis XI's orchard at Plessis-lès-Tours. They were introduced into Anjou by Jean Bourré, Louis XI's Finance Minister *(qv)*. Rivalling the latter are the following varieties: *de Monsieur, William,* a speciality of Anjou, *Passe-Crassane* and *Beurré Hardy*.

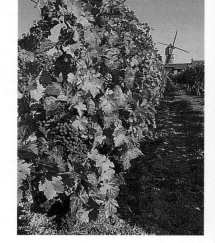

Melons were introduced to the region by Charles VIII's Neapolitan gardener. Already in the 16C the variety and quality of the local fruit and vegetables were much praised by Ronsard among others. The walnut and chestnut trees of the plateaux yield oil, the much-prized wood and the edible chestnuts, often roasted during evening gatherings.

Cultivation under glass, irrigation and new varieties have stimulated an agricultural revival. The Reinette apple from Le Mans has been supplanted by more prolific American varieties such as the Granny Smith or Golden Delicious.

Early vegetables – Early vegetables are a speciality in the Loire Valley since, in general, they are ready two weeks before those of the Paris region. Asparagus from Vineuil and Contres, potatoes from Saumur, French beans from Touraine and artichokes from Angers are despatched to Rungis, the main Paris market. Mushrooms are one of the region's more unusual crops. They are grown in the former tufa quarries near Montrichard, Montoire, Montsoreau, Tours and particularly in the Saumur area.

The Orléans region grows great quantities of lettuce, cucumbers and tomatoes, all in massive greenhouses.

Flowers and nursery gardens – Pots of geraniums or begonias, borders of nasturtiums and climbing wistaria with its pale mauve clusters adorn the houses. The region of Orléans-la-Source, Olivet and Doué-la-Fontaine is famous for its roses and for its hydrangeas, geraniums and chrysanthemums which are grown under glass. Tulips, gladioli and lilies are grown (for bulbs) near Soings.

Nursery gardens proliferate on the alluvial soils of the Loire. The lighter soils of Véron, Bourgueil and the Angers district are suitable for the growing of artichokes, onions and garlic for seed stock. The medicinal plants that were cultivated in the Chemillé region during the phylloxera crisis are attracting renewed interest.

Michelin Maps (scale 1 : 200 000), which are revised regularly provide much useful motoring information.

Keep current Michelin Maps in the car at all times.

Livestock

Cattle, sheep and pigs – In the fodder-growing areas *(champagnes* and *gâtines)* young dairy stock are reared inside while elsewhere beef and dairy cattle feed on the pastures of the Maine, Anjou and Touraine valleys. The most popular breeds are the Normandy, Maine-Anjou and the Pie noire. Charolais cattle are fattened in the neighbourhood of Cholet. Milk production is concentrated in the valleys of Touraine, especially in the wooded farmland of Anjou and Les Mauges where the French Frisian-Pie Noire breed is favoured.

Sheep rearing is limited to the limestone plateaux of the Upper Maine where the black-faced *Bleu du Maine* and *Rouge de l'Ouest* prosper. Pigs are to be found everywhere but especially in Touraine, Maine and Anjou; the production of potted pork specialities – *rillettes* and *rillons* – is centred in Vouvray, Tours, Le Mans and Angers. The ever-growing demand for the well-known goats' cheeses has resulted in an increase in goat keeping. Market days in the west country are colourful occasions: the liveliest are the pig markets in Craon and the calf sales in Château-Gontier as well as the cattle and goat sales in Chemillé and Cholet.

Poultry – Poultry rearing (in the Gâtinais and at Loué in the Sarthe) has grown considerably; its development is linked to the food industry and the cooperatives which have greatly contributed to the agricultural revival which has taken place since the war.

Horses – Numerous studs continue to rear for breeding and racing purposes while the finer arts and traditions of horsemanship are perpetuated by the National Riding School and *Cadre Noir* at St-Hilaire-St-Florent near Saumur. Many a small town still has its racecourse, and local riding clubs and schools keep alive the interest in horses and horseriding and its ancillary crafts.

Industry

Recent growth is noticeable, particularly in the non-polluting indutries such as high technology, research, electronics and fashion, in all the main towns along the Loire Valley and in the development of ancillary industries based on the processing of agricultural produce. With the exception of Châteaudun and Vendôme, the main industrial centres are to be found along the Loire at Gien, Sully, St-Denis-de-l'Hôtel, Orléans, Beaugency, Mer, Blois, Amboise, Tours and Angers. The new industry is therefore not concentrated in the main towns but helps to stimulate the economy in rural areas, eg the region round Cholet. Michelin tyre factories have been set up at Orléans, Tours and Cholet. Nuclear power stations are in operation at Avoine-Chinon, Belleville-sur-Loire, Dampierre-en-Burly and St-Laurent-des-Eaux.

Service industries

Insurance, mainly in Le Mans, conferences, a speciality of Tours and Orléans, as well as the decentralisation of financial institutions, health services and prestigious business and administrative schools, and the great tourist potential are all factors in the attraction of investment into the region.

The cultural heritage, the forests, the 570km - 354 miles of navigable water for leisure craft and the proliferation of leisure parks all play their part in the local economy.

CHÂTEAUX OF THE LOIRE - FROM CHAMBORD TO CHINON

THE MICHELIN GREEN GUIDE - NOW ON VIDEO!

Sit back and enjoy a glimpse of the splendours of the Loire Valley from the comfort of your home.

The majestic course of the Loire from Chambord to Chinon evokes the history of the French kings who, charmed by its natural beauty, had magnificent châteaux built in which they installed the colourful pageantry – and intrigue – of their courts, bringing the ideas and aesthetics of the Renaissance to France.

To echoes of sumptuous court banquets the Loire takes us past the richly stocked game parks of Chambord and Chinon, which once rang to the sound of the hunt, and the famous vineyards and orchards which have earned the Touraine region its reputation as "the garden of France". Mouthwatering images of local gastronomic delights complete this voyage of discovery, ideally suited both as a tempting preview and as a colourful reminder of your holiday in the Loire Valley.

HISTORICAL TABLE AND NOTES *(1)*

Gallo-Roman Era and the Early Middle Ages

BC 52	*Carnutes revolt. Caesar conquers Gaul.*
AD IC-4C	*Roman occupation of Gaul.*
313	*Constantine grants freedom of worship to Christians (Edict of Milan).*
372	St Martin, Bishop of Tours. He dies at Candes in 397.
451	The Huns besiege Orléans.
573-594	Episcopacy of Gregory of Tours, author of the History of the Franks.
7C	Founding of the Benedictine Abbey of Fleury, later to be named St-Benoît.
late 8C	Alcuin of York forms a school for copyists at Tours; Theodulf, Bishop of Orleans.
768-814	*Charlemagne.*
840-877	*Charles the Bald.*
9C	Viking invasions reach Angers, St Benoît and Tours. Rise of the Robertian dynasty.

The Capets (987-1328)

987-1040	Fulk Nerra, Count of Anjou.
996-1031	*Robert II, the Pious.*
1010	Foundation of the Benedictine abbey at Solesmes.
1060-1108	*Philippe I.*
1101	Foundation of Fontevraud Abbey.
1104	First Council of Beaugency.
1137-1180	*Louis VII.*
1152	Second Council of Beaugency; Eleanor of Aquitaine marries Henry Plantagenet.
1154	Henry Plantagenet becomes King of England as Henry II.
1180-1223	*Philippe-Auguste.*
1189	Death of Henry II Plantagenet at Chinon. *Struggle between Capets and Plantagenets.*
1199	Richard the Lionheart dies at Chinon and is buried at Fontevraud.
1202	John Lackland loses Anjou. Last of the Angevin kings, he dies in 1216.
1215	*Magna Carta.*
1226-1270	*Louis IX (St Louis).*
1285-1314	*Philippe IV, the Fair.*
1307	Philippe the Fair suppresses the Order of the Knights Templars *(Arville).*

The Valois (1328-1589)

1337-1453	*Hundred Years War: 1346 Crécy; 1356 Poitiers; 1415 Agincourt.*
1380-1422	*Charles VI.*
1392	The King goes mad *(Le Mans).*
1409	Birth of King René at Angers.
1418	The Massacre at Azay-le-Rideau.
1422-1461	*Charles VII.*
1427	The Dauphin Charles establishes his court at Chinon.
1429	Joan of Arc delivers Orléans; tried and burnt at the stake two years later *(Chinon, Orléans).*
1453	Battle of Castillon: final defeat of the English on French soil.
1455-1485	*Wars of the Roses: Margaret of Anjou leader of Lancastrian cause.*
1461-1483	*Louis XI.*
1476	Unrest among the powerful feudal lords. Royal marriage at Montrichard.
1483	Death of Louis XI at Plessis-lès-Tours.
1483-1498	*Charles VIII.*
1491	Marriage of Charles VIII and Anne of Brittany at Langeais.
1494-1559	*The Campaigns in Italy.*
1496	Early manifestations of Italian influence on French art *(Amboise).*
1498	Death of Charles VIII at Amboise.
1498-1515	*Louis XII. He divorces and marries Charles VIII's widow.*
1515-1547	*François I.*
1519	French Renaissance: Chambord started; Leonardo da Vinci dies at Le Clos-Lucé.
1539	*Struggle against the Emperor Charles V. He visits Amboise and Chambord.*
1547-1559	*Henri II.*
1552	The sees of Metz, Toul and Verdun join France; treaty signed at Chambord.
1559-1560	*François II.*
1560	Amboise Conspiracy; François II dies at Orléans.
1560-1574	*Charles IX.*
1562-1598	*Wars of Religion.*
1562	The Abbey of St-Benoît is pillaged by the Protestants; battles at Ponts-de-Cé and Beaugency.
1572	*The St Bartholomew's Day Massacre in Paris.*
1574-1589	*Henri III.*
1576	*Founding of the Catholic League by Henri, Duke of Guise to combat Calvinism.* Meeting of the States-General in Blois.
1588	The murder of Henri, Duke of Guise and his brother, the Cardinal of Lorraine *(Blois).*

The Bourbons (1589-1702)

1589-1610	*Henri IV.*
1589	Vendôme retaken by Henry IV.
1598	*Edict of Nantes.* Marriage of César de Vendôme *(Angers).*
1600	Henri IV marries Marie de' Medici.
1602	Maximilien de Béthune buys Sully.
1610-1643	*Louis XIII.*
1619	Marie de' Medici flees Blois.
1620	Building of the college by the Jesuits at La Flèche.
1626	Gaston d'Orléans, brother of Louis XIII, is granted the County of Blois.
1643-1715	*Louis XIV.*
1648-1653	*Civil war against Mazarin, the Fronde.*
1651	Anne of Austria, Mazarin and the young Louis XIV take refuge in Gien.
1669	Première of Molière's play *Monsieur de Pourceaugnac* at Chambord.
1685	*Revocation of the Edict of Nantes signed by Louis XIV at Fontainebleau.*
1715-1774	*Louis XV.*
1719	Voltaire exiled at Sully.
1756	Foundation of the Royal College of Surgeons at Tours.
1770	The Duke of Choiseul in exile at Chanteloup.

The Revolution and First Empire (1789-1815)

1789	*Storming of the Bastille.*
1792	*Proclamation of the Republic.*
1793	*Execution of Louis XVI.* Vendée War.
	Fighting between the Republican "Blues" and Royalist "Whites". *(Cholet, Les Mauges).*
1803	Talleyrand purchases Valençay.
1804-1815	*First Empire under Napoleon Bonaparte.*
1808	Internment of Ferdinand VII, King of Spain, at Valençay.

Constitutional Monarchy and the Second Republic (1815-1852)

1814-1824	*Louis XVIII.*
1824-1830	*Charles X.*
1830-1848	*July Monarchy: Louis-Philippe.*
1832	*The first steamboat on the Loire.*
1832-1848	*Conquest of Algeria.*
1848	Internment of Abd El-Kader at Amboise.
1846-1852	*Second Republic. Louis Napoleon-Bonaparte, Prince-President.*

The Second Empire (1852-1870)

1852-1870	*Napoleon III as Emperor.*
1870-1871	*Franco-Prussian War.*
1870	*Proclamation of the Third Republic on 4 September in Paris.*
	Frederick-Charles of Prussia at Azay-le-Rideau. Defence of Châteaudun.
	Tours becomes the headquarters of the Provisional Government.
1871	Battle of Loigny.

The Third Republic (1870-1940) and the Present Day

1873	Amédée Bollée completes his first car, *l'Obéissante (Le Mans).*
1908	Wilbur Wright's early trials with his aeroplane.
1914-1918	*First World War.*
1919	*Treaty of Versailles.*
1923	The first Twenty-four Hour Race at Le Mans.
1936	Louis Renault establishes his first decentralised factory south of Le Mans.
1939-1945	*Second World War.*
1940	Defence of Saumur; historic meeting at Montoire.
1945	*Armistice of Rheims.*
1946	*Fourth Republic.*
1952	First *son et lumière* performances at Chambord.
1958	*Fifth Republic.*
1963	Opening of France's first nuclear power station at Avoine near Chinon.
1970	Founding of the University of Tours.
1989	Inauguration of the TGV (high-speed train) *Atlantique.*

(1) Events of general historical import are printed in italics.

Join us in our constant task of keeping up-to-date.
Please send us your comments and suggestions.

MICHELIN TYRE
Public Limited Company
Tourism Department - The Edward Hyde Building
38 Clarendon Road - WATFORD Herts WD1 1SX

THE RICH HISTORY OF THE LOIRE REGION

Antiquity and the Early Middle Ages

During the Iron Age the prosperous and powerful people known as the **Cenomanni** occupied a vast territory extending from Brittany to the Beauce and from Normandy to Aquitaine. They minted gold coins and put up a long resistance to both barbarian and Roman invaders. They reacted strongly to the invasion of Gaul by the Romans and in 52 BC the **Carnutes,** who inhabited the country between Chartres and Orléans, gave the signal, at the instigation of the Druids, to raise a revolt against Caesar. It was savagely repressed but the following year Caesar had to put down another uprising by the Andes under their leader Dumnacos.

Peace was established under Augustus and a period of stability and prosperity began. Existing towns such as Angers, Le Mans, Tours and Orléans adapted to the Roman model with a forum, theatre, baths and public buildings. Many agricultural estates *(villae)* were created or extended as the commercial outlets developed. They reached their peak in the 2C; by the end of the 3C instability and danger were so rife that the city had been enclosed behind a wall.

At the same time Christianity was introduced by St Gatien, the first bishop of Tours; by the end of the 4C it had overcome most opposition under **St Martin,** the greatest bishop of the Gauls *(qv),* whose tomb later became a very important place of pilgrimage (St Martin's Day: 11 November).

In the 5C the Loire country suffered several waves of invasion; in 451 Bishop Aignan held back the Huns outside Orléans while waiting for help. Franks and Visigoths fought for domination until Clovis was finally victorious in 507.

His successors' endless quarrels, which were recorded by Gregory of Tours, dominated the history of the region in the 6C and 7C while St Martin's Abbey was establishing its reputation. In 732 the Saracens, who were pushing north from Spain, reached the Loire before they were repulsed by Charles Martel.

The order achieved by the Carolingians, which was marked by the activities of **Alcuin** and **Theoduff,** did not last. In the middle of the 9C the Vikings came up the river and ravaged the country on either side, particularly the monasteries (St Benoît, St Martin's). **Robert,** Count of Blois and Tours,

Alcuin and Rabanus Maurus
(National Library, Vienna)

defeated them but they continued their depredations until 911 when the Treaty of St-Clair-sur-Epte created the Duchy of Normandy.

During this period of insecurity the Robertian dynasty (the forerunner of the Capet dynasty) gained in power to the detriment of the last Carolingian kings. A new social order emerged which gave rise to feudalism.

Princely power

The weakness of the last Carolingian kings encouraged the independence of turbulent and ambitious feudal lords. Although Orléans was one of the favourite royal residences and the Orléans region was always Capet territory, Touraine, the county of Blois, Anjou and Maine became independent and rival principalities. This was the age of powerful barons, who raised armies and minted money. From Orléans to Angers every high point was crowned by an imposing castle, the stronghold of the local lord who was continually at war with his neighbours.

The counts of Blois faced a formidable enemy in the counts of Anjou, of whom the most famous was **Fulk Nerra** *(qv).* He was a first-class tactician; little by little he encircled Eudes II, Count of Blois, and seized part of his territory. His son, Geoffrey Martel, continued the same policy; from his stronghold in Vendôme he wrested from the house of Blois the whole county of Tours. In the 12C the county of Blois was dependent on Champagne which was then at the height of its power.

At the same period the counts of Anjou reached the height of their power under the Plantagenets *(qv);* when Henri, Count of Anjou, became King Henry II of England in 1154 his kingdom stretched from the north of England to the Pyrenees. This formidable new power confronted the modest forces of the kings of France but they did not quail under the threat of their powerful neighbours and skilfully took advantage of the quarrels which divided the Plantagenets.

In 1202 King John of England, known as John Lackland *(qv),* lost all his continental possessions to Philippe-Auguste *(qv);* the Loire country returned to the French sphere of interest.

In accordance with the wishes of his father Louis VIII, when Louis IX came to the throne he granted Maine and Anjou as an apanage to his brother Charles, who abandoned his French provinces, including Provence, and tried to establish an Angevin kingdom in Naples, Sicily and the Near East, as did his successors. Nonetheless, Good **King René** *(qv),* the last Duke of Anjou, earned himself a lasting place in popular tradition.

The Cradle of Feudalism

Feudalism flourished in France in the 11C and 12C in the region between the Seine and the Loire under the Capet monarchy.

The system was based on two elements: the fief and the lord. The **fief** was a "beneficium" (benefice), usually a grant of land made by a lord to a knight or other man who became his vassal.

The numerous conflicts of interest which arose from the system in practice produced a detailed code of behaviour embodying the rights of the parties. During the 12C the services due were defined, such as the maximum number of days to be spent each year in military service or castle watch. Gradually the fiefs became hereditary and the lord retained only overall ownership. In the case of multiple vassalage, liege homage was paid to one lord and this was more binding than homage to any other.

An almost perfect hierarchical pyramid was created descending from the king to the mass of simple knights. The more important vassals had the right of appeal to the king in case of serious dispute with their suzerain; it was by this means that King John (John Lackland) was deprived of his French fiefs by Philippe-Auguste early in the 13C.

All the inhabitants of an estate were involved in the economic exploitation of the land; the estate had evolved from the Carolingian method of administration and was divided into two parts: the domain, which was kept by the lord for himself, and the holdings, which were let to the tenants in return for rent. The authority exercised by the lord over the people who lived on his estate derived from the royal prerogative of the monarch to command his subjects which passed into the hands of powerful lords who owned castles. This unlimited power enabled them to impose military service, various duties (road mending, transport, etc) and taxes on their tenants.

Joan of Arc

The Hundred Years War (1337-1453) brought back the English, who became masters of half the country and besieged Orléans; if the town had surrendered, the whole of the rest of the kingdom would probably have passed into the enemy's hands. Then **Joan of Arc** appeared and proclaimed her intention of "booting the English out of France"; national pride was awakened. The shepherdess from Domrémy persuaded Charles VII to give her a command *(see Chinon)*. With her little army she entered beleaguered Orléans, stormed the English strongholds and freed the city *(see Orléans)*. The fleeing enemy was defeated on the Loire, at Jargeau, and in the Beauce, at Patay, and in spite of the betrayal of Compiègne and the stake at Rouen, the enemy's total defeat was assured.

16C: Royal munificence and religious tumult

The 16C saw in the Renaissance, and with it an explosion of new ideas in art and architecture, resulting in one of the liveliest periods in the history of the Loire country.

The Renaissance – The University of Orléans with its long-established reputation attracted a number of **humanists**: Nicolas Béraud, Étienne Dolet, Pierre de l'Estoille, Anne du Bourg. The world of ideas was greatly extended by the invention of printing – the first printing press in the Loire Valley was set up in Angers in 1477 – which made learning and culture more accessible. In the middle of the century the **Pléiade** *(qv)* was formed in the Loire Valley and attracted the best local talent *(qv)*.

By choosing Touraine as their favourite place of residence the kings made a significant contribution to the artistic revival of the region. The chief instigators of the great French Renaissance were **Charles VIII** and particularly **Louis XII** and **François I**, who had all travelled in Italy; they transformed the Loire Valley into a vast building site where the new aesthetic ideals flourished at Amboise, Blois and especially Chambord.

AN OUTLINE OF THE CAMPAIGN OF JOAN OF ARC IN THE LOIRE COUNTRY
FROM MARCH 1 TO JULY 1, 1429

The great lords and financiers followed suit and built themselves most elegant houses (Azay-le-Rideau, Chenonceau) while graceful mansions were erected in the towns.

The Renaissance was the expression of a new way of thinking which redefined man's place in the world and presented a radically different view from that which had been held in the past; this gave rise to the desire for harmony and the cult of beauty in all fields: poetry, music, architecture as an expression of nature shaped by man, etc.

Religious tumult – The Renaissance excited not only intellectual activity but also the need for a moral and religious revival. Despite several local experiments (eg Le Mans), the Roman Church did not succeed in satisfying these aspirations. Naturally the ideas of **Luther** and **Calvin** (who was in Orléans between 1528 and 1533) were well received in cultivated circles. In 1540 the Church responded with

François I in 1525 by Jean Clouet
(Louvre Museum)

repression; several reformers died at the stake but the Reform movement continued to grow; nor was support confined to the elite but extended to the mass of the people, craftsmen and tradesmen. The dispute between Protestants and Roman Catholics inevitably led to armed conflict. In 1560 the **Amboise Conspiracy** *(p 45)* failed disastrously and ended in bloodshed. Catherine de' Medici tried to promote conciliation by issuing edicts of tolerance but in April 1562 the Huguenots rose up and committed many acts of vandalism: damaging places of worship and destroying statues, tombs and relics. The Roman Catholics under Montpensier and Guise regained the upper hand and exacted a terrible vengeance, particularly in Angers *(qv)*. From 1563 to 1567 there was relative peace, but in 1568 the armed struggle broke out anew; the Catholic and Protestant armies, the latter under Condé and Coligny, caused waves of bloodshed. In Orléans the **feast of St Bartholomew** was celebrated with thousands of deaths. During the last quarter of the century the Reformed Churches were much weaker and **Henri III's** struggle with the Catholic League came to the fore. In 1576 Touraine, Anjou and Berry were granted to François d'Alençon, the king's brother and head of the League, as a conciliatory gesture but the Guises would not compromise and conspired against the king who, seeing no other solution, had them assassinated at Blois in December 1588 *(qv)*. The population divided into Royalists, and Leaguers who were powerful in the Loire region. Henri III, who had been forced to withdraw to Tours, allied himself with Henri of Navarre and was marching on Paris when he himself was assassinated on 2 August 1589.

It took Henri IV nearly ten years to restore peace to the region. The brilliant period in the history of the Loire Valley, which coincided with the last years of the Valois dynasty, ended in tragedy.

17C and 18C: Peace is restored

The Loire country ceased to be at the centre of political and religious ferment. There were indeed a few alarms during the minority of Louis XIII and the Fronde, caused by the indefatigable conspirator, Gaston of Orléans *(p 68)*. Order was however restored under Louis XIV. Centralisation under the crown stifled any sign of autonomy: the districts of Orléans and Tours were administered by energetic treasury officials while the towns lost the right to self-government.

In the religious domain the Roman Catholic Church re-established itself: convents and seminaries grew in number, the old monastic foundations underwent reform and the suppression of sorcery went hand in hand with the rise in the intellectual level of the clergy. Protestantism had a struggle to survive, except in Saumur owing to the Academy, and was dealt a devastating blow by the **Revocation of the Edict of Nantes** in 1685.

A developing economy – Human enterprise benefited from the general stability. Agriculture developed slowly: cereals in the Beauce, raw materials for textiles (wool, linen, hemp), market gardening together with fruit growing and wine making in the Loire Valley were a considerable source of wealth while cattle raising remained weak. Rural crafts played an important role together with urban manufacturing: hemp cloth round Cholet, cheesecloth in the district of Le Mans, sheeting in Touraine and Anjou, bonnets in Orléanais. The silk weavers *(qv)* of Tours achieved a firm reputation.

Nevertheless in the 18C, except for sheets from Laval and Cholet, the textile industry went into decline. Orléans, the warehouse of the Loire, specialised in sugar refining and the finished product was distributed throughout the kingdom. The Loire, under the control of the "community of merchants" *(see the Loire Valley: Boats and Boatmen)*, was the main axis for trade; wine from Touraine and Anjou, wool from the Berry, iron from the Massif Central, coal from the Forez, wheat from the Beauce, cloth from Touraine and cargoes from exotic countries – everything travelled by water. On the eve of the Revolution these activities were in decline but the region had about two million inhabitants and several real towns: Orléans (pop 40 000), Angers (pop 30 000), Tours (pop 20 000) and Le Mans (pop 17 000).

The Revolution

Touraine and Orléanais accepted the Revolution but Maine and Anjou rose in revolt.

Social Conflict – At first it was social conflict in which the country peasants were opposed to the townspeople and the weavers from the villages. The townspeople, who had been won over by the new ideas, were enthusiastic about the new political order while the peasants became increasingly disillusioned. Religious reform upset parish life and the administrative reforms provoked criticism and discontent because they favoured the townspeople. The national guards in their blue uniform were more and more disliked: they were sent out from the towns to compel compliance with the revolutionary decisions, if necessary by force. The decree imposing mass conscription in March 1793 was seen as an unacceptable provocation in the country and the peasants rose in a body. Les Mauges *(qv)* in particular was immediately in the forefront of the battle.

The Vendée War – The Angevin rebels appointed leaders from among their number, countrymen like **Stofflet** and **Cathelineau** or noblemen like **Bonchamps.** For four months their armies won several important engagements in support of the Church and the king; they captured Cholet, Saumur and then Angers. The Convention replied by sending in several army units. The royalist Whites were severely defeated at Cholet *(qv)* on 17 October by General Kléber and General Marceau and had to retreat. As they fled they were pitilessly massacred and the remnants of the "great Catholic and royal army" were exterminated in the Savenay Marshes beyond Nantes. By way of reprisal against the local population the Convention appointed General Turreau in January 1794 to "clean up" the country. From February to May his **"infernal columns"** converged on the centre, killing women and children and setting fire to villages.

The Chouans – The war was followed by sporadic outbursts of guerrilla activity: daring exploits, ambushes and even assassinations. Jean **Cottereau,** also known as Jean Chouan, was the leading figure who gave his name to the movement. The country people maintained a relentless resistance. At the end of August a faint peace-making gesture was made under the authority of General **Hoche.** Charette and Stofflet, who continued the struggle, were arrested and shot in February and March 1796. The insurrection in the Vendée came to an end under the Consulate. The war left in its wake much ruin and formidable bitterness which was revealed later in the very rigid political attitudes of the people of Maine and Anjou.

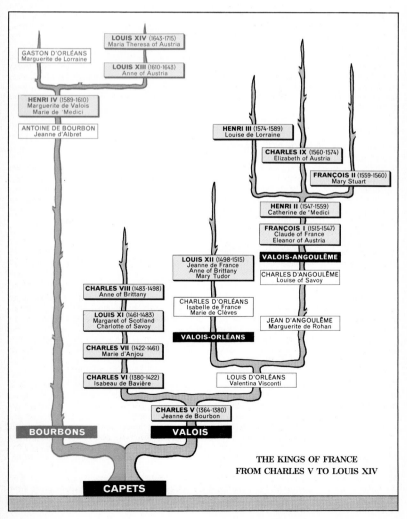

THE KINGS OF FRANCE
FROM CHARLES V TO LOUIS XIV

October 1870 - January 1871 – After the fall of the Empire, France recovered its balance under the stimulus of Gambetta who arrived in Tours by balloon on 9 October. The Bavarians, who were victorious at Artenay, had already captured Orléans (11 October) and indicated that they would link up with the Prussian army at Versailles via the Beauce. Châteaudun *(qv)* put up a heroic resistance for ten hours on 18 and 19 October and was bombarded and set on fire in reprisal.

The army of the Loire was formed under the command of **General d'Aurelle de Paladines;** two corps, the 15th and 16th (Chanzy), formed in the Salbris camp, set out from Blois for Orléans. The engagement took place at Marchenoir and then at Coulmiers on 9 November: the French were victorious and General Von der Thann was forced to evacuate Orléans. Meanwhile the 18th and 20th corps tried to check the advance of the Duke of Mecklenburg on Le Mans and Tours but they were beaten on 28 November at Beaune-la-Rolande by Prince Frederick-Charles who had hastened south from Metz. On 2 December the 16th and 17th corps were defeated at Patay and Loigny where the Zouaves under Lt Col de Charette, the great-nephew of the Famous Royalist, fought with distinction. Although cut in two the first army of the Loire survived. Orléans had to be abandoned while the government retreated to Bordeaux (8 December).

A second Loire army was formed under **General Chanzy;** it resisted every enemy attack and then retrenched on the Loir. On 19 December the Prussians captured Château-Renault and two days later arrived in front of Tours but did not besiege the town. The decisive battle was fought between 10 and 12 January on the Auvours plateau east of Le Mans. Chanzy was forced to retreat towards Laval; Tours was occupied and Prince Frederick-Charles took up residence at Azay-le-Rideau *(qv)*. The armistice was signed on 28 January 1871.

1917-18 – The Americans set up their headquarters in Tours while the first "Sammies" disembarked at St-Nazaire and were billeted along the Loire.

1940-44 – On **10 June 1940** the French Government moved to Tours, and Cangé Château, on the southeast edge of the town, became the temporary residence of the President of the Republic. On 13 June the Franco-British Supreme Council met in Tours; at Cangé the Council of Ministers decided to transfer the government to Bordeaux. During that week of tragedy the bridges over the Loire were machine-gunned and bombarded; floods of refugees choked the roads. The towns were badly damaged. 2 000 cadets from the Cavalry School at Saumur excelled themselves by holding up the German advance for two days along a 25km - 15 mile front *(see Saumur)*. On 24 October 1940 Marshal Pétain met Hitler at **Montoire,** and agreed to his demands; collaboration was born. The Gestapo in Angers established a reign of terror in the region.

The Resistance was born in 1941; the information and sabotage networks, the underground forces and the escape agents (the demarcation line followed the River Cher and ran between Tours and Loches) hampered the movements of the occupying forces who responded with torture, deportation and summary execution. In August and September 1944 the American army and the forces of the Resistance achieved control of the area with heavy losses.

BIRTH AND EVOLUTION OF THE CHÂTEAUX

The first châteaux (5C to 10C) – In the Merovingian period the country was protected by isolated strongholds: some had evolved from Gallo-Roman "villas" (country estates) which had been fortified; others were built on high ground (Loches, Chinon). Generally they covered a fairly large area and served several purposes: residence of important people, place of worship, a place for minting money, an agricultural centre and a place of refuge for the population. This type of stronghold continued under the Carolingians but the growing insecurity in the second half of the 9C introduced a wave of fortification in an attempt to counter the Viking threat. The early castles, which were built in haste, rested on a mound of earth surrounded by a wooden palisade; sometimes a central tower was erected as an observation post. The structure contained very little masonry. Until the 10C castle building was a prerogative of the king but thereafter the right was usurped by powerful lords; small strongholds proliferated under the designation "towers"; the keep had been invented.

The mott castle (11C) – The mott was a man-made mound of earth on which was erected a square wooden tower, the **keep.** An earth bank protected by a ditch supported the perimeter fence, which consisted of a wooden palisade and enclosed an area large enough to contain the people of the neighbourhood. The keep was built either as the last place of refuge or at the weakest point in the perimeter fence; some castles had more than one mott. In several of the Angevin castles built by Fulk Nerra *(qv)* the keep protected a residential building erected at the end of a promontory, as at Langeais, Blois and Loches, which are typical of the Carolingian tradition.

The stone castle (12C-13C) – By the 11C some castles had defensive works built of stone. The keep was still the strongest point and took the form of a massive quadrangular structure. The keeps at Loches, Langeais, Montbazon, Chinon (Coudray) and Beaugency are remarkable examples of 11C architecture.

The 12C keep overlooked a courtyard which was enclosed by a stone **curtain wall,** gradually reinforced by turrets and towers. Within its precincts each castle comprised private apartments, a great hall, one or more chapels, soldiers' barracks, lodgings for the household staff and other buildings such as barns, stables, storerooms, kitchens, etc.

The tendency grew to rearrange the buildings more compactly within a smaller precinct. The keep comprised a storeroom on the ground floor, a great hall on the first and living rooms on the upper floors. The compact shape and the height of the walls made it difficult to besiege and only a few men were required for its defence.

In the 13C, under the influence of the crusades and improvements in the art of attack, important innovations appeared. Castles were designed by experts to be even more compact with multiple defensive features so that no point was unprotected. The curtain wall bristled with huge towers and the keep was neatly incorporated into the overall design.

A circular plan was adopted for the towers and keep; the walls were splayed at the base; the depth and width of the moat were greatly increased. Sometimes a lower outer rampart was built to reinforce the main rampart; the intervening strip of level ground was called the lists. Improvements were made to the arrangements for launching missiles: new types of loophole (in a cross or stirrup shape), stone machicolations, platforms, bratticing, etc. The 13C castle, which was more functional and had a pronounced military character, could be built anywhere, even in open country. At the same time a desire for indoor comfort began to express itself in tapestries and draperies and furniture (chests and beds), which made the rooms more pleasant to live in than they had been in the past.

The late medieval castle – In 14C and 15C castle-building the accent moved from defence to comfort and decoration. The living quarters were more extensive; large windows to let in the light and new rooms (state bedrooms, dressing rooms and lavatories) appeared; decoration became an important feature.

In the military sphere there were no innovations, only minor improvements. The keep merged with the living quarters and was surmounted by a watch tower; sometimes the keep was suppressed altogether and the living quarters took the form of a rectangular block defended by huge corner towers. The entrance was flanked by two semicircular towers and protected by a barbican (a gateway flanked by towers) or by a separate fort. The top of the curtain wall was raised to the height of the towers which were crowned by a double row of crenellations. In the 15C the towers were capped by pointed, pepperpot roofs.

Other fortified buildings – Churches and monasteries, which were places of sanctuary and therefore targets of war, were not excluded from the fortification movement, especially during the Hundred Years War. The towns and some of the villages also turned their attention to defence and built ramparts round the residential districts. In 1398, 1399 and 1401 Charles VI issued letters and ordinances enjoining the owners of fortresses and citizens to see that their fortifications were in good order.

From the end of the 13C fortified houses were built in the country districts by the lords of the manor; they had no military significance but are similar in appearance to the smaller châteaux.

The Renaissance château – In the 16C military elements were abandoned in the search for comfort and aesthetic taste: moats, keeps and turrets appeared only as decorative features as at Chambord, Azay-le-Rideau and Chenonceau. The spacious attics were lit by great dormer windows in the steep pitched roofs. The windows were very large. The spiral turret stairs were replaced with stairs that rose in straight flights in line with the centre of the main façade beneath coffered ceilings. The gallery – a new feature imported from Italy at the end of the 15C – lent a touch of elegance to the main courtyard.

Whereas the old fortified castle had been built on a hill, the new château was sited in a valley or beside a river where it was reflected in the water. The idea was that the building should harmonise with its natural surroundings, although these were shaped and transfigured by man's hand; the gardens, which were laid out like a jewel casket, were an integral part of the design. Only the chapel continued to be built in the traditional style with ogee vaulting and Flamboyant decoration.

The classical style, which dominated the 17C and 18C, introduced a rigorous sense of proportion. The château became a country house set in a beautiful garden (Cheverny and Ménars).

Cheverny — The Armoury

The siege – The attacker's first task was to besiege the enemy stronghold. The defences he constructed (moat, stockade, towers, forts or blockhouses) were intended both to prevent a possible sortie by the besieged and to counter an attack from a relief army. In the great sieges a veritable fortified town encircled the site under attack.

In order to make a breach in the defences of the besieged place the attacker used mines, slings and battering rams. For this he had specialist troops who were experts in siege operations.

Balista.

The projectile is placed in ① and launched by the action of the spring ② on the release of the lever ③, which has been drawn back by the winch ④.

Undermining – When the ground was suitable the attackers would dig tunnels under the ramparts and curtain walls. The cavity was shored up with wooden props which were set on fire when the attackers withdrew; the tunnel and the wall above then collapsed.

The defenders would respond by digging another gallery intersecting the first and the combatants would fight underground. When they could no longer defend the breaches, the besieged withdrew to the keep.

Projectiles – The machines used for launching projectiles worked on a spring or a counter-balance. The most usual were the ballista, the crossbow mounted on a tower, the trebuchet, the mangonel and the stone sling.

The large **mangonels** could launch stones of over 100kg - 220lbs up to 200m - 654ft using an average trajectory. These rocks could smash the merlons, shake the walls or enlarge the breaches made by the battering ram. Other projectiles were used: grape shot, incendiary arrows (Greek fire), flaming faggots and even carrion to spread disease. The crossbow fired shafts 5m - 16ft long which could fell a whole file of soldiers.

The siege tower – This was the most highly developed weapon of attack. It was built of wood – the Middle Ages had marvellous carpenters – and covered with hide; it was about 50m - 160ft tall and could shelter hundreds of men.

To advance it to the foot of a wall it was necessary to fill in a section of moat and build a wooden slipway. The huge structure was placed on rollers and moved with hoisting gear.

Mangonel

The lever ① is brought to ground level by the winch ②. When it is released it returns sharply to the perpendicular by the action of the counter-weight ③ and the men pulling on the ropes. The projectile is launched by the catapult at the end of the lever.

The battering ram – The ram complemented the work of the projectiles. It was manned by a hundred soldiers who maintained the to-and-fro movement of the beam. For breaking down gates there was a smaller version which could be manœuvred by a dozen strong men. The force of the large rams was very great; to cushion the blow the defenders would try to interpose bales of wool. The ram was protected by a stout wooden shield covered with hide which the defenders tried to pierce with stones and flaming faggots.

The assault – The siege towers were equipped with drawbridges which were let down on to the ramparts so that the soldiers could flood over the curtain walls while others rushed in through the breaches. Scaling ladders were erected against the walls. The more agile men threw grappling irons over the battlements and hauled themselves up hand over hand by rope. The defenders unleashed a hail of arrows and projectiles and tried to cut the ropes or throw down the ladders. Boiling pitch and quicklime were poured on the heads of the assault troops. If the attackers succeeded in breaching the walls they still had to capture a succession of individual defences (gates, towers and keep). A determined defence could hold out for a long time by means of narrow twisting stairs, false entrances, traps, chicanes, loopholes and internal machicolations.

The era of the cannon – The bombard increased in effectiveness. Towards the middle of the 15C under the influence of the Bureau brothers, the French royal artillery became the best in the world. In one year Charles VII recaptured from the English sixty places which had resisted sieges of from four to ten months. Siege technique was altered and adapted. The place being besieged was encircled by a ring of fortified camps linked to one another by trenches. The artillery was then drawn up into position and the gunners were protected behind a bank or stockade. The firing rate was not very high and the aim was even less accurate. The defenders also used artillery and made sorties to spike the enemy's guns. Military architecture was completely transformed; towers were replaced by low thick bastions and curtain walls were built lower but much thicker. This new system of defences was perfected by Vauban.

MEDIEVAL CHÂTEAU LIFE

One living room – In the 10C and 11C life in a castle was crude. The whole family lived, ate and slept in the same room on the first floor of the keep. Furniture was rare and tableware rudimentary.

A lonely life – The owner of a castle had to be self-sufficient and lived in great insecurity. When the lord was out hunting or fighting his neighbours or off on a crusade, his lady administered his affairs.

MEDIEVAL PALACE LIFE

The Great Hall – In the 13C living quarters began to improve. In the Near East the crusaders experienced a comfortable way of life and acquired a taste for it. In future public and private life were conducted in separate rooms. The most handsome room in the castle was the Great Hall; here the lord held audience and dispensed justice; feasts and banquets took place in it. The earlier loopholes were replaced by windows, fitted with panes and shutters. The walls were hung with paintings and tapestries, the floor tiles were covered with rush mats or carpets on which one could sit or lie; flowers and greenery were strewn on the floor and, in summer, in the fireplaces.

The bedchamber – The bedchamber opened off the Great Hall. Except in royal or princely households, a married couple slept in the same room. The furnishings grew richer; the bed was set on a dais and surrounded with rich curtains; there were Venetian mirrors, tapestries, costly drapes, benches with backs, a princely chair, a praying-desk, library steps and cushions, a dresser, a table, chests, a cupboard. To entertain the ladies there was an aviary, often a parrot.

Mourning lasted for fifteen days during which the ladies hung their rooms with black and stayed in bed with the shutters closed. For a birth the shutters were also closed; the room was lit with candles and decorated with flowers and the most precious objects which were set on the dresser.

Near to the bedchamber there was a study which was also used for private audiences, a council chamber and an oratory or chapel. A special room was set aside for the guards. In the larger houses there was also a state room where the ceremonial clothes were on display. After making his first toilette in his bedchamber among the close members of his household, the prince would take his place on the bed in the reception room and finish his dressing among a different company. This practice evolved into the solemn "levées" of Louis XIV.

Food – The food was good and the meals gargantuan. When eaten in private the meals were served in the bedchamber or in the Great Hall. Before and after the meal basins and ewers of scented water were provided for the diners to rinse their hands since fingers often took the place of forks. The plates were of silver. At banquets the diners sat along one side of a great table since the central area was used by the jugglers, acrobats and musicians who provided entertainment in the intervals.

Bathing and hygiene – Near the bedchamber or in a separate building was the bath house. Until the 14C bathing was the fashion in France. The common people used to go to the public baths once a week; the upper classes often took a daily bath. The bath house contained a sort of pool which was filled with warm water and a chamber for the steam bath and massage. A barber or a chambermaid was in attendance for it was the fashion to be clean shaven.

In the absence of a bath house, baths were taken in a tub made of wood or bronze or silver. Often people took supper together while bathing. Before a meal guests would be offered a bath. Men and women bathed together without being thought immoral.

These habits of cleanliness disappeared from the Renaissance until the Revolution. The preachers inveighed against the communal baths which they asserted had become places of debauch. In the 13C there were 26 public baths in Paris; in Louis XIV's reign there were only two.

In other respects medieval castles were well enough provided with conveniences.

Entertainment – Castle life had always had plenty of idle hours and a variety of distractions had developed to fill them. Indoors there was chess, spillikins, dice, draughts and, from the 14C, cards. Outdoors there was tennis, bowls and football, wrestling and archery. Hunting with hounds or hawks and tournaments and jousts were the great sports of the nobles. The women and children had dwarfs to entertain them; at court the jester was free to make fun of people, even the king.

There were frequent festivities. Performances of the Mystery Plays, which sometimes lasted 25 days, were always a great success.

Troubadours — Peterborough Psalter (1390)

A Bourgeois Court – The court resided regularly in the Loire Valley under Charles VII whose preference was for Chinon and Loches. These visits ended with the last of the Valois, Henri III. Owing to the straitened circumstances to which the King of France was reduced Charles VII's court was not brilliant; but the arrival of Joan of Arc in 1429 made the castle of Chinon for ever famous.

Louis XI disliked pomp and circumstance. He installed his wife, Charlotte de Savoie, at Amboise but he himself rarely came there. He preferred his manor at Plessis-lès-Tours where he lived in fear of an attempt on his life. His only interests were hunting and dogs.

The queen's court consisted of fifteen ladies-in-waiting, twelve women of the bedchamber and 100 officers in charge of various functions including the saddler, the librarian, the doctor, the chaplain and the lute player. The budget amounted only to 37 000 *livres,* of which 800 *livres* were spent on minor pleasures: materials for

Porcupine (Louis XII) — Cominus et eminus

needlework and embroidery, books, parchments and illuminating. Charlotte was a serious woman and a great reader; her library contained 100 volumes, a vast total for that time. They were works of piety and morality and books on history, botany and domestic science. A few lighter works, such as the *Tales of Boccaccio,* relieved this solemnity. In fact, compared with Charles the Bold, the royal lifestyle seemed homely rather then princely.

A Luxurious Court – With the accession of Charles VIII, "the King of Amboise", at the end of the 15C, the taste for luxury appeared. Furnishings became rich: in the castle were 220 Persian, Turkish and Syrian carpets, 45 beds, 60 chests, 60 tables, numerous Flemish and Parisian tapestries, works of art from Italy and sumptuous silverware. A magnificent aviary contained rare birds. Lions and wild boars, which were made to fight with huge mastiffs, were kept in a menagerie. The armoury contained a fine collection of armour, the battle-axes of Clovis, St Louis and Du Guesclin.

A Gallant Court – Louis XII, who was frugal, was the bourgeois "King of Blois". But under François I (1515-47) the French court became a school of elegance, taste and culture. The Cavalier King invited men of science, poets and artists to his court. Women, who until then had been relegated to the Queen's service, played an important role; the King made them the leaders of a new society. He expected them to dress perfectly and gave them the wherewithal to do so.

The King also took care that these ladies were treated with courtesy and respect. A gentleman who had permitted himself to speak slightingly of them escaped the supreme penalty only by flight – "So great", says a contemporary historian, "was the King's anger, he swore that whoever reflected on the honour of these ladies would be hanged." A code of courtesy was established and the court set an example of good manners. The festivals given by François I at Amboise, where he spent his childhood and the first years of his reign, were of unprecedented brilliance.

Salamander (François I) — Nutrisco et extinguo

Weddings, baptisms and the visits of princes were sumptuously celebrated. Sometimes the festivities took place in the country, as on the occasion when the reconstruction of a siege was organised; a temporary town was built to be defended by the Duke of Alençon while the King led the assault and capture. To increase the sense of realism, the mortars fired large balls. Hunting, however, had pride of place; 125 people were employed in keeping the hounds at a cost of 18 000 *livres* per year while 50 looked after the hawks at a cost of 36 000 *livres.*

The Last Valois – Under Henri II and his sons, Blois remained the habitual seat of the court when it was not at the Louvre. It was Henri III who drew up the first code of etiquette and introduced the title "His Majesty", taken from the Roman Emperors. The queen mother and the queen had about 100 ladies-in-waiting. Catherine de' Medici also had her famous "Flying Squad" of pretty girls, who kept her informed and assisted her intrigues. About 100 pages acted as messengers. In addition there were 76 gentlemen servants, 51 clerks, 23 doctors and 50 chambermaids.

The King's suite included 200 gentlemen-in-waiting and over 100 archers and Swiss guards. There was a multitude of servants. Princes of the blood and great lords also had their households. Thus, from the time of François I, about 15 000 people surrounded the King; when the court moved, 12 000 horses were needed. By comparison, in the 16C only 25 French towns had more than 10 000 inhabitants.

QUEENS AND GREAT LADIES

The official position enjoyed by women at court around the King often enabled them to play an important if not always useful part in the political affairs of the country. It also enabled them to protect and develop the arts.

Agnès Sorel *(qv)* adorned the court of Charles VII at Chinon and at Loches. She gave the King good advice and reminded him of the urgent problems facing the country after the Hundred Years War, while the queen, Marie d'Anjou, moped in her castle.

Louise de Savoie, the mother of François I, had a great devotion to St Francis of Paola. Only this piety, mingled with the superstitions of her astrologer, Cornelius Agrippa, restrained her ambition. She lived only for the accession of her son to the throne and for the disruption of the plans of Anne of Brittany by making him marry Claude, the daughter of Louis XII.

There were many women in the love life of François I including Françoise de Châteaubriant and the **Duchess of Étampes,** who ruled his court until his death.

Diane de Poitiers *(qv),* the famous favourite of Henri II, was a robust and hardy woman. She retained her energy, both physical and mental, well into old age, to the amazement of her contemporaries. She made important decisions of policy, negotiated with the Protestants, traded in Spanish prisoners, distributed honours and magistracies and, to the great humiliation of the queen, saw to the education of the royal children. Such was her personality that almost every artist of the period painted her portrait.

The foreign beauty of **Mary Stuart,** the hapless wife of the young King François II, who died at 17 after a few months' reign, threw a brief lustre over the court in the middle of the 16C. She is recalled in a drawing by Clouet and some verses by Ronsard.

A different type altogether was **Marguerite de Valois,** the famous Queen Margot, sister of François II, Charles IX and of Henri III. Her bold eyes, her exuberance and her amorous escapades caused much worry to her mother, Catherine de' Medici. Her marriage to the future King Henri IV did little to tame her and was moreover annulled.

Catherine de' Medici *(qv)* had married the Dauphin Henri in 1533 and was a figure at court for 55 years under 5 kings. Although eclipsed for a while by the beautiful Diane de Poitiers, she took her revenge on the death of Henri II by taking over Chenonceau.

With the accession of Charles IX she became regent and tried to maintain the authority of the monarchy during the Wars of Religion by manoeuvring skilfully between the Guises and the Bourbons and using diplomacy, marriage alliances and family intrigue. Under Henri III her influence steadily diminished.

FAMOUS NAMES FROM THE LOIRE

LITERATURE

The balance and clarity of the French language first found expression in the Loire Valley; its peaceful landscapes have fostered many French writers.

Middle Ages – In the 6C, under the influence of St Martin, Tours became a centre of great learning: Bishop **Gregory of Tours** wrote the first history of the Gauls in his *Historia Francorum* and Alcuin of York founded a famous school of calligraphy at the behest of Charlemagne, while in the 11C in the Latin poems of **Baudri de Bourgueil** art came under the influence of courtly life. At the beginning of the 13C Orléans witnessed the impact of the popular and lyrical language of the *Romance of the Rose,* a didactic poem by two successive authors – the mannered **Guillaume de Lorris,** who wrote the first 4000 lines, and the realist **Jean de Meung,** who added the final 18000. The poem was widely translated and exercised immense influence throughout Europe. **Charles d'Orléans** (1391-1465) discovered his poetic gifts in an English prison. He was a patron of the arts and author of several short but graceful poems; at his court in Blois he organised poetic jousts. In 1457 **Villon** was the winner.

Hitherto a princely pastime, poetry in the hands of Good King René of Anjou became an aristocratic and even mannered work of art. In Angers **Jean Michel,** who was a doctor and a man of letters, produced his monumental *Mystery of the Passion;* its 65000 lines took four days to perform.

Renaissance and Humanism – When the vicissitudes of the Hundred Years War obliged the French court to move from Paris to Touraine, new universities were founded in Orléans (1305) and Angers (1364). They very soon attracted a vast body of students and became important centres in the study of European humanism. Among those who came to study and to teach were Erasmus and William Bude, Melchior Wolmar a Hellenist from Swabia and the reformers Calvin and Theodore Beza; **Étienne Dolet,** a native of Orléans, preached his atheist doctrines for which he was hanged and burned in Paris.

Rabelais (1494-1553), who was born near Chinon, was surely the most popular native of Touraine. After studying in Angers, he became a learned Benedictine and then a famous doctor. In the adventures of Gargantua and Pantagruel *(qv)* he expressed his ideas on education, religion and philosophy. He was very attached to his native country and made it the setting for the Picrocholine war in his books. His comic and realistic style, his extraordinarily rich vocabulary and his universal curiosity made him the first prose writer of his period.

François Rabelais
(Condé Museum, Chantilly)

The Pleiades (La Pléiade) – A group of seven poets, named after the constellation Taurus, founded a new school in the Loire Valley which was to dominate 16C poetry; their aim was to develop their own language through imitation of Horace and the ancients. Their undoubted leader was **Ronsard** *(qv)* the Prince of Poets from near Vendôme but it was **Joachim du Bellay** *(qv)* from Anjou who wrote the manifesto of the group, *The Defence and Illustration of the French Language,* which was published in 1549. The other members of the group were Jean-Antoine de **Baïf** from La Flèche, Jean Dorat, Étienne Jodelle, Marot and Pontus de Tyard who all held the position of Court Poet; their subjects were nature, women, their native country and its special quality, *"la douceur angevine".*

Classicism and the Age of Enlightenment – At the end of the Wars of Religion, when the king and the court returned north to Ile-de-France, literature became more serious and philosophical. The **Marquis of Racan** composed verses beside the Loir; the Protestant Academy in Saumur supported the first works of **René Descartes**. In the following century, **Néricault-Destouches**, from Touraine, followed in Molière's footsteps with his comedies of character; Voltaire stayed at Sully; Rousseau and his companion Thérèse Levasseur lived at Chenonceau; Beaumarchais, who wrote *The Barber of Seville,* settled at Vouvray and visited the Duke of Choiseul in exile at Chanteloup.

Romanticism – The pamphleteer **Paul-Louis Courier** (1772-1825) and the songwriter **Béranger** (1780-1857), who were active during the second Bourbon restoration, were both sceptical and witty and liberal in politics. **Alfred de Vigny** (1797-1863), a native of Loches who became a soldier and a poet, painted an idyllic picture of Touraine in his novel, *Cinq-Mars.* The greatest literary genius of Touraine was **Honoré de Balzac** (1799-1850) *(qv)*. He was born in Tours and brought up in Vendôme; he loved the Loire Valley and used it as a setting for the numerous portraits in his vast work, *The Human Comedy.*

Contemporary writers – The poet, **Charles Péguy** *(qv)* who was born in Orléans, wrote about Joan of Arc and his beloved Beauce. **Marcel Proust** *(qv)* also returned to the Beauce in his novel *Remembrance of Things Past.* Another poet, **Max Jacob** (1876-1944), spent many years in work and meditation at the abbey of St-Benoît-sur-Loire.
The Sologne calls to mind the young novelist, **Alain-Fournier**, and his famous work, *Le Grand Meaulnes (The Lost Domain).* The character of Raboliot the poacher is a picturesque evocation of his native country by the author **Maurice Genevoix** (1890-1980), a member of the Academy. **Georges Bernanos** (1888-1948), an original Catholic writer, is buried at Pellevoisin. The humourist **Georges Courteline** (1858-1929) was born in Touraine which was also the retreat of several writers of international reputation: Maeterlinck (Nobel prize in 1911) at Coudray-Montpensier *(qv);* Anatole France (Nobel prize in 1921) at La Béchellerie; Bergson (Nobel prize in 1927) at La Gaudinière. **René Benjamin** (1885-1948) settled in Touraine where he wrote *The Prodigious Life of Balzac* and other novels.
Angers was the home of **René Bazin** (1853-1932), who was greatly attached to the traditional virtues and his home ground, and of his great-nephew, **Hervé Bazin,** whose violent attacks on conventional values were directly inspired by his home town.

BOOKS TO READ

Editions of works mentioned below can be obtained through public libraries.

Châteaux of the Loire by Philippe and Gouvion (Thames & Hudson, 1986)

Eleanor of Aquitaine and the Four Kings by Amy Kelly (Harvard University Press, 1974)

Joan of Arc by Marina Warner (Penguin, 1983)

The Loire Valley and Its Wines by J. Selly (Lennard Publishing Ltd, 1989)

The Cathedral's Crusade, The Rise of the Gothic Style in France by Ian Dunlop (Hamish Hamilton, 1982)

The Loire Valley by Henry Myhill (Faber & Faber, 1984)

The Loire by S. Jennett (Batsford, 1975)

Loire Valley by J.J. and J. Wailing (Thomas Nelson Ltd, 1982)

Companion Guide to the Loire by Richard Wade (Collins, 1984)

Loire Gastronomique by Hilaire Wolden (Octopus Books, 1992)

The Châteaux of the Loire by Marcus Binney (Penguin-Viking, 1992)

Access in the Loire (Disabled Tourists' Guide) Obtainable from Access Project (PHSP), 39 Bradley Gardens, London W138HE

The following novels have settings in the Loire region:

Honoré de Balzac: *Eugénie Grandet, Le Curé de Tours, La Femme de Trente Ans, L'Illustre Gaudissart, Le Lys dans la Vallée*

René Benjamin: *La Vie Tourangelle*

Alain-Fournier (Henri-Alban Fournier): *Le Grand Meaulnes*

Maurice Genevoix: *Raboliot*

Émile Zola: *Earth*

Marcel Proust: *A la Recherche du temps perdu, Jean Santeuil*

Charles Péguy: *Jeanne d'Arc*

François Rabelais: *Gargantua and Pantagruel* comprising *Pantagruel, Garguantua, Tiers Livre, Quart Livre*

*The **Michelin Green Guide France.***

A selection of the most unusual and the most typical sights along the main tourist routes.

SCIENCE

The Royal School of Surgery, now the Faculty of Medicine and Pharmacy, was founded in Tours in 1756. It was also in Tours that **Bretonneau** (1778-1862) taught and conducted his research on infectious diseases; his work was brilliantly continued by his pupils **Trousseau** and **Velpeau. Denis Papin** (1647-1714), physicist and inventor, was born near Blois. Another physicist was **Charles** (1746-1823), born in Beaugency, who collaborated with the Montgolfier brothers and in 1783 made the first ascent in a hydrogen balloon in Paris.

FINE ARTS

Clément Janequin (1480-1565), a master of religious and secular music, became an Angevin by adoption and was for many years head of the Angers Cathedral Choir School. **Jean Clouet** from Flanders, who was attached to Louis XII and François I, and his son **François,** who was born in Tours, drew some very fine portraits.
In the 19C the sculptor and engraver, **David of Angers** (1788-1856), achieved fame through his hundreds of medallions which record the profiles of the celebrities of his period.

Painters	Sculptors
Jean Fouquet (*c*1420-80). Portraitist and miniaturist, born in Tours; his backgrounds evoke the Loire Valley.	**Michel Colombe** (*c*1430-1514?). Head of an important studio in Tours; he combined Gothic tradition with Italian novelty.
The Master of Moulins (late 15C). His charm and purity of line are characteristic of the French school. Identified with Jean Perréal (*c*1455-1530).	**Fra Giocondo** (*c*1433-1515). Famous monk from Verona, humanist and engineer who settled in Amboise in 1499.
Jean Bourdichon (*c*1457-1521). Miniaturist who painted Anne of Brittany, with a fluid and seductive style.	**Guido Mazzoni** (*c*1450-1518). An Italian, known as Il Paganino, who specialised in terracotta.
Leonardo da Vinci (1452-1519). Invited to settle in the Loire Valley from 1516 by François I; died in Amboise.	**Domenico da Cortona** (1470-1549). Italian architect, called Il Boccadoro (Golden Mouth), in France from 1495.
François Clouet (1520-72). Born in Tours, he became portrait painter to the Valois kings. His work shows subtlety and penetration.	**The Justes** (16C). Florentine family descended from Antoine Juste (1479-1519) who was naturalised in 1513 and settled in Tours in 1515.
Jean Mosnier (1600-56). Interior decorator and author of religious works. Worked mainly at Cheverny and Beauregard and also in the neighbourhood.	**Girolamo della Robbia** (1488-1566). Arrived in the Orléans region from Florence in 1518 and produced terracotta medallions.
	Michel Bourdin (1585-1645). From Orléans; a realist in style.

Self-portrait of Leonardo da Vinci

THE INHABITANTS OF THE LOIRE VALLEY

The character of the people in the Loire Valley is apparently best illustrated by the following legend which is current in Touraine. The holy relics of St Martin were being carried from Auxerre to Tours. The route was crowded with invalids and cripples who were instantly cured as the relics passed by. Two poor cripples who lived on alms suddenly heard the terrible news – terrible because for them it meant ruin. To escape the miracle which threatened them, they fled as fast as their poor limbs would carry them but they were too slow; the procession overtook them and they were cured. They had to abandon their crutches and begging bowl and work for their living. There was no point in lamenting their lot; it was better to profit from their cure. They went off along the banks of the Loire, praising the Lord and his saint with such enthusiasm that they were able to found a rich chapel and a village, Chapelle-sur-Loire, near Langeais.

The region where the "best French" is spoken – Since the Loire Valley was the cradle of France, it is here that old France is recalled in the sayings which have shaped the French language. It is in this region, so it is said, that the best French is spoken. This does not mean that one hears nothing but the best literary expressions; the local dialect is as unintelligible to the untuned ear as any other.

Fun and games – The young people of the Loire Valley meet at the patronal festivals, the "assemblies" where a special platform is set up for dancing. In the past at the major festivals servants put themselves up for hire and accepted a coin *(le denier à Dieu)* from their new master to seal the contract.
In the fishermen's taverns on the banks of the Loire the old men still play *alouette* or *bigaille,* two games inherited from the boatmen which require 48 cards; declarations are made by signs.
There are about 500 clubs in the Loire Valley, from Bourgueil to Angers, where bowls **(boules de fort)** are played. The bowls are hollow on one side and weighted on the other; the ground is marked out in squares and surrounded by a raised edge. The bowls describe a skilfully judged curve before coming to rest near the jack *(maître),* the small white ball which is the target.

Festivals – Midsummer harvest, threshing and grape-picking are celebrated in a lively manner in the Loire Valley with huge meals and generous supplies of wine. Rabelais greeted the local wine as the "good September brew".

RURAL ARCHITECTURE

The various types of local houses to be found in the Loire Valley are determined by local building materials, local needs and customs.

On the plateaux and in the wooded plains – In the **Beauce,** a wheat-growing plain, the farms are built round a closed courtyard with an imposing entrance. In the towns the houses are rough-cast and roofed with flat tiles.
In the **Dunois** and the **Vendômois** the houses are decorated with a chequered pattern of alternating stone and flint. The long low cottages of the **Sologne** are roofed with thatch or flat tiles; the older houses are built of timber frames filled with cob while the more modern are of brick.
On the plateaux between the Cher, the Indre and the Vienne the country houses are often surrounded by clumps of walnut or chestnut trees. Flat tiles predominate in the country while slates are more common in town. The big house in any locality is usually recognisable by its hipped roof. Between the Sologne and the Loire one often sees red brick buildings with white tufa facings.
In **Anjou** there are two distinct types of building: those constructed of limestone in White Anjou in the east and those constructed of schist in Black Anjou in the wooded farmland of the Mauges, Craonnais and Segréen. The fine blue-black slates are found throughout the province except in the Mauges.
In **Maine** the houses are built of limestone in White Maine on the River Sarthe and of granite or schist in Black Maine in the Mayenne Valley.

In the river valleys – In the valleys of the Loire and its tributaries the typical vine-grower's house consists of the living quarters, the storeroom and the stable under one roof with an external oven and an outside stair beneath which is the entrance to the cellar.
A peculiarity of the valleys is the **troglodyte dwelling** which is hollowed out of the limestone tufa and has a chimney protruding at ground level. Often decorated with flowers and trellises and sheltered from the wind, it is cool in summer and warm in winter.

A troglodyte dwelling

Consult the Index to find an individual town or sight.

ART

ABC OF ARCHITECTURE

To assist readers unfamiliar with the terminology employed in architecture, we describe below the most commonly used terms, which we hope will make their visits to ecclesiastical, military and civil buildings more interesting.

Ecclesiastical architecture

illustration I

Ground plan. – The more usual Catholic form is based on the outline of a cross with the two arms of the cross forming the transept: ① Porch – ② Narthex – ③ Side aisles (sometimes double) – ④ Bay (transverse section of the nave between 2 pillars) – ⑤ Side chapel (often predates the church) – ⑥ Transept crossing – ⑦ Arms of the transept, sometimes with a side doorway – ⑧ Chancel, nearly always facing east towards Jerusalem; the chancel often vast in size was reserved for the monks in abbatial churches – ⑨ High altar – ⑩ Ambulatory: in pilgrimage churches the aisles were extended round the chancel, forming the ambulatory, to allow the faithful to file past the relics – ⑪ Radiating or apsidal chapel – ⑫ Axial chapel. In churches which are not dedicated to the Virgin this chapel, in the main axis of the building is often consecrated to the Virgin (Lady Chapel) – ⑬ Transept chapel.

Romanesque Gothic

◀ illustration II

Cross-section: ① Nave – ② Aisle – ③ Tribune or Gallery – ④ Triforium – ⑤ Barrel vault – ⑥ Half-barrel vault – ⑦ Pointed vault – ⑧ Buttress – ⑨ Flying buttress – ⑩ Pier of a flying buttress – ⑪ Pinnacle – ⑫ Clerestory window.

illustration III ▶

Gothic cathedral: ① Porch – ② Gallery – ③ Rose window – ④ Belfry (sometimes with a spire) – ⑤ Gargoyle acting as a waterspout for the roof gutter – ⑥ Buttress – ⑦ Pier of a flying buttress (abutment) – ⑧ Flight or span of flying buttress – ⑨ Double-course flying buttress – ⑩ Pinnacle – ⑪ Side chapel – ⑫ Radiating or apsidal chapel – ⑬ Clerestory windows – ⑭ Side doorway – ⑮ Gable – ⑯ Pinnacle – ⑰ Spire over the transept crossing.

illustration IV

Groined vaulting:
① Main arch – ② Groin
③ Transverse arch

illustration V

Oven vault:
termination of a barrel
vaulted nave

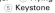

illustration VI

Lierne and tierceron vaulting:
① Diagonal – ② Lierne
③ Tierceron – ④ Pendant
⑤ Corbel

illustration VII

Quadripartite vaulting:
① Diagonal – ② Transverse
③ Stringer – ④ Flying buttress
⑤ Keystone

▼ illustration VIII

Doorway: ① Archivolt. Depending on the architectural style of the building this can be rounded, pointed, basket-handled, ogee or even

adorned by a gable – ② Arching, covings (with string courses, mouldings, carvings or adorned with statues). Recessed arches or orders form the archivolt – ③ Tympanum – ④ Lintel – ⑤ Archshafts – ⑥ Embrasures. Arch shafts, splaying sometimes adorned with statues or columns – ⑦ Pier (often adorned by a statue) – ⑧ Hinges and other ironwork.

illustration IX ▶

Arches and pillars: ① Ribs or ribbed vaulting – ② Abacus – ③ Capital – ④ Shaft – ⑤ Base – ⑥ Engaged column – ⑦ Pier of arch wall – ⑧ Lintel – ⑨ Discharging or relieving arch – ⑩ Frieze.

Military architecture

illustration X

Fortified enclosure: ① Hoarding (projecting timber gallery) – ② Machicolations (corbelled crenellations) – ③ Barbican – ④ Keep or donjon – ⑤ Covered watchpath – ⑥ Curtain wall – ⑦ Outer curtain wall – ⑧ Postern.

illustration XI

Towers and curtain walls: ① Hoarding – ② Crenellations – ③ Merlon – ④ Loophole or arrow slit – ⑤ Curtain wall – ⑥ Bridge or drawbridge.

◀ illustration XII

Fortified gatehouse: ① Machicolations – ② Watch turrets or bartizan – ③ Slots for the arms of the drawbridge – ④ Postern.

illustration XIII ▶

Star fortress: ① Entrance – ② Drawbridge – ③ Glacis – ④ Ravelin or half-moon – ⑤ Moat – ⑥ Bastion – ⑦ Watch turret – ⑧ Town – ⑨ Assembly area.

GLOSSARY OF ARCHITECTURAL TERMS USED IN THE GUIDE

Aisle: illustration I.
Altarpiece: illustration XVII.
Ambulatory: illustration I.
Apse: illustration I.
Apsidal chapel: illustration I.
Arcade: a range of arches within a larger arch.
Archivolt: illustration VIII.
Atlantes: supports in the form of caved male figures.
Axial or Lady Chapel: illustration I.
Bailey: open space or court of stone-built castle.
Barrel vaulting: illustration II.
Bartizan: a battlemented parapet.
Basket-handled arch: depressed arch common to late medieval and Renaissance architecture.
Bastion: illustration XIII.
Bay: illustration II.
Bracket: small supporting piece of stone or timber to carry a beam or cornice.
Brattice: a temporary wooden gallery or parapet for use during a siege.
Buttress: illustration II.
Capital: illustration IX.
Caryatids: supports in the form of carved female figures.
Cheekpiece: illustration XVIII.
Chevet: French term for the altar end of a church; illustration I.
Chi Rho: monogram of Christ comprising the Greek letters X and P.
Clamp: metal clamp joining two pieces of stone.
Coffered ceiling: vault or ceiling decorated with sunken panels.
Corbel: see bracket; illustration VI.
Crypt: underground chamber or chapel.
Curtain wall: illustration X.
Diagonal ribs: illustrations VI and VII.
Embrasure: splay of window or door; illustration VIII.
Entablature: that part of an order above the column comprising the architrave, frieze and cornice.
Flamboyant: latest phase (15C) of French Gothic architecture; name taken from the undulating (flame-like) lines of the window tracery.
Fresco: mural paintings executed on wet plaster.
Gable: triangular upper portion of a wall to carry a pitched roof; illustration III.
Gallery: illustration II.
Gargoyle: illustration III.
Groined vaulting: illustration IV.
Hypocaust: underground heating duct.
Keel vaulting: resembling an inverted ship's hull.
Keep: illustration X.
Keystone: middle and topmost stone in an arch or vault; illustration VII.
Lancet arch: arch with a pointed head.
Lancet window: high and narrow window terminating in a lancet arch.
Lavabo or lavatory: a trough for washing the hands in a monastery.
Lintel: illustration VIII.
Lists: a space enclosed by palisades in which jousting took place.
Machicolations: illustration X.
Mandorla: almond-shaped.
Misericord: illustration XVIII.
Moat: ditch generally water-filled.
Mullion: vertical post dividing a window.
Narthex: vestibule or portico at the west end of some early Christian churches.
Niello: inlaid enamel work.
Nimbus: halo.
Oculus: round window.
Organ case and loft: illustration XIV
Ovan vaulting: illustration V.
Parapet walk: see sentry walk; illustration X.
Parclose screen: screen separating a chapel or the choir from the rest of the church; illustration XVIII.
Pepperpot roof: conical in shape.
Peristyle: a range of columns surrounding or on the façade of a building.
Phylactery: an inscribed scroll; an amulet.
Pier: illustration VIII.
Pietà: Italian term designating the Virgin Mary with the dead Christ on her knees.
Pilaster: engaged rectangular column.
Pinnacle: illustration II and III.
Porch: covered area before the entrance to a building.
Postern: illustrations X and XII.
Rib vaulting: illustrations VI and VII.
Recessed tomb: funerary niche.
Retable: illustration XVII.
Rood beam: illustration XVI.
Rood loft or screen: illustration XV.
Rose window: illustration XVII.
Sentry walk: illustration X.
Spire: illustration III.
Stalls: illustration XVIII.

35

Tau cross: T-shaped.
Telamones: supports in the form of carved male figures.
Torus: large convex moulding semicircular in shape at the base of a column or pedestal.
Tracery: intersecting stone ribwork in the upper part of a window.
Transept: illustration I.
Triforium: illustration II.
Triptych: three panels hinged together, chiefly used as an altarpiece.
Tunnel vaulting: see barrel vaulting.
Twinned: columns or pilasters grouped in twos.
Voussoir: wedge-shaped stone forming part of an arch or vault; illustration XIII.
Wall walk: see sentry walk; illustration X.

illustration XIV

illustration XV

Rood screen : It replaced the rood beam in larger churches and was used for preaching and reading the Epistle and Gospel. From the 17C onwards many were removed as they tended to hide the altar.

Rood beam : It extends across the chancel arch and carries a Crucifix flanked by statues of the Virgin and St John and sometimes other people present on Calvary.

illustration XVI

Organ
① great organ case
② little organ case
③ caryatids
④ loft

illustration XVII

Altar with retable or altarpiece
① retable or altarpiece
② predella
③ crowning piece — ④ altar table
⑤ altar front

illustration XVIII

Stalls
① high back
② elbow rest
③ cheekpiece
④ misericord

Romanesque, Gothic and Renaissance elevations

11C-12C	**13C**	**Late 13C-14C**	**15C**	**16C**
Romanesque	Lancet Gothic	Rayonnant Gothic	Flamboyant Gothic	Renaissance

RELIGIOUS ARCHITECTURE

Romanesque art (11C-12C)

Orléanais – The church in Germigny-des-Prés, which dates from the Carolingian period, and the Benedictine basilica of St Benedict are remarkable.
There are two fine churches in the Cher Valley in St-Aignan and Selles.

Touraine – Various influences from Poitou are evident: apses with column buttresses, domed transepts, doorways without pediments.
The belltowers are unusual: square or octagonal with spires surrounded at the base by turrets.

Anjou – The Angevin buildings are clustered in the region round Baugé and Saumur. Cunault church shows the influence of Poitou in the ogive-vaulted nave buttressed by high aisles with groined vaulting.
The domes roofing the nave of the abbey

Romanesque doorway
Saumur — St Peter's Church

church at Fontevraud and the absence of aisles are features of the Aquitaine school.

From Romanesque to Gothic

The **Plantagenet style,** which is also known as **Angevin,** takes its name from Henry Plantagenet *(qv).* It is a transitional style which reached the height of its popularity early in the 13C and was abandoned before its end.

Angevin vaulting – In ordinary Gothic vaulting all the keystones are at the same level but in Plantagenet architecture the vaulting is curved so that the central keystone was about 3m - 10ft higher than the supporting arches; the best example is St Maurice's Cathedral in Angers.
At the end of the 12C Angevin vaulting grew lighter; slimmer and more numerous ribs sprang from slender round columns. Early in the 13C the high lierne vaulting was decorated with elegant sculptures.
The Plantagenet style spread from the Loire Valley into the Vendée, Poitou, Saintonge and the Garonne Valley. At the end of the 13C it was introduced by Charles of Anjou to southern Italy.

Angevin vaulting

| Mid 12C | Late 12C | Early 13C |

St Maurice's Cathedral, Angers   Chancel of St Sergius' in Angers

Gothic art (12C-15C)

Gothic art is characterised by the use of intersecting vaults and the pointed arch. The triforium, which originally was blind, is pierced by apertures which eventually give way to high windows *(illustrations p 36).* The tall, slender columns, which were topped by capitals supporting the vaulting, were at first cylindrical but were later flanked by engaged columns. In the final development the capitals were abandoned and the roof ribs descended directly into the columns.
The **Flamboyant style** follows this pattern; the diagonal ribs are supplemented by other, purely decorative, ribs called liernes and tiercerons *(illustrations p 33).*
The Flamboyant style (15C) of architecture is to be found in the façade of Holy Trinity in Vendôme and of St-Gatien in Tours, in Notre-Dame de Cléry and in the Sainte-Chapelle at Châteaudun.

Renaissance and Classical Styles (16C-17C-18C)

Italian influence is strong in the decoration of churches in the **Renaissance** period: basket-handle or round-headed arches, numerous recesses for statues. Montrésor church and the chapels at Ussé, Champigny-sur-Veude and La Bourgonnière are of particular interest.
In the **classical** period (17C-18C) religious architecture strove for a majestic effect: superimposed Greek orders, pediments over doorways, domes and flanking vaulting. The church of Notre-Dame-des-Ardilliers in Saumur has a huge dome; St Vincent's in Blois is dominated by a scrolled pediment.

SECULAR ARCHITECTURE

Gothic Period

In addition to the castles built for the Dukes of Anjou, such as Saumur, manor houses and mansions were constructed in the 14C for merchants who had grown rich through trade.

The 15C saw a proliferation in the lively ornate Gothic style of châteaux built of brick with white stone facings, such as the château at Lassay, of manor houses such as Le Clos-Lucé near Amboise, of town mansions with projecting stair turrets and high dormers, and of half-timbered houses. The finest examples of Gothic houses are to be found in Le Mans, Chinon and Tours.

Gardens – Monastic gardens, such as those belonging to the abbeys in Bourgueil, Marmoutier and Cormery, consisted of an orchard, a vegetable patch with a fish pond and a medicinal herb garden.

In the 15C they were succeeded by square flower beds which were created by King René at his manor houses in Anjou and by Louis XI at Plessis-lès-Tours. A fresh note was introduced with shady arbours and fountains where the paths intersected; entertainment was provided by animals at liberty or kept in menageries or aviaries.

Renaissance Period

The Renaissance did not spring into being at the wave of a magic wand at the end of the Italian campaigns. Before the wars in Italy, Italian artists had been made welcome at the French court and the court of Anjou; Louis XI and King René had employed sculptors and medallion makers such as Francesco Laurana, Niccolo Spinelli and Jean Candida.

New blood, however, was imported into local art by the arrival of artists from Naples in 1495 at the behest of Charles VIII.

At Amboise and Chaumont and even at Chenonceau, Azay or Chambord, the châteaux still looked like fortresses but the machicolations assumed a decorative role. Large windows flanked by pilasters appeared in the façades which were decorated with medallions; the steep roofs were decorated with lofty dormers and carved chimneys. The Italian influence is most apparent in the low-relief ornamentation. At Chambord and Le Lude the décor was refined by local masters such as Pierre Trinqueau.

Renaissance Decoration

Azay-le-Rideau Château
Grand staircase frieze
① Shell — ② Urn
③ Scroll — ④ Dragon
⑤ Putto — ⑥ Cupid
⑦ Horn of plenty
⑧ Satyr

The Italian style is most obvious in the exterior of the François I wing at Blois where Il Boccadoro copied Bramante's invention, the rhythmic façade which was composed of alternating windows and niches separated by pilasters. Later, as in Beaugency town hall, came semicircular arches and superimposed orders, then the domes and pavilions which mark the birth of classical architecture.

The Italians created new types of staircases: two spirals intertwined as at Chambord, or straight flights of steps beneath coffered ceilings as at Chenonceau, Azay-le-Rideau and Poncé.

The Renaissance also inspired a number of town halls – Orléans, Beaugency, Loches – and several private houses – Hôtel Toutin in Orléans, Hôtel Gouin in Tours and the Hôtel Pincé in Angers.

Gardens – In his enthusiasm for Neapolitan gardens, Charle VIII brought with him from his kingdom in Sicily a gardener called **Dom Pacello de Mercogliano,** a Neapolitan monk, who laid out the gardens at Amboise and Blois; Louis XII entrusted him with the royal vegetable plot at Château-Gaillard near Amboise.

Pacello popularised the use of ornate flowerbeds bordered with yew and fountains with sculpted basins. The gardens of Chenonceau and Villandry *(qv)* give a good idea of his style.

The extraordinary vegetable garden at Villandry, which is laid out in a decorative pattern in the style popular during the Renaissance, still has certain traditional medieval and monastic features; the rose trees, planted in a symmetrical pattern, symbolise the monks, each digging in his own plot.

Classical Period (17C-18C)

Following the removal of the court to Ile-de-France, architecture in the Loire Valley went into decline. Handsome buildings were still constructed but the designers came from Paris.

In the more austere climate of the 17C the pompous style of the Sun King displaced the graceful fantasy of the Renaissance and the picturesque asymmetry of the medieval buildings. The fashion was for pediments, domes (Cheverny Château, *qv*) and the Greek orders (Gaston d'Orléans wing of Blois Château). Tower structures were abandoned in favour of rectangular pavilions containing huge rooms with monumental chimneys decorated with caryatids and painted ceilings with exposed beams; the pavilions were covered with steep roofs in the French style.

There was a new wave of château building – Ménars, Montgeoffroy – but the main legacy of the 18C is in the towns. Great terraces were built in Orléans, Tours and Saumur with long perspectives aligned on the axis of magnificent bridges which had level roadways.

STAINED GLASS

A **stained-glass window** is made up of pieces of coloured glass fixed with lead to an iron frame. The perpendicular divisions of a window are called **lights.** Metal oxides were added to the constituent materials of white glass to give a wide range of colours.

Details were often drawn in with dark paint and fixed by firing. Varied and surprising effects were obtained by altering the length of firing and by the impurities in the oxides and defects in the glass. The earliest stained-glass windows were made in the 10C but none has survived.

12C-13C — The colours were intense and brilliant with blues and reds predominating; the glass and leading were thick and smoothed down with a plane; the subject matter was naive and confined to superimposed medallions.

The Cistercians favoured grisaille windows which were composed of clear-to-greenish glass with foliage designs on a cross-hatched background which gives a greyish **(grisaille)** effect.

14C-15C — The master-glaziers discovered how to make a golden yellow; lighter colours were developed, the leading became less heavy as it was no longer produced by hand, the glass was thinner and the windows larger. Gothic canopies appeared over the human figures.

16C — Windows became delicately coloured pictures in thick lead frames, often copied from Renaissance canvases with strict attention to detail

13C stained-glass window (detail)
Angers Cathedral

and perspective; there are examples at Champigny-sur-Veude, Montrésor and Sully-sur-Loire.

17C-18C-19C — Traditional stained glass was often replaced by vitrified enamel or painted glass without lead surrounds. In Orléans Cathedral there are windows with white diamond panes and gold bands (17C) and 19C windows depicting Joan of Arc.

20C — The need to restore or replace old stained glass stimulated a revival of the art. Representational or abstract compositions of great variety emerged from the workshops of the painter-glaziers: Max Ingrand, Alfred Manessier and Jean Le Moal.

MURAL PAINTINGS AND FRESCOES

In the Middle Ages the interiors of ecclesiastical buildings were decorated with paintings, motifs or edifying scenes. A school of mural painting akin to the one in Poitou developed in the Loire region. The remaining works of this school are well preserved owing to the mild climate and low humidity. The paintings are recognisable by the weak matt colours against light backgrounds. The style is livelier and less formalised than in Burgundy or the Massif Central while the composition is more sober than in Poitou. Two techniques were used: **fresco work**, which was done with watercolours on fresh plaster thus eliminating any retouching ; and **mural painting,** where the colours were applied to a dry surface and which was therefore less durable.

Romanesque Period – The art of fresco work with its Byzantine origins was adopted by the Benedictines of Monte Cassino in Italy, who in turn transmitted the art to the monks of Cluny in Burgundy. The latter used this art form in their abbeys and priories whence it spead throughout the whole country.

FRESCOES AND MURAL PAINTINGS
Romanesque period
Gothic period
Renaissance
Pilgrim's road

The technique – The fresco technique was the one most commonly used, although beards and eyes were often added when the plaster was dry so that they are usually no longer visible. The figures, drawn in red ochre, were sometimes highlighted with touches of black, green and the sky blue so characteristic of the region.

The subject matter – The subjects, which were often inspired by smaller-scale works, were intended to instruct the faithful in the truths of religion and also to instil a fear of sin and Hell. The most common theme for the oven vaulting was Christ the King enthroned, majestic and severe; the reverse of the façade often carried the Last Judgement; the walls depicted scenes from the New Testament while the Saints and Apostles adorned the pillars. Other frequently-portrayed subjects are the Contest between the Vices and the Virtues, and the Labours of the Months.

The most interesting examples – Good examples of fresco painting are found throughout the Loir Valley in Areines, Souday, St-Jacques-des-Guérets, Lavardin and especially St-Gilles Chapel in Montoire. There is also a fine work in St-Aignan in the Cher Valley. The crypt of Tavant Church in the Vienne Valley is decorated with lively paintings of high quality.

In Anjou a man called Fulk seems to have supervised the decoration of the cloisters in St Aubin's Abbey in Angers. His realistic style, although slightly stilted in the drawing, seems to spring from the Poitou school. More characteristic of the Loire Valley are the Virgin and Christ the King from Ponginé in the Baugé region.

Gothic Period – It was not until the 15C and the end of the Hundred Years War that new compositions were produced which remained in fashion until the mid 16C. These were more truly mural paintings than frescoes and new subjects were added to the traditional repertoire; a gigantic St Christopher often appeared at the entrance to a church *(see Amboise)* while the legend of the Three Living and Three Dead, represented by three proud huntsmen meeting three skeletons, symbolized the brevity and vanity of human life.

The most interesting examples – In the Loire Valley such paintings are to be found in Alluyes, Lassay and Villiers. Two compositions with strange inconography adorn the neighbouring churches in Asnières-sur-Vègre and Auvers-le-Hamon.

Renaissance – In the 16C paintings in churches became rarer. There are however two surviving examples from this period: the Entombment in Jarzé church and the paintings in the chapter house of Fontevraud Abbey.

GEMMAIL

Gemmail*(qv)* is a modern art medium consisting of assembling particles of coloured glass over a light source. The inventor of this art form was **Jean Crotti** (1878-1958). The Malherbe-Navarre brothers, an interior decorator and a physicist, provided the technical expertise; they discovered a bonding agent which did not affect the constituent elements.

TAPESTRIES FROM THE LOIRE WORKSHOPS

Hanging tapestries, which had been in existence since the 8C to exclude draughts or divide up great chambers, became very popular in the 14C. The weavers worked from cartoons or preparatory sketches using wool woven with silk, gold or silver threads on horizontal (low warp – *basse-lisse*) or vertical (high warp – *haute-lisse*) looms.

Religious tapestries – Owing to their value tapestries were used as investments or diplomatic gifts; as well as those commissionned for châteaux or even specific rooms, some were hung in churches or even in the streets. The most famous is the 14C Apocalypse tapestry *(see Angers)*.

Mille-fleurs – The *mille-fleurs* (thousand flowers) tapestries evoke late medieval scenes – showing an idealized life of enticing gardens, tournaments and hunting – against a green, blue or pink background strewn with flowers and plants and small animals. These are attributed to the Loire Valley workshops (*c*1500). Good examples exist in Saumur, Langeais and Angers.

Renaissance to 20C – Paintings replace cartoons and finer weaving techniques and materials render greater detail possible. The number of colours multiplies and panels are surrounded by borders. In the 18C the art of portraiture is introduced into tapestry work.

In the 20C **Jean Lurçat** *(qv)* recommended the use of natural dyes. Contemporary weavers experiment with new techniques and three dimensional effects.

Le Chant du Monde by Jean Lurçat, 1958
(Jean Lurçat Museum, Angers)

FOOD AND WINE

The Loire Valley is a region for good eating, cheerful drinking and calm digestion; it offers the visitor simple healthy cooking.
The following menu lists some of the local specialities and the best wines to accompany them.

Menu

HORS-D'ŒUVRE
Vouvray - Sancerre

Les rillons de Touraine.
Les rillettes du Mans, de Tours ou d'Angers.
Le boudin blanc bourré non de mie, mais de blanc de poulet.

POISSONS
Vouvray - Saumur - Montlouis - Sancerre - Rosés d'Anjou

Le brochet, le saumon, la carpe ou l'alose au beurre blanc.
La friture de Loire.
La brème farcie et surtout la matelote d'anguille au vin vieux.

VIANDES
Bourgueil - Chinon - Saumur-Champigny

Le gibier de Sologne.
Le carré ou la noisette de porc aux pruneaux.
Le cul-de-veau à l'angevine.
Le coq au vin du pays ou la fricassée de poulet.
Le chapon ou la poularde du Mans à la broche.

LÉGUMES

Les choux-verts au beurre.
Les asperges de Vineuil.
Les champignons farcis ou à la crème.
La salade à l'huile de noix.

FROMAGES
Bourgueil - Chinon

Crottins de Chavignol ; Olivet à la cendre.
St-Benoît ; Valençay ; Selles-sur-Cher ; Ste-Maure ; Vendôme.
St-Paulin ; crémets d'Anjou.

FRUITS

Les prunes et pruneaux de Tours, les melons de Tours.
Les fraises de Saumur, les abricots et les poires d'Angers.
Les Reinettes du Mans.

DESSERTS
Vouvray pétillant, Vouvray, Crémant de Loire
Saumur - Coteaux du Layon - Montlouis

Les macarons de Cormery.
Les chaussons aux pommes et toute la cohorte des cotignacs,
des confitures d'Orléans et des pâtisseries de Tours ; les tartes des demoiselles Tatin.
Pour digérer: d'excellents marcs, des liqueurs de fruits dont Angers a le secret.

Hors-d'œuvre: various types of potted pork; sausage stuffed with chicken meat.

Fish: pike, salmon, carp or shad with butter sauce; small fried fish from the Loire; stuffed bream and eels simmered in wine with mushrooms, onions and prunes (in Anjou).

Main course: game from Sologne; pork with prunes; veal in a cream sauce made with white wine and brandy; casserole of chicken in a red wine sauce or in a white wine and cream sauce with onions and mushrooms; spit-roasted capon or large hen.

Vegetables: green cabbage with butter; Vineuil asparagus; mushrooms stuffed or with a cream sauce; lettuce with walnut oil.

Cheese: St-Benoît, Vendôme and St-Paulin are made from cows' milk. Chavignol, Valençay, Selles-sur-Cher, Ste-Maur and crémets are made from goats' milk; the latter are small fresh cream cheeses; Olivet is factory-made with a coating of charcoal.

Fruit: plums and prunes from Tours; melons from Tours; Saumur strawberries; apricots and pears from Angers; Reinette apples from Le Mans.

Dessert: macaroons from Cormery; apple pastries; quince and apple jelly; preserves from Orléans and Tours pastries; caramelised apple turnovers.

Liqueurs: there are excellent marcs and fruit liqueurs, notably those from Angers.

Marcs: pure white spirit obtained from pressed grapes.

Local wines – The best-known white wines are from Vouvray, a dry, mellow wine with the flavour of ripe grapes, and Montlouis, with a delicate fruity flavour; both are made from the Chenin Blanc grape, known locally as the **Pineau de la Loire.**

The best-known red wine, known as Breton, is made from the Cabernet Franc grape which came originally from Bordeaux and produces the fine, light wines of Bourgueil and those from Chinon which have a stronger bouquet; the same grape is used to make a dry rosé which has charm and nobility. Among the wines of Anjou are the Rouge de Cabernet and the Saumur-Champigny which have a fine ruby glow and the subtle taste of raspberries. The Cabernet de Saumur is an elegant dry rosé with a good flavour. Another red wine comes from the Breton vines grown on the Loudun slopes.

The wines of Sancerre, on the eastern fringe of the châteaux country, are made from the Sauvignon grape and are known for their "gun-flint" flavour.

Less famous wines are the *gris meuniers* from the Orléanais and the *gascon,* which are pale and have a low alcohol content.

The slopes of the Loir produce a dry white and an acid-tasting red which improve with keeping. A light and pleasant white wine is made from the Romorantin grape which is grown only in the Sologne. The slopes of the Loire produce 15% of the entire *Muscadet* crop. The Ancenis-Gamay wine, made from Burgundy Gamay vines, is less well-known than the Gros Plant from Nantes *(see Michelin Green Guide Atlantic Coast)* as it is produced in smaller quantities. This light, dry, fruity wine, a perfect accompaniment to cooked pork meats, is produced in an area of about 350ha-865 acres around Ancenis *(qv).*

The character of the region is most apparent in the wine cellars which are often old quarries hollowed out of the limestones slopes at road level. They are therefore easily accessible so that the owner can drive his vehicles straight in. The galleries often extend for several hundred yards. Some open out into chambers where local societies hold their meetings and festivities.

The wine cellars also witness the reunions of the wine producers' brotherhoods *(confréries vineuses)* which preserve the tradition of good wine in the Loire Valley and joyously initiate new members *(chevaliers)* to their brotherhoods: *Les Sacavins* in Angers, *les Entonneurs rabelaisiens* in Chinon, *la Chantepleure* in Vouvray and the *Coterie des Closiers de Montlouis.*

In the temple of Bacchus – Behold the guest facing the barrels of the latest vintage, firmly fixed on their stands; they contain table wine *(vin ordinaire)* which flows into the silver goblet when the plug is drawn. The owner fills the glasses and the ruby-red nectar is held up to the light. The tumblers have no stem or foot so they cannot be set down until they are drained – *Nunc est bibendum* (now is the time to drink).

The wine is not to be swallowed in one draught but savoured first for its bouquet and then, after a knowing glance at one's neighbour, tasted in small sips. When the glass is empty, no words of appreciation are required, just a simple click of the tongue and the owner, his eyes shining, will say *"Ça se laisse boire...".*

From the huge pocket in his grey apron the owner produces an enormous key; the lock grates, the cellar is open. All round, projecting from recesses in the rock, are the coloured bottle tops of red, yellow, blue and white: full-bodied Sancerre; Vouvray which "rejoices the heart"; heady Montlouis; Chinon with its aftertaste of violets; Bourgueil with its hint of raspberries or wild strawberries and its Angevin brothers, sparkling Saumur, lively and spirited, white Saumur, dry and lively, wines from La Coulée de Serrant and the Layon. For the vintage years see the list printed in the current Michelin Red Guide France.

*The annual **Michelin Red Guide France***
revises its selection of establishments which
- *serve carefully prepared meals at a reasonable cost,*
- *include service on the bill or in the price of each dish,*
- *offer a menu of simple but good food at a modest price,*
- *provide free parking.*

It is well worth buying the current edition.

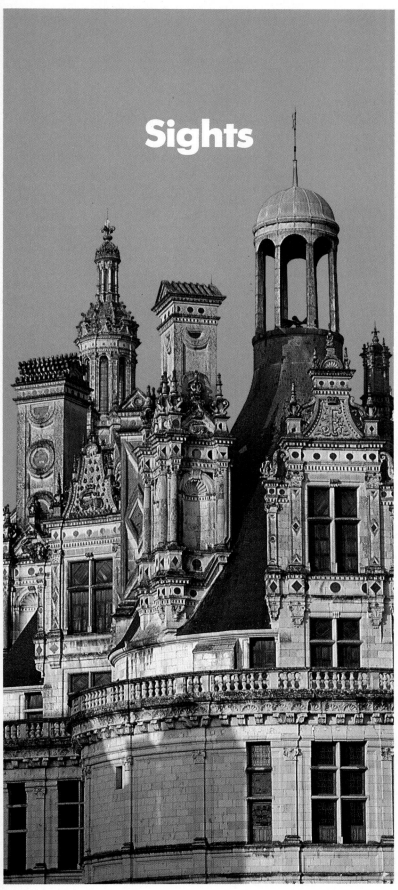

Sights

Michelin map 🟦 fold 16 or 🟦 fold 14 – Local map under LOIRE VALLEY: Orléans-Chinon – Facilities

The town of Amboise, which lies on the south bank of the Loire below the proud remains of its castle, appears at its most picturesque when seen from the bridge or the north bank of the river.

★★ CHÂTEAU

Son et Lumière – *See the Calendar of Events at the end of the guide.*

The rock spur above the town, on which the château ruins stand, has been fortified since the Gallo-Roman period. Before long a bridge was built which brought in revenue from tolls on the passage of goods and increased the strategic importance of Amboise *(1)*.

For a period in the 11C there were two fortresses on the heights and one down in the town; all three were engaged in perpetual warfare. Eventually the Counts of Amboise gained the upper hand and held the domain until it was confiscated by Charles VII (1422-61).

The golden age of Amboise was the 15C when the château was enlarged and embellished by Louis XI and Charles VIII. Although the end of the century (1496) marks the beginning of Italian influence on French art, there is little to see at Amboise, since the new building was by then well advanced. The Italian style was to gain in popularity under Louis XII and flourish under François I.

Charles VIII's taste for luxury – Charles VIII, who was born and grew up in the old castle, had since 1489 dreamed of enlarging and redecorating it in accordance with his taste for luxury.

Work began in 1492 and during the next five years two ranges of buildings were added to the older structure. Hundreds of workmen laboured continuously, if necessary by candle-light, to satisfy the king's desire to move into his new residence without delay. In the interim the king visited Italy where he was dazzled by the artistic standards and the luxurious life-style. He returned to France in 1495 laden with furniture, works of art, fabrics, etc. He also recruited to his service a team of scholars, architects, sculptors, decorators, gardeners and tailors... even a poultry breeder who had invented the incubator.

Charles VIII was particularly impressed by the Italian gardens: "They lack only Adam and Eve to make an earthly paradise". On his return he instructed Pacello to design an ornamental garden on the terrace at Amboise. Among the architects whom he employed were Fra Giocondo and Il Boccadoro; the latter, a leading figure in the introduction of Renaissance ideas into France, had worked at Blois and Chambord and on the Paris Town Hall.

A tragic death – In the afternoon of 7 April 1498 Charles VIII was escorting the queen to watch a game of real tennis in the castle moat when they passed through a low doorway in the outer wall. Although not tall, the king hit his head on the lintel. Apparently unscathed, he chatted unconcernedly as the game progressed. Suddenly, however, he fell back unconscious. He was laid on a bed of straw in an evil-smelling chamber and such was the consternation caused by his collapse that he was left there until 11 o'clock in the evening when he died.

The whirl of gaiety under François I – François d'Angoulême, the future François I, was only 7 when he came to Amboise with his mother, Louise de Savoie, and his sister, who was to become the famous and learned Margaret of Navarre. At Amboise, which Louis XII had appointed as his residence near to his own château at Blois, the young François, who was heir apparent to the throne, was given a thorough intellectual, sporting and military education. He continued to live at the château during the first three years of his reign and this was the most brilliant period in the life of Amboise. Magnificent festivities were organised to celebrate his engagement to Claude of France, his departure for Italy, the birth of the Dauphin, etc. Balls, tournaments, masquerades and wild beast fights followed one another in endless days given up to luxury and pleasure. A bevy of prostitutes was hired by the king to add to the enjoyment of the young noblemen of the court.

Amboise Château in 16C
Only the parts shown in black are extant

---

(1) In the Middle Ages there were only seven bridges between Gien and Angers. Troops then moved very slowly and the possession or loss of a bridge had a great influence on operations. Towns at bridgeheads drew great profit from the passage of merchandise.

The wing of the château begun by Louis XII was completed by François I and his mother between 1517 and 1520 at a cost of 230 000 livres. Such was the king's passion for the arts that he invited Leonardo da Vinci to live at Le Clos-Lucé *(qv)*. After 1519 he grew tired of Amboise and stayed there only for brief periods, as for example on his return from captivity in Italy in 1526.

On 18 October 1534 Amboise was involved in the affair of the placards: a pamphlet inveighing against "the huge, horrible and unbearable abuses of the papal mass" was fixed to the door of the royal chamber. François I was furious and decided to take repressive measures; the religious quarrel became acrimonious.

François returned to Amboise on 8 December 1539 where he received his old adversary, Charles V, with great pomp and ceremony.

At the end of his life François preferred to live at Chambord or Fontainebleau.

Amboise Conspiracy (1560) – The conspiracy casts a bloody reflection on the château. In the turbulent years leading up to the Wars of Religion a Protestant, **La Renaudie,** gathered round him in Brittany a body of reformists who were to proceed to Blois in small groups to ask the young king for the freedom to practise their religion and also no doubt to try to lay hands on the Guises, the bitter enemies of the Huguenots.

The plot was discovered and the court withdrew from Blois, which was indefensible, to Amboise where the king signed an edict of pacification in an attempt to calm things down. The conspirators, however, persisted and on 17 March they were arrested and killed as they arrived, including La Renaudie. The conspiracy was suppressed without mercy; some of the conspirators were hanged from the balcony of the château, some from the battlements, others were thrown into the Loire in sacks, the noblemen were beheaded and quartered. In 1563 there was a truce followed by an Act of Toleration, signed at Amboise, which brought an end to the first war of religion; the country settled down to four years of peace.

Destruction – Together with Blois, Amboise passed into the hands of Gaston d'Orléans, Louis XIII's brother and a great conspirator *(see Blois);* during one of his many rebellions, the château was captured by royalist troops and the outer fortifications were razed in 1631. It reverted to the crown and was used as a prison where Fouquet, his financial adviser, and the Duke of Lauzun, the lady-killer, were imprisoned by Louis XIV.

Later Napoleon granted the château to Roger Ducos, a former member of the Directory. As there were no subsidies for its upkeep, he had a large part of it demolished.

The château now belongs to the St-Louis Foundation which was set up by the Count of Paris to preserve the French national heritage.

TOUR ⏱ *time: 3/4 hour*

Terrace – The château is entered by a ramp which opens on to the terrace overlooking the river. From here there is a magnificent **view★★** of the lazy Loire and its verdant valley, the town's pointed roofs and walls. The Tour de l'Horloge is set above one of the town gates; to the west is silhouetted the Church of St-Denis with its squat bell-tower; and to the southeast Le Clos-Lucé can be seen.

In the time of Charles VIII the terrace was entirely surrounded by buildings. Festivals were held in this enclosed courtyard: tapestries adorned the walls, a sky-blue awning showing the sun, the moon and the stars gave protection from the weather.

St Hubert's Chapel (R E) – Curiously set astride the walls this jewel of Flamboyant Gothic architecture is all that remains of the buildings which once bordered the ramparts.

With pleasing proportions, finely sculpted decoration and crowned by a delicate spire, it is the work of Flemish masters who were brought to Amboise by Louis XI; they were also employed by Charles VIII before his admiration for Italian art began. Built in 1491 it was Anne of Brittany's oratory.

Before entering admire the Gothic door panels and the finely carved lintel: on the left **St Christopher** carries the Infant Christ while on the right **St Hubert**, the patron saint of hunting, looks at a cross which has appeared between the antlers of a stag.

Amboise — St Hubert's Chapel

TOURS N 152 • N 152 BLOIS • D 31, CHÂTEAU-RENAULT • A 10-E 05 • BLOIS, D 751

CHÂTEAU

LE CLOS-LUCÉ

0 — 300 m

Leclerc (Pl.)	B 10	Concorde (R. de la)	B 4	Martyrs-de-la-R. (Av.)	A 12
Nationale (R.)	AB	François-1er (R.)	B 6	Orange (R. d')	B 15
Victor-Hugo (R.)	B	J.-J. Rousseau (R.)	B 7	Voltaire (R.)	A 19

King's Apartments (Logis du Roi) – This is the only part of the château which escaped demolition *(see illustration p 44)*. The Gothic Wing, built against the Minimes Tower – both built by Charles VIII – overlooks the Loire while the Renaissance wing, set at a right angle, was constructed by Louis XII and raised by François I.

The tour includes a visit to the guardroom with its segmental ogive vaulting, the sentry walk with its beautiful view of the Loire, and several rooms, among them Henri II's bedchamber, which are furnished in Gothic or Renaissance style, hung with lovely tapestries and embellished with fine fireplaces.

The first floor apartments arranged for Louis-Philippe contain Empire style furniture and portraits of the royal family by Winterhalter, the official painter.

In the Gothic Wing, the **Hall of States**, restored early this century, is a large room built of brick and stone with ogive vaulting supported by a line of columns in the centre of the room. It was here that the Protestants headed by La Renaudie *(qv)* were judged; most of them were then hanged from the balcony, henceforth called "the Conspirators' Balcony". It was also the prison for nearly five years (1848-52) of the Algerian leader **Abd el-Kader**, the focus of resistance to French presence in the Mahgreb.

Minimes Tower (Tour des Minimes ou des Cavaliers) – This round tower is famous for its ramp which horsemen could ride up, assuring easy access for the provisioning of supplies. The ramp spirals round an empty core which provides air and light. From the top, one overlooks the northern face of the castle and the Conspirators' Balcony and there is a fine extensive view★★ of the Loire and its valley.

Heurtault Tower (Tour Heurtault) (B L) – Set in the château's south wall, this tower also has a spiral ramp. The carving on the sculpted corbels supporting the rib vaulting repays close study.

Gardens – These pleasant gardens lie where parts of the château once stood. The bust of Leonardo da Vinci is on the site of the collegiate church, where he was buried.

★LE CLOS-LUCÉ (B) ⊘ tour: 1 hour

A manor house of red brick relieved by tufa dressings, Le Clos-Lucé was acquired by Charles VIII in 1490. François I, Margaret of Navarre and their mother, the regent Louise de Savoie, also resided here.

In 1516, François I invited **Leonardo da Vinci** to Amboise and lodged him at Le Clos-Lucé where the great Renaissance man organised the court festivities and lived until his death on 2 May 1519; he was 67.

The wooden gallery in the courtyard gives a good view of the manor's main façade. On the first floor is the bedroom, restored and furnished, where Da Vinci died, as well as his studio. This is where he probably worked on schemes like his project for the draining of the Sologne or his design for a palace at Romorantin *(qv)* for Louise de Savoie.

On the ground floor is the oratory built by Charles VIII for Anne of Brittany, the salons with 18C wainscoting where Da Vinci probably had his workshops, the Renaissance reception room and the kitchen with its monumental chimney-piece.

In the basement is the museum of Leonardo's **"fabulous machines"**, a collection of models made by IBM based on the designs of this polymath who was a painter, sculptor, musician, poet, architect, engineer and scholar, and was four centuries ahead of his time. Note the entrance to the secret passageway which the King used on his visits to Da Vinci.

The grounds include gardens laid out in Renaissance style, from the terrace of which there is a view back to the château and over the river.

For visitors who wish to know more about Leonardo, there is a showing of a video describing his life, revealing not only the artist but also the humanist who considered the spiritual dimension in his scientific work.

ADDITIONAL SIGHTS

Postal Museum (Musée de la Poste) (B M¹) ⊘ – Housed in the early 16C Hôtel Joyeuse, the museum has fascinating collections evoking the development of postal services in France. On the ground floor are postillions' uniforms, **badges**, models of coaches and documents dating back to the days when the mail was exclusively "royal". The upper floors are devoted to

Le Clos-Lucé
François I buying the Mona Lisa from Leonardo da Vinci

the story of the letter post, accessible to one and all, and to developments such as the maritime service, air mail, and to systems of communication like Chappe's semaphore telegraph, cat's whisker Gody wirelesses...

The carriage room contains the famous pistols used by the Russian poet Pushkin in the duel that was to end his life in 1837.

Town Hall Museum (Musée de l'hôtel de ville) (B M²) ⊘ – *Entrance on Rue de la Concorde.* The former town hall, which was built early in the 16C for Pierre Morin, treasurer to the king of France, now houses examples of the royal signature, a 14C carving of the Virgin, Aubusson tapestries, portraits of the Duke of Choiseul and six rare 18C gouaches of Chanteloup Château, painted when it was at the height of its splendour.

Clock Tower (Tour de l'Horloge) (B F) – The tower, which is also known as the Amboise Belfry and was recently restored, was built in the 15C at the expense of the inhabitants on the site of a town gateway called l'Amasse. The pedestrian street below is very busy in the summer season.

Nearby on the old town ramparts stands **St Florentine's Church** (B), built at the behest of Louis XI.

St Denis' Church (Église St-Denis) (A) – This compact little church dates mostly from the 12C. Inside there are Angevin vaults and, in the nave, fine Romanesque capitals. The south aisle has a 16C Entombment, the recumbent figure known as the Drowned Woman *(Femme noyée)* and an interesting 17C painting of *Charles VIII welcoming St Francis of Paola to Amboise.*

MICHELIN GUIDES

The **Red Guides** *(hotels and restaurants)*

Benelux - Deutschland - España Portugal - Main Cities Europe - France - Great Britain and Ireland - Italia

The **Green Guides** *(fine art, historical monuments, scenic routes)*

Austria - Canada - England : the West Country - France - Germany - Great Britain - Greece - Ireland - Italy - London - Mexico - Netherlands - New England - New York - Paris - Portugal - Quebec - Rome - Scotland - Spain - Switzerland - Washington

...and the collection of **regional guides for France.**

Michelin map ⬛ fold 20 and ⬛ fold 11 or ⬛ fold 31 — Local maps under LOIRE VALLEY: Chinon-Champtoceaux and MAYENNE VALLEY.
See plan of the conurbation in the current Michelin Red Guide France

The former capital of Anjou stands on the banks of the Maine, formed by the confluence of the Mayenne and the Sarthe, 8km - 5 miles before joining the Loire. Today Angers is a lively town, especially in the pedestrian precinct of the old town and along the Boulevard du Maréchal-Foch.

A flourishing trade is based on Anjou wines, liqueurs, fruit and vegetables, seeds, flowers, medicinal plants and other horticultural products. The Sacavins wine brotherhood *(qv)* which was founded in 1905 organizes an autumn wine festival *(late September)*. There is an thriving electronics and car accessories industry. The **Anjou Festival** *(see Calendar of Events)*, with its many varied events (drama, music, dancing, poetry, art, etc), takes place throughout the Maine et Loire *département* and draws large crowds.

HISTORICAL NOTES

In the 1C BC Angers was at the centre of a community of hunters and fishermen. Their chief was Domnacus, who took to the heaths and forests and never submitted to the Romans who captured the city.

From Romans to Vikings — Angers-Juliomagus, the capital of the Andes tribe, covered 198 acres and flourished in the 2C. Unfortunately few traces of this brilliant past have survived. In the Late Empire the city went into decline and was obliged to confine itself to a small area (22 acres) on a slope above the River Maine; under the combined effect of the German menace of invasion and general impoverishment the population decreased. Christianity, on the other hand, continued to make progress and in 453 AD a church council met in Angers. Bishop Thalaise was one of the important ecclesiastical figures of the period, a scholar who protected and defended his city.

Angers' religious rise was not affected by the bloody quarrels of the Merovingian succession; the abbeys of St Aubin and St Sergius were founded in the 6C and 7C and soon attracted new settlements. Under the Carolingians the town recovered but was soon destabilised by the revolts of the nobility and the Viking invasions. In December 854 the Vikings pillaged Angers and withdrew. In 872 they returned and held the town for over a year. Charles the Bald, assisted by the Duke of Brittany, laid siege to the invaders and succeeded in dislodging them; a more or less legendary tradition says that Charles dug a canal intending to divert the waters of the Maine and when the Vikings realised that their ships would be grounded they fled in panic.

First House of Anjou (10-13C) — Under the early Counts, who were called Fulk, Angers enjoyed a particularly brilliant period.

The founders — The weakness of the throne at the end of the 9C permitted the emergence of independent principalities. The first Angevin dynasty was established in 898 by Fulk the Red, Viscount and then Count of Angers, a title which he handed down to his descendants. Fulk II the Good extended his territory into Maine showing scant regard for the King of France, pale Louis IV of Outre-Mer, whom he openly despised, while Geoffrey I Grisegonelle exacted homage from the Count of Nantes. The Angevins also played a more subtle game manoeuvring between the Robertians (ancestors of the Capets), who were well established in the region, and the Carolingians whose power continued to wane.

Fulk Nerra and his successors — The rise of the Angevin dynasty to the height of its power in the 11C and 12C was due to exceptional political skill, uninhibited by any scruples, remarkable ability in warfare and a keen eye for alliances through marriage. **Fulk III Nerra** (987-1040) was the most formidable of this line of feudal giants. Disruptive and aggressive, he was always making war to extend his territory; one by one he obtained Saintonge as fief of the Duke of Aquitaine, annexed the Mauges, extended his boundaries to Blois and Châteaudun, captured Langeais and Tours (he was expelled from the latter by Robert the Pious), intervened in the Vendômois, took Saumur etc. Ambitious, predatory, covetous, cruel and criminally violent, Fulk Nerra (the Black owing to his very dark complexion) was typical of the great feudal lord in the year 1000. From time to time he had sudden fits of Christian humility and penitence when he would shower gifts on churches and abbeys or take up the pilgrim's staff and depart for Jerusalem.

His son Geoffrey II (1040-60) continued his father's work consolidating the conquest of Maine and Touraine but he died without issue. The succession was divided between his two nephews who lost no time in quarrelling. Fulk IV finally gained the upper hand over Geoffrey III but at the cost of the loss of Saintonge, Maine and the Gâtinais which he was too lazy to recover. In 1092 his second wife, the young and beautiful Bertrade de Monfort, was seduced, abducted and married by King Philip I. For this scandalous behaviour the king was excommunicated *(see Beaugency)*. The position was redressed by Geoffrey IV Martel, who was killed in 1106, and most of all by **Fulk V the Younger** (1109-31), who took advantage of Anglo-French rivalry and made judicious marriage alliances. He recovered Maine through his own marriage in 1109; two years later with the family's approval he married his two daughters to the kings of France and England. His greatest success however was the marriage in 1128 of his son Geoffroy to Mathilda of England, daughter and heir to Henri I and widow of the German Emperor Henry V. His ultimate achievement concerned himself: in 1129, by then a widower, he married Melisand, daughter of Baldwin II and heir to the kingdom of Jerusalem. He founded a new Angevin dynasty in the Holy Land and consolidated the position of the Frankish kingdoms.

Geoffrey V (1131-51), known as Plantagenet because he wore a sprig of broom *(genêt)* in his hair, ruled with a rod of iron over "Great Anjou" (Anjou, Touraine and Maine) and tried to exercise his wife's rights over Normandy, which he annexed in 1144, and England, where Stephen of Blois had been king since 1135. Geoffrey died in 1151.

Plantagenets and Capets – In 1152 **Henry Plantagenet,** son of Geoffrey *(qv)* and Mathilda, married Eleanor of Aquitaine whom Louis VII had recently divorced. He already held Anjou, Maine, Touraine and Normandy; by his marriage he acquired Poitou, Perigord, Limousin, Angoumois, Saintonge, Gascony and suzerainty of the Auvergne and the County of Toulouse. In 1153 he forced Stephen of Blois to recognise him as his heir and the following year he succeeded him on the throne of England. He was now more powerful than his Capet rival. Henry II of England spent most of his time in France, usually at Angers. "He was a redhead, of medium height, with a square, leonine face and prominent eyes, which were candid and gentle when he was in a good humour but flashed fire when he was irritated. From morning to night he was involved in matters of state. He was always on the go and never sat down except to eat or ride a horse. When he was not handling a bow or a sword, he was closeted in Council or reading. None was more clever or eloquent than he; when he was free from his responsibilities he liked to engage in discussion with scholars." (M. Pacaut).

For the next fifty years there was war between the Plantagenets and the Capets. In the end it was the latter who were victorious: by relying on the subtleties of feudal law, they played upon the separatist tendencies of the individual provinces brought together in the Anglo-Angevin empire and the dissension dividing the Plantagenets. Philippe-Auguste inflicted a harsh blow when he captured the French territory of King John in 1205; this meant that Anjou and Touraine ceased to belong to the English crown but England and France continued to fight one another for supremacy until the end of the Hundred Years War.

Later Anjou Dynasty (13C-15C) – During the regency of Blanche of Castille, Anjou was again lost as a result of the barons' revolt when Pierre de Dreux surrendered the province to Henry III. Taking advantage of a truce in 1231 Blanche and her son Louis began to build the impressive fortress of Angers.

Anjou returned to the Capet sphere of influence and in 1346 St Louis gave it, together with Maine, to his younger brother Charles as an apanage. In 1258 it was confirmed as a French possession by the Treaty of Paris. In 1360 Anjou was raised to a duchy by John the Good for his son Louis. From the 13C to the 15C Anjou was governed by the direct line of Capet princes and then by the Valois. The beginning and end of this period were marked by two brilliant figures, Charles I and King René.

Charles of Anjou – Charles was an unusual personality – steeped in devotion and madly ambitious. At the request of the Pope, he conquered Sicily and the Kingdom of Naples and established his influence over the rest of the Italian peninsula. Intoxicated with success he dreamed of adding the Holy Land, Egypt and Constantinople to his conquests but the Sicilian Vespers returned him rudely to reality: on Easter Monday 1282 the Sicilians revolted and massacred 6 000 Frenchmen of whom half were Angevins.

Good King René – The last of the dukes was Good King René – titulary king of Sicily. He knew Latin, Greek, Italian, Hebrew and Catalan, painted and wrote poetry, played and composed music and was knowledgeable in mathematics, geology and law – one of the most cultivated minds of his day. He had the common touch and liked to talk to his subjects; he organised popular festivities and revived the old games of the age of chivalry. He loved flower gardens and introduced the carnation and the Provins rose. At twelve he married Isabelle de Lorraine and was devoted to her for thirty-three years until her death at 47 when he married Jeanne de Laval who was 21. Despite the odds, it was also a happy marriage. Towards the end of his life René accepted philosophically the annexion of Anjou by Louis XI. As he was also Count of Provence he left Angers which he had greatly enriched, and ended his days in Aix at the age of 72 (1480).

During the period of the Duchy a university was founded in Angers which flourished with from 4 000 to 5 000 students from ten nations.

Henri IV to the present – The Wars of Religion took on a bitter twist at Angers where there was a strong Calvinist church; on 14 October 1560 many people were attacked. Thereafter confrontations grew more frequent and in 1572 there was a massacre in the town.

It was in Angers Château in 1598 that Henri IV finally brought the troubles of the League to an end by promising his son César *(see Vendôme)* to Françoise de Lorraine, daughter of the Duc de Mercœur, the leader of the Catholic party. The marriage contract was signed on 5 April; the bride and groom were six and three years old. A week later the Edict of Nantes came into force; the Protestants had obtained freedom of worship. In 1652, although held by the forces of the Fronde, Angers had to submit to Mazarin; in 1657 the town lost its right to elect its local magistrates. After his arrest in Nantes Louis XIV's Finance Minister, Fouquet, spent three weeks in the château in the governor's apartments, guarded by d'Artagnan. By then the town had about 25 000 inhabitants and was slightly industrialised.

At the outbreak of the Revolution in 1789, Angers declared enthusiastically for the reformers. The cathedral was sacked and turned into a temple of Reason. In 1793 the defection of the Girondin administration allowed the Royalist Vendée party to capture the town between 20 June and 4 July. The Republicans lost no time in retaking it and the Terror claimed many victims.

In the early 19C Angers dozed until awakened by the arrival of the railway line from Paris to Nantes: the station was opened in 1849 by Louis-Napoleon. Modern development had begun and, apart from a pause early in this century, it has continued to increase during recent decades.

★★★ CASTLE (CHÂTEAU) (AZ)
time: 2 hours

Angers Castle

The **fortress** ⊘, which incorporates the former Plantagenet domain, was built by St Louis between 1228 and 1238 and is a fine specimen of feudal architecture in red schist and white stone. The moats, which were dug in 1485 by Louis XI, are now laid out as gardens. The seventeen round towers, strung out over 1km - 1/2 mile, are 40 to 50m - 131 to 164ft high.

Formerly one or two storeys taller they were crowned with pepperpot roofs and machicolations. The towers were lowered to the level of the curtain walls under Henri III during the Wars of Religion. The original order had been to dismantle the fortress, but the governor simply decapitated the towers and laid out terraces − to give the defenders a clear field of fire − and by the King's death most of the building was still intact.

From the top of the highest tower, the Mill Tower **(Tour du Moulin)**, on the north corner, there are interesting **views★** over the town, the cathedral towers and St-Aubin, the banks of the Maine and the gardens laid out at the foot of the castle, and, in the castle precincts, the series of towers on the curtain wall, the careful design of the gardens punctuated with topiary arches, the chapel and the Royal Apartments (Logis Royal), the home of the Dukes of Anjou in the 15C.

Continue by going round the **ramparts**, especially on the east side where a charming medieval garden is laid out with lavender, marguerites and hollyhocks growing in profusion, near vines like those which King René loved to plant.

★★★ Apocalypse Tapestry − Sheltered in a specially designed building this famous

tapestry is the oldest and largest which has come down to us. It was made in Paris between 1373 and 1383, commissioned by Nicolas Bataille for Duke Louis I of Anjou from Hennequin of Bruges' cartoons based on an illuminated manuscript of King Charles V. It was used at the marriage of Louis II of Anjou to Yolande of Aragon in Arles in 1400 and then at religious festivals until the end of the 18C when King René bequeathed it to the cathedral. It was later discarded as a piece of no value but restored between 1849 to 1870.

Originally 130m - 426ft long and 5m - 16 1/2ft high, it consisted of 6 sections of equal size, each with a major figure sitting under a canopy, their eyes turned towards two rows of 7 pic-

Angers
Apocalypse Tapestry (detail)

tures, the alternating red and blue backgrounds of which form a chequered design. Two long borders represent the Sky, filled with angelic musicians, and the Earth, strewn with flowers (first part missing).

The 76 pictures which have come down to us form a superb whole; the biblical text corresponding to each scene appears opposite the tapestries together with a reproduction of the reverse side.

One cannot remain unmoved by the scale of the work, the rigorous composition, as well as its great decorative value and purity of design. The tapestry closely follows the text of St John in the last book of the New Testament; to rekindle the hope of Christians shattered by the violent persecutions, the artist shows the victory of Christ in the form of prophetic visions and, after many ordeals, the triumph of his Church.

Chapel and Royal Apartments (Logis Royal) – These 15C buildings stand inside the enclosure. In the vast and light chapel, note the finely sculptured Gothic leaves of the door, the small separate ducal chapel with a fireplace, and on a keystone, the representation of the Anjou cross *(see Baugé)*. The adjacent staircase, the work of King René, reaches the upper floor of the logis.

★★**The Passion and Mille-fleurs Tapestries** – The Royal Apartments house a beautiful collection of 15 and 16C tapestries including the four hangings of the late-15C **Passion Tapestry**, which are wonderfully rich in colour, and several *mille-fleurs* tapestries. Among them are the **Angels carrying the Instruments of the Passion**, which is unusual in that it has a religious theme, the admirable 16C **Lady at the Organ** and the fragment showing **Penthesilea**, the Queen of the Amazons, from a hanging of the Nine Heroines, women with chivalrous virtues.

★★**OLD TOWN** *time: allow half a day*

Start from the château entrance and take the small Rue St-Aignan.

Crescent Mansion (Hôtel du Croissant) (AY B) – This 15C mansion, with mullion windows and accolade arches, housed the registrar of the Order of the Crescent (Ordre du Croissant), a military and religious chivalrous order founded by King René. The blason on the façade bears the coat of arms of St Maurice, patron of the order, a 4C Christian legionary put to death because he refused to kill his co-religionists. Opposite stand picturesque timber-framed houses.

Continue to the St-Maurice Ascent, a long flight of stairs which leads to the cathedral square (fine view of the cathedral).

★★**St-Maurice's Cathedral (Cathédrale St-Maurice) (BY)** ⊘ – This is a fine 12C and 13C building. The Calvary standing to the left of the façade is by David of Angers.

Façade – It is surmounted by three towers, the central tower having been added in the 16C. The **doorway** was damaged by the Protestants and the Revolutionaries, and in the 18C by the canons, who removed the central pier and the lintel to make way for processions. Notice the fine statues on the splaying. The tympanum portrays Christ the King surrounded by the symbols of the Four Evangelists; the graceful folds of the garments show skilful carving.

Above at the third-storey level are eight niches containing roughly carved, bearded figures in 16C military uniforms, St Maurice and his companions.

Interior – The single nave is roofed with one of the earliest examples of Gothic vaulting which originated in Anjou in the mid 12C. This transitional style known as Angevin or Plantagenet vaulting *(see illustrations p 37)* has the characteristic feature that the keystones of the diagonal (ogive) arches are at least 3m - 10ft above the keys of the transverse and stringer arches giving a more rounded or domical form. In Gothic vaulting all the keys are at roughly the same level. The vaulting of St Maurice covers the widest nave built at that time measuring 16.38m - 64ft across, whereas the usual width was from 9 to 12m - 30 to 40ft; the capitals in the nave and the brackets supporting the gallery with its wrought-iron balustrade are remarkably carved. The gallery is supported by a relieving arch at each bay. The Angevin vaulting in the transept is of a later period than that in the nave, with more numerous and more graceful ribs. The evolution of this style was to continue along these lines.

The chancel, finished in the late 12C, has the same Angevin vaulting as the transept. Its 13C stained glass has particularly vivid blues and reds.

The church is majestically furnished: high 18C organ (**A**) supported by colossal tela-mones, monumental 19C pulpit (**B**), high altar (**C**) surmounted by marble columns supporting a canopy of gilded wood (18C), 18C carved stalls (**D**) in front of which is a marble statue of St Cecilia by David of Angers (**E**). The walls are hung with tapes-tries, mostly from Aubusson.

St-Maurice's **stained-glass windows**★★ allow one to follow the evolution of the art of the master glaziers from the 12C to the present day.

There is a detailed printed description of the windows in the church; they are best examined through binoculars.

ST MAURICE'S CATHEDRAL

1 - St Catherine of Alexandria (12C).
2 - Dormition and Assumption of the Virgin (12C).
3 - The martyrdom of St Vincent of Spain (12C).
4 - Transept rose windows (15C): to the left Christ showing his wounds and to the right Christ in Majesty.
5 - North transept side windows (15C): St Rémi and Mary Magdalene.
6 - Chancel windows (13C) – from left to right: life of St Peter and St Eloi; St Christopher (16C); St Lawrence; the Tree of Jesse; St Julian; the life of Christ, and the lives of Saints Maurille, Martin, Thomas Becket and John the Baptist.

ANGERS

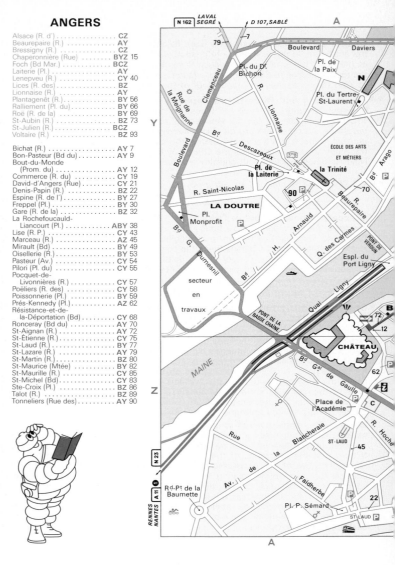

Alsace (R. d') . . . . CZ
Beaurepaire (R.) . . . . AY
Bressigny (R.) . . . . CZ
Chaperonnière (Rue) . . . . BYZ 15
Foch (Bd Mar.) . . . . BCZ
Laiterie (Pl.) . . . . AY
Lenepveu (R.) . . . . CY 40
Lices (R. des) . . . . BZ
Lionnaise (R.) . . . . AY
Plantagenêt (R.) . . . . BY 56
Ralliement (Pl. du) . . . . BY 66
Roë (R. de la) . . . . BY 69
St-Aubin (R.) . . . . BZ 73
St-Julien (R.) . . . . BCZ
Voltaire (R.) . . . . BZ 93

Bichat (R.) . . . . AY 7
Bon-Pasteur (Bd du) . . . . AY 9
Bout-du-Monde
  (Prom. du) . . . . AY 12
Commerce (R. du) . . . . CY 19
David-d'Angers (Rue) . . . . CY 21
Denis-Papin (R.) . . . . BZ 22
Espine (R. de l') . . . . BY 27
Freppel (Pl.) . . . . BY 30
Gare (R. de la) . . . . BZ 32
La Rochefoucauld-
  Liancourt (Pl.) . . . . ABY 38
Lise (R. P.) . . . . CY 43
Marceau (R.) . . . . AZ 45
Mirault (Bd) . . . . BY 49
Oisellerie (R.) . . . . BY 53
Pasteur (Av.) . . . . CY 54
Pilori (Pl. du) . . . . CY 55
Pocquet-de-
  Livonnières (R.) . . . . CY 57
Poëliers (R. des) . . . . CY 58
Poissonnerie (Pl.) . . . . BY 59
Prés-Kennedy (Pl.) . . . . AZ 62
Résistance-et-de-
  la-Déportation (Bd) . . . . CY 68
Ronceray (Bd du) . . . . AY 70
St-Aignan (R.) . . . . AY 72
St-Étienne (R.) . . . . CY 75
St-Laud (R.) . . . . BY 77
St-Lazare (R.) . . . . AY 79
St-Martin (R.) . . . . BZ 80
St-Maurice (Mtée) . . . . BY 82
St-Maurille (R.) . . . . CY 85
St-Michel (Bd) . . . . CY 83
Ste-Croix (Pl.) . . . . BZ 86
Talot (R.) . . . . BZ 89
Tonneliers (Rue des) . . . . AY 90

The modern windows of the chapel of Our Lady of Mercy and the south aisle bear witness to a revival of this art which had been in decline since the 16C.

Walk past the Bishop's Palace to reach Rue de l'Oisellerie.

At nos 5 and 7, there are two lovely half-timbered houses dating from the 16C.

Take the first road on the right.

★**Maison d'Adam** (BYZ D) – Picturesque 16C half-timbered house, with posts decorated with carved figures. It owes its name to the apple tree which appears to hold up the corner turret and was, until the Revolution, flanked by two statues of Adam and Eve. In the 18C this house was inhabited by a consulting judge called Michel Adam.

Continue along Rue Toussaint.

No 37 (BZ L) has a classical doorway, once the entrance to All Saints Abbey (Ancienne abbaye Toussaint). It leads to an elegant little courtyard flanked by a turret.

★**David of Angers Gallery** (Galerie David d'Angers) (BZ E) ⊘ – *33 bis Rue Toussaint.* The restored 13C abbey church houses practically the complete collection of plaster casts donated by the sculptor David of Angers to his native town; its Plantagenet vaulting has been replaced by a vast iron-framed glass roof, so that the appearance of the exhibition is influenced by the weather; it is at its best on a fine day.

The well-displayed collection comprises monumental statues (King René, Gutenberg, Jean Bart whose bronze statue stands in Dunkirk), funerary monuments (eg of General Bonchamps whose tomb is in the church of St-Florent-le-Vieil *(qv)*, busts of famous people of the time (Chateaubriand, Victor Hugo, Goethe, Balzac), and medallions in bronze of the artist's contemporaries.

In the chancel with its square east end lit by a rose window added in the 18C are exhibited terracotta studies, drawings and sketch books as well as the graceful *Young Greek Girl* which adorned Markos Botzaris's tomb. In a windowed recess stands the *Young Shepherd,* ideally placed against the greenery of the gardens of the modern public library.

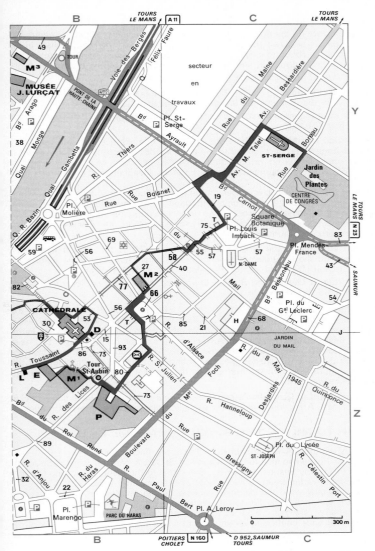

To the south of the church are the 18C cloisters with two remaining galleries *(restored)*.

Go around the east end of the church to reach Logis Barrault.

Logis Barrault (Fine Arts Museum) (BZ **M¹**) ⊘ – This beautiful late-15C residence was built by Olivier Barrault, the King's Secretary, Treasurer to the Brittany States and Mayor of Angers. In the 17C it was taken over by the seminary, whose pupils included Talleyrand *(qv)* the future Bishop of Autun.

On the first floor is a beautiful collection of medieval and Renaissance works: carved chests, statues (16C terracotta Virgin of Tremblay), enamels and ivories. Note the fine 13C mask on the recumbent statue.

The second floor is devoted to paintings: lovely primitives, two remarkable small portraits of Charles IX as a young man and Catherine de' Medici after Clouet; 17C paintings (Philippe de Champaigne, Mignard) and above all the 18C French school (Chardin, Fragonard, Watteau, Boucher, Lancret, Greuze) together with sculptures by Lemoyne, Houdon and Falconet; and 19C works including sketches by David, Ingres Géricault, Delacroix, landscapes by Corot and Jongking. There are also canvases by the local painters Lenepveu and Bodinier, and pastels (separate room) by Alexis Axilette, a native of the region, who was born at Durtal.

St-Aubin Tower (Tour) (BZ **F**) –12C belfry of the former Abbey of St-Aubin, a wealthy Benedictine abbey founded in the 6C. It took its name from St Aubin, Bishop of Angers (538-550), who was buried there.

★**Monastery buildings** (BZ **P**) ⊘ – The 17C abbey buildings are now local government offices. On the left-hand side of the courtyard is a glazed-in **Romanesque arcade★★**, part of the cloisters, with sculptures of remarkably delicate craftsmanship. The door with sculptured arching led to the chapter house; the arcades support a gallery from which those monks who had no voice in the chapter could listen to the proceedings; decorating the twin bay on the right of the door is a Virgin in Majesty with two censing angels while on the archivolt a multitude of angels bustle about; beneath this the scene of the Three Wise Men is painted: on the left Herod sends his men to massacre the innocents, while on the right the star guides the Wise Men.

The last arcature on the right has the best preserved scene of all: in the centre the unequal combat between David armed with his sling and the giant Goliath in his coat of mail is about to start; on the right the victorious David is cutting off the head of the vanquished and on the left he offers his trophy to King Saul.

Take Rue St Martin to reach Place du Ralliement.

Place du Ralliement (BY 66) – This lively square is the centre of town, its shops dominated by the monumental façade of the theatre.

Walk from the square into Rue Lenepveu and then take the first street on the left, Rue l'Espine.

★**Hôtel Pincé** (BY M²) ⊘ – The Hôtel Pincé is a Renaissance mansion built for a Mayor of Angers and bequeathed to the town in 1861. It houses the **Turpin de Crissé Museum,** originally based on the fine personal collection of this local painter (1772-1859) who was chamberlain to the Empress Josephine and a member of the Institut de France.

There are Greek and Etruscan vases on the ground floor and an Egyptian collection on the 1st floor. But the principal attraction is on the 2nd floor, a beautiful collection of Japanese ceramics, masks and engravings, the bequest of the Count of St Genys, nephew of Turpin de Crissé, as well as the Chinese collection (ceramics, bronzes, fabrics).

St-Laud District – The small Rue St-Laud (BY 77) is the axis of a pleasant pedestrian and shopping district, where several ancient façades can be seen: at no 21 Rue St-Laud (15C) and at no 9 Rue des Poëliers (16C) (CY 58).

Take Rue St Etienne and Rue du Commerce, then cross Boulevard Carnot to reach St Sergius' Church.

★**St Sergius' Church** (St-Serge) (CY) ⊘ – Until 1802 it was the church of the Benedictine abbey founded in the 7C. The 13C **chancel**★★ is remarkably wide, elegant and luminous, a perfect example of the Angevin style, with its lierne vaulting descending in feathered clusters on to slender columns. The 15C nave seems narrower because of its massive pillars. At the end the high windows are filled with graceful 15C stained glass depicting the Prophets (north side) and the Apostles (south side). On the rear wall of the chancel is a Flamboyant sacrarium where relics were kept.

Botanical Garden (Jardin des Plantes) (CY) – There are beautiful trees and a pool in the lower part. A section reserved for succulent plants forms an exotic garden.

NORTH BANK OF THE RIVER MAINE *tour: 1 hour*

★★**Lurçat Museum of Contemporary Tapestry** (Musée Lurçat) (ABY) ⊘ – The museum is housed in the former **Hospital of St John**★ (Ancien Hôpital St-Jean); founded in 1174 by Étienne de Marçay, Seneschal to the Plantagenet King Henry I, the hospital provided treatment and care for the sick until 1854.

The vast hospital ward has Angevin vaulting resting on slender columns; to the right of the entrance is the 17C former **Dispensary**★ with earthenware jars and trivets on the wooden shelves (1612). In the central recess stands a splendid pewter vessel (1720) once containing an antidote to snake bites.

The room is hung with a series of Lurçat tapestries called **Le Chant du Monde**★★ (The Song of the World). Jean Lurçat (1892-1966), who revived the art of tapestry, had discovered the *Apocalypse Tapestry (see Angers)* in 1938 and had been profoundly impressed by it; 19 years later he started the work displayed here, which constitutes his masterpiece. It consists of ten compositions with a combined length of 80m - 260ft, the fruit of years of research carried out by the artist himself; it is coarsely woven and characterised by an almost total lack of perspective and deliberate restriction of the range of colours. Evoking the joys and agonies of humanity in the face of Life and Death, it is an extraordinary synthesis of forms, colours and rhythms.

The doorway in the west wall leads to the Romanesque cloisters with a little garden and a collection of stonework.

The adjacent chapel has Angevin vaults and a Baroque high altar and gallery. Further west still is the former **granary** (N) with its twin bays. An annexe contains the Simone Lurçat bequest of paintings, ceramics and other tapestries made by her husband.

The extension to the museum has meant that the permanent exhibition with works by Gromaire, Daquin and Matégot, may now be displayed. The exhibits are shown in chronological order. One of the rooms is devoted to tapestries by T. Gleb. The ground floor is used for temporary exhibitions.

A short distance away, at no 3 Boulevard Daviers, the **Regional Textile Art Centre** (Centre Régional d'Art Textile) (BY M³) ⊘, which consists of a group of workshops for about twenty warp-weavers, organises exhibitions.

One may also watch artists working at their looms and in particular witness what is known as a *tombée* by well-known weavers. This is the important moment when the tapestry they have completed, which has been rolled up section by section over the long months of its creation, is finally unrolled in its entirety for the very first time.

★**La Doutre** (AY) – The district "across the Maine" (d'outre Maine) has kept its old timber-framed houses in good repair: in pretty Place de la Laiterie (AY), in Rue Beaurepaire which runs from the square to the bridge (no 67, which is ornamented with statues and dates from 1582, was the house of the apothecary Simon Poisson) and along Rue des Tonneliers (AY 90).

Holy Trinity Church (La Trinité) (AY) is a 12C building with a 16C belfry.

EXCURSIONS

Cointreau Distillery (Distillerie Cointreau) ⊘ *—Take the Le Mans road, northeast on the plan; turn right into Boulevard de la Romanerie to the St-Barthélémy industrial area.*
The famous orange-flavoured liqueur was invented by the Cointreau brothers in 1849. Various attempts to fake it are on display in the museum, as is the firm's own publicity material. There is an audio-visual presentation *(12 mins)* and the production area with its stills as well as the maturing floors can be visited.
The annual output of the plant amounts to some 28 million litres, three quarters of which is exported.

Pignerolle Château *– 8km - 5 miles east of Angers by D 61; on the outskirts of St-Barthélémy-d'Anjou.* The castle, which stands in a large public park of over 70ha - 173acres, is a replica of the Petit Trianon in Versailles. It was built in the 18C by an Angevin architect, Bardoul de la Bigottière, for Marcel Avril, King's Equerry and Master of the Riding Academy of Angers. During the Second World War the castle served successively as the seat of the Polish government in exile, the headquarters of the German admiral, Doenitz, and, after the liberation of France, the quarters for American units under General Patton.

Now thoroughly restored and redecorated, the castle houses the **European Museum of Communication**★ ⊘. The rich collection of scientific apparatus displayed in an instructive and lively manner traces the fascinating history of communication, the major steps in its development and the various modes of expression employed. The ground floor, dedicated to Leonardo da Vinci, shows the origins of communication – language, the written word, the measurement of time, music, the invention of printing (through which cultural exchanges took place for the first time), the history of electricity, and the advent of telegraphy with its impact on man from a sociological and cultural point of view. A modern sculpture composed of several elements representing locomotion announces the presence of another aspect of communication which is shown in the former stables under the name Phan-

European Museum of Communication
Aeroplane radio receiver (1918)

tasmagoria *(Fantasmagorie)*. On the first floor is an extensive retrospective of radio – which made instantaneous communication possible – (an entire room is devoted to radio sets from 1908 to 1960) and television (there is a reconstruction of a 1950s recording studio). The second floor displays reconstructions of the salon in Jules Verne's *Nautilus* and Armstrong's landing on the moon. The future is represented by a couple of Venusians.

Les Ponts-de-Cé *– Pop 11 032. 7km - 4 miles to the south by N 160.*
This is a straggling town about 2 miles long; its main street crosses a canal and several arms of the Loire, affording some fine views from the bridges. The history of this small town includes many bloody episodes. Under Charles IX 800 camp-followers were thrown into the Loire; when the château was taken from the Huguenots in 1562, any surviving defenders were treated to a similar fate. In 1793 numerous Royalists were shot on the island that surrounds the château.
On the edge of the road, overlooking the Loire, stand the remains of a château, an ancient 15C fortress crowned with machicolations.

St-Aubin's Church – This church, which was built in the Gothic style, has recently been restored after being gutted by fire in 1973. Some interesting items survived: altarpieces and statues (Christ in Captivity).

Trélazé *– Pop 10 539. In the eastern suburbs, road to Saumur.*
Trélazé is famous for its slate which has been quarried since the 12C. When the Loire was still a commercial highway, the blue-grey slates were carried upstream in boats to provide roofs for all the châteaux, manor houses and more modest residences which lined the banks of the river.

Slate Museum ⊘ – The museum, which is near a former quarry, presents the geological formation of slate, the old tools used in quarrying, the life of the men who worked in the quarries and the modern techniques.
There is a demonstration of old-style slate splitting given by former slatemen.

*The annual **Michelin Red Guide France***
offers comprehensive up-to-date information in a compact form.
An ideal companion on holidays, business trips or weekends away.

It is well worth buying the current edition.

AREINES

Michelin map **64** fold 6 or **238** fold 2 – 3km - 2 miles east of Vendôme – Local map: under LOIR VALLEY: Bonneval-Vendôme

Areines, a village in the Loir plain, was an important town in the Roman era.

Church – The plain façade is adorned by a 14C Virgin; the church itself is 12C. The interior is decorated with a group of **frescoes,** gracefully drawn and freshly tinted.
In the apse a majestic Christ is surrounded by evangelical symbols: the lion of St Mark, in stylised Byzantine manner; below are the Apostles with sky-blue haloes, typical of Loire Valley art *(p 39);* in the central window are warrior saints also with haloes.
The chancel vault shows the Lamb adored by angels; on the sides are the Annunciation and the Visitation, elegantly depicted, and the Nativity, partially effaced. The frescoes on the walls of the chancel seem to be of a later period: the Marriage of the Virgin is on the right.

ARGENT-SUR-SAULDRE

Michelin map **65** north of fold 11 or **238** northwest of fold 19

Print works, clothing factories, potteries and brickworks contribute to the commercial activity of this little town on the River Sauldre in the Sologne.

Château – The château was built on the banks of the Sauldre by the Sully family in the 13C; it now houses two interesting museums.

Trades and Traditions Museum (Musée des Métiers et Traditions de France) ⊘ – The museum's collections illustrate the life of country people from the 18C onward. There are reconstructed workshops (shoemaker, coppersmith, cooper) as well as agricultural implements, tools and household objects as made and used in the various regions of France. Leisure activities are evoked too with displays devoted to seasonal festivities. Particularly notable is a late-19C sorcerer's chair from Berry and a compass elaborately decorated with, the suits from playing cards.
The museum also houses a large collection of late-19C Gien faience.

Vassil Ivanoff Museum ⊘ – The Bulgarian ceramicist Vassil Ivanoff (1897-1973) worked in Borne *(east of Henrichemont),* a village with a number of potteries. The examples of his work exhibited here *(in the Intendance building)* demonstrate the richness of his imagination and his commitment to extracting the most from his raw material, clay. Vases, pots, cups, plates and strange tubular constructions take on a diversity of forms in an almost sculptural way; some of Ivanoff's most successful work is characterised by the use of copper oxide, giving an oxblood colour.

St Andrew's Church – The former château chapel is entered by a stout porch-belfry (16C) with a spire rebuilt in the 17C. In the keystone of the choir-vault is the crucified figure of St Andrew himself, while the baptismal chapel has a stunning 16C group of the Trinity.

EXCURSIONS

★**Étang du Puits, Cerdon** – *16km - 10 miles northwest. Cross the Sauldre and turn left into D 176.*

★**Étang du Puits** – The large and shining expanse of water covers 175ha - 309 acres in the heart of an oak and pine forest; there is a fine view from the road along the retaining dyke. There are facilities for regattas as well as a beach, pedaloes, rowing boats and a playground. There is plentiful fishing for carp, bream and pike which can weigh up to 15 pounds. The reservoir feeds the Sauldre Canal.
Go round the reservoir on D 765 and then continue to Cerdon.

Cerdon – Pop 929. A peaceful, well-kept village in the Sologne. In the 15C church are several paintings and handsome modern stained glass in the chancel.

★**Blancafort** – *8km - 5 miles southeast by D 8. See Blancafort.*

ARVILLE

Michelin map **60** southwest of fold 16 or **237** fold 37 – Local map under MONDOUBLEAU

The D 921 running south from Le Gault-Perche gives a good view of the Templar commandery which later passed to the Knights of St John of Jerusalem. The ironstone building in its rural setting makes an attractive picture.

The Templars – The order, which was both military and monastic, was founded in 1119 near the site of Solomon's Temple in Jerusalem. The members wore a white mantle bearing a red cross and were bound by their vows to defend the Holy City from the Moslems and protect all Christians making a pilgrimage to Jerusalem. To this end they built fortified commanderies on the main roads. A pilgrim would deposit a sum of money at his local commandery before setting out and in exchange for the receipt could draw the same sum on arrival in the Holy Land; thus the commanderies came to serve as banks in the 13C.
The Templars lent money to the Popes and to kings and princes, and grew rich and powerful. Early in the 14C the order of Templars numbered 15 000 knights and 9 000 commanderies. It had its own judicial system, paid no tax and took its authority directly from the Pope. Such wealth and independance created many enemies and brought about the order's downfall.

In 1307 Philip the Fair persuaded the Pope that the Templars should be brought to trial; he had every member of the order in France arrested on the same day. The Grand Master, Jacques de Molay, and 140 knights were imprisoned in Chinon castle; the following year they were brought to Paris. A trial was held in which they were accused of denying Christ by spitting on the Cross in their initiation ceremonies; 54 of them, including Jacques de Molay, were burned alive on one of the islets in the Seine. It was a brutal punishment although the order had sometimes acted degenerately.

Arville Commandery

The Commandery – The 12C chapel is crowned by a gable belfry which is linked to a flint tower, once part of the town walls. The town gateway (late 15C) is decorated with two brick turrets with unusual conical roofs made of chestnut slats.

*The **Practical Information** section at the end of the guide lists :*
- *information on travel, motoring, accommodation, recreation*
- *local or national organisations providing additional information;*
- *calendar of events*
- *admission times and charges for the sights described in the guide.*

★ ASNIÈRES-SUR-VÈGRE   Pop 338

Michelin map **64** northwest of fold 2 or **232** northeast of fold 20

Asnières lies in an attractive setting, deep in the picturesque Vègre Valley. The D 190 from Poillé provides an attractive view over the old houses with their pitched roofs, the church and a mansion called the Cour d'Asnières.

Bridge – This medieval hump-backed structure provides a charming **view★** of the river, of the old mill still in working order, in its setting of fine trees, and of the elegant mansion with its turret and dormer windows on the right bank. Close to the mill stands a château known as the Moulin Vieux dating from the 17C and 18C.

Church – The interior is decorated with Gothic **wall paintings★** – 13C in the nave and 15C in the chancel. The most famous, on the inside wall of the main façade, shows Hell. On the left Christ is preparing to release the souls trapped in Limbo by attacking the three-headed dog, Cerberus, with a lance; in the centre Leviathan is swallowing up the Damned; finally canine-headed demons are stirring a cauldron of the Damned in which one can see the wimple of the lady of the manor and the bishop's mitre.

The scenes on the north wall of the nave represent the Adoration of the Magi, Jesus' Presentation in the Temple and the Flight into Egypt. Note in the chancel a Baptism of Christ, a Flagellation and a Crucifixion.

Cour d'Asnières – Standing a little to the south of the church is a large, elongated Gothic building, with attractively paired windows. It was here that the canons of Le Mans, the one-time lords of Asnières, exercised their seigneurial rights, hence the name *cour* meaning court.

Verdelles Château ⊘ – *2.5km - 1 1/2 miles by the D 190 in the direction of Poillé.* This late-15C château has remained unaltered since its construction by Colas Le Clerc, Lord of Juigné. It marks the transition between the feudal castle and the stately home; four towers grouped closely together surround the central part of the château which has moulded windows. Note the attractive suspended turret decorated with Gothic arcades.

★ AUBIGNY-SUR-NÈRE   Pop 5 803

Michelin map **65** fold 11 or **238** folds, 18, 19
See town plan in the current Michelin Red Guide France

On the borders of Berry and the Sologne, little Aubigny is a busy place on the River Nère which here flows partly underground. Local activity centres on the fairs, the electric motor and precision instrument factories and the sports ground.

The Stuart City – In 1423 Charles VII gave Aubigny to a Scotsman, John Stuart, his ally against the English. He was succeeded by Béraud Stuart, who effected a reconciliation between Louis XI and his cousin, the future Louis XII, and then by Robert Stuart, known as the Marshal of Aubigny, who fought in Italy under François I.

Gentlemen and craftsmen from Scotland settled here. They established glass-making and weaving using the white wool from the Sologne. Before the 19C the importance of cloth manufacture was so great that the town was known as Aubigny-les-Cardeux or the Carders' Aubigny. Rue des Foulons recalls the days when cloth was dressed by fulling in the waters of the Nère.

SIGHTS

★**Old houses** – A number of early-16C half-timbered houses have survived. The oaks used in their construction were given by Robert Stuart from the nearby Forest of Ivoy. There are several along Rue du Prieuré and its continuation, Rue des Dames, charming and busy streets hung with shop signs from the Town Hall to the church, as well as in Rue du Charbon and Place Adrien-Arnoux. No 10 Rue du Pont-Aux-Foulons is the only house to have survived the fire of 1512. In Rue du Bourg-Coutant stands the **Maison du Bailli**★ with its carved beams, and almost opposite, at the corner of Rue de l'Eglise, the pretty **François I House.**

St Martin's Church – The church is built in Gothic style, marking the arrival of Ile-de-France influences in Berry. At the entrance to the chancel two 17C painted statues represent a charming Virgin and Child and a dramatic Christ Reviled, while in the chancel a 16C stained glass window depicts the life of St Martin. In the third chapel to the right there is an admirable 17C wood *Pietà*.

Stuart Château ⊘ – This 16C building was the work of Robert Stuart; altered by Louise de Keroualle, Duchess of Portsmouth, it now serves as Aubigny's town hall. The entrance gatehouse, dating from the time of Robert Stuart, is flanked by attractive brick bartizans; the keystone of the vault is emblazoned with the Stuart coat of arms. Pass into the charming irregular courtyard with its mullioned windows and round or polygonal turreted staircases. One of the rooms of the château is devoted to the life and work of **Marguerite Audoux** (1863-1937), the local writer whose novel about a shepherdess *Marie-Claire* is based on her own childhood.
In summer, the château hosts both the Festival of Mural Poetry and the Sologne Art Exhibition.

Duchess of Portsmouth's Park – These gardens, still called the Grands Jardins, were laid out in the 17C and adorned with clipped hedges, arbours and fine trees. They are named after Charles II's favourite who lived at La Verrerie Château *(see below)*.

Ramparts – The line of the old town wall, built originally by Philippe-Auguste, is marked by the streets enclosing the town centre and the two round towers overlooking the Mall which runs parallel to the Nère spanned by footbridges.

EXCURSIONS

★**La Verrerie Château** ⊘ – *11km - 7 miles southeast by D 89.*
The château stands in an isolated but beautiful **setting**★ near the Forest of Ivoy beside a lake formed by a broad stretch of the Nère. It is thought to have inspired Alain-Fournier for one of the episodes in his novel *Le Grand Meaulnes*.
The château originally consisted of four ranges of buildings round a courtyard; the oldest part was built by Charles VII who gave it to John Stuart at the same time as Aubigny-sur-Nère. At the end of the 15C Béraud Stuart built a château (house and chapel) which was completed during the Renaissance by his nephew Robert, Maréchal d'Aubigny. In 1670 the château reverted to the crown; in 1673 Louis XIV gave it to the Duchess of Portsmouth, the favourite mistress of Charles II of England.
The graceful **Renaissance gallery**★ was erected by Robert Stuart in 1525, the date when the frescoes were painted in the 15C chapel; the tabernacle in carved wood dates from the Renaissance. The 19C wing added behind the Renaissance gallery contains some fine furniture from the Renaissance to the Louis XVI period; two 18C Beauvais tapestries hang in the dining room; the Renaissance cupboard in the salon contains four remarkable 15C alabaster **weepers**★ from the tomb of Jean de Berry.
The boudoir displays a collection of 19C dolls together with their furniture as well as the library of **Melchior de Vogüé** (1829-1916), a member of the Académie Française, a diplomat and archaeologist who directed excavations in Palestine and Syria.

Join us in our constant task of keeping up-to-date.
Please send us your comments and suggestions.
MICHELIN TYRE
Public Limited Company
Tourism Department - The Edward Hyde Building
38 Clarendon Road - WATFORD Herts WD1 1SX

Michelin map ▨▨ fold 14 or ▨▨▨ fold 35 – Local map under LOIRE VALLEY: Orléans-Chinon – Facilities

Strategically sited at a bridging point on the Indre on the main road from Tours to Chinon, Azay was soon fortified. It is named after one of its lords, Ridel or Rideau d'Azay, who was knighted by Philippe-Auguste and built a strong castle.

The most tragic incident in its history was the massacre of 1418. When Charles VII was Dauphin he was insulted by the Burgundian guard as he passed through Azay. Instant reprisals followed. The town was seized and burnt and the Captain and his 350 soldiers were executed. Azay was called Azay-le-Brûlé (Azay the Burnt) until the 18C.

A financier's creation (16C) – When it rose from its ruins Azay became the property of **Gilles Berthelot**, one of the great financiers of the time. He had the present delightful mansion built between 1518 and 1527. His wife, **Philippa Lesbahy**, directed the work, as Catherine Briçonnet had directed that of Chenonceau.

But under the monarchy, fortune's wheel turned quickly for financiers. The rich Semblançay ended his career on the gibbet at Montfaucon. Berthelot saw the fatal noose draw near, took fright, fled and later died in exile. François I confiscated Azay and gave it to the Captain of his Guard.

In the 19C one of the many subsequent owners rebuilt the great north tower and added a corner tower on the east.

In 1870, when Prince Frederick-Charles of Prussia was staying in the château, one of the chandeliers crashed down on to the table. The Prince thought that his life was being threatened and Azay barely escaped further retribution. In 1905 the château was bought by the State for 200 000 francs.

★★**Son et Lumière** – *See the Calendar of Events at the end of the guide. Entrance in Rue de Pineau.*

TOUR ⊘ *time: 3/4 hour*

A tree-clad setting on the banks of the Indre provides the backdrop for the Château d'Azay, one of the gems of the Renaissance. Similar to Chenonceau, but less grandiose, its lines and dimensions suit the site so perfectly that it gives an unforgettable impression of elegance and harmony. Though Gothic in outline, Azay is modern in its bright appearance and its living accommodation. The medieval defences are purely symbolic and testify only to the high rank of the owners. The massive towers of other days have given way to harmless turrets with graceful forms. Dormer windows spring from the corbelled sentry walk, the machicolations lend themselves to ornament and the moats are mere placid reflecting pools.

Partly built over the Indre, the château consists of two main wings at right angles. The decoration shows the influence of the buildings erected by François I at Blois: pilasters flank the windows, double entablatures separate the storeys but here there is a strict symmetry throughout the design of the building.

The château's most striking feature is the **grand staircase** with its three storeys of twin bays forming open loggias and its elaborately decorated pediment. At Blois the staircase is still spiral and projects from the façade; at Azay as at Chenonceau which was built a few years earlier, it is internal with a straight ramp.

The reflection in the water and the varnished wooden boats, specially built for the Son et Lumière show and moored at the water's edge, add to the gentle melancholy of the site and, together with the rows of houses and gardens along the River Indre, make excellent subjects for photographs.

Azay-le-Rideau Château

AZAY-LE-RIDEAU CHÂTEAU

The interior is furnished and hung with tapestries. The dining hall has its original beams and linenfold panelling while the room known as François I's bedchamber has a chimneypiece decorated with the royal salamander.

ADDITIONAL SIGHT

St-Symphorien – This curious 11C church, altered in the 12C and 16C, has a double gabled **façade★**. Embedded to the right are remains of the original 5C and 6C building: two rows of statuettes and diapered brickwork. To the left above the basket-handle arched porch, there is a Flamboyant window (restored) which dates from the 16C.

EXCURSION

The Indre Valley from Azay to Pont-de-Ruan – *Round tour of 26km - 16 miles east - about 2 hours.*
Leave Azay going south by the bridge over the Indre which gives an attractive view of the château through the trees of the park.

Bear left immediately into D 17 and then right into D 57.

Villaines-les-Rochers – Pop 930. Wickerwork has always been the mainstay of the village. In the 19C Balzac wrote from the neighbouring Château de Saché: "We went to Villaines where the local baskets are made and bought some very attractive ones". The black and yellow osiers and green rushes are cut in winter and steeped in water until May when they are stripped and woven. This craft is traditionally handed down from father to son who work in troglodyte workshops (several troglodyte houses can be seen).

The Villaines-les-Rochers Cooperative ⊙, which was founded in 1849 by the parish priest, numbers about 80 families; a number of workshops have been set up where young craftsmen are trained, among them students from the national school of osier culture and basketwork at Fayl-Billot in Haute-Marne. The workshops can be visited and the craftsmen's work is on sale.

Return to D 17 by D 217 which runs beside the River Villaine.

Saché – *See Saché.*

Pont-de-Ruan – Pop 536. A beautiful picture appears at the crossing of the Indre: two windmills, each on an island, set among trees. The site is described at length by Balzac in *Le Lys dans la Vallée.*

Return to Azay via the D 84.

Every year
the **Michelin Red Guide France**
revises the town plans:
- *through routes, by-passes, new streets, one-way systems, car parks*
- *the exact location of hotels, restaurants, public buildings...*

Current information for easy driving in towns.

BAUGÉ
Pop 3 748

Michelin map 🔢 folds 2 and 12 or 🔢 fold 21 – Facilities

Baugé, a peaceful town with noble dwellings, is the capital and market town of the surrounding region, a countryside of heaths, forests and vast clearings. There is a good view of the town with its ruined walls from Rue Foulques-Nerra to the west.

Under the sign of the Cross of Anjou – Baugé, which was founded in 1000 by Fulk Nerra *(qv)*, became one of the favourite residences of Yolande of Aragon, Queen of Sicily, and her son, King René *(qv)*, in the 15C. Yolande, who was a faithful supporter of Charles VII and Joan of Arc, repulsed the English from Anjou at the battle of Vieil-Baugé (1421) in which Sir Guérin de Fontaines distinguished himself at the head of the Angevins and Scottish mercenaries.

René painted, wrote verses and hunted the wild boar in its lair *(bauge)* in the adjacent forests; he also prayed before the relic of the True Cross which was venerated at La Boissière Abbey *(qv).*

Once Louis XI had gained possession of Anjou, Baugé went into decline: the saying "I'll give you my rent from Baugé *(je vous baille ma rente de Baugée)*" means "I can give you nothing".

BAUGÉ

Clemenceau (R. G.) ..... Y

Beausse (R. M. de la) .... Y 2
Cygne (Pl. du) .... Z
Cygne (R. du) .... Y 4
Dr-Zamenhof (R. du) ... Y 5
Église (R. de l') .... Z 6
Europe (Pl. de l') .... Z
Foch (Bd Mar.) .... Z
Foulques-Nerra (R.) ..... Z
Gaulle (Av. Gén. de) ... Z 7
Girouardière (R. de la) ... Z 9
Jeanne-d'Arc (Av.) ...... Z
Le-Gouz-de-la-B. (Av.) ... Z 10
Lofficial (R.) .... Y 12
Melun (R. A. de) .... Y 14
Paix (R. de la) .... Y
Pasteur (R.) .... Y
Pau-Brulé (R. du) ...... Y
Renan (R. É.) .... Y 15
République (Pl. de la) .... Y
St-Nicolas .... Z 16
Valboyer (R. du) .... Z
Victor-Hugo (R.) .... Z 17

SIGHTS

Château (Z) ⊘ – This 15C building now serves as the town hall, tourist information centre and **museum** (collections of weapons, porcelain and old coins).
In 1455 King René himself supervised the building of the turrets, dormer windows and the oratory as well as the bartizan on the rear façade, where the master masons are portrayed.
An ogee-arched doorway gives access to the **spiral staircase** which terminates with a magnificent palm tree vault, decorated with the Anjou-Sicily coat of arms and other emblems: angels, tau crosses (T-shaped), symbols of the cross of Christ and stars which, in the Apocalypse, represent the souls of the blessed in eternity.

Chapel of the Daughters of the Heart of Mary (Chapelle des Filles du Cœur de Marie) (ZB) ⊘ – Formerly part of an 18C hospice, the chapel now houses a precious relic.

★★**Cross of Anjou** – The cross with two transoms (the upper one carried the inscription), which was also known as the Cross of Jerusalem, was venerated as a piece of the True Cross by the Dukes of Anjou and in particular by King René. At the end of the 15C after the Battle of Nancy in which René II Duke of Lorraine, a descendant of the Dukes of Anjou, defeated Charles the Bold, the Lorraine troops adopted the Cross of Anjou as their own symbol in order to recognize one another in battle and the cross became known henceforward as the Cross of Lorraine. It is supposed to be made from a piece of the True Cross, brought back from the Holy Land after the crusade in 1241; it is a marvel of the goldsmith's craft, set with precious stones and fine pearls and was created at the end of the 14C for Louis, first Duke of Anjou, by his brother Charles V's Parisian goldsmith. It is unusual in that it has a figure of Christ on both sides.

Hospital (Hôpital public) (Y) ⊘ – The hospice, which was founded in 1643, was run by the nuns of the St Joseph Order of Hospitallers.
The **dispensary**★ with its original parquet floor and wall panelling displays a collection of herb jars which match the colours of the ceiling, glass and pewter vessels and 16C-17C faience pots from Lyon and Narbonne with Italian or Hispano-Moorish decoration. It is best to visit on a bright day as the exhibits cannot be subjected to electric light. Across the corridor is the Chapel; the altarpiece with a gilt wood ciborium is 17C.

Hôtels (Z) – The quiet streets of old Baugé are lined with noble mansions (hôtels) with high doorways: Rues de l'Église, de la Girouardière and Place du Cygne.

St Laurent's Church (Z) ⊘ – Late 16C-early 17C; the organ, dating from 1644, was restored in 1975.

EXCURSION

The Baugeois – Round tour of 38km - 24 miles – about 1 hour – local map p 62. Leave Baugé by D 141 going east along the Couasnon Valley.

Dolmen de la Pierre Couverte – Leave the car at the side of the road 3.5km - 2 miles from Baugé. A signposted path leads to the dolmen standing in a forest clearing.
By car again, take D 141 towards Pontigné, with fine views to the right of the Couasnon Valley and the forested massif of Chandelais.

Pontigné – Pop 192. The **church**, dedicated to St Denis, whose effigy is above the Romanesque portal, is crowned by an unusual twisting spiral bell tower. Inside, Angevin vaulting *(p 37)* covers the nave while the capitals of the transept sport monstrous heads and water leaf motifs and the charming central apse is supported by a complex network of radiating tori.

In the apsidals 13C-14C **mural paintings★** depict Christ the King and the Ressurection of Lazarus on one side and the Virgin Enthroned, surrounded by the Annunciation, the Nativity and the Adoration of the Shepherds on the other.

Follow the road behind the church and turn right into D 766.

The road affords a fine view of the orchards in the valley.

Bear left and then turn right in the direction of Bocé.

★ **Chandelais Forest** (Forêt de Chandelais) – This is a magnificent State-owned property, covering 800 hectares - 2 000 acres. The splendid fully-grown oak and beech trees are replanted every 210 years.

Follow the forest road to the central crossroads before turning right in the direction of Bocé. Then take D 939 to the left towards Cuon.

Cuon. – Pop 416. Behind the church with the curious conical spire is a charming 15C manor house.

Opposite the church an old inn still bears the inscription "Au Soleil d'Or" (The Golden Sun) where travellers on foot or on horseback could find lodging.

From Cuon take the road to Chartrené.

The wooded park on the left marks the site of the Château de la Grafinière.

Beyond Chartrené turn left to D 60. After 4.5km - 3 miles follow D 211 to the right, crossing heaths and woodlands, to reach Fontaine-Guérin.

Fontaine-Guérin – Pop 628. The belfry of the much-altered Romanesque **church** is crowned by a twisting spire.

Inside, the 15C roof is decorated with 126 painted panels (15C-16C) with secular themes.

The D211 towards St-Georges-du-Bois leads to an artificial lake with facilities for swimming, sail-boarding and picnicking.

A "Threshing Fête" with processions in traditional costume is held on the second Sunday in August.

Follow the Couasnon Valley, taking D 144 in the direction of Le Vieil-Baugé and passing within sight of ruins of the Château de la Tour du Pin.

Le Vieil-Baugé – Pop 1 172. Le Vieil-Baugé is the site of a battle in 1421 when the English were defeated by an Angevin army supported by Scottish mercenaries led by John, the Earl of Buchan. He was rewarded with the baton of High Constable of France.

The old village crowns a hilltop overlooking the valley of the Couasnon.

St-Symphorien ⊙, the church, has a slim twisted spire which leans owing to the internal wooden framework.

The nave is partially 11C and the handsome **chancel★** is 13C with Angevin vaulting.

The façade and the south transept are by the Angevin architect, Jean de Lespine, and date from the Renaissance.

Le Vieil-Baugé — Twisted spire

To plan a special itinerary:

- *consult the **Map of Touring Programmes** which indicates the recommended routes, the tourist regions, the principal towns and main sights.*
- *read the descriptions in the **Sights** section which include Excursions from the main tourist centres.*

Michelin Maps nos 60, 61, 63, 64, 65 and 67 indicate scenic routes, interesting sights, viewpoints, rivers, forests...

BAZOUGES-SUR-LE-LOIR

Michelin map 64 fold 2 or 232 fold 21

From the bridge there is a charming **view**★ of the river with its washing places, the castle and the water mill, the church and its tower in the square and the gardens mounting to the roofs of Bazouges.

Château ⊙ – The château of Bazouges, together with its water mill, was built on an attractive site on the banks of the Loir in the 15C and 16C by the Champagne family, one of whom, Baudoin (Baldwin), was chamberlain to Louis XII and François I.

The entrance is flanked by two massive towers, with machicolations and pepper-pot turrets; one of them contains the 15C chapel which is decorated with Angevin vaulting and two old statues of St Barbara and St John.

The guard room over the gateway leads to the sentry walk. Another more imposing guard room with a stone chimneypiece is on view as well as the 18C state rooms and the formal French park which is planted with cypresses and yew trees and surrounded by water.

Church – The building dates from the 12C. A solid tower rises above the crossing. The nave vaulting, which is made of oak shingles, is painted with 24 figures (12 Apostles and 12 angels) separated by trees each bearing an article from the Creed (early 16C).

BEAUFORT-EN-VALLÉE

Pop 5 364

Michelin map 64 fold 12 or 232 folds 32, 33 – Local map under LOIRE VALLEY: Chinon-Champtoceaux

Beaufort is set in the middle of the rich plains of the Anjou Valley. In the 18C-19C it was one of the largest manufacturers of sail cloth in France. The town is dominated by the ruins of the **château,** which was built in the 14C by Guillaume Roger, Count of Beaufort and father of Pope Gregory XI. One of the towers was rebuilt in the 15C by King René. From the top of the bluff on which the ruins stand there is a broad **view** of the surrounding country.

The **church,** which was largely restored in the 19C, has a fine belfry built by Jean de Lespine and completed in 1542 over the 15C crossing.

The interior contains a 17C Adoration of the Shepherds, a carved wooden altar (1617) and the earlier high altar, made of marble, which is now under the great window in the transept.

EXCURSION

Blou – Pop 752. *16km - 10 miles by N 147 towards Longué and D 206.*
The Romanesque **church** with its massive buttresses has curious 11C diapering on its north transept. A 13C belltower rises above the transept crossing.

★ BEAUGENCY

Pop 6 917

Michelin map 64 fold 8 or 238 fold 4 – Local map under LOIRE VALLEY: Orléans-Chinon – Facilities

Beaugency recalls the Middle Ages. It is best to enter the town from the south, crossing the River Loire by the age-old multi-arched bridge (attractive view). The oldest parts of the bridge date from the 14C but there was an earlier bridge as a toll was already in existence in the 12C.

The Two Councils of Beaugency (12C) – Both councils were called to deal with the marital problems of Philippe I and Louis VII.

While visiting Fulk IV in Tours *(qv),* Philippe seduced the Countess Bertrade and repudiated Queen Bertha soon after. The king thought that he would easily obtain the annulment of his marriage by raising a vague claim of consanguinity but Pope Urban II refused him. The king persisted and was excommunicated so that he was unable to join the First Crusade (1099). Eventually the excommunication was lifted by the Council of Beaugency in 1104 and four years later the King died at peace with the church. He was buried according to his wishes at St-Benoît-sur-Loire.

Much more important was the Council of 1152 which annulled the marriage of Louis VII and **Eleanor of Aquitaine.** The beautiful and seductive Eleanor, who was the daughter and heir of the Duke of Aquitaine, had married Louis in 1137. For ten years the royal couple lived in perfect harmony, Eleanor exercising great influence over her husband. In 1147 they set out together on the Second Crusade but once in Palestine their relationship deteriorated.

Louis grew jealous of Eleanor's partiality for Raymond of Poitiers. They had a quarrel and returned to France separately. Divorce became inevitable and on 20 March 1152 the Council of Beaugency officially dissolved the union of Louis and Eleanor for prohibited kinship: both were descended from Robert the Pious.

Eleanor was not without suitors; almost immediately she married Henry Plantagenet *(qv),* the future King of England, so that her dowry, a large part of southwest France, passed to the English crown.

This event, one of the most important in the Middle Ages, was to lead to many centuries of Anglo-French rivalry.

A disputed town – Beaugency commanded the only bridge that crossed the Loire between Blois and Orléans before modern times. For this reason the town was often attacked *(see note 1 p 44).* During the Hundred Years War (1337-1453) it fell into English hands four times: in 1356, 1412, 1421 and 1428. It was delivered by Joan of Arc in 1429.

BEAUGENCY

Cordonnerie
  (R. de la) 6
Maille-d'Or
  (R. de la) 10
Martroi (Pl. du)
Pont (R. du)
Puits-de-l'Ange
  (R. du) 12

Abbaye (R. de l') 2
Bretonnerie
  (R. de la) 3
Châteaudun
  (R. de) 4
Dr-Hyvernaud (Pl.) . . 8
Dunois (Pl.) 9
Sirène (R. de la) 15
Traîneau (R. du) 17
Trois-Marchands
  (R. des) 18

The town was then caught up in the turmoil of the Wars of Religion (1562-98). Leaguers and Protestants held it by turns. At the time of the fire started by the Huguenots in 1567, the abbey was burnt down, the roof of Notre-Dame collapsed and so did that of the keep.

During the 1870-71 war against the Prussians there was fierce fighting not far from the town which was held by General Chanzy.

SIGHTS

★ **Abbey Church** (Église Notre-Dame) – The Romanesque church was built in the 12C as part of an abbey and has been restored. In the chancel a series of twinned arches alternates with the windows and larger arches; the huge round columns in the nave with their massive carved capitals represent the calm strength of the purest Romanesque art, despite the false wooden vaulting in the nave which was put up after the fire in 1567.

The abbey formed the setting for the two Councils of Beaugency.

Near the church are the 18C buildings of the old abbey. At the bottom of the narrow Rue de l'Abbaye stands the **Devil's Tower** (Tour du Diable) which was part of the fortifications defending the bridgehead; in the Middle Ages the Loire flowed at its foot.

Place Dunois, the square in front of the abbey church and the keep, and **Place St-Firmin** make a picturesque combination. Lit by old lanterns, the two squares are equally attractive after dark.

★ **Keep** (Donjon) – This is a fine example of 11C military architecture. At this period, keeps were rectangular and buttressed; later they became circular. The interior is in ruins.

Château Dunois – Formerly a medieval fortress, it was turned into a typical 15C residence, with mullion windows, a stair turret and an arcaded courtyard, by Dunois *(qv)*, Lord of Beaugency.

★ **Orléans District Museum** ⊙ – The rooms of the Château Dunois now house a fine collection of furniture and costumes from the Orléans district. Traditional arts and crafts are evoked as well as souvenirs of local celebrities: Charles, the physician (1746-1823), Eugene Sue, the writer (1804-57). From the loft one can see the 15C timberwork of the roof.

St Firmin's Tower (Tour St-Firmin) – A street used to run under this tower, which is the sole remaining feature of a 16C church which was destroyed during the Revolution.

Templars' House (F) – Interesting Romanesque windows.

Town Hall (H) ⊙ – From Place de la Poste one can admire the Renaissance façade. The Council Chamber on the first floor is hung with eight beautiful pieces of **embroidery★**, executed with incomparable skill. Four of them, depicting the four continents then known, are 17C; the others (gathering mistletoe and pagan sacrifices) are 18C. They belonged to the last but one Abbot of Notre-Dame, who came from a family of shipbuilders in Nantes, which had grown rich importing sugar cane from the West Indies; the sugar cane was shipped up the Loire and processed round Beaugency and Orléans.

Clock Tower (Tour de l'Horloge) (E) – Originally the Exchange Tower, in the 12C it became one of the gateways in the town wall.

Little Mall (Petit Mail) – It dominates the River Loire. Fine view of the valley.

Tavers Gateway (Porte Tavers) (K) – Part of the old town walls.

BEAULIEU-LÈS-LOCHES

Michelin map 🗺 fold 6 or 🗺 fold 14

This old village contains the ruins of a famous abbey founded in 1004 by Fulk Nerra *(qv)*, who was buried there at his wish.

The **abbey church** is dominated by a majestic square Romanesque tower, surmounted by an octagonal spire.

The arms of the transept also date from the Romanesque period but the nave and chancel were rebuilt in the 15C after being destroyed by the English in 1412; beyond the chancel are a few traces of the original Romanesque apse.

The interior is adorned with a 15C *Pietà*, some 18C terracotta statues in the chancel and some 17C portraits and a low-relief carving of the last Supper in the sacristy.

A curious outdoor pulpit adjoins the old abbot's lodgings on the site of the old cloisters to the right of the church.

The former **Church of St-Laurent** has a Romanesque tower and domical Angevin vaulting.

BEAUNE-LA-ROLANDE

Michelin map 🗺 fold 11 or 🗺 fold 42

Beaune-la-Rolande in the Gâtinais takes its name from the River Rolande west of the town. It is a market town where sugarbeet and cereals have replaced saffron and vines.

Church – The building is 15C-16C with an elegant north side in the Renaissance style: there are pilasters with medallions, recesses and doorways with pediments decorated with busts.

To the left is the gate to the former cemetery with an improving sentiment on the lintel. The aisles are almost as wide and high as the nave, so that the building resembles the hall-churches of the late German Gothic period.

At the back of the left aisle there is a painting of the mystic marriage of St Catherine by Frederic Bazille, who fell in the Battle of Beaune-la-Rolande in 1870.

The last side chapel on the left contains a 17C gilt wood altar with panels depicting biblical scenes and a statue of St Vincent de Paul earlier than the stereotyped 19C representations.

★ BEAUREGARD CHÂTEAU

Michelin map 🗺 north of fold 17 or 🗺 fold 15 (8km - 5 miles northwest of Cour-Cheverny)

The château stands in a vast park laid out on geometric lines. The building has kept its Renaissance appearance despite 17C additions and the 19C roof extension.

TOUR ⏱ *time: 3/4 hour*

★★**Portrait Gallery** – Above the ground floor arcade is a gallery which was decorated for Paul Ardier, Lord of Beauregard at the beginning of the 17C and Treasurer of the Exchequer under Louis XIII. The long room has retained its old Delft tiling depicting an army on the march: cavalry, artillery, infantry, musketry...; the panelling and the ceiling were painted by Pierre Mosnier.

The most interesting feature of the gallery is the collection of over 300 historical portraits. They are arranged in bays, each devoted to a different reign making a complete succession of monarchs from the first Valois, Philippe VI, to Louis XIII. Round the portrait of each king are grouped the queen, the chief courtiers and important foreign contemporaries; thus, next to Louis XII are Isabella of Castille, her daughter Joan the Mad and Amerigo Vespucci, the Florentine explorer who gave his name to America. Each reign is complete with its dates and the king's emblem.

★**Cabinet des Grelots** – The work of Scibec de Carpi who was also active at Fontainebleau and Anet, this charming little room was fitted out towards the middle of the 16C for Jean du Thiers, Secretary of State to Henri II and then Lord of Beauregard. His coat of arms, azure with three spherical gold bells *(grelots)*, decorates the coffered ceiling; the bells reappear as a decorative motif on the oak panelling which lines the room and conceals the cupboards where the château archives are kept.

The huge 16C kitchen with two fireplaces is also on show.

★ BÉHUARD

Michelin map 🗺 fold 20 or 🗺 fold 31 – Local map under LOIRE VALLEY: Chinon-Champtoceaux

Béhuard Island has accumulated round a rock on which stands the little church. The old **village ★** with its 15C and 16C houses makes a picturesque ensemble.

In the pagan era there was a shrine on the island dedicated to a marine goddess, which was replaced in the 5C by a small oratory where prayers were said for sailors "in peril on the Loire". In the 15C Louis XI, who had been saved from a shipwreck by the intercession of the Virgin, built the present church which became an even more popular place of pilgrimage than in the past and was dedicated to the Virgin, the protector of travellers, since she herself had experienced the dangers of travel during the Flight into Egypt.

Church (Église Notre-Dame) – The church, which is dedicated to the Virgin, faces the souvenir shop which stands on the site of the old **King's Lodging** (logis du roi) built in the 15C, so it is said, for the visits of Louis XI; a small stairway leads to the church. Part of the nave is composed of the island rock. Votive chains, presented by a lucky man who escaped from the barbarian galleys, hang in the chancel; the 16C stalls have delightfully malicious carved misericords. The statue of Our Lady of Béhuard stands in a niche in the chancel. The late-15C window of the Crucifixion in one of the aisles shows the donor, Louis XI *(left)*; behind the entrance door there is an old medieval chest.

Walk – It is worth exploring such an attractive site; a short path, beside the Calvary where religious ceremonies take place, leads down to the Loire and a broad sandy beach.

Michelin Maps (scale 1 : 200 000) which are revised regularly provide much useful information:
> *- latest motorway developments and changes;*
> *- vital data (width, alignment, camber, surface) of motorways or tracks*
> *- the location of emergency telephones.*

Keep current Michelin Maps in the car at all times.

BELLEGARDE
Pop 1 442

Michelin map 🔠 fold 11 or 🔢 fold 42

The colour-washed houses of Bellegarde are grouped round a huge square and surrounded by rose nurseries, market gardens and wheatfields.
The town was called Choisy-aux-Loges until 1645 when it was bought by the Duke of Bellegarde. In 1692 it passed to Louis-Antoine de Pardaillan, **Duc d'Antin.**

Courtier and patron of the arts – D'Antin was the legitimate son of Madame de Montespan and the Surveyor to the King. He was a model courtier; Voltaire wrote that he had a talent for flattery, not only in words but in actions.
During a visit to Petit-Bourg Château, near Paris, Louis XIV complained about a row of chestnut trees which, although very fine from the garden, obscured the view from the royal apartments. D'Antin had the trees felled during the night and all trace of the work cleared away; on waking the King was astonished to find the view unobstructed.
D'Antin collected works of art and acted as a patron to artists. His mother was a frequent visitor to Bellegarde where he erected a series of brick buildings (1717-27).

SIGHTS

★ **Château** – At the centre of this unusual and picturesque group of buildings stands the square keep, quartered with bartizans and cut off by a moat, which was built in 14C by Nicolas Braque, Finance Minister to Charles V.
The brick **pavilions** with stone dressings which surround the courtyard were built by D'Antin to house the château staff and his guests; from left to right they comprise the Steward's pavilion surmounted by a pinnacle turret, the Captain's massive round brick tower, the kitchen pavilion, the Salamander pavilion, which houses the **Town Hall** ⊙ and contains a salon with Regency wood panelling, and, on the other side of the gate, the Antin pavilion with a mansard roof. A **rose garden** has been laid out round the moat.
A drive skirting the rose garden leads to the stables *(private property)*; the pediment is decorated with three horses' heads sculpted by Coysevox.
> *Turn left to reach the church in Place du Marché.*

Church – The façade of this Romanesque building is a harmonious combination of proportion and decoration. Note the ornamentation of the central doorway: wreathed and ringed engaged piers support carved capitals depicting fantastic foliage and animals.
The nave contains an interesting collection of 17C **paintings**: *St Sebastian* by Annibale Carracci and *St John the Baptist with the Infant Louis XIV as St John* by Mignard (righthand wall) and *The Descent from the Cross* by Lebrun (righthand chapel); Louise de la Vallière *(qv)* may have been the model for the two female characters in these pictures.

EXCURSION

Boiscommun – Pop 923. *7.5km - 5 miles northwest by D 44.*
Of the castle only two towers and other ruins remain and these can be seen from the path which now follows the line of the former moat.
This interesting 13C **church** with its Romanesque doorway has a Gothic nave with a majestic elevation. It is relatively easy to discern the different periods of construction by looking at the changes in the capitals, the form of the high windows and openings of the triforium.
At the end of the aisle, above the sacristy door, is a late-12C stained-glass window showing the Virgin and Child. On leaving glance at the organ loft, ornamented with eight painted figures (16C) in costumes of the period; the figure of Roland, hero of a 12C epic poem, is identified by the inscription.

★ BERCÉ FOREST

Michelin map **64** fold 4 or **232** folds 22, 23

Bercé Forest is all that remains of the great Le Mans Forest which used to extend from the River Sarthe to the River Loir; its foliage covers a fine plateau (5 391ha - 13 322acres) incised by small valleys and natural springs.
The magnificent trees – immensely tall sessile oaks mixed with chestnuts and slim beeches – provide cover for a herd of deer.
In the 16C Bercé Forest was crown property; it is now carefully exploited for high quality oak. The trees, which are felled on a rotation of between 200 and 240 years, yield a pale yellow wood with a fine grain much in demand in cabinet-making (veneers) and for export throughout Europe.
Pines (maritime, Scots) and larches predominate on the poorer soil to the west of the forest.

TOUR ⊙ time: 3/4 hour
16km - 10 miles from St-Hubert to La Futaie des Clos

The trees which are destined to be felled are marked on the trunk; those with a number (oaks and beeches) are to be retained.

Fontaine de la Coudre – The spring, which is the source of the River Dinan, a tributary of the Loir, flows slowly under the tall oaks known as La Futaie des Forges.
A path is marked with instructive notices for children explaining the uses of the forest.

★ **Sources de l'Hermitière** – A deep valley thick with towering oaks and beeches hides the pure waters of these springs.

★ **Futaie des Clos** – This is the finest stand of oaks in the forest. Two violent storms in 1967 caused great gaps among the trees. While some of the giant oaks (300 to 340 years old) are very decrepit, others are splendid specimens.

Park in the car park under the trees.

A path leads to the Boppe oak, or rather to its stump, protected by a roof, since the ancient tree was struck by lightning in 1934 at the venerable age of 262; its circumference was 4.77m - 15 1/2ft at 1.3m - 4ft from the ground. Its neighbour – Roulleau de la Roussière – still flourishes after 340 years; it has grown to a height of more than 43m - 141ft.

★ BLANCAFORT
Pop 991

Michelin map **65** north of fold 11 or **238** fold 19

This is a very picturesque and smart village clustered round the church which has an unusual belfry-porch.

★ **Château** ⊙ – The 15C château is built of red brick and has a uniform and rather plain façade. The courtyard which is flanked by two pavilions was added in the 17C. The visit includes the library with its Regency panelling and the dining room with its walls covered in Flemish leather, painted, gilded and embossed; fine display of pewter.
The park provides a pleasant walk among the scroll-like flower beds laid out in the French style near the château or along woodland paths beside the river where the scents of the garden are strongest at dusk.

MICHELIN GREEN GUIDES

Architecture
Fine Art
Ancient monuments
History
Geography
Picturesque scenery
Scenic routes
Touring programmes
Places to stay
Plans of towns and buildings

A collection of regional guides for France.

Michelin map 🔢 fold 7 or 🔢 fold 3 – Local map under LOIRE VALLEY: Orléans-Chinon

Blois is situated on the Loire between the Beauce to the north of the river and the Sologne to the south. It is the commercial centre of an agricultural region producing mainly wheat in the Beauce and in the valley wine, strawberries, vegetables and bulbs. First among the vegetables is the asparagus which was first cultivated at Vineuil and St-Claude in the Blois region; it has since spread to Contres in the south and into the Sologne where the soil is light.

Blois is built on the north bank of the Loire, on the hillside overlooking the river; many of the medieval streets still remain, steep and twisting and occasionally linked by flights of steps. The terracing of the houses produces the characteristic tricoloured harmony of Blois, the white façades of its buildings contrasting with their blue slate roofs and red brick chimneys.

HISTORICAL NOTES

From the Counts of Blois to the Dukes of Orléans – In the Middle Ages the Counts of Blois were powerful lords with two estates: Champagne and the region of Blois and Chartres. Despite the repeated attacks of their neighbours and rivals, the Counts of Anjou, particularly the mighty Fulk Nerra *(qv)*, who whittled down their Blois domain, they founded a powerful dynasty.

The Count of Blois married the daughter of William the Conqueror and their son, Stephen, became king of England in 1135. At this period the House of Blois was in the ascendant under Thibaud IV. After his death in 1152, attention was concentrated on Champagne, and the Loire land was somewhat abandoned together with England, where the Plantagenets took over in 1154 *(qv)*.

In 1234 Louis IX bought a lease on the County of Blois from the Count of Champagne. In 1392 the last Count, Guy de Chatillon, sold the county to Louis, Duke of Orléans and brother of Charles VI. Thereafter the court of Orléans was held in Blois. Fifteen years later Louis of Orléans was assassinated in Paris on the orders of the Duke of Burgundy, John the Fearless. His widow, Valentine Visconti, retired to Blois where she expressed her disillusion by carving on the walls: *Rien ne m'est plus, plus ne m'est rien* (Nothing means anything to me any more); she died inconsolable the following year.

A poet: Charles of Orléans (1391-1465) – Charles, the eldest son of Louis of Orléans, inherited the castle and spent some of his youth there. At fifteen he married the daughter of Charles VI, but she died in childbirth. At twenty he married again but soon departed to fight the English. He proved a poor general at the Battle of Agincourt where he was taken prisoner but his poetic gift helped him to survive twenty-five years of captivity in England. He returned to France in 1440 and being once more a widower he married, at the age of fifty, Marie de Clèves, who was then fourteen. The château of Blois was his favourite residence. He demolished part of the grim old fortress and built a more comfortable mansion. Charles formed a little court of artists and men of letters. Great joy came to him in old age: at seventy-one he had a son and heir, the future Louis XII.

The Golden Age of the Renaissance – **Louis XII** was born at Blois in 1462 and succeeded Charles VIII in 1498. Blois became the royal residence rather than Amboise. The King and his wife, **Anne of Brittany**, liked Blois and embarked on considerable improvements: the construction of a new wing and the laying out of huge terraced gardens, designed by the Italian gardener, Pacello, who also worked at Amboise. These gardens covered Place Victor-Hugo and extended towards the railway station. Queen Anne had a large suite (ladies-in-waiting, pages, equerries and guards) and lived in high style. She died on 9 January 1514; the king was soon married to a sixteen-year-old English princess but he died on 1 January 1515 in Paris without a male heir. While at Blois he had drawn up the Customs of France, a code of law.

François I divided his time between Amboise and Blois. He commissioned the architect, Jacques Sourdeau, to build a new wing at Blois; it is the most beautiful part of the château and bears the king's name. His wife, **Claude of France**, was the daughter of the late king and was very attached to Blois, where she was brought up and where she died in 1524, barely twenty-five years old, having borne seven children in eight years. As François I was away fighting in Italy, her funeral was not held until November 1526. After that the king came to Blois no more.

Assassination of the Duke of Guise (1588) – The historical interest of the château reached its peak under **Henri III**. The States-General twice met at Blois. The first time was in 1576, when there was a demand for the suppression of the Protestant Church. In 1588 **Henri de Guise**, the Lieutenant-General of the kingdom and all-powerful head of the League in Paris, supported by the King of Spain, forced Henri III to call a second meeting of the States-General, which was then the equivalent of Parliament. Five hundred deputies, nearly all supporters of Guise, attended. Guise expected them to depose the King. The latter, feeling himself to be on the brink of the abyss, could think of no other means than murder to get rid of his rival. The killing took place in the château itself, on the second floor *(see p 70)*. Relieved of the threat, Henry III exclaimed "Now, I am king!". Eight months later he himself succumbed to the dagger of Jacques Clement.

A conspirator: Gaston of Orléans (17C) – In 1617 **Marie de' Medici** was banished to Blois by her son, Louis XIII. A little court in exile grew up in the château; the leading figure was **Richelieu**, the Queen Mother's confidant and cardinal-to-be, but he became involved in intrigues and decided to flee to Luçon hoping for a more favourable occasion to pursue his ambition.

On 22 February 1619 the Queen Mother escaped; despite her size, she climbed down a rope ladder into the moat in the dark. After such a feat she and her son were reconciled... through the mediation of Richelieu!

In 1626 Louis XIII gave the country of Blois and the duchies of Orléans and Chartres to his brother, **Gaston of Orléans**, who was scheming against Cardinal Richelieu. Soon, however, he grew bored with his new estates and turned to conspiracy again but his inconstancy prevented him from carrying any project to its conclusion: one day he would talk of killing Richelieu, the next day he would be reconciled with him. He went into exile, returned to France, started a new conspiracy and then left again. He was reconciled with the king in 1634 and was at last able to devote himself to his residence in Blois for which he had grandiose schemes. He sent for Mansart and commissioned a vast new building which would have entailed the destruction of the old château. Between 1635 and 1638 a new range of buildings was erected but then work had to stop owing to a lack of funds. The birth of the Dauphin released Richelieu from the need to humour the king's brother so the latter returned to his old ways. In 1642 he was a party to the plot hatched by the Duc de Bouillon and the Marquis de Cinq-Mars. He escaped conviction but was deprived of his claim to the throne. From 1650-53 he played an active part in the Fronde against Mazarin and was banished to his estates; after this further failure he finally settled down. He lived in the François I wing, embellishing the gardens, until his death in 1660.

★★★ CHÂTEAU ⏱ *time: 2 hours*

Son et Lumière – *See the Calendar of Events at the end of the guide.*

Place du Château – This vast esplanade is the former "farmyard" of the château. Slightly below, the terraced gardens offer a wide **view** over the roofs behind which can be seen the bridge over the Loire, and at the foot of the retaining wall, an open square, Place Louis XII; to the right the spires of St Nicolas' Church. Immediately on the left the cathedral with its Renaissance tower stands out.

The **façade** of the château on the esplanade has two main parts: on the right the pointed gable of the Chamber of the States-General (**1**), relic of the former feudal castle (13C), and then the pretty building of brick and stone erected by Louis XII (**5**). The latter building shows no symmetry and openings were still placed according to the amiable whims of the Middle Ages.

Two windows on the first floor have balconies. The one on the left opened from Louis XII's bedroom. His Minister, the Cardinal d'Amboise, lived in the nearby house, which was destroyed in June 1940 and has since been rebuilt with only moderate success. When the King and the Cardinal took the air on their balconies they could chat together. The great Flamboyant gateway is surmounted by an alcove containing a modern copy (made in 1857 by Seurre) of an equestrian statue of Louis XII. The window consoles are adorned with spirited carvings. The coarse humour of the period is sometimes displayed with great candour (first and fourth windows to the left of the gateway).

The inner courtyard – Cross the courtyard to reach the delightful terrace (good **view** of St Nicolas' Church and the Loire) on which stands the **Foix Tower** (**2**) which formed part of the medieval wall.

Return to the courtyard lined with buildings from every period, which together make up the château.

St Calais Chapel (**4**) – Of the King's private chapel which was rebuilt by Louis XII, only the Gothic chancel remains. Mansart demolished the nave when he built the Gaston of Orléans Wing. The modern stained glass windows depicting the life of St Calais are by Max Ingrand.

Charles of Orléans Gallery (**3**) – Although called after Charles of Orléans this gallery probably dates from the Louis XII period. Until alterations were made in the 19C the gallery was twice its present length and connected the two wings at either end of the courtyard. Note the unusual basket-handle arches.

Louis XII Wing (**5**) – The corridor or gallery serving the various rooms in the wing marks a step forward in the search for more comfort and convenience. Originally rooms opened into one another. At each end of the wing a spiral staircase gave access to the different floors. The decoration is richer and Italianate panels of arabesques adorn the pillars.

Feudal Period:
① Chamber of the States General (13C)
② Foix Tower (13C)

Gothic-Renaissance Transitional Period:
③ Charles of Orléans Gallery (late 15C-early 16C)
④ St Calais Chapel (1498-1508)
⑤ Louis XII Wing (1498-1501)

Renaissance period:
⑥ François I Wing: Façade des Loges (1515-1524)

Classical period:
⑦ Gaston of Orléans Wing (1635-1638)

Blois Château

François I Wing (6) – The building extends between the 17C Gaston of Orléans Wing and the 13C chamber of the States-General (1). Only fourteen years passed between the completion of the Louis XII Wing and the commencement of the François I Wing, but the progress made was important: it meant the triumph of the Italian decorative style.

French originality, however, persisted in the general plan. The windows were made to correspond with the internal arrangement of the rooms, without regard for symmetry; they were sometimes close together, sometimes far apart; their mullions were sometimes double, sometimes single; and pilasters sometimes flanked the window openings, sometimes occupied the middle of the bay. A magnificent **staircase** was added to the façade and it was to be the first of a series. Since Mansart demolished part of the wing to make room for the Gaston of Orléans buildings, this staircase is no longer in the centre of the façade. It climbs spirally in an octagonal well, three faces of which

Blois Château — François I Staircase

are recessed in the building. This masterpiece of architecture and sculpture was evidently designed for great receptions. The well is open between the buttresses and forms a series of balconies from which members of the court could watch the arrival of important people.

The decoration is varied and elaborate. The royal insignia *(p 28)* are used together with all the customary themes of the Renaissance *(p 38)*.

Gaston of Orléans Wing (7) – This range designed by François Mansart between 1635-38 in the classical style, is in sharp contrast to the rest of the building. Inside, a projecting gallery runs round the base of the cupola crowning the grand staircase, lavishly decorated with trophies, garlands and masks.

Royal Apartments in the François I Wing – The François I staircase climbs to the first floor where various rooms contain splendid fireplaces, tapestries, busts, portraits and furniture. The interior decoration was restored by Duban (19C).

First floor – The most interesting room is that of Catherine de' Medici. It still has its 237 carved wood panels concealing secret cupboards which may have been used to hide poisons, jewels or State papers or may have been made in accordance with the practice of having wall cupboards in Italian-style rooms. They were opened by pressing a pedal concealed in the skirting board.

Second floor – This is the scene of the **murder of the Duke of Guise.** The rooms have been altered and the King's cabinet is now included in the Gaston of Orléans Wing. It is therefore rather difficult to follow the phases of the assassination on the spot.

The plan below shows the lay-out of the rooms at the time of the murder. The account is taken from contemporary witnesses.

It is 23 December 1588, about 8 o'clock in the morning. Out of the 45 impoverished noblemen who are Henri III's men of action, 20 have been chosen to deal with the Duke; 8 of them with daggers hidden under their cloaks are waiting in the king's chamber sitting on the chests and chatting about this and that. The 12 others, armed with swords, are in the old cabinet. Two priests are in the oratory of the new cabinet: the king is making them pray for the success of his enterprise.

The Duke of Guise is in the Council Room together with several important people. He has been up since 6 o'clock having spent the night with one of the ladies of the "flying squad" *(p 28)* and is cold and hungry. First he warms himself at the fire and eats one of the prunes in his comfit box. Then the Council started. Henri III's secretary tells Guise that the king would like to see him in the old cabinet.

To reach this room, Guise has to go through the king's chamber because only two days previously the door between the Council Room and the cabinet had been walled up. The Duke enters the king's chamber and is greeted by the assassins. He turns left towards the corridor outside the cabinet. Guise opens the door and in the narrow passage sees the men waiting for him, sword in hand. He tries to retreat but is cut off by the eight men in the king's chamber. They fall upon their victim, seize him firmly by his arms and legs and wrap his sword in his cloak.

The Duke is very strong; he knocks down four of his assailants and wounds a fifth with his comfit box. He staggers to the door of the chamber and then collapses by the king's bed, riddled with stab wounds, murmuring "Miserere mei Deus". Henri III steps out from behind the tapestry where he has been hiding and walks up to his rival. Some men say he slapped his face crying "My God! isn't he big! He seems bigger now he is dead than when he was alive". They went through the dead man's pockets and found a letter containing the phrase: "it costs 700 000 livres every month to sustain a civil war in France".

Afterwards Henri III went down to his mother, Catherine de' Medici, and told her joyfully: "I've lost my friend, the king of Paris is dead" – "God grant", his mother replied, "that you have not become king of nothing at all"; according to another version, she remained silent. With a quiet conscience, Henri went to hear mass in thanksgiving in St Calais' Chapel.

The next day the duke's brother, the Cardinal de Lorraine, who had been imprisoned immediately after the murder, was also assassinated. His body was put with Guise's in a room in the château that cannot now be identified. Later they were burned and the ashes were thrown into the Loire. The Queen Mother did not long survive the drama but died about twelve days later.

BLOIS CHÂTEAU : 2nd FLOOR IN 1588

0   20m

→ → → Route taken by the Duke of Guise

Part demolished in 17 C for the construction of the Gaston of Orléans Wing

Guard Room — Wall added in 16 C — New cabinet — priests
King's Chamber
Old cabinet — Council Chamber — Guard Room — Oratory Queen's Chamber
Table
Henri III
Wall demolished in 16 C
Great Stair

Take the grand stair-case down to the first floor and cross the Guard Room.

Chamber of the States-General (Salle des États-Généraux) (1)

This is the oldest (13C) part of the château, the feudal hall of the old castle of the Counts of Blois. From 1576 to 1588 the States-General, the French Parliament, used to convene in this hall. The twin barrel vaults are supported on a central row of columns.

Go out into the courtyard.

Archaeological Museum ⊙ – *Ground floor of François I Wing on the right of the grand staircase.* The museum has displays of prehistoric remains from the Loir-et-Cher. Five rooms of items including stone tools, pottery, glassware, weapons and sarcophagi dating from the Palaeolithic to the Merovingian periods are shown in chronological order.

Robert-Houdin Gallery – The gallery is devoted to the famous local conjurer (1805-71), who was also scholar, writer and clockmaker. He invented electric clocks including the master clock (Horloge-mère - 1850) which was exhibited with the Mysterious Clock (Pendule mystérieuse - 1839), a fine piece with three main elements – moving hands, a dial and a glass column (a clock of this type can be seen at Cheverny Château).

To the left of the grand staircase there is an **audio-visual presentation** on the château.

★**Fine Arts Museum** ⊙ – *First floor in Louis XII Wing.*
The main interest lies in the 16C and 17C paintings and portraits which are well presented : portraits of Marie de' Medici as the personification of France by Rubens, of *Louis XIV, Anne of Brittany* and *Gaston of Orléans,* as well as 17C Dutch and Flemish paintings including genre scenes and festivals. The chimney-pieces carry 19C versions of the arms of Louis XII (a porcupine) and Anne of Brittany (Franciscan cords and ermine tails).

Façade des Loges and Gaston of Orléans Façade – These can best be seen at the beginning of the walk through Old Blois which is described below.

★**OLD BLOIS** *time : 2 hours – route shown on plan*

★**Anne of Brittany Pavilion** (Z) ⊙ – This graceful little building of stone and brick is now the Tourist Centre. Note the cable mouldings which emphasize the corners, and the openwork sculptured stone balustrade with the initials of Louis XII and Anne of Brittany, his wife. Originally the Pavilion was in the middle of the château gardens (the Avenue Jean-Laigret was later opened up) and the royal couple often went to say novenas in the small oratory, in order to have a son.
On the right along the Avenue Jean-Laigret, the Pavilion extends into a long half-timbered wing, also built under Louis XII, which was later used as an **orangery.**

Walk along Place Victor-Hugo, which is lined on the north by the façade of the **Church of St Vincent** (Z) (17C) built in the style known as Jesuit, and on the south by the beautiful Façade des Loges of the château.

King's Garden (Jardin du Roi) – This small terraced garden, overlooking the Place Victor-Hugo, is all that remains of the vast château gardens, formerly directly accessible from the François I wing by a footbridge over the moat, and extending as far as the railway station. From near the balustrade there is an excellent **view★** to the left over the high slate roof topping the Anne of Brittany Pavilion which was built in these gardens, as was the neighbouring orangery, and to the right over the Church of St Vincent and Place Victor-Hugo; in the background is the massive square silhouette of the Beauvoir tower, and to its right is the cathedral steeple; on the right rises the Façade des Loges (the François I Wing of the château) and the end pavilion of the Gaston d'Orléans.

Façade des Loges – The interior part of François I's first construction backed on to the feudal wall and had no outside view. This troubled the King and so he decided to add on against the outside of the ramparts a second building which would have a great many apertures. Since from here it is a sheer drop into the gully, the building had to be supported on a stone foundation.
The two storeys of *loges* and the upper gallery of this façade make it very different from other parts of the building. Il somewhat resembles certain Italian palaces. But here again, the asymmetry of the windows, watchtowers, balconies, pilasters and the foundations, is very typically French.

BLOIS

Commerce (R. du) .... Z
Orfèvres (R. des) .... Z 43
Papin (R. Denis) .... Z
Porte-Côté (R.) .... Z 48
Président-Wilson (Av.) ...... Z 51

Abbé-Grégoire
 (Quai H. de l') .... Z 2
Anne-de-Bretagne (R.) ...... Z 3
Beauvoir (R.) .... Y 6
Bourg-St-Jean (R. du) ...... Y 10
Chemonton (R.) .... Y 16

Clouseau (Mail) .... Y 17
Cordeliers (R. des) .... Y 18
Élus (R. F.) .... Z 22
Fossés-du-Château (R.) .... Z 23
Laigret (R. J.) .... Z 32
Lion-Ferré (R. du) .... Z 35
Louis-XII (Pl.) .... Z 38
Maunoury
 (Av. du Mar.) .... Y 39
Monsabre
 (R. du Père) .... Z 41
Papegaults (R. des) .... Y 44
Papin (Escaliers Denis) ...... Y 45
Pierre-de-Blois (R.) .... Z 46
Poids-du-Roi (R. du) .... Z 47

Puits-Châtel
 (R. du) .... Y 52
Remparts
 (R. des) .... Y 53
Résistance
 (Rd-Pt de la) .... Z 55
St-Honoré (R.) .... YZ 59
St-Jean (Q.) .... Y 60
St-Louis (Pl.) .... Y 62
St-Martin (R.) .... Z 63
Trois-Marchands
 (R. des) .... Z 67
Trouessard (R.) .... Y 69
Vauvert (R.) .... Z 70
Villebois-Mareuil (Q.) ...... Z 75

There is an impressive row of gargoyles above the top floor of the *loges*.
Returning to Place des Lices, one can take in at a glance the majestic **Gaston of Orléans Façade** which overlooks the moat, its classical style no longer comparing unfavourably with the gay and lively Renaissance façades.

★**St Nicolas** (Z) – A beautiful building of the 12C and 13C, of great unity, the church was formerly part of the Benedictine Abbey of St Laumer whose sober monastic buildings, in classical style, extend to the Loire. The plan is of characteristically Benedictine type with a large chancel surrounded by an ambulatory and radiating chapels. Note the lovely historiated capitals in the chancel and the unusual 15C altarpiece dedicated to St Mary of Egypt to the left.

Jacobin Convent (Z) – *Rue Anne-de-Bretagne*. The building dates from the 15C-16C. On the first floor is the **Museum of Religious Art** ☉, while on the second floor, beneath a fine timber roof, is the **Natural History Museum** ☉, with good displays on the wildlife of the region.
There is a fine view of the J. Gabriel bridge from the banks of the Loire.

Louis XII Fountain (Z N) – This is a copy of the monument which was erected by Louis XII in the Flamboyant Gothic style; the original, which is badly damaged, is kept in the château.

Hôtel de la Chancellerie (Z K) – This late-16C mansion is one of the biggest in Blois. Behind the 17C carriage entrance note at the back of the courtyard the superb staircase with straight banisters.

Hôtel d'Alluye (YZ E) – *At no 8 Rue St-Honoré*. A fine private mansion built in 1508 for **Florimond Robertet,** Treasurer successively to Charles VIII, Louis XII and François I. When accompanying Charles VIII on his expedition to Naples, the financier took a liking to Italian art. Behind the façade of the mansion with its delicate Gothic Renaissance sculptures, a large **courtyard** ☉ opens up with pure Renaissance Italianate **galleries★**. The building now houses the head office of a group of insurance companies founded in 1820.

Beauvoir Tower (Y S) – This ancient square keep (12C) belonged to a separate fief from the château and was later incorporated into the town's fortifications.
Old half-timbered façades line Rue Beauvoir (nos 3, 15 and 21), surrounding a 15C stone house (no 19).

Denis Papin Steps (ZY 45) – At the top of the steps a long view suddenly opens up towards the south. Dominating the view is the statue of **Denis Papin,** recognized as the father of the steam machine.

Born in Chitenay (12km - 7 1/2 miles south of Blois) in 1647, he was forced into exile by the Revocation of the Edict of Nantes and published his memorandum on "How to soften bones and cook meat quickly and cheaply" in England; his "digester" known as Papin's cooking pot, thus became the forerunner of today's pressure cooker. In Germany under the patronage of the Landgrave of Hesse, Papin discovered "a new way of raising water by the use of fire"; in 1706 in Kassel he carried out public tests demonstrating the motive power of steam. After the death of his patron, he died in poverty in 1714.

Maison des Acrobates (Y V) – *At no 3 Place St-Louis.*
This is a typical medieval house, with its half-timbered façade, its two corbelled storeys, and posts carved with acrobats, jugglers, etc.

St Louis' Cathedral (Y) – Built in the 16C and flanked by a high Renaissance tower with a lantern, the cathedral was almost entirely destroyed in 1678 by a hurricane. Thanks to the intervention of Colbert, whose wife was a native of Blois, it was rapidly reconstructed in the Gothic style. In the nave, above the large arches, one can still see the projecting stones which were to be sculptured like those in the bays of the chancel. The base of the tower (12C) is part of the original collegiate church built by St Solenne, bishop of Chartres in the 5C, who taught Clovis his catechism and assisted at his baptism by St Rémy. The **crypt** ⊙ *(entrance on the right of the chancel)* dates from the 10C and was enlarged in the 11C to accommodate the crowds of pilgrims; it was the largest of its day and contained the tomb of St Comblée.

Town Hall and gardens of the Bishop's Palace (Y H) – *Access by the gate to the left of the cathedral.* Situated behind the cathedral, the town hall is in the former bishop's palace, built at the beginning of the 18C by Jacques-Jules Gabriel, father of the architect of Place de la Concorde in Paris.
Further towards the east, the gardens of the bishop's palace form a terrace overlooking the Loire, with a lovely **view★** (stand near the statue of Joan of Arc) over the river, its wooded slopes and the roofs of the town; to the south is the pinnacle of the Church of St Saturnin, and to the right on the north bank, the pure spires of the Church of St Nicolas. Lovely view also of the cathedral chevet.

Denis Papin House (Y Q) – Also called Hôtel de Villebresme, this lovely Gothic house at the top of Rue Pierre-de-Blois spans the road with a timber-framed foot-bridge.
At the bottom of Rue Pierre-de-Blois on the left a fine Renaissance door stands out bearing the Latin inscription *"Usu vetera nova"* which can be translated "through use, the new becomes old" or on the contrary "the old becomes new again".
Go down Rue des Juifs: at no 3 is the 16C-17C Hôtel de Condé, with its classical courtyard. Lower down on the left, bordering a half-timbered house, is the cross-roads of Rue des Papegaults (16C houses at nos 4, 10 and 14) and Rue du Puits-Châtel.

Rue du Puits-Châtel (Y 52) – Many interior courtyards are worth a glance through half-open entrance doors.
At no 3 there is an outside staircase with a half-timbered balcony (16C); at no 5 the staircase turret is in stone and there are vaulted galleries and sculptured balconies on the landings (early 16C); next door at no 7 the Hôtel Sardini has a courtyard with Renaissance arcades, and above the door of the staircase turret is Louis XII's porcupine.

ADDITIONAL SIGHTS

St Saturnin Cloisters ⊙ – *Entrance indicated on the Quai Villebois-Mareuil.*
This former cemetery with timber-roofed galleries, was built under François I. It serves as a lapidary museum, containing fragments of sculptures from the houses of Blois destroyed in 1940.

Basilica of Our Lady of the Trinity (N.-D. de la Trinité) – *Northeast of the plan. Take Rue du Prêche.*
This building designed by the architect Paul Rouvière, built between 1937 and 1949, has some fine stained glass and a Stations of the Cross sculptured out of cement by Lambert-Rucki. The 60m - 200ft high campanile affords an extensive view of the surrounding countryside (240 steps). The carillon consists of 48 bells, the largest weighing over 5.3 tonnes - 5 tons. It is one of the best in Europe.

EXCURSION

Maves ⊙ – *19km - 12 miles north.* 15C pivotal windmill.

*The current edition of the annual **Michelin Red Guide France** offers a selection of pleasant and quiet hotels in convenient locations. Their amenities are included (swimming pools, tennis courts, private beaches and gardens...) as well as their dates of annual closure.*

The selection also includes establishments which offer excellent cuisine : carefully prepared meals at reasonable prices, Michelin stars for good cooking.

*The current annual **Michelin Camping Caravaning France** lists the facilities offered by many campsites (shops, bars, restaurants, laundries, games rooms, tennis courts, miniature golf courses, playgrounds, swimming pools...)*

La BOISSIÈRE

Michelin map **64** south of fold 3 or **232** – fold 22

The name of La Boissière is linked with a precious relic: the Cross of Anjou *(see Baugé)*. The cross was brought from the Middle East in the 13C by a crusader and given to the Cistercians at La Boissière who built a chapel for it. During the Hundred Years War the cross was kept in Angers Château. It returned to La Boissière in about 1456 and remained there until 1790 when it was transferred to Baugé.

La Boissière Abbey ⊘ – In the 18C the abbey buildings became a residence; the 12C church was reduced to the chancel: altarpiece and recumbent Gothic figures.

Chapel of the True Cross – The 13C Chapel *(restored)* stands on the road to Dénezé; the interior comprises three bays of Angevin vaulting.

BONNEVAL   Pop 4 420

Michelin map **60** fold 17 or **237** fold 38 – Local map under LOIR VALLEY: Bonneval-Vendôme

Bonneval grew up in the Middle Ages round the 9C Benedictine monastery of St Florentin on the Loir. The old town walls are reflected in the waters of the surrounding moat.

Former Abbey – A specialist hospital, the Henri Ey psychiatric centre, now occupies the old abbey buildings. The beautiful 13C **forfified gateway ★** with is pointed archway was integrated into the abbot's lodging, which was built by René d'Illiers, bishop of Chartres in the late 15C; it is an attractive building of chequered stonework, flanked by two machicolated towers and capped with pinnacled gables over the dormer windows. In front of the abbey stretches the **Grève**, a large shaded square beside the moat. For an attractive view of the old towers and the church spire go to the end of Rue des Fossé-St-Jacques to the west of the town.

Notre-Dame Church – The early-13C church was built in the pure Gothic style: a fine rose window above the flat chevet, an elegant triforium in the nave, fine woodwork behind the font and a 17C figure of Christ.

From the nearby bridge, Rue de la Résistance, there is a picturesque view.

St Roch Gate and King's Tower (Porte St-Roch and Tour du Roi) – Several pointed arches mark the old houses which line the street, Rue St-Roch, which leads to St Roch Gate with its two round towers. Beside it stands the King's Tower, the old keep, pierced by loopholes and capped with a pepperpot roof. This part of the town wall was built in the 15C when the Mall Moat (Fossés du Mail) was dug to cut the town in two since the length of the walls made it difficult to defend.

Boisville Gate and Mill Bridge (Porte Boisville et Pont du Moulin) – To the west of the town, between the railway and the by-pass, stands the Boisville Gate (13C); the only remaining part of the first town wall, it was reduced in size in the 15C.

EXCURSION

Alluyes – Pop 577. *7km - 5 miles northwest.*
Formely one of the five baronies of Le Perche-Gouët *(qv)*, Alluyes at the end of the 15C belonged to Florimond Robertet *(qv)*. All that is left of the old **castle** is the great round tower of the keep and a fortified gate across the moat.
On the left bank of the river stands the **church** (15C-16C); the south side presents a succession of pointed gables corresponding to the bays of the south aisle – a common architectural feature in this region. On the left wall of the nave are two Gothic murals depicting *St Christopher* and the *Legend of the Three Living and the Three Dead (p 40)*. On the left of the nave is a 16C Virgin bearing a representation of the Trinity on her breast and the arms of Florimond Robertet at her feet.

CHÂTEAUX OF THE LOIRE - FROM CHAMBORD TO CHINON

THE MICHELIN GREEN GUIDE - NOW ON VIDEO!

Sit back and enjoy a glimpse of the splendours of the Loire Valley from the comfort of your home.
The majestic course of the Loire from Chambord to Chinon evokes the history of the French kings who, charmed by its natural beauty, had magnificent châteaux built in which they installed the colourful pageantry – and intrigue – of their courts, bringing the ideas and aesthetics of the Renaissance to France.
To echoes of sumptuous court banquets the Loire takes us past the richly stocked game parks of Chambord and Chinon, which once rang to the sound of the hunt, and the famous vineyards and orchards which have earned the Touraine region its reputation as "the garden of France". Mouthwatering images of local gastronomic delights complete this voyage of discovery, ideally suited both as a tempting preview and as a coulourful reminder of your holiday in the Loire Valley.

★ BOUMOIS-CHÂTEAU

Michelin map 🔲 fold 12 or 🔲 – fold 33 (7km - 4 miles northwest of Saumur)

Boumois Château ⊙ is hidden among the trees some 300m - 330 yards from the D 952; the apparently feudal exterior of the 16C château conceals a graceful residence in the Flamboyant and Renaissance styles.

The drive leads to the main entrance; on the left stands a 17C dovecot still with its rotating ladder and nesting-places for 1 800 birds. A massive gate leads into the main courtyard which is protected by a fortified wall, formerly reinforced by a moat.

Boumois Château

The house itself, which is late 15C, is flanked by two huge machicolated towers. The entrance to the stair turret in the inner courtyard is closed by a door with detailed Renaissance motifs and the original and most unusual wrought-iron lock. The armoury on the first floor displays a collection of 15C and 16C weapons (mostly Germanic in origin), a marble effigy of Marguerite de Valois, a full-length portrait of Elizabeth I of England and an Indian screen from Coromandel. The tour also takes in a second floor room with a wooden ceiling, the parapet walk and a chamber containing a fine 16C bed from the Vosges. In the beautiful Flamboyant chapel is a *Virgin and Child* by Salviati and a 15C Burgundian sculpture of the Holy Family. Boumois was the birthplace in 1760 of Aristide Dupetit-Thouars. This highly experienced naval officer took part in the French expedition to Egypt. In the course of the Battle of the Nile, fought between the British (commanded by Nelson) and the French off Aboukir, Dupetit-Thouars preferred to die a hero's death on the quarterdeck of his ship, the *Tonnant,* rather than haul down his flag.

★ La BOURGONNIÈRE CHAPEL

Michelin map 🔲 fold 18 or 🔲 fold 29, 30 (9km - 6 miles southeast of Ancenis) – Local map under LOIRE VALLEY: Chinon-Champtoceaux

South of D 751, between Bouzillé and Le Marillais, is the modest entrance to La Bourgonnière.

★**St Saviour's Chapel** ⊙ – Towers, turrets and buttresses adorn the chapel which is decorated with shells, the initials LC and tau-crosses (T-shaped) – all symbols of the Antonians, properly known as the Hospital Brothers of St Antony. The order was protected by Charles du Plessis and Louise de Montfaucon who had the sanctuary built between 1508 and 1523. The Antonians nursed people afflicted with ergotism, a violent fever, also known as St Antony's Fire since St Antony was invoked to relieve the suffering.

The beautiful doorway is surmounted by a sculpted lintel and the door panels are marked with tau-crosses. The star vaulting above the nave is ornamented with coats of arms and pendants. The oratory (right) contains a rare feudal bench decorated with 16C Italianate grotesques. Above the high altar is a remarkable statue of the Virgin, attributed to Michel Colombe, between St Sebastian and St Antony the Hermit.

The **altarpiece★** (left), decorated with foliated scrolls and cherubs, as well as the central altarpiece, is probably the work of an Italian artist. There is a remarkable Christ in Majesty, clothed in a long tunic, crowned and nailed to a cross, against a painted background depicting the Angels bearing the instruments of the Passion, as well as Charlemagne and St Louis, the patrons of the donors.

BOURGUEIL   Pop 4 001

Michelin map 🔲 fold 13 or 🔲 fold 34 – Local map under LOIRE VALLEY: Chinon-Champtoceaux

Bourgueil is well situated in a fertile region between the Loire and the Authion at the eastern end of the Anjou Valley where the hillsides are carpeted with vines. Ronsard *(p 30)* was a frequent visitor and it was there that he met the "Marie" of his love songs. Nowadays the little town's renown derives from the full-bodied red wines produced by the ancient Breton vines found only in that area. Rabelais mentions them in his works. A Wine Fair is held on the 1st weekend in March.

Parish Church ⊙ – Illuminated by lancet windows, the large Gothic chancel is divided into three and covered with Angevin vaulting of equal height. Its width contrasts with the narrow and simple 11C Romanesque nave.

Halles – Opposite the church backing on to the former Town Hall is the elegant market place with stone arcades.

Abbey ⊘ – *East of the town on the road to Restigné.*
The abbey was founded at the end of the 10C by the Benedictines and was one of the richest in Anjou. Its vineyards stretched over the entire hillside and its woods reached down to the Loire. In the 13C and 14C it was fortified and surrounded by a moat. The elegant building by the roadside containing the **cellar** and **granary** dates from the same period; the gable is flanked by two turrets surmounted by an octagonal stone spire. The wine cellars were on the ground floor and the abbey's grain was stored on the floor above.
The tour includes the building constructed in 1730: dining room with 18C panelling, monumental staircase with wrought-iron banisters and huge vaulted hall. On the first floor the monks' cells have been made into a museum with displays of costumes, bonnets and tools from the early years of this century.

Blue Windmill (Moulin bleu) ⊘ – *2km-1 1/4 miles north.*
The windmill, which is built over a cellar, is of a similar type to the one at La Herpinière near Turquant *(see Montsoreau)*; the cap is mounted on a conical structure supported on a stone vault so that the cap can pivot to bring the sails into the wind. The miller manœuvres the cap by means of the tail or ladder which also serves as a counterweight to the sails. The sails have been restored according to a 15C model.
The tannin obtained from grinding the bark of the chestnut tree was used in the tanneries in Bourgueil.
There is a fine **view** down on to the vineyards of Bourgueil and south to the Loire Valley.

Cave touristique de la Dive Bouteille ⊘ – The cool chamber, hollowed out of the rock, contains a collection of old presses – one is 16C – and of photographs of the vineyard. Wine tasting.

EXCURSIONS

Restigné – Pop 1 187. *5km - 3 miles east.*
The wine-growing village lies just off the main road clustered round the **church.** The façade is decorated with a diaper pattern and the lintel of the south doorway is carved with fantastic beasts and Daniel in the lion's den. The Angevin Gothic chancel ending in a flat chevet, is similar to the one in Bourgueil; the keystones in the high vaults are decorated. The 11C nave is roofed with 15C timberwork; the beams are decorated with the heads of monsters.

Les Réaux – *4km - 2 1/2 miles south.*
In the 17C this charming **château** ⊘ dating from the late 15C belonged to Tallement des Réaux, who wrote a chronicle, *Historiettes,* of early 17C French society. The château is surrounded by a moat and the entrance pavilion is flanked by two machicolated towers; the defensive features have however been subordinated to the decorative: chequerwork in brick and stone; gracefully carved ornamentation in the shell-shaped dormer windows, the salamander above the entrance; soldiers for weather vanes.

Chouzé-sur-Loire – Pop 2 124. *7km - 4 miles south.*
The attractive village on the north bank of the Loire was once a busy port; the deserted dockside where the mooring rings are rusting and the **Nautical Museum** ⊘ recall the past. The charming 15C **manor house** in Rue de l'Église is where Marie d'Harcourt, wife of Dunois, the famous bastard of Orléans *(see Châteaudun),* died on 1 September 1464.

Varennes – Pop 214. *15km - 9 miles southwest.*
From the old river port on the Loire there is a very attractive **view** of Montsoreau Château *(qv).* The towpath makes a pleasant walk.

Brain-sur-Allonnes – Pop 1 801. *10km - 6 miles west.*
Excavations in a 14C house have uncovered the medieval site of the Painted Cellar **(Cave Peinte)** ⊘. Some beautiful faience tiles are displayed in the adjoining **museum.**

BREIL
Pop 303

Michelin map 🔢 fold 13 or 🔢 fold 34 (6km - 3 1/2 miles southeast of Noyant)

The path to Breil through Baugeois Wood makes a pleasant walk.

Church – The semicircular apse and the tall stone spire above the nave make the exterior Romanesque; fine Plantagenet vaulting *(see p 37)* in the chancel.

Le Lathan Château ⊘ – Facing the church, the château has a well-restored 17C formal park with an ornamental canal terminating in an elegant 18C pavilion.

Every year
the Michelin Red Guide France
revises its selection of starred restaurants
which also mentions culinary specialities and local wines.
It also includes a selection of simpler restaurants
offering carefully prepared dishes which are often regional specialities
at a reasonable price.

It is well worth buying the current edition.

★★ BRISSAC CHÂTEAU

Michelin map **64** fold 11 or **232** fold 32 – Local map under LOIRE VALLEY: Chinon-Champtoceaux

The château is set in a fine park shaded by magnificent **cedar trees ★**. The building is unusual both for its height and for the juxtaposition of two buildings which were not meant to stand side by side; the later building was supposed to replace the earlier.

The main façade is flanked by two round towers with conical roofs, ringed by graceful machicolations, traces of the medieval castle which was built c 1455 by Pierre de Brézé.

The castle was bought by René de Cossé in 1502 and has remained in the family ever since. It was severely damaged by the Wars of Religion. René's grandson, **Charles de Cossé**, Count of Brissac, was one of the leaders of the League, the Catholic party which supported the Guises *(see Blois)* in the 16C; in 1594, as Governor of Paris, he handed the keys of the city to Henri IV who was encamped outside the city; in gratitude the king raised him to the status of duke. The new duke began to rebuild his house following the plans of Jacques Corbineau, the architect responsible for the Port-Louis Citadel at Lorient; the work ceased at his death in 1621 and the château was left in its present state.

Brissac Château — Central Pavilion

The **château** ⊙ *(time: 1 hour)* has an incomplete main façade flanked by medieval towers; it consists of the central pavilion and the left wing, abundantly ornamented with pilasters and statues in niches. The right wing, which would have replaced the Gothic tower, was never built.

TOUR ⊙ *time: 1 hour*

The 17C French painted **ceilings** are often embellished with sculptures; the walls are hung with superb tapestries and the rooms are full of fine furniture. The dining room has a large painting of the old Bercy château and park in Paris while in the grand salon there are fine 18C furnishings, Venetian crystal chandeliers and a pastel portrait of the 8th Duke of Brissac by Elisabeth Vigée-Lebrun.

The Louis XIII staircase leads to the imposing guard room, as well as to the bedchamber where Louis XIII and his mother, Marie de' Medici, were at least temporarily reconciled after the Battle of Ponts-de-Cé in 1620, and to the Hunt Room (Chambre des Chasses) hung with magnificent 16C Flemish tapestries from the collection of Louis-Philippe.

Beyond the picture gallery, with its portrait of the famous Widow Cliquot in the company of her grand-daughter Anne de Mortemart, is the chapel; here there is a moving bas-relief by David of Angers as well as finely-worked choir-stalls in the Italian Renaissance style.

On the second floor there is a delightful 17C-style theatre (restored), built in 1883 by the Vicomtesse de Tredern, who had a true soprano voice.

The tour ends in the cellars of the château.

North of Brissac on the road to Angers stands a handsome windmill with a chamber hollowed out below ground level.

BROU   Pop 3 803

Michelin map **60** fold 16 or **237** folds 37, 38

Although Brou was once a barony in Le Perche-Gouët, it is more characteristic of the Beauce; it is a market town centred on its market place where poultry and eggs are the main commerce.

There are many old street names which have remained unchanged since the Middle Ages.

Market Place (Place des Halles) – On the corner of Rue de la Tête-Noire stands an old house with jutting upper storeys, which dates from the early 16C; the timberwork is decorated with carved motifs.

In Rue des Changes near the market place there is another 16C house with a curved façade; the corner post bears the figures of St James and a pilgrim, since Brou is on the route from Chartres to Santiago de Compostela in Spain.

EXCURSIONS

Yèvres – Pop 1 676. *1.5km - 1 mile east.*
The **Church** dates mainly from the 15C and 16C. The elegant Renaissance doorway is framed by carved pilasters (instruments of the Passion) and surmounted by a double pediment.
The interior contains some remarkable classical **woodwork★**: the pulpit which is decorated with effigies of the Virtues, the retable on the high altar, the altars in the side chapels and an eagle lectern. The door into the baptismal chapel is beautifully carved with scenes of the martyrdom of St Barbara and the baptism of Christ.
There is a fine ceiling of carved wood and note the cupboards in which the oil for Holy Unction is kept. Behind the churchwardens' pew there is a collection of 18C and 19C vestments.
The sacristy contains Louis XIII woodwork and collections of 18C and 19C sacred vessels.

Frazé – *See Frazé.*

Tour of Le Perche-Gouët – *See Le Perche-Gouët.*

BUEIL-EN-TOURAINE Pop 341

Michelin map **64** fold 4 or **232** fold 23

Set above the valley of the River Long, Bueil-en-Touraine is the cradle of the Bueil family which has supplied France with an admiral, two marshals and a poet, Honorat de Bueil, Marquis de Racan *(qv)*.
At the top of the hill there is a curious group of buildings formed by the juxtaposition of the Church of St Peter in Captivity (left) and the Collegiate Church of St Michael.

Church of St Peter in Captivity – The church is built against a large but incomplete square tower; steps lead up to the door. Within there is a remarkable **font** in the Renaissance style: small statues of Christ and the Apostles in the panels. At the end of the nave there are traces of early 16C frescoes and old statues. A door leads into the collegiate church.

Collegiate Church of the Holy Innocents and St Michael – The church was built by the Bueil family to contain their tombs. The recumbent figures of the Lords of Bueil and their ladies are laid in the recesses: the first wife (right) of John V of Bueil is wearing a headdress *(hennin)* and an emblasoned surcoat.

★ CANDES-ST-MARTIN Pop 244

Michelin map **64** southwest of fold 13 or **232** fold 33 – Local map under LOIRE VALLEY: Chinon-Champtoceaux

The village of Candes stands on the south bank of the Vienne at its confluence with the Loire; the church was built on the spot where St Martin died in 397 and it was from here that the Saint's body was taken on its miraculous journey up the Loire to Tours *(qv)*.

★Church – The building was erected in the 12C and 13C and provided with defences in the 15C. The roadside façade is remarkable for its combination of military architecture and rich decoration. The vault of the porch is supported by a central pillar on to which the ribs fall in a cluster. The doorway is framed by sculptures (damaged).
Within, the nave is buttressed by aisles of the same height. The Angevin vaulting *(see p 37)* rests on soaring piers; the whole structure gives an impression of lightness. The nave was built at an angle to the older chancel.
On leaving the church look up at the west façade which is also fortified.
A narrow path on the right of the church leads to the top of the slope *(1/4 hour on foot Rtn)*; fine **view** of the rivers; meeting.
Another walk via Rue St-Martin, below the church, and then Rue du Bas ends by a plaque showing the distances between the various ports on the Loire, recalling how much the river was used for transporting goods in former days.

MICHELIN GREEN GUIDES

Art and Architecture
History
Geography
Ancient monuments
Scenic routes
Touring programmes
Plans of towns and buildings

A selection of guides for holidays at home and abroad.

★★★ CHAMBORD CHÂTEAU

Michelin map **64** south of folds 7 and 8 or **238** fold 3 – Local map under LOIRE VALLEY: Orléans-Chinon

Chambord, which covers an area of 21,829 sq yards, is the largest of the Loire country châteaux. Its scale foreshadows Versailles. Its sudden appearance at the end of an avenue and the sight of its white mass gradually widening and becoming clearer in detail, make a deep impression, even more striking at sunset. To this must be added the fine structural unity of the building, the rich decoration it owes to the Renaissance, then at its height, and finally two marvellous features: the great staircase and the roof terrace.

Chambord Château

HISTORICAL NOTES

Grandiose creation of François I (16C) – The Counts of Blois had built a small castle in this lonely corner of the Forest of Boulogne, which was excellent hunting country only four leagues from their capital. As a young man François I liked to hunt in the forest and in 1518 he ordered the old castle to be razed to the ground to make room for a sumptuous palace.

Several designs were proposed and no doubt Leonardo da Vinci, the King's guest at Le Clos-Lucé *(qv)*, drew a plan which was made into a model by Il Boccadoro. In 1519 the surveyor, François de Pontbriant, who had worked at Loches and Amboise, took charge of the project. As the work progressed, the original plans were altered and large sums of money were swallowed up but the king did not stint. Even when the Treasury was empty and there was no money to pay the ransom for his two sons in Spain, when he was reduced to raiding the treasuries of the churches or to melting down his subjects' silver, the work went on. It suffered only one interruption, from 1524 to 1525 when the King was a prisoner after the Battle of Pavia. In his enthusiasm the King even proposed in 1527 to re-direct the course of the Loire so that it should flow in front of the château but the task would have been enormous and a smaller river, the Cosson, was diverted instead.

By 1537 the major work was completed – the towers and body of the keep, the terraces; over 1800 men had been employed under the direction of Sourdeau and Trinqueau, master masons. Only the interior decoration was lacking. In 1538 the King decided to build a pavilion linked to the keep by a two-storey building, and a second symmetrical wing was added to the west side. In 1545 the royal pavilion was finished but François I, who till then had lived in the northeast tower, had little time to enjoy it as he died two years later. Henri II continued his father's work by building the west wing and the chapel tower while the curtain wall was completed. At his death in 1559 the château was still unfinished.

The château is a jewel of the Renaissance, the result of the "veritable mathematisation of architecture" (Jean Jacquart); it has 440 rooms, 365 fireplaces, 13 main stairs and 70 backstairs.

Royal visits – In 1539 the King was able to receive **Charles V** at Chambord. A group of young women dressed as Greek divinities went to meet the Emperor and strewed flowers at his feet. The visitor, charmed by this reception and amazed by the mansion, said to his host: "Chambord is a summary of human industry".

Henri II continued the building. It was at Chambord, in 1552, that the treaty with three German princes was signed, bringing the three bishoprics of Metz, Toul and Verdun to the French crown; it was ratified in 1648 by the Treaty of Westphalia. François II and Charles IX often came to hunt in the forest. Henri III and Henri IV hardly appeared at Chambord, but Louis XIII renewed the link.

The sport of kings – The domain was rich in game and lent itself to hawking. At one time there were more than three hundred falcons. The royal packs received every attention, and for breeding purposes the best dogs were brought from the four corners of Europe to improve the strain.

Hunting was the favourite medieval sport and princes were brought up to it from their earliest days. Louis XII took 5m - 16ft ditches in his stride. Despite his delicate constitution Charles IX used to hunt for as long as ten hours at a stretch, tiring five horses in the process and often spitting blood such were his exertions. He it was who accomplished the feat of stalking a stag without the help of the hounds.

La Grande Mademoiselle (17C) – Chambord was part of the county of Blois which Louis XIII granted to his brother, Gaston of Orléans *(see Blois)*. One can be both a conspirator and a good father: Gaston's daughter, "La Grande Mademoiselle", relates that her favourite game as a child was to make her father go up and down one of the double spiral staircases while she passed him in the opposite direction, without ever meeting him.
Later, it was at Chambord that she declared her love to the Duke of Lauzun. She led him to a looking glass, breathed on it and traced the name of the irresistible charmer with her finger.

Louis XIV and Molière – Under Louis XIV the property reverted to the crown. The King stayed at Chambord nine times between 1660 and 1685 and had considerable restoration work done.
Molière wrote *Monsieur de Pourceaugnac* at Chambord in a matter of a few days. At the first performance the King never smiled. Lully, who had written the music and was playing the role of apothecary, had an inspiration: he jumped feet first from the stage on the harpsichord and fell through it. The King burst out laughing and the play was saved.
Le Bourgeois Gentilhomme caused Molière renewed anguish. The King was icy at the first performance. The courtiers who were made fun of in the play were ready to be sarcastic. But after the second performance the King expressed his pleasure and the whole court changed their criticisms into compliments.

Maréchal de Saxe (18C) – Louis XV put the château at the disposal of his father-in-law, Stanislas Leszczynski, the deposed King of Poland. Then he presented the domain, with 40 000 *livres* revenue, to the Marshal de Saxe as a reward for his victory over the Dutch and English at the Battle of Fontenoy in 1745. Was this a coincidence or a piece of mischief by the son-in-law? Maurice de Saxe was the natural son of Auguste of Poland, the lucky rival of Stanislas and the man who drove him from the throne.
The luxury-loving, proud and violent Marshal filled the château with life and excitement. To satisfy his taste for arms he found quarters there for two regiments of cavalry composed of Tartars, Wallachians and even Negroes, whom he brought from Martinique. These strange troops rode fiery horses from the Ukraine which were trained to assemble at the sound of a trumpet. The Marshal imposed iron discipline. For the least fault he hanged the culprits from the branches of an old elm.
More by terror than by courtship Maurice de Saxe won the favours of a well-known actress, Mme Favart, and compelled her to remain at Chambord. He re-erected Molière's stage for her amusement. Monsieur Favart played the triple role of director, author and consenting husband.
The Marshal died at fifty-four, some said, in a duel with the Prince de Conti whose wife he had seduced. Others ascribed his death to a neglected chill. Vainglorious even in death, Maurice de Saxe had given orders that the six cannon he had placed in the main courtyard of the château should be fired every quarter of an hour for sixteen days as a sign of mourning.

From the Revolution to the Restoration – After the Marshal's death the château was neglected and gradually fell into disrepair. What furniture was left was destroyed during the Revolution.
In 1809 Napoleon gave Chambord as an entailed estate to Marshal Berthier. Berthier sold the timber and left the estate unoccupied. After his death the Princess was authorized to sell it.
It was bought by public subscription in 1821 for the Duke of Bordeaux, heir to the throne and posthumous son of the Duke of Berry who had just been assassinated. Paul-Louis Courier *(p 30)* wrote such a trenchant pamphlet against the subscription that he was sentenced to two months in prison. He was so passionate in his politics that he even proposed that Chambord should be demolished.

The Affair of the White Flag (1871-73) – In 1871 Henri, Count of Chambord and, since the fall of Charles X in 1830, legitimate heir to the French throne, was close to achieving his purpose; it was in 1871, following the disruption of the war that the French elected a monarchist assembly in favour of the restoration of the monarchy. The monarchists were, however, divided into two groups: the legitimists who supported the traditional monarchy; and the Orléanists, more modern in their outlook, who upheld the principles of 1789. Eventually both parties agreed on the name of the heir: **Henri V**, the last of the Bourbon line. As he had lived in exile for forty years, he was not aware of the realities of French politics when he returned to his native soil. He went to live at Chambord where on 5 July 1871 he proclaimed his convictions in a manifesto which ended with these words: "Henri V will not abandon the white flag of Henri IV".
The effect of this declaration on public opinion was a disaster: the royalists lost the partial elections. The Count of Chambord stubbornly refused to reconsider the matter and returned to Austria. Two years later in October 1873 a final attempt to compromise – a tricolour flag dotted with fleurs de lys – failed. The National Assembly accepted the situation and voted for the Republic. Henri did not succeed to the throne and died in 1883. Chambord Château, which had witnessed the final hours of the monarchy, passed to his nephew, the Duke of Parma. In 1932 his descendants sold it to the State for about 11 million francs.

TOUR ⊘ *time: 1 1/2 hours*

★**Son et Lumière** – *See the Calendar of Events at the end of the guide.*

> *Visitors enter through the Royal Gate (Porte Royale). It is advisable to obtain a plan of the château.*

Although the ground plan of Chambord is feudal – a central **keep** with four towers, which is in itself a veritable castle, set in an enclosed precinct – the architecture is Renaissance and evokes no hint of war. The château is a royal palace built for pleasure. During the construction two wings were added, one containing the royal apartments and the other the chapel; the northwest façade is particularly impressive, its attractiveness deriving from the Italian influence in the sculptures and wide bays.

Chambord is the personal creation of François I. The name of the architect has not been recorded but the architecture seems to have been inspired by the spirit of Leonardo da Vinci who had been staying at the French court and died in the spring of 1519 when work on the château began. François I never saw the château finished; it was Henri II who raised the second storey of the chapel and Louis XIV who completed the building.

Main Courtyard – From the entrance there is a fine view of the keep linked to the corner towers by two arcades surmounted by galleries. A gallery was added to the façade towards the end of the reign of François I at the same time as the two external spiral stairs in the north corners of the courtyard.

Double Staircase – The famous double staircase stands at the intersection of the cross formed by the four guard rooms. The two flights of steps spiral round one another from the ground floor to the roof terrace. The stonework at the centre and round the outside is pierced by many openings so that one can see from one flight across to the other and admire the splendid vaulting adorned with salamanders in the rooms which form a cross on the second floor. The pillars and capitals are beautifully decorated in the style of the early French Renaissance.

State Rooms – The rooms on the ground floor and on the first floor have been restored and refurbished to evoke memories of the king and the many visitors to Chambord.

Ground floor: the Sun Room (Salle des Soleils) is named after the sunbursts decorating the shutters; the painting by Baron François Gérard shows the *Recognition of the Duke of Anjou as King of Spain;* the Brussels tapestry portrays the *Call of Abraham.* François I's Hunting Room is hung with a series of late-16C tapestries after cartoons by Laurent Guyot.

First floor: Although at first François I had his rooms in the north tower of the keep, they were moved to the outer north tower when the chapel was added to the symmetrical west tower. In the king's bedchamber the bedspread and hangings are of gold embroidered velvet (16C Italian); it was on one of the window panes that the king is supposed to have engraved a melancholy couplet: *Souvent femme varie, bien fol est qui s'y fie* (Woman often changes, he who trusts her is a fool). In François I's dressing room the salamander, the king's emblem, and the letter F alternate in the coffers of the barrel-vaulted ceiling; the room was used as an oratory by Queen Catherine Opalinska, wife of Stanislas Leszczynski. The Queen's Room in the François I Tower at the north corner of the keep is hung with Paris tapestries relating the History of Constantine, after cartoons by Rubens.

The king's suite, which follows, is decorated with tapestries and historic portraits; the rooms in the centre of the northwest façade of the keep were furnished by Louis XIV. The Royal or State Bedchamber, which was used successively by Louis XIV, Stanislas Leszczynski and Marshal de Saxe, was panelled in the Regency style in 1748 for the Marshal; the next room at the exact centre of the building has a remarkable view of the park. Marshal de Saxe left his mark in the King's Guard Room in the form of a huge porcelain stove. The Dauphin's Suite in the East Tower, contains many mementoes of the Count of Chambord: paintings, the state bed presented by his supporters, statues of Henri IV and the Duke of Bordeaux, the first and last Counts of Chambord, as children, and a collection of miniature artillery given to the young Prince for his amusement and instruction; the cannon fired shot which could pierce a wall. Also on display is his third manifesto dated 5 July 1871 in which he declared "Henri V will not abandon the white flag of Henri IV".

Second floor: the rooms are devoted to hunting: weapons, trophies and other related items; among the tapestries there is the *Story of Meleager* after cartoons by Lebrun (F. Sommer Room) and the *Story of Diana* after cartoons by Toussaint Dubreuil (Diana Room).

Roof Terrace – *Illustration p 43*. The terrace, a direct inspiration from castles such as Méhun-sur-Yèvre and Saumur, is unique: a maze of lanterns, chimneys, stairs and dormer windows, all intricately carved and curiously decorated with a sort of mosaic of inset slates cut in various shapes – lozenges, circles and squares – in imitation of Italian marble. The stair continues above the terrace in a single spiral enclosed a magnificent lantern 32m - 105ft high.

It was here that the court spent most of its time watching the start and return of the hunts, military reviews and exercises, tournaments and festivals. The thousands of nooks and crannies of the terrace invited the confidences, intrigues and assignations which played a great part in the life of that brilliant society. One of the terrace pavilions contains a permanent **exhibition** of 61 paintings explaining the history of the château.

Park – Since 1948 the park has been a national hunt reserve covering 5 500ha - 13 591 acres of which 4 500ha - 11 120 acres are forest; it is enclosed by a wall, the longest in France, 32km - 20 miles long and pierced by six gates at the end of six beautiful rides.

Walkers are admitted to a restricted area (520ha - 250 acres) on the west side. Four observation hides have been built so that people can watch the herds of deer and sounders of wild boar browsing for food (before sunrise and after sunset).

★ CHAMPIGNY-SUR-VEUDE   Pop 859

Michelin Map **67** fold 10 or **232** south of fold 34 (6km - 4 miles north of Richelieu)

Champigny lies in the green Valley of the Veude and still has some 16C houses (Rue des Cloîtres and Route d'Assay). The most interesting sight, however, is the chapel, with its fine Renaissance windows, of the now vanished château.

★**Sainte-Chapelle** ⊙ – The chapel, which is a remarkable example of Renaissance art at its height, was part of a castle built from 1508 to 1543 by Louis I and Louis II de Bourbon-Montpensier. The castle itself was later demolished on the orders of Cardinal Richelieu who felt that its magnificence outshone his nearby Château de Richelieu. Only outbuildings remain but even these give some idea of the size and splendour of the château that was pulled down. The Sainte-Chapelle, which owed its name to the portion of the True Cross which was kept there, was saved by the intervention of Pope Urban VIII.

Louis I of Bourbon, who had accompanied Charles VIII to Naples, wanted the chapel to be in the transitional Gothic-Renaissance style.

The peristyle, which was built later, is decidedly Italian in character: the detailed sculptured ornament is based on the insignia of Louis II of Bourbon and includes crowned and plain Ls, lances, pilgrims' staffs, flowers, fruit, etc. The porch has a coffered ceiling.

A fine wooden door dating from the 16C, carved with panels depicting the Cardinal Virtues, leads to the nave which has ogive vaulting with liernes and tiercerons. There also the visitor will see at prayer the figure of Henri de Bourbon, last Duke of Montpensier, carved by Simon Guillain at the beginning of the 17C.

★★**Stained-glass windows** – Installed in the middle of the 16C, these windows are the chapel's most precious jewel. The windows all together form a remarkable example of Renaissance glasswork.

The subjects portrayed are: at the bottom – thirty-four portraits of the Bourbon-Montpensier House from the time of St Louis; above – the principal events in the life of St Louis; at the top – scenes from the Passion. The window in the centre of the chevet shows a moving representation of the Crucifixion. The vividness and delicate combination of colours throughout should be noticed, particularly the purplish blues with their bronze highlights which are beyond compare.

★ CHANTELOUP PAGODA

Map **64** fold 16 or **238** fold 14 (3km - 2 miles south of Amboise) – Local map under LOIRE VALLEY: Orléans-Chinon

The **pagoda** ⊙ stands on the edge of Amboise Forest, all that remains of the splendid château built by the **Duke of Choiseul,** one of Louis XV's ministers, in imitation of Versailles. It was later abandoned and demolished in 1823 by estate agents.

When Choiseul was exiled to his estates to please Madame du Barry, he turned Chanteloup into an intellectual and artistic centre. He commissioned the pagoda (1775-78) from the architect, Le Camus, as a memorial to his friends' loyalty. This unusual building *(illustration at the end of index)* looks somewhat out of place on the banks of the Loire but it shows how popular such "chinoiserie" was in the 18C.

The **setting★** of the pagoda evokes the sumptuous surroundings of Choiseul's exile; there is a plan of the whole structure inside the building. The large fan-shaped pool, now overgrown, and the traces of the alleys in the park, which can be discerned from the balconies of the pagoda, help to resurrect the original design.

The pagoda is 44m - 144ft high and consists of seven storeys, each smaller than the one below.

From the top (149 steps) there is a fine **panorama** of the Loire Valley as far as Tours and of the Amboise Forest.

Michelin map 60 fold 17 or 237 fold 38 – Local map under LOIR VALLEY: Bonneval-Vendôme – Facilities

Châteaudun and its castle stand on a bluff, indented by narrow valleys called *cavées,* on the south bank of the Loir at the point where the Perche region joins the Beauce.

Fairs and Markets – In the 18C and 19C Châteaudun was an important centre for the grain trade. The farmers came in from the Beauce with samples of their harvest which was sold and delivered to the grain merchants; they then sold it on to the millers, cattle farmers and horse dealers.

On Thursdays the main square was a picturesque sight thronged with people conducting their business. Among the blue shirts, goffered bonnets, light carts and sheep-dogs, moved the porters, wearing the plaque, the sign of their function, which they had paid for in gold. Traders and farmers feasted at the "Good Labourer" (Bon Laboureur) in Rue Gambetta where Zola went to observe them when he was writing his novel *The Earth* and tasted the local Beauce cheese accompanied by the traditional draught of beer.

The poppies of the Beauce were crushed in the presses to yield poppy seed oil. The Beauce sheep provided wool for the textile industry which is recalled in certain street names: Rue des Filoirs and Rue des Fouleries.

HISTORICAL NOTES

In the 10C Châteaudun was seized by Thibaut the Trickster and so passed into the hands of the Counts of Blois. In 1392 the last of the Counts sold the counties of Blois and Dunois to Louis of Orléans, Charles VI's brother; Châteaudun passed by succession to Charles of Orléans, the poet, who offered it to his half-brother John, the Bastard of Orléans, whose descendants, the Orléans-Longueville family, owned Châteaudun until the end of the 17C.

Birth of the Alexandrine – It was at Châteaudun in the 12C that the poet Lambert Licors was born. He was one of the authors of the *Story of Alexander,* a heroic poem inspired by the legend of Alexander the Great which was very popular in the Middle Ages. Its 22 000 lines were written in the heroic metre, with 12 feet to the line, which subsequently came to be known as the Alexandrine metre.

Dunois, the Bastard of Orléans (1402-56) – Handsome Dunois, the faithful companion of Joan of Arc, was the bastard son of Louis of Orléans and Mariette d'Enghien. He was brought up by Valentine Visconti, Louis of Orléans' wife, who loved him as much as her own children. From the age of 15 Dunois fought the English for several decades. In 1429 he rallied the army to the defence of Orléans and delivered Montargis. He took part in all the great events of Joan of Arc's career. At the end of his life, crowned with honours, he founded the Sainte-Chapelle and in 1457 retired to Châteaudun where he received the poet François Villon.

Dunois was buried in the church of Notre-Dame at Cléry *(qv).* He was well educated and well read and Jean Cartier, the chronicler, described him as "one of the best speakers of the French language".

A Financier – Dodun, a native of the county of Dunois, started out with nothing and became Financial Controller under the Regency. In 1724 his portrait was painted by Rigaud; in 1727 Bullet built him a magnificent mansion in Rue de Richelieu in Paris; the château and the marquisate of Herbault also came into his possession.

Dodun made up for his ill-gotten gains by finding the money for rebuilding Châteaudun after the town burnt down in 1723. Reconstruction was directed by Jules Hardouin, nephew of Jules Hardouin-Mansart; he was responsible for the part of the town which is laid out on the grid system.

A Heroic Defence – On 18 October 1870 the Prussians attacked Châteaudun with 24 cannon and 12 000 men. Confronting them were only 300 national guards from the county of Dunois and 600 free fighters; although they held out all day behind their barricades, despite a heavy bombardment from midday to half past six, they were outnumbered and had to retreat. The Germans set fire to the town and 263 houses were destroyed. In recognition for services to France, Châteaudun received the Legion of Honour and adopted the motto "Extincta revivisco" (I rise again from the ashes).

CHÂTEAU ⊙ *time: 1 hour*

Châteaudun is the first of the Loire châteaux on the road from Paris and stands on a bluff rising steeply above the River Loir (there is an excellent view from the north bank level with an old mill near the bridge). The buildings, which date from the 12C and 16C, have been restored with care and taste and the rooms have been provided with furniture and hung with 16C and 17C tapestries.

Fortress-like from the outside, from the courtyard the buildings resemble a stately mansion.

The roofless keep, which is 31m - 102ft high, dates from the 12C; it is one of the earliest round keeps, also one of the most impressive and best preserved.

The **basement rooms** which extend into the Dunois Wing are always open *(entrance at the bottom of the Gothic staircase).* Two large adjoining rooms, beautifully decorated with intersecting ribbed vaulting, were the kitchens, with a double chimney extending the whole width of the room. The small rooms on the north side were occupied by the guards in charge of the exiguous prison cells, some of which have ogival vaulting.

Sainte-Chapelle –

Dunois was responsible for this graceful 15C building; it is flanked by a square belfry and two oratories and the chancel ends in a three-sided apse. The upper chapel, which was provided for the servants, has a panelled wooden ceiling; the lower chapel has ogival vaulting.

The south oratory is decorated with a well-preserved 15C mural of the Last Judgement. The charming collection of fifteen **statues★★** is an excellent example of the work produced in the workshops in the Loire

Valley in the late 15C. Twelve of them are life-size and painted, and date from the time of Dunois; they represent St Elizabeth, St Mary the Egyptian, deliciously clothed with her own hair, St Radegund with her sceptre, St Apollonia with forceps gripping a tooth, St Barbara with her tower, St Genevieve, St Catherine holding the wheel and the sword that killed her, a Magdalen, St John the Baptist and St John the Evangelist, Dunois' patron saints St Martha with a dragon at her feet and a majestic Virgin and Child; Mary was the patron saint of Marie d'Harcourt, Dunois' wife. The three smaller statues are of Dunois himself, St Francis and St Agnes and were added by François d'Orléans-Longueville and Agnès de Savoie, son and daughter-in-law of the Bastard.

Dunois Wing –

It was started in 1460 and is in the true Gothic tradition but the internal fittings suggest the desire for comfort which followed the Hundred Years War.

The huge living rooms have massive overhead beams and are hung with tapestries, including, on the first floor, a superb series from Brussels depicting the life of Moses; the Court Room (Salle de Justice), where the Lord of the Manor gave judgment, was panelled in the 17C and painted with the arms of Louis XIV when the king visited Châteaudun; it served as a revolutionary tribunal in 1793. On the top floor a vertiginous parapet walk beside the machicolations leads to the guard room.

Longueville Wing –

In completing his father's work, François I de Longueville had a staircase built in the Gothic style; it rises through three floors and opens on to the main courtyard through a double bay like an Italian loggia; the decoration is in the Flamboyant style. The design is in transition between the medieval turreted staircase of the Dunois Wing and the Renaissance at the east end of the Longueville Wing.

The Longueville Wing was built between 1511 and 1532 by François II de Longueville and then by his brother the Cardinal on foundations which date from the preceding century; it was never completed. At roof level an Italian cornice supports a Flamboyant balustrade. The staircase at the east end is richly decorated with Renaissance motifs in a Gothic setting. The ground floor rooms, among them the Renaissance gallery, are hung with 17C Paris and Amiens tapestries. In the grand salon on the first floor there are carved 16C chests and, facing each other, two monumental chimney-pieces, one in the Gothic and one in the Renaissance style.

OTHER SIGHTS

Old town (Vieille ville) (A) – *To visit the old town follow on foot the route shown on the plan opposite.*

Rue du Château, which is lined by overhanging houses, opens into a charming little square with two old houses: the one with pilasters, beams and carved medallions is 16C, the other, much restored, is a corner house with a carved corner post showing the Virgin and St Anne (badly deteriorated).

Rue de la Cuirasserie, which contains a fine 16C house with a corner turret, opens into a square named after Cap-de-la-Madeleine, a town in the province of Quebec in Canada founded in 17C by a priest from Châteaudun. On the right is the workhouse (Hôtel-Dieu), founded in 1092 and modernised in 1762; on the left is the Law Court (Palais de Justice) housed in a former Augustinian abbey, built in the classical style.

★Magdalen Church (Église de la Madeleine) (A) – The church is built into the ramparts; its north façade is topped by pointed gables, a common regional feature. The interior is vast; it was built in the 12C to an ambitious plan and never completed owing to a lack of funds. The south door, overlooking a steep drop, is Romanesque with human figures and fantastic animals carved over the arch.

Continue down Rue des Huileries to Rue de la Porte-d'Abas; on the left, near the ruins of a Roman gate, stands the 16C Porters' Lodge (Loge aux Portiers) decorated with a carefully restored statue of the Virgin.

Walk up Rue St-Lubin with its central water channel to return to the front of the château. Go through the arch at the beginning of Rue de Luynes and into Impasse du Cloître St-Roch, then turn right into a narrow and winding street, Venelle des Ribaudes, which opens into a small square on the edge of the bluff; from here there is a pleasant view of the Loir and the river valley. On the right of the square stands a 15C house with a Flamboyant door and mullion windows.

Take Rue Dodun back to the château.

Mall Walk (Promenade du Mail) (A) – The walk, which parallels the edge of the bluff above the river valley, has been widened and turned into a public garden. The **view★** extends westward across the two branches of the Loir, the St-Jean suburb and beyond to the hills of the Perche region.

Museum (A M) ⊘ – This is worth visiting for its remarkable **stuffed bird collection★** on the first floor and for its fine Oriental objects including French East India Company porcelain, Buddhist statuary and Islamic weapons.
On the ground floor, the Egyptian room has mummies and funerary objects from the Early Dynastic Period discovered at Abydos in the late 19C by the French Egyptologist Amelineau. Here too is a mummy mask of the Graeco-Roman period found at Antinoe.
There are also displays of archaeological finds from the Châteaudun area while more recent local history is evoked by souvenirs from the 1870 war.
Other collections include a series of local 19C landscape paintings and a fine 16C carving in polychrome wood, entitled Circumcision, from Antwerp.

St Valerian's Church (St-Valérien) (B) – The late 12C-early 13C church has a tall square tower and crocketed spire; on the south side there is a fine Romanesque multifoil doorway.

Our Lady of Champdé Chapel (Notre-Dame-du-Champdé) (B) – All that remains of this chapel is a Flamboyant façade with finely worked ornamentation; a delicate balustrade is supported by sculpted consoles at the base of the gable which holds an effigy of the Virgin.

Church of St John of the Chain (Église St-Jean-de-la-Chaîne) – *Exit* ⑤ *on the plan.*
In the suburb of St John on the north bank of the Loir stands an early-16C ogee arched gate at the entrance to the churchyard.
St John's Church was built mainly in the 15C but the apses date from the 11C and 12C.
From this side of the river there is a fine view of the north front of the château.

Foulon Caves (A B) ⊘ – *35 Rue des Fouleries.* Bordering the roadside like the many other caves in the area, and clearly visible, these caves owe their name to the activity of the fullers *(fouleurs)* who used to work here. Hollowed out in the Senonian limestone by the waters of the Loir, the cave roofs have flinty concretions which in places have been transformed into geodes of chalcedony or quartz by the effects of crystallisation.

CHÂTEAUDUN

Gambetta (R.) .... **AB**	Cap-de-la-Madeleine (Pl.) .... **A 3**	Huileries (R. des) .... **A 8**
République (R.) .... **AB**	Château (R. du) .... **A 4**	Luynes (R. de) .... **A 10**
18-Octobre (Pl. du) ...... **A 21**	Cuirasserie (R. de la) ...... **A 5**	Lyautey (R. Mar.) .... **A 12**
	Dunois (Pl. J. de) .... **A 6**	Porte d'Abas (R. de la) ... **A 14**
	Guichet (R. du) .... **A 7**	St-Lubin (R.) .... **A 18**
		St-Médard (R.) .... **A 19**

EXCURSIONS

Lutz-en-Dunois – Pop 422. *7km - 4 miles by* ②, *towards Orléans.*
Lutz has a charming Romanesque **church** with a low belltower crowned by a saddleback roof. The interior is decorated with 13C **murals** in red, yellow and ochre: those in the apse depict Apostles and Bishop Saints; on the walls of the nave are Christ's Entry into Jerusalem, the Entombment, the Resurrection, and the Descent into Purgatory.

Bois de Nottonville Abbey – *18km - 11 miles by* ②; *take the D 927 to Varize and then follow the signs.* The 11C priory (restored in the 15C) belonged to Benedictine monks from Marmoutier. Note, in particular, the fortified doorway, the barn with a roof shaped like an inverted hull, and the dovecot.

CHÂTEAU-GONTIER   Pop 11 085

Michelin Map ▓ fold 10 or ▓▓ fold 19 – Local map under MAYENNE VALLEY. – Facilities

On the border between Brittany and Maine, Château-Gontier is a picturesque old town, the capital of the Mayenne country. It was founded in the 11C by Fulk Nerra, Count of Anjou *(qv);* he constructed a castle on the rocky spur overlooking the river and put it in the charge of one Gontier, an officer in his army. The area around belonged to the Benedictines of the Abbey of St Aubin at Angers, and it was they who built the 11C Priory of St John the Baptist by the side of the castle.
The town is divided into two distinct areas: the upper town bisected by Grande Rue on the west bank of the river, and the area around St Julian's Hospital on the east bank. The town suffered much damage in the course of the Hundred Years War (the castle was destroyed in 1368) and was one of the centres of Royalist resistance to the French Revolution. The Royalist leader and friend of Cadoudal, **Pierre-Mathurin Mercier,** was born here in Rue Trouvée, the son of an inn-keeper. They passed through the town in October 1793 with the forces of the Vendée. Mercier became a general and then Marshal of the Royal Armies in Brittany, meeting his death at the Battle of Loudéac in 1801, aged only 26.
The town has always been a great centre for fairs and markets, and its St-Fiacre Park (B) is the traditional location for the Thursday sale of sheep and calves, one of the continent's most important markets of its kind.
The quaysides are a reminder of the days when Château-Gontier was a port on the canalised Mayenne (**boat trips** ⊘ and houseboat hire at the Relais nautique).

UPPER TOWN *time: 1 1/2 hours*

World's End Gardens (Jardin du Bout-du-Monde) (A) – Laid out in the grounds of the old priory, these attractive gardens give glimpses of the river and the far bank.

St John's Church (Église St-Jean-Baptiste) (A) – The church is built in flint and red sandstone.
The **interior**★ is remarkable for its forceful yet pure Romanesque style. The nave has modern stained glass and irregularly-spaced columns supporting impressive arcades, while the crossing is roofed by an unusual dome resting on pendentives ending in colonnettes. There are remains of 13C and 14C frescoes in the nave while those in the transepts date from the 12C; in the north transept they illustrate God's creation of the birds, domestic animals and Adam and Eve, and the figures of the Three Wise Men can be discerned in St-Benoît's chapel. In the south transept are representations of Noah and the Ark.
The beautiful crypt is roofed with groined vaulting supported on two rows of culumns.
The walk down to Place St-Just gives a glimpse of the steep rise known as Montée du Vieux-Collège.

Viewpoint – From under the elm trees on the terrace built on the old ramparts there is a fine view of the far bank of the river.
Go down Montée St-Just to the Grande Rue.
At the corner of Grande Rue and Rue de la Harelle there is a fine 15C timber-framed house (B **L**), and opposite, the old salt-store, built in tufa and with a turret dating from the 16C.
Go up the Grande Rue and turn left into Rue de Thionville, then right into Rue d'Enfer.
The cobbled street is bordered on the left by the basement of the Church of St John the Evangelist.
To the right, Rue Lierru leads to Rue Jean-Bourré, a reminder of the fame that this son of the town acquired as Financial Secretary and Treasurer of France in the reign of Louis XI *(see Le Plessis-Bourré Château).*

Museum (A **M**) ⊘ – Housed in the lovely 17C Hôtel Fouquet, the museum has a number of good paintings and sculptures as well as Greek and Roman remains; an unfinished painting by Le Brun of the *Battle of Constantine and Maxentius;* 17C Dutch pictures; a fine wooden statue of St Martha (15C French) and a 14C marble Virgin. Local artists are represented by engravings by Tancrède Abraham and watercolours by Louis Renier (19C).
Go up Rue du Musée (the building on the corner with Rue Bruchemotte has an elegant turret) and into Rue Chevreul.

Hôtel de Lantivy (A **F**) – This town house (no 26) has a particularly interesting 16C façade.
Take Rue René Homo to the left, then on the right Rue Fouassier and Rue de l'Allemandier to Place St-Jean.

CHÂTEAU-GONTIER

Alsace-Lorraine
  (Q. et R. d') . . . . B 2
Bourg-Roussel (R.) . . . . A 5
De Coubertin (Q. P.) . . . . . . B 7
Foch (Av. Mar.) . . . . B 9
Fouassier (R.) . . . . A 10

Français-Libres
  (Pl. des) . . . . A 12
Gambetta (R.) . . . . A 14
Gaulle
  (Quai Ch. de) . . . . B 15
Homo
  (R. René) . . . . A 18
Joffre (Av. Mar.) . . . . A 20
Leclerc
  (R. de la Division) . . . . . . A 22

Lemonnier (R. Gén.) . . . . B 24
Lierru (R. de) . . . . B 25
Olivet (R. d') . . . . A 29
Pasteur (Q.) . . . . B 31
Pilori (Pl. du) . . . . A 33
République (Pl.) . . . . A 36
St-Jean (Pl.) . . . . A 39
St-Just (Pl.) . . . . B 40
Thionville
  (R. de) . . . . B 45

EAST BANK *time: 1/2 hour*

There are fine views of the upper town from the Pierre-de-Coubertin quayside (**B**).

Trinity Church (Eglise de la Trinité) (B) – This former Ursuline chapel was built in the 17C by Pierre Corbineau and his son Gilles, architects from Laval. A statue of St Ursula adorns the pilastered façade. Inside there is a monumental 18C altarpiece and the convent parlour grille.
To the right of the church is the elegant 15C manor house known as the **Manoir de la Touche (B N)** ⊙.

Notre-Dame-du-Genneteil Church (B E) ⊙ – Once a college chapel, this severe little Romanesque edifice is built of schist; it is now used to house temporary exhibitions.

EXCURSIONS

La Maroutière Château ⊙ – *3km - 2 miles by ③ on the plan.*
Built in the 13C and 14C, the château is set in a superb park containing one of the last private racecourses.

St-Ouen Château – *7km - 4 1/2 miles by ④ on the plan.*
Just before **Chemazé** this 15C-16C château appears on the right of the road; the great square tower which contains the stairs bears a crown-like superstructure and the dormer windows are pedimented.

CHÂTEAU-LA-VALLIÈRE   Pop 1 482

Michelin map 🔢 northwest of fold 14 or 🔢 fold 22

This calm, small town ideal for tourists seeking a quiet haven is situated in a wooded region interspersed with many stretches of water.
Louise de la Baume le Blanc, better known as the Duchess of La Vallière, spent her childhood at La Vallière Manor, near the village of Reugny to the northeast of Tours.
Lady-in-waiting to Charles I of England's widow, Henrietta Maria, the gentle, gracious Louise captured the heart of the Sun King, Louis XIV, at Fontainebleau in 1662. She remained the royal mistress for five years before being ousted by the haughty Mme de Montespan. Following her fall from favour, she retired to the Carmelite Convent in Rue St-Jacques in Paris and eventually took the black veil from the hands of Queen Maria-Theresa; the preacher was Bossuet. For the thirty-six years of her stay her piety, modesty and tolerance never failed her.

Happy Valley Lake (Étang du Val Joyeux) – This vast stretch of water *(bathing and sailing facilities)*, formed by the River Fare, lies in an attractive wooded setting. The nearby hill is crowned by a church.

Château-la-Vallière Forest – The town is surrounded, except on the north side, by a vast forest of pines and oaks, interspersed with stretches of heath, which covers about 3 000ha - 11sq miles and is ideal for hunting.

Vaujours Château – *3.5km - 2 miles.*
The romantic ruins of this château are preceded by a fortified barbican and a rampart wall marked out at intervals by round towers; only one of the once-battlemented towers stands in its entirety. The courtyard is bordered by the remains of the chapel and main building dating from the 15C. Louis XI came to the château several times to stay with his half-sister, Jeanne, the daughter of Charles VII and Agnès Sorel. Louise de La Vallière also held the title of the Duchess of Vaujours but only visited the château once in 1669.

CHÂTEAUNEUF-SUR-LOIRE   Pop 6 558

Michelin map **64** fold 10 or **237** fold 41 or **238** fold 6

Châteauneuf has made good the damage caused by the bombardments that shattered the town in 1940.
On the site of the former fortified castle, where Charles IV the Fair died in 1328, Louis Phelypeaux de la Vrillière, Secretary of State to Louis XIV, built a small-scale imitation of Versailles. After the Revolution the château was sold to an architect from Orléans who had it demolished; only the 17C rotunda and gallery, the outbuildings and the pavilions in the forecourt, some of which are used as the Town Hall, remain.

Château Grounds – The park is bordered by a moat; the western section is filled with water and crossed by a graceful stone footbridge. It is at its best at the end of May or in early June when the exotic plants and giant **rhododendrons** are in flower.

Loire Nautical Museum ⊙ – The museum on the ground floor of the château contains collections made up for the most part of donations from descendents of boatmen, which testify to the importance of the great river through the ages. Among the displays are anchors and carpentry tools as well as furniture, clothes, jewellery and a beautiful collection of Nevers faience. Here are also presentations on river floods and pack ice.
A documentation centre supplies detailed information about river navigation and transport on the Loire.

St Martial's Church – The church was built late in the 16C in the Gothic style but lost its nave in a fire in 1940; all that remains is a double arch through which the old market hall can be seen. Within stands the marble **mausoleum**★ of Louis Phelypeaux de la Vrillière who died in 1681; it is an imposing Baroque monument, framed by two skeletons acting as caryatids, and was carved in Italy by a pupil of Bernini.

St Peter's Market Hall (Halle St-Pierre) – Next to the church stands this picturesque building supported on wooden columns; originally built as a boat-house, it became the corn market in 1854.

EXCURSION

Orléans Canal: Loire Reach – *The Seine Reach is described under the excursions of Lorris. 24km - 15 miles to the lake.*
The Orléans Canal, which links the Loire to the Loing just north of Montargis, was built between 1677 and 1692. The 79km - 49 mile long canal was the scene of intense activity, mainly the transport of timber and coal to Paris, for 250 years. The canal was closed in 1954 with the decline of river traffic on the Loire and the competition from the railways. Repairs are now being made to the canal to make it navigable again for pleasure boats. The stretch between Fay-aux-Loges and Combreux is now open to boats and barges.

Leave Châteauneuf-sur-Loire by D 11.

Fay-aux-Loges – Pop 2 597. This little village on the banks of the Orléans Canal has a handsome low **church** (11C-13C). Although the vaulting is ogival the building gives the impression of a stout Romanesque church which is accentuated by the use of the hard Fay stone as a facing right up to the pyramidal spire. The modern stained glass blends well with the austere architecture. The fortified house behind the church is the vicarage.

Continue on D 9 to the northeast.

Combreux – Pop 142. The town clusters picturesquely on the south bank of the Orléans Canal. On the north side of the town and the canal, east of D 9, stands the spectacular **château** (16C-17C), built of brick with stone dressings and surrounded by a moat.

Cross the canal to reach the leisure park.

★ **Étang de la Vallée** ⊙ – The reservoir which feeds the Orléans Canal is on the eastern fringe of the Orléans Forest in a wild setting of dense trees and tall reeds where ducks and moorhens cackle and quack. There are facilities for bathing, fishing, sail boarding, sailing, camping and picnics.

CHÂTEAU-RENAULT Pop 5787

Michelin map 64 folds 5, 6 or 238 fold 1 – Facilities

Château-Renault was founded in 1066 by Renault, son of Geoffroi de Château-Gontier, on a tongue of land between the River Brenne and the River Gault at the point where they meet. The town has now extended well beyond its original confines. The main street runs in a large curve down to the river bank. Chemical and electronics industries have replaced the traditional activity of leather working.

Leather and Tanning Museum (M) ⊘ – Housed in an old tannery, the museum displays the various stages in the traditional tanning process and has a collection of old currying machinery.

Château – A 14C gate, surmounted by a hoarding (to enable the defenders to protect the entrance) leads in to the lime-planted terraces which offer an attractive **view**★ over the town.

The 12C **keep (B)** has been slighted; the old 17C château is now occupied by the Town Hall. The château belonged to the owners of the château in Châteaudun and then to two illustrious sailors: the Marquis of Château-Renault under Louis XIV and, under Louis XVI, the Count of Estaing who died at the guillotine in 1793.

EXCURSION

St-Laurent-en-Gâtines – Pop 690. *11km - 7 miles west.*
At the roadside stands a massive edifice in brick and stone. Long known as **"la Grand' Maison"** (the Big House), it was formerly the residence of the abbots of Marmoutier, who owned the land of St-Laurent-en-Gâtines. The building was constructed in the 15C and converted into a church in the 19C: a spire was raised on the polygonal tower which housed the stairs and two large Flamboyant windows were inserted on one side.

★★ CHAUMONT-SUR-LOIRE CHÂTEAU

Michelin map 64 folds 16, 17 or 238 fold 14 – Local map under LOIRE VALLEY: Orléans-Chinon

The former fortress of Chaumont was demolished twice; it was rebuilt between 1465 and 1510 by Pierre d'Amboise, by the eldest of his seventeen children, Charles I d'Amboise, and by his grandson, Charles II. The latter, thanks to his uncle, Cardinal Georges d'Amboise, who was in great favour with King Louis XII, became Grand Master of the King's Household, Marshal, Admiral of France and Lieutenant-General in Italy.

In 1560 Catherine de' Medici, the widow of Henri II, acquired the castle only as a means of revenge against **Diane de Poitiers,** the mistress of the late King. The Queen compelled her rival to give up her favourite residence of Chenonceau in exchange for Chaumont. Diane de Poitiers never lived at Chaumont but retired to Anet where she died in 1566.

Catherine de' Medici's stay at Chaumont and the existence there of a room connected by a staircase with the top of a tower have given rise to conjecture. The room was said to be the study of **Ruggieri,** the Queen's Astrologer, and the tower, the observatory from which Catherine and her master plotter consulted the stars. It was apparently at Chaumont that Catherine read in the future the grim fate awaiting her three sons, François II, Charles IX and Henri III, and the accession of the Bourbons with Henri IV of Navarre.

Mass-produced medallions – In the 18C one of the proprietors of the castle, Le Ray, Governor of the Invalides in Paris, retained the famous Italian artist **Nini,** a glass engraver and potter, for 1 200 *livres* a year, plus lodging and heating. Nini fitted out a workshop in the stables and an oven in a dovecot.

Using a hollow mould he reproduced many copies of medallions of more than a hundred famous people of the time, including Benjamin Franklin who spent some time at the château. Le Ray made a large profit from this new industrial method of portraiture.

19C – Exiled from Paris by Napoleon, Madame de Staël spent some time in 1810 at Chaumont as a guest of Le Ray's son. She worked there, surrounded by her "court" which included Benjamin Constant and Madame Récamier. When her guests praised the landscape of the Loire, she replied sadly: "Yes, it's an admirable scene, but how much I prefer my gutter in the Rue du Bac."

In 1875 the castle was bought by **Mlle Say,** heiress to an industrial fortune, who soon became the Princesse de Broglie; for Chaumont this was an era of luxury and magnificent festivities.

Since 1938 Chaumont has belonged to the State.

TOUR *time: 3/4 hour*

Chaumont Château is as well sited as Amboise on the south bank of the Loire, overlooking the town and the river; the view★ from the terrace is admirable. The feudal austerity of the buildings is softened by the Renaissance influences and complemented by the magnificent stables, a reminder of coaching days.

The park ⊙ – An uphill walk along a shady avenue giving glimpses of the Loire leads to the castle. This is a pleasant walk and will give an idea of the fine park with its centuries-old cedars.

The building – The outer west façade, which is the oldest, is severely military. Most of the windows that can be seen now did not exist originally. The two other façades, though they still have a feudal look, show the influence of the Renaissance.

At ground floor level there is a frieze bearing the interlaced Cs of Charles d'Amboise and his wife, Catherine, alternating with the rebus of the castle: a volcano or *chaud mont* (Chaumont). The emblem of Diane de Poitiers is carved in front of each machicolation: it consists of intertwined Ds or of the hunting horn, bow and quiver of Diana the Huntress.

Beyond the drawbridge, the entrance gate is adorned with the arms of France and the initials of Louis XII and Anne of Brittany on a field of fleurs de lys and ermine. The hat of the Cardinal d'Amboise is carved on the tower on the left, and the arms of Charles d'Amboise, Admiral and Marshal of France, on the righthand tower. These emblems are protected by small structures in a mixed Gothic and Italian Renaissance style. On entering the courtyard go first to the terrace. It was built in the 18C on the site of the north wing, which had been demolished by an owner who liked the view. A magnificent Loire landscape can be seen from it.

Chaumont Château
Spiral staircase

The apartments ⊙ – Note the room of the two rivals, Catherine de' Medici and Diane de Poitiers, and also Ruggieri's study and the Council Room, which is paved with Renaissance majolica tiles brought from Palermo in Sicily by the Princesse de Broglie. They contain fine tapestries, good furniture and a collection of the terracotta medallions made by Nini.

The stables ⊙ – *About 50m from the château.* Their size and appointments give an idea of the part played by horses in the lives of princely families.

Built in 1877 by the Prince de Broglie and lit by electricity in 1906, the stables were used until 1917, when the Prince went bankrupt and was forced to sell his horses. In a corner of the stables note the double-roofed tower, the former dovecot, transformed into an oven for Nini *(see above),* which later became the riding school for the children at the château.

Every year
the Michelin Red Guide France
revises its selection of hotels and restaurants which
        - are pleasant, quiet, secluded;
        - offer an exceptional, interesting or extensive view;
        - have a tennis court, swimming pool or private beach;
        - have a private garden...

It is worth buying the current edition.

★★★ CHENONCEAU CHÂTEAU

Michelin map **64** fold 16 or **238** fold 14 (7km - 4 1/2 miles east of Bléré) – Local map under LOIRE VALLEY: Orléans-Chinon

The beautiful château of Chenonceau stretches across the River Cher in a perfect harmony of water, greenery, gardens and trees in a fine natural setting. To this perfection is added the elegance of the architecture, the interior decoration and magnificent furniture *(1)*.

View of Chenonceau in 1850 *(Lithograph by Leroy)*

The château shaped by women – The first castle was built between 1513 and 1521 by Thomas **Bohier,** Collector of Taxes under Charles VIII, Louis XII and François I. Bohier's acquisition of Chenonceau and the château's frequent change of owner make up an eventful tale. For 400 years the women involved – wives, mistresses and queens – played the role of heroine, happy or sad.

Catherine Briçonnet, the builder – The Chenonceau estate, comprising a manor and a simple mill, belonged to the lords of Marques; they sold it in ruins to Bohier in 1499 but an heiress exercising her lineal right of redemption bought it back. Bohier however did not give up and patiently acquired all the adjoining fiefs and manors until the property was encircled. Eventually in 1512 Chenonceau was seized and put up for sale; Bohier bought it for 12 400 *livres.* Immediately he demolished all the old buildings except for the keep. As he was kept busy by his duties and often had to be with the army near Milan, he could not supervise the building of his new residence. It was his wife Catherine, from a family of great financiers in Touraine, who took charge and was the moving spirit. In the site chosen for the building and its simple plan one feels a feminine influence and an eye for convenience and comfort: the four rooms on each floor are arranged round a central hall and, another novelty, the stairs rise in a straight line.

The new building was completed in 1521 but Bohier and his wife had little time in which to enjoy it as they died in 1524 and 1526 respectively. A few years later, Bohier's accounts were examined and he was shown to owe a large sum of money to the Treasury. In order to pay his father's debts, Antoine Bohier transferred the château in 1535 to François I who used it as a hunting lodge.

Diane de Poitiers, the everlasting beauty – When Henri II came to the throne in 1547 he gave Chenonceau to Diane de Poitiers. She was twenty years older than he but very attractive. "I saw her" wrote a contemporary "at the age of 70 (in fact she died at 67) as beautiful to look at and as attractive as at 30. She had a very white skin and wore nothing on her face". She was the widow of Louis de Brézé, for whom she had a splendid tomb built in Rouen Cathedral, and she always wore the colours of mourning: black and white. Her influence over Henri II was such that in addition to all the other favours she received, she made him wear mourning too, to the despair of the rejected and humiliated queen.

Diane was an able manager and intended to exploit her estate and her position; she took an interest in agriculture, in the sale of wine, in her financial income and in anything that earned money. She found an excellent source of revenue in the 20 *livres* tax on bells, of which she received a good share; Rabelais said "The king has hung all the bells of the kingdom round the neck of his mare". Diane was a woman of taste; she created a beautiful garden and had a bridge built linking the château with the north bank of the Cher.

Diane made provision for the future; the 1535 act by which Chenonceau became part of the royal estates was repealed and the château temporarily restored to Thomas Bohier but as he was in debt to the crown it was seized automatically and put up for auction; Diane had only to buy it officially and thus became the legal owner.

---

(1) The town of Chenonceaux has an x but not the château.

Despite these precautions, when Henri II was killed in a tournament in 1599, Diane found herself face to face with Catherine de' Medici who was now regent. While her husband was alive the queen had been patient and dissembling and had accepted the situation but now she wanted vengeance. Knowing that Diane was very attached to Chenonceau, she forced her to give up the property in exchange for Chaumont. After a brief attempt at resistance, Diane gave in, left the banks of the Cher and retired to Anet Château where she died seven years later.

Catherine de' Medici, the magnificent – With her love of the arts Catherine de' Medici also had a love of magnificence, and she satisfied both on a grand scale at Chenonceau. She had a park laid out, built a graceful two-storey gallery on the bridge and added vast outbuildings.

Grand festivals were frequent and the people marvelled at them. One was given for the arrival of François II and Mary Stuart; another for Charles IX was even more brilliant. Young women disguised as mermaids welcomed the visitors from the moats along the avenue leading to the château. Their singing was matched by that of the nymphs emerging from the thickets. But the appearance of satyrs scattered the graceful chorus. Nothing was lacking from these festivities. There were banquets, dances, masquerades, fireworks and a naval battle on the Cher.

Henri III presided over a sylvan festival that cost 100 000 *livres* and made a sensation. "The most beautiful and virtuous ladies of the court", we are told, "appeared half naked, with their hair loose, like brides, and with the Queen's daughters, waited on the guests".

Louise de Lorraine, the inconsolable (end of 16C) – Catherine bequeathed Chenonceau to her daughter-in-law, Louise de Lorraine, wife of Henri III. After the King's assassination by Jacques Clément, Louise retired to the château, put on white mourning according to royal custom and wore it to the end of her life; she was therefore known as the "White Queen" or the "White Lady". Her bedroom, her bed, her carpets and chairs were covered with black velvet, and the curtains were of black damask; crowns of thorns and Franciscan girdles were painted in white on black ceilings.

For eleven years, faithful to the memory of her husband, Louise divided her time between prayer, needlework and reading.

Madame Dupin, an intellectual (18C) – From Louise de Lorraine Chenonceau passed to her niece, Françoise de Lorraine, wife of César de Vendôme, the son of Henri IV and Gabrielle d'Estrées who had themselves stayed at the château in 1598. In 1733 it became the property of Dupin, the farmer-general who was the tax collector. Madame Dupin kept a salon which was attended by all the celebrities of the period. **Jean-Jacques Rousseau** was her son's tutor and it was for the benefit of this boy that he wrote his treatise on education, *Émile*. In the *Confessions* the philosopher wrote warmly of that happy time: "We had a good time in that beautiful place, we ate well, I became as fat as a monk."

Madame Dupin advanced into old age surrounded by the affection of the villagers so that the château survived the Revolution unscathed. At her wish she was buried in the park.

Madame Pelouze, lover of antiquity (19C) – In 1864 Madame Pelouze bought Chenonceau and made it her life's work to restore the château to its former glory. Catherine de' Medici had altered the main façade by doubling the windows and placing caryatids between them. The new openings were walled up and the caryatids were moved into the park. A building which had been added between the chapel and the library was removed. Madame Pelouze proceeded boldly with refurbishments in the debatable taste of the 19C.

The château now belongs to the Menier family.

Son et lumière – *See the Calendar of Events at the end of the guide.*

TOUR ⏱ *time: 2 hours*

Approach – A magnificent avenue of plane trees leads to the château. The tourist who likes to indulge his fancy can try to imagine the entry of Charles IX, among mermaids, nymphs and satyrs. Standing back on the left, at the end of a path, you will see the caryatids moved from the façade by Mme Pelouze; the outbuildings erected to the plans of Philibert Delorme are on the right. After crossing a drawbridge you reach a terrace surrounded by moats. To the left is Diane de Poitiers' Italian garden; to the right, that of Catherine de' Medici, bounded by the great trees in the park. On the terrace stands the keep of the original château remodelled by Bohier. Here you will read the initials "TBK" (Thomas Bohier and Katherine). You will find them again in the château, with the motto: *S'il vient à point, me souviendra.* The meaning of this motto is rather obscure. It may be: "If the building is finished it will preserve the memory of the man who built it."

CHENONCEAU

0 ___ 100 m

CHER

Diane de Poitiers' Garden

CHÂTEAU

Catherine de' Medici's Garden

Keep

Waxworks Museum

Orangery

N

CHENONCEAUX

The château – The château consists of a rectangular mansion with turrets at the corners. It stands on two piers of the former mill, resting on the bed of the Cher. The library and the chapel project on the left. Catherine de' Medici's two-storeyed gallery stands on the bridge over the river. This building by Philibert Delorme has a classical simplicity contrasting with the rich, gay appearance given to the older portion by the sculptures on the balustrades, roof and dormer windows.

Ground floor – The four main rooms lead off the hall whose ribbed vaults have keystones aligned along a broken axis. The former guardroom *(left)* is paved with majolica tiles and adorned with 16C Flemish tapestries; in the chapel is a 16C marble bas-relief of a Virgin and Child; the fireplace in Diane de Poitiers' bedroom was designed by Jean Goujon; pictures hang in Catherine de' Medici's Green Cabinet as well as an Oudenaarde tapestry.

The great gallery overlooking the Cher is 60m - 197ft long and has black and white chequered paving; incorporated in its ceiling is the ceiling of Louise de Lorraine's bedroom; during the First World War the gallery was converted into a military hospital and from 1940 to 1942 the demarcation line ran right through the middle. In François I's bedroom hang paintings by Van Loo *(Three Graces),* Il Primaticcio *(Diane de Poitiers as the Huntress Diana),* and a handsome 15C Italian piece of furniture inlaid in ivory and mother-of-pearl is worth noting; in a salon with a magnificent French-style ceiling are works by Rubens *(Jesus and St John),* Mignard, Nattier *(Mme Dupin)* and a portrait of *Louis XIV* by Rigaud, richly framed.

First floor – This is reached by a straight staircase, which at the time it was built was an innovation in France. From the vestibule, with its Oudenaarde tapestries depicting hunting scenes and Carrara marble statues of Roman emperors brought by Catherine de' Medici from Florence, walk through to Gabrielle d'Estrées' bedroom, the Royal, or Five Queens' Bedroom, the bedroom of Catherine de' Medici and finally to that of César de Vendôme. All the rooms are furnished and adorned with fine Gobelins tapestries.

A small convent for Capuchin nuns was established in the attics, complete with a drawbridge which was raised at night to separate the nuns from the castle's other occupants.

Kitchens – There is an attractive dresser and a series of brass containers.

Waxworks Museum ⊙ – The Dômes building, so called because of the shape of the roof, presents fifteen scenes evoking life in the château and the person-alities connected with it.

The park – The gardens and the banks of the Cher provide picturesque views of the château.

EXCURSION

Montlouis-sur-Loire along the Cher Valley – *Round trip of 50km - 31 miles – time: 1 3/4 hours.*

> *Leave Chenonceaux eastwards (towards Montrichard), immediately turn south across the Cher and take N76 west towards Tours.*

Bléré – Pop 4388. Facilities. Place de la République at the entrance to Bléré was once a cemetery; the only monument now remaining was erected in 1526 and elegantly carved in the Italian style; it was the **funerary chapel** of Guillaume de Saigne, Treasurer of the Royal Artillery under François I.

Leugny Château ⊙ – This elegant château on the Cher was built by the architect Portier, a pupil of Gabriel, for himself. It is furnished in the Louis XVI style.

Véretz – Pop 2709. This smart little town nestles between the Cher and the hillside. It presents a charming picture from the north bank of the river: the houses and church lead the eye west to the tree-lined paths and terraces of the château. Among those who walked in the château park were the Abbé de Rancé (1626-1700) who reformed the Trappist order, the Abbé d'Effiat and Madame de Sévigné, the Princess de Conti and the Abbé de Grécourt who wrote light verse; Voltaire stayed at the Château de Véretz in his youth. In the village square stands a monument to **Paul-Louis Courier** (1772-1825), who spent his childhood near Luynes and served as an officer under the Empire. In 1816 he bought the Chavonnière estate with its large house on the Véretz plateau and made his home there with his young wife. From his country retreat he began to harass the government with caustic and witty pamphlets including the famous "A petty village tyrant under the Restoration". Despite his talent he was disliked for his quarrelsome and unbridled temper; on 10 April 1825 he was assassinated in the Larçay Forest in mysterious circumstances.

> *Take D85 north across the River Cher to Montlouis.*

Montlouis-sur-Loire – See Montlouis-sur-Loire.

> *Take D751 east (direction Amboise) and turn right into D40 to St-Martin-le-Beau.*

St-Martin-le-Beau – Pop 2427. The **church** has a finely-sculpted Romanesque doorway.

> *Return to Chenonceaux by D40.*

The Michelin Green Guide France...

makes tourism in France easier and more enjoyable by highlighting the outstanding natural features and the works of man.

Never visit France without a Michelin guide.

Michelin map 🔲 fold 17 or 🔲 fold 15

Not far from the châteaux of Blois and Chambord, Cheverny stands on the edge of the Sologne Forest. Its classical façade is built of white stone from the Bourré quarries *(28km - 17 miles southwest)* and is crowned by a splendid slate roof. Built without interruption between 1604 and 1634 by Count Hurault de Cheverny, the château has a rare unity of style, both in its decoration and in its architecture.

The symmetry and majesty of the façade are characteristic features of the period of Henri IV and Louis XIII; on either side of the single bay containing the main entrance and staircase are steep-roofed central sections, themselves flanked by massive corner pavilions with square domes topped by open belfries. At first floor level there are oval niches containing the busts of Roman emperors, while the Hurault coat of arms above the main doorway is surrounded by two concentric collars, one of the Order of the Holy Ghost, one of the Order of St Michael.

The interior is sumptuously decorated with furniture, sculpture, gilt, marble, multicoloured panelling...

Son et Lumière – *See the Calendar of Events at the end of the guide.*

Cheverny Château

APARTMENTS ◷ *tour: 3/4 hour*

Dining-Room – To the right of the hall is the dining-room hung with a fine 17C Flemish tapestry and refurbished in the 19C when the passage and the chimney with the bust of Henri IV were installed. The room has retained its painted ceiling and small painted wall panels depicting the story of Don Quixote; both are by Jean Mosnier (1600-56), a native of Blois. The walls are covered with Cordoba leather embossed with the Hurault coat of arms.

Private apartments in the West Wing – Access is by the splendid main staircase with its straight flight and rich sculptural decoration. The apartments consist of eight rooms, all magnificently furnished.

Armoury – *Illustration p 25.* This is the largest room in the château. The ceiling, the wainscoting and the shutters were painted by Mosnier, who also did the painting on the gilt wood chimneypiece, flanked by statues of Mercury and Venus. A collection of arms and armour from the 15C and 16C is displayed on the walls as well as a tapestry from the Gobelins (1610) showing the Abduction of Helen.

King's Bedroom – This is the most splendid room in the château. The ceiling is coffered in the Italian style, gilded and painted by Mosnier, as is the rich Renaissance chimneypiece, which is decorated with telamones, cherubs and plant motifs. The walls are hung with tapestries from the Paris workshops (1640) after Simon Vouet; beneath them are wainscots decorated with small pictures. The canopied bed is covered with Persian silk embroidered with flowers (1550).

Grand Salon – The ceiling of the Grand Salon on the ground floor is entirely covered, as is the wall panelling, with painted decoration enhanced with gilding. Among the paintings are, on either side of the mirror, a portrait of *Jeanne d'Aragon* from the School of Raphael and, on the chimneypiece, a portrait by Mignard of *Marie-Johanne de Saumery,* Countess of Cheverny.

Gallery, Petit Salon, Library – The **Gallery** is furnished with magnificent Regency chairs and contains several paintings, including a canvas by François Clouet of *Anne de Thou,* Countess of Cheverny, a portrait of *Jeanne d'Albret* by Miguel Oñate and a self-portrait by Rigaud. The **Petit Salon** is hung with 16C, 17C and 18C paintings; the furniture includes a small gaming table inlaid with different types of Carrara marble. The woodwork and the beautiful parquet floor of the **Library** are worthy of note; there are some very fine bindings too.

Tapestry Room – The smaller salon, which follows, is hung with five 17C tapestries from Flanders after cartoons by Teniers. Both rooms contain Louis XIV and Louis XV period furnishings: Louis XV Chinese lacquered commode and Louis XV clock.

The outbuildings – There is **kennelling** for a pack of 70 hounds, cross-breeds between English fox-hounds and the French Poitou, and the **trophy room** displays 2 000 deer antlers.

The château is still the home of the descendants of the Hurault de Cheverny family who have maintained the tradition of deer hunting; between autumn and Easter each year the hunt rides out in the surrounding woodland.

Orangery – Some 220 yards from the northern steps, on the way out of the castle grounds, stands a magnificent, early-18C building, now entirely restored. Receptions are held here all the year round and, in summer, exhibitions.

EXCURSION

Troussay Château ⊘ – *3.5km - 2 miles west skirting the Cheverny park as far as D 52; turn left and take the first right fork.*

This small Renaissance château was refurbished in the late 19C by the historian Louis de la Saussaye with features from other historic buildings of the region then in a state of neglect. Note particularly the stone carving of a **porcupine,** the emblem of Louis XII, on the rear façade taken from the Hurault de Cheverny mansion in Blois and the beautiful **chapel door**★ carved with delicate scrolls. The tiles on the ground floor date from Louis XII's reign, the Renaissance windows came from the Guise mansion in Blois and the grisailles on the ceiling in the little salon are attributed to Jean Mosnier *(p 31).* The château is lived in and is furnished with fine pieces dating from the 16C to the 18C. The outbuildings round the courtyard house a small museum evoking past domestic and agricultural life in the Sologne.

The towns and sights described in this guide
are indicated in black lettering on the local maps and town plans.

★★ CHINON   Pop 8 627

Michelin map **37** fold 9 or **232** fold 34 – Local maps see below and LOIRE VALLEY: Orléans-Chinon – Facilities

Chinon lies at the heart of a well-known wine region and is surrounded by the fertile **Véron countryside** *(qv)* and the beautiful **Chinon Forest.** To the tourist it looks like a medieval town dominated by the walls of its ruined castle which comes to life again each year during the **medieval market** *(see Calendar of Events).*

Approach from the south for the best **view**★★ of the town and the castle brooding over the River Vienne.

Park in Quai Danton to inspect the castle in detail.

From the Quai the differents parts of the castle are clearly visible: on the left – Coudray Fort; in the centre – the massive Middle Castle (Château du Milieu) extending to the narrow Clock Tower (Tour de l'Horloge) with its roof and machicolations; on the right – St George's Fort, now dismantled.

A walk along the banks of the Vienne is especially agreeable, particularly in the landscaped **English garden** (Jardin Anglais) **(B)** where palm trees flourish in the mild climate of the Loire Valley.

Gargantua's Father – François Rabelais (1494-1553) was born near Chinon at La Devinière *(qv)* and grew up in Chinon where his parents had a house in Rue de la Lamproie. He was the author of the spirited adventures of Pantagruel and his father Gargantua, two giants whose earthy realism always delights the reader. When Gargantua was born his first baby cry was for "A drink, a drink!"; fed on the milk of 17 913 cows, he grew rapidly and "became fat in the face with about eighteen chins". The good-natured giants were fond of feasting and drinking and are freely invoked in the wine cellars of Chinon when the vintage is being tasted.

River Vienne at Chinon

HISTORICAL NOTES

Chinon was originally a Gallo-Roman camp and then a fortress belonging to the Counts of Blois. In the 11C it passed to their enemies, the Counts of Anjou, one of whom, Henry Plantagenet, built the major part of the present castle. In 1154 he became King of England but Chinon, at the heart of his continental possessions, was one of his favourite residences; he died there on 6 July 1189. It was during the Angevin period from 1154 to 1204 that Chinon thrived.

John Lackland, dispossessed vassal – John, the youngest son of Henry II, inherited the Plantagenet empire on the death of his elder brother Richard the Lionheart, who was killed at Châlus in 1199. His deceitful character and his underhand plotting brought him many enemies. First he quarrelled with his nephew Arthur of Brittany who sought refuge at the French court. Then he abducted Isabelle d'Angoulême, the fiancée of the Count of La Marche, and married her at Chinon on 30 August 1200. Discontent with the behaviour of their overlord caused the knights of Poitou to appeal to the royal court in Paris. John refused to attend the hearing; he was condemned to forfeit his French fiefs.

John was reduced to being King of England only and one by one Philippe Auguste captured all the former English strongholds in France; in 1205 Chinon passed to the French crown. John tried to fight back but in vain; after the truce of 26 October 1206 he was forced to give up. He sought, nonetheless, to gain his revenge and in 1213 he took part in the Anglo-German coalition against Philippe Auguste. He was defeated the following year by the future Louis VIII at the Battle of La Roche-aux-Moines near Angers. The French victory was confirmed by the Treaty of Chinon on 18 September 1214. John, who had alienated all the knights in his kingdom and fully deserved his nickname of Lackland, died two years later.

The Court of the "King of Bourges" (early 15C) – With the accession of **Charles VII** Chinon moved into the limelight. France was in a desperate situation. Henry VI, King of England, was also "King of Paris"; Charles VII was only "King of Bourges" when he established his little court at Chinon in 1427. The following year he called a meeting of the States-General of the central and southern provinces which had remained faithful to him. They voted 400 000 *livres* to organize the defence of Orléans, then besieged by the English *(see Orléans)*.

Joan of Arc at Chinon (1429) – Escorted by six men-at-arms, Joan travelled from Lorraine to Chinon, arriving on 6 March, without encountering any of the armed bands which were ravaging the country. The people took this as a clear sign of divine protection. Waiting to be received by Charles VII, Joan spent two days at an inn in the lower town, fasting and praying.

When the peasant girl of eighteen was admitted to the palace, an attempt was made to put her out of countenance. The great hall was lit by 50 torches; 300 gentlemen in rich apparel were assembled there. The King hid among the crowd. A courtier wore his robes.

Joan advanced shyly, immediately recognized the King and went straight to him. "Gentle Dauphin", she said – for Charles, not having been crowned, was only the Dauphin to her – "my name is Jehanne la Pucelle (Joan the Maid). The King of Heaven sends word by me that you will be anointed and crowned in the city of Reims, and you will be the Lieutenant of the King of Heaven, who is the King of France."

Charles was obsessed with doubts about his birth owing to the scandalous behaviour of his mother, Isabella of Bavaria. When the Maid said to him: "I tell you in the name of Our Lord Christ that you are the heir of France and the true son of the King", he was reassured and almost believed in the heroine's mission.

His advisers were more stubborn. The poor girl was made to appear before the court at Poitiers. A bench of doctors and matrons was to decide whether she was bewitched or inspired. For three weeks she was cross-examined. Her naïve replies, her swift repartee, her piety and her confidence in her heavenly mission convinced the most sceptical. She was recognized as the "Messenger of God". She returned to Chinon, where she was equipped and given armed men and left on 20 April 1429 to accomplish her miraculous and tragic destiny *(see map p 21)*.

★★OLD CHINON (VIEUX CHINON) (A) *time: 3/4 hour*

Chinon was once surrounded by high walls which earned it the name Ville Fort (Fortified Town); the old town with its pointed roofs and winding streets nestles between the quays on the River Vienne and the castle bluff. There are many medieval houses with picturesque details: half-timbered houses with carved beams, stone gables with corner turrets, mullioned windows and carved doorways.

Start from Place Charles-de-Gaulle.

Take **Rue Voltaire,** formerly called **Rue Haute St-Maurice,** which is the main axis of the old town.

Wine and Cooperage Museum (A M¹) ⊙ – Housed in a wine cellar, the museum uses life-size automata and a recorded commentary to present the work of a vineyard, the wine-making process and the cooper's art.

In a righthand turning, Rue des Caves-Peintes, which leads up to the hillside, is the **Caves Peintes** where, according to Rabelais, Pantagruel drained many a glass of cool wine; the paintings have disappeared but since Rabelais' time these old quarries have always been devoted to the Sacred Bottle since it is here that the annual ceremony of the Entonneurs Rabelaisiens (the wine growers' brotherhood) is held. No 19 Rue Voltaire is a 14C half-timbered house. Rue Jeanne-d'Arc climbs steeply up to the castle; a plaque marks the **well** where, according to tradition, Joan of Arc placed her foot when she dismounted from her horse on arriving in Chinon.

A

Commerce (R. du) .... **A** 4
Gaulle (Pl. Gén. de) ... **A** 8
J.-J.-Rousseau (R.) ... **B**
Jeanne-d'Arc (Q.) ... **AB**
Rabelais (R.) .... **AB** 17

Carnot (R.) .... **A** 2
Caves Peintes
  (Imp. des) .... **A** 3
Courances (R. des) .. **B** 5
Diderot (R.) .... **B** 6
Dr-Gendron (R.) ..... **A** 7
Grand-Carroi (R.) ... **A** 9
Jacques-Cœur (R.) ... **A** 10
Jeanne-d'Arc (R.) .... **A** 13
Lamproie (R. de la) .. **B** 14
Voltaire (R.) .... **A** 20

Hôtel Torterue de Langardière (18C) – *Rue Jeanne-d'Arc.*
The classical façade is enhanced by handsome wrought-iron balconies.

★★ **Grand Carroi (A B)** – (*carroi* = crossroads). Despite its restricted size, which hardly merits such a grand name, this was the centre of the town in the Middle Ages, where Rue Haute St-Maurice, an old Gaulish road, intersected Rue du Grand-Carroi which led down to the bridge over the Vienne. This is the setting for the annual "Medieval Market" *(see Calendar of Events).*
The picturesque courtyards of the old houses are open to the public; the prettiest are not far from one another: no 38, called the Red House (**Maison Rouge** – 14C) is half-timbered with brick and an overhanging upper storey; another half-timbered house, no 45, is decorated with statues serving as columns; no 44, the States-General House (**Hôtel des États-Généraux**) is a handsome 15C-16C brick building, which houses the Museum of Old Chinon, and the broad stone doorway of no 48, the 17C Government House (**Hôtel du Gouvernement**), opens into an attractive courtyard lined with graceful arcades.

Museum of Old Chinon and of River Transport (A M²) ⊘ – The museum is housed in the States-General House, where Richard the Lionheart is said to have died in 1199 after being at the siege of Châlus in the Limousin, and where the States-General – the French Parliament – met in 1428 at the request of Charles VII to provide him with the money to continue the war against the English.
The ground floor exhibits are mainly concerned with folk art and archaeological finds. There are beautiful rooms: the main hall on the first floor has a full portrait of Rabelais by Delacroix; and the second floor, where the roof is in the form of a ship's hull, contains the collections of a local historical society. There are also ceramics including Langeais ware, St Mexme's cope brought back from the Holy Land during one of the Crusades, as well as Gothic chests and wooden statues of the Virgin.
There are various exhibits connected with the traffic on the Vienne and the Loire and models of the different kinds of vessels: flat-bottomed barges, lighters and expendable pinewood boats *(see Loire Valley).*

Bailiff's Court (Palais du Bailliage) – *No 73 Rue Haute St-Maurice.*
Walk round into Rue Jacques-Cœur to admire the southern façade of this building which houses the Hostellerie Gargantua: the corbelled turret and the crocketed gable.

St Maurice's Church (12-16C) (A E) – The vaulting in the nave and the chancel are in the pure Angevin style.
Further west in **Rue Haute St-Maurice** is the **Bodard de la Jacopière House** (no 81), a 15C-16C building with a town gateway (15C) picked out in nails on the wooden façade; no 82 is a 16C building (**Hôtel des Eaux et Forêts**) with a corner turret and elegant dormer windows.

★★ **CASTLE (CHÂTEAU)** ⊘ *time: 1 hour*

It is best to approach the castle by the Route de Tours (D 751) which skirts the massive walls on the north side. Note the reconstructions of ancient machines including a balista (catapult for launching stones) and a trebuchet, used in siege warfare until the 14C.
Built on a spur overlooking the Vienne, this vast fortress (400m by 70m - 1 312ft by 230ft) dates mostly from the reign of Henry II (12C). Abandoned by the court after the 15C and bought in the 17C by Cardinal de Richelieu, the castle was dismantled little by little until Prosper Mérimée undertook to preserve it. The grandiose ruins evoke eight centuries of history.
It was composed of three sections separated by deep dry moats.

CHINON CASTLE

St George's Fort – The eastern fort, which is now dismantled, protected the vulnerable side of the castle which was accessible from the plateau.

Middle Castle (Château du Milieu) – The entrance to the Middle Castle is across the moat and through the 14C **Clock Tower** (Tour de l'Horloge) which is unusually shallow (only 5 m - 16 ft deep). Inside, there are four rooms with displays evoking the great moments in the life of Joan of Arc. A bell, the Marie Javelle, which is dated 1399, sounds the hour from the lantern at the top of the tower. One is free to stroll in the gardens and explore the ruined towers; from the south curtain wall there is a very picturesque **view**★★ of the slate roofs of Old Chinon, the Vienne and the river valley.

Coudray Fort – West of the gardens another bridge crosses the moat to Coudray Fort on the point of the rock spur. Coudray keep (right) was built by Philippe Auguste early in the 13C; the Templars *(see Arville)* were imprisoned here by Philip the Fair in 1308 and it was they who carved the famous graffiti on the north wall of the present entrance. Joan of Arc lodged on the first floor, now roofless, in 1429.

Royal Apartments (Logis royal) – Joan of Arc was received in the great hall on the first floor; only the fireplace remains. The guard room on the ground floor displays a large model of the castle as it was in the 15C; in the kitchens there is a fine Aubusson tapestry (17C) depicting Joan of Arc recognizing the Dauphin together with two Flemish tapestries *(Bear Hunt* and *The Judgement of Paris)*. A small lapidary museum leads to the 13C **Boissy Tower;** here, in a vaulted chamber once used as a chapel, there is the family tree of the Capets, the Valois and the Plantagenets, as well as a map of France in 1420 explaining the position of the Dauphin when Joan of Arc arrived.

ADDITIONAL SIGHTS

St Stephen's Church (St-Étienne) (B) – Built around 1480 by Philippe de Commines, the church has a Flamboyant door carved with his coat of arms.

Rue Jean-Jacques Rousseau (B) – Several picturesque medieval houses can be seen, especially nos 71 and 73 at the crossroads with Rue du Puy-des-Bancs.

St Mexme's Church (B) ⊘ – Two imposing towers overlooking Place St-Mexme and the nave and the narthex are all that is left of this 10C-11C church.

St Radegund's Chapel (B) ⊘ – *Access on foot by the steep path which begins northeast of St Mexme's Church.*
The steep rise is bordered by troglodyte houses. In the 6C a pious hermit had his cell built in the cave. Radegund, the wife of King Chlotar I, came to consult the hermit about her intention to leave the court and founded the convent of the Holy Cross (Ste-Croix) in Poitiers – the cell was later enlarged into a chapel where the hermit was buried. A Romanesque portal leads into the chapel. On the left is a Romanesque fresco depicting a Royal Hunt; on the right 17C paintings recount St Radegund's life. One can also visit the **cave** dwelling, adjoining the chapel, and the **Folk Museum** (Musée des Arts et Traditions populaires).

EXCURSIONS

Steam Railway ⊘ – A steam train dating from the 1920s runs from Chinon to Richelieu via Ligré and Champigny-sur-Veude. *See Richelieu.*

★⓵ **Vienne Valley** – Michelin map **67** folds 9, 10 or **232** folds 34, 35. *Round tour of 60km - 38 miles – about 3 hours. Leave Chinon to the east by Rue Diderot and D 21.*

The road follows the chalky slope through the well-known vineyards of Cravant-les-Côteaux.

Vieux-Bourg de Cravant – *1 km - 1/2 mile north of Cravant-les-Côteaux.*
The **church** ⊘ of this old town is particularly interesting because of its age. The nave is a rare example of the Carolingian style (early 10C). The 11C south portal is adorned with a twisted fringe; just at the entrance to the chancel two rectangular pillars have been adorned with Merovingian interlacing. These pillars used to support the roof of the south portal.

In the south chapel, added in the 15C, there are remains of a fresco (on the west wall) representing the chapel's donors, who were probably Georges de La Trémoille, Minister to Charles VII, Catherine de l'Ile-Bouchard, his wife, and their children. There is also a lapidary museum.

Follow D 21 to Panzoult and then take D 221 to Crouzilles.

Crouzilles – Pop 540. Built in the 12C and covered with Angevin vaulting in the 13C, the **church** is fascinating owing to the way in which the statues have been incorporated into the church's structure. The buttresses on either side of the Romanesque door have been carved with a niche to hold a statue; in the apse, statues have been placed at the springing line of the vault: St Peter, the Virgin, St John, St Paul and in the southeast corner of the south transept the "beau Dieu de Crouzilles".

Take D 760 west to L'Ile-Bouchard.

L'Ile-Bouchard – See L'Ile-Bouchard.

The road passes in front of the church of St-Gilles, then crosses the Vienne to the other half of the town.

Take D 18 east to Parçay-sur-Vienne.

Parçay-sur-Vienne – Pop 512. This 12C **church** has a fine Romanesque doorway flanked by blind arcades. It is decorated with carved archivolts representing bearded faces (33 in total), foliated scrolls and palmettes, and the ensemble is adorned with a motif resembling fish scales. The capitals in the chancel are decorated with fantastic animals of amazing ugliness inspired by the Apocalypse of St John the Divine.

Return to L'Ile-Bouchard and take D 760 westwards along the south bank of the Vienne.

Tavant – Pop 227. This Romanesque **church** ☉ is of special interest owing to its 12C **frescoes★** which adorn the vaulting, the apse and crypt. More marked in the crypt than in the church, the figures show a power of expression and a degree of realism extremely rare during the Romanesque period. Note the capitals in the chancel.

About 2 miles further on, beyond Sazilly, D 760 passes **Bretignolles Château** (left), a Louis XII-style building with turrets.

Turn left into D 749.

★Rivau Castle – See Rivau Castle.

Return to Chinon by D 749 and ③ on the plan.

2 Rabelais Country – *25km - 15 miles by ③ on the plan. The road runs through a tunnel of tall plane trees to St-Lazare; turn right into D 751; after 3 km - 2 miles turn left into D 759; then turn right into D 24 and fork right into D 117.*

La Devinière ☉ – This house was the birthplace of **François Rabelais** (1494-1553). He was the son of a Chinon lawyer and after a studious childhood, he became a monk, fell in love with ancient Greek and studied the humanists. He transferred to the secular clergy, studied medicine at Montpellier and became a famous doctor, under the patronage of such great names as Cardinal Jean du Bellay and his brother the Governor of Piedmont; in 1551 the Cardinal obtained the living at Meudon for Rabelais.

With the publication of *Pantagruel* in 1532 Rabelais, the distinguished Hellenist, revealed the humourous side of his character by choosing burlesque farce and every kind of comedy to express his philosophy.

At La Devinière one sees Rabelais' room and a small museum illustrating his life and work; there is an interesting study on the origins of his hero Gargantua.

Return to D 117 going south.

On the opposite side of the valley stands the beautiful **Coudray-Montpensier Château** (15C) with its myriad roofs. In between lies **Seuilly-Côteaux**, a long straggling street of troglodyte houses.

It was in the abbey at Seuilly that Rabelais was educated; he used it as the setting for one of his characters in *Gargantua*.

Lerné – Pop 330. Picturesque village built of yellow tufa. In Rabelais' book this was the village from which the bakers *(fouaciers)* of a special sort of bread set out to sell their goods *(fouaces)* in Chinon market; it was a dispute between them and the shepherds from Seuilly that sparked off the comic Picrocholean War between Picrochole, king of Lerné, an aggressive fighter, and Grandgousier, the wise prince of Seuilly, who was Gargantua's father.

Return to Chinon, taking D 224 which runs through Seuilly-Bourg at the bottom of the slope; near the road junction with D 749 (right) stands **La Roche-Clermault Château** which was taken by assault by Picrochole and his men in Rabelais' story.

Chinon Nuclear Power Station ⊙ – *12 km - 7 miles northwest by* ④ *on the plan. Entrance near Port-Boulet bridge.*

It was here on the banks of the Loire that the first of France's many nuclear power stations was built in 1963. Chinon A used natural uranium for fuel, graphite as moderator, and carbon dioxide as cooling medium, and has now ceased production. Chinon B, with its four low cooling towers, is of the pressurised water reactor type. Chinon A, nicknamed "the Bubble" (Boule) became the **Nuclear Industry Museum** ⊙ in February 1986; an **audio-visual presentation** features a TV camera's view of the core of the reactor and the whole of the power station can be seen through the four portholes at the top of the great sphere.

CHOLET   Pop 55 132

Michelin map 🔢 folds 5, 6 or 🔢 fold 30.
Town plan in the current Michelin Red Guide France

Cholet is a spacious modern town, which thrives on its various industries: textiles, shoes, fashion, plastics, electronics, agricultural machinery and a Michelin tyre factory. The town is surrounded by the pastures of Les Mauges *(qv)* and is also an important cattle market.

Ravages of War – There is scarcely a building in Cholet which dates from before the Revolution since the town suffered sorely in the Vendée wars *(qv)*. At the beginning to the peasant insurrection the town was captured by the Whites (15 March 1793) who then regrouped before marching victoriously on Saumur and Angers. On 17 October Cholet was captured by Kléber after a bloody battle in which 40 000 Whites faced 25 000 Blues; the victor described it as a "battle between lions and tigers"; the dead numbered 10 000. On 10 March 1794 after hand to hand fighting in the streets Stofflet was victorious but a few days later the "infernal columns" under General Turreau put Cholet to fire and the sword. On 18 March Stofflet returned but was soon repulsed by General Cordelier; the town was left in ruins.

Cholet handkerchiefs – Cholet has been involved in the cultivation of hemp and flax since the 11C; spinning and weaving are long-established industries. In the 16C the handkerchief was introduced into France from Italy; in the 18C Cholet cloth was part of the cargo of manufactured goods which the shipowners of Nantes and La Rochelle traded on the coasts of Africa in exchange for slaves who were then sold in the West Indies; the money was spent on rum which was imported into France; this was the "triangular trade". Despite the devastation of the town in the revolutionary wars, Cholet was not destroyed; it re-established its crafts and tenaciously fostered the textile industry throughout the 19C. Cholet table linen is now well known as is the traditional red handkerchief.

SIGHTS

★**History and Art Museum** (Musée d'Art et d'Histoire) ⊙ – *2 Avenue de l'Abreuvoir*. The collections have been reorganised in a building opposite the town hall.

History Gallery: Exhibits of maps, prints, and weapons trace the course of the tragic conflict of Revolutionary times and then the Vendée Wars which ravaged the town and left it in mourning. Features of the collection include Girardet's painting *The Rout of Cholet,* a cast of the Bonchamps mausoleum *(see St-Florent-le-Vieil)* and above all the series of famous full-length portraits of some of the leaders of the Vendée resistance commissioned by Louis XVIII for the Guard Room of the old St-Cloud château, prominent among them one of Cathelineau *(illustration p 147)*.

Art Gallery: 18C works include paintings by the local artist Pierre-Charles Trémolières, Carle van Loo, N Hallé, Nattier, de Troy and Loutherbourg. The 19C is represented by a large number of sculptures by Hippolyte Maindron as well as canvases by Troyon, Diaz de la Peña and Maufra. Geometric Abstraction is well represented with pictures by Vasarely, Gorin, Nemours, Herbin, Claisse, Gleizes, Valmier, Honegger, Magnelli, Heurtaux and Morellet.

Old Houses – A pedestrian precinct has been created in the town centre, where Place Rougé, Rue du Devau and its continuation Rue du Commerce have a number of old houses with rare 18C wrought-iron balconies. On the south side of the street the **Mall Garden** makes a pleasant setting for the Law Courts.

EXCURSIONS

Lake Ribou – *3.5km - 2 miles southeast by D 20 (towards Maulévrier) and then D 600 to the right.* The vast artificial lake encircled by hills provides facilities for a variety of water sports (windsurfing, rowing, sailing, etc.) and fishing. The gently sloping shores are suitable for other sports such as archery, golf and riding. There is also a campsite.

La Goubaudière Farm ⊙ has been converted into a **Rural Museum** showing a typical late-19C interior of the Cholet region: furniture, everyday articles, collection of tools and farm machinery from 1900-50.

Le Verdon Lake – *7km - 4 miles southeast.* This lies immediately downstream from Lake Ribou and covers an area of 280ha - 692 acres. One end of the lake stretches into the hills. The lake has become a nature reserve for the migratory birds that flock here in their thousands.

Maulévrier – *13km - 8 miles southeast (see Maulévrier).*

Coudray-Montbault Château ⊘ – *25km - 15 1/2 miles east by N 160 and D 960.* The moated 16C château with its two massive round towers of brick and stone and green lozenge decoration was built on the ruins of a 13C castle. A ruined chapel in the park contains a recumbent figure and an Entombment.

CINQ-MARS-LA-PILE   Pop 2 370

Michelin map 64 fold 14 or 232 fold 35 (5km - 3 miles northeast of Langeais)

The place name is derived from a curious monument in the shape of a slim tower *(pile),* dating from the Gallo-Roman period, which dominates the ridge east of the village. The structure is 5m - 16 1/2ft square and 30m - 98 1/2ft high and is topped by four small pyramids, one at each corner. It could be a funerary monument or a navigation light but it is most likely a mausoleum built in the 2C AD.

Castle ⊘ – Two round towers (11C and 12C) on the hillside mark the site of the medieval castle where Henri d'Effiat, Marquis of Cinq-Mars, was born. He was the favourite of Louis XIII but was convicted of conspiring against Richelieu and beheaded in Lyon in 1642 at the age of 22.
Each tower contains three rooms, one above the other, roofed with eight-ribbed ogive vaulting. From the top there is an extensive view of the Loire Valley. The surrounding **park**★ is particularly beautiful: here a romantic garden, there a complicated maze, elsewhere dense woodland. The bushes are clipped and the paths neatly edged but with a light touch that does not spoil the naturel charm.

★ CLÉRY-ST-ANDRÉ   Pop 2 506

Michelin map 64 fold 8 or 238 fold 4 – Local map under LOIRE VALLEY: Orléans-Chinon

The present **church** had its origin in a humble chapel to which, in 1280, some ploughmen carried a statue of the Virgin found in a thicket. The cult of this statue spread throughout the district, and the chapel, too small to accommodate the pilgrims, was transformed into a church served by a college of canons. This was destroyed in 1428 by the English commander Salisbury, during his march on Orléans. A popular **pilgrimage** is held on 8 September and the following Sunday.
Charles VII and Dunois supplied the first funds for rebuilding, but the great benefactor of Cléry was **Louis XI.** During the siege of Dieppe, while still only the Dauphin, he vowed to give his weight in silver to Notre-Dame de Cléry if he were victorious. His prayer was answered and he kept his vow. When he became King, Louis XI dedicated himself to the Virgin and his attachment to Cléry was strengthened thereby. He was buried there by his wish and the building was completed by his son, Charles VIII.
The house (now a school) in which Louis XI stayed during his visits to Cléry is on the south side of the church opposite the transept entrance.

★ BASILICA ⊘ time: 1/2 hour

Notre-Dame de Cléry is a 15C building with the exception of its square tower abutting the north side of the church which is 14C and alone escaped destruction by the English. *Entrance in the transept.*
The interior of the church is austere yet elegant; it should be imagined in the warm light of its former stained glass windows and hung with tapestries.

The Tomb of Louis XI – The tomb stands on the north side of the nave and is aligned with the Virgin's altar, so that it lies at an oblique angle to the axis of the church.
The marble statue of the King is the work of an Orléans sculptor, Bourdin (1622). It took the place of the original bronze statue melted down by the Huguenots.

Louis XI's Vault – Louis XI's bones and those of his wife, Charlotte de Savoie, are still in the vault which opens on to the nave near the tomb. The two skulls, sawn open for embalming, are in a glass case. Note the decorative mourning band *(litre)* which runs round the vaulting.
Tanguy de Châtel, who was killed during a siege while saving the life of Louis XI, is buried under a flagstone alongside the royal vault. Further to the right another stone covers the urn containing the heart of Charles VIII. The inscription on this urn is repeated on the nearest pillar.

★**St James's Chapel** – *South aisle.* The church dean, Gilles de Pontbriand, and his brother built this chapel to serve as their tomb. The Gothic decoration is very rich. The vaulting is decorated with girdles and pilgrims' purses, for Cléry is on the pilgrimage route to St James's shrine in Santiago de Compostela, Spain. The walls are studded with ermines' tails and bridges (the arms of the Pontbriands). There are three fine statues of which two are of wood: St James in a pilgrim's cloak is 16C, St Sebastian is 17C, and the Virgin with the very delicate features is 16C and of stone. The Breton-style wooden grille was offered by Louis XIII in 1622.

101

Dunois Chapel – *From the St James's Chapel the second door to the left.* Dunois and his family lie here *(see Châteaudun).* The church at Cléry was finished when this chapel was added (1464) so that the construction of the vaulting was complicated by the presence of a buttress.

Stalls – These were presented by Henri II. Their seats are carved with human masks and the initials of the donor and his mistress, Diane de Poitiers (see cheekpieces – *see p 36* – of second row on the right).

Chancel – On the modern high altar is a statue in wood of Notre-Dame de Cléry. In the central window a fine piece of 16C stained glass represents Henri III founding the Order of the Holy Spirit.

Sacristy and Oratory of Louis XI – In the second ambulatory bay on the right is the beautiful door to the sacristy, in pure Flamboyant style. Above it a small opening leads to an oratory *(spiral staircase in the sacristy)* from which Louis XI could follow mass.

CLOYES-SUR-LE-LOIR   Pop 2593

Michelin map 𝟨𝟘 southwest of fold 17 or 𝟤𝟥𝟩 fold 38 – Local map under LOIR VALLEY: Bonneval-Vendôme – Facilities

Cloyes, once a fortified town, bestrides a bend in the Loir on the southern edge of the Beauce; it was also a staging post on the pilgrim road to Santiago de Compostela. It is a welcoming town with several old houses and a church with a 15C belfry. In 1883 **Zola** stayed in Cloyes to study the local customs for his novel – *The Earth* – which is set in Cloyes and Romilly-sur-Aigre *(see below).*

The Children's Crusade – In 1212 a young shepherd from Cloyes, called Estienne, gathered a following of about 20 000 children on a pilgrimage to the Holy Land. Neither their parents nor their friends could deter them. The expedition was doomed to failure: some children died on the road, others perished at sea and a few were even sold to the Saracens.

Yron Chapel – *1km - 1/2 mile south on N 10 (towards Vendôme), then turn right into D 8¹; entrance in the garden of the old people's home.* The Romanesque chapel is decorated with well-preserved **mural paintings** in red and ochre tones. Those in the nave are 12C and depict the Flagellation and the Offering of the Magi (left), Judas' Kiss and a priest (St Bernard) (right) and the Apostles (apse) below a delicate portrayal of Christ in Majesty (14C).

EXCURSIONS

★**Montigny-le-Gannelon Château** – *2km - 1 1/2 miles north by D 23. See* Montigny-le-Gannelon.

Aigre Valley – *Round trip of 20km - 12 1/2 miles. Leave Cloyes-sur-le-Loir by D 8 going east.* The road climbs on to a plateau overlooking (right) the Aigre Valley.

Romilly-sur-Aigre – Pop 405. The quiet country village climbs the slope on the south bank of the Aigre. Above the village on the edge of the plateau *(D 8³ towards Ouzouer-le-Doyen)* stands an unusual church adjoining a fortified building. Romilly appears in **Zola's** novel *The Earth* under the name of Rognes; the large Beauceron farm described by Zola is probably based on La Touche about 500 m - 550 yards beyond the church.

Return through the village to D 8; turn right.

La Ferté-Villeneuil – Pop 394. Drive through the village down to the banks of the Aigre where a fortified Romanesque church with a solid tower complements the charming scene.

Take the road back to Cloyes.

CORMERY   Pop 1 323

Michelin map no 𝟨𝟦 fold 15 or 𝟤𝟥𝟪 fold 15

Cormery, which is famous for its macaroons, is prettily sited beside the Indre with inns on either bank. Near the bridge, half-hidden under the weeping willows is an **old mill;** downstream the river feeds the ancient washing place.

Old Abbey – The Benedictine Abbey, which was founded in 791, was suppressed a thousand years later in 1791; the buildings were confiscated and sold and mostly demolished. The few remains conjure up a picture of the complete abbey; the model shows it as it was in the 14C and 15C.

Rue de l'Abbaye, which begins the Town Hall *(on N 143)* passes under a tall ruined tower, **St Paul's Tower,** the huge 11C belltower above the entrance to the church; note the Romanesque low-reliefs and the decorative effect below the upper windows. The **Prior's Lodging** at the foot of the tower is marked by an elegant staircase turret. In the street on the left are the arches of the **former refectory** (13C). Of the church itself nothing remains on the far side of the tower; the street follows the line of the nave. The graceful Gothic chapel (left) which was reserved for the Abbot was originally next to the apsidal chapel of the church and linked to the **Abbot's Lodging** which has a turret and a half-timbered penthouse.

Notre-Dame-du-Fougeray – The church of Our Lady of Fougeray, which dominates the valley, is a Romanesque building with elements typical of the Poitou region: a large apse with three apsidal chapels, historiated brackets, a frieze and a dome on pendentives over the transept crossing.

In the cemetery opposite the church there is an altar and a 12C lantern of the dead.

COURTANVAUX CHÂTEAU

Michelin map **64** fold 5 or **238** fold 1 (2km - 1 1/4 miles northwest of Bessé-sur-Braye)

The **château** ⊙, a Gothic building sheltering in the valley, was the seat of a marquisate held successively by the Louvois and Montesquiou families; one of the owners was Michel Le Tellier, Marquis de Louvois and Louis XIV's Minister for War. In 1815, when Napoleon fell from power, the château came to life again after 150 years of neglect and became the residence of the **Countess of Montesquiou** who had been governess to the King of Rome, Napoleon's son by Marie-Louise.

An avenue of plane trees leads to the charming Renaissance gatehouse. The buildings have typical 15C and 16C features: tall roofs, mullioned windows and pointed dormer pediments. The courtyard is dominated by two terraces. The main block, called the "grand château", has a suite of four rooms (47m - 154ft long) on the first floor; they were re-decorated in 1882.

CRAON   Pop 4 767

Michelin map **63** fold 9 or **232** fold 18

Craon (pronounced Cran) is a quiet Angevin town on the River Oudon surrounded by woodland and pastures, devoted to arable farming and castle raising. It is famous for its horseraces (August and September).

Craon was the birthplace of Volney (1757-1820), the philosopher, who enjoyed great fame in his lifetime.

Château ⊙ – Built c1770 in the local white tufa, this elegant château has a curvilinear pediment and windows adorned with festoons characteristic of the Louis XVI period. The courtyard façade is in a severe neo-classical style. Several 18C rooms with fine woodwork and Louis XVI furnishings are on show.

The attractive landscape park in the English style running down to the river has a laundry building as well as an underground ice house, built in the 19C. In winter it was filled with ice and packed snow to serve as a cold chamber for the preservation of food in the summer.

EXCURSIONS

★**Robert Tatin Museum** ⊙ – *14km - 9 miles northeast. Take D 126 to the southeast at Cosse-le-Vivien.*

It was here, around the old farmhouse known as "La Frénouse", that the painter and ceramicist **Robert Tatin** (1902-83) allowed his architectural fantasies free rein. The place is approached via an avenue lined with strange statues leading to the Giants' Gate and the figure of a dragon with jaws agape. Then come three major coloured structures made of reinforced concrete, representing Our Lady of the Whole World, the Moon Gate and the Sun Gate, which stand reflected in a pool shaped like a cross and lined by representations of the twelve months of the year. The architecture, painting and ceramics of the place seem to have been drawn from experience of a symbolic, initiatory nature.

The museum as a whole takes the visitor into the fantastic world of this self-taught artist, whose naive and visionary creations draw on Oriental, Pre-Colombian and even Celtic sources, fusing them into an art of universel significance – a bridge between East and West.

Renazé – *Pop 2 860. 10km - 6 miles southwest.*

With their heyday in the early years of this century, the quarries at Renazé continued to produce their finely-grained slate up until 1975. The Longchamp site has now been turned into a **Slate Museum** ⊙, with displays of tools and machinery, demonstrations of the slate-worker's skills and a slide-show *(1/4 hour)* evoking the dark world of the underground workings which gradually replaced conventional quarrying.

Mortiercrolles Château ⊙ – *11km - 7 miles southeast by D 25 and a path to the left.*

This beautiful château was built in the late 15C by Pierre de Rohan, Marshal of Gié. A broad moat surrounds the long curtain wall with its four corner towers, which is guarded by a remarkable **gatehouse**★ with alternating courses of brick and stone and fine machicolations in tufa. In the courtyard the building containing the main apartments (right) is decorated with superb dormer gables. At the rear of the courtyard an elegant chapel of brick with stone courses was re-roofed in 1969: note the pretty Renaissance side door and the piscina adorned with shells.

Michelin Maps (scale 1 : 200 000) which are revised regularly,
indicate:

- *golf courses, sports stadiums, racecourses, swimming pools, beaches, airfields,*
- *scenic routes, public footpaths, panoramas,*
- *forest parks, interesting sights...*

The perfect complement to the Michelin Green Guides for planning holidays and leisure time.

Keep current Michelin Maps in the car at all times.

★★ CUNAULT CHURCH

Michelin map **64** fold 12 or **232** fold 32 (12km - 8 miles northwest of Saumur) – Local map under LOIRE VALLEY: Chinon-Champtoceaux

Cunault Abbey was founded in 847 by monks from Noirmoutier fleeing from the Normans; in 862 they had to move from Cunault and take refuge further away in Tournus in Burgundy where they deposited the relics of St Philibert. Cunault therefore became a rich Benedictine priory dependant of Tournus Abbey. The monastic church is a beautiful Romanesque structure dating from the 11C-13C.

The huge 11C belltower has been extended by a 15C stone spire; the broad façade is simply decorated with arches at the base and three windows above. In contrast the tympanum over the door is richly decorated with a Virgin in Majesty in generous high relief.

Interior – On entering one is struck by the size and height of the pillars. Cunault church was built in the regular Benedictine style to provide for the liturgical ceremonies (seven per day in the Rule of St Benedict) and for the crowds which attended the pilgrimage on 8 September. The ambulatory with its radiating chapels which circumscribed the chancel and the side aisles were broad enough to take the traditional processions, and the raised chancel enabled the faithful to see the celebrant. The church is now doubly impressive for its clean lines and for the rich decoration (11C-12C) of the 223 **capitals.** Only two, at the entrance to the chancel, are visible without binoculars: (right) nine monks standing and (left) St Philibert welcoming a sinner. The ambulatory chapels contain (starting on the left) a 16C *Pietà,* a 16C ash vestment wardrobe (for stiff copes) and a rare 13C carved and painted **shrine** belonging to St Maxenceul who converted Cunault in the 4C. In the 15C the church was deco-

Cunault Church — Detail of the doorway

rated with frescoes; a few fragments and a fine St Christopher remain. The four bells in the tower come from Constantine Cathedral in Algeria. Opposite the church stands the prior's lodging, an attractive 16C house.

DAMPIERRE-EN-BURLY   Pop 915

Michelin map **65** fold 1 or **238** fold 7 (13km - 8 miles west of Gien)

The flat tiled roofs of Dampierre present an attractive spectacle to anyone approaching from the west on D 952 from Ouzouer-sur-Loire; as the road crosses the tree-lined lake by a causeway, the ruins of a château come into view; beyond what remains of the towers and curtain wall of the castle rises the church tower. In the square by the church stands one of the château gatehouses, an elegant early-17C building, in brick and stone, decorated with bossed pilasters beneath a pyramidal roof.

Nuclear Power Station ☉ – *3km - 2 miles south; signposted.*
The four gigantic cooling towers (165m - 541ft high and 135m - 443ft diameter at the base) rising out of the flat Loire Valley belong to the nuclear power station which, like those at Chinon *(qv)* and St-Laurent-des-Eaux *(qv),* uses the river to supply water to the cooling system. The Dampierre complex, which was commissioned in 1980 and 1981, consists of four production units with an output of 900 MW using enriched uranium in pressurized water reactors.
The way in which the reactors work is described in the information centre, named after **Henri Becquerel** (1852-1908), physicist, whose family lived at Châtillon-Coligny 30km - 21 miles east.

DANGEAU   Pop 742

Michelin map **60** fold 17 or **237** fold 38 (9km - 6 miles west of Bonneval)

The village square is bordered by old houses of brick and timber construction (15C).

St Peter's Church – The church, which was built early in the 12C by monks from Marmoutier, is a vast, well-arranged structure in a very pure Romanesque style. The buttresses and facings are of ironstone. The door in the south porch is decorated with scrolls and strange symbols carved on the lintel: the cross appears between the sun and the moon which have human faces, avarice is shown as a demon holding a purse, luxury as a female figure.
The wooden ceiling in the nave is supported on archaic pillars. There are several statues in the aisles: the two figures on horseback are typical of popular 15C-17C religious art. The baptistry contains a marble triptych of the Passion and the Resurrection, dated 1536.

DESCARTES
Pop 4 120

Michelin map 68 fold 5 or 232 fold 48

It was in Descartes, formerly known as La Haye, that **René Descartes** (1590-1650), the famous French philosopher, physicist and mathematician was baptised, although the family home was in the neighbouring town of Châtellerault. At the age of eight he was sent to the Jesuit College of Henri IV in La Flèche where he received a semi-military education, before joining the army under the Prince of Nassau. While pursuing his military career, he travelled widely in Europe, devoting most of his time to study, and the pursuit of his life's mission as it was revealed to him on 10 November 1619. In 1629 he went again to Holland where he stayed for twenty years, studying at various universities and writing and publishing some of his most famous works. In 1649 he accepted an invitation to the Swedish royal court, where he died on 11 February 1650.

Cartesian thought – Written in French rather than in the Latin of all philosophical or scientific works published hitherto, Descartes' *Discourse on Method* (1637) was intended to be accessible to all. Published four years after Galileo's condemnation by the Inquisition, this seminal work met with a quite different reception and was destined to confound the sceptics; it marked the beginning of modern thought and scientific rationalism. In it, Descartes broke with scholasticism and founded a way of thinking based entirely on reasoned methodology and the systematic application of doubt, even to the extent of querying one's own existence, which he however resolved in the following way: "I who doubt, I who am deceived, at least while I doubt, I must exist, and as doubting is thinking, it is indubitable that while I think, I am." Descartes' work gave birth to an intellectual revolution, one of whose first fruits was analytical geometry.

Descartes Museum ⊘ – *29 Rue Descartes*. This house is where Descartes was born. Documents recounting his life and works are displayed.

EXCURSIONS

Balesme – *2km - 1 mile to the northwest*. Standing amidst this charming village with its houses roofed in rose-coloured tiles, the church presents an attractive belfry over the transept crossing.

Ferrière-Larçon – *16km - 10 miles to the east*.

Château du Châtellier – Standing on a rocky outcrop, commanding the Brignon Valley, this castle (rebuilt 15C and 17C) has preserved some of its medieval fortifications: moats, drawbridges and to the east of its rampart, an imposing round keep.

Ferrière-Larçon – Pop 292. The picturesque tile roofs of this village climb haphazardly up the valley slopes. The **church** is an interesting mixture of styles with a narrow Romanesque nave (12C) and a vast, luminous Gothic chancel (13C). The elegant Romanesque belltower has an octagonal stone spire with a pinnacle at each corner.

★ DOUÉ-LA-FONTAINE
Pop 7 260

Michelin map 67 fold 8 or 232 fold 32 – Local map under LAYON VALLEY

Doué and its outskirts are built on a chalk plateau which is riddled with caves; some are old quarries, others were excavated to provide housing or storage, as a wine cellar or a stable. The caves are invisible from the street since they were not hollowed out of the hillside as in the valley of the Loire and its tributaries, but were below ground level and opened laterally into a broad ditch forming a courtyard. Some are still in use but most were abandoned long since.

Doué still has a number of old houses with turrets and external stairs. The town's main activities are nursery gardening and rose growing; examples of these arts are on display at the famous flower show, **Journée de la Rose**, which takes place each year in mid-July in the arena, and at the **Rose Garden**, a large park on the Soulanger road. At the end of the park, some late-18C stables belonging to Baron Foullon have been converted into an Old Trades Museum.

A windmill marks the entrance to Doué in the Saumur road, the lone survivor of the many that used to cover the region.

★★**Zoo (Parc zoologique des Minières)** ⊘ – The zoo is situated on the western edge of Doué on the road to Cholet (D 960); the **setting** ★ is a series of old quarries, now over-grown. The tunnels, caverns and smaller cavities have been used to provide the animals with a natural outdoor habitat, to enable as much contact with the public as possible (in summer some of the monkeys roam freely while the macaws perch in the trees).

Doué-la-Fontaine Zoo

The way of life and the characteristics of the various creatures living in the zoo are explained on the notices. There are several threatened species which would not survive unless they were bred in captivity: snow panthers, Sumatra tigers, wolves, gibbons, the lemurian colobus and Andean condor. A quarry has been turned into a "Vulture Safari" where the visitor can walk among the birds of prey; the "Emu Safari" enables one to see these huge birds at close range. 18 families of monkeys roam freely on as many islands.

There are several displays, including those in the **"Naturoscope"** on wildlife conservation and environmental protection, housed in an old farm. The importance of sound to animals is explained in an immense "sound cave". The "Faluna" *(p 14)* gallery contains animal fossils from the park itself.

Arena ⊘ – In the 15C an old quarry in the **Douces** district was transformed into an arena when terraces of seats were cut out of the solid rock. It is now used for theatrical and musical performances and the flower show *(see above)*. Beneath the terraces are vast caves which were for a long time inhabited, and kitchens and other rooms are still visible. Royalists were imprisoned here during the revolutionary wars.

Carolingian House (Maison Carolingienne) – *Boulevard du Docteur-Lionnet, on the southern outskirts of the town near the road to Argenton-Château (D 69).*
This 9C fortified dwelling was later transformed into a keep.

EXCURSIONS

Rochemenier Troglodyte Village (Village troglodytique de Rochemenier) ⊘ – *6km - 3 1/2 miles north by D 69 and D 177.* The underground village of Rochemenier, an example of troglodytic settlement adapted to the conditions of the plain, was dug out of the marly deposit known as faluna. Though extending over a wide area, it is now hidden by the new above-ground dwellings where the majority of the local people live. Two troglodytic farmsteads, abandoned around 1930, are open to the public.

La Fosse Troglodyte Hamlet (Hameau troglodytique de la Fosse) ⊘ – *5.5km - 3 miles north by D 214.*
Excavations in 1979 revealed this fine example of a type of rural architecture which was formerly unappreciated; the hamlet used to house three families until it was abandoned in the 1940s. Like the *bories* of Provence it shows how the peasants adapted to living underground. The various chambers were hollowed out below ground around a sunken courtyard, similar to the troglodyte dwellings in Tunisia; only the chimneys protruded above ground level. Ovens and chimneys were dug straight into the earth; so were stores for grain and vegetables.

Sculpted Cavern (Caverne sculptée) ⊘ – *5.5km - 3 miles north by D 69.*
This cave at **Dénezé-sous-Doué** is most unusual; its walls are carved with hundreds of strange figures. From the attitudes and dress and musical instruments the archaeologists have dated the carvings to the 16C; they are probably the work of a secret society of stonemasons and depict their initiation rites. The guides are at hand to give a detailed explanation of the different scenes.

Coudray-Montbault Château – *24km - 15 miles west by D 960. See under Cholet: Excursions.*

Admission times and charges for the sights described are listed at the end of the guide.
Every sight for which there are times and charges is identified by the symbol ⊘ in the Sights section of the guide.

DURTAL

Michelin map ⁵⁴ fold 2 or ²³² fold 20

Durtal is attractively sited in the shelter of its château on the Loir. The **Chambiers Forest** on the southern edge of the town provides 1 300ha - 5sq miles of walks among the oak and pine trees; broad rides radiate from the King's Table (table au roy). The racecourse is a popular meeting place for the sporting fraternity.

Château ⊘ – This lordly stronghold on the Loir belonged to François de Scepeaux, Marshal of Vieilleville, who was host to Henri II, Charles IX and Catherine de' Medici. It came through the Revolution relatively unscathed and is now a retirement home.
The six-storey keep and the round towers with machicolations and pepperpot roofs are 15C and 16C. The sentry walk provides a view of the Loire Valley and the Chambiers Forest. The main range and the other buildings are in the Louis XIII style. Note the tapered dormers framed with twisted columns in the courtyard. The tour of the interior includes the kitchens, the dungeons, the 15C round tower and the great hall which is decorated with frescoes.

Verron Gate – This 15C gate flanked by two turrets is part of the original curtain wall of the castle.

Old Bridge – View of the River Loir, the watermills, the pointed roofs of the town and a medieval round tower upstream.

FAYE-LA-VINEUSE

Michelim map 🔢 south of fold 10 or 🔢 fold 46 (7km - 4 miles south of Richelieu)

Faye-la-Vineuse stands on a rise once covered in vineyards overlooking the valley formed by a tributary of the Veude. During the Middle Ages it was a prosperous walled city of five parishes and 11 000 inhabitants. It was ruined during the Wars of Religion.

St George's Church ⊙ – The Romanesque church was once a collegiate church surrounded by cloisters and conventual buildings. Although it has suffered from excessive restoration it still retains some interesting features: a tall transept crossing with a cupola on pendentives, two side aisles typical of churches in the Berry region, a chancel with a very high elevation and an ambulatory, and carved capitals well worth close inspection – apart from the many plant motifs and imaginary animals there are also battle scenes. The 11C **crypt** is unusually large and its vaulting high. Note the two carved capitals of the Adoration of the Magi and jousting knights.

★ La FERTÉ-BERNARD

Michelin map 🔢 fold 15 or 🔢 folds 11, 12 – Local map under Le PERCHE-GOUËT

La Ferté-Bernard is a lively commercial town at the centre of an agricultural region. The old houses cluster round the Church of Our Lady of the Marshes. The lush pastures of the Huisne valley are watered by this river, its tributary the Même and several smaller streams.

The old fortified town, which grew up round the castle *(ferté)* was built on stilts in the middle of the marshes. It was distinguished by the name of the first feudal lord, Bernard, whose descendants held the domain until the 14C. Under Louis XI it was the property of the Guise family; in the 16C it enjoyed a period of economic prosperity which produced some remarkable buildings which contribute to the charm of the town. After taking the side of the League and being defeated by the troops of Henri IV, La Ferté was sold to Cardinal de Richelieu in 1642; his heirs held it until the Revolution.

La Ferté-Bernard was the birthplace of the poet **R. Garnier** (1544-90); he wrote seven tragedies of which the best-known, *The Jews,* echoes Corneille and foreshadows Racine. His play *Bradamante* is an early tragi-comedy while his modernism links him to Voltaire.

The lambs of La Ferté – "It needs only two to strangle a wolf" so it was said. In 1590 the troops of Henri IV under the Prince de Conti were besieging La Ferté which was defended by the supporters of the League who were commanded by a descendant of the Emperor of Byzantium, Drago Comnenos.

As food was in short supply, Comnenos decided to get rid of the surplus population and expelled a number of women to fend for themselves, to the great delight of the besiegers. Comnenos then disguised 200 of his ruffians as young women and expelled them. The besiegers approached with great expectations but when they came within range the "lambs" threw off their bonnets and petticoats and turned into hardened old troopers who put the credulous suitors to flight.

SIGHTS

★★ **Church of Our Lady of the Marshes** (Notre-Dame-des-Marais) (B) – This magnificent building is a fine example of the Flamboyant style with early touches of the Renaissance. The nave and transept and the square tower were built between 1450 and 1500; from 1535 to 1544 Mathurin Delaborde worked on the church and between 1550 and 1590 the Viet brothers were in charge of the construction of the spacious chancel (completed in 1596); the ambulatory serves the radiating chapels which have galleries, flying buttresses and solid buttresses topped with crocketed pinnacles.

Exterior – There are Renaissance motifs in the carved decoration of the chancel; the south side is ornamented with scroll work and busts of Roman emperors in the spandrels; there are niches in the buttresses. The low gallery is supported on a carved cornice of shells and busts in relief between the corbels. On the balustrade stand some unusual little statues of the King of France and his twelve peers, etc; in the spaces are the words "Regina Coeli". The upper gallery spells out the letters of "Ave Regina Coelorum". The height of the chancel compared with the original tower on the lefthand side reveals the ambitiousness of the plans drawn up in the late 16C.

The entrance is the Flamboyant south door.

Interior – At the west end are the original Renaissance holy water stoups; the nave contains the organ pipes supported on a Flamboyant corbel.

The very elegant chancel consists of soaring arches, each one surmounted by a small statue on a dais, a light and simple Renaissance triforium and tall windows filled with light 16C and 17C glass.

The three **apsidal chapels ★** are of particular interest. The righthand chapel has an astonishing ceiling of ogive vaulting meeting in a crown-shaped pendant; the windows, the delicate carved cartouches and the stoup are all 16C. In the central chapel the spaces between the ribs are decorated with stalactites and honeycombs; the Renaissance window (left) shows the meal at Bethany with Mary Magdalene at Jesus' feet. The lefthand chapel has an unusual ceiling. The altarpiece in the side chapel on the left of the chancel shows the instruments of the Passion.

Bourgneuf (R.) . . . . B 5
Denfert-
Rochereau (R.) . . . . . . B 12
République (Pl. de la) . . . B 25
Thiers (R.) . . . . B 28
Victor-Hugo (R.) . . . . A
4-Septembre (R. du) . . . . . A 33
8-Mai-1945 (Av. du) . . . . . A 35

Abreuvoir (R. de l') . . . . . . B 2
Bert (R. P.) . . . . A 3
Carnot (R.) . . . . B 6
Château (R. du) . . . . B 7
Châteaudun (R. de) . . . . . . B 8
Florant (R.) . . . . AB 13
Grand-Mail
(Promenade du) . . . . . . B 15

Huisne (R. du Quai d') . . . B 16
Huisne (R. d') . . . . B 18
Marchand (R. A.) . . . . B 21
Petit-Mail (Promenade du) B 24
St-Julien (Pl.) . . . . A 26
Viet (R.) . . . . B 30
Voltaire (R.) . . . . A 32

St Julian's Gate (Porte St-Julien (A)) – The gate which is protected by two round towers and machicolations was built in the 15C under Louis XI; the moat was fed by the River Huisne. There was a postern and a double gate for vehicles guarded by a portcullis and a drawbridge.

Old Houses – East of St Julian's Gate in Rue de l'Huisne (**B 18**) are a few Renaissance houses (no 15 - telamone).
There are several old houses in Rue Carnot including a pilgrim inn (15C) on the road to Santiago de Compostela and a house (butcher's shop) decorated with painted telamones representing a pilgrim (ground floor) being stared at by a madman and a grimacing Moor and two people (first floor) stoning St Stephen.
The Tourist Information Office (syndicat d'initiative) in Cour du Sauvage is housed in the town's former salt store.

Market (B B) – The market hall *(restored)* in Place de la Lice and Rue Carnot was built in 1535. The façade overlooking the square is decorated with Guise lions on each gable and an extensive tile roof pierced by dormers and supported by very fine woodwork.

Fountain – The granite fountain (15C-16C) is fed by a spring in Les Guillottières district which is channelled beneath the Huisne.

St Lyphard's Chapel (B) ⊙ – Thorough restoration work has revealed the former chapel of an 11C feudal castle that was built between two arms of the River Huisne and then partly demolished on the orders of Charles VI. The outbuidings *(private property)* also remain. The chapel, which was originally built against the main body of the castle and given a small side oratory in which a Virgin in Majesty may be seen, is decorated with modern stained-glass windows of Louis, Duke of Orléans, and his wife Valentine Visconti, lord and lady of La Ferté-Bernard to whom the castle was endowed in 1392.

EXCURSIONS

Ceton Church – *8km - 5 miles northeast.*
St Peter's Church (recently restored) derives its importance from the Cluniac priory to which it belonged from 1090. The tower is Romanesque, the Gothic nave and chancel were built in the 13C-16C. Each bay in the side aisles has its own roof at right angles to the nave in the Percheron manner.
A touchingly naive 16C Entombment stands out in the interior among the fine statues.

Le Perche-Gouët Round Trip – *See Le Perche-Gouët. From Ceton drive 5km - 3 miles east to Les Etilleux.*

*The chapter on art and architecture in this guide gives an outline of artistic creation in the region, providing the context of the buildings and works of art described in the **Sights** section.*

This chapter may also provide ideas for touring.

It is advisable to read it at leisure.

La FERTÉ-ST-AUBIN

Michelin map **64** fold 9 or **238** fold 5

The town extends north-south between the N 20 and the railway line. A sawmill and a garment factory are the only remaining examples of the town's past commercial activity. The old district by the château has a few typical local houses: low, timber-framed with brick infill, huge roofs of flat tiles.

Château ⊙ – Built on the banks of the Cosson in brick relieved with courses of stone, this is an impressive edifice, albeit an asymmetrical one; to the left is the "Little Château" still with its 16C diamond-patterned brickwork, to the right the "Big Château", built in the mid-17C with a classical façade topped by sculpted dormers. The centrepiece is formed by a pedimented portal flanked by domed pavilions.

Inside *(access via the ramp)*, the dining room and the Grand Salon have kept their 18C furnishings as well as a number of portraits including one of the *Marquis de la Carte* attributed to Largillière and another of *Louis XV* at the age of 54. The Marshals' Room is devoted to the memory of Marshal de la Ferté, who distinguished himself at the Battle of Rocroi, and of Ulrich de Lowendal, a contemporary of Marshal de Saxe, his neighbour at Chambord *(qv)*.

On the first floor of the righthand wing *(access on the right)*, are 17C, 18C and 19C state apartments and the Guard Room with its fine French-style ceiling. On the second floor are a number of rooms with displays on traditional trades of the Sologne, and the basement kitchens can also be visited.

The main courtyard is defined by two identical buildings; the one on the left houses the **stables** and the **saddlery**, the one on the right the orangery in which receptions are held.

In the grounds is a **menagerie** with a little model farm. There are also 30ha - 75 acres of English-style parkland with a network of islands and an "enchanted house" for children.

St Aubin's Church – 12C-16C. The tall tower over the entrance dominates the Cosson Valley.

EXCURSION

Le Ciran Domain – *7km - 5 miles east*. The domain is a stretch of typical Sologne country: forest, scrub, meadows, streams, pools. The château and the old storehouse contain a little **museum** ⊙ devoted to the Sologne and its former way of life.

★ La FLÈCHE

Michelin map **64** fold 2 or **232** fold 21 – Local map under LOIR VALLEY: Vendôme-La Flèche – Facilities

This charming Angevin town, pleasantly situated on the banks of the Loir, is renowned for its *Prytanée*, a military college which has trained generations of officers.

Market town for the varied fruit produce from the Maine, La Flèche has recently experienced an industrial expansion with the building of several large factories, including the printing works of the paperback publishers *Livre de Poche*.

Students tend to group around the Henri IV Fountain (on the square of the same name); and yet a stroll along the Boulevard Latouche and Carmes Gardens is also pleasant.

Henri IV – La Flèche was given as part of a dowry to Charles de Bourbon-Vendôme, the grandfather of Henri IV of Navarre, of "Paris is well worth a Mass" fame.

It was here that the young Prince Henri happily spent his childhood and where in 1604 he founded a Jesuit college, which was to become the *Prytanée*.

Cradle for Officers – The Jesuit college grew rapidly and by 1625 there were 1 500 pupils. Full of their success, the good fathers started a dispute with the Governor of the town who wanted to prevent them fishing in their moat; the dispute became known as the "war of the frogs". Following the expulsion of the Jesuits from France in 1762, the college became a military school and then an imperial military academy *(prytanée)* in 1808. The pupils were nicknamed *"brutions"* owing to their lack of good manners but the college produced some famous people: Descartes, La Tour d'Auvergne, the Dupetit-Thouars and several generals and marshals: Davout, Junot, Jourdan, Bertrand, Gallieni.

Missionaries in Canada – Jérôme le Royer de la Dauversière, a native of La Flèche, was one of the founders of Montreal. The paganism of the Canadian Indians moved him to create the "society of Our Lady for the conversion of the Savages" which started a little colony in 1642, now the capital of Quebec. In 1646 several Jesuit priests from La Flèche, working as missionaries in the Huron country, were martyred by the Iroquois Indians: Jogues, Lalemant and Brébeuf. Another old pupil of the college in La Flèche, **François de Montmorency-Laval**, became the first bishop of Nouvelle-France in 1674.

Unhappy exile – Under the monarchy La Flèche was a peaceful town with nothing to offer by way of entertainment but a hairdresser's, two billiard halls and a café. **Gresset** (1709-77), the poet whose playful spirit produced the adventures of the parrot Vert-Vert, composed his heroic-comic masterpiece while in exile in La Flèche for indiscreet use of his tongue and his pen.

LA FLÈCHE

0   400 m

Carnot (Rue) .... Y 3
Grande-Rue .... Y
Grollier (Rue) .... YZ 10
Marché-au-blé (Pl.) .... Y 13

Boierie (R. de la) .... Z 2
Collège (R. du) .... Y 4
Dauversière (R. de la) ..... Y 5
Foch (Prom. du Mar.) ...... Z 8
Gallieni
    (R. du Mar.) .... Z 9
Henri-IV (Pl.) .... Y 12
Montréal (Bd de) .... Z 14
Moulin (Bd Jean) .... Y 16
Ravenel (R.) .... Y 17
Rhin-et-Danube
    (Av.) .... Y 18
Thury-Harcourt
    (Av. de) .... Z 19
Verdun (R. de) .... Y 20

SIGHTS

★ **Military College (Prytanée national militaire)** (Y) ⊘ – Essentially it is a school for the children of officers or civil servants who are working for the baccalauréat; they are selected after taking an entrance exam at the age of 15. The school also takes young students from any background, whose school record is acceptable, to prepare them for entrance to the national service academies *(grandes écoles);* there is a cavalry section. A monumental Baroque doorway, surmounted by a bust of Henri IV, marks the entrance to the former Jesuit college. It opens into the main courtyard, also known as the Austerlitz courtyard; at the far end stands a Louis XVI-style house (1784) which houses the staff. The school has an excellent library of some 45 000 volumes; some date from the 15C.

★ **St Louis's Chapel** – 1607-37. The chapel is in the Sebastopol Court where the architecture is austere. It is arranged in the typical Jesuit manner: nave bordered by side chapels, large galleries, plentiful light. The Baroque décor is impressive from the great retable on the high altar to the magnificent organ (1640) in its graceful loft. Set in an upper niche in the left transept is a heart-shaped lead gilt urn which contains the ashes of the hearts of Henri IV and Marie de' Medici.

Chapel of Our Lady of the Virtues (Notre-Dame-des-Vertus) (Y) – This is a charming Romanesque chapel with a semicircular-arched doorway and oven-vaulted apses. The wooden vaulting in the nave is completely decorated with 17C paintings (scrolls and medallions). The Renaissance **woodwork★** came originally from the chapel of Le Verger Château *(qv);* note the "Muslim warrior" on the back of the main door; the panels are Renaissance. The carvings in the nave include medallions and religious attributes.

Château des Carmes (Z H) – The 17C buildings erected on the ruins of a 15C fortress now house the Town Hall. The façade facing the Loir consists of a steep gable flanked by two machicolated turrets. The **Carmes Garden,** which is open to the public, reaches down to the river; from the bridge there is a fine view of the calm water reflecting the garden and the château.

EXCURSION

★ **Le Tertre Rouge Zoo (Parc zoologique)** ⊘ – *5 km - 3 miles east. Leave La Flèche by ② on the plan and turn into D 104; continue for 1 km - 1/2 mile after the third level crossing.*
The zoo covers 7ha - 17 acres in a forest setting. There are mammals (wild animals, monkeys, deer, elephants, etc), many birds, and numerous reptiles housed in two vivariums (pythons, boas, crocodiles, tortoises, etc). The **Natural Science Museum** presents a diorama of the regional fauna. The 600 animals in the collection of the naturalist Jacques Bouillault can be seen in their natural habitats.

Michelin map ⬛ southwest of fold 13 or ⬛ fold 33 – Local map under LOIRE VALLEY: Chinon-Champtoceaux

Fontevraud Abbey is on the borders of Anjou, Touraine and Poitou. Despite the ravages of history, it remains the largest group of monastic buildings in France. Major restoration works are now being carried out, including the gardens of the Bourbon Apartments. There is a good view of the abbey from the Loudon road on the south side of the village.

Foundation (1101) – The order at Fontevraud was founded by **Robert d'Arbrissel** (*c* 1045-1117) who had been a hermit in the Mayenne Forest before being appointed by Urban II to preach in the West. He soon gained a large group of disciples of both sexes and chose this place to found a mixed community.

From the beginning the abbey was unique among religious houses in that it had five separate buildings accommodating priests and lay-brothers (St-Jean-de-l'Habit), contemplative nuns (St Mary), lepers (St Lazarus), invalids (St Benedict) and lay-sisters (St Mary Magdalene).

Each body led its own life, with its own church and cloister, chapter house, refectory, kitchen and dormitory. Robert d'Arbrissel had ordained that the whole community should be directed by an Abbess chosen from among the widows; she was later designated as "Head and General of the Order" and this arrangement continued unaltered right up to the French Revolution. In 1119 Pope Calixtus II came to bless the cemetery and consecrate the church.

The Order had dependent houses in both England and Spain. The one at Amesbury in Wiltshire was founded by Henry II in 1177 in repentance for the murder of Thomas Becket.

An Aristocratic Order – The success of the new Order was immediate and it quickly took on an aristocratic character; the abbesses, who were members of noble families, procured rich gifts and powerful protection for the abbey. The Plantagenets showered it with wealth and ten of their number elected to be buried in the abbey church. The abbey became a refuge for repudiated queens and daughters of royal or exalted families who, voluntarily or under compulsion, retired from the secular world. There were thirty-six abbesses, half of whom were of royal blood including five from the House of Bourbon, between 1115 and 1789. Louis XV entrusted the education of his four younger daughters to the Abbess of Fontevraud.

There were however periods of laxity caused by difficulties in recruiting nuns and the fact that the monks were disinclined to obey a woman, but an energetic abbess was always found to redress the situation. Marie de Bretagne (15C) was the first reforming abbess. Renée and Louise de Bourbon in the 16C and in the 17C Jeanne-Baptiste de Bourbon, daughter of Henri IV, and Madame de Montespan's sister, Gabrielle de Rochechouart de Mortemart, the "queen of the abbesses", made the abbey a spiritual and cultural centre of great renown.

In the 18C Fontevraud owned 75 priories and about 100 estates; the community consisted of 100 nuns and 20 monks.

Plantagenet Tombs – As a family the Plantagenets heaped wealth on the abbey and fifteen of them were buried in the abbey church. Henri II, his wife Eleanor of Aquitaine and their son Richard the Lionheart are buried in the crypt.

FONTEVRAUD ABBEY

Later transfers to the crypt include the hearts of John Lackland and of his son Henry III, who rebuilt Westminster Abbey which in the 13C became the traditional burial place of English sovereigns.

Violation of the Abbey – The Huguenots desecrated the abbey in 1561; in 1792 the Order was suppressed by the Revolutionaries who completely destroyed the monks' priory in the following year.

In 1804 Napoleon converted the remaining buildings into a state prison which was closed only in 1963.

Cultural Vocation – In 1975 the Abbey embarked on a new vocation as a **Cultural Centre of the West** ⊙ which conserves the buildings and organises concerts, exhibitions, seminars and lectures. Accommodation for visitors is provided in St Lazarus' Priory, a short distance away from Fontevraud's other buildings.

★★ABBEY ⊙ time: 2 hours

Among the buildings around the entrance court, most of which date from the 19C are, on the left, the vast 18C stables *(la fannerie)* and on the right, the 17C and 18C abbess's house adorned with garlands and low-reliefs.

★★Abbey church – This vast 12C church, divided into storeys at the time it served as a prison, has again found its original purity.

The wide nave with its delicately carved capitals is roofed by a series of domes, a characteristic of churches found in the southwest of France (Cahors, Périgueux, Angoulême, etc). Fontevraud is the northernmost example of these curious domed churches and this can be explained by the important links between the Anjou and Aquitaine during the Plantagenet reign.

Built several decades earlier than the nave, the transept and chancel resemble the Benedictine plan: an ambulatory and radiating chapels where the luminosity and repetition of vertical lines – slender columns, arcades, pillars – signify the aspiration to reach up to heaven.

The building houses **Plantagenet tombs★**, polychrome recumbent figures representing Henry II, Count of Anjou and King of England *(qv)*, his wife Eleanor of Aquitaine, who died at Fontevraud in 1204, their son Richard the Lionheart and lastly Isabella of Angoulême, second wife of their son, King John of England. In the 16C these recumbent figures were laid in the kings' cemetery (cimetière des rois) of which only the base still stands in the nave to the left of the chancel's entrance.

St Mary's Cloisters (Cloître Ste-Marie) – The cloisters in the nuns' convent have Renaissance vaulting except on the south side, which is Gothic-inspired. A richly carved doorway in the east gallery, paved with the Bourbon coat of arms, opens into the **chapter house★** which has 16C murals representing the abbesses.

St Benedict's Cloisters (Cloître St-Benoît) ⊙ – The 17C-18C cloisters lead to the infirmary and the warming-room. The north wing includes the 12C St Benedict's Chapel.

Refectory – This large hall (45m - 148ft long) with its Romanesque walls is roofed with Gothic vaulting which replaced a timber ceiling in 1515.

★★Kitchen – This is the only Romanesque kitchen which has been conserved over the centuries – despite its alterations. In many respects it resembles the kitchen at Glastonbury.

The technical skill of Magne, the architect, backed by his artistic feeling combines to form a most intriguing building. The kitchen is roofed with overlapping stones and topped by a number of chimneys, inserted in 1904; built on an octagonal plan and capped by an octagonal hood, the building was originally flanked by eight apsidal chapels, three of which were destroyed in 16C, when the kitchen was attached to the Refectory. The kitchen's large size can be explained by the great number of people it served and the large amount of smoked meat and fish (it was also used as a smoke room) consumed as part of the daily diet.

Fontevraud Abbey — Kitchen chimneys

ADDITIONAL SIGHTS

★St Michael's – A low lean-to gallery was built against the walls of this parish church in the 18C, giving it an unexpected character and sheltering a beautiful 12C door with Romanesque paintings. Although the church was enlarged and remodelled in the 13C and 15C, an inner arcade with small columns and typical Angevin vaulting remain from the original Romanesque building.

The church contains numerous **works of art★**. The high altar of carved and gilded wood was made at the behest of the Abbess, Louise de Bourbon, in 1621 for the abbey church. In a north side chapel is a 15C wooden Crucifix simultaneously tormented and at peace, and an impressive 16C Crowning with Thorns by the pupils of Caravaggio. In a Crucifixion painted on wood in an archaic style by Étienne Dumonstier, the artist sought to portray the pitiful waste of the struggles between Catholics and Protestants by depicting the protagonists at the foot of the Cross. One can make out Catherine de' Medici as Mary Magdalene, Henri II as the soldier piercing the heart of Christ, and their three sons, François II, Charles IX and Henri III. Mary Stuart is the Holy Woman with a crown; the Virgin has the features of Elizabeth of Austria. The modest nun in the foreground is the Abbess, Louise de Bourbon who was host to Mary Stuart in 1548, Charles IX in 1564 and Catherine de' Medici in 1567.

St Catherine's Chapel – This 13C chapel stands in what was originally the churchyard; it is crowned by a lantern of the dead.

★ FOUGÈRES-SUR-BIÈVRE CHÂTEAU

Michelin map 🔢 fold 17 or 🔢 fold 15 (8km - 5 miles northwest of Contres)

In the charming village of Fougères, surrounded by nursery gardens and fields of asparagus, stands the austere yet noble north façade of the feudal-looking **château** ⊘ of Pierre de Refuge, Louis XI's Chancellor.
Without much difficulty you can pick out the moats, drawbridge, arrow slits – replaced in the 16C by windows – and the keep's battlements *(p. 34)* which disappeared when the roof was added.
The building was begun in 1470. Already, twenty years before, Charles d'Orléans had pulled down the old fortified castle at Blois and built a more cheerful residence in its place. The builder of Fougères did not follow the new fashion. He built a true stronghold round the square 11C keep.
However, when completed by his son-in-law, Jean de Villebresme, the château acquired a certain grace: the east wing in the main court has a gallery of arcades with lovely dormer windows; the attractive turreted staircase in the northwest corner with its windows flanked by pilasters with Renaissance motifs; the large windows added in the 18C to the south wing which made it ideal as a spinning mill in the 19C.
The size of the rooms seen from within is impressive; so are the wooden roof-frame of the main building which is shaped like a ship's hull, and the conical roof-frame of the towers.

EXCURSION

Roujoux Leisure Park ⊘ – *5km - 3 miles east by D 7 towards Fresnes.*
The grounds of Roujoux Château, which was rebuilt by René de Maille in the reign of Louis XIII, are arranged for leisure activities with picnicking, games and mini-golf in a 7ha - 17 acre park.
Inside the château there is an historical **museum** where puppets re-enact the life of the château since the coming of the Vikings.

FRAZÉ   Pop 489

Michelin map 🔢 fold 16 or 🔢 north of fold 37 (8km - 5 miles northwest of Brou)

Frazé is a little village in the valley beside the River Foussarde. Its origins are Gallo-Roman; later it was fortified and surrounded by water. The square, Place de la Mairie, provides a charming view of both the church and the château.
Frazé is a good starting point for an excursion into Le Perche-Gouët *(qv)*.

Château ⊘ – The château was begun to a square plan in 1493 and protected by a moat and a pool; it was completed in the 16C and 17C with the outbuildings which form an entrance porch.
The surviving buildings include a watch tower; two towers of which one stands alone and is decorated with machicolations and a moulding; a fort flanked by towers and ornamented with sculpted corbels; an interesting chapel with historiated ornaments. An old well, gardens, canals and terraces enhance the courtyard and the park.

Church – The church has an attractive Renaissance doorway.

---

*The annual **Michelin Red Guide France***
revises its selection of establishments which
        - serve carefully prepared meals at a reasonable cost,
        - include service on the bill or in the price of each dish,
        - offer a menu of simple but good food at a modest price,
        - provide free parking.
It is well worth buying the current edition.

GENNES Pop 1 867

Michelin map **64** fold 12 or **232** folds 32, 33 – Facilities – Local map under LOIRE VALLEY: Chinon-Champtoceaux

Among the wooded hills hereabouts are numerous megaliths including the **Madeleine Dolmen** south of the Doué road. Discoveries including an aqueduct, baths, an amphitheatre and the figure of a nymph indicate the existence here of a Gallo-Roman shrine dedicated to a water cult. There is a small **archaeological museum** ⊙.

Amphitheatre ⊙ – Discovered as long ago as 1837 and still being excavated, this is assumed to have been the structure serving as the local amphitheatre between the 1C and 3C. It is set into a terraced slope cut into on the northeast by a podium and has an elliptical arena whose principal axis measures 44m - 145ft. On the north side is the boundary wall built of sandstone, tufa and brick paralleled by a paved drainage corridor.

St Eusebio's Church ⊙ – On its hill-top overlooking the Loire, the church has kept only its transept and tower from the 12C. From the tower there is a vast **panorama** over Gennes and the valley of the Loire from the Avoine nuclear power station to Longue and Beaufort. The churchyard has a memorial to the cadets of the Saumur Cavalry School who fell defending the Loire crossing in June 1940.

EXCURSIONS

Le Prieuré – *6.5km - 4 miles west by D 751, turn left in Le Sale-Village.* The hamlet clusters around this charming priory whose **church** (12C and 13C) has a delightful square Romanesque tower and, inside, a fine painted wooden altar (17C).

Les Rosiers – Pop 2 204. *1 km - 1/2 mile north.* Linked to Gennes by a suspension bridge, this village has a church whose Renaissance tower was built by the Angers architect Jean de l'Espine; the staircase turret flanking it is pierced by pretty, pilastered windows. In the church square is a statue of Jeanne de Laval, second wife of René of Anjou *(see Angers)*.

★ GERMIGNY-DES-PRÉS CHURCH

Map **64** fold 10 or **238** fold 6 (4km - 2 1/2 miles southeast of Châteauneuf-sur-Loire)

The little church in Germigny is a rare and precious example of Carolingian art; it is one of the oldest in France and can be compared with the imperial rotunda in Aix-la-Chapelle.

Theodulf, a clergyman at Charlemagne's court – Theodulf was a Visigoth from Spain who came to Neustria after 782 and joined Charlemagne's erudite circle. Before 798 he became Bishop of Orléans and then Abbot of Micy and of St-Benoît-sur-Loire. He was a brilliant scholar, a poet steeped in the ancient culture and a weighty theologian; he was very active in his diocese, promoting schools and fostering study and the intellectual life.

He had a villa (country estate) not far from Fleury; Germigny Church is the oratory, all that now remains. The house was sumptuously decorated: murals representing the Earth and the World, marble floors and superb mosaics in the oratory which date from about 806. On Charlemagne's death, Theodulf fell into disgrace, accused of plotting against Louis the Pious; he was deposed in 818 and exiled; he died in Angers in 821. His villa was set on fire and destroyed by the Vikings in the 9C. Much of the original rich decor was destroyed by Lisch's clumsy restoration in the 19C.

Germigny-des-Prés Church — Apsidal mosaic

TOUR ⓧ *time: 1/2 hour*

The east apse – the only original remnant – is in the form of a Greek cross similar to Echmiadzin Cathedral in Armenia; it has a remarkable **mosaic**★★ on the roof representing the Ark of the Covenant surmounted by two cherubim flanked by two archangels; between them appears the hand of God. The use of gold and silver in the design of the archangels links this mosaic to the Byzantine art of Ravenna. Other elements in the décor – the stucco blind arcades, the triumphal arch (destroyed) and the capitals – show the combination of several artistic influences: the Umayyads, the Mozarabs and the Lombards. The work was discovered under a thick layer of distemper in 1840 when some archaeologists saw children playing with cubes of coloured glass which they had found in the church and decided to investigate. The early church, built on the Greek cross plan, had four identical apses; the interior would have been sumptuously decorated with mosaics and stucco ornamentation and the floor paved with inlaid marble and porphyry. The altar is lit by a square lantern above the crossing fitted with panes of translucent alabaster (the technique for fitting glass panes was not then widespread). The present nave, which dates from the 15C, has replaced the fourth apse.

For a quiet place to stay

*Consult the annual **Michelin Red Guide France** (hotels and restaurants)
and the **Michelin Guide Camping Caravaning France**
which offer a choice of pleasant hotels and quiet campsites
in convenient locations.*

★ GIEN
Pop 16 477

Michelin map 🟦65 fold 2 or 🟦238 fold 7 – Facilities

Built on a hill overlooking the north bank of the Loire, Gien, a small town with many flowers, is well known for its faience. Respect for the traditional forms of regional architecture and a careful use of local materials have given the areas rebuilt after the last war an original and attractive appearance. From the bridge there is a lovely **view**★ of the château, the houses along the quays and the Loire.

Gien is a very old town which grew up round a castle, said to have been built by Charlemagne. It was here in 1410 that the Armagnac faction was set up in support of Charles of Orléans against the Burgundians in the civil war which led up to the last episode in the Hundred Years War. The castle was later rebuilt by **Anne de Beaujeu** (1460-1522), the Countess of Gien, who was Louis XI's eldest daughter.
Aged 23 when her father died, she was appointed regent during the minority of her brother Charles VIII (1483-91), a position which she held with success and firmness, revealing qualities of great statesmanship acknowledged by those around her.

In 1652 during the **Fronde,** the armed revolt mounted by the great princes (Condé, Beaufort and Madame de Longueville) against the king forced Anne of Austria, Mazarin and the young Louis XIV to flee from Paris; they took refuge in Gien while Turenne, at the head of the royal troops, defeated the enemy at Bléneau *(25km - 15 1/2 miles east of Gien).*

GIEN

Gambetta (R.)	Z 6
Thiers (R.)	Z 23
Victor-Hugo (R.)	Z 24
Anne-de-Beaujeu (R.)	Z 2
Bildstein (R.)	Y 3
Briqueteries (R. des)	Y
Château (Pl. du)	Z
Clemenceau (R. Georges)	Z 5
Curie (Place)	Y
Hôtel-de-Ville (R. de l')	Z 7
Jean-Jaurès (Pl.)	Z 9
Jeanne-d'Arc (R.)	YZ
Joffre (Q. du Mar.)	Z
Leclerc (Av. du Mar.)	Z 12
Lenoir (Quai)	Z
Louis-Blanc (R.)	Z 13
Marienne (R. de l'Adj. Chef)	Z 15
Montbricon (R. de)	YZ
Noé (R. de)	Y
Paris (R. de)	YZ
Paul-Bert (R.)	Z 16
Président-Wilson (Av. du)	Y 17
République (Av. de la)	Y 19
Verdun (Pl. de)	Y
Vieille-Boucherie (R.)	Z 25
Villejean (Av. J.)	Y

SIGHTS

★★**International Hunting Museum** (Musée International de la Chasse) (Z M) ⊘ – Gien Château on the eastern fringe of Orléans Forest and the Sologne, a region abounding in game, is an ideal setting for a hunting museum.

The **château**★ which dominates the town was built in 1484 of red brick with a slate roof. The decoration is restrained: a pattern of contrasting dark bricks and bands of white stone and a few stair turrets.

The rooms of the château with their beamed ceilings and fine chimneypieces make a worthy setting for the exhibition of fine art inspired by hunting: tapestries, porcelain, cut glass, paintings, etc. The other displays are devoted to the weapons and accessories used in hunting since the prehistoric era: powder flasks, strip cartoons, porcelain plates and jugs, decorated pipes, hunting knives, fashion plates, chimney plaques, crossbows, harquebuses, pistols and guns with detailed ornamentation.

Hunting scenes depict mythological and Christian legends: Diana surprised in her bath by Acteon whom she turned into a stag which was devoured by his own dogs; numerous portrayals of the legend of St Hubert *(qv)*. There are displays on the fashioning of a gun flint and the making of a pistol with Damascene decoration, while the falconry gallery explains the significance of the different coloured hoods. Beneath its superb roof the great hall is devoted to the work of **François Desportes** (1661-1743) and **Jean-Baptiste Oudry** (1686-1755), great animal painters attached to Louis XIV; another room contains the uncluttered art of Florentin Brigaud (1886-1958), a sculptor and engraver of animals. The Daghilhon-Pujol Room displays a collection of jacket buttons decorated with hunting motifs. There is also a collection of hunting horns and the trophy room contains the 500 antlers given to the museum by the great hunter, Claude Hettier de Boislambert.

From the château terrace there is an extensive **view**★ of the River Loire and the slate roofs of the town, reconstructed in the traditional style with pointed gables and diaper patterning in the brickwork.

On the north side of the château stands the **Church of St Joan of Arc;** it was rebuilt in brick in 1954 adjoining the 15C belltower which is all that remains of the collegiate church founded by Anne de Beaujeu. The slender round pillars of the interior create an atmosphere conducive to meditation such as is found in Romanesque churches.

Faience Factory (Faïencerie) ⊘ – *West of the town (exit ④ on the plan). Access by Quai or Rue Paul-Bert.*

When the factory was founded in 1821 Gien was chosen because it was near the deposits of clay and sand needed for the paste, had plentiful supplies of wood to fire the kilns and the Loire provided transport of the finished product. Gien was well known for its dinner services and objets d'art when at the end of the 19C it developed a new technique called Gien blue *(bleu de Gien)* which produced a deep blue glaze enhanced with golden yellow decoration. As well as continuing the old expensive handmade pieces, the factory produces modern services at reasonable prices. An old paste store has been converted into a faience **museum;** some of the very large pieces were made for the Universal Exhibition in 1900. There is also a display of current production.

EXCURSION

St-Brisson-sur-Loire – Pop 1 021. *6km - 4 miles southeast.* Here in the borderlands between Berry and the Orléans country stand the remains of a 12C hilltop **fortress** ⊘ minus its keep and crenellated south wall. The east wing and the staircase tower were restored in the 19C. The cellars of the old castle are open to the public, as is a suite of rooms with mementoes of the D'Estrades and Séguier families. In the library is a letter written by Rousseau.

GIZEUX   Pop 510

Michelin map **64** centre of fold 13 or **232** fold 34

On the east side of the village stands the **church** which contains 17C tombs of the Du Bellay family. On the right are two kneeling figures in white marble: René du Bellay (d 1611) in armour, and his wife Marie in an open-necked dress and bonnet. On the left is Martin du Bellay, their son, and his wife, both wearing ruffles.

EXCURSION

Vernantes – *12km - 7 1/2 miles west.*

Vernoil – Pop 1 296. The **church** has a massive belltower. Enter the priory yard (right) to see the solid octagonal turret and mullioned windows of the old prior's lodging.

Vernantes – Pop 1 749. A 12C tower marks the site of the **church;** only the chancel is still standing. The nave, destroyed by lightning in the 19C, has been replaced by a simple porch. A new church has been built on the other side of the square.

Michelin Maps (scale 1 : 200 000) which are revised regularly,
-   *highlight towns cited in the Michelin Red Guide France for their hotels or restaurants*
-   *indicate which towns in the Red Guide are accompanied by a town plan.*

Michelin makes it so easy to choose where to stay and to find the right route.

Keep current Michelin Maps in the car at all times.

Le GRAND-PRESSIGNY
Pop 1 120

Michelin map 68 fold 5 or 232 fold 48 - Facilities

Le Grand-Pressigny stands in a picturesque position facing the confluence of the Claise and Aigronne rivers. It was once protected by its hilltop castle.
The site is well-known in the field of prehistory on account of its many flint workshops where large numbers of blades were made at the end of the Neolithic era. These have been found far afield; some even in Switzerland.

★ **Prehistory Museum** (Musée Départemental de Préhistoire) ⊙ – The **castle**, a fine setting for the museum, retains aspects of a medieval fortress: 13C walls punctuated by round towers, a fortified gatehouse, and, at some distance, the two remaining sections of walls that belonged to the square 12C keep. Standing amidst well-tended gardens is the 16C seigneurial home, adorned on the donjon side with an elegant façade of Renaissance arches.
The **museum**, founded in 1910 by Dr Edouard Chaumié, traces the different stages of prehistoric evolution through displays of discoveries made in major sites in the Touraine.
There are special facilities for the blind.
Gallery 1 outlines the main periods of prehistory; Gallery 2, the very early and Lower Palaeolithic Ages; there is a sample film of sediment from a sand quarry in Abilly. Gallery 3, exhibits from two sites in the Touraine, Roche Cotard in Langeais and Reignoux in Abilly, represent the Middle Palaeolithic era as does a model depicting the life of Mousterian hunters. Gallery 4 contains displays of the Upper Palaeolithic era, particularly Solutrian hunters. Gallery 5 is devoted to the Neolithic Age, especially the late Neolithic period when knapped flint artefacts were widely used.
Gallery 6 contains exhibits of the age of metals including a bronze seal from Azay-le-Rideau and presentations of sites in the Creuse Valley.
A computer program may be consulted for further information.
A coach-house containing a section on palaeontology displays fossils from the Touraine, in particular those found in deposits from the Faluns Sea to the north and south of the Loire.

EXCURSION

La Celle-Guenand – Pop 365. *8.5km - 5 miles northeast*. La Celle-Guenand has a harmoniously proportioned church with a sober Romanesque façade. The covings in the façade's central doorway have been finely carved with masks and imaginary figures. In the transept crossing, which has a dome on squinches, note the interlacing work carved on the abacuses above the solid, rough-hewn capitals. To the right of the entrance, an enormous monolith decorated with masks serves as a stoup (12C).

GUÉ-PÉAN CHÂTEAU

Michelin map 64 fold 17 or 238 fold 15 (13km - 8 miles east of Montrichard)

Gué-Péan Château ⊙ is isolated in a quiet wooded valley; there are riding stables in the outbuildings and a picnic area in the grounds. The château was built as a country house in the 16C and 17C but the plan is that of a feudal castle: three ranges of buildings round a closed courtyard with a huge round tower at each corner, surrounded by a dry moat and reached by a stone bridge. The detail is more decorative; the tallest tower (the other three were never completed) is capped with a bell-shaped roof and delicate machicolations; the other buildings, with arcades and elegant windows flanked by pilasters, are roofed in the French manner.

Interior – The rooms are furnished in the style of Louis XV and Louis XVI; Germain Pilon designed the Renaissance chimneypiece in the Grand Salon. The library houses autographs and historic souvenirs. Access to the sentry walk.

L'ILE-BOUCHARD
Pop 1 800

Michelin map 68 north of fold 4 or 232 folds 34, 35 – Local map under Vienne Valley near Chinon

Formerly one of the ports on the River Vienne, the ancient settlement of L'Ile-Bouchard derives its name from the midstream island where in the 9C the first known lord, Bouchard, is said to have built a fortress which was destroyed in the 17C. The estate was bought by Cardinal Richelieu and belonged to his descendants until 1789.

St Leonard's Priory (Prieuré de St-Léonard) ⊙ – *South of the town, signposted.*
The priory church stood on the lower slopes of the valley; little now remains standing: the 11C Romanesque apse in white tufa, an ambulatory and radiating chapels. The arcades were reinforced by additional arches a century later.
The historiated **capitals**★ *(left to right)* represent:
1st pillar, Annunciation and Visitation, Nativity, Adoration of the Shepherds, Adoration of the Three Wise Men;
2nd pillar, Circumcision, Massacre of the Innocents, Flight into Egypt, Jesus in the midst of the doctors;
3rd pillar, Judas' Kiss, Crucifixion, Last Supper;
4th pillar, Jesus' Entry into Jerusalem, Descent into Hell, Beheading of St John the Baptist.

St Maurice's Church ⊘ – The octagonal tower, dating from 1480, is capped by an openwork stone spire. The main building is in the transitional Flamboyant-Renaissance style and supported on pilasters decorated with Renaissance medallions. The very beautiful replica of an early-16C **cathedra★** (bishop's throne) in the chancel is adorned with most graceful Renaissance carvings portraying the Annunciation, the Nativity and the Flight into Egypt; the sculptors are shown on the cheekpieces *(p 36)*.

Beside the church stands a charming early-17C manor house with pedimented dormers.

St Giles' Church (St-Gilles) – This 11C church on the north bank of the Vienne was enlarged (nave) in the 12C and altered again (chancel) in the 15C. The two attractive Romanesque doorways have no tympanum but are decorated with plants and geometric figures. The dome on squinches over the transept crossing supports a Romanesque tower.

St Maurice's Church
16C Cathedra (detail)

ILLIERS-COMBRAY   Pop 3 329

Michelin map 🔲 fold 17 or 🔲 south of fold 26

Illiers, on the upper reaches of the River Loire, is a market town serving both the Beauce and the Perche regions.

"Combray" – It was under this name that **Marcel Proust** (1871-1922) portrayed Illiers in his novel *Remembrance of Things Past* in which he analysed his feelings and those of the people he had known.

Marcel Proust spent his holidays in Illiers where his father Dr Proust had been born; the impressions young Marcel experienced here, like the taste of madeleine cake dipped in tea, were later to become "that great edifice of memories".

In town one can recognise the bourgeois district – *le côté de chez Swann* – facing the rich wheatfields of the Beauce and the aristocratic district – *le côté de Guermantes* – overlooking the Perche region and its horses. In the novel the Loir becomes the Vivonne.

SIGHTS

"Aunt Léonie's House" ⊘ – *4 Rue du Docteur-Proust.*
Some of the rooms (kitchen, dining room) in the house belonging to Proust's uncle, Jules Amiot, are still as they were in the novel. The bedrooms have been arranged to accord with Proust's descriptions of them. The **museum** evokes the writer's life, work and relationships, and has portraits and mementoes as well as a number of photographs by Paul Nadar.

Catelan Meadow (Pré Catelan) – *South of the town on D 149.*
Designed by Jules Amiot, the landscaped gardens, which include a "serpentine", a dovecot, a pavilion and some fine trees, make a pleasant walk beside the Loir. The garden is evoked by Proust in *Jean Santeuil,* its hawthorn hedge in *Swann's Way.*

★ INDROIS VALLEY

Michelin map 🔲 folds 16, 17 or 🔲 folds 13 to 15

The River Indrois winds its picturesque way westwards through the clay and chalk of the Montrésor marshland *(gâtine)* to join the Indre. Its course is lined by willows, alders and poplars and lush green meadows. The sunny slopes are planted with fruit trees, in orchards or espaliers, and a few vines.

FROM NOUANS-LES-FONTAINES TO AZAY-SUR-INDRE
33km - 20 miles – about 2 hours

Nouans-les-Fontaines – Pop 828. The 13C church harbours a masterpiece of primitive art: the **Deposition★★** or *Pietà of Nouans* (behind the high altar) by Jean Fouquet. The vast painting on wood (2.36m by 1.47m) is one of the finest late-15C French works. The deliberately neutral colours employed, the resigned expressions of the figures, and their majestic attitudes make this a moving composition.

Coulangé – At the entrance of this pleasant hamlet stands (right) the belltower of the former parish church (12C). On the opposite bank of the river a round tower and part of a wall are all that remain of the fortifications which once protected the former Benedictine abbay of Villeloin.

★ **Montrésor** – *See Montrésor.*

Beyond Montrésor the D 10 offers scenic views of the lake at Chemillé-sur-Indrois and the country east of Genillé.

Genillé – Pop 1 428. The houses climb up from the river to the late-15C château with its angle towers and dovecot. Dominated outside by its belfry the interior of the church possesses a 16C Gothic chancel.

St-Quentin-sur-Indrois – Pop 405. The town occupies one of the best sites in the valley.

East of the village the road (D 10) offers a fine view south of Loches Forest before joining the course of the River Indre at Azay-sur-Indre.

Azay-sur-Indre – *See Loches: Excursions.*

*For historical information on the region consult the table and notes in the **Introduction**.*

INGRANDES   Pop 1 410

Michelin map 🔢 fold 19 or 🔢 fold 30 – Local map under LOIRE VALLEY: Chinon - Champtoceaux

In the 17C and 18C Ingrandes was a major port on the River Loire. From the south bank of the river one can see the low walls which protect the town when the river is in spate.

Its position just south of the Breton border made Ingrandes an important centre for smuggling salt: Anjou was subject to the salt tax *(gabelle)* which was particularly unpopular since salt was the only means of preserving food; Brittany was exempt.

Church – The church was designed in 1956 in the regional style. It is built of granite with a slate belltower; the modern stained glass windows were made by the Ateliers Loire after cartoons by Bertrand.

EXCURSION

Champtocé-sur-Loire – Pop 1 333. *6km - 4 miles east on N 23.*

On the northeast side of the town stand the ruins of the castle of **Gilles de Rais** (1404-40), a sinister personality who may have inspired Charles Perrault to write his story about Bluebeard. He was a powerful lord, a Marshal of France and the faithful companion of Joan of Arc whom he attempted to rescue from prison in Rouen; for many years he hid his criminal instincts. When he was brought before the court in Nantes and charged with alchemy, raising the devil and the massacre of children, he confessed his crimes in great detail, hesitating only about the number of his victims: a hundred, two hundred or more. On 26 October 1440 Gilles de Rais was hanged between two of his accomplices.

JARZÉ   Pop 1 434

Michelin map 🔢 southwest of fold 2 or 🔢 southeast of fold 20

The countryside is measured out in pasture, crops and woodland round Jarzé-en-Baugeois which belonged to Jean Bourré *(qv)*. The castle, which was built in 1500 and burnt down in 1794, was restored in the 19C.

Church – This was originally a collegiate church built in the Flamboyant style on the foundations of an 11C building.

The seigneurial chapel (right) is covered with lierne and tierceron vaulting. The 16C stalls in the chancel are decorated with amusing carvings. A niche in a pillar on the right of the chancel contains a late-15C statuette of St Cyr, in robe and bonnet, holding a pear in his hand; St Cyr, the son of St Juliette of Tarsus, was martyred at the age of 3. This young child is more likely the son of Jean Bourré, reminding us that his father introduced the Bon-Chrétien pear into Anjou *(see p 16)*.

At the back of the apse are traces of a beautiful early-16C **mural** of the Entombment.

EXCURSION

Chapel of Our Lady of Montplacé ⊘ – *Round trip of 4km - 2 1/2 miles by D 82 north towards La Flèche; take the first turning on the right. Return by D 766.*

The chapel, standing alone on its bluff, is visible from afar. The neighbouring farm buildings add a touch of simplicity to its noble appearance; there is a fine 17C western doorway dedicated to the Virgin.

In about 1610 the previous chapel on this site was being used as a sheepfold although it still contained an ancient statue of the Virgin. One day when the shepherdess brought in her sheep the statue was illuminated. Next day the whole neighbourhood came to see; miraculous healings occurred; religious fervour grew; soon the pilgrims' offerings were such that the present chapel was built and completed towards the end of the 17C. A tradition was established of making a pilgrimage to the Protector of the Baugeois region, and there is still a great annual Marian festival held on 15 August.

Entrance by the side door.

The three large altars are in the purest 17C style. In the niche in the lefthand altar is the ancient statue venerated by the pilgrims. It is a *Pietà* carved in walnut showing traces of its original colouring. The walls are hung with many votive offerings.

Michelin map ⁶⁴ fold 14 or ²³² folds 34, 35 – Local map under LOIRE VALLEY: Orléans-Chinon – Facilities

The town's white houses nestle below the château's walls. Facing the château there is a lovely Renaissance house decorated with pilasters; the church's tower is also Renaissance.

Louis XI's château – It was Fulk Nerra, Count of Anjou *(qv)*, who, at the end of the 10C, built the **keep,** the ruins of which still stand in the gardens – it is the oldest existing keep in France.

The château itself was built by Louis XI from 1465-69 as a strongpoint on the road from Nantes, the route most likely to be taken by an invading Breton army. This threat vanished after the marriage of Charles VIII and Anne of Brittany was celebrated at Langeais itsef in 1491.

★★ CHÂTEAU ⊘ *time: 1 hour*

The château was built in one piece – a rare event – and has not been altered since – an even rarer event. It is one of the most interesting in the Loire Valley owing to the patient efforts of Mr Jacques Siegfried, the last owner, who refurnished it in the style of the 15C.

From the outside it looks like a feudal fortress: high walls, round towers, a crenellated and machicolated sentry walk and a drawbridge over the moat. The façade facing the courtyard is less severe, suggesting a manor house with mullioned windows and pointed dormers decorated like the doors of the stair turrets. The buildings consist of two wings set at a right angle; on the west side of the courtyard a terraced garden rises to the Siegfried tomb at the foot of the keep.

★★★ **The apartments** – Well presented with period furnishings the atmosphere is more alive than in most other old castles and gives an accurate picture of aristocratic life in the 15C and early Renaissance. There are many fine tapestries mostly Flemish but with some *mille-fleurs.* Note the many examples of the girdle of the Franciscan Tertiaries and the repetition of the monogram K and A for Charles VIII and Anne of Brittany.

The guard room has a monumental chimneypiece the hood of which represents a castle with battlements manned by small figures.

One of the first-floor bedchambers has an early four-poster bed, a credence table and Gothic chest. The room where Charles VIII and Anne of Brittany cele-

Langeais Château
Diptych of Charles VIII and Anne of Brittany

brated their marriage is hung with a series of tapestries portraying the Nine Heroes, and there are also 15 waxwork figures, authentically clad, evoking the events which led to the union of Brittany with France. Charles VIII's chamber has a fine Gothic chest and a curious 17C clock. The upper great hall, rising through two storeys, has a chestnut timber roof in the form of a ship's keel. The Creation is the theme of the Renaissance tapestries hanging here. The sentry walk, a covered gallery the length of the façade, offers views of the Loire and the town.

ADDITIONAL SIGHT

Crafts Museum (Musée de l'Artisanat) ⊘ – *800m - 1/2mile north, in the direction of Hommes*. Housed in the old Church of St Lawrence, this exhibition is devoted to traditional trades and crafts; there are the booths and workshops of coopers, farriers, saddlers, clog-makers, carpenters...

EXCURSIONS

Cinq-Mars-la-Pile – *5km - 3 miles northeast by N 152. See Cinq-Mars-la-Pile.*

St-Étienne-de-Chigny – *7.5km - 4 1/2 miles northeast by N 152; fork left into D 76 and left again into D 126 towards Vieux-Bourg. See St-Étienne-de-Chigny.*

Luynes – *Pop 4 128. 12km - 7 1/2 miles northeast by N 152 and then left into D 49.* The road (N 152), along the Loire embankment, offers a good view of this picturesque village on the hillside, where the cellars are hollowed out of the rock. The **market hall** (halles) is of wood with a high roof of flat tiles. There are several timber-framed houses; opposite the church in Rue Paul-Louis-Courier there is a house with carved beams depicting St Christopher, a *Pietà* and the Virgin.

From the road, D 49, which climbs north through the vineyards, there is a fine view south of the 13C **castle** guarding the community.

LASSAY-SUR-CROISNE   Pop 168

Michelin map 64 fold 18 or 238 fold 16 (11km - 7 miles west of Romorantin)

Lassay is a village in the Sologne, a region of woods and vast pools of water.

St Denis' Church – The charming little 15C church has a beautiful rose window and a slender spire.

In the left transept, above the recumbent figure of Philippe du Moulin, there is an attractive early-16C **fresco** of St Christopher; on the right the artist has painted Lassay church and on the left in the background Le Moulin Château.

★**Le Moulin Château** ⊙ – *1.5km - 1 mile west by a track beside the River Croisne.*
Le Moulin Château stands in a rural setting, its red-brick walls reflected in the water of the moat.

It was built between 1480 and 1506 by **Philippe du Moulin,** an important noble devoted to the service of Charles VIII and Louis XII, who saved the life of Charles VIII at the Battle of Fornoue in 1495. It follows the square fortress plan surrounded by a curtain wall reinforced with round towers.

In 15C fashion the buildings are decorated with the diaper pattern and bands of stone; the effect is more elegant than military. The keep or residence has large mullioned windows and is furnished in contemporary style: in the dining room there are a 15C sideboard and a chandelier, both from the Sologne; there is a painted ceiling in the salon; the bedrooms contain tester beds and Flanders tapestries; 19C comfort is represented by the central heating. Near the entrance is the vaulted kitchen with its great chimney; the spit was turned by a dog.

★ LAVARDIN   Pop 245

Michelin map 64 fold 5 or 238 fold 1 – Local map under LOIR VALLEY: Vendôme-La Flèche

The romantic ruins of this feudal fortress rise in a jagged silhouette on a rocky promontory above the village and the River Loir spanned by a Gothic bridge. The castle was the principal stronghold of the Counts of Vendôme in the Middle Ages and its strategic importance greatly increased as early as the 12C owing to its position between the kingdom of France under the Capets and the possessions of the Angevin kings. In 1188 Henry II of England and his son Richard the Lionheart besieged the castle in vain.

In 1589 the troops of the League *(see p 18)* captured the castle but the following year it was besieged by Henri IV's soldiers under the Prince de Conti and surrendered. The King ordered the castle to be slighted.

Castle ⊙ – The path skirting the south side of the castle offers a good view of the gatehouse and the keep.

Although well worn by the weather and the passage of time, the impressive ruins give a good idea of the three lines of defence, of the gatehouse (12C-15C) and of the rectangular 11C keep (26m - 85ft high) which was reinforced in the following century with towers of the same height. The innermost defensive wall is the best preserved.

St Genest's Church – The church was built in an archaic Romanesque style with a square belfry porch. Low-relief sculptures have been re-used in the structure; those in the apse represent the signs of the zodiac.

LAVARDIN

Interior – The church is divided into three parts by square piers capped by delicately-carved early-12C imposts. The chancel, which is entered through a triumphal arch, ends in an oven-vaulted apse, where curious Romanesque pillars, probably part of an earlier building, support roughly-hewn capitals. The windows in the north aisle are framed by delightful twisted Romanesque colonnettes.

The **mural paintings** date from the 12C to 16C. The oldest, most stylized and majestic ones are on the pillar at the entrance to the left apsidal chapel: Baptism of Christ and a Tree of Jesse. The well-conserved group in the chancel and apse shows scenes from the Passion: the Washing of the Feet *(right)* and *(left)* Christ in Majesty surrounded by the symbols of the Evangelists. In the right apsidal chapel note a St Christopher and Last Judgement (15C) where Paradise (above) and Hell are colourfully portrayed. On the pillars in the nave and aisles are 16C figures of saints venerated locally. Note the Martyrdom of St Margaret on the wall of the south aisle and the Crucifixion of St Peter on a pillar on the north side of the nave.

Old houses – One is 15C and half-timbered while the other is Renaissance with an overhanging oratory, pilastered, mullioned dormer windows and a loggia overlooking the courtyard.

The **Town Hall** (Mairie) (H) ⊙ contains two beautiful 11C rooms with handsome 15C vaulted ceilings; the one on the ground floor is used for exhibitions.

The 13C **bridge** gives an attractive view of the lush green banks of the river.

LAYON VALLEY

Michelin map **67** folds 6, 7 or **232** folds 31, 32

The Layon, which was canalized under Louis XVI, follows the trough which runs northwest between the Mauges schists *(qv)* and the Saumur limestone escarpments, except between Beaulieu and St-Aubin where the river has traversed the ancient massif. In the clear air, the deeply incised meanders sometimes create an impression of a hilly terrain.

The region has a certain attraction with its vineyards, its crops sometimes interspersed with fruit trees (walnut, peach, plum, etc), its hillsides crowned with windmills, its wine growers' villages with their cemeteries planted with cypresses.

The "Coteaux du Layon" – The delicious mellow white wines of the Layon vineyards are produced by the *chenin,* often known as *pineau,* variety of grape. They are harvested in late September when the grapes begin to be covered with a mould known as Noble Rot *(pourriture noble).*

Bonnezeaux and **Quarts de Chaume** are well-known wines.

FROM PASSAVANT TO CHALONNES-SUR-LOIRE
67km - 41 1/2 miles – about 3 hours

Passavant-sur-Layon – Pop 155. This attractive village on the edge of a lake formed by the Layon, is enhanced by the romantic ruins of its château. The church has a Romanesque chancel.

Take *D 170 to Neuil-sur-Layon, turn right after the church into D 77; after the bridge over the Layon bear left into D 69 towards Doué-la-Fontaine.*

The landscape at this point is still typical of the Poitou with its hedgerows, sunken roads and farmsteads roofed with Roman tiles. The vineyards are grouped on the exposed slopes and at Neuil slate roofs appear.

Beyond Les Verchers bear left into D 178 towards Concourson.

The road runs parallel with the Layon through fertile country; beyond Concourson it offers an extensive view of the river valley.

In St-Georges-sur-Layon take the road north towards Brigné, turning left into D 83 to Martigné-Briand.

Martigné-Briand – Pop 1 689. This vineyard village clusters round its ruined château, which was burnt down during the Vendée War *(qv)*. Built in the early 16C, its north façade has glazed bays with Flamboyant motifs.

Take D 748 southwest towards Aubigné, turning right to Villeneuve-la-Barre.

Villeneuve-la-Barre – Drive through this picturesque village, which is gaily decorated with flowers in season, to the **Benedictine monastery,** a handsome edifice with a courtyard. The rather austere chapel, in a former barn, has white stained-glass windows with abstract motifs.

Aubigné – Pop 263. This picturesque village has preserved several elegant town houses. Near the 11C church stands an old fortified gateway where the remains of the portcullis and drawbridge can be seen.

Leave Aubigné on D 408 to Faveraye-Mâchelles and turn right into D 120 which passes through the village. After crossing D 24 bear left into D 125.

Rablay-sur-Layon – Pop 571. This is a well-sheltered attractive wine village; in Grande Rue there is a brick and half-timbered house (15C) with an overhanging upper storey. A building dating from the 17C now houses artists' studios.

This road, D 54, crosses the Layon, then skirts a vine-covered cirque; from the plateau there is an extensive view of the valley.

Beaulieu-sur-Layon – Pop 981. This wine grower's village *(panoramic table)* in the midst of the Layon vineyards has attractive mansard-roofed houses. The town hall building was once the residence of the steward of the Abbess of Ronceray. There are 13C frescoes in the **church.**
To the west of Beaulieu on D 55 *(right)* in a low building is a **Caveau du Vin** ⊘ with a collection of old Angevin wine bottles and glasses.
The road descends into the valley; its steep sides are riddled with caves and quarries. At Pont-Barré there is an attractive view of the narrow course of the Layon and a ruined medieval bridge, scene of a bloody struggle between Royalists and Revolutionaries on 19 September 1793.

St-Lambert-du-Lattay – Pop 1 203. A **Museum of the Grape and the Wine of Anjou** ⊘ was established in the Coudraye cellars in 1978. It describes the phylloxera which ravaged the vineyards in the late 19C. Vineyard tools and barrels, illustrations and commentaries embody the living memory of a people who have always been engaged in the cultivation of the grape.
The road winds its way up and down the slopes which produce the Quarts de Chaume wine *(qv)*.

Before entering St-Aubin turn left into D 106 and soon after turn right.

Château de la Haute-Guerche ⊘ – The castle was built in the reign of Charles VII and burnt down in the Vendée wars *(qv)*; only its ruined towers now dominate the valley. Extensive view of the countryside.

Return to D 125 and continue west to Chaudefonds; turn right into D 121 which leads to Ardenay on the Angevin corniche road.

★**Angevin Corniche Road** – *See Loire Valley: From Angers to Champtoceaux.*

Chalonnes-sur-Loire – *See Loire Valley: From Angers to Champtoceaux.*

Le LIGET CHARTERHOUSE

Michelin map **68** north of fold 6 or **238** fold 14 (10km - 6 miles east of Loches)

On the eastern edge of Loches Forest, bordering the road, stands the great wall of the **charterhouse** ⊘. The noble 18C **gateway**★ is flanked by numerous outbuildings which give an idea of the size and wealth of the house just before the Revolution. The monastery was founded in the 12C by Henry II of England in expiation, so it is said, of the murder of Thomas Becket, Archbishop of Canterbury; it was sold as state property at the end of the 18C and mostly demolished. Nonetheless the few traces which remain suggest how large and impressive the buildings must have been.

Walk past the outbuildings (carpenter's shop, forge, locksmith's shop, bakery, etc) and descend the central path.

In front of the house are the ruins (left) of the 12C church; behind it still stands one side of the great cloister which was built in 1787: in the cell walls are the hatches through which the monks received their meals.

St John's Chapel ⊘ – *Return to the Loches road; 1km - 1/2 mile east turn left.* Standing alone in the middle of a field is an unusual round 12C building where the first monks of the charterhouse probably lived. The interior is decorated with some Romanesque frescoes: the Deposition and the Entombment.

La Corroirie – Eastwards towards Montrésor, in the bottom of a small valley, behind a screen of trees (left) stands another building belonging to the charterhouse which was fortified in the 15C. Clearly visible are the fortified gate and the square machicolated tower with drawbridge.

Le LION D'ANGERS   Pop 3 095

Michelin map **63** fold 20 or **232** fold 19 – Local map under MAYENNE VALLEY

The town is picturesquely sited on the west bank of the River Oudon just north of its confluence with the Mayenne. It is a horse breeding centre, particularly of halfbreeds; the horse racing and competitions held here are famous throughout Anjou.

St Martin's Church – The tracery decoration above the door is pre-Romanesque; the nave with its wooden vaulting is Romanesque. On the left wall of the nave above the entrance door are some 16C murals showing the Devil vomiting the Seven Deadly Sins, a Crucifix and St Christopher. In a recess there is a diptych of an Ecce Homo.

★**L'Isle-Briand National Stud** ⊘ – *1km - 1/2 mile east of Le Lion-d'Angers.*
The national stud at L'Isle-Briand, which was transferred from Angers in 1974, is an ultra-modern establishment; about 80 selected horses are stabled here. The tour includes the barns, the harness room, the forge and the riding school. The loose boxes are grouped according to the different types of horses: Normandy cob, Breton or Percheron draught horses, Anglo-Arabs, pure-bred Arabs, saddle horses, trotters, etc.

Michelin map **63** fold 18 or **232** fold 29 (3km - 1 1/2 miles south of Ancenis) – Local map under LOIRE VALLEY: Chinon-Champtoceaux

Liré, a village in the Loire Valley, owes its fame to **Joachim du Bellay** (1522-60), the poet, who was born in the vicinity. Du Bellay, like his friends the poets of the Pléiade *(p 30)*, was brought up on Greek and Latin poetry, and he sought to provide the French language with literary works of the same stature as those he admired in the ancient languages; he was the author of the group's manifesto, *The Defence and Illustration of the French Language*, which appeared in Paris in 1549.
He signed it IDBA which stands for Ioachim du Bellay Angevin and shows his affection for his native province. In 1553 he went to Rome with his cousin, the Cardinal, and wrote his finest work *The Regrets*.

Joachim du Bellay Museum ⊙ – The museum occupies a 16C house *(restored)* in the middle of the town. Souvenirs of the poet are displayed on the first floor; the ground floor is devoted to local traditions and customs.

★★ LOCHES

Pop 6 544

Michelin map **68** fold 6 or **238** south of fold 14 – Facilities

Loches is a small town on the south bank of the Indre; its military past is most evident in the old town, which is huddled on the slopes of a bluff above the river and still resembles a medieval fortified town, with two of its original three defensive walls quite well preserved. Fine **views★** of the castle from the public garden on the north bank. Loches was the birthplace of the romantic poet, **Alfred de Vigny** (1797-1863), whose mother's family had been closely involved with the town's history since the Renaissance. The poet *(qv)* left the town when only an infant.

A thousand-year-old fortress – Loches is built on a natural strongpoint which has been occupied since at least the 6C when Gregory of Tours spoke of a fortress commanding a monastery and a small town. From the 10C to 13C Loches was under the sway of the Counts of Anjou who altered the fortress by building a residence and a moated keep on the end of the promontory. Henri II of England *(qv)* reinforced the defences. On his death in 1189 his son Richard the Lionheart took possession of the land before leaving on the crusade with Philippe-Auguste. In the Holy Land Philippe-Auguste, an artful schemer, abandoned Richard and hurried back to France (1191) where he began an intrigue with John Lackland, Richard's brother, who agreed to give up the fortress (1193). When Richard was ransomed – he had been held captive in Austria – he hastened to Loches and captured the castle in less than three hours (1194); his exploit was celebrated in all the chronicles of the day. When Richard died, Philippe-Auguste re-captured the castle by way of revenge but less brilliantly: the siege lasted a whole year (1205). Loches was given to Dreu V and repurchased by Louis IX in 1249.
Loches became a royal residence. In 1429, after her victory at Orléans, Joan of Arc rejoined Charles VII at Loches and insisted that he should set out for Rheims.

Agnès Sorel – She was the owner of Beauté Castle (at Nogent-sur-Marne) near Paris and also a great beauty, so that her title, La Dame de Beauté, had a double meaning. She was born at Fromenteau Castle in the Touraine in 1422 and became Charles VII's favourite; when the Dauphin, the future Louis XI, made life at court in Chinon impossible for her, she came to live in Loches. Her influence on the King was often beneficial – she cured him of his depression and encouraged him in his effort to save his kingdom – but her taste for luxury coupled with great generosity was a heavy burden on the slender royal purse. She died on 9 February 1450 at Jumièges where she had gone to be with Charles VII. Her body was brought back to Loches and buried in the collegiate church. Some years later the canons, who had benefited from her largesse, asked Louis XI to transfer her tomb to the castle. He agreed on condition that the gifts went too. The canons let the matter drop.

Louis XI's Cages (late 15C) – A tour of the castle will include the dungeons and barred cells but not the cages in which Louis XI liked to confine his prisoners; these "monuments of tyranny" were destroyed by the inhabitants of Loches in 1790. The cages were made of a wooden framework covered with iron. The more comfortable measured 2m - 6 1/2ft cubed but there was a shallower model in which the prisoner could only lie or sit. Legend has it that the prisoner never came out alive; it seems however that the cages were used only at night or to transport the prisoner. Cardinal Jean Balue, who is said to be the inventor of these cages, knew them well. He was greatly in favour under Louis XI who covered him with honours but he plotted secretly with the Duke of Burgundy; in 1469 he was discovered and imprisoned in Loches until 1480; he died 11 years later.

Loches Château — Recumbent figure of Agnès Sorel

★★ MEDIEVAL CITY (LA CITÉ MÉDIÉVALE) ⊙
Time: 2 hours – park the car in Mail Droulin

★ **Royal Gate (Porte Royale)** (Z) – 11C. It had powerful defences; it was flanked by two towers in the 13C; the machicolations and the slots for the drawbridge chains are still visible.

Go through the gateway; turn left into Rue Lansyer to reach the museums.

The **Lansyer Museum** (Z **M**) ⊙ contains works by Lansyer (1835-93), a local painter who was a pupil of Courbet and a friend of Delacroix; and objects from the Far East.

Le Terroir Museum ⊙ houses a reconstruction of a local interior and enables the visitor to see the inside of the Royal Gate. View over Loches.

★ **St Ours' Church** (Z) – In 1802 the old collegiate church of the Virgin became the parish church dedicated to St Ours, a local apostle in the 5C. The roof of the nave rises in two octagonal pyramids and is flanked by two towers. The Angevin porch shelters a Romanesque doorway, richly decorated with strange carved animals; the upper part (badly damaged) represents the Virgin and the Wise Men. A holy water stoup has been hollowed out in a Gallo-Roman column.

The famous pyramid vaulting in the nave was built by Prior T. Pactius in the 12C. The transept, which was designed for a chapter of 12 canons, opens into the aisles.

★★ **Castle (Château)** (YZ) ⊙ – The tour begins in the **Agnès Sorel Tower** (B) which dates from the 13C and has been known since the 16C as the "Beautiful Agnès Tower".

Royal Apartments (Logis Royaux) – From the terrace which provides a fine view of Loches and the Indre Valley, it is clear that the château was built at two different periods. The Vieux Logis (14C), the older, taller building, is heavily fortified with four turrets linked by a sentry walk at the base of the roof. It was enlarged under Charles VIII and Louis XII by the addition of the more recent Nouveau Logis, in the manner and style of the Renaissance.

Enter the **Vieux Logis** by the room known as Charles VII's ante-chamber where a copy of the manuscript of the proceedings of Joan of Arc's (1431) is on display. On the wall hang a 16C tapestry narrating a allegorical depiction of music as well as a portrait of *Charles VII,* a copy of the painting by Jean Fouquet. Then enter the great hall with the large fireplace where on 3 and 5 June 1429 Joan of Arc came to urge Charles VII to go to Rheims. She was accompanied at the time by Robert Le Masson, Chancellor of France, who died in 1443, Dunois *(qv)* and Gilles de Rais *(qv)*. Lovely tapestries *(Verdures and Oudenaarde)* adorn the walls.

The **recumbent figure of Agnès Sorel★**, placed in the Charles VIII Room, is of special interest. During the Revolution, soldiers of the Indre battalions, whose historical knowledge was not equal to their Revolutionary zeal, took the favourite of Charles VII for a saint, chopped up her statue, desecrated her grave and scattered her remains. The alabaster monument was restored in Paris under the Empire and again on the occasion of its transfer to the Nouveau Logis. Agnès is shown recumbent, with two angels supporting her lovely head and two lambs – the symbol of gentleness and her name – lying at her feet. In the same room is displayed the portrait by Fouquet of the Virgin, whose face is that of the beautiful Agnès, amidst red and blue angels (the original is in Antwerp).

Another room contains an interesting **triptych★** from the school of Jean Fouquet (15C), which originally came from St Antony's church, with panels evoking the Crucifixion, Carrying of the Cross and Deposition.

The tour ends in Anne of Brittany's oratory, a tiny room finely worked and decorated with the ermine of Brittany and the girdle of St Francis. The canopy opposite the altar originally surmounted the royal pew and the only door was the one to the right of the altar.

Return to the Church of St-Ours and by way of Rue Thomas-Pactius, make for the Mail du Donjon. Turn round, after a bend to the right, to get a view of the church.

★★ **Keep (Donjon)** (Z) ⊙ – The keep was built in the 11C by Fulk Nerra *(qv)* to defend the fortified town from the south. It is a powerful square construction which, together with the towers Ronde and Martelet, forms an imposing fortified group. Early in the 13C the promontory was defended by a moat, a rampart and the keep which comprised a residence and its outbuildings, a collegiate church and houses for the canons.

On the outside can still be seen the putlog holes in which the timbers supporting the hoardings rested. To the left of the entrance, in Philippe de Commines's dungeon, is an iron collar weighing 16kg - 35lb.

The floors of the three storeys have vanished but three sets of fireplaces and windows can still be seen on the walls. A staircase of 157 steps climbs to the top of the keep from which there is a fine view of the town, the Indre Valley and Loches Forest.

Round Tower (Tour Ronde) (D). – This round tower was in fact another keep. Like the Martelet it was built in the 15C to complete the fortifications at the point where three walls met: the keep wall, the castle wall and the town wall.

Known as the Louis XI Tower, the round tower contains two large rooms; on the walls of one is some interesting 16C graffiti. A cell has been reconstructed to illustrate the incarceration of a prisoner in the late 15C. Below the torture chamber is a vaulted cell which is traditionally attributed to Cardinal Balue. 102 steps lead up to a terrace from which there is a view of the moat, and beyond, a vast panorama of Loches.

Martelet (E) – The most impressive dungeons, occupying several floors below ground, are to be found in this building. The first was that of **Ludovico Sforza** the Moor, Duke of Milan, who was taken prisoner by Louis XII.

LOCHES

Descartes (R.)	Y 9
Grande-Rue	Y 13
Picois (R.)	Y
République (R. de la)	Y
Auguste (Bd Ph.)	Y
Balzac (R.)	ZY
Bas-Clos (Av. des)	Y 2
Blé (Pl. au)	Y 3
Château (R. du)	YZ 5
Cordeliers (Pl. des)	Y 6
Delaporte (R.)	Z 8
Donjon (Mail du)	Z
Droulin (Mail)	Z
Foulques-Nerra (R.)	Z 10
Gaulle (Av. Gén. de)	Z 12
Lansyer (R.)	Z 14
Marne (Pl. de la)	Y
Moulins (R. des)	Y 15
Pactius (R. R.)	Z 16
Poterie (Mail de la)	Z
Ponts (R. des)	Y 18
Porte-Poitevine (R.)	Z 19
Quintefol (R.)	YZ
Ruisseaux (R. des)	Z 20
St-Ours (R.)	Z 21
Tours (R. de)	Y
Verdun (Pl. de)	Y
Victor-Hugo (R.)	Y
Vigny (R. A.-de)	Y
Wermelskirchen (Pl. de)	Y 29

For eight years (1500-08) at Loches, he paid for his tricks and treacheries. On the day of his release the sunlight was so bright and the excitement of freedom so great that he fell down dead. Ludovico, who was Leonardo da Vinci's patron, covered the walls of his prison with paintings and inscriptions. Next to the stars, cannons and helmets may be seen a phrase, hardly surprising in the circumstances: *celui qui n'est pas contant* (he who is not content).

Below, lit by a solitary ray of light, is the dungeon where the Bishops of Autun and Le Puy, both implicated in the Constable of France or Charles, Duke of Bourbon's change of allegiance to the Emperor Charles V, found leisure to hollow out of the wall a small altar and a symbolic Stations of the Cross. In another cell was interned the Count of St-Vallier, father of Diane de Poitiers *(qv)*. He was sentenced to death and informed of his reprieve – on the intervention of his daughter – only when on the scaffold.

On the same underground level as the dungeons, galleries open off to quarries, which in the 13C provided stone for the small fortified covered passageways flanking the ramparts.

Tourists who are pressed for time should turn right on leaving the Martelet to reach the Mail de la Poterie and their cars. For those with another hour to spare, we would recommend a walk round the outside of the ramparts.

★**Walk round the outside of the ramparts and the old town** – *Turn left on coming out of the Martelet.*

This walk *(3/4 hour on foot)* shows one that this medieval town was in fact an entrenched camp, complete with all its own defences. The perimeter wall is more than 1km - 3/4 mile long and is pierced by only two gateways.

Note first the three spur towers built in the 13C in front of the keep, then walk in the moat to Rue Quintefol before coming up on to the ramparts; good view of the chevet of St Ours' Church. This section within the second perimeter wall follows Rue St-Ours around picturesque old houses.

On emerging through the perimeter wall take one of the narrow pedestrian streets opposite which leads to the late-15C **Porte des Cordeliers** (Y F); this and the Porte Picois *(see below)* are the only two remaining gates of the town's original four. It was the main gate of the city on the road to Spain. Go through the gate to see its riverside façade with machicolations and flanked by bartizans.

Bear north to the 16C **St Antony's Tower** (Tour St-Antoine) (Y K) one of the rare belfries in central France; then to the 15C **Porte Picois** (Y N) also with machicolations; it is adjacent to the **town hall**★ (Y H) a dignified Renaissance building adorned with flowered balconies. Continue to the **Chancellerie** (Y R) of the Henri II period (mid-16C), embellished with fluted columns, pilasters and wrought-iron balconies.

EXCURSIONS

Beaulieu-lès-Loches – *See Beaulieu-lès-Loches.*

Bridoré – Pop 461. *14km - 9 miles southeast by ③ on the plan.*
The late-15C **church**, dédicated to St Roch, contains a monumental 15C statue of the Saint (nave right). The legend of St Hubert *(qv)* is evoked on a 16C low-relief sculpture. The **Castle** *(not open to the public)*, which belonged to Marshal Boucicaut in the 14C, was altered in the 15C by Imbert de Bastarnay, Secretary to Louis XI. It is an imposing pile, bordered by towers, caponiers and a deep dry moat on three sides. The most interesting parts are the gatehouse, flanked by a machicolated round tower, and the rectangular keep with a Louis XII-style dormer window and lateral bartizans with pepperpot roofs; the main apartments adjoin the keep.

★Indre Valley – Michelin maps ▨ fold 15, 16 or ▨ folds 13, 14 – *27km - 16 miles northwest by* ①, *N 143 and D 17 – about 1 hour.*
From Chambourg-sur-Indre to Esvres D 17 takes a picturesque route beside the Indre which meanders lazily past a windmill or a boat moored in the reeds.

Azay-sur-Indre – Pop 309. Azay stands in a pleasant site at the confluence of the Indre and the Indrois *(qv)*. Adjoining is the park of the château that once belonged to La Fayette.

Reignac – Pop 909. Visible from the bridge over the Indre (on the road to Cigogné), in a pastoral setting, is the Reignac windmill.

Cormery – *See Cormery.*

Cross the Indre and follow N 143 towards Tours for 1km - 1/2 mile then bear left into D 17.

The trip ends at Esvres, located in lovely surroundings.

*Local maps and town plans in **Michelin Guides** are oriented with north at the top.*

★★ LOIR VALLEY

Michelin map ▨ fold 17 and ▨ folds 2 to 7, or ▨ folds 21 to 24, ▨ folds 37 and 38 and ▨ folds 1 and 2

The Loir winds placidly from the Ile-de-France to Anjou through a peaceful landscape bordered by gentle hills. Green meadows, smart towns and charming villages justify the title Gentle France *(la Douce France)*. From its source to its confluence with the Sarthe (350km - 218 miles) the Loir has made its way through a chalky terrain, flowing under steep bluffs on the outside of its many bends. Since the Neolithic period men have hollowed caverns in these bluffs and these troglodyte dwellings are one of the charms of the valley.

Originally the river was navigable up to Château-du-Loir but now the only boats are occupied by fishermen who appreciate the variety and abundance of the fish and the trembling poplars and silvery willows at the water's edge. It is a pastoral region devoted to raising cattle and poultry and growing grapes on the slopes *(coteaux du Loir)* between Vendôme and Château-du-Loir.

In the Middle Ages pilgrims on the road to Santiago de Compostela followed the upper reaches of the river before turning south to Tours; their religious fervour has left its mark in the priories, commanderies, churches and chapels which are often decorated with frescoes.

127

UPPER REACHES

☐1 From Bonneval to Vendôme *77km - 47 miles – allow one day*

Bonneval – *See Bonneval.*

Leave Bonneval to the south.

Uninterrupted views as the road crosses the plateau. Before **Conie** the road crosses the river of the same name and follows it (D 110) downstream to **Moléans** with its 17C castle. In the pretty village of **St-Christophe** the road rejoins the slow waters of the Loir which it follows (D 361) to Marboué.

Marboué – Pop 1 052. Once a Gallo-Roman settlement, the village is known for its tall 15C belltower and crocketed spire and for its bathing beach on the river.

★★ **Châteaudun** – *See Châteaudun.*

★ **Montigny-le-Gannelon** – *See Montigny-le-Gannelon.*

Cloyes-sur-le-Loir – *See Cloyes-sur-le-Loir.*

Leave Cloyes by D 81 east to Bouche-d'Aigre.

A picturesque road (D 145[7]) follows the east bank of the Loir south though **St-Claude** with its pointed church on the hill.

St-Jean-Froidmentel – Pop 385. On the west bank is the village of St-Jean Froidmentel. Its church has an attractive Gothic-Renaissance doorway; above the basket-handle arch is an accolade and two small pediments.

Return to the east bank.

Only a row of poplars separates the road from the river. Between Morée and Fréteval there are fishing huts on the bank and a few smart houses.

Fréteval – Pop 848. The ruins of a **medieval castle** *(1/4 hour on foot Rtn)* look down from their bluff on the east bank to Fréteval on the far bank which is a favourite rendez-vous of fishermen.

Areines – *See Areines.*

★★ **Vendôme** – *See Vendôme.*

MIDDLE REACHES

☐2 From Vendôme to La Chartre
78km - 49 miles – allow one day – Local map below

★★ **Vendôme** – *See Vendôme.*

Villiers-sur-Loir – Pop 976. The village overlooks the sloping vineyards facing Rochambeau Castle. The church is decorated with some very attractive 16C murals: on the left wall of the nave there is a huge St Christopher carrying the child Jesus and the Legend of the Three Living and the Three Dead. 15C stalls.

Take road towards Thoré. Immediately after crossing the Loir turn left.

Rochambeau – The road runs along the foot of the cliff through the semi-troglodyte village up to the castle where Marshal Rochambeau (1725-1807) was born; he commanded the French expeditionary force in the American War of Independence and is buried in Thoré.

Return to the west bank of the river and turn left into D 5.

Le Gué-du-Loir – The hamlet was built where the Boulon joins the Loir amid lush meadows and islands ringed by reed beds, willows, alders and poplars. On leaving the hamlet the road (D 5) skirts the wall of **Bonaventure Manor**, which was probably named after a chapel dedicated to St Bonaventure. In the 16C it belonged to Henri IV's father, Antoine de Bourbon-Vendôme who entertained his friends there, including some of the poets of the Pléiade. Later Bonaventure came into the possession of the de Musset family. The poet, **Alfred de Musset**, whose father was born at the Manor, used to spend his holidays as a child with his godfather, Louis de Musset, at the Château de Cogners, since the Manor had by then been sold.

Continue west along D5 (direction Savigny); then take the second turning to the right (C13) at a wayside cross.

A wooded valley leads to the picturesque village of **Mazangé** clustered round the pretty church with its Gothic door.

Return to Gué-du-Loir; turn right into D24 (direction Montoire-sur-le-Loir).

The road cuts off a large loop in the river where, in cutting its course, the Loir had revealed a cliff face in which the inhabitants of Asnières hollowed out their troglodyte houses.

Turn right into D82 to Lunay.

Lunay ⊙ – Pop 1213. Lunay is grouped in a valley round the main square where some old houses have survived. St-Martin's **church** is huge and Flamboyant with an attractive doorway. The stones of the arch are carved with ivy and pampres; in one of the niches with decorated canopies is a charming little statue of the Virgin and Child.

Les Roches-l'Évêque – Pop 302. The village is confined between the river and the cliff. The troglodyte dwellings are well known locally, festooned with wistaria and lilac.

Cross the Loir (D917 - follow the arrows); turn right to Lavardin.

★ **Lavardin** – *See Lavardin.*

Take the minor road along the south bank of the river to Montoire.

Montoire-sur-le-Loir – *See Montoire-sur-le-Loir.*

Soon Troo and its church appear on the skyline.

Troo – *See Troo.*

At Sougé turn left into the signed tourist road to Artins.

Vieux-Bourg d'Artins – The village is situated right on the river bank. The **church** has Romanesque walls with Flamboyant windows and a pointed-arched doorway.

From Artins take D10 east; then turn right to l'Isle Verte; after 100m - 110 yards turn left into a road which runs in front of the Château du Pin.

From the bridge opposite the château one can see **l'Ile Verte** (the Green Island) a little way upstream where the Braye joins the Loir. It was here, where the row of poplars tremble in the breeze and the willows mark the edges of the meadows, that the poet Ronsard wanted to be buried; nowhere is more evocative of his genius.

Couture-sur-Loir – Pop 450. The **church** has a Gothic chancel with Angevin vaulting and 17C woodwork in the Rosary Chapel (on right of chancel). The recumbent figures in the nave are Ronsard's parents; note the costume detail.

In Couture-sur-Loir take D57 south to La Possonnière.

★ **La Possonnière Manor** – *See La Possonnière Manor.*

Return to Couture and continue north (D57) crossing the Loir below the Château de la Flotte on its wooded hill.

Poncé-sur-le-Loir – *See Poncé-sur-le-Loir.*

In Ruillé turn left into D80 which crosses the Loir.

The road is very picturesque particularly south of Tréhet; the hillside is riddled with caves.

Villedieu-le-Château – Pop 462. This village has a pleasant **setting** in a valley with troglodyte dwellings hollowed out in its slopes. Houses, gardens, ruined ramparts and the remains of the belfry of St John's Priory compose a charming picture.

Return to Tréhet and turn left into D10.

La Chartre-sur-le-Loir – Pop 1074. Facilities. On the north bank of the river are the Bercé Forest *(qv)* and the Jasnières Vineyard which produces a little-known mellow white wine which ages well.

LOWER REACHES

③ From La Chartre to La Flèche
74km - 46 miles – 1/2 day – Local map p 128

La Chartre-sur-le-Loir – *See above.*

The road from La Chartre to Marçon (well-known wine) passes through quiet countryside.

> *In Marçon turn right into D 61 which crosses the river valley to the foot of the slope on which St Cecilia's Chapel (Chapelle de Ste-Cécile) stands. Turn left into D 64 skirting the hillside which is riddled with troglodyte dwellings.*

Château-du-Loir – Pop 5 473. The keep in the public gardens is all that remains of the medieval castle which gave the town its name. Underneath it are the old cells occupied briefly by the many convicts who passed through here bound for the penal colony of Cayenne via the ports of Nantes or La Rochelle. In the chancel of the **church of St Guingalois** is a monumental 17C terracotta *Pietà;* Mary's features are particularly expressive. In the south aisle is a mounted figure of St Martin and in the north transept, a pair of Flemish Mannerist wooden panels showing the Nativity (15C) and the Resurrection (late 15C). Below the chancel there is a Romanesque crypt and, in the **sacristy** ⊘, a fine wooden figure (16C) depicting the Scourging of Christ.

> *Leave Château-du-Loir by D 10 going south (direction Château-la-Vallière). After crossing the bridge in Nogent turn right immediately into C 2.*

La Bruère – Pop 218. The **church** contains several statues in the nave: St Fiacre holding his spade, St Roch and St Sebastian; the graceful chancel vaulting is in the Renaissance style, the windows are 16C.

> *Leave La Bruère by D 11 towards Vaas.*

Vaas – Pop 1 564. On the left, just before the bridge leading into town, stands an old **corn mill** ⊘, the Moulin de Rotrou. The riverside, with its houses, tiny garden plots, church and washing place makes a most attractive scene.

The road passes through meadows, nursery gardens and conifer forests thick with gorse and broom.

> *Follow the signed tourist route, turning left into D 188 to La Chapelle-aux-Choux.*

Cherré Archaeological Site – This site had already been identified in the 19C but it was aerial photography which speeded up research in the 1970s. The Gallo-Roman settlement dates from the 1C and 2C AD and comprises a temple, baths, two other buildings and a theatre of pointed reddish sandstone which has been completely excavated. During the excavations a necropolis from the Hallstatt period (the protohistoric period - 8C to 5C BC) was discovered under the *cavea* (the seating area).

> *Continue south, bearing left over the river and then turn right into D 141 which skirts the grounds of Le Lude Château.*

★★ Le Lude Château – *See Le Lude Château.*

> *Leave Le Lude to the northeast towards Mansigné.*

Soon after the turn and before reaching La Grifferie Château there is a view over the valley which is laid out in fruit orchards, asparagus beds, potato fields and maize plantations.

> *Bear left into D 214 to Luché-Pringé. After crossing the River Aune, turn right into D 13 to Vénevelles Manor.*

Vénevelles Manor ⊘ – 15C-17C. The manor is set in a quiet valley and surrounded by a broad moat.

Luché-Pringé – Pop 1 486. Facilities. The exterior of the **church** (13C-16C) is unusual: the many ornamented gables and the musicians sitting on the edge of the roof on either side of the façade. Above the entrance door is a low-relief of St Martin *(qv)* on horseback.

The interior contains an early-16C *Pietà* (right) carved in walnut. The wide chancel (13C) ends in a square chevet; the Angevin vaulting is supported on tall slim columns in the traditional Plantagenet style. Next to the church stands an elegant priory (13C-15C) with an octagonal turret.

Pringé – The tiny Romanesque **church** at Pringé was altered in the 15C. The doorway in the façade is Romanesque. The interior is decorated with 16C murals showing St Hubert, St George and St Christopher.

Gallerande Château ⊘ – The road (D 13) skirts the moat enclosing the park which is romantic and deserted; it is planted with huge trees: cedars, limes and oaks border the vast lawns. From the courtyard gate there is a fine view of the northeast façade of the château which has four machicolated round towers and an unusual octagonal keep.

★ La Flèche – *See La Flèche.*

The star ratings are allocated for various categories :
> *- regions of scenic beauty with dramatic natural features*
> *- cities with a cultural heritage*
> *- elegant resorts and charming villages*
> *- ancient monuments and fine architecture*
> *- museums and picture galleries.*

★★★ LOIRE VALLEY

Michelin map 🔢 🔢 and 🔢 or 🔢 and 🔢

The Loire, so often celebrated by the poets since Ronsard and Du Bellay, for long brought life to the countryside, but today no river traffic plies the great waterway. Nonetheless, the river still gives its character to the region and the finest landscapes are those it adorns with its long vistas and graceful curves.

GEOGRAPHICAL NOTES

The Loire, a former tributary of the Seine – The longest river in France – 1 020km - 634 miles – rises at the foot of the Gerbier-de-Jonc peak on the southern edge of the Massif Central. Only its middle course is described here. Originally the Loire followed the course of the River Loing and flowed into the Seine but, when an arm of the Atlantic penetrated inland as far as Blois, the river left its old bed and turned west. North of the loop thus formed extends the Orléans Forest thriving on the granite sand carried down by the river from the Massif Central.

A fickle river – The Loire with its irregular and capricious regime is sometimes furious and sometimes indolent. In summer, only a few rivulets *(luisettes)* trickle between the sand or gravel banks *(grèves)*. In these conditions it has the appearance of a "sandy river", but in autumn, during the rains, or at the end·of winter, when the snow melts, it is in spate and its swirling waters then run high. It sometimes bursts the dykes, known as *levées* or *turcies,* built to protect the countryside from floods. The waters spread over the valley floor like a huge yellow blanket pierced here and there by tiled roofs or a few poplar trees.

Many village walls bear the tragic dates of great floods: 1846, 1856, 1866 and 1910.

BOATS AND BOATMEN

Shipping on the Loire – Up to the mid-19C, in spite of disadvantages – sandbanks, whirlpools, floods, mills and tolls – the Loire and its tributaries, particularly the Cher, were much used as a means of communication. As early as the 14C navigation was organised by a guild of mariners centred on Orléans who charged a toll and kept the channel clear. In the 17C-18C a canal was built from the River Loing to Orléans which developed into a large port with warehousing. In addition to merchandise – wood and coal from the Forez, pottery from Nevers, grain from the Beauce, wines from Touraine and Anjou – there was a great flow of travellers who preferred the river to the road. The journey from Orléans to Nantes by river took six days, and from ten to twenty for the return journey with a good-wind. Coaches and their passengers were transported on rafts.

The river traffic comprised flat bottomed barges (scows or lighters) with large square sails. **Toues**, barges without rigging, are still used today to transport hay and livestock; **sapines** with a greater capacity and rudely made of fir planks, were destroyed at the end of the voyage; **gabarres** were much larger vessels with sails up to 20m - 66ft high. The boats travelled in groups with a mother ship pulling two decreasingly smaller boats, one of which carried the bargee's cabin. The convoy was preceded by a wherry or punt to sound the river bed. The bargees had to be skilled on the upstream voyage to negotiate the bridges; the punt anchored beyond the bridge and the barges were hauled through with their sails lowered. At Ponts-de-Cé and Beaugency, where the current flowed obliquely through the arches, ropes from the bridge were used to guide the boats.

The "Unexplodables" – In 1832 the first steamboat service was started between Orléans and Nantes. It caused a sensation. Two days were enough for the journey, but there were accidents, for boilers exploded. Enthusiasm died down. The appearance of new steamboats nicknamed "unexplodables" restored confidence so much so that in 1843 more than 100 000 passengers were carried on the Loire and the Allier by the various steamboat companies which ran the services between Moulins and Nantes. With the development of the railway, navigation on the Loire declined. In 1862 the last shipping company closed down.

The Boatmen – Dressed in blue, with a red scarf and belt and gold earrings, the boatmen were a rough crew, given to frequent drinking and teasing the barmaids. While waiting for a favourable wind they would savour an eel stew and a glass or two of wine before embarking on a chorus of their favourite songs.

An "unexplodable" steam boat at Amboise

VIEWS OF THE LOIRE

The itineraries described below link the sights of prime importance with the most picturesque stretches of road. Car drivers should not allow the natural beauty of the countryside to distract them from the dangers of the winding roads.

On the **north bank**, N 152 offers only rare glimpses of the Loire before Blois but after Blois the road follows the embankment closely and lovely vistas succeed one another as far as the outskirts of Tours; between Tours and Angers the road continues along the river offering picturesque stretches of road.

On the **south bank**, D 751 wanders slightly from the Loire. Nevertheless, scenic views may be enjoyed a couple of miles downstream from Blois as well as between Amboise and Tours; also further downstream below Saumur and along the Angevin Corniche Road. The traffic-free country lanes parallel to the main road which follow the river bank more closely also offer superb views: D 88 west of Tours; D 16 downstream from Villandry; D 132 beginning at Gennes; and D 210 from Montjean-sur-Loire to St-Florent-le-Vieil.

★★DOWNSTREAM TO BLOIS

1 From Orléans to Blois

84km - 52 miles – about 6 hours not including the St-Laurent-des-Eaux Nuclear Power Station – local map above

★**Orléans** – See Orléans.

Leave Orléans by Avenue Dauphine (south of the plan).

Nursery gardens and rose gardens line both sides of the road as far as the Loiret which flows between wooded banks.

Olivet – See Orléans: Olivet.

In Olivet turn left into D 14 which leads to La Source Floral Park.

★★**La Source Floral Park** – See Orléans: Olivet.

Take D 14 westwards.

Smart little houses with pretty gardens line the road to Cléry.

★**Cléry-St-André** – See Cléry-St-André.

★**Meung-sur-Loire** – See Meung-sur-Loire.

Take N 152 to Beaugency; soon the large towers of the St-Laurent Nuclear Power Station are visible on the horizon.

★**Beaugency** – See Beaugency.

Leave by ③. Turn right just before St-Laurent-Nouan to the power station.

St-Laurent-des-Eaux-Nuclear Power Station ⊘ – The complex is sited on a peninsula projecting into the Loire. St-Laurent "A", using the natural uranium/graphite/carbon dioxide process, consisted of two units with a combined capacity of 500 MW.

It closed in June 1992. St-Laurent "B" is of the pressurised water reactor type and consists of two units with an annual output of 10 billion kWh. The power station's waste water is used to heat an extensive area of greenhouses.

St-Dyé-sur-Loire – Pop 762. Facilities. Legend has it that this little place was founded in the 6C by St Deodatus (also known as St-Dié or St Dyé). There are many reminders of the days when St Dyé's riverside was busy with the activity associated with the construction of the great Château of Chambord *(qv);* walls looming above the quayside, little houses in Rue de Chambord and a number of grander buildings of the 15C, 16C and 17C where the craftsmen and their masters resided. The **church** ⊘, with its impressive belfry-porch, contains the tombs of St Deodatus and his companion, St Baudemir, and has a revolutionary inscription in the chancel.

The **Maison de la Loire** ⊘ in the 17C Hôtel Fonteneau houses the tourist information centre as well as exhibits relating to the Loire and its valley.

The road enters the walled Chambord Estate.

The sudden appearance of the stately façade of the Chambord Château on the River Cosson makes for an unforgettable experience.

★★★ **Chambord Château** – *See Chambord Château.*

Take D 84 northwest to Montlivault on the banks of the Loire.

The road which follows the embankment offers beautiful **views**★ of this verdant setting: poplars, fields of asparagus, tulips and gladioli. On the north bank stand the silhouettes of Ménars Château *(qv),* then Blois with its basilica, cathedral and castle.

★★ **Blois** – *See Blois. About 1/2 day.*

Dried Apples

The technique for preserving fruit, which was in use at the time of the Revolution and continued until the beginning of 1914, reached its height in about 1880 when winegrowers forced to abandon their vines on account of phylloxera, turned to the drying of apples. With the advent of machines for peeling and drying, the activity developed from a craft into an industry and tonnes of dried apples were exported to Belgium, Great Britain and Sweden.

Historical archives on the Loire Valley show that a similar method for preserving fruit was used at Rivarennes near Ussé, where the making of dried pears became a veritable industry.

★★★ DOWNSTREAM TO TOURS

② From Blois to Tours
89km - 55 miles − about 4 hours − local map p 132.

★★ **Blois** − *See Blois. About 1/2 day.*

Leave Blois by ⑤, N 152.

The road offers numerous views of the Loire which is strewn here with sandbanks which are a lush green in summer. The Chaumont metal bridge leads to Chaumont Château on the south bank.

★★ **Chaumont-sur-Loire Château** − *See Chaumont-sur-Loire Château.*

Return to the north bank.

Shortly after Le Haut-Chantier, Amboise Château is visible from the road.

★★ **Amboise** − *See Amboise.*

Leave Amboise on D 81 then at Civray de Touraine bear left to Chenonceau.

★★★ **Chenonceau Château** − *See Chenonceau Château.*

Return by D 40; at La Croix de Touraine bear right into D 31 to Amboise.

★ **Chanteloup Pagoda** − *See Chanteloup Pagoda.*

In Amboise cross the river and turn left into N 152 towards Tours.

Négron − Standing below N 152 this village has a charming square overlooked by the church and a Gothic house with a Renaissance front.

Vernou-sur-Brenne − *See Vouvray: Excursion.*

Vouvray − *See Vouvray.*

Continue west along N 152 towards Tours.

On approaching **Rochecorbon**, a small town at the foot of a bluff riddled with troglodyte dwellings, note the **lantern,** a watchtower on the top of the hill. Further on, at the end of a long wall (right) stands an imposing 13C doorway, part of **Marmoutier Abbey**, which was founded by St Martin in 372 and fortified in the 13C and 14C.

Enter Tours by ④ on the plan.

★★ **Tours** − *See Tours. About 1/2 day.*

★★★ DOWNSTREAM VIA CHINON TO SAUMUR

③ From Tours to Chinon
61km - 38 miles - about 5 hours - local map p 132

★★ **Tours** − *See Tours. About 1/2 day.*

Leave Tours by D 88 going west.

The road runs along the Loire embankment passing gardens and vegetable plots and St Cosmas' Priory *(See Tours: St-Julien District)*. Fine views of the south bank of the river.

In L'Aireau-des-Bergeons turn left into D 288 to Savonnières.

Savonnières − *See Savonnières.*

★★★ **Villandry** − *See Villandry.*

After Villandry take the road south (D 39) out of troglodyte country and into the Indres Valley.

★★★ **Azay-le-Rideau Château** − *See Azay-le-Rideau Château.*

The road (D 17) runs west between Chinon Forest *(left)* and the River Indre, which divides into several channels.

A charming but narrow road winds between hedges and spinneys with occasional glimpses of the river. A bridge spanning the Indre provides one of the best views of Ussé Château.

★★ **Ussé Château** − *See Ussé Château.*

After Rigny-Ussé, the road crosses the **Véron,** a tongue of highly-fertile alluvial soil at the confluence of the Loire and the Vienne. It yields grain, grapes and fruit in abundance; the plums used in the famous *"pruneaux de Tours"* are grown here.

★★ **Chinon** − *See Chinon. Tour: 2 hours.*

4 From Chinon to Saumur
38km - 23 1/2 miles – about 3 hours – local map below

★★ **Chinon** – *See Chinon. Tour: 2 hours.*

Leave Chinon by ③ on the plan and then turn right into D 751 west to Saumur.

Just before entering Candes turn right into D 7 on to the bridge over the Vienne to view the attractive **setting**★ of the village at the Loire-Vienne confluence.

Return to the south bank of the Vienne.

★ **Candes-St-Martin** – *See Candes-St-Martin.*

Montsoreau – *See Montsoreau.*

★★ **Fontevraud-l'Abbaye** – *See Fontevraud-l'Abbaye.*

Return to Montsoreau.

From the bridge over the Loire west of Montsoreau there is a fine view upstream of Montsoreau and Candes and downstream of Saumur Château which is just visible. The road (D 947) is bordered by troglodyte dwellings and white Renaissance houses.

Small wine villages nestle between the road and the limestone cliffs, which are riddled with caves and old quarries – some are now used for growing mushrooms. At **Saut-aux-Loups** ⊘ just beyond Montsoreau on the Maumenière hillside, galleries display the different stages of mushroom growth and some of the rarer varieties, like the blue-stalk *(pied-bleu)* which smells lightly of aniseed, are exhibited. In season, one may also taste the famous "somersault" mushrooms known as *"galipettes"*. These large button-mushrooms, picked when fully mature and cooked in bread ovens hollowed out of the tufa, probably owe their name to the fact that in the olden days they were grown in stacks and when they reached a certain stage of maturity fell to the ground, somersaulting as they went.

The sloping vineyards produce a dry or medium dry white wine, a Cabernet rosé called **Cabernet de Saumur**, and a red wine called **Champigny**.

Troglo'Tap ⊘ at Val-Hulin in the Turquant district is another example of local agricultural heritage. The art of dried apples *(pommes tapées)* has been revived in an enormous cave decorated with ancient farm implements. The apples are peeled, placed in flat wicker baskets, dried for five days in tufa ovens and when flattened for preservation may be kept for several months. They are eaten in a preparation made with local red wine flavoured with cinnamon. There is a slide presentation *(10 mins)*.

Continue along the D 947 to Saumur past the elegant Church of Our Lady of Ardilliers *(see under Saumur: Additional Sights)*.

★★ **Saumur** – *See Saumur. About 1 1/2 hours.*

★ DOWNSTREAM TO ANGERS

5 From Saumur to Angers
48km - 30 miles – about 3 1/2 hours – local map below

★★ **Saumur** – *See Saumur. About 1 1/2 hours.*

Leave Saumur by ⑤ on the plan.

St-Hilaire-St-Florent – *See Saumur: Additional sights.*

On the right extend huge meadows bordered by trees and protected by dykes.

Chênehutte-les-Tuffeaux – The village **church** stands beside the road on the north side of the village. It is an attractive Romanesque building with a handsome doorway in the same style; the arch stones are carved.

Trèves-Cunault – A 15C crenellated tower is all that remains of the old castle. Tucked in beside it is the little **church ★** of Trèves. The beauty of its interior derives from the great arches of the broad Romanesque nave; the chancel arch frames the rood beam bearing a Crucifixion. The holy water stoup by the entrance is of porphyry with primitive carvings; to the right is a recumbent figure; to the left stands a tall stone reliquary pierced with Flamboyant arches.

★★ **Cunault Church** – *See Cunault Church.*

Gennes – *See Gennes.*

> *Re-cross the bridge and bear right immediately into D 132 along the south bank.*

Le Thoureil – Pop 355. This quiet, spruce little village was formerly a very active river port for the handling of apples. Inside the **church**, on either side of the choir there are two beautiful wooden reliquary shrines dating from the late 16C, which originally belonged to the Abbey of St Maurus of Glanfeuil *(see below)*; they are adorned with statuettes of Benedictine monks (Maurus, Roman) and saints who were popular locally.

St-Maur-de-Glanfeuil Abbey ⊙ – This ruined Benedictine abbey *(now an international ecumenical centre as well as a religious community of Augustinians)* is named after St Maurus, a hermit who came from Angers and founded a monastery in the 6C on the site of the Roman villa of Glanfeuil on the Loire.
Excavations in the first courtyard have revealed a 4C Gallo-Roman temple (nymphaeum) dedicated to the water goddesses (Nymphs). St Maurus converted the temple into a chapel; the column bases are clearly visible.
Follow the sign "Chapelles" to the raised second courtyard. To the left are two chapels, St Martin's (13C) containing the tomb of St Maurus, and a modern edifice (1955), built up against the west front of the 11C abbey church, its austere appearance relieved by the use of sparkling stained glass. Continue to the second floor; carved into the gable of the old west front is a superb **Carolingian cross** with fine strapwork ornamentation.

★★★ **Angers** – *See Angers. About 1/2 day.*

★ DOWNSTREAM TO CHAMPTOCEAUX

6 **From Angers to Champtoceaux**
83km - 50 miles – about 4 hours – local map p 134

★★★ **Angers** – *See Angers. About 1/2 day.*

> *Leave Angers by Boulevard du Bon-Pasteur going west and turn left into D 111 going south to Bouchemaine.*

Beyond the riverside settlement of La Pointe the road leaves the Loire to wind through the vineyards to Épiré and then descends into the valley of a stream which joins the Loire at Savennières.

Savennières – Pop 1 164. The attractive village **church** has a Romanesque chevet ornamented with modillions and carved friezes; the south door is also Romanesque. The walls of the nave are built of schist decorated with a herringbone pattern in brick (10C). Two well-known, dry, white Savennières wines are "La Coulée de Serrant" and "La Roche aux Moines".

★ **Béhuard** – *See Béhuard.*

Rochefort-sur-Loire – Pop 1 877. Rochefort lies in a rural setting on the Louet, a side stream of the Loire. The neighbouring slopes produce the famous **Quarts de Chaume**, a distinctive and heady white wine.
The are several old houses, with turrets or watchtowers, in the main square below the D 751. A plaque in the church square commemorates the formation of the Rochefort Poetry School (École de Poésie) in 1941, which comprised a number of modern poets from the west of France.

★ **Angevin Corniche Road** – For the next 5 miles the road along the south bank of the Loire turns and twists through many tight bends cut into the cliff face. Beyond Haie-Longue are superb views of the riverside villages lying in the broad valley.

La Haie-Longue – In a bend in the road at the entrance to La Haie-Longue stands a chapel dedicated to **Our Lady of Loretto,** the patron saint of aviators; legend has it that her house was carried by the breeze from Nazareth to the Dalmatian coast and thence to Loretto on the Italian coast where it is venerated as the Holy House (Santa Casa). Opposite stands a monument in honour of René Gasnier, a pioneer in aviation. Behind the monument is a viewing table. From here there is a remarkable **view ★** of the River Loire and its back-waters *(see p 15)* glinting silver in the light; the turreted manor houses set about with meadows and sloping vineyards make a charming picture. The wine from these vineyards in known as "Coteaux du Layon" *(qv)*.

Chalonnes-sur-Loire – Pop 5 354. Chalonnes, which was the birthplace of St Maurille, Bishop of Angers in the 5C, is pleasantly situated. From the quayside on the Loire there is an attractive view of the river. The old port now harbours more pleasure craft than fishing boats.
West of Chalonnes the road (D 571) skirts the edge of the plateau from which small streams flow north to join the Loire.

Montjean-sur-Loire – Pop 2 469. The narrow streets of Montjean (pronounced Montejan) are confined on a rocky promontory overlooking the Loire. The buildings of the old forge house an interesting **museum** ⊙ devoted to traditional local activities like the hemp industry, navigation on the Loire, lime-burning, coal-mining... From the terrace near the church there is a wide **view** of the Loire Valley, of the suspension bridge over the river and of numerous villages with their grey slate roofs.

> *From Montjean to St-Florent take D 210.*

The **road**★ along the river embankment provides views over the Loire (right) and of the slopes rising to the south of the Thau, an old side stream of the Loire (left). Beautiful **view** on reaching Ingrandes.

Ingrandes – *See Ingrandes.*

St-Florent-le-Vieil – *See St-Florent-le-Vieil.*

West of St-Florent-le-Vieil the road (D 751) winds through gently rolling hills.

★**La Bourgonnière Chapel** – *See La Bourgonnière Chapel.*

Liré – *See Liré.*

Ancenis – Pop 6 896. Town plan in the Michelin Red Guide France. Facilities.
The houses of Ancenis are built of schist and roofed with slate and rise in tiers on the north bank of the Loire overlooking the suspension bridge which is 500 m - 550 yards long.
The town fortifications and the castle ramparts, now in ruins, commanded the valley so that Ancenis was known as "the key to Brittany". The town was once a busy port in the shipment of wine and was active in the sailcloth industry.
Ancenis is still an important agricultural market and has one of the largest cooperatives in France, the CANA (Cooperative Agricole La Noëlle à Ancenis), which is involved in many activities. The Vignerons de La Noëlle group of producers grows 350ha - 865 acres of vines for the wines of Nantes and Anjou.
The vineyards of the district around Ancenis, Carquefou, Champtoceaux, Ligné, St-Florent-le-Vieil and Varades produce good wines including **Muscadet des Coteaux de la Loire** whites, and **Coteaux d'Ancenis Gamay** and **Coteaux d'Ancenis Cabernet** reds and rosés.

Leave Ancenis by ④ on the plan, N 23 going west.

Oudon – Pop 2 353. The dominant feature is the medieval keep, built between 1392 and 1415. From the top of the **tower** ⊙ there is a beautiful view of the valley.

★**Champtoceaux** – Pop 1 333. Facilities. Champtoceaux is built on an impressive **site**★ on the top of a ridge overlooking the Loire Valley.
The terrace behind the church (**Promenade de Champalud**★★) is like a balcony above the Loire which divides into several channels round the islands in midstream (viewing table).
Beyond the terrace are the ruins of the fortress which was demolished in 1420 and an old toll bridge over the river. The local white wines are to be recommended.

★ LORRIS   Pop 2 620

Michelin map 🗺 fold 1 or 🗺 fold 42 or 🗺 fold 7

Lorris is famous for its charter of freedom which was granted in 1122 by Louis VI. The town was a hunting seat for the Capet kings and a place of residence for Blanche of Castille and her son Louis IX of France.
In 1215 it was the birthplace of Guillaume de Lorris, who wrote the first part of the *Romance of the Rose (Roman de la Rose) (qv)*, a poem of courtly love which influenced Chaucer in his writings.

★**Church of Our Lady (Notre-Dame)** – The church is noteworthy not only for the purity of its architecture (12C-13C) but also for its furnishings.
The elegant Romanesque door leads into the luminous Gothic nave. High up in the nave are a **gallery** and the early-16C **organ loft**★ which is carved with pilasters and medallions. The late-15C **choir stalls**★ are decorated with the Prophets and Sibyls on the cheekpieces and scenes from The Golden Legend, the New Testament and everyday life on the misericords. Above the old altar hang two 18C angels. Also worth noting are the polychrome statues in the ambulatory and an alabaster Virgin (late-15C) near the baptismal font.
A **museum** about the organ and old musical instruments has been created under the eaves.

Museum of the Resistance and Deportations (Musée Départemental de la Résistance et de la Déportation) ⊙ – The museum stands in a green setting, housed in the former station now restored. Its rich collection of audio-visual documents relates the history of the Second World War and its consequences on the region. The order of events, from the deeper causes of the war to the liberation of France, is thoroughly illustrated through authentic documents, moving accounts of memories, dioramas (the exodus of refugees and a reconstruction of a camp of members of the resistance movement in a forest) armed figures and a variety of other models.

Place du Matroi – The 16C **town hall,** of brick with stone courses and heavily ornamented dormer windows, stands in the main street overlooking the spacious square; opposite is the **market** (halles) covered with an oak roof (1542).

EXCURSION

Orléans Canal: Seine Reach – *For the Loire Reach of the canal see under the Excursions of Châteauneuf-sur-Loire. Round trip of 15km - 9 miles by D 44 to the northwest and then a left turn into D 444.*

Grignon – The hamlet is set deep in the countryside on the banks of the canal. It makes a most attractive picture with its tow-paths, locks and lock-keeper's house. Continue south to **Vieilles-Maisons** where the church has a timber-framed porch.

Étang des Bois – *Due south of Vieilles-Maisons.* This is another of the reservoirs associated with the Orléans Canal. The little lake is fringed with oak, beech and chestnut trees and is a popular spot in summer (campsite, bathing, fishing, sail boarding, canoeing and picnic areas).

★★ Le LUDE CHÂTEAU

Michelin map 64 fold 3 or 232 fold 22 – Facilities

Le Lude lies on the south bank of the Loir which is the border between Maine and Anjou; since the erection of the first fort, La Motte, it has seen a thousand years of history. The Son et Lumière, which was started in 1957, has proved a great attraction to visitors.

The 11C fortress of the Counts of Anjou was replaced in the 13C-14C by a castle which withstood several assaults by the English before it fell in 1425; it was recaptured two years later by Ambroise de Loré, Beaumanoir and Gilles de Rais *(qv)*.

In 1457 the castle was acquired by Jean de Daillon, a childhood friend of Louis XI. His son built the present château on the foundations of the earlier fortress: it kept the traditional square layout with a massive tower at each corner but the large windows and the delicate decoration make it a country house in the contemporary taste.

★★★**Son et Lumière** – *See the Calendar of Events at the end of this guide.*

Skilful lighting, the projection of large-scale images and the play of water enhance the beautiful design of the château and its park on the banks of the Loir; a natural plateau provides a superb stage for the cast of 135 in scintillating costumes, who present a succession of tableaux from a Renaissance pavane to the waltzes of the Second Empire.

Tour ⊙ – The U-shaped early-17C courtyard was closed off in the late 18C by an arched portico.

Façades – Facing the park, to the right, is the François I Wing. Its façade is a mixture of the fortress style, with its round medieval towers, and Renaissance refinement, with its windows framed by pilasters, pedimented dormer windows, medallions and carved ornamentation. Overlooking the river, the Louis XVI Wing in white tufa stone exemplifies the classical style: it is severe and symmetrical and the façade's central projecting part is topped by a carved pediment. The north wing *(visible from Rue du Pont which skirts the château)* is the earliest wing (early-16C); it was rearranged in the 19C when the stone balconies and equestrian statue of Jean de Daillon were added.

Interior – The Louis XII Wing houses a large 19C library with 2 000 books that belonged to the Duke of Bouillon, and a ballroom restored in the 15C and 16C style. The 18C building contains a fine suite of rooms including a splendid oval saloon in pure Louis XVI style with woodwork and mirrors, an 18C bedroom and a 16C painting studio decorated with murals from the school of Raphael illustrating Biblical scenes and the *Triumphs* of Petrarch; note the ceiling painted in the Italian grotesque style. In the François I Wing a small library has a 17C Gobelins tapestry; in the dining room, where the window recesses reveal the thickness of the medieval walls, there is a vast chimneypiece with a carved salamander and ermine tufts *(p 28)*, while on the walls hang three Flemish tapestries including a *verdure* showing a red parrot.

The underground passages and 13C guardroom beneath the parterre of the former fortress are now open to the public *(access from the outside)*.

Architects' House (Maison des Architectes) – *3 Rue du Marché-au-Fil near the entrance to the château.*

The house, which was built in the 16C by the architects of the château, presents the ornamentation typical of the Renaissance priod: mullioned windows, pilasters with Corinthian capitals, decorated with roundels and lozenges, and friezes running between the floors.

EXCURSION

Genneteil; La Boissière – *Round trip of 28km - 17 miles – about 1 1/2 hours.* Leave Le Lude by D 257 going southwest.

Genneteil – Pop 342. The Romanesque **church** has a 13C belltower with a stair turret and a beautiful 11C doorway; the arch stones are carved with the signs of the zodiac and human faces. The lefthand chapel is decorated with Romanesque frescoes.

Take D 138 southeast.

Chigné – Pop 302. The fortified **church** (12C-15C) presents an interesting façade flanked by a tower. Above the triple-arched doorway note the line of carved brackets and the primitive carvings which have been incorporated, much altered, in the building.

Continue via les 4 Chemins to La Boissière.

La Boissière – *See La Boissière.*

Take D 767 north; in La Croix-de-Beauchêne take D 138 right.

Broc – Pop 331. The attractive **church** has a squat Romanesque tower and a row of carved brackets on the chevet. The broad nave is roofed with lierne and tierceron vaulting; the Romanesque apse is decorated with 13C frescoes: Christ in Majesty (on half-dome), the Annunciation (left) and the Virgin in Majesty (right). On the nave wall is a very beautiful wooden Crucifix of the Louis XIII period.

Return to Le Lude via La Croix-de-Beauchêne and D 307.

The key on p 2 explains the abbreviations and symbols used in the text or on the maps.

★★ Le MANS
Pop 145 465

Michelin map **60** fold 13 or **232** folds 10, 22
Plan of the conurbation in the current Michelin Red Guide France

Le Mans, a large modern town, stands on the banks of the Sarthe at its confluence with the Huisne; it is a thriving provincial capital, its calendar marked by frequent fairs: Spring Fair (end or March or early April); the Grand Exhibition called the Four-Day Fair (mid-September); the Onion Fair (first Friday in September). It is also one of the most important insurance centres in France. Its industry is closely involved with the construction and racing of cars (24-hour Le Mans circuit, Bugatti circuit).

The citizens of Le Mans are fond of good food: potted pork *(rillettes),* plump pullets *(poulardes dodues),* capons *(chapons)* accompanied by sparkling cider and the famous Reinette apple.

River Sarthe at Le Mans

HISTORICAL NOTES

In the 4C the ancient town of Vundunum surrounded itself with ramparts to resist the barbarian invasions; this was the period when St Julian began to convert the people of the region.

The Plantagenet Dynasty – The Plantagenet connections with this town were beneficial. When **Geoffroy Plantagenet**, Count of Anjou, married Matilda, the grand-daughter of William the Conqueror, he added Normandy and Maine to his domains. Geoffroy often resided at Le Mans and on his death in 1151 he was buried here. His son, who in 1154 became **Henry II** of England, was the founder of the Coëffort Hospital and it was to Le Mans, his birthplace, that he retired in his old age only to be expelled by one of his rebellious sons **Richard the Lionheart,** then in alliance with the French king.

While on the Third Crusade Richard married Queen Berengaria of Navarre and it was to her in her widowhood that Philippe-Auguste gave the county of Maine which he had reconquered from Richard's younger brother, John Lackland. Berengaria founded Epau Abbey *(see Excursions)* where she was buried. During the Hundred Years War Le Mans was under English control until 1448.

The drama of 5 August 1392 – In the summer of 1392 King **Charles VI** of France launched an expedition against the Duke of Brittany, who supported the English. On 5 August the king left Le Mans with his troops and rode westwards. Suddenly, as they approached a leper house, an old man, disfigured and in tatters, blocked his road and cried "Don't go any further, noble king, you have been betrayed!"

Charles was deeply affected by this incident but continued on his way. A little later, when they paused to rest under the hot sun, a soldier let his lance fall against a helmet, causing a strident clang in the silence. Charles jumped. Gripped by a sudden fury and believing he was being attacked, he drew his sword and shouted out that he was being delivered to his enemies. He killed four men, gave his horse free rein and galloped about wildly without anyone being able to intervene. Finally he was worn out and one of his knights was able to mount behind and bring the horse under control. They laid the king in a wagon and tied him down; then they took him back to Le Mans convinced that he was about to die.

This terrible onset of madness in the middle of the Hundred Years War had serious consequences. Deprived of its ruler and a prey to princely rivalries, the kingdom grew weak. From time to time Charles VI would regain his reason only to sink again soon after into madness. Henry V of England took advantage of the situation: in 1420 he imposed the famous treaty of Troyes by which Charles VI disinherited his son and recognized Henry as his heir.

Charles VI died in 1422; the drama begun near Le Mans had lasted thirty years.

The Comic Novel – The cathedral chapter in Le Mans had several members of note: Arnould Gréban, author of a *Mystery of the Passion* (c 1450) a poem of 30 000 lines; Ronsard, who was a canon in 1560; Jacques Pelletier, a friend of Ronsard; and Paul Scarron.

Scarron (1610-60) became an unordained canon of Le Mans Cathedral and also a poet; he enjoyed excellent health, a prebend and a house attached to the cathedral.

Unfortunately for him, since he preferred city life, he had from time to time to spend some time in Le Mans where he consoled himself with food and wine. In 1638 Scarron fell victim to a noxious drug dispensed by a charlatan and was paralysed. His hard lot was mitigated by Marie de Hautefort, a former mistress of Louis XIII who had been exiled to Le Mans and who offered her friendship, and by the Muse which inspired the Comic Novel *(Le Roman Comique),* a burlesque work relating the adventures of a troop of actors in Le Mans and its neighbourhood.

In 1652 Scarron married **Françoise d'Aubigné,** grand-daughter of the Calvinist poet Agrippa d'Aubigné, who said "I would rather marry a legless cripple than the convent". When she was widowed she was elevated to the rank of Marquise de Maintenon before her secret marriage to Louis XIV (1683) over whom she had a great influence.

In the vanguard of progress – Before the Revolution Le Mans had several flourishing industries: candle making, tanning, making sailcloth from locally-grown hemp and weaving a coarse black woollen material used for clerics' and lawyers' gowns. A dozen merchants in the town controlled about 2 000 jobs in the district which produced 18 000 items of which two thirds were exported.

In the second half of the 19C the town entered the first rank of industrial centres when **Amédée Bollée** (1844-1917), a local bell-founder, began to take an interest in the infant motor car industry.

His first car *(l'Obéissante)* was finished in 1873; it was a 12-seater break with two engines each driving one back wheel; it weighed just over 4 tonnes empty and had a maximum speed of over 40km - 25 miles per hour.

Later he built the *Mancelle,* the first car to have the engine placed in front under a bonnet and to have a transmission shaft. The Austrian emperor, Franz-Joseph went for a ride in the *Mancelle.*

Bollée's son Amédée (1867-1926) devoted himself mainly to racing cars; they were fitted with Michelin tyres and reached 100km - 62 miles per hour. After the First World War he began to produce an early form of piston rings which became the main line of manufacture in his factory.

On 27 June 1906, the first prize on the Sarthe circuit was won by Szisz driving a Renault fitted with Michelin detachable rims.

In 1908 his brother, Léon Bollée, invited **Wilbur Wright** to attempt one of his first flights in an aeroplane at Les Hunaudières. When asked how the aircraft had performed Wright replied "Like a bird".

In 1936 Louis Renault set up his first decentralized factory south of Le Mans in the Arnage plain.

Le Mans 24 Hour Race – In 1923 Gustave Singher and Geroges Durand launched the first Le Mans 24 hour endurance test which was to become a sporting event of universal interest and an ideal testing-ground for car manufacturers.

The difficulties of the circuit and the duration of the race are a severe test of the quality of the machine and of the endurance of the two drivers who take turns at the wheel of each car. The track has been greatly improved since the tragic accident in 1955 when several spectators died.

Whether seen from the stands or from the fields or pine woods which surround the track, the race is an unforgettable experience: the roaring of the engines, the whining of the vehicles hurtling up the Hunaudières section at more than 350km - 200 miles per hour, the smell of petrol mingled with the resin of the pine trees, the glare of the headlights at night, the emotion and excitement of the motor car fanatics.

In May 1991, the 24 hour circuit was thoroughly modernised, with a new sports module and refuelling pits, making it one of the leading tracks of its kind in the world.

Every year there is a Le Mans 24 hour motorcycle race and a Le Mans 24 hour truck race. Every other year there is a Grand Prix de France motorcycle race.

Course Records – The first 24 hour race in 1923 was won by Lagache and Léonard from Chenard and Walcker; they covered 1 109.536km at an average of 92.064km per hour; the fastest circuit time was achieved by Clément in a Bentley: 107.328km per hour. The most famous names in motor racing have taken part in the 54 trials held since then.

23 May 1923 — Departure of first Le Mans 24-Hour Race
(Lithograph by Géo Ham)

In 1971 when the track was 13.469km long H. Marko and G. Van Lennep covered 5 335.313km in a Porsche 917 at an average of 222.304km per hour; Siffert drove the fastest lap, also in a Porsche 917, at an average of 243.905km per hour.
From 1972 to 1978 the circuit was 13.640km long; D. Pironi and J.-P. Jaussaud hold the course record with 5 044.530km in a Renault Alpine A 442 Turbo in 1978. The circuit was altered in 1979 (13.626km) and again in 1986 (13.528km). Between 1981 and 1987, Porsches had an uninterrupted run of victories.
In 1988 Lammers, Wallace and Dumfries put an end to Porsche's leadership by winning in a Jaguar XJR 9LM and in 1989 Mass, Reuter and Dickens carried off the first prize in their Mercedes. In 1990 Jaguar won again, with Cobb, Nielsen and Brundle. An important change was made to the track that year: for reasons of security, two slow sections were added to the Hunaudières straight, bringing the length of the circuit to 13.600km.
1991 was marked by Peugeot's competitive comeback but is was Mazda that won with Gachot, Herbert and Weidler who set a new course record. They covered 4 923.200km on the 13.600km track at an average of 205.333km per hour.

★★ ST JULIAN'S CATHEDRAL *time: 1 hour*

The magnificent edifice, dedicated to St Julian the first Bishop of Le Mans, rises proudly above the impressive tiered arrangement of the Gothic **chevet**★★★, amazing for its system of Y-shaped two-tiered flying buttresses. The present building comprises a Romanesque nave, Gothic chancel and Radiant or Middle Gothic transept flanked by a tower. Interior illumination.

Exterior – Overlooking the charming Place St-Michel the south porch has a superb 12C **doorway**★★ contemporary with the Royal Doorway of Chartres. A comparison of the two doorways shows that they portray the same themes: Christ in Majesty, the Apostles and a series of statue columns.
The doorway is flanked by statue columns: on the jambs are Sts Peter and Paul while the figures on the splay embrasures represent Solomon and the Queen of Sheba, a Prophet, a Sibyl and the ancestors of Christ. The Apostles in serried ranks occupy the niches of the lintel with Christ the King on the tympanum, surrounded by the symbols of the Evangelists, being sprinkled with incense by the angels of the first recessed arch.
Among the other scenes on the arches are the Annunciation, Visitation, Nativity, Presentation in the Temple, Massacre of the Innocents, Baptism of Christ and the Wedding Feast at Cana.
Looking to the right of the porch note the transept pierced by immense windows and the 12C-14C tower (44 m - 210 ft high).
The west front, overlooking the Place du Cardinal-Grente, bordered by Renaissance dwellings, is in an archaic Romanesque style. One can clearly distinguish the original 11C gable embedded in the gable added the following century when the new vaulting was being built.
At the righthand corner of the west front is a pink-veined sandstone menhir. Tradition has it that visitors should place their thumb in one of the holes to be sure of having visited Le Mans.

Nave – The Romanesque main building rests on great 11C round arches which were reinforced in the following century by pointed arches. The dominical vaults or Plantagenet-style vaulting *(p 37)* springs from majestic capitals which show great finesse of detail. In the side aisles are eight Romanesque stained glass windows ; the most famous one represents the Ascension (1). The great window of the west front, heavily restored in the 19C, evokes the Legend of St Julian.

Transept – The 14C-15C transept, pierced by a small columned gallery and immense windows, with its ethereal quality and its bold elevation is in striking contrast to the nave.
The south arm is dominated by the 16C organ loft (2), while the north arm is suffused with light transmitted by the beautiful 15C stained glass. Three 16C tapestry hangings (3) represent the Legend of St Julian.

ST JULIAN'S CATHEDRAL

0 —— 30 m

CHEVET ★★★ Pl. des Jacobins
Lady Chapel
10
9
CHANCEL Sacristy
7 7
Baptismal 6 7 8
Chapel 4 5 7
7 7
TRANSEPT 2
3
Tower
Pl. St-Michel
N
NAVE **Doorway**★★
1
Menhir
R. des Chanoines
WEST FRONT
Pl. du Cardinal-Grente

At the entrance to the baptismal chapel (Chapelle des Fonts), which opens into the north arm, facing one another are two remarkable Renaissance **tombs**★★. The one on the left (4), that of Charles IV of Anjou, Count of Maine, the brother of King René *(qv)*, is the work of Francesco Laurana. The recumbent figure lies, in the Italian style, on an antique sarcophagus and the delicacy of the facial features recalls Laurana's talents as a portraitist.

On the right the magnificent monument (5) to the memory of Guillaume Du Bellay, cousin of the poet, shows the figure holding a sword and a book and reclining on one elbow in the antique manner on a sarcophagus which is adorned with an attractive freize of aquatic divinities.

The tomb of Cardinal Grente (6) was placed here in 1965.

Chancel – This lofty and soaring Gothic chancel (13C) is one of the finest in France – 34m - 112ft high (compare Notre-Dame in Paris 35m - 115ft); it is encircled by a double ambulatory with a crown of apsidal chapels.

The serried ranks of the tall upward-sweeping columns support lancet arches showing a definite Norman influence. In the high windows of the chancel and first ambulatory and in the low windows of the chapels, the 13C **stained glass**★★ is a blaze of colour dominated by vivid blues and reds. Binoculars are needed to identify the rather rigid and wild figures of the Apostles, bishops, saints and donors.

Hanging above the 16C choir stalls is the famous series of **tapestries** (7) of the same period depicting the lives of Sts Gervase and Protase.

Chancel precincts – In the first chapel on the right (8) is a moving 17C terracotta Entombment.

The sacristy door beyond was formerly part of the 17C rood screen. The beautiful 16C woodwork, in the sacristy, originally formed the high backs of the choir stalls.

The 14C Canons' Doorway (9) has a tympanum with an effigy of St Julian.

The Lady Chapel dates from the 13C; it is closed by a delicate 17C wrought-iron grille. The stained glass windows are of the same period; they depict the Tree of Jesse (10) and the story of Adam and Eve.

The vaulting is covered with paintings dating from 1380. The scene, illustrating an Angels' Concert, displays great delicacy of draughtsmanship.

★★THE MEDIEVAL TOWN (LE VIEUX MANS) time: 1 hour

Closely packed inside the Gallo-Roman ramparts (visible from the quays), the medieval town is built on a hill dominating the Sarthe. Restaurants and craft shops animate this picturesque ensemble of winding streets, cut by stepped alleys, bordered by 15C half-timbered houses, Renaissance town houses and 18C *hôtels* graced with wrought-iron balconies.

From Place des Jacobins follow on foot the itinerary indicated on the plan below.

Place St-Michel – Standing in the cathedral precincts is the Renaissance house (W) where Paul Scarron lived during his period as a member of the Chapter. The presbytery, no 1*bis,* has retained a 15C staircase turret.

★**Queen Berengaria's House (Maison de la Reine Bérengère) (M²)** – *No 9 Rue Reine-Bérengère.* This elegant house was built around 1460 for an alderman of Le Mans; Queen Berengaria, wife of Richard the Lionheart, would not have known it since she lived in the 13C. The decoration consists of an accolade above the door, beams supported on historiated brackets and sections of carved woodwork on the façade. No 7, which dates from *c*1530, has statues of St Catherine and St Barbara.

Museum of History and Ethnography ⊘ – Queen Berengaria's House is now a museum of history and ethnography. A Renaissance room on the ground floor is devoted to regional furniture.

THE MEDIEVAL TOWN

Assé (Cour d')	2
Boucheries (R.)	16
Bouquet (R.)	18
Chanoines (R. des)	22
Chapelains (R. des)	23
Écrevisse (R. de l')	36
Pans-de-Gorron (R. des)	57
Pilier-Rouge (R. du)	61
Reine-Bérengère (R. de la)	64
St-Honoré (R.)	72
St-Pavin-de-la-Cité (R.)	75
Truie-qui-file (R. de la)	79

On the first floor, the glazed pottery of the Sarthe region (Ligron, Malicorne, Bonnétable and Prevelles) is lively and imaginative; the strikingly fresh colours — yellow, green and brown — are used lavishly on the statuettes, altarpieces, chafing-dishes, pots, roof finials, etc. On the second floor are paintings by 19C artists from the Sarthe region including Hervé-Mathé, Dugasseau and Gizard. *The third floor is currently being renovated.*

House of the Two Friends (Maison des Deux-Amis) (**Y**) — *Nos 18-20.* The two friends are shown supporting a coat of arms. Built in the 15C, two centuries later it was the home of Nicolas Denizot, the poet and painter and friend of Ronsard and Du Bellay.

On the opposite side of Rue Wilbur-Wright, which was cut through the hillside to relieve traffic congestion, is the **Red Pillar House** (Maison du Pilier Rouge) (**B**), a half-timbered house containing the tourist information centre; its corner post is decorated with a death's head.

At the beginning of the Grande-Rue stands *(right)* the Green Pillar House (Maison du Pilier Vert) (**E**) and further on the former 16C Hôtel d'Arcy (**F**).

Return to the Maison du Pilier Rouge and turn right into the street of the same name which ends on Place St-Pierre lined with half-timbered houses.

Town Hall (Hôtel de Ville) (**H**) — The town hall was built in 1760, within the walls of the palace of the Counts of Maine. Take the steps to Rue Rostov-sur-le-Don from where there is a view of the old town's southeast ramparts; on one side of the steps is a 14C tower (**K**) and on the other the former Collegiate Church of **St-Pierre-la-Cour** (**L**), now an exhibition and concert hall.

Hôtel de Vignolles (**N**) — This 16C mansion with tall French-style roofs stands at the beginning of Rue de l'Écrevisse on the right.

Adam and Eve House (Maison d'Adam et Ève) (**R**) — *No 71 La Grande-Rue.* This superb Renaissance mansion was the home of Jean de l'Épine, an astrologer and physician.

At the corner of **Rue St-Honoré** (**72**) a column shaft is decorated with three keys, the sign of a locksmith. The street is lined with half-timbered houses. The picturesque Cour d'Assé opens opposite Rue St-Honoré. From here onwards Grande-Rue descends between noble classical mansions. Bear right into the more popular Rue St-Pavin-de-la-Cité; on the left is the Hôtel d'Argouges (**S**) which has a lovely 15C doorway in its courtyard. Continue along Rue St-Pavin-de-la-Cité; after a vaulted passageway turn left into Rue Bouquet. At the corner of Rue de Vaux a 15C niche shelters a Mary Magdalene; at no 12 the Hôtel de Vaux (**V**) is late 16C.

Further on to the left there is a view of the Great Postern steps (**X**), part of the Gallo-Roman ramparts.

Return along Rue de Vaux to Rue Wilbur-Wright; cross it and climb the steps turning left into Rue des Chanoines. At no 26 stands the St-Jacques' canon's residence (**D**) built around 1560.

Turret House (Maison de la Tourelle) (**Ω**) — This Renaissance dwelling, with its windows and dormers decorated with delicate scrollwork, has a turret on the corner of the Pans-de-Gorron alley.

Hôtel du Grabatoire (**Z**) — On the other side of the steps, facing the Romanesque doorway of the cathedral, this 16C mansion stands on the side of what was originally the infirmary for sick canons; it is, today, the episcopal palace. On its right, note the Pilgrim's House (Maison du Pèlerin) decorated with cockleshells, the symbol adopted by pilgrims who had visited the shrine of St James at Compostela *(see Michelin Green Guide to Spain).*

ADDITIONAL SIGHTS

★**Tessé Museum** (BV **M¹**) ⊙ — The museum is housed in the former bishop's palace, which was built in the 19C on the site of the Tessé family mansion; its collections seized in 1793 and its fine 19C paintings, now form the nucleus of the museum.

Ground floor — A small room (left) contains a superb enamelled copper plaque, called the **Plantagenet enamel**★, a unique piece representing Geoffroy Plantagenet, Count of Anjou and Maine from 1129 to 1151, Duke of Normandy in 1144 and father of Henry II of England; originally it adorned the tomb (no longer extant) of this powerful knight in the cathedral.

The Italian paintings include an interesting series of 14C-15C altarpieces with gold backgrounds, a delightful female saint with slit eyes by Pietro Lorenzetti from Siena, two panels from a marriage chest by Pesellino of Florence (the Penitence of David and the Death of Absalom) and a very touching Virgin suckling the Infant Jesus.

In the Renaissance room there is a half-relief in enamelled terracotta from the Della Robbia workshop; also two panels by the Master of Vivoin, part of an altarpiece from Vivoin Priory (Sarthe).

There are classical paintings by Philippe de Champaigne (*The Dream of Elijah,* the famous *Vanity* exhibited in the Tessé room), Georges de la Tour *(St Francis in Ecstasy)* and Nicolas Tournier (*The Drinking Party* — in the entrance). The 18C room contains a superb bookcase by Bernard Van Risenburgh.

First floor — The Northern school of painting is represented by Van Utrecht, Kalf *(Still Life with Armour),* several bambocciata (on peasant subjects) and landscapes. A whole room is devoted to *The Comic Novel* by Scarron: as well as a portrait of the author there are paintings by Coulom and engravings by Oudry and Pater.

Second floor — This floor is reserved for temporary exhibitions of other collections belonging to the museum, as well as a section on Egyptian archaeology.

Blondeau		
(R. Claude)	BX	9
Bolton (R. de)	BX	13
Gambetta (R.)	AX	
Marchande (R.)	BX	50
Minimes (R. des)	AX	
Nationale (R.)	BY	
Perle (R. de la)	BX	58
St-Jacques (R.)	BX	73
Barbier (R.)	AX	5
Barillerie (R. de la)	AX	6
Courthardy (R.)	BX	28

Dr-Gallouëdec (R.)	AV	32
Eichthal (R. d')	AY	37
Éperon (Pl. de l')	AX	38
Galère (R. de la)	AX	42
Grande-Rue	AVX	46
Levasseur (Bd René)	BX	48
Mendès-France		
(R. Pierre)	BX	51
Mission (R. de la)	BY	53
Préfecture (Av. de la)	BX	63
Reine-Bérengère		
(R. de la)	BV	64
Rhin-et-Danube (Av.)	AV	65

Roosevelt		
(Pl. Franklin)	AX	68
Rostov-s-le Don		
(Av. de)	BX	69
Triger (R. Robert)	BV	77
Wilbur-Wright (R.)	AV	80
Yssoir (Pont)	AV	82
33ᵉ Mobiles (R. du)	BX	83

Horticultural Garden (Jardin d'horticulture) (BV) – This beautiful garden with its rockery and cascading stream was designed in 1851 by Alphand, the landscape gardener responsible for the Blois de Boulogne, Montsouris Park and Buttes-Chaumont in Paris. From The Mall on the terrace there is a fine view of the cathedral.

Place and quinconces des Jacobins (BV) – The square, Place des Jacobins, which is famous for its view of the chevet of the cathedral, was laid out on the site of a former Dominican convent. At the entrance to the tunnel through the old town stands a monument to Wilbur Wright by Paul Landowski and an unusual floral clock.

Directly opposite, a modern concert hall has been built; the interior is decorated with a tapestry by Picart le Doux.

The quincunx, Quinconces des Jacobins, is made up of a series of terraced avenues of lime trees.

Yssoir Bridge (AV 82) – View of the cathedral, the old town, the Gallo-Roman wall with its geometric decoration and a riverside walk past traces of medieval fortifications.

Close to the bridge on the north bank is the church of Notre-Dame-du-Pré.

144

Church of Our Lady in the Fields (Notre-Dame-du-Pré) (AV) – In a square planted with magnolia trees stands the old abbey church of the Benedictine convent of St Julian in the Fields (St-Julien-du-Pré); the column capitals and chancel are Romanesque.

Church of the Visitation (AX) – This church, which stands in the main square, Place de la République, at the heart of the modern town, was originally a convent chapel; it was built in about 1730. The main façade, in Rue Gambetta, is lavishly decorated with a portico of Corinthian columns sheltering a Rococo door; the interior decor, of the same date, is also Baroque.

★**La Couture Church (Église de la Couture) (BX B)** – The church, now in the centre of the town and next to the Préfecture housed in the old convent buildings (18C), was originally the abbey church of the monastery of St-Pierre-de-la-Couture (a corruption of 'culture' which referred to the fields that used to surround the church). The façade is 13C. The door is framed by the Apostles putting down the forces of evil; on the pediment is Christ, between the Virgin and St John, presiding over the Last Judgement; on the arch stones, making up the Heavenly Host, are rows of Angels, patriarchs, prophets (1st row), martyrs (2nd row) and Virgins (3rd row).
The wide single nave, built in the late 12C in the Plantagenet style (p 37), is lit by elegant twinned windows surmounted by oculi. Note in the first bay the forms of the Romanesque arches of the original nave on the blind walls of the great pointed arches which support a narrow ledge below the windows. To the left on entering is a curious 11C pilaster sculptured with a Christ in Benediction. The enchanting white marble **Virgin**★★ (1571), on the pillar directly opposite the pulpit, is by Germain Pilon and originally came from the now-vanished retable of the high altar. The blind arcades are hung with 17C **tapestries** and 16C panels painted by one of the monks. The massive round 11C columns of the chancel, with squat capitals showing Eastern influence in the decoration, support very narrow round arches. Above, the vaulting ribs spring from fine Plantagenet-style statues.
The 11C crypt, altered in 1838, has pre-Romanesque or Gallo-Roman columns and capitals; an inverted antique capital serves as a base for one of the pillars. The 6C-7C shroud of St Bertrand, Bishop of Le Mans and founder in 616 of the monastery, is exposed at the entrance (automatic time switch for lighting). The presumed burial place of St Bertrand is marked by a reclining plaster figure in a wall alcove.

★**Joan of Arc's Church (Ste-Jeanne-d'Arc) (BY E)** – This, the former Coëffort Hospital, was founded about 1180 by Henry II of England in atonement, so it is said, for the murder of his former Chancellor, Archbishop Thomas Becket in Canterbury Cathedral. The 12C great hall or ward for the sick is now the parish church. A similar institution, the former Hospital of St John in Angers was built by the same monarch. The plain façade, pierced by an arched doorway, above which are twinned windows, opens into a vast room divided into three naves of equal height. The elevation is elegant with slender columns with finely carved capitals, supporting Plantagenet vaulting. In the Middle Ages wide canopied beds for several patients at a time were aligned down the side aisles with an altar in the central passage.

EXCURSIONS

★**L'Épau Abbey** ⊙ – 4km - 1 1/2 miles by Avenue Léon-Bollée (BX); turn right into the ring road, cross the railways and follow the arrows.
In 1229 a Cistercian abbey was founded on the south bank of the Huisne by Queen Berengaria, the widow of Richard the Lionheart, who spent her last days here.
The cloister, which was destroyed in 1365 by bands of mercenaries who were ravaging Maine, was surrounded by the monastic buildings.
On the right is the **refectory** wing with the arcades of the washing place (lavatorium). Opposite are the monks' quarters, including the writing room (**scriptorium** – right) and the **chapter house** (left) with elegant ogive vaulting and the tomb of Queen Berengaria; the first floor consisted of the **dormitory** with wooden vaulting.

On the left is the **church,** which was built in the 13C and 14C and repaired after the ravages of 1365 early in the 15C; this is the date of the huge chancel window which is delicately carved. The church was designed to the traditional Cistercian plan: a square east end with three chapels facing east in each arm of the transept.

Motor racing circuits – To the south of Le Mans between N 138 and D 139.

24 hour circuit – *13.6km - 8 1/2miles.* The circuit begins at the Tertre Rouge bend on N 138. The road, which is about 10m - 33ft wide, is marked in kilometres. The double bend on the private road and the Mulsanne and Arnage hairpin bends are the most exciting hazards on the 24 hour course. In 1972 the course was realigned to provide the public with a better view.

Within the confines of the circuit is Les Hunaudières race course for horses where Wilbur Wright made his first flight; commemorative stele.

From the main entrance to the track on D 139 a tunnel leads to the Bugatti circuit and the museum.

Bugatti permanent circuit ⊙ – Apart from being used by its school for racing drivers, the track is also a permanent testing ground for teams of racing car drivers and motorcyclists who use it for private trials.

★★**Motor Museum** (Musée de l'Automobile de la Sarthe) (**M**) ⊙ – *Access by the principal entrance to the Le Mans circuit (D 139 north of D 921).*

The museum's array of more than 100 vehicles follows the evolution of the motor car from its very beginnings.

Among the vintage exhibits are the De Dion-Bouton Trépardoux steam car of 1855, a Léon-Bollée oil-engined three-wheeler of 1896, a front-wheel drive electrically-powered Krieger of 1908 and a Lorraine-Dietrich of 1912. From the interwar years are a number of prestige cars like a Hispano-Suiza chauffeur-driven drop-head coupé of 1929, a Voisin "aerodyne" of 1935 and an 8-cylinder Bugatti of 1939 as well as a 1931 Citroën half-track which took part in the renowned *"Croisière Jaune"*, the first trans-Asia journey by automobile (1931-32) form Beirut to Beijing. Among the veterans of the Le Mans 24 hours are the Chenard Tank of 1925, a Ferrari Barquette of 1925 which won the 1949 event with the Chinetti-Selsdon team, the D.B. Panhard of 1960 which won on performance rating, a Porsche 904 GTS (1964) and a Rondeau (1983).

Cycles and motorcyles complete this remarkable collection.

Montfort-le-Gesnois – Pop 2 657 – *20km - 12 1/2 miles east of Le Mans by Avenue Léon-Bollée (**BX**) and N 23; after 16km - 10 miles bear left.*

Just west of **Connerré** (pop 2 545), a small town which is famous for its potted pork *(rillettes),* lies the ancient commune of Pont-de-Gennes which grew on a picturesque site near the Roman bridge over the River Huisne. The present narrow hump-back **bridge** was built of sandstone in the 15C and spans the expanding river where it flows between the trees. View of the 13C church of St Giles, a ruined mill covered with creepers and overshadowed by weeping willows and a little weir where the water tumbles and races.

Loudon Woods (Bois de Loudon) – *18km - 11 miles southeast by Avenue Jean-Jaurès (**BY**), N 223 and D 304; fork left into D 145^E and turn left again into D 145.*

Woodland tracks branch off (right) D 145 into the coniferous forest; in the autumn the sandy soil is covered with a thick carpet of heather.

Spay – Pop 2 314. *10km - 6 miles southwest by N 23 and D 51 turning near Arnage.* The 9C-12C Romanesque **church** ⊙ (restored) has a Baroque high altar richly decorated and a very elegant 14C Virgin and Child. The precious pyx (1621) is part of the church's treasure.

★ MANSE VALLEY

Michelin map 232 fold 35 or 64 folds 14, 15 and 68 fold 4

The River Manse flows west through quiet picturesque countryside away from the main roads to join the Vienne at L'Ile-Bouchard.

FROM L'ILE-BOUCHARD TO N 10   *27km - 17miles – about 2 hours*

L'Ile-Bouchard – *See L'Ile-Bouchard.*

Leave L'Ile-Bouchard to the north.

Avon-les-Roches – Pop 560. The 12C-13C **church** has a stone spire over the right transept. The arches of the porch and the door are decorated with archivolts and delicately carved capitals; an inscription in the porch (left) tells of the death of Charles the Bold.

Take the road east towards Crissay; after 1 km - 1/2 mile turn left.

Roches-Tranchelion Collegiate Church – The ruins of this Gothic collegiate church (1527) are visible from afar. *Cars may use the steep earth track which leads up to the church.* The ruins perched on a height overlooking the surrounding countryside bear witness to past greatness. Little remains of the vaulting but the elegant façade is still standing, decorated with delicate carving; note the seated figure above the great window under the triumphal arch, and the Renaissance decoration of pilasters and medallions representing the local lords.

Crissay-sur-Manse – Pop 97. The ruins of the 15C castle (left), the stone spire of the village church (right) and the several 15C houses with square turrets compose a charming picture.

St-Épain – Pop 1 336. The village **church** (12C, 13C and 15C) is capped by a 13C square tower; the **fortified gate**, adjoining it, is all that remains of the 15C curtain wall. Note the **Hôtel de la Prévôté** with its mullioned window and overhanging upper storey. Pass through the doorway to admire the hôtel's other façade, which is flanked by a round tower.

On the other side of the main street stands a house with a watch turret where the road bends southeast to Ste-Maure.

This road climbs up the verdant Manse valley.

After passing under the railway, bear left.

★ **Courtineau Road** – This small picturesque road winds between the stream hidden amidst the trees and the cliff dotted with troglodyte dwellings. The chapel of **Our Lady of Loretto** (N.-D.-de-Lorette), a small 15C oratory, has been carved into the cliff face beside a small troglodyte dwelling of the same period.

Les MAUGES

Michelin map **63** folds 18, 19 and **67** folds 5, 6 or **232** folds 30, 31

The southern part of Anjou on the borders of the Vendée and Poitou, which is known as Les Mauges, is a silent secret region bordered by the Loire to the north, by the Layon valley to the east and the departments of the Vendée and Deux-Sèvres to the south and west. The terrain consists of schist rock, an extension of the Armorican massif culminating in Puy de la Garde (210m - 689ft); Les Mauges is a mixture of woodland and pasture used for cattle raising, where the Durham-Mancelle breed is fattened before being sold in thousands at the markets in Chemillé and Cholet.

The straight main roads, which were created during the Revolution and under the Empire for strategic reasons, are superimposed on a network of deep lanes well-suited to ambushes which played a prominent part in the Vendée War; the windmills which still crown the heights were often used by the Whites to send signals.

The Vendée War (1793-96) – The execution of Louis XVI had been a shock; the persecution of the priests caused discontent; the decision of the Convention in February 1793 to impose conscription provoked a revolt. To the cry "Long live God and Long live the King" the peasants of the Vendée and Les Mauges, who were not receptive of the new ideas, rose against the Republic and banded together under the white flag of the monarchy, hence their name, the Whites. They chose leaders from their own kind – Stofflet, the gamekeeper and Cathelineau, the pedlar – or from among the nobles – Elbée, Bonchamps, La Rochejaquelein and Charette.

Cathelineau by Girodet-Trioson (1824)
(Cholet Museum)

147

On 15 March they captured Cholet and soon held Les Mauges. The Blues (blue was the colour of the Republican uniform) counter-attacked and pushed the Catholic and Royalist army back to the Sèvre; but the Whites regained the advantage and captured the whole of Anjou (June 1793). Alarmed at this turn of events, the Convention sent the Mayence army under Kléber and Marceau.

At first it was beaten at Torfou (19 September 1793) but then it was victorious at Cholet (17 October) after a bloody battle in which the Whites were forced to retreat to St-Florent *(see St-Florent-le-Vieil)*. The following day 80 000 Whites crossed the Loire. The survivors were massacred in their thousands, shot down or drowned in the Loire. General Westermann wrote to the Convention: "The Vendée is no more, it has died under our free sword... I have crushed the children under the horses' feet and massacred the women. I have not one prisoner with which to reproach myself." At the end of January 1794 the Convention sent Turreau's **"infernal columns"** but the extermination plan failed. Insurrection rose again in Les Mauges and in the Poitou marshes; this was the period of the **Chouans.** They weakened, however, and entered into a parley under General Hoche. A treaty was signed on 17 February 1795 but the peace was precarious and often violated; the treaty was finally confirmed under the Consulate.

Memorials of the Vendée War – Throughout the region there are monuments to the events of 1793-96. At **Maulévrier** there is a pyramid commemorating Stofflet and a martyrs' cemetery *(see Maulévrier)*.

At the crossroads on N 149 and D 753 near **Torfou** stands a column celebrating the victory of the Whites over the Mayence army (19 September 1793). Bonchamps was buried at **St-Florent-le-Vieil** *(qv)*. A cross was erected on the road to Nuaillé near **Cholet** where La Rochejaquelein fell on 29 January 1794.

Many churches in Les Mauges and the Saumur region have **stained-glass windows** *(1)* that illustrate forcefully and realistically the Vendée War and relate the great deeds of its heroes. The windows, particularly in Vihiers, La Salle-de-Vihiers, Montilliers, Chemillé, Chanzeaux, St-Laurent-de-la-Plaine, Le Pin-en-Mauges and further north at La Chapelle-St-Florent, were mostly the work of local glass-makers including Clamens, Bordereau, Megen, and more recently, Rollo, who by both restoring and creating stained glass, has continued the tradition in Anjou.

SIGHTS *Local map below*

Beaupréau – Pop 5 937. Beaupréau is a small town built on a steep slope on the north bank of the River Evre. In 1793 it was the headquarters of the Whites; their leader, d'Elbée, owned a manor at St-Martin, on the east side of the town which now houses the public library. The 15C **château** overlooking the Evre (good view from the south bank) is now a clinic. Although it was set on fire in 1793, the entrance has retained its character: two large towers flanking a 17C pavilion which has a pyramidal roof flanked by two small slate cupolas.

Chemillé – Pop 6 016. The town, which extends along the valley of the Hyrôme, is an important centre for stock-raising and for the production of medicinal plants (demonstration garden in the grounds of the town hall). In July 1793 Chemillé was the scene of a fierce struggle between Blues and Whites, in the course of which 400 Blues who had been taken prisoner were saved from death only by the intervention of General d'Elbée. In the Place du Château there is a 13C doorway with honeycomb decoration, a vestige of the old citadel. The disused church of Notre-Dame has an interesting Romanesque **tower** with blind arcading and two richly decorated Romanesque bays.

The 12C **Church of St Peter** ⊙, which was thoroughly restored at the beginning of this century, has a fine stained glass window (1917) by Jean Clamens. It illustrates the **Vendée Pater** incident when Elbée, one of the great leaders of the Vendée War, made his soldiers, who were pressing to kill their prisoners, recite the Our Father. They were thus encouraged to "forgive them their trespasses" and the men were spared.

(1) For further information on stained glass in the Vendée area, read Les Vitraux vendéens et les maîtres verriers angevins by J. Boisleve (Maulévrier, Hérault) or enquire at the Mauges Environmental Centre (Carrefour touristique et culturel des Mauges) in St-Florent-le-Vieil (qv).

3.5km - 2 miles east of Chemillé *(by the Saumur road then D 124)* stands the little **La Sorinière Chapel** ⊘, built in 1501 by the local lords of the manor. It still retains its interesting **murals★** dating from the beginning of the 16C; full of fascinating detail, they depict the Nativity, the Adoration of the Magi and St Christopher. The altar has a Mary in Mourning, supported by St John (16C). In an adjoining room there are mementoes of the area's troubles during the Vendée War.

Cholet – See Cholet.

Le Fuilet – Pop 1 796. Le Fuilet and the neighbouring hamlets – les Challonges, Bellevue, les Recoins, etc. – lie on an excellent clay soil which has given rise to the many brickworks and potteries which produce a variety of articles (ornamental, horticultural or artistic).

The potteries are open to the public during working hours: preparation and shaping of the clay by hand or by machine according to the work.

Maulévrier Forest – See below.

St-Laurent-de-la-Plaine – Pop 1 387. The **museum of old crafts** ⊘ is housed in three groups of buildings, among them the 18C vicarage, one of the two houses in the village which survived the ravages of the Republicans in 1794. About fifty trades are illustrated with implements collected from all over France (weaving equipment from St-Étienne, a saw from the Vosges, a paddle-wheel...). In addition to the traditional exhibition rooms (lace), a number of **workshops** – clog-maker, oil dealer, blacksmith, wax chandler, laundry – have been reconstructed inside a magnificent timber-built barn.

MAULÉVRIER   Pop 2 650

Michelin map **67** fold 6 or **232** fold 30

The name Maulévrier is believed to date from the Merovingian period and means "bad greyhound" *(mauvais lévrier)*. Fulk Nerra *(qv)* built the first castle here in 1036 and set up a barony which, under Louis XIV, was passed on to Colbert's brother; his descendants owned it until 1895. **Stofflet** *(qv)*, the famous Vendée leader, was gamekeeper to one of them in 1774. He is commemorated by a stele in the park. The castle, which was partly destroyed during the Revolution, was rebuilt to its original plan in the 19C. At the end of the century, a manufacturer from Cholet called upon the architect **Alexandre Marcel** to restore it and lay out an oriental-style park in the grounds. Today Maulévrier is well-known for its greyhound races.

Maulévrier Oriental Park ⊘ – The terraces of Colbert Castle overlook the park of 28ha - 70 acres that was laid out by A. Marcel between 1899 and 1910. Like a Japanese garden, it was planned around a peaceful lake to represent the changing seasons and the progression of living things, with symbols (rising and setting sun) of the life process from birth to death.

A path with Japanese lanterns leads around the lake through exotic species of shrubs and trees (Japanese maples, magnolia stellatae, cryptomerias, flowering cherries and aucubas) to a pagoda and garden with a spring, the symbol of birth and light. There is also a Khmer temple (used by Buddhists) approached by steps adorned with lions, a red bridge leading to the Crane and Tortoise islands (symbols of paradise), a hill of meditation, a rise of azaleas, and so on.

Beyond the shadowy lanes of conifers are a bonsai exhibition and a Raku earthenware workshop.

EXCURSION

Maulévrier Forest – The **Martyrs' Cemetery**, which is situated between Yzernay and Chanteloup beside the D 196, is surrounded by a forest of tall oak trees. During the Vendée War, Stofflet used its inaccessibility to conceal his headquarters where the wounded were brought for treatment. On 25 March 1794, however, the Blues penetrated the forest and massacred 1 200 of the Whites; two days later they took their revenge with a second massacre. The commemorative chapel standing alone in the forest is now a peaceful place.

Alexandre Marcel (1860-1928)

The Parisian achitect Alexandre Marcel restored many old buildings before gaining recognition and becoming famous for his thermal baths (Grands Thermes) in Chatelguyon, private mansions in Paris and Cholet, and a magnificent palace for the Maharajah of Kapurthala.

His love for the Orient resulted in the "Pagoda" in Rue Babylone in Paris and acclaimed buildings for several international exhibitions. He designed the Round the World Panorama (Panorama du Tour du Monde) hall for the French shipping company Messageries Maritimes, and the Cambodian Pavilion, in which he reproduced parts of the Temple of Angor Vat, for the Universal Exhibition in 1900.

Thanks to these constructions he was brought to the notice of King Leopold II of Belgium who asked him to rebuild, in Laeken Park (Brussels), the Japanese Tower and Chinese Pavilion which would otherwise have been demolished (see Michelin Green Guide Belgium/Luxembourg).

★ MAYENNE VALLEY

Michelin map 📖 folds 10, 20 or 📖 folds 19, 31

The quiet Mayenne follows a picturesque and winding course between steep wooded banks as it flows south to join the Loire. The river was made navigable in the 19C when a total of 39 locks was built between Laval and Angers and is now ideal for pleasure craft.

The valley is too steep for any villages to be built beside the river so it has been preserved in its natural state. The route described below passes through the villages of low red stone houses with slate roofs which crown the top of the slopes. There are good views of the river, some from a bridge and some from the by-roads which lead down to a picturesque site on the river bank to a mill or an isolated château.

The birds of the lower Angevin valleys – The 5 000ha - 12 355 acres of flood plains to the north of Angers at the confluence of the Mayenne, Sarthe and Loir, form a haven for migrating black-tailed godwits. From February to March, up to 30 000 of the birds gather here from West Africa before heading north to the Netherlands where they nest. Several weeks later, these same meadows shelter the largest French population of a species that is dying out, the land-rail.

FROM CHÂTEAU-GONTIER TO ANGERS

71km - 44 miles – allow one day – local map below

Château-Gontier – *See Château-Gontier.*

Daon – Pop 408. The village and its 16C manor house are superbly sited on a slope above the Mayenne. Daon was the birthplace of Abbé Bernier who negotiated the peace between the Chouans and the Republicans.

> *In Daon take D 213 eastward, then take the second turning on the left.*

A long avenue of lime and plane trees leads straight to the attractive 16C moated **l'Escoublère manor house.**

> *Return to Daon and take D 22 southeast, bearing right into D 190 to Marigné and D 78 to Chenillé-Changé.*

Chenillé-Changé – Pop 150. This is one of the most attractive villages in the Segréen region with its **fortified water-mill** ⊙ dating from the turn of the century and still in use, as the white trails of flour on the schist walls show. The old houses, 11C church and a **river boat centre** ⊙ with small barges moored along the shady banks of the Mayenne, all add to the peace and beauty of the scene *(photograph p 215).*

> *Take the road across the river to Chambellay and turn right into D 187.*

La Jaille-Yvon – Pop 239. The village is perched on the cliff above the river. From the east end of the church there is an extensive view of the fields and meadows in the valley.

> *Take D 189 west and turn left into N 162 going south.*

Shortly after the turning to Chambellay one sees (left) the imposing 15C-17C buildings of the **Château du Bois-Montbourcher,** surrounded by lawns and woods on the edge of a vast lake.

Le Lion d'Angers – *See Le Lion d'Angers.*

★**L'Isle-Briand National Stud** – *See Le Lion d'Angers.*

Grez-Neuville – Pop 1 040. The picturesque village in the heart of the Maine basin slopes gently down to the banks of the Mayenne, its slate spire reflecting in the water. Grez-Neuville is the departure point for **river cruises** ⊙ along the Mayenne and Oudon. In season, a Percheron may be seen on the tow-path pulling a boat for about 1km - 1/2 mile.

The road down the east bank (D 191) sometimes overhangs the river; it passes (left) **Le Sautret Château,** an impressive building with a dry moat.

> *In Feneu take D 768 south across the river to Montreuil-Juigné.*

★★★**Angers** – *See Angers. About 1/2 day.*

150

★ MÉNARS CHÂTEAU

Michelin map **64** fold 7 or **238** fold 3 (8km - 5 miles northeast of Blois)

The 17C château *(not open to the public)* on the north bank of the Loire was bought in 1760 by the Marquise de Pompadour, who had been Louis XV's mistress. She had extensive alterations carried out by the architect, Gabriel; the furniture and decoration were of the very best but the Marquise had little enjoyment of them since she died in 1764. Her brother, the Marquis of Marigny, who inherited the marquisate of Ménars, invited the architect Soumot to lay out the gardens.

The entrance court is bordered by the service **buildings** which the famous Marchioness had built; their elegance belies their humble purpose. An underground passage enabled the servants to reach the château without crossing the courtyard.

The terrace faces the Loire; in the Marchioness' time it was the main entrance to the château: visitors arrived at Ménars by river in the days before the road was built. The steep slope between the château and the water is laid out in **terraces ★** decorated with statues, vases, grottoes, fountains, temples of Venus and avenues of hundred-year old trees.

★ MEUNG-SUR-LOIRE   Pop 5 993

Michelin map **64** fold 8 or **238** fold 4 – Local map under LOIRE VALLEY: Orléans-Chinon

This picturesque fortified village extends up the slope from the Loire which laps at the roots of the tall trees in the Mall to the main road (N 152) which is up on the plateau away from the old town. From the **old market** a narrow and twisting street, **Rue Porte-d'Amont,** climbs up to an archway; little lanes skirt **les Mauves,** a stream with many channels which runs between the houses (Rue des Mauves, Rue du Trianon). The town has raised a statue to its most famous son, **Jean de Meung.** In about 1280 he added 18 000 lines to the *Romance of the Rose (Le Roman de la Rose)* which had been written some forty years earlier by Guillaume de Lorris *(qv)* and consisted of 4 000 lines. The allegorical narrative was the greatest literary achievement of a period which did not lack readers of stamina. Chaucer translated part of the work and was much influenced by it throughout his poetic career.

The bridge at Meung was often fought over during the Hundred Yars War; it was captured by the English in 1428 and retaken by Joan of Arc on 14 June 1429.

★**St Liphard's Church** – The plain building with its tower and spire dates from the 11C and 13C; the chevet is semicircular and the transept has unusual rounded ends. From beyond the chevet there is a good view of the church and the château.

Château ⊙ – The venerable building is a curious mixture of styles. The entrance front (13C), where there are traces of the drawbridge which spanned the dry moat, is medieval; the main entrance was created on the opposite front in the 16C, when the medieval entrance was walled up, and altered in the 18C.

The interior owes much to the 19C. After visiting the rooms in the château the tour goes **underground** to the 12C chapel with its palm tree vaulting and the dungeons where prisoners were put to the "question".

Until the 18C the château belonged to the Bishops of Orléans, who administered justice in their diocese but, being men of God, they did not have the right to put men to death. Prisoners sentenced to lifelong confinement were lowered on ropes into an underground tower, **oubliette,** with a well at the bottom; each day they received the same quantity of bread and water, however many they were, until they died of starvation or illness.

François Villon *(qv)*, who had powerful patrons, was the only one ever to come out alive; he suffered only one summer of imprisonment before Louis XI released him during a visit to Meung.

MIRÉ   Pop 958

Michelin map **64** fold 1 or **232** fold 20 (10km - 6 miles north of Châteauneuf-sur-Sarthe)

The **church** is roofed with wooden keel vaulting decorated with 43 late-15C painted panels depicting the four Evangelists, angels bearing the instruments of the Passion and the Apostles presenting the Creed.

Vaux Château ⊙ – *3.5km-2 miles northwest by D 29 towards Bierné.*
The picturesque château stands well back from the road to the right. The ruined curtain wall enclosed an elegant building with a stair turret and mullioned windows. This manor house was built at the end of the 15C by Jean Bourré *(qv)*, Lord of Miré. Happy in the knowledge that he had provided the Angevin orchards with a delicious fruit, he urged his steward "above all" to "take good care of the *Bonschrétiens* pears" which he was gathering.

To plan a special itinerary:

*- consult the **Map of Touring Programmes** which indicates the recommended routes, the tourist regions, the principal towns and main sights.*

*- read the descriptions in the **Sights** section which include Excursions from the main tourist centres.*

*Michelin Maps nos **60, 61, 63, 64, 65** and **67** indicate scenic routes, interesting sights, viewpoints, rivers, forests...*

MONDOUBLEAU

Michelin map 🔟 south of folds 15, 16 and 🔢 north of folds 5, 6 or 🔢 fold 1

Approached from the west Mondoubleau appears clustered on the east bank of the River Grenne. Perched at a crazy angle on a bluff to the south of the road to Cormenon are the ruins of a red sandstone **keep**, the remains of a fortress built at the end of the 10C by Hugues Doubleau from whom the town has taken its name. Partly hidden among the houses and trees are the remains of the curtain wall which protected the keep and the several precincts of the castle.

Old houses – 15C. On the corner of Rue du Pont de l'Horloge and the castle ramp.

Mall Walk – Rue Gheerbrant leads to the post office and the square, Place St-Denis; go through the public garden behind the post office to reach the Grand Mall (Grand Mail), a long shady avenue providing a pleasant view of the valley.

EXCURSIONS

Arville –*Round trip of 26km - 16 miles north by D 921 – about 1 hour.*

St-Agil Château ⊙ – An interesting château encircled by a moat. The part of the building dating from the 13C was altered in 1720. The early-16C entrance pavilion is flanked by two towers decorated with a diaper pattern in red and black bricks. The machicolations guard the sentry walk and the pepperpot roofs. The main building has a dormer window with a medallion of the lord of the manor, Antoine de la Vove. The park was landscaped by Jules Hardouin-Mansart and transformed in 1872 in the English style. The splendid lime trees were planted in 1720.

Arville –*See Arville.*

Souday –Pop 567. The nave of the **church** is extended by an interesting 16C two-storey chancel. Two flights of stairs, with wrought-iron railings which date from 1838, lead to the upper floor which is lit by Renaissance stained glass depicting the Passion and the Resurrection of Christ. The elegant ogive vaulting in the crypt springs from columns without capitals. The south transept is decorated with 16C paintings of St Joseph, St Joachim and four scenes from the life of John the Baptist; on the ceiling are the symbols of the four Evangelists.

Sargé – *Round trip of 24km - 15 miles –about 1 hour – leave Mondoubleau by D 151 going southeast.*

Le Temple – Pop 150. All that is left of the Templar commandery is a 13C church with a squat belltower and a square chevet nestling pleasantly by a pool.

Turn right into D 156.

Sargé-sur-Braye – Pop 988. St Martin's **church** was built in the 11C and 15C. The painted wainscoting dates from 1549. The murals discovered in the nave are 16C (*Pietà*, St Martin) and in the chancel 14C (Christ in Majesty and the Labours of the Months; note the three faces of Janus symbolizing January).

Baillou – Pop 230. The little village is picturesquely clustered below a great 16C-17C château.

The beautiful early-16C **church** stands alone on a mount. The Renaissance doorway is flanked by scrolled pilasters, surmounted by figures of Adam and Eve.

The south transept contains a carved altarpiece (1618) depicting the death of the Virgin surrounded by the Apostles and the donor, a priest called Gaultier.

Take D 86 back to Mondoubleau. Fine view of the town on arrival.

★ MONTGEOFFROY CHÂTEAU

Michelin map 🔢 folds 11, 12 or 🔢 fold 32 (24km - 15 miles east of Angers)

The regular plan of this beautiful château can be appreciated from the entrance with its Rococo scrolls; it consists of an imposing central block linked by terraced pavilions to two wings set at right angles. The two round towers attached to the wings, the curvilinear moat defining the courtyard and the chapel to the right are the only remains of the original 16C building.

The Montgeoffroy estate came into the possession of Erasme de Contades in 1676; the buildings owe their present appearance to his grandson, the famous Marshal who commanded the German army in the Seven Years War and who was Governor of Alsace for 25 years. His architect was the Parisian Nicolas Barre.

The **château** ☉ has remained in the family, and has consequently kept its original furnishings and decor, giving an effect of great charm. There are signed pieces of furniture by Gourdin, Blanchard, Garnier and Durand (each in the place it was designed to occupy), pictures by Drouais, Rigaud, Pourbus the Younger, Van Loo, Desportes and Louis Vigée, together with tapestries and hangings of the 18C. Documents bearing the signatures of Louis XV, Napoleon and Louis XVIII add to the interest, while in the kitchens is a display of 260 tin and copper pots and pans.
The **chapel** has Angevin vaulting *(p 37)* and 16C glass depicting the kneeling figure of the previous owner of Montgeoffroy, Guillaume de la Grandière.
In the **stables** is a collection of horse-drawn vehicles and a magnificent harness room fitted out in Norway spruce.

MONTIGNY-LE-GANNELON   Pop 388

Michelin map 🗺 60 south of fold 17 or 🗺 237 fold 38 (2km - 1 mile north of Cloyes-sur-le-Loir) – Local map under LOIR VALLEY: Bonneval-Vendôme

This fortress on the north bank of the Loir can be seen from afar on the N 10. The name Montigny comes from Mons-Igny meaning Signal Hill; Gannelon evokes the traitor who betrayed Roland to his enemies, or more likely the priest of Saint-Avit de Châteaudun who inherited the fortress in the 11C.
The small town, which lies between the river and the bluff, was once fortified; the Roland Gate (12C) still stands on the side facing away from the river.

★ **Château** ☉ – A second wall with five gates enclosed the château; the composite west façade faces the approach through the park. The combination of brick and stonework is striking.
The Ladies' Tower (Tour des Dames) and the Clock Tower (Tour de l'Horloge – whose portal carries the coats of arms of the Montmorencys – on the right – and of the Lévis – on the left) are the only remains of the Renaissance château which was rebuilt in 1495 by Jacques de Renty.
The château contains interesting information on the illustrious Lévis-Mirepoix family. To the right of a large Renaissance staircase adorned with portraits of Marshals of Lévis in medallions are the Gothic cloisters with a fine collection of 16C Italian faience plates. The richly-furnished rooms that follow contain numerous portraits and mementoes of the Montmorency and Lévis-Mirepoix families.

Column Room – Documents relate the founding of the town of Lévis-Lauzon in Quebec, which in 1861 was named after François-Gaston, Duke of Lévis, who had defeated the English at Sainte-Foy in 1760. Other displays evoke the tender esteem in which the Prince de Montmorency, Duke of Laval, held Madame Récamier.

Ladies' Chamber – Portraits of the women of the family. Fine secret cabinet in the Italian Renaissance style.

Grand Salon – Portrait of Gilles de Montmorency-Laval whose life remains wrapped in mystery and who inspired Charles Perrault for his character Bluebeard.

Montmorency Dining Hall – The Montmorency Pavilion to the north of the Clock Tower was built in 1834 by the Prince de Montmorency, Duke of Laval, to house the full-length portraits of the rulers to whom he was attached as French ambassador as well as those of Pope Pious VII and Léon XII.
In the grounds, a colourful collection of ostriches, emus, nandus, waterfowl and pheasants (Amherst's and a splendid tufted monal) roams through a cluster of 150-year-old trees. Hidden behind a screen of greenery is the former riding school and stables for coach teams, a vast shelter on a frame of steel girders which was built at the same time as the Eiffel Tower. Today it contains old farm implements, carriages and stuffed animals.

Church ☉ – The church dedicated to St Giles and St Saviour contains the shrine of St Felicity.

MONTLOUIS-SUR-LOIRE   Pop 8 309

Michelin map 🗺 64 fold 15 or 🗺 232 fold 36 or 🗺 238 fold 13 – Facilities

Montlouis rises up a hillside of tufa which is riddled with caves. Its vineyards on the south-facing plateau between the Loire and the Cher produce a heady and fruity white wine made from the famous Pinot de la Loire grape. Beside the church stands a Renaissance mansion (now the clergy house); the dormer windows are decorated with shells.

The Babou Family – In the 16C Montlouis was ruled by the Babous of La Bourdaisière, a turbulent family whose main residence, the Château de la Bourdaisière, lay a few miles to the south on the banks of the Cher. Montlouis was built *c*1520 by Philibert Babou, silversmith to François I, and lived in by Marie Babou, his wife, who was called *"la belle Babou"* and had a roving eye: she boasted of having "known", in the biblical sense of the word, François I, Charles V and many others. Gabrielle, the beautiful daughter of Antoine d'Estrées and Françoise Babou, who was born in 1573, also enjoyed the royal favour: she was the mistress of Henri IV and when she died the King turned to another Babou for consolation.

Loire House (La Maison de la Loire) ☉ – *Quai A. Baillet.* Exhibitions on the fauna and flora of the region are displayed here.

MONTOIRE-SUR-LE-LOIR

Pop 4 065

Michelin map ⓺⓸ fold 5 or ⓶⓷⓶ fold 24 or ⓶⓷⓼ fold 1 − Local map under LOIR VALLEY: Vendôme-La Flèche − Facilities

Montoire developed round St Giles' Priory which was founded in the 7C. In the 9C Charles the Bald had a fort built to protect the country from Viking incursions. Pilgrims making for Tours to pray at the tomb of St Martin used to stay the night in Montoire which was also on the route to Compostela in Spain. At this period leper houses were set up in Montoire and Troo.

A self-made man − In the 16C Montoire passed into the possession of the Bourbon family. Early in the 18C the Regent sold the manor of Montoire to Louis Fouquet, son of the Minister of Finance, who sold it in his turn to the Count of Les Noyers de Lorme. In fact the count's name was **Amédée Delorme** and his father was an innkeeper in Blois. Originally employed as a footman in Paris, he met the Regent in a brothel and lent him some money. He continued to serve the Regent as a moneylender and after making a tidy sum he increased it considerably speculating in Rue Quincampoix at the time of John Law *(qv),* a Scots financier who founded a bank in 1719 which crashed in 1720.

A momentous meeting − In mid-October 1940 German uniforms appeared in large numbers, convoys of machine guns roved the streets, anti-aircraft batteries were set up on the hills, military patrols erected barbed wire barriers on the roads and made house-to-house searches, the electricity and telephones were cut off, German railwaymen replaced the staff of the SNCF, people living in houses beside the railway line were ordered to close their shutters and stay indoors, a squadron of Messerschmidts frightened the cattle in the fields, two armoured trains bristling with guns patrolled the line from Vendôme to La Chartre.
On 22 October Hitler and Pierre Laval met in Montoire Station; in the event of an attack Hitler's train could have withdrawn into the tunnel at St-Rimay to the east. The following day saw the famous meeting between Hitler and Marshal Pétain in which the German Chancellor tried to persuade the French Head of State to make war against the United Kingdom.

SIGHTS

Bridge − Beautiful **view**★ of the Loir flowing past old houses covered with wistaria where weeping willows trail their tendrils in the water among the fishing boats moored to the banks.

★**St Giles' Chapel (St-Gilles)**
⊘ − At the beginning of the lane leading to the chapel stands a Renaissance house (Maison du "Jeu de Quilles" − **D**) which bears a plaque dedicated by a guild *(see Tours, Trade Guild Museum)* to one of its members who was a native of Montoire.
The main gate opens on to the apse of a graceful Romanesque chapel which belonged to a Benedictine priory of which Ronsard was once head. He left in October 1585 to visit his other priories, St Madeleine de Croixval and St Cosmas, near Tours, where he died two months later. The chapel and the prior's lodging are pleasantly set about with lawns and yew trees.

MONTOIRE

★★**Mural paintings** − The paintings are to be found in the apse and transepts which are shaped like a clover leaf. Each half-dome bears a figure of Christ painted at a different date. The oldest (first quarter of the 12C) in the apse shows a very majestic Christ surrounded by angels; this is the **Christ of the Apocalypse**.
In the south transept is another 12C Christ, offering the keys to St Peter (missing); this figure shows Byzantine influence in the tight and symmetrical folds of the garments.
The third figure in the north transept dates from the 13C and shows Christ with the Apostles recalling Pentecost; the unnatural attitudes and the colours − white, ochre and the blue of the haloes − are typical of the local school *(see p 39).* Note too the paintings on the arches of the crossing, particularly the Battle of the Virtues and Vices on the western arch.

Castle (Château) ⊘ − A stone and flint wall encloses the 11C square keep which stands on a spur of rock.
There is a fine view of the Loir Valley and the keep at Lavardin.

Renaissance Houses (B) − Two Renaissance houses stand side by side in Place Clemenceau; the larger, with mullioned windows and high dormer windows, is also the older. There are two others in Rue St-Oustrille (Maison du "Jeu de Quilles") and Rue St-Laurent (Antoine-Moreau Hospital).

154

★ MONTPOUPON CHÂTEAU

Michelin map 🔢 fold 16 or 🔢 fold 14 (12km - 7 1/2 miles south of Montrichard)

Of the old 13C fortress only the towers remain; the main building, which has mullioned windows and Gothic-style gables, was built in the 15C while the entrance pavilion, which is decorated in the Renaissance style on the rear façade, is early 16C.

The **outbuildings** ★ ⊘ contain an excellent demonstration of the way the castle was run in the last century. The kitchen, with its oven and copper pans, was still in use in 1978; the laundry displays delicate garments, decorated with pleats and edged with lace, such as were worn in the 19C. The hunting museum presents hunting costumes and hunting souvenirs and the guide demonstrates the different notes of several horns and tells the story of the Montpoupon Hunt. There are carriages on display in the stables and the equipment used by the château owners in the saddle and harness rooms.

★ MONTRÉSOR   Pop 362

Michelin map 🔢 south of folds 16, 17 or 🔢 southeast of fold 14

The sloping site of Montrésor on the north bank of the River Indrois is reflected in the water. The old market in the town is a timber-frame construction; the handsome 16C house with a watch tower in the main street is now the police station.

★ **Château** ⊘ – The curtain wall with its ruined towers belongs to the fortress built by Fulk Nerra *(qv)* in the 11C; within it at the centre of a charming, half-wild park stands the residence built in the early 16C by **Imbert de Bastarnay,** lord of Montrésor from 1493. This building has mullioned windows on the south front facing the river, gabled dormers and two machicolated towers. In 1849 the château was restored by **Count Xavier Branicki,** a Polish emigré who accompanied Prince Napoleon to Constantinople during the Crimean War and tried to raise a Polish regiment.

The furnishings are as they were at the time of Branicki: his shooting trophies decorate the entrance hall; military souvenirs and medals and pictures by Polish and French painters are exhibited throughout. Also worthy of note are low-reliefs in wood representing the battles of John III Sobieski of Poland (17C), a boudoir containing Italian Primitives and gold and silver plate. From the curtain wall above the river there is an attractive view of the valley and the houses of the town.

Church – The church was built between 1519 and 1541 in the Gothic style – only the doorway is Renaissance; it was originally a collegiate foundation set up by Imbert de Bastarnay, who built the church to house his tomb. The **Bastarnay tomb** ★ in the nave consists of three recumbent figures in white marble – Imbert, his wife and son – resting on a base decorated with statues of the twelve Apostles. Of the same date are two windows and the choir stalls, the latter in Renaissance style and richly decorated with medallions and misericords. In the chancel chapel (left) is a painting of the *Annunciation* by Philippe de Champaigne (17C).

★ MONTREUIL-BELLAY   Pop 4 041

Michelin map 🔢 south of fold 12 or 🔢 fold 33 – Facilities

The little town of Montreuil-Bellay possesses a very lovely **site** ★ beside the Thouet on the border of the Poitou and Anjou regions. From the east bank of the river and bridge there are good views of the château and church. The gardens along the west bank are an agreeable place for a stroll as is the picturesque square, Place des Ormeaux, in front of the château entrance.

Long stretches of the medieval wall are still standing: **St John's Gate** (Porte St-Jean), which is flanked by two large rusticated towers, dates from the 15C.

Recalcitrant vassals – In 1025 Fulk Nerra *(qv),* Count of Anjou, gave this stronghold to his vassal **Berlay** (distorted into Bellay), who made it into a powerful fortress. A century later, safe behind their stout walls, his successors plotted and intrigued against their overlord. In 1151, one of them, Giraud, held out for a whole year before he capitulated to Geoffroy Plantagenet, who then razed the keep which he had just reduced by means of an early incendiary bomb: a vessel full of oil was sealed, heated to incandescence and launched by a mangonel *(p 26).*

When the Plantagenets acceded to the throne of England and thus became the main enemy of the king of France, the Berlays (who later became the du Bellays) pledged their allegiance to their immediate overlord; Philippe-Auguste thereupon besieged their castle and dismantled it.

SIGHTS

★★ **Château** ⊘ – Imposing walls, pleasant gardens and remarkable furnishings are the main features of Montreuil Château. Behind the fortress aspect, within the fortified gateway, stands the graceful residence built by the Harcourt family in the 15C. From the courtyard terrace fine views of the church, the château and the grounds which descend in great steps down to the river.

The **medieval kitchen** with its central chimney like the one at Fontevraud *(qv)* was slightly altered in the 15C and is still in perfect condition: copper pans and kitchen range (18C) with seven fire boxes fuelled by charcoal.

The 15C **Canons' Lodge** has four stair turrets with conical roofs serving four separate sets of rooms, each consisting of living rooms over a store room (one was transformed into a steam-room) for the canons who served in the castle chapel.

Montreuil-Bellay Château

The **New Château** was built in the 15C; it has a beautiful stair turret decorated with mullioned windows protected by delicately-carved mock balustrades. The loggia with its ogee arch is 19C; on its right stands a 12C-13C tower. In the vaulted **cellar** the brotherhood of the Sacavins holds its meetings; it was founded in 1904 by the then owner of the castle, Georges de Grandmaison, to advertise Anjou wine. The winepress, into which the grapes were poured directly from the courtyard through a trap door, was still in use at the beginning of this century.

The rooms in the château are 7m - 23ft high and fully furnished. The dining-room (49m² - 527sq ft) has painted ceiling beams; the little **oratory** decorated with frescoes is late 15C: the angelic musicians on the vaulting are playing a motet of which the guide plays a recording. Visitors see the bedroom of the Duchess of Longueville, Condé's sister, who was the prime mover behind the Fronde *(qv)* and was exiled by Louis XIV to Montreuil where she lived in brilliant style. In the Great Salon there is a Brussels tapestry and a German marquetry cupboard; in the small music salon there is a superb bureau made by the famous cabinet maker Boulle (1642-1732), inlaid with copper and tortoise-shell.

Church of Our Lady (Notre-Dame) – It was built as the seigneurial chapel between 1472 and 1484 and has astonishingly strong walls and buttresses. Note the black mourning band in the nave and the private oratory for the owner of the castle.

Maison Dovalle ⊘ – *69 Rue Dovalle.* The façade of this 16C house was altered in the 18C. There is a fine view of the towers of the château, the Thouet Valley and in the far distance, Puy-Notre-Dame *(qv)*, from the watch tower in the garden.

The building is named after the Romantic poet **Charles Dovalle** (1807-29) whose collected works *Le Sylphe* were published posthumously with a preface by Victor Hugo.

The attic floor, in which the original timber-work is visible, houses the **Charles Léandre Museum.** Originally from Normandy, Léandre (1862-1934), who lived in Montmartre, Paris, was a talented draughtsman, painter, pastellist *(Woman with a Dog)* and engraver, combining classicism and impressionism in his work. He is best known for the acid caricatures of his contemporaries which appeared in the satirical magazines of the Belle Époque like *Le Rire* and *L'Assiette au beurre.* He was also famous for his posters.

Les Nobis – Deep in the vegetation beside the Thouet are the ruins of St Peter's Church which was burnt down by the Huguenots in the 16C; the Romanesque apse is decorated with carved capitals. Nearby are two wings of a 17C cloister.

EXCURSION

La Salle Water-Mill (Moulin de la Salle) ⊘ – *1km - 1/2 mile northeast by N147 towards Saumur.* This is the last water-mill still in use on the River Thouet. The different stages for the conversion of wheat into flour are explained; a water-wheel and various grinding and sifting utensils may be seen working.

Asnières Abbey ⊘ – *7.5km - 5 miles northwest.*
On the northern edge of Cizay Forest are the romantic ruins of what was once an important monastery founded in 12C. The tall and graceful **chancel**★ with its delicately ribbed vaulting is, like the chancel of St Sergius' Church in Angers, the most perfect specimen of Angevin Gothic art *(see p 37).* The Abbot's chapel, which was added in the 15C, has a pointed recess decorated with trefoils and festoons and 14C crucifix.

*Consult the **Map of Places to Stay** at the beginning of the guide to choose a suitable location.*

Michelin map 🆖 folds 16, 17 or 🆖 fold 14 – Facilities

From the riverbank and bridge over the Cher there is a good **view** of the town and its medieval houses clustered around the church below the crumbling keep.

The north bank above the town is pitted with quarries (**Bourré** is a village 3km - 2 miles to the east; its stone has been used for the construction of the nearby châteaux) which have been transformed into troglodyte dwellings, caves for growing mushrooms or cellars maturing wine by the **Champagne method** ⊘.

SIGHTS

★**Keep** ⊘ – The square keep which stands on the edge of the plateau above the River Cher is enclosed by the remains of its curtain wall *(p 34)* and by a complex system of ramparts which protected the entrance. It was built *c*1010 by Fulk Nerra *(qv)*, reinforced with a second wall in 1109 and then with a third in 1250. Despite being reduced in height by 4m - 13ft on the orders of Henri IV in 1589 for being in the possession of the Leaguers *(qv)*, the keep recalls the distant past. From the top (tiny platform: 4 people only) there is a panoramic **view**★★ of the town and the Cher Valley.

St Cross Church – The church which was originally the castle chapel stands below the keep at the top of the Great St Cross Steps (Grands Degrés Ste-Croix). The façade is decorated with elegant Romanesque arches; the arches of the porch are ornamented with a twisted torus. The elegant doorway is also Romanesque.

Jeanne de France, the daughter of Louis XI, and her young cousin, the Duke of Orléans, were married in this chapel in 1476.

The bride, who was 12, was ugly and deformed and had no attraction for Louis d'Orléans who had been forced into the marriage by the king. Knowing that his daughter could not bear a child, Louis XI hoped in this way to bring to an end the Orléans line, which was a junior branch of the Valois family which chafed at the royal authority. Events, however, took a different course. In 1498 Louis XI's son, Charles VIII, died accidentally at Amboise *(qv)* leaving no heir since his sons had died in infancy. As the king's nearest relative Louis d'Orléans acceded to the throne as Louis XII. In his will Charles VIII had stipulated that the new king should marry his widow, Anne of Brittany. Repudiated, Jeanne devoted herself to a life of good works; she retired to Bourges where she founded a religious order.

Old houses – There are several picturesque old façades up by the keep. **Hôtel d'Effiat** in Rue Porte-au-Roi, which was built in the late 15C-early 16C, has a Gothic décor with a few Renaissance elements; in the 16C it was the residence of Jacques de Beaune, Treasurer to Anne of Brittany and then to Louise de Savoie, the mother of François I; the mansion has retained the name of its last owner, the Marquis d'Effiat, who at his death (1719) presented it to the town to be converted into an old people's home.

There are two old timber-framed houses in the square, Place Barthélemy-Gilbert, and on the corner of Rue du Pont stands **Ave Maria House** (16C) which has three gables and finely carved beams. Opposite are the Lower St Cross Steps (Petits Degrés Ste-Croix) which lead to some troglodyte dwellings.

Further on, at the corner of Rue du Prêche, stands the 11C stone façade of the Sermon House (**Maison du Prêche**).

Nanteuil Church – *On the road to Amboise (D 115)*. The church is a tall Gothic building with a Flamboyant doorway; the apses are Romanesque decorated with carved capitals. The tall and narrow nave has Angevin vaulting. Above the entrance porch is a chapel built by Louis XI; it is approached by external and internal steps. There is a long-established tradition of a pilgrimage to the Virgin of Nanteuil on Whit Monday.

EXCURSION

Thésée – Pop 1 074. *10km - 6 miles east*. West of the village stand the remains of the Gallo-Roman settlement of Tasciaca beside the Roman road from Bourges to Tours; it owed its 1C-3C prosperity to the making and selling of ceramics. Known as "Les Maselles", the settlement extended over the area of present-day Thésée and Pouillé; it is built out of the soft local limestone laid conventionally or in herringbone pattern and reinforced with brick at base and corners.

Archaeological museum ⊘ – Housed in the town hall (an 18C wine-grower's property in the middle of a splendid 7ha - 18acre park), the museum's collection consists of objects excavated from the sanctuary *(fanum)* and from the numerous potteries unearthed on either side of the river; ex-votos, statuettes, coins, jewellery, buckles as well as ceramics, some of them signed, all help to evoke the life of those who once dwelt here on the banks of the Cher.

Join us in our constant task of keeping up-to-date.
Please send us your comments and suggestions.

MICHELIN TYRE
Public Limited Company
Tourism Department
The Edward Hyde Building
38 Clarendon Road
WATFORD - Herts WD1 1SX

Michelin map ▐64▐ folds 12, 13 or ▐232▐ fold 33 – Local map under LOIRE VALLEY:
Chinon-Champtoceaux – Facilities

Montsoreau is famed for its castle which dominates the confluence of the Loire
and the Vienne.

Montsoreau

Castle ⊙ – The castle was built in the 15C by a member of the Chambes family
which produced bold warriors and enterprising women. One of the ladies of
Montsoreau seduced the Duke of Berry, brother of Louis XI and through him
formed the League for the Public Good (Ligue du Bien Public) which the king
defeated only by the assassination of the pretender and his mistress. A century
later one of the most active executioners in the massacre of the Huguenots on
St Bartholomew's Day was a Chambes. An event in the history of the family and
the castle was used by Alexandre Dumas in one of his novels, *La Dame de
Montsoreau*. The heroine was forced by her jealous husband to meet her lover,
Bussy d'Amboise, at the Château de la Coutancière (on the north bank of the Loire)
where he was assassinated. After this outburst, husband and wife lived in perfect
harmony until they died forty years later.
The river front, which was once at the water's edge, is an impressive example of
military architecture.
The castle houses a **Goum Museum** about the conquest of Morocco, Marshal Lyautey
and the history of the cavalry regiments *(goums)* recruited in Morocco. The
collections, formerly in Rabat, were brought to France in 1956 when Morocco
became independent.

★★**Panorama** – *1km - 1/2 mile by the road to the right of the castle up the hill;
signposts*. There is a belvedere in the vineyards on the cliff top: view downstream
of the town, the castle and the Loire Valley, upstream of the tree-lined confluence
of the Loire and the Vienne.

La Herpinière Windmill – *1.5km - 1 mile southwest by V3.*
There used to be a number of windmills on the plateau; this one in the commune
of Turquant dates from the 15C. The milling chamber is hollowed out of the tufa
below ground level.

MOULIHERNE   Pop 951

Michelin map ▐64▐ folds 12, 13 or ▐232▐ fold 33

Mouliherne stands on a rock on the north bank of the quiet Riverolle.

Church – The church, which is built on a mound, has a beautiful square 13C
belltower with splayed windows and a twisting spire typical of the Baugé region.
The interior vaulting demonstrates the evolution of the Angevin style *(see p 37)*: in
the chancel barrel vaulting; in the south transept an early example of quadripartite
vaulting; in the north transept and on the transept crossing a more elaborate
version of the former, supported on beautiful Romanesque capitals decorated with
water lily leaves and fantastic animals; in the nave, wide and soaring Gothic
vaulting. Behind the high altar in the nave are 9C-10C Carolingian sarcophagi.

EXCURSION

Linières-Bouton – *Pop 87. 5km - 3 miles east by D 62.*
This is a quiet village just off the main road. The **church** has a beautiful **chancel** built
in the Plantagenet style; there is a painting of the Annunciation (1677), a huge
Baroque cross in gilded wood and a sculpture of the Holy Family, probably 17C.

MULSANS

Michelin map **64** fold 7 or **238** fold 3 (14km - 9 miles northeast of Blois)

Mulsans is a small farming village on the edge of the Beauce with the traditional walled-in farmyards of the region. The charming **church** has Flamboyant windows and a fine Romanesque belltower decorated with blind arcades and twin bays. There is a Renaissance gallery supported on carved wood columns extending the full width of the nave and incorporating the porch; this is a regional feature known as a *"caquetoire"* where people pause to talk after church.

NOYANT-LA-GRAVOYÈRE

Michelin map **63** fold 9 or **232** fold 18

The Noyant-la-Gravoyère district, in the heart of the Upper Anjou Segréen region, once had a flourishing fine-slate industry for which the poet Du Bellay held great affection.

★**The Blue Mine** ⊙ – *Either take D 775 towards Pouancé and then D 219, or the tourist train from St-Blaise leisure park.* The St-Blaise slate quarries in La Gatelière, which overlook La Corbinière lakes, were closed in 1936. They have since been cleared and opened to the public.

Noyant-la-Gravoyère — The Blue Mine

The 126m - 413ft **descent into the bottom of the mine** is done by funicular railway (visitors must wear helmets). Once down, a small train passes through cleared galleries to the enormous extraction chambers, some of which are 80m - 262ft deep. There, a *son et lumière* show illustrates the life of miners in the 1930s, the dangers to which they were exposed and the daily round of work at the bottom of the pit. The last chamber evokes the myths that man's imagination has conjured up about the world underground. Before leaving the pit, there is a demonstration of a blast with explosives.

Back above ground, standing amongst birch-trees, are some restored **slate cleavers' cabins.** These huts once used by splitters or cleavers, who were also known as "lords of the hill", now house tools for making roofing tiles. Sound effects illustrate the splitting process applied to the blocks of schist brought up from the pit. The **Slate Museum** in the old boiler room relates the history of the slate industry, its operating methods and the technical progress made over the years thanks to improved machinery.

The birds of the Loire

The Loire, the "last wild river in Europe", with its islands, back-waters, long sand banks and grassy shores, is one of the natural regions in France where the flora and fauna are particularly abundant and diverse. Among the birds that build their nests along its banks are the common and little tern, the little ringed plover and the common sandpiper.

From March to the end of June, Parney Island below Montsoreau is home to over 750 pairs of gulls — black-headed, Mediterranean, common and Iceland — and common and little terns. Lastly, in August and September, among the many migratory species on the river is the osprey which makes spectacular dives into the slow waters.

Michelin map 🔢 fold 9 or 🔢 fold 40 or 🔢 fold 5 – Local map under LOIRE
VALLEY: Orléans-Chinon
Plan of the conurbation in the current Michelin Red Guide France

Orléans has always been an active business centre, trading in the wheat of the
Beauce, the honey, poultry and potatoes of the Gâtinais, the game of the Sologne
and the wines of the Loire Valley; the town has several industrial zones such as
Chapelle-St-Mesmin; in between there is an unbroken network of garden centres,
nursery gardens and market gardens which have made Orléans the "city of roses"
and one of the poles of the "garden of France" as the Loire Valley is called.

Orléans is the capital of the Central region of France (an economic division) and an
important administrative and university town. These activities are mostly concentrated in the satellite town of **Orléans-la-Source.**

The **Festivals of Joan of Arc** in spring *(see Calendar of Events)* go back to 1435; every
year the inhabitants celebrate their deliverance from the English.

From the Carnutes to Joan of Arc – The Gauls considered the land of the
Carnutes to be the centre of their territory, Gaul; each year the Druids held their
great assembly there and it was at Cenabum (Orléans) that the signal was given to
revolt against Caesar in 52 BC.

A Gallo-Roman city soon rose from the Gaulish ruins. In June 451 it was besieged
by Attila the Hun, but the inhabitants, inspired by their bishop, St Aignan,
succeeded in driving off the invaders.

In the 10C and 11C Orléans was one of the focal points of the Capet monarchy.

THE SIEGE OF 1428-29

This memorable siege was one of the great episodes in the history of France; it
marks the rebirth of a country which was sinking into despair.

The forces engaged – From the
beginning of the 15C the
defence of Orléans had
been organised to repulse
an English attack. The city
wall was composed of two
parts *(see plan);* on the
east side was the old
square wall of the Gallo-
Roman camp and on the
west a longer wall, enclosing more ground, which
was built in the 14C. There
were 34 towers and the
wall was divided into six
sections each defended by
50 men. All the inhabitants
took part in the defence of
the city whether as soldiers

or by maintaining the walls and ditches. In all about 10 000 men were involved
under the orders of the Governor of Orléans, Raoul de **Gaucourt,** and his captains.
During the summer of 1428 the commander of the English army, the **Earl of Salisbury,**
had destroyed the French strongholds along the Loire and gained control of the
river downstream from Orléans, thus preventing the city from being relieved from
the west. After the fall of Beaugency on 25 September he began to march on
Orléans. His army consisted of 400 men-at-arms, 2 250 archers, together with
400 lancers and 1 200 archers recruited in France, in all over 4 000 men.

The struggle began on 17 October when the English pounded the city with
bombards and heavy cannon; their chief aim however was to cut the city off from
any contact with the surrounding contryside. On the south side of the town there
was a bridge spanning the Loire which was defended at its southern end by Les
Tourelles Fort. The people of Orléans had earlier demolished all the buildings in this
district to make the enemy's approach more difficult. On 24 October, however, the
English captured Les Tourelles Fort but, as Salisbury was inspecting the grounds he
was killed by a cannon ball fired, it was thought, from the tower of Notre-Dame
Church. The French defenders blew up an arch and built a hasty wooden outwork
in front of St Antony's Fort on an island in the river. By way of counteraction the
besiegers demolished two arches in front of Les Tourelles Fort and raised a high
earth bank.

Orléans was now cut off from the rest of the French Kingdom. On 8 November the
majority of the English forces withdrew to Meung-sur-Loire and the French took
the opportunity to raze the other suburbs to prevent the English from re-
establishing themselves there. The besiegers were not, however, inactive. They
surrounded the town with a series of trenches commanded by small forts but their
lines were not impenetrable particularly in the northeastern sector where sorties
were still possible. Dunois (also known as the Bastard of Orléans), who had arrived
with his troops on 25 October, looked down from the top of the walls on the
English forts without being able to intervene.

The two sides settled down to a war of attrition punctuated by skirmishes outside
the gates. From time to time feats of arms raised the morale of the besieged. The
prowess and cunning of Master-Gunner Jean de Montesclerc became famous: he
killed many English soldiers and would often pretend to die so that when he re-
appeared the dismay and alarm of the English were redoubled. Two bombards
called Rifflart and Montargis rose to fame owing to their fire power and their range
which caused great damage on the south bank of the Loire.

The months of misery and waiting seemed, however, to grow longer and longer; food grew scarce and in February 1429 part of the garrison left. The English were close to victory. Dunois, however, remained optimistic.

The Arrival of Joan of Arc – In April 1429 Joan of Arc persuaded the future **Charles VII** to rescue Orléans. She left Blois with the royal army, crossed the river and approached Orléans by the south bank so as to take the English by surprise but the river was too high and the army had to return to the bridge at Blois. Meanwhile, Joan and a few companions crossed by boat a few miles upstream of Orléans at Checy and entered the town on 29 April by the Burgundy Gate (Porte de Bourgogne). She was greeted by an enthusiastic crowd and issued her famous ultimatum to the English, that they should surrender the keys of all the good French towns that they had captured and violated to her the Maid who had been sent by God to boot them out of France.

The Orléanais rallied and prepared for battle while Joan confronted the hostility of the captains and the Governor.

On 4 May the royal army, which Dunois had rejoined, attacked St-Loup Fort without warning Joan. When she learned of it she made a sortie, raising her banner, and the French were victorious. The following day Joan, who was excluded from the captains' council, suggested pressing forward the attack against Les Tourelles Fort and on the morning of 6 May, although efforts were made to fault her, Joan herself led the attack against the Augustinian monastery. A second time her forceful intervention upset the English who were engaged in pursuing the retreating French troops. This second victory increased her popularity and made the captains look ridiculous. The English troops grew alarmed. Joan called on them again to withdraw and when they refused she went on the offensive again on 7 May against the advice of the Governor who tried to bar her way. While fighting in the front line outside Les Tourelles Fort she was wounded in the shoulder by a crossbow bolt. The English thought she was done for and Dunois suggested postponing the attack to the following day but, after having the wound dressed and praying to the saints, Joan returned to the attack bearing her standard. With renewed vigour the French hurled themselves against the English, and the remaining French made a sortie from the town on to the bridge. The English garrison in the fort were caught in the crossfire; they were forced to abandon the fort and surrendered. On Sunday 8 May the English withdrew from the last forts and lifted the siege: Joan received a triumph in Orléans for her victory.

This check to the English advance had enormous repercussions; it threw their plans into disarray, since they had counted on taking not only the town itself but also the bridge over the Loire, as its capture would have enabled them to join forces with the English troops stationed in central and southwestern France under the terms of the 1360 Treaty of Brétigny; it also weakened the position of the Duke of Bedford, the regent in England, but above all it gave new confidence to the Dauphin and his army. On 18 June the French forces won the Battle of Patay.

THE CITY CENTRE

★**St Cross Cathedral (Ste-Croix** – **EFY)** – The Cathedral of the Holy Cross was begun in the 13C and its building went on until the 16C, but it was partly destroyed by the Protestants in 1568. Henri IV, the first Bourbon King, being grateful to the town for having supported him, undertook to rebuild the cathedral, not in the style of the 17C, but in a composite Gothic style. The work went on throughout the 18C and 19C. The old Romanesque towers still standing before the Wars of Religion (1562-98) were replaced by pseudo-Gothic towers.

The **West Front** has three large doorways with rose windows above them crowned by a gallery with openwork design. The skill of the masons can be seen in the unusually fine quality of the stonework. At the base of the two towers admire the delicacy of the spiral staircases, also with openwork design, at each of the four corners.

The vast **doorway** has four gigantic statues of the Evangelists.

The Siege of Orléans

ORLÉANS

Bannier (R.)	**DY**
Jeanne-d'Arc (R.)	**EY**
République (R. de la)	**EY**
Royale (R.)	**EZ** 125
Tabour (R. du)	**EZ** 145
Antigna (R.)	**DY** 4
Bourgogne (R. Fg de)	**FZ** 15
Bretonnerie (R. de la)	**EY** 16
Briand (Bd A.)	**EY** 19
Champ-de-Mars (Av.)	**DZ** 25
Châtelet (Square du)	**EZ** 32
Charpenterie (R. de la)	**EZ** 34
Chollet (R. Théophile)	**EY** 36
Claye (R. de la)	**FY** 38
Coligny (R.)	**FZ** 39
Croix-de-la-Pucelle (R.)	**EZ** 43
Dauphine (Av.)	**EZ** 47
Dolet (R. Étienne)	**EZ** 49
Dunois (Pl.)	**DY** 52
Dupanloup (R.)	**EY** 53
Escures (R. d')	**EY** 55
Étape (Pl. de l')	**EY** 56
Ételon (R. de l')	**FY** 57
Folie (R. de la)	**FZ** 58
Fort-des-Tourelles (Q.)	**EZ** 60
Gaulle (Pl. Gén. de)	**DZ** 65
Hallebarde (R. de la)	**DY** 70
Madeleine (R. Fg)	**DZ** 88
Motte-Sanguin (Bd de)	**FZ** 95
Notre-Dame-de-Recouvrance (R.)	**DZ** 97
Oriflamme (R. de l')	**FZ** 98
Parisie (R.)	**EZ** 100
Poirier (R. du)	**EZ** 106
Pte-Madeleine (R.)	**DY** 108
Pte-St-Jean (R.)	**DY** 109
Pothier (R.)	**EZ** 112
Prague (Quai)	**DZ** 113
Rabier (R. F.)	**EY** 117
St-Euverte (Bd)	**FYZ** 126
St-Euverte (R.)	**FY** 127
Ste-Catherine (R.)	**EZ** 138
Ste-Croix (Pl.)	**EYZ** 139
Secrétain (Av. R.)	**DZ** 140
Tourneuve (R. de la)	**FZ** 147
Trévise (Av. de)	**DZ** 148
Verdun (Bd de)	**DY** 152
Vieux-Marché (Pl.)	**DZ** 159

Interior – The vast main body of the cathedral comprises five aisles. On the north side of the chancel, in the Chapel of St Joan of Arc, is the statue of Cardinal Touchet (1894-1926), who made incessant efforts to propagate the cult of the Maid. In the central chapel of the apse is a fine marble Virgin by Michel Bourdin (early 17C), a sculptor born in Orléans.

Splendid early-18C **woodwork**★★ adorns the chancel. It was made to the designs of Mansart, Gabriel and Lebrun by Jules Degoullons, one of the decorators of Versailles and designer of the stalls in Notre-Dame, Paris; the carved medallions and the panels of the high backs of the choirstalls are particularly fine.

In the **crypt** ⊘ are traces of the three buildings which preceded the present cathedral, and two sarcophagi; one belonged to Bishop Robert de Courtenay (13C) who collected the most precious items in the **Treasury** ⊘. Among these are two gold medallions (11C) decorated with cloisonné enamel in the Byzantine manner, which used to adorn the gloves worn by the Bishop of Orléans for ceremonies and processions; 13C gold and silverware; and 17C paintings by Vignon and Jouvenet.

North Transept and East End – In the north transept is a rose window with the emblem of Louis XIV at the centre. Excavations at the base have revealed the old Gallo-Roman walls and part of a tower.

The **east end** with its flying buttresses and pinnacles is clearly visible from the gardens of the former episcopal palace (**FY Q**), an 18C building which now houses the municipal library.

Campo Santo (**EY**) – To the left of the modern Fine Arts School (École Régionale des Beaux-Arts) is a graceful Renaissance portal and on the north side of this same building is a garden edged with an arcaded gallery. The garden was a cemetery outside the walls in the 12C, the galleries were added in the 16C (exhibitions).

★★**Fine Arts Museum** (Musée des Beaux-Arts) (**EY M¹**) ⊘ – In the primitives gallery is an outstanding 15C painting from the Sienese school, a *Virgin and Child* with two angels by Matteo di Giovanni. The 14C-16C sculptures include a marble Virgin and Child (1370) and a fine bust of Cardinal Morvillier by Germain Pilon. The Italian, Flemish and Dutch schools are represented by works by Correggio *(Holy Family)*, Tintoretto *(Portrait of a Venetian)*, Annibale Carracci *(Adoration of the Shepherds)*, Pourbus the Younger and Ruysdaal. Velasquez' remarkable *St Thomas* (*c*1620) dates from the period the artist spent in Seville.

On the first floor is displayed the 17C-18C French school (note the delicate 12C-16C **ivories** ★ displayed in the corridor): vast religious paintings inspired by the Counter-Reformation, *St Charles Borromeo* by Philippe de Champaigne, *Triumph of St Ignatius* by Claude Vignon. The chiaroscuro technique is exemplified in *St Sebastian* from Georges de La Tour's studio. Among the 17C canvases are *Bacchus and Ariadne,* a rare mythological work by Le Nain, and a good portrait of *Le Nôtre* from Claude Lefevre's studio. Masterpieces from Richelieu's château include the graceful *Four Elements* by Deruet and *Louis XIV as a Child.*
The collection of 18C portraits includes: *Mme de Pompadour* by Drouais; *Moyreau,* the engraver by Nonotte; the *Marquis of Lucker* by Louis Tocqué. Paintings by Hubert Robert *(Landscape with Ruined Tower, The Wash House)* and Boucher *(The Dovecote)* are noteworthy.
In the Pastel Gallery there are 18C portraits including works by Perronneau and Nattier as well as expressive busts by Pigalle and Houdon and French ceramics and medallions.
The 19C is represented by artists such as Gros, Cogniet, Courbet *(The Wave),* Boudin, Antigna, a native of Orléans, and Gauguin *(Fête Gloanec).*
20C art is illustrated by paintings by artists like Soutine, Rouault, la Fresnaye, Gromaire and Max Jacob. There are also sculptures by Bourdelle, Maillol Zadkine, Charles Malfray and Gaudier-Breszka and the museum also houses a number of contemporary works.

Hôtel Groslot (EY H) – Built in 1550 by the bailiff Jacques Groslot, this large Renaissance mansion in red brick with diapering in black was subject to extensive remodelling in the 19C. Admire the delicate scrollwork on the staircase pillars and the two main entrances flanked by caryatids. This was the king's residence in Orléans: François II, who died here after opening in 1560 the States-General, Charles IX, Henri III and Henri IV all stayed here.
On the other side of the building is the **garden** where the façade of the former chapel of St-Jacques (15C) has been re-erected.
On the other side of the road stand the **Pavillons d'Escures** (EY N), town houses in brick with stone courses dating from the early 17C.

Place Ste-croix (EYZ 139), a vast symmetrical esplanade, bordered by classical façades and arcades, was laid out *c*1840 when Rue Jeanne-d'Arc was opened up.

On the south side of the square there is a bronze statue of the Loire holding the fruits of the river valley in the folds of her dress. The 15C **Hôtel des Créneaux** (EZ **R**) was the town hall from the 16C to 1790.

★**Historical Museum** (EZ **M²**) ⊘ – It is housed in an elegant little mansion, **Hôtel Cabu** (1550), beside another Renaissance façade.
On the ground floor is the astonishing **Gallo-Roman treasure**★ from Neuvy-en-Sullias (31km - 19 miles east of Orléans) which consists of a series of expressive statues, a horse and a wild boar in bronze as well as a number of statuettes which once graced a pagan temple.
The first floor is devoted to the Middle Ages and to the classical period; there are sculptures from Germigny-des-Prés and St-Benoît-sur-Loire, souvenirs of Joan of Arc (15C German tapestry, 17C standard from the Joan of Arc Festival), as well as typical local ceramics. The second floor is occupied by local folklore, gold and silverware and clocks.

Place du Martroi (EY) – This square is the symbolic centre of the town by virtue of the presence here of the statue of Joan of Arc by Foyatier (1855). The name is derived from the Latin word *martyretum* which was used to refer to the 6C Christian cemetery. On the west corner of Rue Royale stands the old Chancellery Pavilion (**Pavillon de la Chancellerie**) which was built in 1759 by the Duke of Orléans to house his archives.

Rue Royale (EZ **125**) – This broad street, lined with arcades, was opened up c1755 when the Royal Bridge (**Pont George V**) was built to replace the old medieval bridge which had stood 100m - 100yds upstream in line with St Catherine Street, the old north-south axis of the city.

Charles Péguy Centre (EZ **D**) ⊘ – The centre is housed in the old **Hôtel Euverte Hatte,** which is also known as Agnès Sorel House, because Charles VII's favourite may have lived there as a child; the present building was erected later in the reign of Louis XII. The rectangular windows are framed with Gothic friezes; the Renaissance arcade in the courtyard was added in the reign of François I.
The centre traces the life and career of **Charles Péguy** (1873-1914), poet and campaigner, who was born in Orléans and died on 5 September 1914 at the beginning of the Battle of the Marne. His writings reflect the causes he adopted and defended with intransigence: Dreyfus, socialism, patriotism, Catholicism. He wrote about the life of Joan of Arc: a long play in 1897 and a series of mysteries in 1911-12. There is a library devoted to Péguy, his work and his literary, political and social environment including the Dreyfus affair. The Péguy museum on the second floor contains manuscripts and souvenirs.

★**Joan of Arc House** (DZ **E**) ⊘ – The tall timber-framed façade contrasts with the modernity of the square, Place du Général-de-Gaulle, which was badly bombed in 1940. The building is a faithful reconstruction of the house of Jacques Boucher, Treasurer to the Duke of Orléans, where Joan stayed in 1429. An audiovisual show on the first floor recounts the lifting of the siege of Orléans by Joan of Arc on 8 May 1429; there are reproductions of period costumes and weapons of war.

Joan of Arc Centre (EY **L**) ⊘ – The centre's resources include a library, microfilm and photographic archives.
Beyond the house and the two adjacent Renaissance façades on the right there is an arch leading into Jacques Boucher Square. Standing alone in the garden is the **Pavillon Colas des Francs,** an elegant little Renaissance building, where Boucher's grandson conducted his business; a room on the ground floor houses the archives, while another room upstairs was where the silver was kept.

Hôtel Toutin (DZ **K**) ⊘ – The house was built in 1540 for Toutin, manservant to François I's son. In the small courtyard is a double Renaissance arcade covered in Virginia creeper and a statue of François I.

Quai Fort-des-Tourelles (EZ **60**) – Opposite a statue of Joan of Arc standing in a small square is a commemorative cross and an inscription on the low wall beside the Loire which mark the site of the southern end of the medieval bridge and the Tourelles Fort in the 15C; its capture by Joan of Arc led to the defeat of the English and the lifting of the siege. Fine **view**★ of the whole town.

Quai du Châtelet (EZ) provides a quiet shady walk beside the river. In Sully's time, early in the 17C, this was one of the busiest parts of town; it was from here that goods bound for Paris from the Loire valley and the Massif Central were transferred from river to road, and from here that the 6-day voyage downstream to Nantes was begun.

Rue de Bourgogne (EFZ) – This was the main east-west axis of the old Gallo-Roman city. Now largely pedestrianised, it is ideal for window shopping. There are several old façades: no 261 is a 15C stone house with a half-timbered gable.
Along the street is the **Préfecture** (EZ **P**), housed in a 17C Benedictine convent. Opposite in Rue Pothier is the façade of the old Thesis Hall (**Salle des Thèses**) (EZ **X**), a 15C library, which is the only remnant of the University of Orléans where Jean Calvin, the religious reformer, studied law in 1528.

Church of St-Pierre-le-Puellier (EFZ) – The 12C Romanesque church, which has been deconsecrated, is at the heart of an old district of pedestrian streets.

St-Aignan's Church (FZ) – The nave of this huge Gothic church, which was consecrated in 1509, was burnt down during the Wars of Religion leaving only the choir and the transepts.

★**Natural History Museum** (EY **M³**) ⊘ – The old museum, which has been completely restored and to which an extension has been added, now houses local and regional displays of a scientific and cultural nature.

Temporary exhibitions are held regularly on the ground floor. Four floors of the museum are devoted to the marine world, aquatic ecosystems (aquarium), reptiles and amphibians (vivarium), higher vertebrates (diorama on the Sologne region), mineralogy, geology, palaeontology and botany (greenhouses of temperate and tropical plants on the top floor). There are simultaneous displays in scientific workshops and a geology laboratory explaining various techniques including the art of keeping aquaria, stuffing animals and pressing plants. Complementary information may be obtained from a library and audio-visual and computer aids.

OLIVET

Like the southern suburbs of Orléans between the Loiret and the Loire, the greater part of Olivet (Pop 17 572 - Facilities) is given over to growing flowers, roses and ornamental plants. It is also a pleasant summer resort on the south bank of the Loiret, composed of elegant houses and old water mills, where people come for the fishing and canoeing.

Mill Walk − *Round trip of 5km - 3 miles from the bridge by the side road along the north bank of the Loiret going west and returning by D 14 going east.*
Two old mills straddle the river over their millraces between the wooded banks of the Loiret; ducks and swans glide up and down on the quiet stream.

★★ **La Source Floral Park** ⊘ − The huge park (30ha - 74 acres) is divided into a great variety of styles of planting: symmetrical beds, rock gardens, wooded parkland, evergreen and flowering shrubs. The display changes with the seasons: in spring − tulips and daffodils followed by irises, rhododendrons and azaleas; from mid-June to mid-July − roses; in July and August − summer flowers; in September − before the dahlias a second flowering of the roses; at the end of the season − chrysanthemums in the exhibition hall.
The park is a delight for everyone, very instructive to the amateur gardener and a showcase for the local horticulture. From the **mirror**★, a semicircular pool, there is a fine view of the château and the delicate "Louis XIII embroidery" which decorates the lawns.
The **Loiret Spring**★ which bubbles up from the ground is supplied by water which branches off from the Loire at St-Benoît-sur-Loire, some 36 miles upstream.
Throughout the year flamingoes stalk by the Loiret while flocks of cranes and emus and herds of deer roam the park.

MICHELIN GUIDES

The **Red Guides** *(hotels and restaurants)*

Benelux - Deutschland - España Portugal - Main Cities Europe - France - Great Britain and Ireland - Italia

The **Green Guides** *(fine art, historical monuments, scenic routes)*

Austria - Canada - England : the West Country - France - Germany - Great Britain - Greece - Ireland - Italy - London - Mexico - Netherlands - New England - New York - Paris - Portugal - Quebec - Rome - Scotland - Spain - Switzerland - Washington

...and the collection of regional guides for France.

Le PERCHE-GOUËT

Michelin map 60 folds 15, 16 − Local map p. 166

Le Perche-Gouët, which is sometimes known as Lower Perche, was named in the 11C after William Gouët who owned five baronies within the jurisdiction of the Bishop of Chartres: Alluyes la Belle, Brou la Noble, La Bazoche, la Gaillarde, Authon la Gueuse and Montmirail la Superbe. Before the Revolution the administration of Le Perche-Gouët was divided between the authority in the Orléans district and that of the Upper Maine. Le Perche-Gouët describes a sort of crescent between the Loir and the Huisne; the soil is composed of chalk marl and banks of sand or clay. Much of the immense forest which once covered the land has been replaced by fields and orchards.
The eastern part of Le Perche-Gouët is very similar to the Beauce but is distinguished by its scattered farms and the abundance of hedges and trees. The western border is marked by a range of wooded hills, only 250m - 820ft high, indented by a network of alluvial valleys and agricultural villages. Most of the streams flow east into the Loir; only the Rhône drains north-west into the Huisne at Nogent-le-Rotrou.
The farms which are hidden in the deep lanes were originally built of wattle and daub or within a brick framework. Their owners raise cattle, particularly dairy herds, which have replaced the breeding of the Percheron draught horses, their coats dappled grey, roan or black.
Maize is the modern crop grown for cattle fodder; its tall stems provide excellent cover for the game which used to shelter in the hedges before they were pulled up, to the alarm of the hunting fraternity.

ROUND TRIP STARTING FROM BROU
97km - 60 miles — about 1/2 day

Brou — *See Brou.*

Take D 15 northwest.

Frazé — *See Frazé.*

Thiron — Pop 489. The village has grown up on the south bank of the Thironne, which flows out of the Monks' Pool (Etang des Moines) near the old abbey founded by St Bernard in 1114 and dedicated to the Holy Trinity. Tiron Abbey (it was spelt without an h in those days) was especially thriving in the 12C and 13C. Among the abbots in the 16C were Charles de Ronsard, the poet's brother, and Philippe Desportes, himself a poet. In 1629 the Benedictines of St-Maur moved in. The **abbey church** is still a huge building even though the chancel collapsed in 1817. Near the entrance (left) is the tombstone of John II of Chartres, Abbot of Tiron in the 13C; the old monks' stalls in the nave are 14C; the woodwork and stalls in the present chancel date from 1740. A few buildings from the 17C college still exist.

Rougemont Farm — From the road (D 371³) passing the farm there is an extensive **view** of the Ozanne river valley.

Les Étilleux — Pop 184. South of the village near a small farm on the D 13 take the path (signpost) which climbs to the top of a mound (270m - 886ft; from the foot of the television aerial) there are beautiful **views** of the Ozanne Valley, the hills of Perche and the Huisne Valley.

St-Ulphace — Pop 185. Halfway up the slope stands the **church** (15C-16C); its powerful façade is flanked by a tower; Renaissance doorway.

Courgenard — Pop 412. The **church** door is carved with low-relief statues in the Renaissance style. The right wall of the nave is decorated with 16C murals depicting Hell and the Legend of the Three Living and the Three Dead; there is also a Baroque altarpiece.

Courtangis Château — Among the tall trees (beech, oak and ash) in an idyllically isolated valley are the turrets, dormers and French roofs of a graceful early-16C manor house.

Bouër — Pop 185. Bouër is a tiny little village hidden in the hills overlooking the Huisne Valley. The slate spire of the **church** is joined to the belltower by scrolls. There are two attractive wooden altars in front of the chancel.
From the terrace a fine view of the Huisne Valley.

Semur-en-Vallon — Pop 429. An attractive village by a man-made lake. In the valley on the western edge of Vibraye Forest stands a 15C moated and turreted **castle;** the entrance front, which is flanked by round towers with lanterns, was altered in the 17C; steep French roofs. A Decauville **train** ⊙ for tourists runs on a 1.5km - 1 mile long circuit.

Montmirail — Pop 447. The little town of Montmirail, once strongly fortified, was built on a site with excellent natural defences.
The **castle** ⊙, constructed in the 15C on top of a medieval mound, was altered in the 18C by the Princesse de Conti; it still has underground works dating from the 11C and 14C. On 9 January 1169, it was the scene of a memorable encounter between the kings of both England and France in the course of which the exiled Archbishop of Canterbury, **Thomas Becket,** reaffirmed the primacy of the Church. The apartments of the Princesse de Conti including the Louis XV Grand Salon are open to the public, as are the dungeons and armouries.

The classical west façade, contrasting with the medieval south and east fronts, can be viewed from the terrace, which also gives a vast **panorama**★ over the countryside of Le Perche-Gouët.

The **church** (12C-16C) has a 16C stained glass window in the chancel and an early-17C painted sepulchre in the left aisle. Opposite is a carved stone which, until the Revolution, contained a reliquary.

A picturesque road (D 927) runs through Montmirail Forest.

La Bazoche-Gouet − Pop 1 279. The **church**, 12C or 13C, was altered early in the 16C by the addition of Flamboyant windows in the side aisles: the one on the south side is remarkable; fine doorway with niches resting on spiral columns. Inside, a square tower supports the 16C belltower. The Renaissance windows in the chancel were the gift of the Bourbons-Conti, who owned the estate; the detail and realistic expressions are remarkable; the subject is the Passion copied from German engravings.

PITHIVIERS Pop 9 325

Michelin map 🔟 fold 20 or 🔟 fold 41
Town plan in the current Michelin Red Guide France

Pithiviers is situated on the border between the Beauce and the Gâtinais. Its main activities are related to the local products − cereals and sugar beet (sugar refinery at Pithiviers-le-Vieil) − but other industries are being introduced.

The rectangle containing the old town is enclosed on four sides by a shady Mall; it is pleasant to wander in the quiet old streets which radiate from Place du Martroi, an irregular triangle of open space in the shadow of the great tower of St Salomon's church.

Transport Museum ⊘ − The railway museum was founded by amateurs in the old terminus of a line which until 1951 used to deliver sugar beet to the refineries and carry passengers between Pithiviers and Toury 32km - 20 miles to the west; the track is 0.60m - approximately 2ft wide, the same gauge as the prefabricated light railway developed by Decauville.

The museum contains several locomotives, some in working order, and various items of narrow gauge rolling stock from a minute 2-axle machine built in 1870 (3 tonnes unloaded weight) to a powerful locomotive (1895) from the regional railway which was 1m - over 3ft gauge. There are many reproductions on display as well as items of equipment and uniform, old tickets, lamps, and other railwayana.

Municipal Museum ⊘ − Local souvenirs are attractively displayed on the first floor; the first room on the South Sea Islands adds a touch of the exotic. Another room is devoted to famous local people, to the more or less legendary origins of the culinary specialities of Pithiviers and to saffron, the strongly-coloured aromatic derived from the crocus; the west Gâtinais was the first place in Europe to cultivate saffron.

It is discourteous to visit a church during a service.

★ Le PLESSIS-BOURRÉ CHÂTEAU

Michelin map 🔟 fold 20 or 🔟 fold 19 (20km - 12 miles north of Angers)

Le Plessis-Bourré ⊘ stands far away at the end of a vista of meadowland, a white building beneath blue-grey slate roofs, bringing to the mind's eye the seigneurial life of the 15C.

Le Plessis-Bourré Château

Born in Château-Gontier **Jean Bourré** (1424-1506) first entered royal service under the Dauphin Louis, the son of Charles VII, whom he served faithfully. When Louis XI assumed the crown in 1461, Bourré was given the important post of Financial Secretary and Treasurer of France. In addition to building several châteaux – Jarzé *(qv)* and Vaux *(qv)* among others – he bought the estate of Plessis-le-Vent and in 1468 ordered work to begin on the new château. The design was inspired by the château at Langeais which he had supervised during its construction, and has a magnificent unity of style.

Among the many illustrious guests that Bourré welcomed to his new residence were Pierre de Rohan *(qv)*, Louis XI and Charles VIII.

Le Plessis, isolated by a wide moat spanned by a many-arched bridge 43m - 47yd long looks, from outside, like a fortress protected by a gatehouse with a double drawbridge and four flanking towers. The largest of these is battlemented and served as a keep. A platform 3m - 10ft wide at the base of the wall provided for artillery crossfire.

The chapel's slender spire rises above the roof to the left of the gatehouse.

Beyond the entrance archway, Le Plessis is transformed into a country mansion with a spacious courtyard, low wings, an arcaded gallery, turret staircases and the high dormer windows of the seigneurial wing.

On the ground floor the visitor will see the St-Anne Chapel and the Hall of Justice before visiting the richly furnished and decorated state apartments, which have a charming view of the gentle countryside.

The first floor has among other rooms a great vaulted chamber with a fireplace. The guardroom has a coffered wooden **ceiling**★★★ painted at the end of the 15C with such allegorical figures as Fortune, Truth, Chastity (a unicorn) and Lust, the Musician Ass, etc. Humorous and moral scenes depict the unskilled barber at work on a patient, the overweening man trying to wring the neck of an eel, a woman sewing up a chicken's crop, etc. There is a large collection of fans in the library. The cellars and attics are also open to visitors ⊘. The palm tree ceiling of the tower staircase rests on carvings inspired by alchemy more truculent than the paintings on the first floor. The attic under the beautiful chestnut keel roof gives access to the sentry walk.

The castle grounds have recently been laid out as a park and make for a pleasant walk.

EXCURSION

La Hamonnière Manor ⊘ – *9km - 5 1/2 miles north via Écueillé.*
The architecture of the manor house, which was built between 1420 and 1575, shows the evolution of the Renaissance style. The buildings round the courtyard consist of a plain residential block (right) with a stair turret, a Henri III section (left) with a window bay framed by pilasters and capitals following the classical progression of the orders, and at a right angle a low wing with two twisted columns supporting the dormer. To the rear stands the keep, probably the last addition made in the 16C; it has a stair turret running from top to bottom and round arched windows.

Le PLESSIS-MACÉ CHÂTEAU

Michelin **58** fold 20 or **232** fold 19 (13km - 8miles northwest of Angers)

Hidden amidst greenery this château is surrounded by a wide moat. Started in the 11C by a certain Macé, the **château** ⊘ became the property in the mid-15C of Louis de Beaumont, the Chamberlain and favourite of Louis XI, who transformed it into a residence fit to accommodate his royal master. The year 1510 saw the beginning of a 168-year-old ownership by the Du Bellay family.

From the exterior Le Plessis still has the appearance of a fortress with its tower-studded wall and rectangular keep, dismantled but still battlemented and surrounded by a moat.

Once inside the great courtyard, the country residence becomes apparent: the decorative elements in white tufa stone enhance the grey of the schists, while windows let in the light.

To the right are the outbuildings housing the stables and guardroom. To the left are the chapel, an unusual staircase turret, and the main dwelling surmounted by pointed gables. In the angle of the main dwelling

Le Plessis-Macé — A balcony

is a charming **balcony** where the ladies watched the jousting tournaments and other entertainments.

The balcony opposite, in the outbuildings, was reserved for the servants.

The tour includes the dining room, the large banqueting hall, several bedrooms, one of which was the king's, and the **chapel**, which has kept its rare Gothic panelling of the 15C and forms two floors of galleries, the first reserved for the lord and his squires, the second for the servants.

PONCÉ-SUR-LE-LOIR Pop 436

Michelin map **64** fold 5 or **232** fold 23 – Local map under LOIR VALLEY: Vendôme-La Flèche

Beside the road (D 197) leading into Poncé from the east stands a Renaissance château. On the west side of the town, south of the main road and the railway line, is the **Craft Centre** ⊙ "Les Grès du Loir". It is housed in the 18C buildings of the old Pallard paper mill on the river bank and consists of the studios of several independent craftsmen: pottery, glassware, ironwork, weaving, woodwork and candle making.

Château ⊙ – It originally consisted of two pavilions flanking the central staircase tower, one of which was destroyed in the 18C and replaced by a characterless wing. Ionic pilasters flanking the windows and pronounced horizontal cornices give a balanced but geometrically severe aspect to the façade. The north front, formerly the entrance front, has an elegant Italian-style arcade which forms a terrace at first-floor level.

The stone **Renaissance staircase★★** is one of the most remarkable in France; in front of it are the remains of a former loggia. The coffered ceilings of the six flights are sumptuously sculptured, with a delicacy, fantasy and art of perspective rarely attained. Over 130 motifs portray realistic, allegorical and mythological subjects.

One can also stroll in the well-kept **gardens,** with their highly effective symmetrical layout: on the edge of the square lawn, the tree-lined walk makes a long vaulted path on one side, and on the other is a labyrinth conducive to tranquillity and meditation; overlooking the entire scene runs a terrace with a mall of lime trees.

The dovecot remains with its 1 800 holes and revolving ladders for gathering the eggs.

The outbuildings house a **museum of Sarthe folklore.**

PONTLEVOY Pop 1 423

Michelin map **64** fold 17 or **238** folds 14, 15

A small town situated in the agricultural region to the north of Montrichard, Pontlevoy is fortunate in having retained a number of charming old houses with stone dressings.

★ABBEY *time: 1 1/4 hrs*

The **former abbey** ⊙ is mainly interesting for its noble 18C buildings (including two wings of the cloisters) and a 15C Gothic church. The foundation dates from 1034, when, according to a legend, Gelduin de Chaumont, vassal of the Count of Blois, established a Benedictine community here as a token of gratitude to the Virgin for surviving a shipwreck. In the 17C, when a reform of monastic life became essential, the abbey was entrusted to the Benedictines of Saint-Maur and the Abbot Pierre de Bérule, who opened an educational establishment in 1644 which made Pontlevoy famous until the 19C. Proclaimed the École Royale Militaire in 1776, the college added to its secular teaching the military training of scholars chosen by the king from among the gentry.

The abbey now houses two centres for transport studies.

Abbey Church – The church, which was rebuilt in the 2nd half of the 15C after being damaged during the Hundred Years War, now consists of only the chancel of the imposing edifice which was planned but never completed. It comprises two bays flanked by aisles where fragments of 15C wall-paintings have been exposed.

In 1651 two large stone retables with marble columns were added to the high altar and to the axial chapel where Gelduin de Chaumont and his immediate descendants are buried.

Conventual buildings – Among these, the 18C refectory decorated with a monumental stove of Delftware, one of four which the Maréchal de Saxe had commissioned for Chambord *(qv),* the remarkable staircase leading to the upper floor, and the majestic façade giving on to the gardens, with emblasoned pediments at regular intervals.

Road Transport Museum ⊙ – Some 20 vehicles built between the very beginnings of motorized road transport and the 1950s are displayed under the fine timber roof of the old riding school.

Municipal Museum ⊙ – Housed in the west wing of the conventual buildings, the museum is devoted to key themes of the early 20C in which local people played an important part.

Firstly, advertising, one of the pioneers of which was **Auguste Poulain,** born in Pontlevoy in 1825 and founder of the famous chocolate factory at Blois. There are old posters (among them ones signed by Cappiello and Firmin Bouisset), chromolithographs and other publicity items.

Then there are some hundred photographs from the collection of 10 000 plates taken by Louis Clergeau, a watchmaker with a passion for photography, and by his daughter Marcelle; they constitute a marvellous record of life in Pontlevoy between 1902 and 1960.

Finally, the heroic beginnings of aviation (1910-14), are evoked by models of the aerodrome and of four training aircraft as well as by photos from the Clergeau collection.

★ La POSSONNIÈRE MANOR

Michelin map **64** fold 5 or **232** west of fold 24 (1km - 1/2 mile south of Couture-sur-Loir) — Local map under LOIR VALLEY: Vendôme-La Flèche

When Louis de Ronsard, soldier and man of letters, returned from Italy in the early 16C he undertook to rebuild his country seat in the new Italian style; he created La Possonnière and the profusion of mottoes engraved on the walls.

The Prince of Poets — In 1524 **Pierre de Ronsard,** Louis' son, was born at the manor. He was destined for a brilliant future in the army or the diplomatic service and at 12 became a page at the court of François I. An illness, however, left him half deaf at 15 and he had to relinquish his ambitions. He took holy orders and turned to poetry and the study of the ancient authors; Pindar in Greek and Horace in Latin became his models. He excelled in composing sonnets in which he described the beauty of Cassandra Salviati *(see Talcy)* and Marie *(see Bourgueil)*. He was the leader of the Pléiade group of poets *(p 30)* and in 1558 was appointed Poet Laureate but, afflicted with gout, he withdrew to his priories at Ste-Madeleine de Croixval *(6km - 4 miles southeast of la Possonnière)* and at St-Cosme-lès-Tours *(see Tours: St-Julien District)* where he died in 1585 leaving a considerable body of work.

★**Manor** ⊘ — The manor house is built against the hillside on the northern fringes of the Gâtines Forest and enclosed with a wall. The name comes from the word *posson* (*poinçon,* a measure of volume) and has sometimes been altered to Poissonnière under the influence of the family coat of arms.

The main façade has mullioned windows in the style of Louis XII on the ground floor but the windows on the first floor are flanked by pilasters with medallions, clearly in the Renaissance style.

Projecting from the rear façade is a graceful stair turret; the elegant doorway is capped by a pediment adorned with a bust. The pediment dormer at the top of the turret bears the arms of the Ronsard family, three silver fishes on a blue ground.

POUANCÉ
Pop 3 279

Michelin map **63** fold 8 or **232** fold 17

Pouancé in its protective ring of lakes is on the border between Anjou and Brittany. In the Middle Ages it played an important economic role owing to its iron foundries which were supplied with ore from the Segré basin. The surrounding woods provided shelter for the Chouans during the Revolution. The main road through the town (N 171) passes at the foot of the ruined **castle** ⊘ (13C-15C). The towers and curtain wall of dark schist are impressive and reinforced by a firing caponier linked to the keep by a postern.

EXCURSIONS

Pierre Frite Menhir — *5km - 3 miles south by D 878, bearing left into D 6 in La Previère and then a track to the right (signpost).* In woodland surroundings, the menhir is 6m - 20ft high.

La Motte-Glain Château ⊘ — *17km - 10 1/2 miles south.*
The red stone château with its strong lines was built late in the 15C by **Pierre de Rohan** *(qv),* Counsellor to Louis XI and then one of the commanding officers of the armies of Charles VIII and Louis XII in Italy.

A reminder of the château's location on the pilgrimage route from Mont-St-Michel to Compostela is given by the scallops and pilgrims' staffs decorating the courtyard façade. The gatehouse is flanked by two round towers.

In the chapel is a fresco from the early 16C representing the Crucifixion. 15C and 16C furniture and Renaissance fireplaces embellish the interior of the château, together with hunting trophies, most of them of African origin.

Le PUY-NOTRE-DAME
Pop 1 322

Michelin map **64** fold 12 or **232** fold 32 (7km - 4 miles west of Montreuil-Bellay)

★**Church** — The church is a remarkable example of Angevin architecture and was built in the 13C. The tower with its stone spire above the south transept is decorated with mouldings forming a recess containing a very beautiful statue of the Virgin (16C). On the north side of the church, enclosed in a cylindrical building, is the well. In the Middle Ages people came from all over France to venerate the Virgin's Girdle, a relic brought from Jerusalem in the 12C, which is kept in the church. The tall, slim nave and aisles lend majesty to the interior; the vaulting in the chancel is rich with lierne and tierceron ribs. The carved stalls beyond the high altar are 16C.

Every year
*the **Michelin Red Guide France***
revises its selection of starred restaurants
which also mentions culinary specialities and local wines.
It also includes a selection of simpler restaurants
offering carefully prepared dishes which are often regional specialities
at a reasonable price.

It is well worth buying the current edition.

★ RICHELIEU Pop 2 223

Michelin map **67** southeast of fold 10 or **232** fold 46

Lying on the southern limits of Touraine, bordering on Poitou, Richelieu is a quiet town which comes to life on market days.

La Fontaine called the place "the finest village in the universe". It is a rare example of classical town planning, the project of one man, the statesman and churchman **Cardinal de Richelieu,** who was eager to lodge his court near his château which was then under construction. The building of the town itself started in 1631 at a time when Versailles was still only an idea.

HISTORICAL NOTES

Cardinal de Richelieu – In 1621 when Armand du Plessis (1585-1642) bought the property of Richelieu it consisted of a village and manor on the banks of the Mable. Ten years later the estate was raised to the status of a duchy. On becoming Cardinal and First Minister of France Richelieu commissioned Jacques Le Mercier, the architect of the Sorbonne and Cardinal's Palace, now Palais-Royal, in Paris, to prepare plans for a château and a walled town. Built under the supervision of the architect's brother, Pierre Le Mercier, the project was considered at the time to be a marvel of urban planning which Louis XIV was to visit at the age of twelve.

Determined not to have his creation outstripped in grandeur, Richelieu created a small principality around his masterpiece and jealously razed entirely or partially many other châteaux in the vicinity. He already owned Bois-le-Vicomte and was to add to his estates Champigny-sur-Veude, L'Ile-Bouchard, Cravant, Crissay, Mirebeau, Faye-la-Vineuse and even the royal residence of Chinon, which he was to allow to fall into disrepair. The great fortress of Loudon also suffered destruction but only after its owner, Urbain Grandier, an arch enemy of the Cardinal, had perished at the stake.

Past splendour – One may call it retribution or the hazard of fate but little has survived of the Cardinal's magnificent residence.

An enormous park originally surrounded a marvellous palace filled with great works of art. Two vast courtyards surrounded by outbuildings preceded the château proper, which was protected by moats, bastions and watchtowers. The entrance porch was adorned with a statue of Louis XIII and surmounted by an allegorical figure of Fame, both the works of Guillaume Berthelot. The pavilion at the far end of the château's main courtyard was originally graced by obelisks, rostral columns (in the form of ships' prows) and Michelangelo's famous group, The Slaves, once intended for the tomb of Pope Julius II.

The apartments, gallery and chapel were hung with works by Poussin, Claude Lorrain, Champaigne, Mantegna, Perugino, Bassano, Caravaggio, Titian, Giulio Romano, Dürer, Rubens and Van Dyck.

The gardens were dotted with copies of antique statues and artificial grottoes which concealed the then-popular water farces. It was in these gardens that the first poplar trees from Italy were planted.

The dispersal of the riches gathered here began in 1727 when the then Marshal de Richelieu, the Cardinal's great-nephew, transported some back to his Parisian town house and sold others. Confiscated in 1792 the château was visited by Tallien, a collector of silverware, and then Dufourni and Visconti who took all that was suitable for the Museum of French Monuments. After the Revolution the descendants of Richelieu ceded the château to a certain Boutron who demolished it for the sale of the building materials.

The works of art were dispersed: the Louvre has *The Slaves* by Michelangelo, Perugino's paintings and a marble table encrusted with precious stones; the series of twelve paintings depicting the victories of Louis XIII are in Versailles; the local museums in Tours and Azay-le-Ferron have several paintings and sculptures; the Fine Arts Museum in Poitiers has Berthelot's statue of Louis XIII. The Orléans Fine Arts Museum has the work of Fréminet and Deruet in its Richelieu Gallery. The obelisks are now at Malmaison and the rostral columns in the Maritime Museum, Paris.

RICHELIEU

Cardinal (Pl. du) 2
Collège (R. du) 3
Marché (Pl. du) 5
Religieuses (Pl. des) . . 6

SIGHTS

★**The town** – The walled town which Richelieu planned at the gates of his château was in itself a fine example of the Louis XIII-style designed by Jacques Le Mercier.

The town embodies the sense of order, balance, regularity and symmetry which characterised the 17C in France. The rectangular plan (700 m - 766 yds long by 500m - 547yds wide) was surrounded by ramparts and a moat. The impressive entrance gates are flanked by rusticated and pedimented gatehouses surmounted by high French roofs.

171

Grande-Rue – The main street traverses Richelieu from north to south. In addition to the gateways note the Louis XIII-style *hôtels* with the decorative elements in white tufa stone, especially no 17, Hôtel du Sénéchal, which has retained its elegant courtyard with busts of Roman emperors.

There are two squares, one at each end of the main street.

Place du Marché (5) – In the southern square, opposite the church, stands the 17C **covered market,** its slate roof supported by a fine chestnut timber frame.

A **museum** ⊘ in the Town Hall (**H**), which was originally built as the Law Courts, contains documents and works of art pertaining to both the Richelieu family and the château.

The **Church of the Virgin** (Notre-Dame), which is built of white stone in the classical, so-called "Jesuit" style, has a certain harmony and nobility. The niches in the façade contain statues of the Evangelists; the chancel is flanked by two towers capped by obelisks, a rare arrangement. The interior exhibits the same architectural features: elegant 18C high altar.

Park ⊘ – A magnificent statue of Richelieu by Ramey stands at the southern end of the main street. It precedes the park (475ha - 1 174 acres), which is criss-crossed by straight avenues of chestnut and plane trees.

Of the many splendid buildings there still exists a domed pavilion, once part of the outbuildings, which houses a small **museum** ⊘ containing models of the château and historical documents on Richelieu. The canals also remain as do two pavilions, the orangery and wine cellar, at the far end of the formal gardens *(southeast).*

The former château entrance is on the D 749 *(southwest).*

EXCURSIONS

Steam Railway ⊘ – Steam trains run on the 20km - 13 miles of track from Richelieu to Chinon via Champigny-sur-Veude and Ligré. The **museum** in Richelieu Station recaptures some of the aura of the days of steam with its collection of locomotives, carriages and other items.

Faye-la-Vineuse – Pop 409. *7km - 4 miles south by D 749. See Faye-la-Vineuse.*

Bois-Aubry Abbey ⊘ *16km - 10 miles east by D 757.* The 12C Benedictine abbey in the middle of the countryside is heralded by its stone spire which may be seen standing on the horizon. The best-preserved feature of the ruins is the square 15C bell-tower. The vaulting in the 13C nave has a keystone decorated with a carved coat of arms. There are twelve finely carved capitals in the early-12C chapter house.

★ Le RIVAU CASTLE

Map 🖲 fold 10 or 🖾 fold 34 (11km - 7 miles north of Richelieu) – Local map under the VIENNE VALLEY near Chinon

The 13C **castle** ⊘ was fortified in the 15C by Pierre de Beauvau, Charles VII's chamberlain. Joan of Arc found horses for her soldiers here on her way to the siege of Orléans. Rivau is mentioned by Rabelais; Gargantua gave the castle to one of this knights after the Picrocholean War. The drawbridge in the keep leads into the main courtyard.

The **interior** is paved with white tufa; the elegant rooms contain Gothic and Renaissance furniture: there is a fine 15C Gothic credence table bearing the royal arms in the guard room (huge fireplace) and the bedroom next to the oratory contains a tester bed with Renaissance columns. Exhibition of contemporary paintings by Pierre-Laurent Brenot.

Use Michelin Maps with Michelin Guides.

La ROCHE-RACAN CHÂTEAU

Michelin map 🖾 fold 4 or 🖾 fold 23 (2km - 1 mile southeast of St-Paterne-Racan)

The Château de la Roche-Racan stands perched on a rock *(roche)* overlooking the Escotais Valley which together with the nearby Loir, were a constant source of inspiration to the first owner and poet, **Racan** (1589-1670).

Born at Champmarin near Aubigné, Honorat de Bueil, Marquis de Racan (1589-1670), was a member of the well-known local family, the Bueils *(qv).* Little inclined to the life of a soldier and unlucky in love, Racan retired to his country seat for the last forty years of his life, a period described in his work, *Stances à la retraite.*

There he strolled by his fountains or hunted hare or deer or visited Denis de la Grelière, the Abbé of la Clarté-Dieu, who invited him to put the Psalms into verse. He brought up his children, pursued his lawsuits, grew beans and rebuilt his château.

Château ⊘ – In 1634 Racan commissioned a local master mason, Jacques Gabriel, a member of a long-established family of architects, to build this château. The main building was originally flanked by two pavilions only one of which remains standing today, pedimented and adorned with a corner turret and caryatids. Long balustered terraces, above mask-decorated arcades, overlook the park and Escotais Valley.

Michelin map 🔢 fold 18 or 🔢 fold 16 – Facilities

The point where the River Sauldre divides into several arms is the site of the former capital of the Sologne. Always an important market town, Romorantin-Lanthenay has gained a new impetus from modern industries such as electronics, refrigeration plants and cameras and other activities such as flour-milling and sheet-iron and steel-plate rolling. In 1968 a Matra factory was opened on the east side of the town for the mass production of saloon cars.

Royal associations – In the 15C Romorantin was the fief of the Valois-Angoulême branch of the French royal family and it was here that François d'Angoulême, later **François I**, spent his turbulent childhood and where his wife-to-be Claude of France, the daughter of Louis XII, was born in 1499. The king loved Romorantin and in 1517 he commissioned Leonardo da Vinci, then at Amboise *(qv)*, to draw up plans for a palace destined for his mother Louise de Savoie. Leonardo envisaged a palace astride the Sauldre, to be built with prefabricated units, but the death of Louise put an end to the project. Da Vinci also studied the possibility of creating a canal to link Romorantin to the Loire.

In France, the Feast of the Epiphany *(la Fête des Rois)* is celebrated by eating a cake *(la Galette des Rois)* which contains a bean. The finder of this bean is the bean king of Twelfth Night. On 6 January, Epiphany, 1521, François I led a mock attack on the Hôtel St-Pol, where a bean king reigned. The occupants of the house were defending themselves when some ill-advised person threw out a glowing log which landed on the royal cranium. To dress the wound the doctors shaved his head; the King then grew a beard. His courtiers followed suit.

SIGHTS

★**Old Houses (B)** – On the corner of Rue de la Résistance and Rue du Milieu stands **La Chancellerie**, a corbelled Renaissance house, of brick and half-timber construction, where the royal seals were kept when the King stayed in the town. The corner post portrays a coat of arms and a musician playing the bagpipes. Opposite stands **Hôtel St-Pol**, built of stone and glazed bricks with window mouldings.

Standing at the junction of Rue du Milieu and Rue de la Pierre is the charming **Maison du Carroir d'Orée** ⊘ (archaeological museum) with its remarkable carved corner posts showing the Annunciation *(left)* and St George killing the Dragon *(right)*.

★**Sologne Museum (H)** ⊘ – The museum introduces the visitor to this formerly insalubrious region. The well-presented exhibits illustrate local ethnography and traditional practices – land, housing, crafts and costume. There is a remarkable reconstruction of the living room of a country cottage as well as a clog maker's workshop.

★**View from the bridges** – From the north branch of the river there is a **view** of the Chapter Mill (**Moulin du Chapitre** – **D**) opposite the old Royal Château (**Château royal** – **P**) which dates from the 15C and 16C and now houses the sub-Prefecture. The narrow southern branch presents a row of attractive half-timbered houses (**V**).

Public Garden (Square Ferdinand-Buisson) – This is a pleasant park with tall trees and footbridges over the river; there are views of the banks and the fulling mill (**E**).

St Stephen's Church (St Etienne) – Over the transept crossing rises a Romanesque tower with delicate sculptures. Beyond the nave with its Angevin vaulting is the sombre chancel which is also roofed with Angevin vaulting springing from powerful Romanesque pillars; each rib of the apsidal vault supports the statue of an evangelist.

St Roch Chapel – At the entrance to the St-Roch district. The graceful building is flanked by turrets with round-arched windows typical of the Renaissance.

Motor Racing Museum (M) ⊘ – Exhibition of Matra racing cars, including the Formula 1 car which was world champion in 1969, and a series of displays tracing the technical developments in car construction.

The museum also has a specialist library.

ROMORANTIN-LANTHENAY

Clemenceau (R. Georges) 6
Trois-Rois (R. des) 34
Verdun (R. de) 35

Brault (R. Porte) 2
Capucins (R. des) 4
Four-à-Chaux (R. du) 8
Gaulle (Pl. Gén. de) 10
Ile-Marin (Quai de l') 13
Jouanettes (R. des) 14
Lattre-de-Tassigny (Av. du Mar. de) 15
Limousins (R. des) 17
Mail de l'Hôtel-Dieu 18
Milieu (R. du) 20
Orléans (Fg d') 22
Paix (Pl. de la) 23
Pierre (R. de la) 24
Prés-Wilson (R. du) 26
Résistance (R. de la) 28
St-Roch (Fg) 30
Salengro (Av. R.) 32
Sirène (R. de la) 33

SABLÉ-SUR-SARTHE

Pop 12 178

Michelin map **64** fold 1 or **232** fold 21 – Local map under the SARTHE VALLEY – Facilities

Situated at a point where two tributaries, the Vaige and the Erve, flow into the Sarthe, Sablé is dominated by the austere façade of its château, which once belonged to the Colbert family and now houses the National Library's restoration and book-binding workshops.

In the 17C the fief belonged to Laval-Bois-Dauphin, Marquis de Sablé. In 1711 Colbert de Torcy, the nephew of the great Jean-Baptiste Colbert, Louis XIV's Minister, rebuilt the château and radically changed the aspect of the town; many houses and the hospital date from this period. Since 1990 development on Place Raphaël-Elizé has highlighted a fine group of 19C buildings in Rue Carnot.

The small port on the canalized part of the Sarthe used to receive sand-laden barges from the Loire. Today it harbours about twenty craft for hire and there is also a **river boat** ⊙, for cruises along the Sarthe.

The town, which is famous for its shortbread biscuits, is the second largest economic centre in the Sarthe region. A favourable environment and pronounced dynamism have helped develop the foodstuff industry and diversity the local economy.

EXCURSIONS

Solesmes – *3km - 2 miles northeast. See Solesmes.*

★**Asnières-sur-Vègre** – *10km - 6 miles northeast. See Asnières-sur-Vègre.*

Auvers-le-Hamon – *Pop 1 197. 8.5km - 5 miles north.*
The **church's** nave is ornamented with 15C-16C **mural paintings** depicting a series of local saints: to the right St Hamès holding his intestines, St Martin on horseback, St Cénéré as a Cardinal, St Eutropius, St Andrew on his cross, St Luke riding a bull, the Nativity and the Flight into Egypt. To the left a Dance of Death, St Avertin, St Apollonia whose teeth were pulled out by her torturers, St James and the Sacrifice of Isaac.

La Chapelle-du-Chêne – *6km - 4 miles southeast. In Les Noës turn left.*
The basilica acts as a centre for religious activities as well as being the object of pilgrimages to Notre-Dame-du-Chêne (Our Lady of the Oak), represented by a 15C terracotta statue. In the park there is a small scale model of the Holy Sepulchre and the Stations of the Cross.

St-Denis d'Anjou – *Pop 1 278. 10.5km - 6 1/2 miles southwest.*
The village, which is covered with flowers in season, has a 12C **fortified church** with keel vaulting and 12C and 15C **frescoes** which were discovered in 1947 and have been gradually restored: St Christopher (west wall); the martyrdom of John the Baptist, the legends of St Nicholas, St Giles and St Hubert on two levels. Opposite the church, which belonged to the Chapter of Angers, stands the 15C canons' house, which is now the Town Hall, and the 16C market, which has a very steep slate roof under which wine was bought and sold.

Varennes-Bourreau Chapel – *6km - 4 miles southeast of St-Denis d'Anjou (D 615).*
The chapel nestles in the lush vegetation beside the River Sarthe; it is decorated with beautiful 12C and 15C frescoes: a mandorla surrounds Christ, His hand raised in blessing. The village of Varennes was formely a small port engaged in the transport of wine to Angers before the vines were destroyed by phylloxera.

SACHÉ

Pop 868

Michelin map **64** fold 14 or **232** fold 35 (6.5km - 4 miles east of Azay-le-Rideau)

Saché is well known because **Balzac** *(see p 30)* often went to stay there. A more recent famous resident was the American sculptor, **Alexander Calder** (1898-1976), who created mobiles and stabiles in abstract forms; one of his mobiles is displayed in the main square of Saché which bears his name.

Saché Château ⊙ – The 16C and 18C château is set in a pleasant park. In the last century it belonged to M. de Margonne, a friend of Balzac. The writer loved to escape to Saché from the bustle of Paris and the dunning of his creditors; in the peaceful surroundings of the château he wrote easily and the action of one of his novels, *Le Lys dans la Vallée*, is set in the Indre Valley between Saché and Pont-de-Ruan. The room where Balzac worked remains as it was in his lifetime. Other rooms in the château contain portraits, manuscripts, first editions and souvenirs of the 1850s. There is an audio-visual presentation on the author's life and works.

★ ST-AIGNAN

Pop 3 672

Michelin map **64** fold 17 or **238** fold 15 – Facilities

St-Aignan stands on the south bank of the Cher at the heart of a region of woods and vineyards: Coteaux du Cher is the wine produced in Seigy and Couffy.

There is a picturesque view of the little town on its sloping site from the bridge or from the north bank on D 675 north of Noyers. Both the church and the château are interesting; so too is Rue Constant-Ragot which contains two Gothic houses and provides the best view of the chevet of the church. A stroll in the narrow streets and neighbouring square will reveal some 15C carved stone or half-timbered houses.

★ **St Aignan's Church** ⊘ – The collegiate church is a Romanesque building dating from the 11C and 12C with an impressive tower over the transept. A spacious tower-porch with delicately-carved capitals leads into the high light nave; the capitals are finely carved into acanthus leaves and fantastic animals; the chancel and ambulatory have historiated capitals showing the Flight into Egypt *(north ambulatory)*, the Sacrifice of Isaac and King David *(south side)*.

★★ **Lower Church** – *Entrance in north transept.* Known formerly as St John's or the Church of the Grottoes, it was probably the early Romanesque church which was used as a stable and store during the Revolution. It is similar in plan to the chancel and decorated with **frescoes** (from the 12C to 15C): St John the Evangelist (15C) in the central chapel of the ambulatory; the legend of St Giles in the south chapel. A great Christ in Majesty in a double mandorla (1200) fills the half dome of the chancel and spreads his blessing through the mediation of St Peter and St James to the sick who are prostrate; the vault over the transept crossing shows the figure of Christ in Judgement resting on a rainbow.

Château ⊘ – A great flight of steps starting from the church porch leads up to the château courtyard; pleasant view of the roofs of the town, one or two of slate amongst the tiles. The château consists of two buildings at right angles, mostly built in the 16C and backing on to the remains of the medieval fortifications on the east side of the courtyard. The elegant Renaissance dwelling has pilasters flanking the windows, carved dormer gables and a handsome stair in an octagonal turret terminating in a lantern. The terrace overlooks the turbulent Cher passing under the bridge.

Provost's House (Maison de la Prévôté) (B) ⊘ – *On leaving the church cross the main street, Rue Constant-Ragot.* The 15C building is used for temporary exhibitions.

EXCURSIONS

St Lazarus' Chapel (Chapelle St-Lazare) – *2km - 1 mile northeast on the road to Cheverny.* On the north side of the road stands a chapel with a gable belfry which was once part of a leper house.

Beauval Zoological Park (Zoo Parc) ⊘ – *4km - 2 1/2 miles south.* There is a fine view of vineyards as the road descends to Beauval Park. Its 8ha – 20 acres of undulating woodland provide a haven for animals, birds and flowers. By turn an old-style rose garden, African savannah and Amazonian forest, the park is home to an exceptional collection of exotic birds including parrots (cockatoos), hornbills, touracos and toucans. There are also many species of apes and monkeys such as chimpanzees and marmosets and several varieties of wild animals including two extremely rare white tigers with blue eyes.

Chémery Château ⊘ – *13km - 8 miles northeast by D 675 bearing right in St-Romain-sur-Cher into D 63.* The château (15C and 16C) is a mixture of medieval and Renaissance architecture. It was raised on the site of a 12C fortress. In the grounds is a dovecot with spaces for 1 200 birds.

★★ ST-BENOÎT-SUR-LOIRE   Pop 1 880

Michelin map 64 fold 10 or 238 fold 6 (10km - 6 miles southeast of Châteauneuf)

The basilica of St Benedict on Loire (St-Benoît-sur-Loire) is one of the most famous Romanesque buildings in France.

Foundation (7C) – According to Celtic tradition St-Benoît-sur-Loire was the place where the local Carnute druids assembled *(qv)*.
In 645 or 651 a group of Benedictine monks led by an abbot from Orléans came to this spot and founded a monastery which very soon gained the favour of the great as is shown by the gift of a shrine by Mumma. In about 672 the Abbot of **Fleury,** as the monastery was called, learned that the body of St Benedict, the father of western monasticism who died in 547, was buried beneath the ruins of the Abbey of Monte Cassino in Italy; he gave orders for the precious relic, a source of miracles and cures, to be transported to the banks of the Loire where it attracted great crowds of people and brought increasing success to the monastery.

Theodulf, Odo, Abbo and Gauzlin – Charlemagne gave Fleury to his adviser and friend, **Theodulf** *(qv)*, the brilliant bishop of Orléans, who founded two famous monastic schools, an external one for secular priests and an internal one for postulant monks. The scriptorium produced some beautiful work.
The death of Theodulf and the Viking invasions upset the courses of study and the smooth running of the monastery; discipline suffered.

In the 10C a spectacular change took place. In 930 **Odo,** a monk from the Touraine, became Abbot of Cluny; he imposed the Cluniac rule at Fleury and reopened the abbey school. St Benedict's regained its prosperity: students flocked to the school, particularly from England, and the French king and princes offered gifts and patronage. The Archbishop of Canterbury, Odo, received the Benedictine habit from Fleury.

The late 10C was dominated by **Abbo,** a famous scholar and teacher, who enjoyed the favour of the Capets. He entered Fleury as a child, studied in Paris and Rheims where he was under the celebrated Gerbert, who had himself been at Fleury, and then returned c975 to Fleury as head of studies. He added to the already extensive library and extended the area of study; in his reign as Abbot (from 988) the Abbey was at the forefront of western intellectual life with a particularly strong influence in England and the west of France. He was also a very able organizer of the monastic life of the Abbey.

Abbo was very influential with Robert II and commissioned a monk called Aimoin to write a **History of the Franks,** which became the official chronicle expounding the "ideology" of the Capet monarchy. Abbo was assassinated in 1004 in a revolt.

The reign of Abbot **Gauzlin,** the future Archbishop of Bourges, early in the 11C is marked by the production of the so-called Gaignières **Evangelistary,** an illuminated manuscript − gold and silver lettering on purple parchment − which is the work of a Lombard painter, and by the construction of the handsome porch belfry.

The present church (crypt, chancel, transept) was built between 1067 and 1108; the nave was not completed until the end of the 12C.

Middle Ages to the present − In the 15C St-Benoît passed *in commendam:* this meant that the revenues of the abbey were granted by the monarch to "commendatory abbots", often laymen, who were simply beneficiaries and took no active part in the religious life of the community.

The monks did not always make such abbots welcome. Under François I they refused to receive Cardinal Duprat and shut themselves up in the tower of the porch. The King had to come in person, at the head of an armed force, to make them submit.

During the Wars of Religion (1562-98) one of these abbots, Odet de Châtillon-Coligny, the brother of the Protestant leader Admiral Coligny, was himself converted to Protestantism. He had the abbey of St-Benoît looted by Condé's Huguenot troops.

The treasure was melted down − the gold casket containing the relics of the Saint alone weighed 17.5kg - 39lb − the marvellous library was sold and its precious manuscripts, about 2000 in number, were scattered to the four corners of Europe. Some are now to be found in Berne, Rome, Leyden, Oxford and Moscow.

The celebrated Congregation of St-Maur, introduced to St-Benoît in 1627 by Cardinal Richelieu, restored its spiritual and intellectual life. The abbey was closed at the Revolution, its archives transferred to Orléans and its property dispersed. At the beginning of the First Empire the monastic buildings were destroyed *(1)* and the church fell into disrepair. In 1835 it was registered as an historical monument, and it was restored on various occasions between 1836 and 1923. Monastic life was revived there in 1944.

The poet and artist **Max Jacob** (1876-1944) retired to the abbey in St-Benoît-sur-Loire, before he was arrested in 1944.

★★ THE BASILICA ⊘

time: 3/4 hour

This imposing edifice was built between 1067 and 1218. The towers were originally much taller.

★★**Belfry Porch** − The belfry originally stood by itself, and is one of the finest examples of Romanesque art. The richly carved capitals are worthy of the visitor's detailed attention with their abaci and corbels delicately carved in the beautiful golden stone. Stylised plants and, particularly, flowing acanthus leaves alternate with fantastic animals, scenes from the Apocalypse, and events in the life of Christ and the Virgin Mary. On the porch (second column from the left), one of the capitals is signed *Umbertus me fecit.*

St Benoît-sur-Loire
The porch of the Basilica

Nave − It was completed in 1218 in the transitional Romanesque style. It is very luminous with its white stone-work and high vaulting which let in plenty of light. The organ loft was added about 1700.

(1) Only a small façade belonging to the former students' chapel remains. It is in the village opposite the war memorial in Place de l'Université.

Transept – Like the chancel, this was finished in 1108. The dome, built on superimposed squinches, carries the central belltower. Under the dome are the stalls dated 1413, and the remains of a choir screen in carved wood presented in 1635 by Richelieu, when he was Commendatory Abbot of St-Benoît.

In the north transept is the precious 14C alabaster statue of Notre-Dame-de-Fleury. A plaque on the right recalls that the poet Max Jacob, who used to pray before this statue, lies in the village cemetery.

★★ **Chancel** – The very long Romanesque chancel was built between 1065 and 1108; note the decor of blind arcades with sculptured capitals forming a triforium. The ambulatory with radiating chapels is typical of a church built for crowds and processions; this plan can be found in most Benedictine churches.

The floor is paved with a Roman mosaic which was transported from Italy in 1531 by Cardinal Duprat; it is similar to the style popular in the eastern part of the Roman Empire. The recumbent figure is that of Philippe I, the fourth Capet King, who died in 1108.

★ **Crypt** – An impressive masterpiece of the second half of the 11C, it has kept its original appearance. Large round columns form a double ambulatory with radiating chapels round the large central pillar containing the modern shrine of St Benedict, whose relics have been venerated here since the 8C.

ST-CALAIS   Pop 4063

Michelin map **64** fold 5 or **238** fold 1

St-Calais, on the border between Maine and the Vendôme region, is a market town dominated by the ruins of a medieval château. A few old gables still look down on the narrow streets.

Five bridges span the River Anille. The district on the west bank grew up round the Benedictine abbey which was founded in the reign of Childebert (6C) by Calais, a coenobite monk from Auvergne. The monastery was destroyed during the Revolution but the few 17C buildings which survived are now occupied by the library, the theatre and the museum.

Apple Turnover Festival (Fête du chausson aux pommes) – This great festival has taken place every year since 1581 (first weekend in September) to commemorate the end of the plague.

SIGHTS

Notre Dame Church – Construction began in 1425 with the chancel; the building is a mixture of the Flamboyant and the Renaissance styles. The belltower is surmounted by a crocketed stone steeple.

The Italian **façade★** was finished in 1549 and is typical of the second Renaissance. The carved panels of the twin doors portray scenes from the life of the Virgin; above in the transom are two horns of plenty framed by a semicircular arch. The whole doorway is flanked by two Ionic pilasters. The charming side doors are surmounted by curvilinear pediments and niches. A pedimented window and an oculus are set in the upper part of the gable which is surmounted by five pinnacles ornamented with statues.

The first three bays of the interior are Renaissance; the vaulting with pendentives springs from majestic columns with Ionic capitals. The 17C loft came from the abbey and the organ itself is of the same date. Restored in 1974, it is the pride and joy of the church's organists. A Baroque retable adorns the high altar; a strong cupboard to the right of the chancel contains the "Shroud of St-Calais" which is made of Sassanid (6C Persian) material.

Riverside (Quais de l'Anille) – Pleasant views of the riverside wash houses, now covered in moss, and gardens of flowers against a background of picturesque roofs.

ST-CALAIS

Coursimault (R.) 2
Dauphin (R. du) 3
Dr-Baudrillard (R. du) 4

Dr-Ollivier (R. du) 5
Guichet (R. du) 9
Image (R. de l') 13
Maubert (R. H.) 17
Poignant (R. Fernand) 18
Sadi-Carnot (R.) 20

ST-ÉTIENNE-DE-CHIGNY
Pop 1 164

Michelin map 🟦 fold 14 or 🟦 fold 35 (13km - 8 miles northeast of Langeais)

Set back from the village which is on the Loire embankment is the **Vieux Bourg** nestling in the Bresme Valley; there are several old houses with steep gables.

★ **Church** – The church was built in 1542 by Jean Binet, major-domo to François I and Mayor of Tours, whose arms appear both within and without in the form of a mourning band. The nave is covered by a remarkable **hammerbeam roof;** the tie beams are carved with enormous grotesque masks and, in the chancel, Jonah in the belly of the whale. The 16C **stained glass window** in the chevet shows the Crucifixion flanked by the figures of the donors, Jean Binet and his wife, Jeanne de la Lande. In the north transept hangs a 16C painting of the *Virgin and Child* by the French school; there is also a mural of St Clement, Pope and patron saint of boatmen. The font dates from the 16C.

ST-FLORENT-LE-VIEIL
Pop 2 511

Michelin map 🟦 fold 19 or 🟦 fold 30 –Local map under LOIRE VALLEY: Chinon-Champtoceaux

The hill on which St-Florent is built is visible from a distance. From the bridge over the Loire there is a good **view** of the town and its hilltop church.

The Mercy of Bonchamps – The revolt in the Vendée *(see Les Mauges)* began in St-Florent on 12 March 1793. The Whites were defeated at Cholet and retreated to St-Florent on 18 October with their prisoners and their wounded, including **Bonchamps** who was near to death. Incensed by the atrocities committed by Westermann and the Mayence Army, the Whites prepared to avenge their leader by massacring the Republicans imprisoned in the church. Hearing by chance of their impending fate, Bonchamps begged his cousin Autichamps to obtain a reprieve for the prisoners. Autichamps therefore ran to the church shouting that Bonchamps wanted the prisoners to be spared and they were spared. Among their number was the father of David of Angers, the sculptor who, in gratitude, created the moving monument in the church.

Church – The church stands at the top of Glonne hill; boasting towers and west front in forthright classical style, it was once the church of the old Benedictine monastery. In one of the north chapels is the white marble **tomb of Bonchamps★** (1825) with David of Angers' presentation of the White leader as a hero of old. Like the chancel, the crypt was restored in the 19C; it has a 15C painted sculpture of the Virgin Mary.

Esplanade – The tree-lined esplanade near the church ends in a column which was erected in honour of the Duchess of Angoulême, daughter of Louis XVI. From the terrace there is an extensive **view★** of the Loire Valley.

Local History Museum ⊙ – Housed in the 17C Sacré-Cœur Chapel, the museum has documents, costumes, uniforms and weapons mostly relating to the Vendée War and its leaders.

Les Coteaux Abbey Farm ⊙ – These once-fortified buildings now house an **Environmental Centre** (Carrefour touristique et culturel des Mauges) with good displays on the natural and man-made heritage of the Mauges region.

ST-GEORGES-SUR-LOIRE
Pop 3 101

Michelin map 🟦 folds 19, 20 or 🟦 fold 31 – Local map under LOIRE VALLEY: Chinon-Champtoceaux

St-Georges on the north bank of the Loire is situated not far from some famous vineyards, "La Coulée de Serrant" and "La Roche aux Moines" where some of Anjou's finest white wines are produced.

Old Abbey – The Abbey was founded in 1158 by the Augustinian Order. Up to 1790 it was occupied by a scholarly community which emerged in 1635 as the result of an effort to bring together the different Augustinian communities: the Genovefans, who were regular canons belonging to the Abbey of St Geneviève in Paris.
The handsome building, which dates from 1684 and is occupied by the Town Hall, contains a grand staircase with a remarkable wrought-iron banister and the chapter house with its original wainscoting where temporary exhibitions are held.

EXCURSION

★★ **Serrant Château** – *2km - 1 mile by N 23 towards Angers. See Serrant Château.*

*Five **Michelin Green Guides for North America:***

Canada
New England
New York
Quebec
Washington.

ST-PATERNE-RACAN

Michelin map 64 south of fold 4 or 232 fold 23

St-Paterne stretches out along the Escotais, which is bordered by riverside wash houses and weeping willows.

Church – The church contains interesting works of art, some of which came from the nearby Abbey of La Clarté-Dieu. The 16C terracotta group to the left of the high altar portrays the Adoration of the Magi; at the centre is a charming **Virgin and Child★**.

In the nave, 18C polychrome statues represent the four great Latin Doctors of the Church – Ambrose, Augustine, Jerome and Gregory the Great – while in the south chapel a large retable (the Virgin of the Rosary) of the same period is accompanied by a 16C terracotta group of St Anne and the Virgin.

EXCURSIONS

La-Roche-Racan Château – *2km - 1 mile south by D 28. See La Roche-Racan Château.*

St-Christophe-sur-le-Nais – Pop 925. *2.5km - 1 1/2 miles north by D 6.* Also in the Escotais Valley this village is the scene of a pilgrimage to St Christopher (penultimate Sunday in July). The **church** is in reality composed of two separate buildings, a former 11C-14C priory chapel and the parish church with its 16C nave and belfry.

On the threshold of the nave a gigantic St Christopher welcomes the visitor. To the right in a recess is a reliquary bust of the saint.

To the left of the chancel, the door leading to the Prior's oratory is surmounted by a fine 14C statue of the Virgin and Child. Two Renaissance medallions decorate the church's wooden roof.

Neuvy-le-Roi – Pop 1 001. *9km - 6 miles east by D 54.* The **church** which dates from the 12C and 16C has a Romanesque chancel and a nave covered with Angevin vaulting *(p 37)*; note in the north aisle the complex pattern of vaulting with projecting keystones (16C), and to the south of the chancel the elegant seigneurial chapel, also with projecting keystones.

On the outside of the north aisle there are many lateral gable ends, frequently to be seen in the region.

ST-VIÂTRE

Pop 1063

Michelin map 64 north of fold 19 or 238 fold 17

This smart little town in the Sologne was formerly a place of pilgrimage containing the relics of St Viâtre, a hermit who retired here in the 6C and, so the legend says, made himself a coffin from the trunk of an aspen tree.

Church – The 15C transept gable is built of brick with a black diaper pattern and edged with spiral rosettes.

The belltower porch shelters the 14C door.

At the chancel step stands a remarkable carved wood desk (18C) of surprising size. In the south transept are four **painted panels★** dating from the early 16C: a realistic evocation of the life of Christ and of St Viâtre.

St-Viâtre Wayside Altar – A brick building (15C) at the north entrance to the village.

STE-CATHERINE-DE-FIERBOIS

Pop 539

Michelin map 64 southwest of fold 15 or 232 fold 35

The spirit of Joan of Arc hovers this village which lies east of the N 10 grouped round its church.

Church – On 23 April 1428, following instructions given by Joan of Arc, a sword was found here, marked with five crosses; Charles Martel was supposed to have placed it there after his victory over the Saracens at Poitiers in 732. The chapel was rebuilt in 1479 and completed in the reign of Charles VIII, whose arms together with those of Anne of Brittany appear on the building. It is in the Flamboyant style with an interesting door beneath a pierced pediment; it was restored in 1859.

The interior vaulting springs directly from the piers. Hanging under a glass cover on the north wall of the nave is a small but very realistic 15C Entombment. The south transept contains an unusual 15C altar; on it stands a 15C statue of St Catherine whose image is also carved on the front. Opposite is a rare confessional in the Flamboyant style, very delicately carved.

Dauphin's House (Maison du Dauphin) – 1415. The door of the house to the left of the church is flanked by two sphinxes. Charming carving on the lip of the well in the courtyard.

Boucicault Almonry ⊙ – 1415. *On the opposite side of the street to the Dauphin's House.*

Once a guest house with dormitories and a chapel dedicated to St James for pilgrims on the way to Compostela in Spain, the building is now a **museum** of local history.

STE-MAURE-DE-TOURAINE Pop 3 969

Michelin map 📖 north of folds 4, 5 or 🔲 fold 35

This small town occupies a sunny site on a knoll commanding the Manse Valley. Roman in origin, the settlement developed in the 6C round the tombs of St Britta and St Maurus, then round the keep built by Fulk Nerra.

The Rohan-Montbazon family were the overlords from 1492 to the Revolution.The town is known for its busy poultry markets and its local goats' milk cheeses. A national Cheese Fair is held annually in June.

Church – The church dates from the 11C but its original appearance was altered when it was restored in 1866. A chapel to the right of the chancel has an attractive 16C white marble Virgin by the Italian school. In the central apse there are two painted panels, one depicting the Last Supper (16C), and the other, Christ on a gold background; the relics of St Maurus are venerated here. The crypt (11C and 12C) has a curious series of archaic Romanesque arcades and a small lapidary museum.

Covered market – The 17C covered market at the top of the town was built by the Rohan family.

STE-MAURE PLATEAU

Round trip starting from Ste-Maure *56km - 35 miles – about 1 hour*

The plateau is dissected by the green valleys of two rivers – the Manse and the Esves – and bordered by three others – the Indre (north), the Vienne (west) and the Creuse (south). It is composed of lacustrine limestone which is easily eroded by running water; in the south there are bands of sand and shell, deposited during the Tertiary era by the Faluns Sea and formerly used to improve the soil.

Ste-Maure – *See above.*

Leave Ste-Maure by D 59 going southeast.

The line of the road running through the valleys between limestone bluffs is often marked by a row of poplars.

Bournan – Pop 200. The village **church** is Romanesque; it has a beautiful apse and a tower over the side chapel topped by a facetted spire.

Liguiel – Pop 2 426. Liguiel is a small town built of white stone; there are a few old houses. The decorated wooden washing place, now restored, is on the edge of the town on the road to Loches (D 31).

Esves-le-Moutier – Pop. 161. The village, which lies on the south bank of the Esves, takes its name from a priory which was surrounded by a wall; the **church** (10C-12C) has a massive square tower with bartizans. The interior contains a 17C wooden gilt altarpiece.

Grillemont Château – The huge white château stands halfway up a slope overlooking an attractive **valley★** of meadows round a lake; the slopes are capped by oak and pine woods. The huge round towers of the castle with their pepperpot roofs were built in the reign of Charles VII for Lescoet, the governor of Loches Castle; in 1765 the 15C curtain wall was replaced by magnificent classical buildings.

SARTHE VALLEY

Michelin map 📖 folds 1 to 3 or 🔲 folds 20 to 22

The River Sarthe flows slowly southwest through the beautiful Maine countryside, describing its meanders in the soft soil of the Upper Cretaceous rocks. Around Sablé the water had to make its way through a granite outcrop. The river is navigable as far as Le Mans with lateral canals running parallel. Woodland alternates with meadows and fields of cereals, potatoes and cabbages.

FROM LE MANS TO SABLÉ *73km - 45 miles – about 3 hours*

★★Le Mans – *See Le Mans; allow a day.*

Leave Le Mans by N 23.

Spay – *See Le Mans: Excursions.*

Take D 51 to Fillé.

Fillé – Pop 836. The village is on the north bank of the Sarthe; the **church,** which was rebuilt after the Second World War, contains a large painted statue of the Virgin (late 16C), glazed somewhat by the fire of August 1944.

La-Suze-sur-Sarthe – Pop 3 614. The bridge over the Sarthe provides a good view of the river, the remains of the castle (15C) and the church.

Leave La-Suze by the D 79 going west through woods towards Fercé.

Fercé-sur-Sarthe – Pop 512. Attractive views from the bridge and from the road up to the church.

Return across the river and turn right into V5 to St-Jean-du-Bois; turn right into D 229.

The road passes a troubadour-style castle (left) and provides several glimpses of the Sarthe before reaching Noyen.

Noyen-sur-Sarthe – Pop 2 192. Noyen is built in terraces on the sloping north bank overlooking the canal which at this point runs parallel to the broad Sarthe. From the bridge there is an attractive **view** of a weir, a mill, an island of poplars, a jumble of roofs and little gardens, the beach and another island.

Take D 69 north to Pirmil.

Pirmil – Pop 367. The **church**, a Romanesque building with buttresses, dates from 1165. The capitals are finely carved. The springers of the ogive vaulting are decorated with figures of saint, a bishop, a priest and a grotesque head.

Return south through Noyen taking D 41 to Malicorne-sur-Sarthe.

Malicorne-sur-Sarthe – Pop 1 659. Malicorne is pleasantly situated at the water's edge. From the bridge there is a pretty view of a mill and the poplars along the bank. On the eastern side of the town, on the D 133 to Mézeray, there is a working **pottery** ⊙ which produces pieces in the perforated Malicorne style and also reproductions of period pieces. The 11C **church** contains a recumbent figure of one of the lords of Chaources (chapel on the right of the nave), a *Pietà* (south transept) and an attractive 16C piscina (left wall on the nave).

Downstream, set back from the south bank of the river in a beautiful park, stands the 17C **château** (altered) where Madame de Sevigné liked to stay, which belonged to the Marquise de Lavardin. The château has turrets and mansard roofs and is surrounded by a moat which is spanned by a charming hump back bridge.

Take D 8 west towards Parcé, making a detour (V1) to the right via Dureil, which provides attractive glimpses of the River Sarthe before rejoining D 8.

Parcé-sur-Sarthe – Pop 1 640. Parcé is a charming little village grouped round a Romanesque tower with a mill on the river. The cypress-girt cemetery at the entrance to the village makes a peaceful setting for the chapel with its gable-belfry.

After crossing the river and the canal, turn left into D 57. On leaving Avoise note, on the left, La Perrigne de Cry (private property), a 16C manor overlooking the river. Take V4 to Juigné which crosses the River Vègre before joining D 22 ; bear left.

Juigné-sur-Sarthe – Pop 1 091. Juigné is a pleasant village set on a promontory which juts south across the valley. There are 16C and 17C houses and the 18C château which belonged to the Marquis of Juigné. From the church square there is a view of the river below and of Solesmes Abbey downstream.

Solesmes – See Solesmes.

Take D 22 beside the canal and the old marble quarries to Sablé.

Sablé – See Sablé.

★★ SAUMUR

Michelin map 64 fold 12 or 232 fold 33 – Local map under LOIRE VALLEY: Chinon-Champtoceaux – Facilities

Saumur is famous for its cavalry school, its wines – especially its sparkling *(mousseux)* wines – and its mushrooms; local production of mushrooms represents 70% of the national figure. These activities have been joined by the manufacture of toys and knitwear and mechanical and electrical firms. Saumur also has the largest factory making carnival masks in Europe.

Each year a tattoo using horses and motor transport is given by the **Cadre Noir** on the vast Place du Chardonnet *(see Calendar of Events)*. Repeat performances are given in the Riding School of the National Equitation Centre in Terrefort *(see below)*.

On summer evenings there are **Tuffolies** performances by strolling players in the streets. Local inhabitants dress in period costume in honour of the famous people such as King René, Philippe Duplessis-Mornay, Rabelais, Balzac and Jeanne Delanou who have made the town famous. Spectators are encouraged to join in.

An eventful history – Charles the Bald built a fortified monastery in the 9C to house the relics of St Florent who converted the region to Christianity in the 4C; it was soon destroyed by the Vikings. In the 11C Saumur was the subject of numerous conflicts between the Count of Blois and the Count of Anjou. In 1203 the town was captured by Philippe-Auguste.

On several occasions the castle was destroyed and then restored or rebuilt. From the time of Louis IX (13C) Saumur shared the destiny of the House of Anjou *(qv)*.

In the late 16C and early 17C the town enjoyed its greatest glory. It was one of the great centres of Protestantism. Henri III gave it as a stronghold to the King of Navarre. The future Henri IV appointed as Governor Duplessis-Mornay, a great soldier, great scholar and fervent Reformer, who was known by the Roman Catholics as the Huguenot Pope. He founded a Protestant academy which gained great renown. In 1611 a general assembly of the Protestant churches was held there to confirm their organisation following the death of Henri IV and the departure of Sully. Louis XIII grew alarmed at the Protestant danger and ordered the town walls to be demolished in 1623. The Revocation of the Edict of Nantes in 1685 dealt Saumur a fatal blow; many of the inhabitants emigrated; the temple was demolished.

Armoured Corps and Cavalry Academy (École d'application de l'Arme blindée et de la Cavalerie) (AY) – In 1763 the Carabiniers Regiment, a crack corps recruited from the best horsemen in the army,

Rider of the Cadre Noir performing the croupade

was sent to Saumur. The present central building was constructed between 1767 and 1770 as their barracks. It now houses the Cavalry School which trains the elite of the French cavalry and took its modern title in 1943.

Distinct from the military school is the **National Equitation Centre** (École Nationale d'Équitation) which comprises the **Cadre Noir** (Black Squad) situated at St-Hilaire-St-Florent on the Terrefort and Verrie plateaux near Saumur.

Saumur Cadets – In June 1940 the officers and cadets of the Cavalry School made it a point of honour to defend the passage of the Loire. For three days, from 18 to 20 June, although inferior in number and having only training equipment they performed many heroic feats and succeeded in holding the Germans in check on a 20km - 12 miles front between Gennes and Montsoreau.

★★ CHÂTEAU (BZ) ⊙ *Time: 1 1/2 hours*

The château is compact and massive but the vertical lines of its pointed and ribbed towers lend it grace. Despite being a fortress it is decorated as if it were a country house with sculptured machicolations and balustrades at the windows overlooking the courtyard. It stands high above the Loire Valley on a sort of pedestal created by the star-shaped 16C fortifications.

A succession of fortresses has been built on the promontory. The present building, which succeeds Louis IX's castle, was rebuilt at the end of the 14C by Louis I, Duke of Anjou and completed by Louis II. The interior was altered in the 15C by René d'Anjou and external fortifications were added at the end of the 16C Duplessis-Mornay. Under Louis XIV and Louis XV it was the residence of the Governor of Saumur; afterwards it became a prison and then barracks; now it houses three museums. From the château terrace there is a fine **panorama★** of the town and the valleys of the Thouet (south) and the Loire (east, west).

★★ Museum of Decorative Arts (Musée d'Arts décoratifs) – The exhibits, which include

the Lair Collection, form a fine display of works of art from the Middle Ages and the Renaissance period: Limoges enamels, alabaster and wooden sculptures, tapestries, furniture, paintings, church ornaments and a collection of faience and

SAUMUR

Beaurepaire (R.) .... **AY**
Bilange (Pl. de la) ...... **BY** 2
Gaulle (Av. Gén. de) ... **BX**
Leclerc (R. du Mar.) .... **AZ**

Orléans (R. d') .... **ABY**
Portail-Louis (R. du) ..... **BY** 10
Roosevelt (R. Fr.) .... **BY** 13
St-Jean (R.) .... **BY** 15

Cadets (Pont des) ...... **BX** 3
Dr-Bouchard (R. du) .... **AZ** 4

Dupetit-Thouars (Pl.) ... **BZ** 5
Fardeau (R.) .... **AZ** 6
Nantilly (R. de) .... **BZ** 7
Poitiers (R. de) .... **AZ** 9
République (Pl. de la) .. **BY** 12
St-Pierre (Pl.) .... **BY** 16
Tonnelle (R. de la) ..... **BY** 17

French porcelain (17C and 18C) together with furniture and tapestries from the same period. The 15C and 16C tapestries include the Return from the Hunt, the Coronation of Vespasian and the Capture of Jerusalem.

★ **Equine Museum (Musée du Cheval)** – The museum depicts the history of the saddle horse and equitation in different countries down the years: collections of saddles, bits, stirrups and spurs, fine engravings referring to the Saumur Cavalry School, horse racing and famous thoroughbreds as well as splendid harness from the world over (Asia, North America and Africa).

Toy and Figurine Museum ⊙ – The collection of old toys in the château's powdermill will delight both young and old by the great variety of displays. Among them are the *Vertuni* series from the early 20C, made of plaster dipped in lead and representing the kings of France, *Lucotte* lead soldiers, late-19C toys made of plaster and flour, small unbreakable *Quiralu* soldiers dating from 1933 and various other compositions.

ADDITIONAL SIGHTS

★ **Old town** (BY) – The narrow twisting streets between the castle and the bridge still follow their original line; in some areas the old houses have been preserved while in others new constructions have been built in the medieval style or are resolutely modern but full of surprises (south of St Peter's Church).
Along the main shopping street, Rue St-Jean, and in the square, **Place St-Pierre**, half-timbered hues and 18C mansions with wrought-iron balconies stand side by side. The new market in the corner (1982) blends with the older styles.

★ **St Peter's Church (St-Pierre)** (BY) – The church is Romanesque except for the west front which collapsed in the 17C and was rebuilt. The beautiful Romanesque door *(illustration p 37)* in the south transept leads into the interior which is hung with two series of 16C **tapestries**★ depicting the life of St Peter and the life of St Florent (starting on the left side of the nave). Regular concerts of organ music.

★ **Town Hall** (BY H) – Only the lefthand section of the building is old (16C). Originally the Loire flowed past the foundations and the building was a bridgehead and part of the town walls, hence its military aspect. The façade facing the courtyard, however, is not at all military; it is in the Gothic-Renaissance transitional style with some fine carving.

★ **Church of Our Lady of Nantilly** (BZ) – This is a fine Romanesque building. Louis XI, who had a great devotion to the Virgin, added the right aisle; his oratory is used as a baptismal chapel. A pillar on the left in the same aisle, bears an epitaph composed by King René d'Anjou for his nurse Tiphaine. Opposite stands the enamelled cross which belonged to Giles, Archbishop of Tyre and keeper of the Seals under Louis IX.

The 12C painted wooden statue of Our Lady of Nantilly was placed in the apse on the right of the chancel. There is a Tree of Jesse in the left transept and the eighteen capitals are of interest. The organ case, which is supported by telamones, dates from 1690.

There are fine **tapestries**★★ dating from the 15C and 16C except for eight in the nave which were made at Aubusson in the 17C and show scenes from the life of Christ and the Virgin.

★ **Cavalry School Museum** (AY M¹) ⊘ – *Entrance in Avenue Foch.*

The very rich presentation of souvenirs, created in 1936 from Barbet de Vaux collections, traces the history of the school and the heroic deeds of the French cavalry and the armoured corps since the 18C.

The exhibits include ornamental swords inlaid with mother-of-pearl, ebony or tortoiseshell and incised sabres which belonged to Egyptian Mamelukes or to marshals and generals of the French Empire: two damascened sabres which were the property of Kellermann, pistols which belonged to Augereau and Daumesnil, the baton of Brune and varius items of equipment used by Kléber and Bertrand.

The uniforms of Napoleon's Grand Army and the Imperial Guard are illustrated by a collection of Sèvres and Meissen porcelain figures, and a series of helmets, cuirasses and sabres which were used by dragoons and hussars.

It is interesting to note the names of some of those men who served in the cavalry of the African Army between 1830 and 1962: Bugeaud, Gallieni (the saviour of Paris in 1914), Charles de Foucault, who was an officer before he became a missionary, Lyautey, de Lattre de Tassigny.

Finally the history of the French cavalry is traced from 1870 through the two World Wars and the Indo-Chinese and Algerian campaigns.

★ **Tank Museum** (Musée des Blindés) (AY M²) ⊘ – It contains over 150 vehicles showing the development of the Armoured Corps, the modern cavalry, since 1918. The hall presents French equipment including one of the first light tanks to appear on the battlefield, the 1918 Renault tank, surrounded by American armoured vehicles used in the liberation of Europe.

Displays of foreign equipment include British tanks, type T34 Soviet tanks and German 1939-45 Panzers.

Church of Our Lady of Ardilliers – *On the eastern edge of the city, Quai L.-Mayaud by ② on the plan, D 947.*

This beautiful 17C building is one of the most popular places of pilgrimage in France. Devotion to Our Lady of Ardilliers began to develop in the reign of François I owing to the discovery of a miraculous statue on this spot by a farm labourer in the last century, but it reached its height in the 17C when the number of pilgrims exceeded 10 000 a year.

St-Hilaire-St-Florent – *2km - 1 mile northwest by D 751.*

The village consists of one long street straggling at the foot of the hill beside the River Thouet. It is a suburb of Saumur devoted to the production of a famous sparkling white wine made by the Champagne method; on either side of the road there is one cellar after another (all the famous makes are open to visitors for tasting).

★ **National Equitation Centre** ⊘ – The school was opened in 1972 on the Terrefort and Verrie plateaux. It is a modern establishment consisting of several units each comprising a granary where foodstuffs are stored, a large dressage arena that can seat 1 200 spectators and stabling for 400 horses with harness rooms and showers. One of the vocations of the school, which comes under the auspices of the Ministry for Youth and Sport, is to maintain the level of French horsemanship and further its renown.

In 1984 the **Cadre Noir** (Black Squad) was established here. A fundamental part of the school, it is involved in all its missions and gives traditional repeat performances of Manège (dressage) and "Airs above the ground" in France and abroad.

Mushroom Museum ⊘ – *2km - 1 mile west by D 751.*

The ancient tufa quarries which pit the hillsides round Saumur are extensively used for cultivating mushrooms which need humidity and a constant temperature (between 11°C and 14°C).

Mushrooms have been grown in the quarries since the time of Napoleon I; production is now on an industrial scale and occupies 800km - 497 miles of galleries yielding some 120 000 tonnes per annum.

The various methods of culture are presented in a working environment; the oldest method in mushroom beds is being replaced by more modern techniques using wooden crates, plastic bags, bales of straw and the trunks of trees.

Apart from button-mushrooms, new types of cultivated mushroom such as *shiitake, pleurote* and *pied-bleu* are also on show.

The museum gives an historical account of tufa, the fine delicate stone in which a great variety of ammonites and sea urchins have fossilised.

Bagneux – Pop 3 968. *South of Saumur by ③ on the plan.* Bagneux, which lies in the heart of the oldest inhabited region of Anjou, is an old village on the banks of the Thouet.

Engine Museum ⊙ – *No 18 Rue Alphonse-Cailleau (second street on the left after Fouchard bridge)*. The engines displayed have been collected by mechanics enthusiasts most of whom attended the Saumur Industrial School and wish to preserve and restore old and contemporary engines.

Return to Rue du Pont-Fouchard for a short distance. Beyond the Town Hall, bear left into Rue du Dolmen.

Dolmen ⊙ – The Great Dolmen, situated in the village itself, is one of the most remarkable megalithic dolmens in Europe. It measures 20m - 22yds long and 7m - 8yds wide and consists of 16 vertical stones forming a passage and supporting a roof 3m - 10ft high which is composed of four capstones; one of them is broken and is held up by an interior prop.

EXCURSIONS

★**Boumois Château** – *7km - 4 1/2 miles northwest by ① on the plan. See Boumois Château.*

St-Cyr-en-Bourg – *Pop 1 169. 8km - 5 miles south by D 93.*
The vine growers of Saumur (**Cave des Vignerons de Saumur**) ⊙ conduct the whole wine-making process, from the grape to the finished product, in a series of underground galleries reaching 25m - 82ft below the ground; a motorised vehicle circulates in the galleries. There is a commentary and wine tasting in a special chamber.

SAVONNIÈRES   Pop 2 030

Michelin map 🔢 fold 14 or 🔢 fold 35 (2.5km - 1 1/2 miles east of Villandry) – Local map under LOIRE VALLEY: Orléans-Chinon

The church has a beautiful Romanesque doorway decorated with animals and doves.

Petrifying Caves ⊙ – *On the western edge of the town on the road to Villandry, D 7.*
The caves were formed in the Secondary Era. In the 12C they were used as quarries and then partially flooded with water. The continuing infiltration of water saturated with limestone is slowly creating stalactites, pools and curtains. There is reconstruction of the prehistoric fauna and a **museum of petrification** with lithographic stones and 19C copper matrices.
Wine tasting takes place in the caves.

SEGRÉ   Pop 6 434

Michelin map 🔢 south of fold 9 or 🔢 fold 18

The schist houses of Segré cascade down the slope to the river which is bordered by quays and spanned by picturesque bridges.
The town is the capital of the Segréen, a region of woods and meadows devoted to mixed farming and also known for its high-grade iron ore.

Old Bridge – The humpback bridge over the River Oudon offers attractive views of the old parts of the town.

St Joseph's Chapel – Views of the old town and the Oudon Valley.

EXCURSIONS

★**La Lorie Château** ⊙ – *2km - 1 mile southeast; signpost on the road to Angers.*
La Lorie is an imposing 18C château approached by a long avenue of trees which meet overhead. The château stands in a setting of formal French gardens.
A dry moat surrounds a square courtyard which is bordered on three sides by ranges of buildings with white tufa tiles; a statue of Minerva "the Bearer of Peace" adorns the central range, which was built in the 17C by René Le Pelletier, Provost General of Anjou; the château's imposing dimensions are due to the addition of the two wings and the symmetrical outbuildings.
The same nobility of line and form is to be found in the interior: the great gallery decorated with beautiful Chinese vases, the late-18C marble salon, the adjoining chapel and the 18C woodwork in the dining room. The great Salon is the most unusual; it is sumptuously decorated with Sablé marble and was designed by Italian artists in 1779; the musicians played in the overhead rotunda.

Le Bourg d'Iré; Nyoiseau – *Round trip of 21km - 13 miles – leave Segré by D 923 going southwest towards Candé; beyond the level crossing turn right into D 181.*

Le Bourg d'Iré – *Pop 782. 8km - 5 miles west.* The town stands in the valley of the River Verzée. From the bridge there is a most attractive **view** of the river.

Noyant-la-Gravoyère – *3km - 2 miles north of Le Bourg d'Iré by D 219. See Noyant-la-Gravoyère.*

From Noyant-la-Gravoyère to Nyoiseau (5km - 3 miles northeast), take D 775 towards Segré and then the first road on the left.

The road runs through a schist gorge, partially flooded by small lakes which make this the most picturesque section of the excursion. The land surrounding the two lakes – St-Blaise and La Corbinière – has been laid out as a **leisure park.**

Nyoiseau – Pop 1 233. The village – its name is a corruption of Niosellum meaning little nest – perched on the slopes of the Oudon Valley has the remains of a Benedictine Abbey for women, now used as a farm as well as housing the town hall. Along the road leading to L'Hôtellerie-de-Flée stands an old Gallo-Roman bridge.

Return to Segré by D 71 and D 775.

Raguin Château ⊙ – *8.5km - 5 miles southwest by D 923; in St-Gemmes-d'Andigné bear left into D 183.*
The old 15C castle was replaced c1600 by Guy du Bellay, son of Pierre du Bellay (cousin of the poet), with a Renaissance-style building.
Although a marshal in the king's army, du Bellay had a taste for luxury and he made Raguin a luxurious and elegant château. When his son, Antoine, married in 1648, he had the first-floor salon and another room fitted with wainscots and had the walls and ceiling entirely redecorated; in the second room, "Chambre des Amours", the cherubs play with the initials of the newly-wed couple.
After the death of his father and then of his wife in 1666, Antoine du Bellay sold the château which changed hands several times.

SELLES-SUR-CHER
Pop 4 751

Michelin map **64** fold 18 or **232** fold 16

Selles-sur-Cher is prettily situated in a bend of the River Cher; the towers of its castle are reflected in the river. The town developed round the abbey which was founded by St Eusice, a hermit who lived in that spot. Only the abbey church now remains.

SIGHTS

St Eusices' Church – The church, which dates from the 12C and 15C, was burned by Coligny in 1562; it was partially restored in the 17C and then more thoroughly in the last century. The façade, which is almost entirely Romanesque, has re-used the columns and capitals from an earlier church which was destroyed by the Normans in about 903.
The **chevet**, which is well built, is ornamented with two friezes of figures; those below the windows are rough, simple and heavy but those above are better proportioned and more elegant. The lower frieze depicts scenes from the New Testament; the upper one illustrates the life of St Eusice.
Near the north wall are low-relief carvings of the Labours of the Months; higher up and further to the right there is a beautiful Visitation, protected by the transept chapel. It is however all very worn.
In the north wall, which was built late in the 13C, there is a charming door decorated with carved capitals supporting tori separated by a chain of flowers and wild rose leaves.
The crypt contains the tomb of St-Eusice (6C).

Castle ⊙ – Hidden on the south bank of the Cher are the remains of an austere 13C fortress, within a rectangular moated enclosure, approached by four bridges.
In contrast, framing the present entrance on the east side are two light 17C buildings joined together by a long arcaded wall, which is pieced by oculi and topped by a parapet walk. These were built by **Philippe de Béthune**, Sully's brother *(see Sully-sur-Loire)* who bought the castle in 1604.
Beyond the magnificent cedar and mulberry trees of the inner park, in the old part on the west side, is the gilded pavilion **(Pavillon Doré)**, an elegant building, decorated in the Italian Renaissance style, which Philippe de Béthune introduced into the old 13C fortress. It has magnificent gilded chimneypieces, wall paintings and coloured coffered ceilings; all have retained their lustre. Also on view are the study containing souvenirs of the **Count of Chambord** (1820-83), pretender to the French throne after the death of Charles X, the little oratory and the bedroom. While living in the gilded pavilion, Philippe de Béthune had a new château built in the contemporary style in red brick outlined in white stone. Here grandeur and generous proportions replace the intimate charm of the gilded pavilion. The tour includes the guard room with its great chimney, the bedroom of Maria Sobieska, the queen of Poland, in which the bed with its twisted columns stands on a dais, and the attractive games room.

Cher Valley Museum ⊙ – The exhibits are varied: documents about Selles' past, tools used by vine growers, basket makers, coopers and watermen, and an interesting section on the preparation of gunflint, a thriving industry in the region from the middle of the 18C until the invention of the percussion cap *(see also Meusnes and Luçay-le-Mâle).*

EXCURSIONS

Châtillon-sur-Cher – Pop 1 395. *5km - 3 miles west by N 75 towards St-Aignan and a turning to the left.*
The little village stands on the north slope of the Cher Valley. **St Blaise's Church** – contains (left wall of chancel) a **panel**★ by the school of Leonardo da Vinci showing St Catherine between two cherubs: the treatment of the hands, a little mannered but very attractive, and the facial expression are typical of da Vinci's style.
A statue of St Vincent, patron of vine-growers, is surrounded by the batons of their brotherhood which are carried in their processions.

Meusnes – Pop 1 009. *6.5km - 4 miles southwest by D 956 briefly towards Valençay and then D 17 west.*
The **church** is in the pure Romanesque style. There is a triumphal arch in the transept surmounted by three charming openwork arcatures. Several beautiful 15C and 16C statues have been reinstated.
A small **gunflint museum** ⊙, housed in the town hall, describes this industry which flourished in the region for three hundred years.

Chabris – Pop 2 627. *8km - 5 miles southeast by D 51.*
Chabris, which is Roman in origin, is set on the south bank of the River Cher; it produces good wine and goat cheese.
The **church**, which is dedicated to St Phalier, a 5C hermit who died in Chabris, is a very old place of pilgrimage (feast day third Sunday in September). The chevet has unusual primitive sculptures of fantastic animals, the Annunciation and sections of stone laid in a diaper pattern which come from an earlier church which was rebuilt in the 15C. The porch, which has a double arcade and gallery, shelters a Gothic door with carved panels. The chancel contains two naive panels depicting the life and miracles of St Phalier who was thought to help women conceive. The **crypt**, which is probably 1C, contains the sarcophagus of the saint.

★★ SERRANT CHÂTEAU

Michelin map 🔢 fold 20 or 🔢 fold 31 (2km - 1 mile northeast of St-Georges-sur-Loire)

Although built over a period of three centuries, 16C to the 18C, this sumptuous moated mansion has great unity of style. Its massive domed towers and the contrast between the dark schist and the white tufa give it considerable character.

Serrant Château ⊙ was begun in 1546 by Charles de Brie, bought by Hercule de Rohan, Duke of Montbazon, in 1596, and sold in 1636 to Guillaume Bautru whose granddaughter married the Marquis of Vaubrun, Lieutenant-General of the king's army. On the death of her husband, who was killed beside Turenne at the Battle of Altenheim, the Marchioness continued the building work until 1705. She commissioned J. Hardouin-Mansart to build the beautiful chapel to the memory of her husband, and Coysevox to design the white marble mausoleum. In 1749 her daughter, the Duchess of Estrées, sold the estate to an Irishman, Francis Walsh, who was made Count of Serrant in 1755 by Louis XV as a reward for his family's support for the Stuart cause; they provided the ship which carried Bonnie Prince Charlie to Moidart in 1745. Two generations earlier another Walsh had enabled James II to flee to exile in France. In 1830 the château came into the ownership of the Duc de la Trémoille, a forebear of the present occupant, Prince Jean-Charles de Ligne.

Tour – The **apartments** are magnificently furnished. Sumptuous Flemish tapestries hang in the dining room. Of particular note are the great Renaissance staircase, the coffered ceilings on the first floor, the library with its ten thousand volumes and the state rooms where both Louis XIV and Napoleon were received. There are many works of art: Flemish and Brussels tapestries, a very beautiful Italian cabinet, a bust of the Empress Marie-Louise by Canova, portraits.

SOLESMES   Pop 1 277

Michelin map 🔢 folds 1, 2 or 🔢 fold 20 – Local map under SARTHE VALLEY

A few miles upstream from Sablé lies Solesmes which has achieved fame through the Benedictine Order. From the north bank of the Sarthe and from the bridge there is an impressive **view**★ of the north front of the abbey, a dark wall, about 50m - 164ft high, which was built at the end of the 19C in the Romanesque-Gothic style and is reflected in the stream. Next to it stands the earlier 18C priory.

Under the Rule of St Benedict – The Benedictine priory founded in 1010 by the Lord of Sablé was served by monks from St-Pierre-la-Couture in Le Mans *(see Le Mans: Additional Sights)*. It grew rapidly and by the early 16C was rich; in the 17C it fell into decline and was taken over by the monks of St-Maur.
The Revolution brought ruin but a new community was established in 1833 by a priest from Sablé, Dom Guéranger, and in 1837 the abbey became the headquarters of the Benedictine Order in France. In 1901 a law was passed expelling all religious orders from France but they returned when it was repealed twenty years later.
Since then the name of Solesmes has been linked with the restoration of the liturgy and the revival of the Gregorian chant in France.
The abbey **services** ⊙ to which the public is admitted demonstrate the beauty of the liturgy celebrated in Benedictine monasteries.

St Peter's Abbey – *Only the abbey church (in the main courtyard) is open.*
The **church**★ comprises the nave and transept which date from the 11C and 15C and the domical-vaulted chancel which was added in 1865. The famous groups of sculpture, which are known as the **"saints of Solesmes"**★★, are in the transept.
The works in the south transept were commissioned by Prior Guillaume Cheminart: a monumental Entombment (1496) with a beautiful representation of Mary Magdalene at prayer; on the left a terracotta *Pietà* from an earlier period.
The works in the north transept, which is dedicated to the Virgin, were commissioned by Prior Jean Bougler between 1530 and 1556; the composition is rather crowded but the detail is interesting. The main scene is the Entombment of the Virgin; Jean Bougler is shown holding one end of the shroud; overhead are the four Fathers of the Church and the Assumption. On the sides are Jesus among the Doctors (left) and scenes from the life of the Virgin (right).

The SOLOGNE

Michelin map **64** folds 8, 9, 18, 19 or **238** folds 3 to 7 and 16 to 19

The Sologne is a paradise for hunters and fisherman. Its immense, flat yet attractive heathland stretches as far as the eye can see covering an area of 490 000ha - 1 892sq miles.

The region, which is given over to farms, forests and a great many solitary pools (accounting for 11 000ha - 27 000 acres), is punctuated by towns whose red brick, stone and timber add colour to the landscape.

Lying between the Loire and the Cher, the Sologne is bordered to the east by the Sancerre Hills and to the west by a curved line running north from Selles-sur-Cher via Chemery, Thenay and Sambin to Cheverny.

The Sologne terrain, which is composed of clay and sand, slopes very gently westwards as can be deduced from the direction in which the main rivers – Cosson, Beuvron and Petite and Grande Sauldre - flow.

Development – In the past the region was a desolate waste ravaged by fevers caused by the stagnant water of the huge lakes but it changed radically in the reign of Napoleon III who had acquired the Lamotte-Beuvron estate and instigated improvements. The Sologne Central Committee started to plant birch and Norway pine trees, to dig canals, to construct roads, to clear and drain the pools and to improve the soil.

The fevers disappeared, the population increased; the Sologne acquired something like its present appearance.

The Sologne countryside – The area under cultivation is about 140 000ha - 540sq miles. Much maize is grown (about 21 500ha - 83sq miles); it is particularly useful crop because it is not only fodder for the livestock but also provides good cover for the game, thus reconciling the interests of both farmers and hunters.

The fodder produced feeds 35 000 cattle, 25 000 sheep and 10 000 goats. Many farms have taken up pheasant rearing or other activities connected with the provision of game. Wherever the farmer has been able to drain the land, one finds fruit orchards and also farms involved in the intensive rearing of cattle, sheep and goats.

The region round Contres produces vegetables and fruit which are sold locally or sent to the central markets or to the canneries. The Sologne and the Loire

Pheasant in the Sologne

Valley near Blois form one of France's leading asparagus-growing areas. The cultivation of strawberries has become very specialised leading to an increase in production. Along the Cher Valley and in the neighbourhood of Blois the production of wine has improved owing to the introduction of the Sauvignon and Gamay grapes. Markets are held in certain small towns such as Gien, Sully, Romorantin-Lanthenay and Lamotte-Beuvron which is the geographical centre of the Sologne.

The traditional local industries (sawmills and packaging materials) have been joined by other manufacturers: porcelain at Lamotte-Beuvron, armaments at La-Ferté-Saint-Aubin and Salbris, commercial vehicles at Romorantin and the cultivation in the area of gladiolus bulbs, dahlias and yams.

The recent improvement in fish farming on the lakes has increasingly rationalised traditional methods of production. Pike, sauger, eel, carp and more recently *meerval* are a delight to fishermen and gourmets alike.

Sologne forests – These form a unique region in central France. Their history and soil type, which is often sandy and water-laden, are comparable to those of forests in Scandinavian countries. Forests cover an area of over 200 000ha - 772sq miles, with an afforestation rate of about 60% especially in the east, and have been spreading each year for a century and a half. Private owners, who possess 90% of the wooded area and all the fallow land (40 000ha - 154sq miles), have improved the forests by introducing new species such as the Scots pine, the larch and the Douglas fir.

These coniferous trees have gradually replaced the maritime pine which was grown for its resin and timber but which died out after the terrible winter of 1879-1880 when the temperature dropped by almost 40 degrees in a matter of hours.

Stag in the Sologne

The trees are thinned out for the manufacture of paper pulp and chipboards. Recent development in the industry has led to the building of a large factory in Sully-sur-Loire and the modernisation of local sawmills where the sawn timber is now converted on the spot.

The thick cover provided by the forest, together with the general peace of the area and the presence of water, attracts a wide variety of fauna. This has to be regulated and larger members of the Cervidae family as well as roe deer and rabbits protected from predators. The region is also a favoured shooting ground on account of the abundance of migratory birds.

The Sologne is well described by Maurice Genevoix in *Raboliot,* the story of a poacher.

TOWNS AND SIGHTS

The Sologne is at its most attractive in the early autumn, when the russet of the falling leaves mingles with the evergreen of the Norway pines above a carpet of bracken and purple heather, broken by the occasional melancholy pool. The bursts of firing which announce the shooting season can detract a little from the charm of the region.

The nature of the Sologne is best appreciated by taking a walk. Owing to the many enclosures, prohibited areas and animal traps it is best to keep to the marked paths such as the GR31 and the GR3c *(see p 11).*

Another picturesque trip of the Sologne requiring less exertion is provided by the **train** ⊙ which runs between Romorantin and Salbris and is operated by the "Compagnie du Blanc Argent".

The "Sologne Scenic Route", (D 922) between Romorantin and La Ferté-St-Aubin, passes through typical Sologne landscapes.

Argent-sur-Sauldre – *See Argent-sur-Sauldre.*

Aubigny-sur-Nère – *See Aubigny-sur-Nère.*

★ **Blancafort** – *See Blancafort.*

Bracieux – Pop 1 157. Facilities. Bracieux is a smart village on the border of the Sologne and the region round Blois. The houses are grouped round the 16C market on the south bank of the Beuvron which is spanned by a picturesque bridge.

Cerdon – *See Argent-sur-Sauldre: Excursions.*

★★★ **Chambord Château** – *See Chambord Château.*

Chaumont-sur-Tharonne – Pop 901. The line of the former ramparts can be traced in the lay-out of the town which is picturesquely situated round its 15C-16C church on a bluff in the centre of the Sologne region.

★★★ **Cheverny Château** – *See Cheverny Château.*

La Ferté-St-Aubin – *See La Ferté-St-Aubin.*

Fontaines-en-Sologne – Pop 520. The **church,** which dates for the most part from the 12C, shows how widespread was the Angevin style *(see p 37):* flat chevet, nave with remarkable domed vaulting. It was fortified in the 17C.
Beside the church there are half-timbered houses with roofs of small flat tiles, commonly found in the region.

Gy-en-Sologne – Pop 419. This typical Sologne cottage, **Locature de la Straize** ⊙, dates from the 16C.

Lanthenay Church – The church contains a painting of the Virgin between John the Baptist and St Sebastian, dating from 1523 and attributed to Timoteo Viti from Urbino who influenced Raphael in his early days. There is also a 17C canvas of the dead Christ with the Virgin and St John and 16C wooden painted statues of St Francis and St Claire.

Lassay-sur-Croisne – *See Lassay-sur-Croisne.*

★ **Le Moulin Château** – *See Lassay-sur-Croisne.*

Neuvy – Pop 288. Neuvy is located on the southern edge of the Boulogne Forest on the north bank of the River Beuvron.
The village **church** stands on its own in its graveyard near a farm built of half timber and half brick on the opposite bank. It was partially rebuilt in 1525. The rood beam supports 15C statues; in the south transept there is a 17C painting of the dead Christ supported by two angels.

★ **Romorantin-Lanthenay** – *See Romorantin-Lanthenay.*

St-Viâtre – *See St-Viâtre.*

Salbris – Pop 6 083 – Facilities. Salbris, on the south bank of the Sauldre, is a busy crossroads and a good centre for excursions into the forest.

St George's Church was built of stone and brick in the 15C and 16C. The centre of the retable on the high altar is occupied by a *Pietà* (16C). The transept chapels are remarkable for the coats of arms of the donors on the keystones of the vault and the attractive pendant sculptures representing the Three Wise Men and the Virgin and Child (south) and the symbols of the Evangelists (north).

Selles-St-Denis – Pop 1 199. The village lies on the north bank of the Sauldre. The **chapel,** which dates from the 12C and 15C and has side chapels and an apse in the Flamboyant style, is decorated with 14C murals of the life of St Genoulph to whom it is dedicated.

Villeherviers – Pop 533. The village is set among asparagus fields in the broad valley of the Sauldre. There is Plantagenet vaulting in the 13C **church.**

Villesavin Château – *See Villesavin Château.*

SUÈVRES

Pop 1 360

Michelin map **64** southeast of fold 7 or **238** fold 3

The ancient Gallo-Roman city of Sodobrium hides its picturesque façades below the noisy main road (N 152) on the north bank of the Loire. **St Chistopher's Church** beside the road is entered through a huge porch *(caquetoire)* where the parishioners could pause to engage in conversation. The stonework is decorated with various fishbone and chevron patterns characteristic of the Merovingian period.

The houses at no 9 and no 14b in Rue Pierre-Pouteau date from the 15C. Turn right into a picturesque dead-end, Rue des Moulins, running beside the stream which is spanned by many footbridges and reflects the tamarisk and weeping willow trees. *Go back to the turning and cross the stone bridge.* The washing place is at the corner of Rue St-Simon; on either side of the street are traces of an old fortified gate. Further on through the trees (left) one sees the two-storey Romanesque tower of **St Lubin's Church** with its attractive south door (15C).

★ SULLY-SUR-LOIRE

Pop 5 806

Michelin map **65** fold 1 or **238** fold 6 – Facilities

Sully Castle commanded one of the Loire crossings. Its history is dominated by four great names: Maurice de Sully, Bishop of Paris who commissioned the building of Notre-Dame, Joan of Arc, Sully and Voltaire.

The Determination of Joan of Arc – In 1429 Sully belonged to Georges de la Trémoille, a favourite of Charles VII. The King was living in the castle when Joan of Arc defeated the English at Patay and captured their leader, the famous Talbot, Earl of Shrewsbury. Joan hastened to Sully and at last persuaded the indolent monarch to be crowned at Rheims. She returned to the castle in 1430 after her check before Paris, and there felt the jealousy and hostility of La Trémoille gaining influence over the King. She was detained almost as if a prisoner but escaped to continue the struggle.

Sully's capacity for work – In 1602 Maximilien de Béthune, the Lord of Rosny, bought the château and the barony for 330 000 *livres*. Henri IV made him Duke of Sully, and it was under this name that the great Minister passed into history.

Sully had begun to serve his King at the age of twelve. He was a great soldier, the best artilleryman of his time and a consummate administrator. He was active in all the departments of State: Finance, Agriculture, Industry and Public Works.

A glutton for work, Sully began his day at 3am and kept four secretaries busy writing his memoirs. He entitled them: *Wise and Royal Economies of State.* Fearing indiscretions, he had a printing press set up in one of the towers of the château and the work was printed on the spot, although it bore the address of a printer in Amsterdam. The old Duke had a mania for orderly accounts. Every tree to be planted, every table to be made, every ditch to be cleaned was the subject of a legal contract.

Sully had an awkward character and he often went to law, especially with the Bishop of Orléans.

Since the Middle Ages it had been the custom for the Lord of Sully to carry the Bishop's chair on the day of his entry into Orléans. The Minister, very much the ducal peer and a Protestant into the bargain, refused to comply with this custom. Finally he obtained permission to be represented at the ceremony.

Sully embellished his castle. The building originally stood on the Loire itself. He separated it from the river by an embankment, dug moats which he filled by deflecting a nearby river laid out the park and enlarged the buildings.

Sully's career came to an end with the assassination of Henri IV in 1610. The Minister retired but he assured Louis XIII of his loyalty and encouraged his co-religionists to do the same. Richelieu made him a Marshal of France.

The spirit of Voltaire (18C) – Exiled from Paris by the Regent for his biting epigrams, Voltaire spent several seasons with the Duke of Sully who surrounded himself with philosophers and free thinkers. Voltaire was 22. His gaiety and wit made him the life and soul of the castle. In the shade of the park among the trees which he described as "carved upon by urchins and lovers", young François-Marie Arouet (he had not then adopted his pen name) indulged in flirtations which he transferred to the stage. A theatre was built for him in the castle where he produced his tragedies and comedies, with his friends playing the roles.

SULLY SUR-LOIRE

Grand-Sully (R. du) 6
Porte-de-Sologne (R.) . . . 12

Abreuvoir (R. de l') 2
Champ-de-
Foire (Bd du) 3
Chemin de Fer (Av. du) . . 4
Jeanne-d'Arc (Bd) 7
Marronniers (R. des) 9
Porte-Berry (R.) 10
St-François (R. du Fg) . . . 15
St-Germain (R. du Fg) . . . 16

★ CASTLE (CHÂTEAU) ⊘ time: 3/4 hour

The castle is an imposing feudal fortress dating largely from before 1360. The keep, which faces the Loire, is rectangular with round towers at the four corners. The wing added to the living quarters by Sully was remodelled in the 18C and 19C.

Several apartments in the 14C keep can be visited, notably the large guard room on the ground floor, another immense hall (portraits of the Dukes of Sully) on the first floor where Voltaire's plays were performed and the oratory in which there is an excellent copy of the funerary group showing Sully and his wife (original at Nogent-le-Rotrou). Finally, on the second floor, there is the unique chamber with its famous timber roof. The visit ends with a tour of the sentry walk facing the Loire.

★★ **The timber roof** – The upper half of the keep has one of the finest timber roofs to have survived from the Middle Ages. Built around 1400, it is 15m - 50ft in height. Its good state of preservation is due to the infinite pains taken by its builders, both in treating the timber and in the way it was put together. Felled in winter under a waning moon, the trees were squared off, getting rid of the sap-wood, and sawn up following the grain. Immersion in water for a period of several months eliminated the sap. Subsequent air-drying would take many years, after which the precious material would be smoked or cured to protect it from rot and decay. The final treatment consisted of coating with an alum-based solution.

Renaissance pavilion – This contains Sully's study and, on the first floor, the great salon with its painted ceiling which was the Minister's bedroom.

ADDITIONAL SIGHTS

Collegiate Church of St-Ythier (Collégiale de St-Ythier) – Built in 1529, the Chapel of Notre-Dame-de-Pitié was enlarged in 1605; it then became the Collegiate Church of St-Ythier. There are two 16C **stained-glass windows:** the one at the end of the south aisle shows pilgrims on their way to St James's shrine in Compostela; the second, showing the Tree of Jesse with the Virgin and the Infant Jesus, is in the central apse. In the north aisle is a 16C *Pietà* above the high altar.

Renaissance House (D) – Above the façade decorated with medallions and pilasters, the dormer windows in the roof with twin bays are surrounded by caryatids.

St-Germain – The 13C church has been severely damaged several times over the centuries and was last restored in 1944. Its remarkably fine spire, 38m - 125ft high, was re-erected in 1960.

★ TALCY   Pop 240

Michelin map 🟦 fold 7 or 🟥 fold 3

Talcy is a remote village in the Beauce; the road south to Mer on the Loire is bordered here and there with rose trees.

★ **Castle** ⊘ – The castle is austere in appearance but interesting for its literary associations, for its furniture and, on a more humble level, for two little masterpieces: the dovecot and the wine press.

This 13C manorial dwelling was bought in 1571 by a rich Florentine, Bernardo Salviati, a cousin of Catherine de' Medici. The Salviati family, so famous in literary history, retained the estate until 1667. Bernardo was the father of Cassandra, to whom **Ronsard** *(see La Possonnière Manor)* dedicated so many sonnets, and of Giovanni Salviati, whose daughter, Diana, similarly inspired the young Agrippa d'Aubigné. Cassandra's daughter married Guillaume de Musset and one of her direct descendants was the great poet Alfred de Musset (1810-57).

Fine furniture (16C-18C) and Gothic tapestries soften the severity of the feudal halls which are roofed in the French style with fine Renaissance beams. The 15C keep with its double doorway (postern and carriage gate) has two corner turrets and a crenellated sentry walk which looks medieval but dates from 1520. The fenestration at the first-floor level was modified in the 18C.

The first courtyard owes its charm to a graceful gallery and an attractive well. In the second courtyard is a large 16C **dovecot;** its 1500 pigeonholes are admirably preserved.

The old **wine press** is still in working order after 400 years of use. The carefully-balanced mechanism enables two men to obtain ten barrels of juice at a single pressing.

MICHELIN GREEN GUIDES

Art and Architecture
History
Geography
Ancient monuments
Scenic routes
Touring programmes
Plans of towns and buildings

A selection of guides for holidays at home and abroad.

Michelin map 🔢 fold 15 or 🔢 folds 35, 36 and 🔢 fold 13 – Local map under
LOIRE VALLEY: Orléans-Chinon

Tours, the capital of Touraine, is traditionally a centre for excursions into the
châteaux country but it has many attractions of its own: its clear light, the orderly
street plan, the squares and gardens, the churches, monasteries and museums.

HISTORICAL NOTES

Gallo-Roman Metropolis – During the Roman period the settlement known as
Turons became a prosperous and free city with the name Caesarodunum (Caesar's
Hill) and extended over a densely populated area of about 40ha - 100 acres. Late in
the 3C however, invasions obliged the inhabitants to take refuge in the present
cathedral district which included the arena. A wall was built to enclose the city and
traces of it can still be seen near the castle and in the nearby street, Rue des
Ursulines.
In 375 the town, which had reverted to its former name Turones, became the seat
of government of the third Lyonnaise, a province comprising Touraine, Maine,
Anjou and Armorica.

St Martin's City (4C) – The man who became the greatest bishop of the Gauls
started as a legionary in the Roman army. At the gates of Amiens the young soldier
met a beggar shivering in the cold wind. He cut his cloak in two with his sword and
gave half to the poor man. The following night in a dream he saw Christ wearing
half his cloak; he was bap-
tised and began his mis-
sion. At Ligugé in Poitou he
founded the first monastery
on Gallic soil. His faith and
charity spread his fame far
afield. In 372 the people of
Tours begged him to
become their bishop.
Although Christianity has
arrived in Gaul a century
earlier, paganism was still
rife. St Martin fought it
with vigour; idols, statues
and temples were systema-
tically destroyed. The ico-
noclast was, however, also
a builder and he covered
Touraine with churches and
chapels. The monastery of
Marmoutier was built at the
gates of Tours.

St Martin cutting his cloak (14C Missal, Tours)

St Martin died in Candes in 397. The monks of Ligugé and Marmoutier quarrelled
over his body; while the men of Poitou slept, the men of Tours transferred the
saint's body to a boat and rowed hard upstream for home. Then a miracle
occurred; although it was November, the trees turned green, the plants burst into
flower and the birds sang – a St Martin's summer. In 471 a basilica was built over
his tomb; it measures 50m × 20m – 164ft × 66ft and has 120 columns, 32 windows
in the apse and 20 in the nave.

A popular pilgrimage – In 496 or 498 **Clovis** came to St Martin's Basilica to
meditate and promised to be baptised if he defeated the Alamanni. He returned in
507 during the war against the Visigoths and commanded his army not to despoil
the territory of Tours but out of respect for St Martin. After his victory at Vouillé,
near Poitiers, he did not forget to visit the basilica on which he bestowed many
presents in thanksgiving. For the occasion he wore the insignia of the consulship
which the Emperor of the East had conferred on him. These visits of Clovis' were
the beginning of the special protection which the Merovingians accorded to the
prestigious sanctuary.
In 563 a young deacon in poor health, who was heir to a noble Gallo-Roman family
in the Arverne (later Auvergne), visited St Martin's tomb. His name was Gregory.
He was cured and settled in Tours. Owing to his piety and probity, coupled with the
renown of several of his relatives (he was the great-nephew of St Nizier of Lyons)
he was elected bishop in 573. **Gregory of Tours** produced many written works,
especially the **History of the Franks** which has been the main source of information
about the Merovingian period: he also wrote eight *Books of Miracles* and the *Lives
of the Fathers*. Under his enlightened direction the town developed and an abbey
grew up round St Martin's Basilica. Gregory died in 594.
For many years pilgrims had been flocking to Tours for cure or counsel. The shrine
of St Martin acquired a great reputation, which was assisted by skilful propaganda
about the numerous miracles which had taken place round his tomb. Among the
ordinary pilgrims in search of the supernatural were kings and princes and powerful
lords seeking absolution for their crimes and abuses. The sanctuary was also a
place of asylum, an inviolable refuge for both the persecuted and the criminal.
The popularity of the cult of St Martin brought the abbey great riches; its estates,
the result of many donations, extended as far as Berry and Bordelais.
Royal favour was expressed in the abbey being granted the right to mint money.

Abbot Alcuin – At the end of the 8C Tours added to its fame by becoming an
intellectual and artistic centre under the influence of Alcuin, a monk of Anglo-
Saxon origin, originally from York in England, who had met **Charlemagne** in Italy and
accompanied him back to France.

The French king wanted to raise the level of learning in his kingdom and he opened a large number of schools to train a well-informed clergy capable in its turn of instructing the population. At his palace in Aix-la-Chapelle he organised a meeting of a group of scholars led by the great figure of Alcuin, the inspirer of the Carolingian Renaissance.

After serving energetically at court Alcuin decided to retire; Charlemagne offered to appoint him abbot of St Martin of Tours (796). Although the community counted over 200 monks, it was not very active. Alcuin undertook to renew its prestige. He reformed the abbey school creating two cycles of study: one was elementary, the other consisted of the seven "liberal arts" (grammar, rhetoric, logic, arithmetic, geometry, music and astronomy). Students came from all over Europe. He revived the scriptorium where the copyists design a new calligraphy for the illuminated manuscripts. He also produced a revised version of the **Vulgate Bible** which became the authorised text throughout the kingdom. He remained in close touch with **Charlemagne** who sought his advice and visited him just before his coronation in December 800. Alcuin died on Whit Sunday 804 at about 75 years of age.

For fifty years after his death Tours continued to be a brillant cultural centre. In 813 a council met in Tours and ordained that the clergy should comment on the Bible in French rather than Latin.

In the 840s the **scriptorium** of St Martin's Abbey produced some splendid masterpieces: the so-called Alcuin Bible, the so-called Moutier-Grandval Bible and the famous Bible of Charles the Bald. Artists from Aix-la-Chapelle and Rheims renewed and enriched the illustrative technique of the abbey scriptorium.

From the early Capets to Louis XI – The Viking invasions reached Tours in 853: the cathedral, the abbeys and the churches were set on fire and destroyed. The relics of St Martin were removed and hidden in the Auvergne. The ancient abbey fell into decline and passed to the Robertians who were lay priests. In 903, after further attacks, the abbey was surrounded by a wall and a new town grew up to the west of the old city; it was called Châteauneuf or Martinopolis.

The Robertians in charge of St Martin's Abbey held immense temporal power and the opportunity to pursue ecclesiastical careers; abbots, bishops and archbishops were appointed from among the 200 canons attached to the abbey. The surname **"Capet"** by which King Hugh was known at the end of the 10C comes from an allusion to the "cappa' (cloak) of St Martin, thus proving that the success of the new royal dynasty owed much to the famous monastery. One of Hugh Capet's vassals, Eudes I, Count of Blois and Tours, obtained from his king c984 the neighbouring Abbey of Marmoutier which was to acquire greater importance in the 11C.

In 997 a huge fire destroyed Châteauneuf and St Martin's Abbey which had to be completely rebuilt, including the basilica which dated from 471. The rivalry in the 11C between the houses of Blois and Anjou, whose domains met in Touraine, ended with the Angevins victorious.

When Pope Alexander III held a great council in Tours in 1163, Touraine belonged to the Plantagenets but in 1205 **Philippe Auguste** captured the town which then remained French.

The 13C was a period of peace and posperity; the **denier tournois,** the money minted in Tours and thereafter in other cities in the kingdom, was adopted as the official currency in preference to the *denier parisis.* Early in the 13C a monk from Marmoutier, John, author of the *History of the Counts of Anjou* and of the *Life of Geoffroi le Bel,* painted a very flattering portrait in his *In Praise of Touraine* of the citizens of Touraine and their wives. "They are always celebrating and their meals are of the very best; they drink from gold and silver cups and spend their time playing at dice and hunting. The women are astonishingly beautiful, they make up their faces and wear magnificent clothes. Their eyes kindle passion but they are respected for their chastity."

In 1308 Tours played host to the Etats-Généraux (French Parliament). Less welcome events soon followed; the arrival of the **Black Death** (1351) and the beginning of the Hundred Years War forced the citizens to build a new wall in 1356 enclosing Tours and Châteauneuf. Touraine, which had been coveted by the great royal vassals, was raised to a Duchy for the future Charles VII and he solemnly entered the town of Tours in 1417. In 1429 Joan of Arc stayed in Tours while her armour was being made. Charles VII settled in Tours in 1444 and on 28 May he signed the Treaty of Tours with Henry VI of England.

Under **Louis XI** Tours was very much in favour; the city acted as the capital of the kingdom and a mayor was appointed in 1462. The king liked the region and lived at Plessis Château *(see below).* Once again life became pleasant and the presence of the court attracted a number of artists of which the most famous was **Jean Fouquet** (born in Tours c1415) who painted the magnificent miniatures in the *Great Chronicle of France* and *Jewish Antiquities.*

The Abbey once again enjoyed the royal favour and recovered some of its former prestige. Louis XI died in 1483 at Plessis; the court moved to Amboise.

Silk weaving and Wars of Religion – Louis XI had promoted the weaving of silk and cloth of gold in Lyons but the project had not met with much enthusiasm so the weavers and their looms were moved to Touraine. The industry reached its highest output in the midldle of the 17C when 11 000 looms were at work and there were two fairs each year. In 1680 decline set in under the effect of competition from Lyons; in 1789 only 1 000 looms were at work in Tours. The silk industry has experienced a modest recovery in the 20C *(see below).*

In this world of craftsmen, intellectuals and artists, the **Reformation** found its first supporters and Tours, like Lyons or Nimes, became one of the most active centres of the new religion. In 1562 the Calvinists caused great disorder, particularly in St Martin's Abbey.

TOURS

Alouette (Av. de l') ...... X 2
Bordiers (R. des) .... U 8
Boyer (R. Léon) .... V 9
Brulon (R. Léon)
  St-Avertin .... X 14
Chevallier (R. A.) .... V 19
Churchill
  (Bd Winston) .... V 20
Delaroche (R.) .... U 30
Eiffel (Av. Gustave) ... U 33
Entraigues (E. d') ...... U 35
Gaulle (Av. Gal de) ..... V 38
Giraudeau (R.) .... V 39

Grammont (Av. de) ..... V 41
Grand Sud (Av.) .... U 45
Groison (R.) .... U 47
Jaurès (bd Jean)
  St-Pierre-des-Corps ... V 51
Lac (Av. du)
  St-Avertin .... V 53
Larçay (R. de)
  St-Avertin .... X 54
Marmoutier (Q. de) .... U 60
Martyrs (R. des)
  Joué-les-Tours .... X 63
Moulin (R. Jean)
  St-Pierre-des-Corps ... V 70
Pas-Notre-Dame
  (R. du) .... U 75

Paul-Bert (Q.) .... U 76
Portillon (Q. de) .... U 79
Proud'hon (Av.) .... V 81
République (Av. de la) ... U 84
République (Av. de la)
  Chambray-lès-Tours ... X 85
St-Avertin (Rte de) ...... X 87
St-Cyr (Q. de)
  St-Cyr-s-Loire .... V 88
St-Sauveur (Pont) ...... V 90
Sanitas (Pont du) ...... VX 93
Tranchée (Av. de la) .... U 96
Vaillant (R. E.) .... V 98
Verdun (Bd de)
  Joué-les-Tours .... X 100
Wagner (Bd R.) .... V 105

The Roman Catholics were merciless in their revenge; ten years before Paris Tours had its own St Bartholomew's massacre: 200 to 300 Huguenots were drowned in the Loire. In May 1589 Henri III and the Parliament retreated from Paris to Tours which once again resumed its role as the royal capital. In the early 17C, a new wall, the lay-out of which may be seen in large boulevards such as Heurteloup and Béranger, doubled the space inside the city. In the latter half of the 18C, extensive town-planning by royal decree opened up a wide road on a north-south axis along which Tours was to develop in the future.

Nevertheless, in the 17C and 18C Tours lost its political and economic importance and in 1801 the population had dropped to only 20 000 inhabitants, less than Angers and Orléans. In the 19C development was slow; there was some building and improvement but little industry. The railway acted as a stimulant and the station at St-Pierre-des-Corps was the focus of renewed activity. In 1921 Tours had overtaken Orléans with 75 000 inhabitants.

Wars – Owing to its communications facilities Tours was chosen in 1870 as the **seat of the Government for the National Defence** but three months later, in the face of the Prussian advance, the government withdrew to Bordeaux. In June 1940 the same chain of events took place but at greater speed. The town was bombed and burned for three days from 19 to 21 September. In 1944 the bombardments began again: 136 people were killed on 20 May. In all, between 1940 and 1944, 1 543 buildings were destroyed and 7 960 were damaged; the town centre and the districts on the banks of the Loire were the most afflicted.

LIFE IN TOURS

Tours has now overflowed from its original site between the Loire and the Cher and consists of a huge conurbation (250 000ha - 965sq miles). The course of the Cher has been straightened and canalised for 7km - 1/2 miles to provide two residential areas, an artificial lake (25ha - 62 acres) and water sports facilities.

Tour has many light industries: processing, pharmaceutical laboratories, printing works. A factory making tyres has been built by Michelin in Joué-lès-Tours on the southwest edge of the city. Tours has not abandoned its traditional livelihood; Jacquard still has 100 looms producing silk and velvet cloth, which is exported throughout the world or used to refurbish the many châteaux and houses in France.

Tours is an important centre for both road and rail trafic; it is also the economic centre for the west central region of France and a market for the wine and agricultural products of the area; there are two fairs, in May and September. The recent Tours-Val de Loire International Congress Centre, or **Vinci** building, beside the SNCF railway station, should further the city's international image. The glass and metal construction with a bold interior design is by the architect Jean Nouvel who was also responsible for the highly innovative Arab Institute (Institut du Monde Arabe) in Paris.

In July on St Anne's day the picturesque garlic and basil fair is held, while an important flower market takes place every Wednesday and Saturday on Boulevard Béranger.

The varied cultural and intellectual life of the city is supported by the university with its 22 000 students, the Centre for Advanced Studies of the Renaissance, the National Conservatory of Music, the Regional School of Fine Arts, a National Centre for Urban Archaeology and by the various specialist institutes of higher education, including a business school.

★★OLD TOURS time: 1 1/2 hours

The vast restoration work begun about 1970 around Place Plumereau and the building of the Faculty of Letters beside the Loire have brought the old quarter to life; its narrow streets, often pedestrian precincts, have attracted shops and craftsmen, and the whole quarter, near the university, has become one of the liveliest parts of town.

★**Place Plumereau** – This picturesque and animated square, formerly the hat market (Carroi aux Chapeaux), is lined with fine 15C timber-framed houses alternating with stone façades.

On the corner of Rue du Change and Rue de la Monnaie there is a lovely house with two slate-hung gables with posts decorated with sculptures; close attention to the corner post will reveal a representation of the Nativity (15C).

Continue down Rue du Change to the corner of Rue de la Rôtisserie where there is an old façade with wooden lattice work. Retrace your steps to Place Plumereau.

To the north of the square a vaulted passageway opens on to the attractive little **Place St-Pierre-le-Puellier,** with its pleasant gardens; excavations have uncovered, among others, a 1C Gallo-Roman public building, 11C and 13C cemeteries and the foundations of the old church after which the square is named. Part of the nave is still visible on one side of the square and from the Rue Briçonnet. To the north, a large ogive-vaulted porch opens on to a small square where four centuries of architecture are harmoniously represented together.

★**Rue Briçonnet** – This charming street is bordered by houses showing a rich variety of local styles: from the Romanesques façade to the 18C mansion. No 35 by the narrow Rue du Poirier has a Romanesque façade, no 31 has a Gothic façade (late 13C); opposite (no 32) is a Renaissance house with lovely wooden statues. Not far away an elegant stair tower marks the entrance to Place St-Pierre-le-Puellier. Further north on the left, nos 23 and 21 have classical façades. No 16 is **Tristan's House** (Maison de Tristan – **K**) ⊘, a remarkable brick and stone construction with a late-15C pierced gable; one of the window lintels in the courtyard bears the inscription *Prie Dieu Pur,* an anagram of the name of Pierre Dupui, who built the mansion.

Gemmail Museum (Musée du Gemmail) (M³) ⊘ – *Entrance no 7 Rue du Mûrier.* A beautiful Restoration building with columns, **Hôtel Raimbault** (1835) contains an exhibition of non-leaded stained-glass windows which have the luminosity of ordinary stained glass and the brilliance of precious stones *(see p 40).*

The 70 pieces on display are the work of master craftsmen whose art is that of a colourist working from a cartoon; the 12C underground chapel is decorated with stained glass and a studio has been reconstructed in the old stables.

Rue Bretonneau – No 33 is a 16C mansion with a fine décor of Renaissance foliage; the north wing was added about 1875.

Rue des Cerisiers – To the west of Rue Bretonneau, no 21 is a 15C house with a Gothic façade.

Rue Paul-Louis Courier – In the inner courtyard, above the doorway of the 15C-16C Hôtel Binet (no 10) is an elegant wooden gallery served by two spiral staircases.

Petit-St-Martin District – In this pedestrian zone, there are numerous art and craft workshops, particularly around the charming **Place Robert-Picou**, formerly the Herb market (Carroi aux herbes).

Place de Châteauneuf – There is a fine view of the **Charlemagne Tower (Q)**, and the remains of the **old Basilica of St-Martin** built in the 11C and 13C over the tomb of the great Bishop of Tours, after the Vikings had destroyed the 5C sanctuary. The new building was as famous as the old for its size and splendour. Sacked by the Huguenots in 1562 it fell into disrepair during the Revolution and its vaulting collapsed. The nave was pulled down in 1802 to make way for the construction of the Rue des Halles. Charlemagne Tower which dominated the north transept, isolated since that time, partially collapsed in 1928, but carefully restored, still has its noble appearance. From the Rue des Halles, note a fine sculptured capital dating from the 12C. At the top of the tower a low-relief dating from the restoration work depicts St Martin sharing his mantle.

Further along Rue des Halles stands the **Clock Tower** (Tour de l'Horloge – **V**) marking the façade of the basilica; in the 19C it was crowned with a dome.

The **new Basilica of St-Martin**, built between 1886 and 1924 in neo-Byzantine style, has the shrine of St Martin in the crypt; it is still the object of pilgrimages.

OLD BASILICA OF ST MARTIN

0 — 40 m

Extant — Demolished

R. de Châteauneuf — Charlemagne Tower — Pl. de Châteauneuf

R. des 3 Pavés Ronds — R. du Change — St Martin's Tomb — NEW BASILICA OF ST MARTIN

Rue des Halles — Descartes

Clock Tower — Rue Julien Leroy — ST MARTIN'S CLOISTERS

★**Hôtel Gouin (M⁴)** ⊘ – This mansion, a perfect example of living accommodation during the Renaissance, is one of the most interesting in Tours. Burnt out in 1940, the north façade with the staircase tower and the **south façade**★ with finely-sculpted Renaissance foliage scrolls were, however, spared.

It houses the **museum** of the Touraine Archaelogical Society which has a very varied collection of exhibits from the Prehistoric era through the Gallo-Roman, medieval and Renaissance periods to the 19C.

Displayed against a background of 18C panelling are the instruments from the medicine chest at Chenonceau Château designed by Dupin de Francueil and Jean-Jacques Rousseau as part of the education of the former's son.

Other items in the artistic display are an Archimedes' screw, an inclined plane, a vacuum pump, etc.

Tours - Hôtel Gouin

Museum of St Martin (M⁶) ⊙ – The museum in Rue Rapin is housed in the 13C Chapel of St John, a former outbuilding of St Martin's Cloisters. Texts and engravings evoke the main events of the life of the saint and his influence on the Christian world borne out by the many churches dedicated to him not only in France, where about 4 000 bear his name, but throughout Europe. The museum also displays remains from the basilicas built in succession over the saint's tomb. Among them are carved marble items from the one built in about 470 as well as murals and mosaics from the 11C Romanesque basilica. There is also a model of the last edifice, showing its appearance before it was destroyed between 1797 and 1802.

Before leaving Rue Rapin, note the old houses, particularly the one at no 6 which is the Centre for Advanced Studies of the Renaissance.

★★ CATHEDRAL DISTRICT *time: 2 hours*

★★ St Gatien's Cathedral (CY) – The cathedral was begun in the mid-13C and completed in the 16C.

It demonstrates the complete evolution of the French Gothic style; the chevet is typical of the early phase, the transept and nave of the development and the Flamboyant west front belongs to the final phase. The first traces of the Renaissance are visible in the tops of the towers.

Despite the mixture of styles the soaring **west front** is a harmonious whole. Monotony is avoided by the slight asymmetry of detail. The foundations of the towers are a Gallo-Roman wall; the solid buttresses show that the bases are Romanesque. The rich Flamboyant decoration was added to the west front in the 15C: pierced tympana, festooned archivolts, ornamented gables over the doorways; the buttresses, which reach to the base of the belfries, were decorated at the same period with niches and crocketed pinnacles.

The 15C superstructure of the north tower is surmounted by an elegant lantern dome in the early-Renaissance style. The south belfry, which was built in the 16C on the Romanesque tower, is also surmounted by a lantern dome in the late Renaissance style.

The **interior** of the cathedral is striking for the purity of its lines. The 14C and 15C nave blends perfectly with the **chancel** which is older, one of the most beautiful works of the 13C.

The **stained-glass windows★★** are the pride of the cathedral. Those in the chancel with their warm colours are 13C. The rose windows in the transept are 14C; the south window is slightly diamond-shaped and the north one is divided by a supporting rib. The windows in the third chapel in the south aisle and the great rose window in the nave are 15C.

The chapel which opens into the south transept contains the **tomb★** of the children of Charles VIII, a graceful work by the school of Michel Colombe (16C), mounted on a base carved by Jerome de Fiesole.

★ The Psalette (Cathedral Cloisters) (CY F) ⊙ – This is an elegant Gothic-Renaissance building where the canons and choir master met, hence the name Psalette – where the psalms were sung.

The cloisters, which are on the north side of the cathedral, have three ranges: the west range (1460) supports the first-floor library while the north and east ranges (1508-24) are almost completely covered by terraces. A graceful Renaissance spiral stair leads up to the tiny archive room (1520) next to the library, a beautiful room with ogive vaulting and an exhibition of the 13C-14C frescoes from the church in Beaumont-Village.

★ Place Grégoire-de-Tours (CY 46) – Fine view of the east end of the cathedral and the Gothic flying buttresses;

to the left is the medieval gable of the **archbishop's palace** (now the Fine Arts Museum): the decisions of the ecclesiastical court were read out from the Renaissance gallery. Note, in Rue Manceau, a 15C canon's house with two gabled dormers and at the beginning of Rue Racine, a tufa building with a 15C pointed roof which housed the Justice-des-Bains – the seat of jurisdiction of the metropolitan chapter. This had been built over the ruins of a Gallo-Roman amphitheatre which, during the Renaissance, was mistakenly believed to have been baths.

A little further along Rue Racine is the **Contemporary Arts Centre** (Centre de Création Contemporaine) (CY N) ⊙ which organises temporary exhibitions of all forms of contemporary art.

> *Continue to Place des Petites Boucheries and take Rue Auguste-Blanqui, then bear right into Rue du Petit Cupidon.*

On the corner of Rue du Petit Cupidon and Rue des Ursulines is an arched passage through buildings which leads into the garden of the Archives of the Indre-et-Loire. This spot contains the best preserved part of the Gallo-Roman walls and the ancient city of *Caesarodunum* with one of its defence towers, known as the Tour du Petit Cupidon and, carved out of the wall, the southern postern which would have been the entrance to a Roman road.

Further along the Rue des Ursulines, on the left, is the 17C **Chapel of St-Michel** in which Mary of the Incarnation is remembered. She was an Ursuline nun who left Tours to spread to Gospel in Canada and founded the first Ursuline convent in Quebec in 1639. *(See Michelin Green Guide Quebec).*

> *Continue to the end of the street to Place François-Sicard.*

The square is named after the sculptor François Sicard who was born in Tours in 1862 and who made a number of sculptures for his home town. A statue of another artist from Tours, Michel Colombe *(qv),* stands in the middle of the square.

★★ Fine Arts Museum (Musée des Beaux-Arts) (CY M²) ⊙ – The museum is housed in the old archbishop's palace (17C-18C);

a gigantic cedar of Lebanon, of perfect shape, was planted in the main courtyard in 1804.

The round tower (left) is recognizable as part of the Gallo-Roman wall from its alternate bands of brick and stone. From the formal garden there is a good **view** of the front of the museum and the cathedral.

The rooms, which are decorated with Louis XVI panelling and silks made in Tours, make a perfect setting for the works of art, some of which used to adorn the châteaux of Richelieu and Chanteloup (now demolished) and the abbeys of Touraine: the Duke of Choiseul's desk, a lacquer commode, paintings by Boucher, Nattier and Rigaud, portraits by Largillière, Tocque, Perronneau and Vestier, sculptures by Le Moyne and Houdon, 17C Flemish and Dutch paintings including a famous ex-voto by Rubens and a *Flight into Egypt* by Rembrandt.

Among the 14C and 15C paintings on the ground floor are some Italian primitives and the museum's masterpieces, *Christ in the Garden of Olives* and *The Resurrection* both by **Mantegna.** There is also a room devoted to Greek and Etruscan ceramics.

The second floor is devoted to 19C and 20C work: Delacroix, Chasseriau, Boulanger's portrait of Balzac, Impressionist canvases and works by Calder *(qv);* one room is devoted to the

Bordeaux (R. de) . . **BZ**
Commerce (R. du) **AY 22**
Grammont (Av. de) **BZ**
Halles (Pl. et R.) . . . **AY**

Marceau (R.) . . . . . . **ABYZ**
Nationale (R.) . . . . **BYZ**
Scellerie (R. de la) . . . . **BY**

Bretonneau (R.) . . . . . . **AY 10**
Briçonnet (R.) . . . . **AY 12**
Carmes (Pl. des) . . . . . **AY 16**

contemporary painter Oliver Debré. There is also a display of **ceramics** by Avisseau (19C), a native of Touraine: plates decorated with motifs in relief in the style of Bernard Palissy.

Castle (Château) (CY) – A tree-lined walk beside the Loire skirts the heterogeneous buildings of the castle, reminders of past ages. The Guise Tower **(Tour de Guise)**, with machicolations and a pepperpot roof, was part of the 13C fortress; it owes its name to the young Duke of Guise who was imprisoned in the castle after the assassination of his father *(see Blois)* and then escaped. Next to it stands the **Mars Pavilion**, which was built in the reign of Louis XVI and is flanked on the south side by a 13C round tower.

★ **Historial Museum (Historical de Touraine)** ⊘ – The museum, which is housed in the rooms of the Mars Pavilion and the Guise Tower, recalls the great moments in the history of Touraine in some 30 waxwork tableaux with 165 figures in rich apparel. The most spectacular scenes show the marriage of Charles VIII and Anne of Brittany, the workshop of Jean Chapillon and his companion smiths, a ball at the court of the Valois, etc. A tropical **aquarium** ⊘ presents over 150 varieties of tropical fish. On the quay stands the **Governors' Lodging (CY L)**, a 15C building with gable dormers. At its base and running towards the Guise Tower is the Gallo-Roman wall, composed of courses of brick alternating with small stones, typical of the period. On the second floor, the **Tours History Workshop** (Atelier Histoire de Tours) ⊘, which was founded in close collaboration with the National Urban Archaeology Centre and Laboratory, contains archaeological and historical documents as well as models and audio-visual presentations which explain the history of Tours and the development of its townscape. In conjunction with these permanent displays there are temporary exhibitions about living in Tours (Vivre à Tours) which highlight its history.

★ **ST-JULIEN DISTRICT** (BY) *time: 1 hour*

The streets near the bridge over the Loire suffered considerable bomb damage in the Second World War; behind the regular modern façades in Rue Nationale some picturesque little squares have still survived.

Wilson Bridge (AY) – The stone bridge was built in the 18C when the route from Paris to Spain passed through Tours rather than Amboise.

St Julian's Church (BY) – The 11C belfry porch is set back from the street in front of the 13C church; the sombre Gothic interior is lit by windows (1960) by Max Ingrand and Le Chevalier. Originally it had adjoining cloisters (now a garden) and conventual buildings. The Gothic chapter house still exists, and **St Julian's Cellars** (12C), is a huge vaulted chamber which now houses the **Touraine Wine Museum (BY M¹)** ⊘.

Châteauneuf (R. de) ...	**AY** 18	Grand-Marché (R. du) .. **AY** 44	Monnaie (R. de la) .... **AY** 68

Châteauneuf (R. de) ... **AY** 18   Grand-Marché (R. du) .. **AY** 44   Monnaie (R. de la) .... **AY** 68
Constantine (R. de) .... **AY** 23   Grégoire-de-Tours (Pl.) . **CY** 46   Paix (R. de la) .... **AY** 73
Courier (R. P.L.) .... **AY** 25   Grosse-Tour (R. de la) . **AY** 49   Petit-Cupidon (R. du).. **CY** 77
Courteline (R. G.) ...... **AY** 27   Lavoisier (R.) .... **BY** 57   Picou (Pl. R.) .... **AY** 78
Cygne (R. du) .... **BY** 28   Manceau (R.) .... **CY** 59   Racine (R.) .... **CY** 82
Descartes (R.) .... **AY** 32   Merville (R. du Prés.) .. **AY** 65   Rapin (Rue) .... **AZ** 83
Grand-Marché (Pl. du) . **AY** 43   Meusnier (R. Gén.) .... **CY** 66   Victoire (Pl. de la) .... **AY** 102

★★**Trade Guild Museum** (Musée du Compagnonnage) (BY M⁵) ⊘ – *Entrance through a porch, 8 Rue Nationale, and a footbridge.*
The museum is housed in the Guest Room (11C) and the **monks' dormitory** (16C) above the chapter house of St Julian's Abbey. It traces the history, customs and skills of the trade guilds which provided training for their members and protected their interests. Both current and obsolete trades are represented through their tools, historical documents and the many **masterpieces** which the **companions** (derived from *cum panis* and meaning someone with whom one shares one's bread) had to produce to become master craftsmen.

★**Beaune-Semblançay Garden** (BY B) – *Entrance through a porch, 28 Rue Nationale.* The Hôtel de Beaune-Semblançay belonged to the unfortunate Minister of Finance who was beheaded during the reign of François I. Bombs destroyed most of the Renaissance mansion except for an arcaded gallery supporting a chapel, a beautiful façade decorated with pilasters and surrounded by plants, and the charming and finely-carved **Beaune Fountain.**
In Rue Jules-Favre stands the sober and elegant façade of the chamber of commerce (**Palais du Commerce** – BY C) which was built in the 18C for the merchants of Tours; the courtyard is more elaborately decorated.

Rue Colbert (BY) – Before Wilson Bridge was built, this street together with its extension, Rue du Commerce, was the main axis of the city. The half-timbered house at no 41 bears the sign "A la Pucelle armée" (The Armed Maid); Joan of Arc's armour is believed to have been made by the craftsman living here in April 1429. Rue Colbert and Rue de la Scellerie, which is reached via Rue du Cygne, are full of antique dealers.

Place Foire-le-Roi (BY) – This was the site of the free fairs established by François I; it was also the stage for the mystery plays which were performed when the kings visited Tours. The north side is lined by 15C gabled houses. The beautiful Renaissance mansion (no 8) belonged to Philibert Babou de la Bourdaisière *(see Montlouis-sur-Loire).* On the west side a side street leads into the narrow and winding "Passage du Cœur-Navré" (Broken-Heart Passage) which leads into Rue Colbert.

★**St Cosmas' Priory** (V) ⊘ – *Plan p 194. 3km - 2 miles west via Quai du Pont-Neuf and its continuation Avenue Proudhon, then along the riverside embankment.* The priory, not much more than a ruin, is situated in a peaceful place in the middle of well-cared-for gardens; there remain a few traces of the church at ground level, as well as the chevet wall, the chancel and the ambulatory (11C and 12C); the poet **Ronsard** *(qv)* was buried here in 1585. He was Prior of St Cosmas' from 1565 until his death; a stone slab with a flowering rose bush covers his tomb.

In the monks' refectory, a large 12C building, note the reader's pulpit decorated with columns and sculptured capitals. The **Prior's lodging**, where Ronsard lived and died, is a charming small 15C house; in Ronsard's time an outside staircase led to the first floor of the residence, which only had one great room on each level; this staircase was pulled down in the 17C when the inside staircase was built. The "lodging" now houses a small **lapidary museum;** a collection of drawings, plans, photos, engravings and an audio-visual presentation evoke the poet's life.

Plessis-lès-Tours Château (V B) ⊘ – *Plan p 194*. This modest brick building is only a small part of the château built by Louis XI in the 15C, which consisted of three wings in a U-shape. The visit includes the room where Louis XI died, surrounded by linenfold panelling, popular in the 15C; various other rooms evoke the memory of Louis XI.

Son of Charles VII and Marie of Anjou, **Louis XI** was born in Bourges in 1423 and acceded to the throne in 1461. He spent a lot of time at Plessis-lès-Tours. Anxious to encourage the economic expansion of his kingdom after the ravages of the Hundred Years War, he developed industry and trade. His struggle with the Duke of Burgundy, Charles the Bold, who had designs on the crown, ended in the defeat and death of the Duke in 1477, and annexation of part of the Duchy in 1482. Louis XI's last years were clouded; fearing an attack on his life and imagining that he had leprosy, he lived in a fog of mistrust and superstition. The betrayal of Cardinal **Jean Balue** appeared in this context: a favourite of Louis XI who showered him with honours, the cardinal secretly conspired with the Duke of Burgundy; he was unmasked in 1469 and imprisoned at Loches until 1480, but lived another 11 years after his release.

On the first floor there are paintings and sculptures recalling the memory of St Francis of Paola, a Calabrian hermit, whom Louis XI called to his side at the end of his life. St Francis was the founder of the ascetic Minim Order; he established his first French community on the royal estate at Plessis.

EXCURSIONS

★**Meslay Tithe Barn (Grange de Meslay)** ⊘ – *10km - 7 miles northeast by ② on the plan, N 10 and a road to the right.*
This former fortified farm belonging to Marmoutier Abbey has a beautiful porch, the remains of a perimeter wall and a remarkable **barn.** The barn is a very good example of 13C secular architecture. The rounded main door is set in a pointed gable and the 15C timber roof is supported by 4 rows of oak heartwood pillars. Touraine music concerts *(see Calendar of Events)* and art exhibitions are held in this barn.

Montbazon – Pop 3 354. Facilities. *9km - 5 1/2 miles south by ⑨ on the plan.*
This is one of the twenty fortresses built by Fulk Nerra *(qv)*. From the ruined **keep** which dominates the village there is a good view *(Rue des Moulins on the left of the Town Hall and a path on the right beyond the old gateway)*.

Mettray Dolmen – *12km - 8 miles northwest by ⑭ on the plan, N 138 turning right into D 76 to Mettray.*
In a spinney in St-Antoine-du-Rocher to the north of Mettray on the right bank of the Choisille *(access by a stone path: sign)* stands the beautiful dolmen of the "Fairy Grotto", one of the most skilfully constructed megalithic monuments in France; it is 11m - 37ft long and 3.7m - 12ft high and consists of twelve evenly-cut stone slabs.

*Some hotels have their own tennis court, swimming pool, private beach or garden. Consult the current edition of the annual **Michelin Red Guide France.***

TROO
Pop 320

Michelin map 🔢 fold 5 or 🔢 fold 24 or 🔢 fold 1 – Local map under LOIR VALLEY: Vendôme-La Flèche

Troo, which perches on a steeply-rising slope and is distinguished from afar by its belfry tower, still has numerous troglodyte dwellings. The houses rising in tiers, one above the other, are linkéd by narrow alleys, stairways and mysterious passages. A labyrinth of galleries, called *caforts* (short for *caves fortes*), exists underground in the white tufa rock. In times of war these *caforts* served as hideouts.

SIGHTS

★**The "Butt" (Butte)** – This is a feudal motte which provides a splendid **panorama** (viewing table and telescope) of the sinuous course of the River Loir and of the small church of St-Jacques-des-Guérets on the far bank.

St Martin's Collegiate Church – The collegiate church was built in 1050 and altered a century later. It is dominated by a remarkable square tower pierced by openings; the splays are ornamented with small columns in characteristic Angevin style. The windows in the Romanesque apse are Gothic. The nave and chancel are covered by a convex vault. The historiated capitals at the transept crossing are Romanesque. The choir stalls and communion table are 15C. The 16C wooden statue is of St Mamès who is invoked against all stomach ailments.

Great Well (Grand puits) – It is known also as the "talking well" because of its excellent echo; it is 45m - 148ft deep and covered by a wooden shingle roof.

St Catherine's Leper-house (Maladrerie Ste-Catherine) – On the eastern edge of the town on the south side of D 917 stands a 12C building with fine Romanesque blind arcades. Originally it was a hospice for sick pilgrims travelling to Tours or Compostela; there was also a leper-house to the west of Troo. When the latter disappeared the hospice took over its goods and its name.

Petrifying Cave (Grotte pétrifiante) ⊘ – The cave which continually streams with water contains stalactites and lime-encrusted objects.

Church of St-Jacques-des-Guérets – The services in this church were

conducted by the Augustinians from the abbey of St George in the Wood (St-Georges-des-Bois) southeast of Troo.

The murals★ were painted between 1130 and 1170 and show Byzantine influence; the drawing and the freshness of the colours are particularly attractive. The most beautiful are in the apse: the Crucifixion, in which the half-figures represent the sun and the moon, and the Resurrection of the Dead (left); Christ in Majesty, surrounded by the symbols of the Evangelists; and the Last Supper (right). Statues of St Augustine and St George adorn the embrasure of the central window. On the right side of the apse appears the Martyrdom of St James who was beheaded by Herod, with Paradise above: the elect shelter in niches like pigeonholes. High up on the south wall of the nave is St Nicholas performing a miracle: the saint is throwing three gold pieces to three sisters whose father was about to sell them; below is the Resurrection of Lazarus. Further on is a vast composition representing the Descent into Hell: Jesus, majestic, delivers Adam and Eve. The left wall of the church was painted at different times from the 12C to 15C: Nativity and Massacre of the Innocents. In the church are two painted wooden statues (16C): in a niche (left) St James on a base which bears the arms of Savoy; in the chancel (left) St Peter.

For a quiet place to stay

*Consult the annual **Michelin Red Guide France** (hotels and restaurants)*
*and the **Michelin Guide Camping Caravaning France***
which offer a choice of pleasant hotels and quiet campsites
in convenient locations.

★★ USSÉ CHÂTEAU

Michelin map 64 fold 13 or 232 fold 34 (14km - 8 miles northeast of Chinon) – Local map under LOIRE VALLEY: Orléans-Chinon

The château stands with its back to a cliff on the edge of Chinon Forest and looks down over its terraced gardens to the River Indre. Its impressive bulk and fortified towers contrast with the white stone, the myriad roofs, the turrets, dormers and chimneys which rise against a green background. The best places for a good view are on the bridge, some 200m - 220yds from the château, or on the Loire embankment. According to tradition, when Perrault, the great writer of fairy tales, was looking for a setting for the Sleeping Beauty, he took Ussé as his model. This story is illustrated by waxwork tableaux in the attics *(access by the sentry walk)*.

From the Bueils to the Blacas. – Ussé is a very old fortress; in the 15C it became the property of a great family from Touraine, the Bueils who had distinguished themselves in the Hundred Years War (1337-1453). In 1485, Antoine de Bueil, who had married one of the daughters of Charles VII and Agnès Sorel, sold Ussé to the Espinays, a Breton family who had been chamberlains and cupbearers to the Duke of Brittany, Louis XI and Charles VIII. It was they who built the courtyard ranges and the chapel in the park. The château often changed hands. Among its owners was Vauban's son-in-law; the great engineer often stayed at Ussé. The estate now belongs to the Marquis of Blacas.

TOUR ⊘

The outside walls (15C) have a military aspect while the buildings overlooking the courtyard are more welcoming and some even have a touch of the Renaissance style; they have been much restored. The courtyard is enclosed by three ranges: the east wing is Gothic, the south is partly Gothic and partly classical, the west is Renaissance; the north wing was removed in the 17C to open up the view of the Loire and Indre Valleys from the terrace. The west wing is prolonged by a 17C pavilion.

The interior has several fine features: a fine 17C *trompe-l'œil* ceiling and a collection of oriental arms; a chapel with a Mazarin writing-desk; the kitchens with an opening to the cellars beneath; the great gallery hung with Flemish tapestries; the grand staircase (17C); an antechamber containing a beautiful 16C Italian ebony cabinet inlaid in the interior with ivory and mother-of-pearl; the State Bedchamber (chambre du roi) with its 18C furniture and hangings; the great gallery on the first floor with its paintings. There is also an

Ussé Château
Flemish tapestry after Teniers the Younger

exhibition of historic costumes. The chapel, which stands alone in the park, was built between 1520 and 1538. It is a pure Renaissance building; the west façade is the most remarkable.

The letters C and L, which appear elsewhere and are one of the decorative elements, are the initials of Charles d'Espinay, who built the chapel, and of his wife, Lucrèce de Pons.

The light and soaring interior is decorated with a beautiful pendant keystone and 16C carved stalls in the chancel, and an attractive Virgin in enamelled earthenware by Luca della Robbia in the south chapel which has ogive vaulting.

★★ VALENÇAY CHÂTEAU

Michelin map 🟥 fold 18 or 🟥 fold 16

Geographically Valençay is in the Berry region but the château belongs to the Loire Valley owing to the period of its construction and its huge size in which it resembles Chambord.

A Financier's Château – Valençay was built c1540 by Jacques d'Estampes, the owner of the castle then existing. He had married the daughter of a financier, who brought him a large dowry, and he wanted a residence worthy of his new fortune. The 12C castle was demolished and in its place rose the present sumptuous building.

Finance has often been involved in the history of Valençay; among its owners were several Farmers-General and even the famous **John Law** *(qv)* whose dizzy banking career was an early and masterly example of inflation.

Charles-Maurice de Talleyrand-Périgord, who had begun his career under Louis XVI as Bishop of Autun, was Foreign Minister when he bought Valençay in 1803 at the request of Napoleon, so that he would have somewhere to receive important foreign visitors. Talleyrand managed his career so skilfully that he did not finally retire until 1834.

Son et Lumière – *See the Calendar of Events at the end of the guide.*

TOUR ⊘ *time: 1 hour*

The entrance pavilion is a huge building, designed like a keep but for show not defence with many windows, harmless turrets and fancy machicolations. The steep roof is pierced with high dormer windows and surmounted by monumental chimneys. Such architecture is also found in the Renaissance châteaux of the Loire Valley but here there are also the first signs of the classical style: superimposed pilasters with Doric (ground floor), Ionic (first floor) and Corinthian (second foor) capitals.

The classical style is even more evident in the huge corner towers: domes take the place of the pepperpot roofs which were the rule on the banks of the Loire in the 16C.

West Wing – This wing was added in the 17C and altered in the 18C. At roof level mansard windows alternate with bulls' eyes (circular apertures). The tour of the ground floor includes the great Louis XVI vestibule; the gallery devoted to the Talleyrand-Périgord family; the Grand Salon and the Blue Salon which contain many works of art and sumptuous Empire furniture including the famous "Congress of Vienna" table; the apartments of the Duchess of Dino. On the first floor the bedroom of Prince Talleyrand is followed by the room occupied by Ferdinand VII, King of Spain, when he was confined to Valençay by Napoleon from 1808 to 1814; the apartments of the Duke of Dino and those of Mme de Bénévent (portrait of the princess by Elisabeth Vigée-Lebrun); the great gallery (with a *Diana* by Houdon) and the great staircase. Something of the spirit of the festivities organised by Talleyrand and his master chef, Marie-Antoine Carème, still lingers in the great dining-room and the kitchens beneath.

VALENÇAY

Blois (R. de) 4
Château (R. du) 7
Halle (Pl. de la) 8
République (R.) 16

Abreuvoir (R. de l') 2
Auditoire (R. de l') 3
Chabris (Rte de) 5
Châtaigniers (R. des) . . 6
Hymans (R. Max) 9
Marnières (R. des) 10
Nationale (R.) 12
Résistance (Av. de la) . 18
St-Maurice (R.) 19
Talleyrand (R. de) 20
Tournebride (R. de) . . . 23

Park ⊘ – Black swans, ducks and peacocks strut freely in the formal gardens near the château. Under the great trees in the park deer, llamas, camels and kangaroos roam in vast enclosures.

Car Museum (Musée de l'Automobile du Centre) (M) ⊘ – The museum is concealed in the park; it contains the collection of the Guignard brother, the grandsons of a coach-builder from Vatan (Indre). There are over 60 old cars (the earliest dating from 1898), perfectly maintained in working order, including the 1908 Renault limousine used by Presidents Poincaré and Millerand; there are also road documents from the early days of motoring, old Michelin maps and guides from before 1914.

EXCURSIONS

Luçay-le-Mâle – Pop 2 159. *10km - 6 miles southwest by the D 960.*
This quiet village contains an interesting **Gunflint Museum** ⊘. Like Selles-sur-Cher and Meusnes *(qv)*, Luçay contributed for many years to the local production of gunflint which came from a deposit of high-quality flint. The museum displays documents on the extraction, the processing and sale of gunflint from the 17C to 19C when the percussion cap was invented. The way of life of the craftsmen is shown, their tools and techniques, the sale price and the export market of the product.

★★ VENDÔME   Pop 17 525

Michelin map 🔢 fold 6 or 🔢 fold 2 – Local maps under LOIR VALLEY: Bonneval-Vendôme and Vendôme-La Flèche – Facilities
Town plan in the current Michelin Red Guide France.

At the foot of a steep bluff, which is crowned by a castle, the River Loir divides into sevral channels which flow slowly under the many bridges of Vendôme (**boat trips**) ⊘. The belfries, gables and steep slate roofs of the old town huddle on the islands in the river while the more recent districts now extend to the bluff. The traditional glove making which started in the Renaissance period has been joined by printing, the manufacture of car components, machine and aircraft controls and plastics.

A troubled history – Although the origins of Vendôme go back to the neolithic and Gaulish periods and the town received its name, Vindocenum, in the Gallo-Roman period, it only began to acquire importance under the Counts, first the Bouchard family, who were faithful supporters of the Capet dynasty, and particularly under the son of Fulk Nerra *(qv)*, Geoffrey Martel (11C), who founded Holy Trinity Abbey.
Since the Count of Vendôme was a vassal of the Plantagenets, his domain was involved in the Hundred Years War: its position on the border between the French and English possessions made it particularly vulnerable. In 1371 the royal house of Bourbon inherited Vendôme and in 1515 François I raised it to a duchy. In 1589 the town sided with the League but was captured by its overlord, Henri IV, and suffered for its disloyalty; the town was sacked and only Holy Trinity Church was left standing.

Henri IV's son, César – Henri IV gave Vendôme to César, his son by Gabrielle d'Estrées. César de Vendôme often lived in his domain during his years of conspiracy, first during the minority of Louis XIII and then against Richelieu. For four years he was imprisoned at Vincennes before being exiled. Finally he lent his support to Mazarin and died in 1655.

Balzac's schooldays – On 22 June 1807 the College of the Oratorians in Vendôme registered the entry of an eight-year-old boy, Honoré de Balzac. The future novelist was an absent-minded and undisciplined pupil. In those days the college discipline was severe as Balzac himself recalled: "once entered the pupils did not leave until the end of their studies... the traditional leather ferula still played its terrible role... letters to parents were obligatory on certain days, so was confession."
Balzac had little aptitude for riding the hobby-horse, the forerunner of the modern bicycle, and was laughed at by his fellow-pupils. He regularly got put into detention in order to read in peace. Such a regime undermined his health and his parents had to take him away. When he returned home his grandmother exclaimed in consternation: "look how the college returns the pretty children we send there".

HOLY TRINITY ABBEY

★**HOLY TRINITY ABBEY (LA TRINITÉ)** *time: 1 hour*

One summer night, Geoffrey Martel, Count of Anjou, saw three fiery spears plunge into a fountain and decided to found a monastery which was dedicated on 31 May 1040 to the Holy Trinity. Under the Benedictine Order the abbey grew considerably so that eventually the abbot was automatically made a cardinal also; in the 12C this office was held by the famous Geoffrey of Vendôme.

Until the Revolution pilgrims flocked to Holy Trinity to venerate the Holy Tear which Christ had shed on Lazarus' tomb and which Geoffrey Martel had brought back from Constantinople. The knights of Vendôme would rally to the cry of the "Holy Tear of Vendôme". The relic was venerated on "Lazarus' Friday" and its curative powers were invoked in the case of eye diseases; this explains the repeated use of the theme of the resurrection of Lazarus in the decoration of the church.

★★**Abbey Church** – The church is a remarkable example of Flamboyant Gothic architecture. The entrance to the abbey precinct is in Rue de l'Abbaye. On either side of the wall stand the Romanesque arcades of the Abbey granary which have been incorporated into more modern buildings; in fact from the 14C onwards the monks allowed the citizens to build their shops against the abbey walls.

Romanesque Belltower – Standing alone (right) is the 12C belltower, 80m - 262ft high, which served as a model for the Old Belltower of Notre-Dame de Chartres. The bays and arcades, which are blind at ground level, grow larger as the embrasures also increase in size. The transition from a square to an octagonal tower is made by means of openwork mini-belltowers at the corners. The base of the first storey is decorated with grinning masks and animals.

West Front – The astonishing Flamboyant west front, which is accentuated by a great incised gable, was built early in the 16C by Jean de Beauce, who designed the New Belltower of Chartres Cathedral; the decorative openwork is like a piece of lace and contrasts with the plainer Romanesque tower.

Interior – The nave, which was started at the transept end in the middle of the 14C was not completed until after the Hundred Years War; the transept, all that is left of the 11C building, leads to the chancel and ambulatory with its five radiating chapels.

The nave is remarkable for the width of the triforium and the height of the windows. The transition from the 14C to 15C phase of construction is achieved without spoiling the unity of conception: the capitals cease, the design of the frieze changes as does the decoration of the triforium and the ribs. The baptismal chapel (1) in the north aisle contains a beautiful Renaissance font in white marble supported by a carved foot from the gardens of Blois Château.

The primitive capitals of the transept crossing are surmounted by polychrome statues (13C) of the Virgin, the Archangel Gabriel, St Peter and St Eutropius who was venerated in the abbey church. The transept vaulting with its historiated keystones was altered in the 14C in the Angevin style *(see p 37)*; in the left transept are statues of John the Baptist (14C) and the Virgin (16C).

The 14C chancel, which is lit by windows of the same date, is decorated with beautiful late-15C stalls (2). The choir screen (3) enclosing the chancel shows Italian influence. To the left of the high altar is the base, decorated with tears, of the famous monument of the Holy Tear with a small aperture through which the relic was exposed by one of the monks.

The chapels radiating from the ambulatory are decorated with 16C stained glass which has been much restored: the best section, which shows the meal in Simon's house, taken from a German engraving, is in the first chapel to the left of the axial chapel containing a **window** dating from 1140 depicting the Virgin and Child (4).

Vendôme — 15C stalls in the Abbey Church

Conventual buildings – Only the east side of the 14C cloister exists in its entirety. In the 14C-15C **chapter house** ⊘ a number of wall-paintings have been exposed; they depict episodes from the life of Christ. The classical-style buildings now house a museum *(see below)*.

Take the passage through the south range of buildings to admire the monumental south front which was built between 1732 and 1742; the pediments bear the royal fleur de lys, the device (Pax) and the emblem (Lamb) of the Order of St Benedict.

★**Museum (M)** ⊘ – The collections are displayed in the abbey's monastic buildings which are reached by a majestic stairway.

The most interesting rooms on the ground floor are devoted to **mural painting**★ in the Loire valley and to **religious art**★ in the Vendôme area from the Middle Ages to the Renaissance. There are remains of the 16C tomb of Marie de Luxembourg and François de Bourbon-Vendôme, fragments of the funerary sculptures of Catherine and Jean VII de Bourbon, keystones from the cloister vaults, and an octagonal stoup which once formed part of the Holy Tear monument.

On the upper floors are the sections on archaeology and natural history. Certain rooms are devoted to 16C-19C paintings and furniture and to earthenware; there is a superb late-18C **harp**★, the work of Nadermann, Marie-Antoinette's instrument-maker, together with contemporary sculptures by the local artist Louis Leygue. Another room displays the tools used in the old local crafts and a reconstruction of a Vendôme rural interior.

ADDITIONAL SIGHTS

Public Garden (Jardin Public) – Running down to the riverside, the garden gives a good view over the town, the abbey and the 13C-14C **Water Gate** (Porte d'Eau or Arche des Grands Prés – **B**).

From the open space on the opposite bank, Place de la Liberté, there are views of the Water Gate from a different angle as well as of the 13C **Islette Tower (D)**. Together with St George's Gate (Porte St-Georges – *see below*) these structures are all that is left of the old ramparts.

Ronsard Park – Round this shady open space are the Lycée Ronsard (formerly the College of the Oratorians where Balzac was a pupil and now occupied by the offices of the Town Hall), the late-15C Hotel de Saillant (now the tourist information centre) and the municipal library with its important collection of old books including 11 incunabula. A 16C two-storeyed wash-house (**L**) is sited on the arm of the river running through the park. The *"Fallen Warrior"* on the lawn is a bronze by Louis Leygue *(see above)*.

St James' Chapel (Chapelle St-Jacques) – Rebuilt in the 15C, and subsequently attached to the College of the Oratorians, the chapel once served the pilgrims on their way to Compostela. It now houses temporary exhibitions.

Church of Mary Magdalen (La Madeleine) – 1474. The bell-tower is surmounted by an elegant crocketed spire.

VENDÔME

Change (R. du) 5
Poterie (R.)
République (Pl. de la) 14
St-Martin (Pl.) 19
Saulnerie (R.) 22

Abbaye (R. de l') 2

Béguines (R. des) 3
Bourbon (R. A.) 4
Chartrain (Fg) 6
Chevallier (R.) 7
Gaulle (R. du Gén.-de) 8
Grève (R. de la) 9
Guesnault (R.) 12
St-Bié (R.) 15
St-Jacques (R.) 18
Verdun (Av. de) 23

Place St-Martin (19) – Until the 19C St Martin's Church (15C-16C) stood here; only the belltower remains. There is also a fine 16C timber-framed house called the "Grand St-Martin"; it is ornamented with figures and coats of arms and has a statue of Marshal de Rochambeau *(qv)*.

St George's Gate (E) – This gate was the entrance to the town from the River Loir; it is flanked by towers which were mostly built in the 14C although the front facing the bridge is decorated with machicolations and carvings of dolphins and Renaissance medallions which were added early in the 16C by Marie de Luxembourg, Duchess of Vendôme. The gate was enlarged under the Empire to accommodate the passage of Napoleon's armies. Inside is the Council Chamber, in use since the 16C.

Castle (Château) ⊘ – Access by car via St-Lubin district and the Temple, a hamlet which grew up round a Templar commandery *(qv)*. The ruined castle is set on the top of "the Mountain" (la Montagne) which overlooks the Loir; it consists of an earth wall and ramparts with 13C and 14C machicolated round towers at intervals; the great Poitiers Tower **(F)** on the east side was reconstructed in the 15C.
The early-17C Beauce Gate **(K)** leads into the precinct which is now a huge garden. There are traces of the Collegiate Church of St George which was founded by Agnès of Burgundy and where the Counts of Vendôme were buried: Antoine de Bourbon and Jeanne d'Albret, the parents of Henri IV, were buried here.

The Mountain Walk (Promenade de la Montagne) – From the terraces there are picturesque **views**★ of Vendôme and the Loir Valley.

EXCURSIONS

Areines – 3km - 2 miles east by D 917 and the first turning left. See Areines.

Nourray – Pop 140. *11km - 7 miles south by N 10 and the third road on the left.*
The little **church** which stands alone in the square has a row of Romanesque arcades beneath carved corbels on the chevet; note the polylobed arch of the central window. In the interior the apse is surrounded by arcading with carved capitals.

Villemardy – Pop 241. *14km - 9 miles southeast by D 957; turn left to Périgny and bear right to Villemardy.*
The **church** dates from the 12C; the simple nave ends in a Gothic chancel. The interior decoration in carved oak is remarkably uniform; the high altar and tabernacle, which are surmounted by an altarpiece, are in the classical style, as are the two small symmetrical altars in the nave. The left wall of the chancel is decorated with a fresco (16C), the Adoration of the Magi, flanked by columns and a pediment in *trompe l'œil;* note the Virgin's headdress which helps to determine the date of the work.

Rhodon – Pop 79. *19km - 12 miles southeast by D 917 (direction Beaugency); in Villetrun turn right to Selommes (D 111) and then left (D 161).*
The internal walls and Gothic vaulting of the **church** bear traces of 14C and 15C mural paintings: Christ in Majesty in the apse and the Months of the Year on one of the transverse arches of the nave.

VERGER CHÂTEAU

Michelin map 64 south of fold 1 or 232 fold 20 (3km - 2 miles north of Seiches)

A great moat, flint towers with dressings and machicolations in white tufa, a gatehouse and imposing outbuildings *(private)* recall the huge residence which **Pierre de Rohan-Guéménée**, Marshal of Gié, started to build in 1482 and where he received Charles VIII whose life he had saved at Fornoue. De Rohan was a marshal of France at 25 and Louis XII's head of Council. In 1506 he intercepted the luggage of Anne of Brittany which he suspected of containing crown property; the king was thought to be dying. The queen had de Rohan banished to Verger.
In 1776 Cardinal de Rohan ordered the château to be demolished; the precious works of art which it contained were dispersed.

Michelin map 🟦 or 🟦 fold 35 — Local map under LOIRE VALLEY: Orléans Chinon

Villandry is one of the last great Renaissance châteaux to be built on the Loire; it has features unusual in Touraine, like rectangular pavilions (instead of the previous round towers) as well as the layout of the esplanade and its moat.
Villandry's international fame is however based not so much on its château as on its gardens, which are among the most fascinating in France.

★★★ THE GARDENS ⊘ time: 1/2 hour

The gardens at Villandry *(illustration p 209)* are the most complete example in France of the formal Renaissance style adopted under the influence of the Italian gardeners brought into the country by Charles VIII; French traditions nevertheless assert themselves in many of the details *(see p 38)*.
When Joachim de Carvallo, founder of the French Historic Houses Association, acquired Villandry in 1906, he set about restoring the gardens to their original state, previous owners having altered them beyong recognition.
The best overall **view** of the gardens is from the terraces to the rear of the château or from the top of the keep.
There are three terraces one above the other: the highest, the water garden has a fine sheet of water acting as a reservoir; below it is the flower garden, consisting of geometric designs outlined in box, one representing allegories of love, the other symbolising music; further designs are based on the Maltese, Languedoc and Basque crosses.
At the lowest level is the fascinating ornamental kitchen garden, a multi-coloured chequerboard of vegetables and fruit trees arranged in nine squares and enclosed by clipped hedges of box and yew. Between this and the church a herb garden has been laid out.
Canals, fountains, cascades, vine-covered pergolas, and the Romanesque village church all combine to make a charming background to the scene.
The flowers, shrubs and fruit trees known in the 16C were more or less the same species as today, though the potato had not yet arrived (introduced by Parmentier in the 18C). The art of gardening was already well-advanced, with pruning, grafting, the use of greenhouses and the raising of early vegetables.

★★ CHÂTEAU ⊘ time: 1/2 hour

Nothing remains of the early fortress except the keep, a square tower incorporated in the present structure which was built in the 16C by Jean Le Breton, Secretary of State to François I.
Three ranges of buildings enclose the courtyard which is open on the north side overlooking the Cher and the Loire in the valley.
Joachim de Carvallo, a Spaniard, furnished the château with Spanish furniture and an interesting collection of paintings (16C, 17C and 18C Spanish schools). The great salon and the dining room on the ground floor have Louis XV panelling. The grand staircase with its wrought-iron banister leads to the picture gallery and to the room with the 13C **Mudejar ceiling** which came from Toledo; the coffers are painted and gilded with typical Moorish motifs, an unexpected sight under northern skies; there are two 16C Italian paintings on wood (St Paul and St John) in lively colours and a portrait of the Infanta by the Velasquez school.
An audiovisual display in the picture gallery shows the astonishingly varied aspect of the gardens according to the season and the time of day.
From the keep there is a splendid view over the terraces of the gardens towards the Rivers Cher and Loire.

VILLESAVIN CHÂTEAU

Michelin map 🟦 fold 18 or 🟦 folds 18, 16 (3km - 2 miles west of Bracieux)

Villesavin derives from Villa Savinus, the name of a Roman villa which stood beside the Roman road built by Hadrian which passed through Ponts d'Arian (Hadrian's Bridges) on the south side of the River Beuvron. The villa's existence is attested by the number of sarcophagi which have been found on the land; one is displayed in the château.
The **château** ⊘ was built between 1526 and 1537 by Jean Le Breton, Lord of Villandry and superintendent of works at Chambord. It is a charming Renaissance building with certain classical tendencies and consists of a central block flanked by symmetrical pavilions.
The handsome dormer windows in the attics and the inscription on the rear façade add to the beauty of the harmonious proportions. The 16C Italian **basin** in the courtyard, which is made of white marble, is a very fine example of Renaissance decorative sculpture.
Pewterware — plates, jugs, etc — is on display in some of the furnished rooms.
There are some vintage cars in the outbuildings.
To the left of the château stands a large 16C **dovecot** — with 1 500 pigeonholes; it is well preserved, including the revolving ladder.
The right to keep pigeons was one of the privileges that disappeared with the Revolution.
The size of the dovecot depended on the extent of the estate: there was one pigeonhole containing a couple of birds for each acre of land.
It is thought that the practice of keeping pigeons was brought back by the Crusaders from the Middle East where the land has always been fertilized with pigeon manure.

VOUVRAY

Pop 2598

Michelin map 🔲 fold 15 or 🔲 fold 36 or 🔲 fold 13 – Local map under LOIRE
VALLEY: Orléans-Chinon

At the heart of the famous vineyard is the village of Vouvray which is set on the
south-facing slopes of the hills that dominate the north bank of the Loire above
Tours. There are one or two old troglodyte houses. The still or sparkling white
wines are some of the most famous produced in Touraine.

The cellars **(caves)** of the wine producers and wine merchants are open the public.
In Vouvray there stands a statue of the famous Gaudissart, the travelling salesman
whom Balzac *(p 30)* described in one of his novels. **Balzac** was born in Tours and
often visited friends in Vouvray. The atmosphere and characters of 1830 have gone
but the charm of the landscape described in his novels still remains.

EXCURSION

Vernou-sur-Brenne – Pop 2197. *4km - 2 1/2 miles east by D 46.*
The picturesque old houses of the village are surrounded by the Vouvray vineyard
and backed by a hillside which is riddled with caves.

YÈVRE-LE-CHÂTEL

Pop 210

Michelin map 🔲 fold 20 or 🔲 fold 41 (6 km - 4 miles east of Pithiviers)

The position of Yèvre – on a promontory of the Beauce plateau overlooking the
natural trench of the Rimarde, a tributary of the River Essone – cries out for a
castle. The present ruins, the kernel of a fortified town, seem to belong to a royal
castle built in the 13C by Philippe-Auguste.

A fortified gate under the elm trees in the main square opens into the outer bailey
of the castle.

Fortress ⊘ – The fortress is diamond-shaped with a round tower at each corner
containing hexagonal rooms with ogive vaulting.

The unprotected sentry walk linking the towers is dangerous.

Platforms in the northwest and south towers provide a **view** of the Beauce and the
Gâtinais. On a clear day the spire of Pithiviers church is visible. To the south the
treetops of Orléans Forest darken the horizon.

St Lubin's Church – On the south side of the village among the tombstones
stands the unfinished stone shell of a huge Gothic church. Its vast size seems to
have been dictated by the need for a place of refuge rather than a place of
worship. The church's great elegance and the speed of its construction (the first
quarter of the 13C) suggest the intervention of a royal hand.

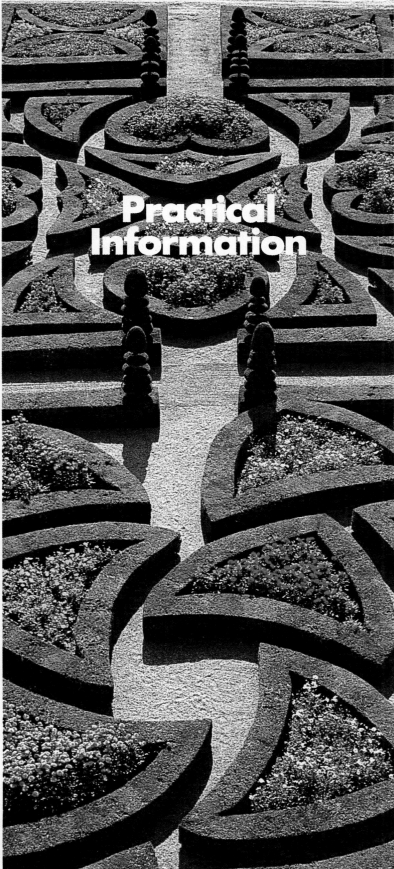

Practical
Information

Villandry Gardens

TRAVELLING TO FRANCE

Passport – Visitors entering France must be in possession of a valid national **passport** (or in the case of the British, a Visitor's Passport). In case of loss or theft report to the embassy or consulate and the local police.

Visa – An **entry visa** is required for Canadian and US citizens (for a stay of more than 3 months) and for Australian citizens in accordance with French security measures. Apply to the French Consulate (visa issued same day; delay if submitted by mail). US citizens should obtain the booklet *Your Trip Abroad* ($1) which provides useful information on visa requirements, customs regulations, medical care etc for international travellers. Apply to the Superintendent of Documents, Government Printing Office, Washington DC 20 402-9325.

Customs – Apply to the Customs Office (UK) for a leaflet on customs regulations and the full range of duty-free allowances. The US Treasury Department (☎ 202 566 8195) offers a publication *Know before you go* for US citizens. There are no customs formalities for holidaymakers bringing their caravans into France for a stay of less than 6 months. No customs document is necessary for pleasure boats and outboard motors for a stay of less than 6 months but the registration certificate should be kept on board.

By air – National and independent airlines operate services to Paris (Charles de Gaulle and Orly) and to the major provincial airports – Nantes and Tours – for the Loire Valley). There are also package tour flights with a rail or coach link-up as well as Fly-Drive schemes. Information, brochures and timetables are available from the airlines and from travel agents. The domestic network (Air Inter) operates frequent services covering the whole country. There are transfer buses to town terminals and to rail stations. Roissy-Rail and Orly-Rail operate fast rail links to the centre of Paris.

By sea – The are numerous **cross-Channel services** (passenger and car ferries, hovercraft, SeaCat) from the United Kingdom and Eire. For details apply to travel agencies or to:

P&O European Ferries, Channel House, Channel View Road, Dover CT17 9TJ; ☎ 0304 203388. Ticket collection: Russell St, Dover, Kent CT16 1QB.

The Continental Ferry Port, Mile End, Portsmouth, Hampshire PO2 8QW; ☎ 0705 827677.

Sealink, Charter House, Park Street, Ashford, Kent TN24 8EX; ☎ 0233 647047.

Hoverspeed, International Hoverport, Marine Parade, Dover, Kent CT17 9TG; ☎ 0304 240241.

Maybrook House, Queen's Gardens, Dover CT17 9UQ; ☎ direct line from London 554 7061, Birmingham 021 236 2190 or Manchester 061 228 1321.

Brittany Ferries, Millbay Docks, Plymouth, Devon PLI 3 EW; ☎ 0752 221321.

The Brittany Centre, Wharf Road, Portsmouth, Hampshire PO 2 8RU; ☎ 0705 827701.

Sally Line, 81 Piccadilly, London WIV 9HF; ☎ 071 409 2240.

Argyle Centre, York St, Ramsgate, Kent CT11 9DS; ☎ 0843 595522.

By rail – British Rail offers a range of services to the Channel ports and French Railways operates an extensive network of lines including many high speed passenger trains and motorail services throughout France. There are rail passes (France Vacances Pass) offering unlimited travel and group travel tickets offering savings for parties. Eurorail Pass, Flexipass and Saver Pass are options available in the US for travel in Europe and must be purchased in the US – ☎ 212 308 3103 (information) and 1 800 223 636 (reservations).

Tickets bought in France must be validated *(composter)* by using the orange automatic date-stamping machines at the platform entrance.

Information and bookings from French Railways, 179 Piccadilly, London WIV OBA; ☎ 071 409 3518 and from principal British and American Rail Travel Centres and travel agencies.

Baggage trolleys (10F coin required-refundable) are available at main line stations.

By coach – Regular coach services are operated from London to Paris and to large provincial towns:

Hoverspeed, Maybrook House, Queens Gardens, Dover CT17 9UQ. ☎ 0304 240241.

Euroways/Eurolines, 52 Grosvenor Gardens, Victoria, London SWIW OAU. ☎ 071 730 8235.

Join us in our constant task of keeping up-to-date.
Please send us your comments and suggestions.

MICHELIN TYRE
Public Limited Company
Tourism Department - The Edward Hyde Building
38 Clarendon Road - WATFORD Herts WD1 1SX

MOTORING IN FRANCE

Documents – Nationals of EC countries require a valid national **driving licence:** nationals of non-EC countries require an **international driving licence** (obtainable in the US from the American Automobile Club).
For the vehicle it is necessary to have the **registration papers** (log-book) and a **nationality plate** of the approved size.

Insurance – Insurance cover is compulsory and although an International Insurance Certificate (Green Card) is no longer a legal requirement in France it is the most effective proof of insurance cover and is internationally recognised by the police and other authorities.
Certain UK motoring organisations (AA, RAC) run accident insurance and breakdown service schemes for members. Europ-Assistance (252 High St, Croydon CRO 1NF) has special policies for motorists. Members of the American Automobile Club should obtain the brochure *Offices to serve you abroad*. Affiliated organisation for France: Association Française des Automobile-Clubs, 9 Rue Anatole-de-la-Forge, 75017 Paris. ☎ (1) 42 27 82 00.

Highway Code – The minimum driving age is 18 years old. Traffic drives on the right. It is compulsory for the front-seat passengers to wear **seat belts:** all back seat passengers should wear seat belts where they are fitted. Children under the age of ten should be on the back seat.
Full or dipped headlights must be switched on in poor visibility and at night; use sidelights only when the vehicle is stationary.
In the case of a **breakdown** a red warning triangle or hazard warning lights are obligatory.
Drivers should watch out for unfamiliar road signs and take great care on the road. In built-up areas priority must be ceded to vehicles joining the road from the right. However, traffic on main roads outside built-up areas and on roundabouts has priority. Vehicles must stop when the lights turn red at road junctions and may filter to the right only where indicated by an amber arrow.
The regulations on **drink-driving** and **speeding** are strictly enforced – usually by an on-the-spot fine or confiscation of the vehicle.

Speed limits – Although liable to modification these are as follows:
– toll motorways 130kph-80mph (110kph-60mph when raining);
– dual carriage roads and motorways without tolls 110kph-68mph (100kph-62mph when raining);
– other roads 90kph-56mph (80kph-50mph when raining) and in towns 50kph-31mph;
– outside lane on motorways during daylight, on level ground and with good visibility minimum speed limit of 80kph (50mph).

Parking Regulations – In town there are restricted and paying **parking zones** (blue and grey zones); tickets must be obtained from the ticket machines (*horodateurs* – small change necessary) and displayed (inside windscreen on driver's side); failure to display may result in a heavy fine.

Route Planning – For 24-hour road traffic information: dial 48 94 33 33 or consult Minitel *(see below)* 3615 Code Route.
See page 13 for the full range of **Michelin maps** covering France.
The road network is excellent and includes many motorways, mostly toll-roads *(autoroutes à péage)*. The roads are very busy during the holiday period (particularly weekends in July and August) and to avoid traffic congestion it is advisable to follow the recommended secondary routes *(Bison Futé-itinéraires bis)*.

Car Rental – There are car rental agencies at airports, air terminals, railway stations and in all large towns throughout France. European cars usually have manual transmission but automatic cars are available on demand. An **international driving licence** is required for non-EC nationals.
Fly-drive schemes are operated by major airlines.

36 15 MICHELIN Minitel Service

Michelin Travel Assistance (AMI) is a computerised route finding system offering integrated information on roads, tourist sights, hotels and restaurants.
36 15 MICHELIN is one of the French Telecom videotex services.
36 15 MICHELIN: access code to connect with the service.

Route planning: give your point of departure and destination, stipulate your preference for motorways or local roads, indicate the sights to see along the way and it will do the rest.

Lunchtime or overnight stops: now look for that special restaurant, secluded country hotel or pleasant camp site along the chosen route.

Where to find the Minitel terminals: public terminals are usually to be found in all post offices, some petrol stations and hotels (over 6 million terminals in France). The cost of consulting 36 15 MICHELIN is 1.27F per minute. This user-friendly travel service is available round the clock.

Access for users outside France: foreign subscribers can access French Telecom videotex services; consult your documentation.

Field of operation: this outstanding European and road tourist data base covers most European countries.

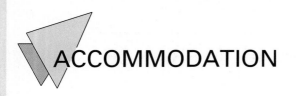

ACCOMMODATION

Places to stay – The map on p 10 indicates recommended places for overnight stops and may be used in conjunction with the **Michelin Red Guide France. Loisirs Accueil** is an officially-backed booking service which has offices in most French départements. For information contact Réservation Loisirs Accueil, 2 Rue Linois, 75015 Paris, ☎ 40 59 44 12 or Loisirs-Accueil Loiret, 8 Rue d'Escures, 45000 Orléans, ☎ 38 62 04 88. The "Accueil de France" Tourist Offices which are open all year make hotel bookings for a small fee for personal callers only. The head office is in Paris (127 Avenue des Champs-Élysées; ☎ 149 52 53 54 for information only) and there are offices in many large towns and resorts.
The brochure *Logis et Auberges de France* is available from the French Government Tourist Office.

Rural accommodation – Apply to Maison des Gîtes de France, 35 Rue Godot-de-Mauroy, 75009 Paris (☎ 47 42 20 20) or 178 Piccadilly, London W1V OAL (☎ 071 493 3480) for a list of relevant addresses.
The French Federation for Green Holiday Resorts, Fédération Française des Stations Vertes de Vacances, Hôtel du Département de la Côte-d'Or, BP 1601, 21035 Dijon Cedex, ☎ 80 49 94 80, publishes an official guide of green resorts in all approved rural areas with details on accommodation, recreation facilities, beauty spots, etc.

Bed and Breakfast – Gîtes de France *(see above)* publishes a booklet on bed and breakfast accommodation *(chambre d'hôte)*.

Youth Hostels – There are many youth hostels throughout France. Holders of an International Youth Hostel Federation card should apply for a list from the International Federation or from the French Youth Hostels Association, 38 Boulevard Raspail, 75007 Paris, ☎ 45 48 69 84.
Members of American Youth Hostels should call 202 783 6161 for information on budget accommodation.
For further information on local youth hostels, apply to:
Youth Hostel Federation, Fédération Unie des Auberges de Jeunesse (FUAJ) Pays de Loire, 44000 Nantes, ☎ 40 20 57 25.
French Youth Hostel League, Ligue Française pour les Auberges de Jeunesse (LFAJ) Pays de la Loire, 1 Rue Darwin, 49000 Angers, ☎ 41 48 14 55.
Loire Ocean Association for Accommodation and Tourist Itineraries, Association Loire Océan Gîtes et Itinéraires (LOGI), 2 Rue de la Loire, Ile Beaulieu, 44000 Nantes, ☎ 40 35 62 26.

Troglodyte Accommodation – For information on troglodyte accommodation or *troglogîtes* contact the Relais des Gîtes du Maine et Loire, BP 2147, 49021 Angers Cedex 02, ☎ 41 20 09 99 or the Centre International de Séjour des Perrières (UCRIF), 49700 Doué-la-Fontaine, ☎ 41 59 77 08.

Camping – There are numerous officially graded sites with varying standards of facilities throughout the Loire region. The **Michelin Guide Camping Caravaning France** lists a selection of camping sites. An International Camping Carnet for caravans is useful but not compulsory; it may be obtained from the motoring organisations or the Camping and Caravanning Club (11 Lower Grosvenor Place, London SW1).

Electricity – The electric current is 220 volts. Circular two pin plugs are the rule – an electrical adaptor may be necessary.

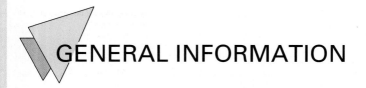

GENERAL INFORMATION

Medical treatment – First aid, medical advice and chemists' night service rota are available from chemists (*pharmacie* – green cross sign).
It is advisable to take out comprehensive insurance cover as the recipient of medical treatment in French hospitals or clinics must pay the bill. Nationals of non-EC countries should check with their insurance companies about policy limitations. Reimbursement can then be negotiated with the insurance company according to the policy held.
American Express offers a service, "Global Assist", for any medical, legal or personal emergency – call collect from anywhere ☎ 202 554 2639.
British citizens should apply to the Department of Health and Social Security for **Form E111,** which entitles the holder to urgent treatment for accident or unexpected illness in EC countries. A refund of part of the costs of treatment can be obtained on application in person or by post to the local Social Security Offices (Caisse Primaire d'Assurance Maladie).

Currency – There are no restrictions on the amount of currency visitors can take into France. To facilitate the export from France of currency in foreign banknotes in excess of the given allocation visitors are advised to complete a currency declaration form on arrival.

Banks – Banks are open from 0900 to 1200 and 1400 to 1600 and are closed on Monday or Saturday (except if market day); some branches open for limited transactions on Saturday. Banks close early on the day before a bank holiday. A passport is necessary as identification when cashing cheques in banks. Commission charges vary and hotels usually charge more than banks for cashing cheques for non-residents.

Most banks have cash dispensers which accept international credit cards.

Credit Cards – American Express, Carte Bleue (Visa/Barclaycard), Diners Club and Eurocard (Mastercard/Access) are widely accepted in shops, hotels and restaurants and petrol stations.

Post – Post Office open Monday to Friday 0800 to 1900, Saturday 0800 to 1200. Postage via air mail to; UK letter 2.80F; postcard 2.40F; US aerogramme 5.00F; letter (20g) 4.30F; postcard 3.70F. Stamps are also available from newsagents and tobacconists.
Poste Restante mail should be addressed as follows: Name, *Poste Restante, Poste Centrale,* département's postal code followed by town name, *France.* The **Michelin Red Guide France** gives local postal codes.

Telephone – Public phones using pre-paid phone cards *(télécarte)* are in operation in many areas. The cards (50 or 120 units) which are available from post offices, tobacconists and newsagents can be used for inland and international calls. Calls can be received at phone boxes where the blue bell sign is shown.
Internal calls – When calling within either of the two main zones (French provinces and Paris and its region) dial only the 8 digit correspondent's number. From Paris to the provinces dial 16 + 8 digit number. From the provinces to Paris dial 16 + 1 + 8 digit number.
International calls – For Paris dial the country code 33 + 1 + 8 digit number. For the provinces the country code 33 + 8 digit number.
When calling abroad from France dial 19, wait until the continuous tone recurs then dial the country code and dialling code and number of your correspondent. For international enquiries dial 19 33 12 + country code.
Telephone rates from a public telephone at any time are: Paris-London: about 5.60F for 1 minute; Paris-New York: 10.30F for 1 minute. Cheap rates with 50 % extra time are available from private telephones on weekdays between 2230 and 0800, at weekends starting 1400 on Saturdays.

Shopping – The big stores and larger shops are open Monday to Saturday, 09 00 to 18 30 – 19 30, Smaller, individual shops may close during the lunch hour. Food shops – grocers, wine merchants and bakeries – are open from 0700 to 1830 – 1930; some open on Sunday mornings. Many food shops close between 1200 and 1400 and on Mondays. Hypermarkets usually open until 2100 – 2200.

Public holidays – The following are days when museums and other monuments may be closed or may vary their hours of admission:

New Year's Day	France's National Day (14 July)
Easter Sunday and Monday	Assumption (15 August)
May Day (1 May)	All Saints' Day (1 November)
VE Day (8 May)	Armistice Day (11 Novembre)
Ascension Day	Christmas Day
Whit Sunday and Monday	

National museums and art galleries are closed on Tuesdays whereas municipal museums are closed on Mondays.
In addition to the usual school holidays at Christmas and in the spring and summer, there are long mid-term breaks (10 days to a fortnight) in February and early November.

Embassies and Consulates

Australia	Embassy	4 Rue Avenue Jean-Rey, 75015 Paris, ☎ 40 59 33 00.
Canada	Embassy	35 Avenue Montaigne, 75008 Paris, ☎ 47 23 01 01.
Eire	Embassy	4 Rue Rude, 75016 Paris, ☎ 45 00 20 87.
UK	Embassy	35 Rue du Faubourg St-Honoré, 75008 Paris, ☎ 42 66 91 42.
	Consulate	16 Rue d'Anjou, 75008 Paris, ☎ 42 66 91 42
		5 Rue Cadeniers, 44000 Nantes, ☎ 40 63 16 02.
USA	Embassy	2 Avenue Gabriel, 75008 Paris, ☎ 42 96 12 02.
	Consulate	2 Rue St-Florentin, 75001 Paris, ☎ 42 96 14 88.
		22 Cours du Maréchal Foch, Bordeaux 33080, ☎ 56 52 65 95.

To plan a special itinerary:

*- consult the **Map of Touring Programmes** which indicates the recommended routes, the tourist regions, the principal towns and main sights.*
*- read the descriptions in the **Sights** section which include Excursions from the main tourist centres.*

Michelin Maps nos 60, 61, 63, 64, 65 and 67 indicate scenic routes, interesting sights, viewpoints, rivers, forests...

TOURIST INFORMATION

French Government Tourist Offices – For information, brochures, maps and assistance in planning a trip to France travellers should apply to the official tourist office in their own country *(see below)*.

French Government Tourist Offices Addresses

Australia
Sydney – Kindersley House, 33 Bligh St, Sydney, New South Wales 2000. ☎ 612 231 52 44.

Canada
Toronto – 1 Dundas St, West Suite 2405 Box 8, Toronto, Ontario M5G IZ3. ☎ 416 593 47 23.
Montreal – 1981 Ave McGill College, Suite 490, Montréal, Québec H3-A2W9. ☎ 514 288 42 64.

Elre
Dublin – c/o 38 Lower Abbey St, Dublin, ☎ (01) 300 777.

United Kingdom
London – 178 Piccadilly, London WIV OAL. ☎ 071 499 6911 (24 hour answering service with recorded message and information) or 071 491 7622 (urgent enquiries only).

United States
Toll-free number – Dial 900 420 2003 for information on hotels, restaurants and transportation.
Middle West: Chicago – 645 North Michigan Avenue, Suite 630, Chicago, Illinois 60611. ☎ 312 337 6301.
East Coast: New York – 610 Fifth Avenue, Suite 222, NY 10020 – 2452. ☎ 212 757 11 25.
West Coast: Los Angeles – 9454 Wilshire Boulevard, Suite 303, Beverly Hills, Cal. 90212. ☎ 213 272 2661.
South: Dallas – 2305 Cedar Spring Road, Suite 205, Dallas, Texas 75201. ☎ 214 720 4010.

Regional Tourist Offices (Comités Régionaux de Tourisme):
Pays de la Loire: Hôtel de Région, 2 Rue de la Loire, 44200 Nantes, ☎ 40 48 24 20.
Centre-Val de Loire: 9 rue St-Pierre-Lentin, 45041 Orléans Cedex (written enquiries only).
The Regional Tourist Offices (Comités Régionaux de Tourisme) publish information brochures on their own region.

Departmental Tourist Offices (Comités Départementaux de Tourisme):
Cher: 5 Rue de Séricourt, 18000 Bourges, ☎ 48 67 00 18.
Eure-et-Loire: 19 Place des Épars, Immeuble du Département, BP 67, 28002 Chartres Cedex, ☎ 37 36 90 90 ext 2815.
Indre: 36 Rue Bourdillon, 36000 Châteauroux, ☎ 54 22 91 20.
Indre-et-Loire: Rue de Bouffon, 37032 Tours (written enquiries only).
Loir-et-Cher: 11 Place du Château, 41000 Blois, ☎ 54 78 55 50.
Loiret: 8 Rue d'Escares, 45000 Orléans, ☎ 38 54 83 83.
Maine-et-Loire: 11 Place du Président-Kennedy, BP 2147, 49021 Angers Cedex 02, ☎ 41 88 23 85.
Mayenne: 84 Avenue Robert-Buron, BP 343, 53000 Laval, ☎ 43 53 18 18.
Orne: 88 Rue St-Blaise, BP 60, 61002 Alençon, ☎ 33 28 88 71.
Sarthe: 2 Rue des Maillets, 72000 Le Mans, ☎ 43 81 72 72.

Tourist Information Centres – The address and telephone numbers of the Tourist Information Centres (Syndicats d'Initiative) of most large towns and tourist resorts may be found among the Admission Times and Charges and in the **Michelin Red Guide France.** They can supply large scale town plans, timetables and local information.

Minitel – The French Telecom videotex service offers a wide variety of information *(fee charged)*. Minitel terminals are installed in hotel chains and some petrol stations. Listed below are some of the telematic services offered:

36 14 ED	electronic service in English
36 15 TCAMP	camping information
36 15 METEO	weather report
36 15 or 36 16 HORAV	general airline information and flight schedules
36 15 BBC	BBC news
36 15 LIBE	USA TODAY
36 15 MICHELIN	Michelin tourist and route information

Tourism for the Disabled – Some of the sights described in this guide are accessible to handicapped people. They are listed in *Touristes quand même! Promenades en France pour les Voyageurs Handicapés* published by the Comité National Français de Liaison pour la Réadaptation des Handicapés (38 Boulevard Raspail, 75007 Paris). This booklet covers nearly 90 towns in France and provides practical information for people who suffer reduced mobility or visual or aural impairment.
Access in the Loire is a guide for the disabled and those who have problems getting around. This carefully researched guide *(see Books to Read p. 30)* gives information about travel, accommodation and tourist attractions in the Loire region.
The **Michelin Red Guide France** and the **Michelin Camping Caravaning France** indicate hotels and camping sites with facilities suitable for physically handicapped people.

RECREATION

Information and brochures outlining the sporting and outdoor facilities available may be obtained from the French Government Tourist Office or from the organisations listed below.

Tourist Routes – The Regional and Local Tourist Offices will give information on tourist routes, pinpointing places of interest.
Tours Tourist Office, Place du Maréchal-Leclerc, ☎ 47 05 58 08.
Chinon Tourist Office, 12 Rue Voltaire, ☎ 47 93 17 85.
Anjou Departmental Tourist Committee, Place du Président-Kennedy, BP 2147, 49021 Angers Cedex, ☎ 41 88 23 85.

Evening Tours – Apply to Tours Tourist Office, Place du Maréchal-Leclerc, ☎ 47 05 58 08 for performances at the castles of Azay-le-Rideau, Amboise and Le Lude.

Crafts – Many arts and crafts studios (weaving, wrought-iron, pottery) are open to visitors in summer. For courses apply to the Tourist Information Centre.

Cycling – The Fédération française de Cyclotourisme: 8 rue Jean-Marie-Jégo, 75013 Paris, ☎ 45 80 30 21 supplies itineraries covering most of France, mentioning mileage, difficult routes and sights to see.
Bicy-Club de France: 8 Place de la Porte Champerret, 75017 Paris.
Lists of cycle hire businesses are available from the Tourist Information Centres.
The main railway stations also hire out cycles which can be returned at a different station.
For information on cycling in the Layon region with mountain bicycles, apply to the Anjou Departmental Tourist Committee, Place du Président-Kennedy, BP 2147, 49021 Angers Cedex, ☎ 41 88 23 85.
There is an IGN map (Institut Géographique National: 1:50 000) of *620 miles cycling around Orléans (1 000 km à vélo autour d'Orléans).*

Rambling – Short, medium and long distance footpath Topo-Guides are published by the Fédération Française de la Randonnée Pédestre (FFRP) – Comité National des Sentiers de Grande Randonnée (CNSGR). These give detailled maps of the paths and offer valuable information to the rambler and are on sale at the Information Centre: 64 Rue de Gergovie, 75014 Paris, ☎ 45 45 31 02; or by mail order from McCarta, 15 Highbury Place, London N5 1QP, ☎ 071 354 16 16.
For further information apply to: Comité de Touraine pour la Randonnée Pédestre, Boulevard Heurteloup, 37042 Tours, ☎ 47 61 02 57 and the Association Départementale du Tourisme Pédestre, 28 Rue de la Tonnelle, 49400 Saumur, ☎ 41 51 31 60.
The Comité Départemental du Tourisme de l'Anjou has published five IGN maps (Institut Géographique National, 1:50 000) of rambling itineraries.

Fishing – Current brochures: folding map *Fishing in France (Pêche en France)* published and distributed by the Conseil Supérieur de la Pêche, 134 Avenue de Malakoff, 75016 Paris, ☎ 45 01 20 20; also available from the Centre du Paraclet, BP 5, 80440 Boves, ☎ 22 09 37 47, and from departmental fishing organisations.
For information about regulations contact the Tourist Information Centres or the offices of the Water and Forest Authority (Eaux et Forêts).
Fishing organisations (Fédérations de Pêche): 25 Rue Charles-Gille, 37000 Tours, ☎ 47 05 33 77; 14 Allée du Haras, 49100 Angers, ☎ 41 87 57 09.

Chenillé-Changé — River boat centre

Cruising – Two publishers produce collections of guides to cruising on French canals. Both series include numerous maps and useful information and are provided with English translations. The publishers are: Navicarte, Éditions Cartographiques Maritimes, 7 Quai Gabriel-Péri, 94340 Joinville-Le-Pont, ☎ 48 85 77 00.

Guides Vagnon, Les Éditions du Plaisancier, 100 Avenue du Général-Leclerc, 69641 Caluire-et-Cuire, ☎ 78 23 31 14.

The table below, though not exhaustive, gives information on boats in the Anjou region which may be hired without a permit and have sleeping accommodation. Day cruises on captained boats are also available. Contact local boat companies for information. Navigation is possible almost year round. Nevertheless, before choosing an itinerary and dates for hire, it is advisable to find out about scouring periods or *écoures (see below)* and locks – which may close at certain times of the day or on public holidays. The cruising speed is 6 to 8kmh - 3.7 to 5mph and sailing is not allowed at night.

Departure points	Rivers	Boat companies
Angers	Mayenne Oudon Sarthe	Maine Réservations Place Kennedy, 49022 Angers Cedex 02 ☎ 41 88 99 38 Concord Plaisance Quai de la Savatte, 49100 Angers ☎ 41 87 93 50
Château-Gontier Malicorne	Mayenne Sarthe	Espace Europe Loisirs Quai Pierre de Coubertin 53200 Château-Gontier ☎ 43 70 34 41
Cheffes-sur-Sarthe Mayenne	Mayenne Oudon Sarthe	Sarthe Fluviale 40 Promenade de Reculée 49100 Angers ☎ 41 73 14 16
Chenillé-Changé	Mayenne Oudon Sarthe	Maine Anjou Rivières Le Moulin 49220 Chenillé-Changé ☎ 41 95 10 83
Daon	Mayenne Oudon Sarthe	France Mayenne Fluviale Le Port, 53200 Daon ☎ 43 70 13 94
Grez-Neuville	Maine Mayenne Oudon Sarthe	Anjou Plaisance Rue de l'Écluse, 49220 Grez-Neuville ☎ 41 95 68 95
Sablé-sur-Sarthe	Mayenne Oudon Sarthe	Anjou Navigation Quai National, 72300 Sablé-sur-Sarthe ☎ 43 95 14 42

During the **scouring periods** when the water level is lowered for maintenance work, the river sections and canals concerned are closed to navigation. Work is usually carried out in autumn from 15 September to 30 October. In the Maine basin, work alternates from river to river, affecting the Sarthe one year and the Mayenne the next. Depending on the year, cruise companies move their pleasure boats to a different river during the scouring period.

Riding and Pony Trekking – Apply to the Fédération des Randonneurs Équestres, 16 Rue des Apennins, 75017 Paris, ☎ 42 26 23 23, or to:

Association Régionale de Tourisme Équestre Val de Loire-Océan; Mr. Cosneau, Le Moulin de la Bille, 44150 St Herblon, ☎ 40 98 05 76; Secretariat: La Senserie, 44522 La Roche Blanche, ☎ 40 98 41 87.

Association Régionale de Tourisme Équestre Val de Loire-Centre; Mr. Legrand-Sourdillon, 66 Rue Devildé, 37000 Tours, ☎ 47 54 51 23.

Délégation Nationale au Tourisme Équestre, Ile St Germain, 170 Quai de Stalingrad, 92130 Issy-les-Moulineaux, ☎ 45 54 29 54, Fax 40 93 52 88.

The Association Nationale de Tourisme Équestre (ANTE), 15 Rue de Bruxelles, 75009 Paris publishes an annual handbook covering the whole of France.

Air Trips – Apply to:

SLA, BP 139, 37171 Chambrey-lès-Tours, ☎ 47 48 37 27.

Tours Aero Services, Tours St-Symphorien and Blois-le-Breuil airports, ☎ 47 51 25 68.

Bombard Balloons, Balloon Trips, Château de Laborde, Meursanges, 21200 Beaune, ☎ 80 26 63 30.

«Les Ailes Tourangelles» Aero-Club, Amboise-Dierre Aerodrome, 37150 Bléré, ☎ 47 57 93 91. Touraine-Hélicoptère, BP 13 Neuvy-le-Roi, ☎ 47 24 81 44.

Saumur Aero-Club, ☎ 41 50 20 27.

Blois-Hélistation, Pont Charles-de-Gaulle, on D 951 out of Blois Vienne, ☎ 54 74 35 52.

Motor boating and water-skiing – Enquire at the local Tourist Information Centre.

Sailing and windsurfing – Apply direct to local sailing clubs or to the Fédération Française de Voile, 55 Avenue Kléber, 75784 Paris Cedex 16, ☎ 45 53 68 00.
Windsurfing, which is subject to certain regulations, is permitted on lakes and in sports and leisure cetres; apply to sailing clubs.

Hunting – For all enquiries apply to Saint-Hubert Club de France, 10 Rue de Lisbonne, 75008 Paris, ☎ 45 22 38 90.

Golf – The **Michelin Golf Map** of France gives comprehensive details of golf courses. An annual guide is published by Éditions Person, 34 Rue de Penthièvre, 75008 Paris. A map showing golf courses and giving the number of holes, addresses and telephone numbers is available from the Fédération Française de Golf, 69 Avenue Victor-Hugo, 75016 Paris, ☎ 45 02 13 55.

Bird Watching – The Délégation Anjou de la Ligue Française pour la Protection des Oiseaux (LPO), 63 bis Rue Barra, 49100 Angers, ☎ 41 87 20 21, organises introductory bird watching excursions in the Maine-et-Loire region.
The Carrefour Touristique et Culturel des Mauges, Ferme Abbatiale des Coteaux, 49410 St Florent-le-Vieil, ☎ 41 72 52 37, organises environmental weekends which include excursions into the countryside to study birds – different species and behaviour – in their natural habitat.
(Both organisations supply binoculars and telescopes).
For further information read the *Guide d'Observation des Oiseaux en Anjou et dans les environs* by J.P. Gislard (La Nouvelle République).

Wind and water mills – Anjou still has a good many mills dotted about the Maine-et-Loire region. About twenty of those that have been restored and are in working condition may be toured in season or by prior arrangement. Apply to the Association des Amis des Moulins de l'Anjou (AMA), 17 Rue de la Madeleine, 49000 Angers, ☎ 41 88 82 23.

Tours of wine cellars – Apply to:
Comité Interprofessionnel des Vins d'Anjou et Saumur, Hôtel de la Godeline, 73 Rue Plantagenêt, 49000 Angers, ☎ 41 87 62 57.
Maison du Vin de l'Anjou, 5 bis Place du Président-Kennedy, 49100 Angers, ☎ 41 88 81 13.
Comité Interprofessionnel des Vins de Touraine, 19 Square Prosper-Mérimée, 37000 Tours, ☎ 47 05 40 01.
For further information contact local Tourist Information Centres, particularly those at Amboise, Angers, Bourgueil, Chinon, Montlouis-sur-Loire, Saumur and Vouvray.

Vendôme — A stall in the Abbey church

CALENDAR OF EVENTS

Holy Saturday
St-Benoît-sur-Loire . . . . Grand Easter Festival (at 2200).

Late April
Saumur . . . . International Competition (☎ 41 51 34 15).

April to September
Saumur . . . . Public display by the "Black Squad" in the dressage arena of the Riders of the National School of Equitation (☎ 41 50 21 35).

March to November
Maulévrier . . . . Greyhound racing at La Tuilerie racetrack (☎ 41 55 05 49/53 50).

Late April/early May
Le Mans . . . . "24 hours": motorcycle race on the Bugatti Circuit *(p. 146)*.

7 and 8 May
Orléans . . . . Joan of Arc Festival: first day – cathedral illuminations; second day – religious ceremony in the cathedral, procession, military parade.

Mid-May
Château-Gontier . . . . Horse Show at La Maroutière Château *(p. 87)*.

Whitsun
Châteauneuf-sur-Loire . . . . Whitsun Festival.

Mid or late June
Le Mans . . . . 24 hour race: car racing on the 24 hour circuit *(p. 146)*.

Chambord . . . . National Hunting and Fishing Show [☎ (1) 47 55 09 16].

Late June-early July
Tours (Meslay Tithe Barn) . . . . Touraine Music Festival with international artists (☎ 47 21 65 08).

Late June to early September
Saumur . . . . Tuffolies Son et Lumière Show in the streets. (*For information and reservations apply to the Tourist Information Centre in Saumur, ☎ 41 51 03 06*).

July
Anjou . . . . Anjou Festival in the impressive setting of the Angevin castles.

First weekend in July
Le Mans . . . . Les Cénomanies Renaissance Festival in Old Le Mans.

July (every day except Monday)
Cléry-St André,
Germigny-des-Prés,
Orléans, Sully-s-Loire . . . . . Music Festival: classical, jazz, dance (☎ 38 36 29 46).

Mid July
Doué-la-Fontaine . . . . Rose Show in the amphitheatre.

Fourth weekend in July
La Ménitré 🖪 fold 3 *(1)* . . . . Headdress Parade involving all the regional folklore groups.
Many young women wear traditional costumes and headdresses (☎ 41 53 63 63).

Last weekend in July
Saumur . . . . Military Tattoo with mounted, motorised and armoured divisions.

First weekend in August
Chinon . . . . Medieval market: reconstitution of Chinon in the Middle Ages; period costumes, entertainers, puppets, old crafts, sampling of old dishes, dancing, concerts, choral singing, traditional art *(admission: 40 F)* (☎ 41 93 17 85).

15 August
Molineuf 64 fold 7 *(1)* . . . . .   Bric-a-brac Fair; with antique-dealers, amateurs and customers.

Early September
Château-Gontier . . . .   Horse Show at La Maroutière Château *(p. 87)*.

Penultimate Sunday in October
Le Lion d'Angers . . . .   International Horse Show.
Demonstrations by the best riders in the world representing 20 nations.

24 December
Anjou . . . .   Les Naulets Mass (in a different rural church each year).
Traditional local groups sing Christmas carols in the local dialect *(Tourist Information Office in Angers: ☎ 41 88 69 93)*.

St Benoît-sur-Loire . . . .   Christmas Eve vigil and mass (at 2200).

_____

(1) The map and fold number are given for places not described in this guide.

For a quiet place to stay

Consult the annual Michelin Red Guide France which offers a selection of pleasant and quiet hotels in a convenient location.

"SON ET LUMIÈRE" SHOWS

This type of show, which was inaugurated at Chambord in 1952 by P. Robert-Houdin, presents the châteaux of the Loire Valley in an original manner.
The information given below is subject to alteration; confirmation of the programmes should be obtained from the Tourist Information Office.

Amboise: At the Court of King François (A la cour du Roy François)
Cinematic evocation of the construction of the château, the arrival of Louise de Savoie, the Campaigns in Italy, everyday life in the château and the rejoicing at Amboise in honour of the king during the Renaissance.
Performances: Wednesdays and Saturdays from the last week in June to the first week in September.
Duration: 1 hour 30min. 30F to 90F. Performances in June and July begin at 2230 and in August and September at 2200 (ticket office opens 1 hour 30min before the show starts). Information from "Animation Renaissance Amboise" (ARA). ☎ 47 57 14 47 or the Tourist Office, ☎ 47 57 01 37.

Azay-le-Rideau: In celebration of Philippa (Puisque de vous nous n'avons autre visage)
The show, which is brought to life by Renaissance personalities, evokes Philippa Les-bahy, the soul of this château.
Performances every evening from late May to late September: May, June and July at 2230; August and September at 2200. Duration: 1 hour. 40F and 50F. Information from the Tourist Office in Tours: ☎ 47 05 58 08 and in Azay-le-Rideau; ☎ 47 45 44 40/47 31 48 05.

Blois: The story of Blois (Ainsi Blois vous est conté)
Evocation of Blois château with texts by Alain Decaux of the Académie Française, narrated by Robert Hossein.
Two performances every evening from 5 June to 22 September at 2230 in French and 2330 in English. 60F. Information and reservations; ☎ 54 78 06 62.

Chambord: Days through the Centuries (Les jours et les siècles)
The show (a walking tour) is based on life in Chambord over the last four centuries.
Performances from 15 April to 15 October, beginning at the meeting point on the south lawn (follow the arrows) at nightfall. Times vary according to the season; approximately 2230 for the first performance in July and 2200 in August. 50F. Information and reservations; ☎ 54 20 34 86.

Chenonceau: The Ladies of Chenonceau (Au temps des Dames de Chenonceau)
Under the influence of six women Chenonceau evolved from a fortified mill into an elegant residence where sumptuous parties were held.
Performances daily from early June to mid-September at 2215. Duration: 45min. 35F. ☎ 47 23 94 45.

Cheverny: Reverie in the Sologne (Rêve en Sologne)
Certain evenings in July at 2215 and in August at 2200. Duration: 1 hour 15min. 80F. Information, ☎ 54 79 96 29.

Le Lude: Spectacular Historical Events (Les Féeries de l'Histoire, *p. 138*)
Performances from mid June to late August, Fridays and Saturdays at 2200 or 2230. A few extra performances in June and August. Duration: 1 hour 45min. 90F. Information, ☎ 43 94 67 27.

Valencay: Beauty and the Beast (La Belle et la Bête)
Fairy tale evocation based on texts by Jean Cocteau.
Performances in July, August and September, Fridays and Saturdays at 2200. Duration: 2 hours. 70F. Information; ☎ 54 00 14 33 and 54 00 04 42 (road to Blois).

ADMISSION TIMES AND CHARGES

As admission times and charges are liable to alteration, the information below is given for guidance only.

The information applies to individual adults. Special conditions for groups are common but arrangements should be made in advance. In some cases there is no charge for admission on certain days, eg Wednesdays, Sundays or public holidays.

Churches are usually closed from 1200 to 1400; they should not be visited during services. Admission times are indicated if the interior is of special interest. Visitors to chapels are usually accompanied by the key-holder; a donation is welcome.

Most tours are conducted by French-speaking guides but in some cases the term "guided tours" may cover group visiting with recorded commentaries. Some of the larger and more frequented sights may offer guided tours in other languages. Enquire at the ticket office or book stall. Other aids for foreign visitors are notes, pamphlets or audio guides.

Enquire at the tourist information centre for local religious holidays, market days etc.

Every sight for which there are times and charges is indicated by the symbol ⊙ in the alphabetical section of the guide. The entries appear in the same order as the sights.

A

AMBOISE   🛈 Quai du Général-de-Gaulle, 37400 ☏ 47 57 02 21

Guided tour of the town organised by the Tourist Information Centre.

Château – Guided tour in summer, 0900 to 1200 and 1400 to 1830 (all day July and August) Closed 1 January, 25 December. 28 F. ☏ 47 57 00 98.

Le Clos-Lucé – Open 23 March to 12 November and public holidays, 0900 to 1900; otherwise, 0900 to 1800. Closed January, 25 December. 31F. ☏ 47 57 62 88.

Postal Museum – Open 1 April to 30 September, 0930 to 1200 and 1400 to 1830; otherwise, 1000 to 1200 and 1400 to 1700. Closed Mondays, January, 1 May, 1 November and 25 December. 15F. ☏ 47 57 00 11.

Town Hall Museum – Guided tour (30min) July and August, 1400 to 1800; otherwise apply in advance. Closed weekends, public holidays. 5F. ☏ 47 57 02 21.

ANGERS   🛈 Place du Président-Kennedy, 49000 ☏ 41 23 51 11 and Place de la Gare, ☏ 41 87 72 50.

Guided tour of the town organised by the Tourist Information Centre. A combined ticket for 35F (valid until 31 December of the year of purchase) gives access to the castle, David of Angers Gallery, Logis Barrault, Hotel Pincé and the Lurçat Museum.

Castle – Open 1 June to 15 September, 0900 to 1900; Palm Sunday to end of May, 0900 to 1230 and 1400 to 1830; otherwise, 0930 to 1230 and 1400 to 1800; guided tour available (1 hour 30min). Closed 1 January, 1 May, 1 and 11 November and 25 December. 31F. ☏ 41 87 43 47.

Cathedral – Open all year, daily except Sunday mornings. Guided tour by prior arrangement July and August daily, otherwise, Sunday afternoons only. ☏ 41 87 58 45.

David of Angers Gallery – Open 15 June to 15 September, 0930 to 1230 and 1400 to 1900; otherwise, 1000 to 1200 and 1400 to 1800. Closed Mondays from 16 September to 14 June, and 1 January, 1 May, 14 July, 1 and 11 November and 25 December. 10F. ☏ 41 87 21 03.

Logis Barrault (Fine Arts Museum) – Open same times as David of Angers Gallery. 5F. ☏ 41 88 64 65.

Monastery Buildings (Hôtel du Département et Préfecture) – Unrestricted access to the Romanesque Arcade; guided tour available, ☏ 41 81 49 49.

Hotel Pincé – Open same times as David of Angers Gallery. 5F. ☏ 41 88 97 27.

St Sergius' Church – Open all year, daily except Sunday mornings. Guided tour (30min) July and August, Sunday afternoons. ☏ 41 43 66 76.

Lurçat Museum of Contemporary Tapestry – Open 15 June to 15 September, daily, 0930 to 1230 and 1400 to 1900; otherwise, daily except Monday, 1000 to 1200 and 1400 to 1800. Closed 1 January, 1, 8 May, 14 July, 1, 11 November, 25 December. 10F. ☏ 41 87 41 06.

Regional Textile Art Centre (Centre Régional d'Art Textile) – Open by prior arrangement Monday, Tuesday, Thursday and Friday from 1000 to 1200 and 1400 to 1700. ☏ 41 87 10 88.

Excursions

Cointreau Distillery – Guided tour (1 hour) 15 June to 15 September, Mondays to Fridays at 1000, 1100, 1400, 1500 and 1600; weekends and public holidays at 1500 and 1630; otherwise, Sundays and public holidays at 1500 and 1630. Closed 23 December to 2 January and 1 May. 20F. ☎ 41 43 25 21.

Pignerolle Château (European Museum of Communication) – Open May and June, 1000 to 1230 and 1400 to 1830; 1 July to 30 September, 1000 to 1230 and 1400 to 1900 (2130 Fridays); guided tour available (1 hour 30 min). Otherwise by prior arrangement. 40F (château and museum), 20F (Phantasmagoria) and 50F (museum and Phantasmagoria).

Trélazé: Slate Museum – Guided tour (2 hours 15 min), 1 July to 15 September, daily except Mondays at 1400; otherwise, on Sundays and public holidays only. Slate splitting demonstration at 1500. 25F. ☎ 41 69 04 71.

ARGENT-SUR-SAULDRE

Trades and Traditions Museum – Open 1 July to 31 August, Monday-Saturday, 1400 to 1830, Sundays and public holidays, 1000 to 1200 and 1400 to 1830; May, June, September and October, daily from 1400 to 1830. 25F. ☎ 48 73 33 10.

Vassil Ivanoff Museum – Open 1 May to 15 October, Mondays to Fridays, 1400 to 1830; weekends and public holidays 1000 to 1200 and 1400 to 1830. 15F. ☎ 48 73 34 02 and (1) 45 89 16 24.

ASNIÈRES-SUR-VÈGRE

Verdelles Château – Ground floor rooms: open 1 May to 30 October by prior arrangement. ☎ 43 95 43 55.

AUBIGNY-SUR-NÈRE

Guided tour of the town: apply to the Tourist Information Centre. ☎ 48 58 00 09.

Stuart Château: Marguerite Audoux Room – Open summer daily, 1000 to 1200 and 1400 to 1800; otherwise, weekends and public holidays only, at the same times. Mural Poetry Festival in June and Sologne Art Festival events in July and August.

Excursion

La Verrerie Château – Guided tour (40 min) daily from mid February to mid November, 1000 to 1200 and 1400 to 1900. 25F. ☎ 48 58 21 25.

AZAY-LE-RIDEAU   ◘ 42 Rue Nationale, 37190 ☎ 47 45 44 40

Château – Open July and August, 0900 to 1900; 1 April to 30 June and in September, 0930 to 1800; otherwise, 1000 to 1230 and 1400 to 1700; guided tour available (45 min). Closed 1 January, 1 May, 1, 11 November, 25 December. 25F. ☎ 47 45 42 04.

Excursion

Villaines-les-Rochers: Co-operative – **Basketwork exhibition:** open April to September, 0900 (1000 Sundays and public holidays) to 1200 and 1400 to 1900. Closed 1 October to 31 March, Sunday and public holiday mornings; 1 January, 25 December. **Workshops:** open Monday to Friday, 0900 to 1700. ☎ 47 45 43 03.

B

BAUGÉ   ◘ Château, 49150 ☎ 41 89 18 07

Château – Guided tour (30 min) mid-June to mid-September, daily except Tuesdays, 1100 to 1200 and 1500 to 1800. 11F. ☎ 41 89 12 12 and 41 89 22 07.

Chapel of the Daughters of the Heart of Mary – Guided tour daily, 1 April to 31 October, 1500 to 1630 (1600 Sundays) and 1800 to 1900; otherwise, Monday to Saturday, 1500 to 1630, Sunday 1500 to 1600 (1630 in November and December). Closed the first Saturday of the month from October to April, Whit weekend and Whit Monday, the first Sunday in July, 24, 25 and 26 July and 15 September. ☎ 41 89 12 20.

Hospital: Dispensary – Open daily except Sunday mornings and Tuesdays, from 1000 to 1200 and 1500 to 1700. 7F.

St Laurent's Church – Closed Sunday afternoons.

Excursion

Le Vieil-Baugé: St Symphorien's Church – Open Monday-Saturday only.

BAZOUGES-SUR-LE-LOIR

Château – Guided tour (45 min) 1 June to 15 September, Tuesdays and Fridays, 1000 to 1200, Thursdays and Saturdays, 1400 to 1700. 14F. ☎ 43 45 32 62.

BEAUGENCY   ◘ 28 Place du Martroi, BP 44, 45190 ☎ 38 44 54 42

Guided tour of the town: apply to the Tourist Information Centre.

Orléans District Museum (Château Dunois) – Open daily except Tuesday, 1000 to 1200 and 1400 to 1830 (1700 October to late March); guided tour (1 hour) available. Closed 1 January, 1 May and 25 December. 18F. ☎ 38 44 55 23.

Town Hall – Guided tour (15 min) 1 May to 30 September, 1000 to 1200 and 1400 to 1700; otherwise, afternoons only, 1400 to 1700. Closed Mondays from 1 October to 30 April, Saturday afternoon, Sundays and public holidays. 6F. ☎ 38 44 50 01.

BEAUREGARD

Château – Open April to late September, 0930 to 1200 and 1400 to 1830; otherwise, 0930 to 1200 and 1400 to 1700; guided tour available (45 min). Closed January, Wednesdays from October to Easter, and 25 December. Restoration work in the Portrait Gallery. 20F. ☎ 54 70 40 05 and 47 47 05 41.

BELLEGARDE

Town Hall: Regency Salon – Guided tour by prior arrangement, Monday to Friday, 0900 to 1200 and 1400 to 1600. ☎ 38 90 10 03.

BERCÉ FOREST

Guided tour (2 hours 30 min) with a nature guide, mid-July to late August, daily except Tuesdays, from the Boppe oak car park at 1000 and 1500. Walking shoes are recommended. 20F.

BLANCAFORT

Château – Guided tour (45 min), 1 April to 2 November, Mondays and Wednesdays-Saturdays, 1000 to 1830, Sundays and public holidays, 1000 to 1200 and 1400 to 1830. 25F. (18F gardens only). ☎ 48 58 60 56 (before 0930).

BLOIS
🛈 11 Place du Château, 41000 ☎ 54 78 55 50

Guided tour of the city: apply to the castle, ☎ 54 78 06 62 or to the Departmental Tourist Committee.

Château – Open 15 March to 1 November, daily, 0900 to 1800; 2 November to 14 March, 0900 to 1200 and 1400 to 1700; guided tour available (1 hour). Closed 1 January and 25 December. There is a Braille brochure and a special itinerary with models and mouldings for the blind. 30F (ticket also valid for the St Saturnin Cloisters). ☎ 54 78 06 62.

Archæological Museum – Same terms and ticket as for the Château.

Fine Arts Museum – Same terms and ticket as for the Château.

Anne of Brittany Pavilion – Open April to September, Monday-Saturday, 0900 to 1900, Sundays and holidays, 1000 to 1300 and 1600 to 1900; October to March, Monday-Saturday, 0900 to 1200 and 1400 to 1800. ☎ 54 74 06 49.

Museum of Religious Art – Open Tuesday-Saturday, 1400 to 1800. Closed public holidays. ☎ 54 78 17 14.

Natural History Museum – Open 1400 to 1800; also 1 June to 31 August, 0900 to 1200. Closed Mondays, 1 January, 1 May, 1 November and 25 December. ☎ 54 74 13 89.

Hôtel d'Alluye Courtyard – Open by prior arrangement. ☎ 54 78 39 80.

Cathedral Crypt – Open daily, 0800 to 1200 and 1400 to 1800.

St Saturnin Cloisters – Open by prior arrangement, 1 June to 30 September, Sundays and public holidays 1000 to 1200 and 1400 to 1830. Same ticket as for Château. ☎ 54 78 06 62.

Excursion

Maves: Windmill – Guided tour (30 min), 3 March to 1 November, 1430 to 1830. Closed Sundays. ☎ 54 87 35 17 and 54 87 31 35.

La BOISSIÈRE

Abbey – Guided tour (30 min), 25 April to 9 May and 1 to 30 August, daily, 1000 to 1200 and 1400 to 1800. 20F.

BONNEVAL
🛈 2 Place de l'Église, 28800 ☎ 37 47 55 89

Guided tour of the town: apply to the Tourist Information centre.

BOUMOIS

Château – Guided tour (45min) July and August, 1000 to 1830; Palm Sunday to 30 June and 1 September to 1 November, 1000 to 1200 and 1400 to 1800. Closed Tuesdays except July and August. 35F. ☎ 41 38 43 16.

La BOURGONNIÈRE

St Saviour's Chapel – Open 1 April to 30 September, Monday-Saturday, 1000 to 1200 and 1400 to 1900, Sundays and public holidays, 1400 to 1900; otherwise, Monday-Saturday, 1000 to 1200 and 1400 to 1700, Sundays and public holidays, 1400 to 1700. Enter through the park and ring the bell at the top of the steps. 10F. ☎ 40 98 10 18.

BOURGUEIL
🛈 Place des Halles, 37140 ☎ 47 97 91 39

Parish Church – Closed Sunday afternoons.

Abbey – Guided tour (1 hour) 1 April to 30 October, weekends and public holidays, 1400 to 1800; also July and August, Mondays, Thursdays, Fridays. 18F. ☎ 47 97 72 04.

Blue Windmill – Open 1 April to 30 September, 1500 to 1900. ☎ 47 97 71 41.

Cave touristique de la Dive Bouteille – Guided tour (30min) 1 April to 30 September, 1000 to 1230 and 1400 to 1830. Closed Mondays except in summer. 12F. ☎ 47 97 72 01.

Excursions

Les Réaux: Château – Interior not open to the public. Literary exhibition "The Loire and its Poets". 15F. ☎ 45 95 14 40.

Chouzé-sur-Loire: Nautical Museum – Open 1 May to 31 August, weekends and public holidays, 1500 to 1800. 10F.

Brain-sur-Allones: Painted Cellar – Guided tour (1 hour) 15 April to 30 September, Monday-Saturday, 1530 to 1800, Sundays and public holidays 1630 to 1800. 10F. ☎ 41 52 87 40.

BREIL

Le Lathan Château – For permission to visit apply to the owners (☎ 41 89 55 06) or the Town Hall (☎ 41 89 55 18).

BRISSAC

Château – Guided tour (1 hour). July and August, 0900 to 1900; 1 April to 30 June and 1 September to 3 November, 0900 to 1200 and 1400 to 1730. Closed Tuesdays except July and August. 35F. ☎ 41 91 22 21.

C

CHAMBORD

Château – Open July and August, 0930 to 1915; 16-30 June and 1-10 September, 0930 to 1815; otherwise, 0930 to 1215 and 1400 to 1815 (1715 2 January to 31 March and 1 October to 31 December). Ticket sales cease 30min before closing time. Closed 1 January, 1 May, 1, 11 November, 25 December. 31F. ☎ 54 20 31 32.
Lecture-tours may be booked in advance, ☎ 54 20 31 50.

CHAMPIGNY-SUR-VEUDE

Sainte-Chapelle – Open 1 April to early October, 1000 to 1200 and 1400 to 1800. 16F. ☎ 47 95 71 46.

CHANTELOUP

Pagoda – Open daily first Sunday in spring to 30 June and 1 to 30 September, 1000 to 1900; 1 July to 31 August, 0900 to 1900; 1 October to 11 November, 1000 to 1200 and 1400 to 1730. 20F. ☎ 47 57 20 97. Walking and picniking permitted in the park.

CHÂTEAUDUN
🚩 1 Rue de Luynes, 28200 ☎ 37 45 22 46

Guided tour of the town: apply to the Tourist Information Centre.

Château – Guided tour (45 min) daily, Palm Sunday to 30 June and 16 to 30 September, 0910 to 1145 and 1400 to 1800; 1 July to 15 September, 0900 to 1930; otherwise, 1000 to 1145 and 1400 to 1600. Closed 1 January, 1 May, 1, 11 November, 25 December. 24F. ☎ 37 45 22 70.

Museum – Open 1 April to 30 September, 1000 to 1230 and 1330 to 1830; otherwise, 1000 to 1200 and 1400 to 1700 (1730 Sundays and public holidays). Closed Tuesdays except July and August; 1 January, 1 May, 25 December. 10F50. ☎ 37 45 55 36.

Foulon Caves – Guided tour (45min) 1 May to 30 September, 1000 to 1200 and 1400 to 1800; otherwise, 1400 to 1800 only. Closed on Mondays in winter. 25F. ☎ 37 45 19 60.

CHÂTEAU-GONTIER
🚩 Mairie, 53200 ☎ 43 07 07 10

Boat trips on the Mayenne – On board the "Duc des Chauvières" with or without meals. Apply to Quai St Fiacre, 53200 Château-Gontier, ☎ 43 70 37 83.

Museum – Open 1 July to 15 September, Wednesday-Saturday, 1400 to 1800; Sundays, 1430 to 1830. ☎ 43 07 26 42.

Manoir de la Touche – Restoration in progress.

Notre-Dame-du-Genneteil Church – Open daily except Tuesdays, 1500 to 1900 (1800 on Sundays).

Excursion

La Maroutière Château – Guided tour (minimum 10 people) on prior application to Château-Gontier Tourist Information Centre. 10F. Riding displays mid-May and early September. ☎ 43 07 07 10 (Château-Gontier Tourist Information Centre) or 43 07 11 91.

CHÂTEAUNEUF-SUR-LOIRE
🚩 Place A. Briand, 45110 ☎ 38 58 44 79

Guided tour of the town: apply to the Tourist Information Centre.

Loire Nautical Museum – Open July and August, daily except Tuesday, 1000 to 1200 and 1400 to 1800; June, Monday, Wednesday-Friday, 1400 to 1800, weekends and public holidays, 1000 to 1200 and 1400 to 1800; 2 January to 31 March, Sunday, 1400 to 1730; October, weekends, 1400 to 1800; otherwise, Sunday and public holidays, 1400 to 1800. Ticket sales cease 30min before closing time. 10F. ☎ 38 58 41 18.

Excursion

Combreux: Étang de la Vallée – Fishing, swimming facilities, boat and pedalo hire.

CHÂTEAU-RENAULT

Leather and Tanning Museum – Guided tour (1 hour) 15 May to 15 September, 1430 to 1730. Closed Monday, Easter, Whitsun and public holidays.

CHAUMONT-SUR-LOIRE CHÂTEAU

Park – Open daily, 0900 to 1120 and 1330 to 1720 (1535, 1 October to 31 March); all day in July and August. Closed 1 January, 1 May, 1, 11 November and 25 December. 25F (ticket also valid for apartments and stables).

Apartments – Open daily, 0915 to 1135 and 1345 to 1735 (1550, 1 October to 31 March); all day in July and August; guided tour (30min) available. Closed 1 January, 1 May, 1, 11 November and 25 December. 25F (ticket also valid for park and stables). ☎ 54 20 98 03.

Stables – Open daily, 0930 to 1215 and 1400 to 1815 (1630, 1 October to 31 March); all day in July and August. Closed 1 January, 1 May, 1, 11 November and 25 December. 25F (ticket also valid for park and apartments).

CHENONCEAU

Château – Open daily, 0930 to 1900 or 1630 (closing time varies according to season). Closed during the lunch hour, mid-November to mid-February. 35F. July and August, child minding and boat trips on the Cher. Refreshments. ☎ 47 23 90 07.

Waxworks Museum – Open same times as the Château. 8F.

Excursion

Leugny Château – Guided tour (30min) 1 April to 31 October; apply in advance to M. Darrasse, Château de Leugny, 37270 Azay-sur-Cher. 25F. ☎ 47 50 41 10.

CHEVERNY

Château – Open 1 June to 15 September, 0915 to 1845; otherwise, 0930 (0915 April and May) to 1200 and 1415 to 1830 (1800 16 to 30 September, 1730 March and October, 1700 November to February). Guided tour available on prior application in writing to Domaine de Cheverny, 41700 Contres. Kennel feeding time 1 April to 15 September, daily except Sundays and public holidays at 1700; otherwise, daily except Tuesdays, weekends and public holidays at 1500. 28F. ☎ 54 79 96 29.

Excursion

Troussay Château – Guided tour (45 min) June to August, 1000 to 1230 and 1400 to 1900; spring holidays 1030 to 1230 and 1400 to 1800; May, September, 1 to 11 November, Sundays and public holidays only, 1030 to 1230 and 1400 to 1800. 20F, 11F outbuildings and Sologne Museum only. ☎ 54 44 29 07.

CHINON
☒ 12 rue Voltaire, 37500 ☎ 47 93 17 85

Guided tour of the town: apply to the Tourist Information Centre or to the "Amis du Vieux Chinon" ☎ 47 93 18 12.

Wine and Cooperage Museum – Guided tour (30min) 1 April to 30 September, 1000 to 1200 and 1400 to 1800. Closed Thursdays. 20F.

Museum of Old Chinon – Open Easter to late September daily except Tuesday, 1000 to 1230 and 1430 to 1800. 15F. ☎ 47 93 18 12.

Castle – Open 1 April to 30 September, 0900 to 1800 (1900 July and August); otherwise, 0900 to 1200 and 1400 to 1700 (1800 15 to 31 March and all October). Closed January, December and Wednesdays from 1 February to 14 March and in November. 21F. ☎ 47 93 13 45.

St Mexme's Church – Closed for repairs.

St Radegund's Chapel – Guided tour (30 min) Easter to late September, 0900 to 1800. 10F.

Excursions

Steam Railway – Train operates late May to early September, weekends; departures 1515, 1615, 1715. 50F (including Locomotive Museum). Information, Richelieu Station ☎ 47 58 12 97.

Vieux Bourg de Cravant: Church – Guided tour (30 min) 1400 to 1900. Closed Tuesdays. 6F. ☎ 47 93 12 40.

Tavant: Church – Guided tour daily except Tuesdays, 1030 to 1200 and 1430 to 1800. 10F (crypt). ☎ 47 58 58 06 (Mme Ferrand) or 47 58 58 01 (Town Hall).

La Devinière – Open 1 May to 30 September, 0900 to 1800; 15 March to 30 April, 0900 to 1200 and 1400 to 1700; otherwise, 0900 to 1200 and 1400 to 1700. Closed Wednesdays out of season; December, January. 17F. ☎ 47 95 91 18.

Chinon Nuclear Power Station – The "Centre d'Information du Public" explains the workings of the power station through audio-visuals aids.
Guided tour (2 hours) July and August at 1000 and 1500; otherwise, (3 hours) at 0915 and 1400. No visits weekends and public holidays. Proof of identity required; apply in advance to Service des Relations Publiques. ☎ 37 98 97 77.

Nuclear Industry Museum – Open all year, Monday-Saturday, 0900 to 1030 and 1400 to 1530 on prior application (see above); 1 May to 31 October, weekends, 0900 to 1030 and 1445 to 1615; 1 November to 30 April, weekends, 1400 to 1530. Closed public holidays.

CHOLET
🏛 Place Rougé, BP 636, 49300 ☎ 41 62 22 35

Guided tour of the town: apply to the Tourist Information Centre.

History and Art Museum – Open daily except Tuesday and public holidays, 1000 to 1200 and 1400 to 1700. ☎ 41 49 29 00.

Excursions

Lake Ribou Leisure Park: La Goubaudière Farm – Open 1500 to 1800. Closed Tuesdays, public holidays. ☎ 41 75 25 94.

Coudray-Montbault Château – Guided tour (1 hour) 1 July to 8 September, 1000 to 1200 and 1430 to 1830. Closed Monday mornings. 20F. ☎ 41 75 80 47.

CINQ-MARS-LA-PILE

Castle – Open daily except Monday, 0900 to sunset. Guided tour (30 min) available. Closed 1 to 15 February and 1 to 22 November. 10F. ☎ 47 96 40 49.

CLÉRY-ST-ANDRÉ

Basilica – For access to Louis XI vault, St James' Chapel and Louis XI oratory, apply to the sacristy or the clergy house (presbytère), 1 Rue du Cloître (near east end of basilica).

COURTANVAUX

Château – Guided tour (1 hour) 1 May to 30 September, 1000 to 1200 and 1400 to 1800; otherwise, Sunday and public holidays only, at same times. 6F50. ☎ 43 35 34 43.

CRAON

Château and Park – Open 1 April to 1 November, daily except Tuesday, 1400 to 1830, July and August only, guided tour (45 min) of the interior. 17F; 10F park only. ☎ 43 06 11 02 and 43 06 34 94.

Excursions

Robert-Tatin Museum – Open daily except Tuesday, 1000 to 1200 and 1400 to 1900 (1730 2 November to 31 March). Closed 24, 25 December. 30F; 40F (including house). ☎ 43 98 80 89.

Renazé: Slate Museum – Open 1 June to 30 September, Tuesday-Saturday 0900 to 1200 and 1400 to 1800; Sunday and public holidays 1400 to 1800; 5 April to 31 May and 1 October to 29 November 1400 to 1800; guided tour (2 hours) available. 20F. ☎ 43 06 41 74 and 43 06 40 14.

Mortiercrolles Château – Guided tour (45min - minimum 4 people) of fortifications and chapel, 14 July to 31 August, daily except Tuesday at 1500, 1600, 1700. 7F.

D

DAMPIERRE-EN-BURLY

Nuclear Power Station – Guided tour (2 hours 30min) at 0900 or 1400. Apply 1-2 weeks in advance to C.P.N. de Dampierre-en-Burly, BP. 18, 45570 Ouzouer-sur-Loire. Proof of identity required. ☎ 38 29 70 04.
Information Centre – Open daily 0845 to 1745.

DESCARTES

Descartes Museum – Guided tour (1 hour) daily except Tuesday, 1400 to 1830. 10F. ☎ 47 59 79 19.

DOUÉ-LA-FONTAINE
🏛 Place du Champ de Foire, 49700 ☎ 41 59 20 49

Zoo – Open 1 April to 30 September, 0900 to 1900. 45F; children (3-10 years) 20F; ticket also valid for the Naturoscope, 1 May to 30 September; otherwise Sunday afternoon only. ☎ 41 59 18 58.

Arena – Guided tour (1 hour) 1 April to 30 October, 1000 to 1200 and 1400 to 1800. Closed Mondays and 5 days around 14 July. 6F. ☎ 41 59 22 28.

Excursions

Rochemenier Troglodyte Village. – Open 1 April to 1 November, 0930 to 1200 and 1400 to 1900. Closed Mondays except July and August. 16F. ☎ 41 59 18 15.

La Fosse Troglodyte Hamlet – Open 1 June to 30 September, 0930 to 1900; 15 March to 30 April and 1 to 15 October, 0930 to 1230 and 1400 to 1800; otherwise, weekends only, 1400 to 1830. Closed January and December as well as Mondays in March, April and October. 17F. ☎ 41 59 00 32.

Sculpted Cavern – Guided tour (30min) July and August, 1000 to 1900; musical evening on Wednesdays at 2100; Palm Sunday to late June and 1 September to 1 November, 1400 to 1800. 17F. ☎ 41 59 15 40.

DURTAL

Château – Guided tour (30min) daily except Monday, 0900 to 1200 and 1400 to 1900. 15F. ☎ 41 76 30 24 (Town Hall).

F

FAYE-LA-VINEUSE

St George's Church, Crypt – Open daily 0900 to 1200 and 1400 to 1900. Apply to M. Paul Baudu opposite the telephone booth. ☎ 47 95 63 32.

La FERTÉ-BERNARD
🅑 Mairie, Rue Carnot, 72400 ☎ 43 93 04 42

St Lyphard's Chapel – Apply to the Tourist Office, ☎ 43 93 25 85 or to the Town Hall, ☎ 43 93 04 42.

La FERTÉ-ST-AUBIN
🅑 Place de la Halle, B.P. 3, 45240 ☎ 38 64 67 93

Guided tour of the town: apply to the Tourist Information Centre.

Château – Open 15 March to 15 November, daily, 1000 to 1900. Unaccompanied tour of stables, menagerie and part of château, guided tour (30min) of ground floor rooms. 30F. ☎ 38 76 52 72.

Excursion

Le Ciran Domain: Museum – Open daily, 1000 to 1200 and 1400 to 1800 (1700 October to April). Closed Tuesdays out of season. 20F. ☎ 38 76 90 93.

La FLÈCHE
🅑 Hôtel-de-ville, 72200 ☎ 43 94 02 53

Military College – Open daily in term time, 0800 to 1200 and 1400 to 1800. 1 July to 31 August, guided tour (1 hour 30min), 1030 to 1230 and 1400 to 1730. 15F. Access from Rue du Collège. Proof of identity required.

Excursion

Le Tertre Rouge Zoo – Open daily, 0900 to 1900. 40F (children 20F). ☎ 43 94 04 55.

FONTEVRAUD-L'ABBAYE
🅑 Mairie, 49590 ☎ 41 51 71 21

Cultural Centre of the West – Details ☎ 41 51 73 52.

Abbey – Extensive restoration work in progress for several years. Open 1 June to 16 September, 0900 to 1900; Palm Sunday to 31 May and 17 September to 31 October, 0930 to 1230 and 1400 to 1800; otherwise 0930 to 1230 and 1400 to 1730. Guided tour available (1 hour). Closed 1 January, 1 May, 1, 11 November, 25 December. 25F. ☎ 41 51 71 41.

St Benedict's Cloisters – Restoration work in progress.

FOUGÈRES-SUR-BIÈVRE

Château – Guided tour (30 min) 1 April to 30 September, 0900 to 1115 and 1400 to 1800; otherwise, 1000 to 1115 and 1400 to 1530. Closed Tuesdays and Wednesdays (except in July and August), 1 January, 1 May, 1, 11 November and 25 December. 18F. ☎ 54 20 27 18.

Excursion

Roujoux Leisure Park – Open Easter to early November, 1100 to 1900 (October weekends only). 40F; children (5-14 years). 18F. ☎ 54 79 53 55.

FRAZÉ

Château – Park only open Easter to late September, Sunday and public holidays, 1500 to 1800. 10F. ☎ 37 29 56 76.

G

GENNES

Archaeological Museum – Open daily except Tuesday, July and August 1000 to 1200 and 1400 to 1800; April, June and September, Sundays and public holidays only, 1000 to 1200 and 1400 to 1800. 15F; ticket also valid for the amphitheatre. ☎ 41 51 83 33.

Amphitheatre – Guided tour (1 hour) same times and ticket, 15F, obtainable from Archaeological Museum, as above. ☎ 41 51 83 33.

St Eusebio's Church – Access to tower July and August, daily, 1500 to 1830; May, June and September, Sunday and public holidays, 1500 to 1830. 10F. ☎ 41 51 84 14.

GERMIGNY-DES-PRÉS

Church – Guided tour available: ☎ 38 58 27 30.

GIEN
🅑 11 Rue Anne-de-Beaujeu, BP 13, 45500 ☎ 38 67 25 28

International Hunting Museum – Open 1 April to 1 November, 0930 to 1830; otherwise, 1000 to 1200 and 1400 to 1700. Closed 1 January to 21 February, 25 December and Mondays from 3 November to 31 March. 23F. ☎ 38 67 69 69.

Faience Factory – **Museum:** open 0900 to 1145 and 1400 to 1745. Closed 1 January, 1 and 11 November, 25 December. 12F. **Factory tours:** individuals may join group tours Monday to Friday midday by prior arrangement. ☎ 38 67 00 05. 15F including admission to museum. **Shop:** open daily except Sundays and public holidays. ☎ 38 67 00 05.

Excursion

St-Brisson-sur-Loire: fortress – Guided tour (1 hour) Easter to 15 November, daily except Tuesdays, 1000 to 1200 and 1400 to 1800. 20F. ☎ 38 36 71 29.

Le GRAND-PRESSIGNY

Prehistory Museum – Open 1 July to 31 August, 0930 to 1200 and 1400 to 1830; 16 March to 30 June and 1 to 30 September, 0900 to 1200 and 1400 to 1800; otherwise, 0900 to 1200 and 1400 to 1700. Closed January and December as well as on Wednesdays from 1 February to 15 March and 1 October to 30 November. 18F. ☎ 47 94 90 20.

GUÉ-PÉAN

Château – Guided tour (45 min) 21 March to 11 November, daily 0900 to 1830; otherwise, 1100 to 1700. 26F. ☎ 54 71 43 01.

I – J

L'ILE-BOUCHARD

St Leonard's Priory – Apply to Mme Berton, 4 Rue de la Vallée aux Nains. ☎ 47 58 60 20.

St Maurice's Church – Apply to St-Gilles parish office. ☎ 47 58 51 03.

ILLIERS-COMBRAY

Aunt Léonie's House – Guided tour (1 hour) at 1500 and 1600. Closed Tuesdays, 1 January, 1 May, 15 August, 1, 11 November and 25 December. 20F. ☎ 37 24 30 97.

JARZÉ

Excursion

Chapel of Our Lady of Montplacé – Apply to Mme d'Orsetti at the clergy house (presbytère).

L

LANGEAIS
🛈 Place du 14-Juillet, 37130 ☎ 47 96 85 75

Château – Open 15 March to 2 November, 0900 to 1830, otherwise, 0900 to 1200 and 1400 to 1700. Guided tour (45min) available. Closed 25 December and Mondays from 3 November to 4 March. 30F. ☎ 47 96 72 60.

Crafts Museum – Open 1 April to 30 September, daily 1000 to 1900; March, October and November, 1000 to 1200 and 1400 to 1800; otherwise, 1400 to 1800 only. 25F. ☎ 47 96 72 64.

LASSAY-SUR-CROISNE

Le Moulin Château – Guided tour (40 min) 1 April to 30 September, 0900 to 1130 and 1400 to 1830; March and 1 October to 15 November, 0900 to 1130 and 1400 to 1730. 25F. ☎ 54 83 83 51.

LAVARDIN

Castle – Open June to September, 0900 to 1800. ☎ 54 85 07 74.

Town Hall – Open Mondays, 1330 to 1700, Wednesdays and Fridays, 1500 to 1900. ☎ 54 85 07 74.

LAYON VALLEY

Beaulieu-sur-Layon: Wine Cellars (Caveau du Vin) – Open 0900 to 1200 and 1400 to 1700. Apply to ☎ 41 78 31 30.

St-Lambert-du-Lattay: Museum of the Grape and the Wine of Anjou – Open 1 April to 31 October, daily, 1000 to 1200 and 1430 to 1830. 18F. ☎ 41 78 42 75.

Château de la Haute-Guerche – Open July and August, 1000 to 1200 and 1400 to 1800.

Le LIGET CHARTERHOUSE

Charterhouse and St John's Chapel – Apply to Mme Arnould, ☎ 47 92 60 02.

Le LION D'ANGERS

L'Isle-Briand National Sud – Open all year, 1400 to 1700 (1630 Sundays and public holidays). ☎ 41 95 82 46.

LIRÉ

Joachim du Bellay Museum – Open 1000 to 1200 and 1400 to 1800. Closed Mondays and Fridays except July and August. 12F. ☎ 40 09 04 13.

LOCHES

Guided tour of the town: apply to the Tourist Information Centre.

Medieval City – Tour by night 1 July to early September except during "son et lumière" shows. Starts 2130 from the Tourist Information Centre. 25F. ☎ 47 59 07 98.

Lansyer Museum – Guided tour (1 hour) 0900 to 1145 and 1400 to 1800 (1700 in March and October, 1600 10 January to late February and in November). Closed Fridays out of season. 12F. ☎ 47 59 05 45.

Le Terroir Museum – Open same times and charges as Lansyer Museum.

Castle – Open July and August, 0900 to 1800; 15 March to 30 June and September, 0900 to 1200 and 1400 to 1800; 1 February to 14 March and 1 October to 30 November, 0900 to 1200 and 1400 to 1700. Closed Wednesdays out of season; January; December. 23F. Ticket also valid for the Keep. ☎ 47 59 01 32.

Keep – Guided tour (45min) July and August, 0930 to 1830; 15 March to 30 June and in September, 0930 to 1230 and 1430 to 1830; 1 February to 14 March and 1 October to 30 November, 0930 to 1230 and 1430 to 1730. 23F; ticket also valid for the Royal Apartments in the Château. ☎ 47 59 07 86.

LOIR VALLEY

Château-du-Loir: St Guingalois'Church – To view the *Christ Reviled* in the Sacristy apply to the clergy house (presbytère), 2 Rue Gendron. ☎ 43 44 01 28.

Vaas: Corn Mill – Guided tour (1 hour 30min). Easter to late September, 1500 to 1800. Closed Tuesday, Thursday and Friday. 15F. ☎ 43 46 70 22.

Vénevelles Manor – Garden only. ☎ 43 45 44 60.

Gallerande Château – Not open to the public but may be viewed from the courtyard gate.

LOIRE VALLEY

St-Laurent-des-Eaux Nuclear Power Station – Information centre open daily. Guided tour of power station (minimum 2 hours 30min) Mondays to Saturdays. 1000 to 1800 by prior appointment. Proof of identity required. Apply to Service des Relations Publiques, B.P. 42, 41220 St-Laurent-Nouan. ☎ 54 44 84 09.

St-Dyé-sur-Loire:

Church – If closed consult directions in doorway.

Maison de la Loire – Open daily, 1400 to 1800. ☎ 54 81 65 45.

Saut-aux-Loups (mushroom galleries) – Open daily, 1 March to 11 November, 1000 to 1830. 15F. Mushroom sampling in season. ☎ 41 51 70 30.

Turquant: Troglo'Tap (dried apples) – Open July and August daily except Mondays, 1000 to 1200 and 1430 to 1830; June and September, 1430 to 1830; Easter to 11 November, weekends, 1000 to 1200 and 1430 to 1830. 20F. Dried apple sampling. ☎ 41 51 48 30.

St-Maur-de-Glanfeuil Abbey – **Two chapels and St Maurus'Cross:** open 1000 to 1130 and 1430 to 1830. Closed January. Guided tour (1 hour) available by prior arrangement. ☎ 41 57 04 16.

Montjean-sur-Loire: Museum – Open Easter to 1 November, daily except Monday, 1500 to 1900 (last tour begins at 1800). Guided tour (1 hour 30min) available. 20F. ☎ 41 39 08 48.

Oudon: Tower – Open July and August, daily, 1000 to 1200 and 1530 to 1730; May, June and 1 to 15 September, weekends and public holidays, 1000 to 1200 and 1530 to 1730. 4F50. ☎ 40 83 60 17 (Town Hall).

LORRIS

Guided tour of the town: apply to the Tourist Information Centre.

Museum of the Resistance and Deportations – Open daily, 1000 to 1200 and 1330 to 1730. Closed Tuesday and Sunday mornings. 20F. ☎ 38 94 84 19.

Le LUDE CHÂTEAU

Château – Open 1 April to 30 September, park 1000 to 1200, interior 1400 to 1800. 22F (park and interior), 18F (park only). ☎ 43 94 60 09.

M

Le MANS

Guided tour of the town: apply to Association des Guides-Conférenciers du Maine, Tourist Information Centre.

Museum of History and Ethnography – Open 0900 (1000 Sundays) to 1200 and 1400 to 1800. Closed public holidays. 10F. ☎ 43 47 38 51.

Tessé Museum – Same times and charges as for the Museum of History and Ethnography.

Excursions

L'Épau Abbey – To visit apply to Le Mans Tourist Information Centre (telephone number above). Guided tour available (30min). Open 0930 to 1200 and 1400 to 1800. 5F; 10F during exhibitions. ☎ 43 84 22 29.

Bugatti Permanent Circuit – Apply to the Director of the Circuit. Guided tour (1 hour) available. ☎ 43 72 50 48 and 43 72 50 25. Fax 43 75 39 10.

Motor Museum – Open Easter to 15 October, 1000 to 1900 (2000 weekends); otherwise, Monday-Friday 1200 to 1800, weekends, 1000 to 1800. Closed early January to beginning of February holidays and Tuesdays out of season. 35F. ☎ 43 72 72 24.

Spay: Church – Open Monday-Saturday, 0900 to 1800 (1700 in winter); Sunday, 1100 to 1800.

Les MAUGES

Chemillé: La Sorinière Chapel – Open 1 June to 30 September, 1500 to 1800. 10F. ☎ 41 30 35 17.

St-Laurent-de-la-Plaine: Museum of Old Crafts – Open 1 April to 1 November, 0900 to 1200 and 1400 to 1800. 25F. 41 78 24 08.

MAULÉVRIER

Oriental Park – Open 1 May to 30 September, 0900 to 1200 and 1400 to 1800 (1900 Sundays and public holidays); otherwise, 1400 to 1800 (1900 Sundays and public holidays). Closed 23 December to 2 January as well as Mondays from 3 January to 1 May. 20F. ☎ 41 55 50 14.

MAYENNE VALLEY

Chenillé-Changé :

Water-mill – Open all year, by prior arrangement. 15F. ☎ 41 05 10 83.

River cruises – Boats may be hired (no permit required) for one or two days. Apply to Maine-Anjou-Rivières, 49220 Chenillé-Changé. ☎ 41 95 10 83.

Grez-Neuville: River Cruises – For information and reservations apply to Anjou Plaisance, Rue de l'Écluse. ☎ 41 88 88 78.

MEUNG-SUR-LOIRE

🛈 42 Rue Jehan de Meung, 45130 ☎ 38 44 32 28

Guided tour of the town: apply to the Tourist Information Centre.

Château – Guided tour (1 hour) 1 July to 31 August, 0945 to 1230 and 1300 to 1730; 1 April to 30 June, 1000 to 1145 and 1400 to 1700; 1 September to 31 October, 1000 to 1130 and 1400 to 1630. 25F. ☎ 38 44 25 61.

MIRÉ

Vaux Château – Restoration in progress; re-opening in 1996.

MONDOUBLEAU

Excursion

St-Agil Château – Exterior only 1000 to 1800.

MONTGEOFFROY

Château – Guided tour (1 hour) 15 June to 15 September, daily, 0930 to 1830; 15 March to 14 June and 16 September to 1 November, 0930 to 1200 and 1430 to 1830. 35F. ☎ 41 80 60 02.

MONTIGNY-LE-GANELON

Château – Park and Agricultural Museum: open mid-March to 1 November, daily, except Sunday mornings, 1100 to 1800. **Château interior:** guided tour (1 hour) June, July, August and September, daily, 1400 to 1900; otherwise, weekends and public holidays 1400 to 1900. 25F (park, château and museum); 10F (park and museum). ☎ 37 98 30 03.

Church – Apply to the château.

MONTLOUIS-SUR-LOIRE

Loire House – Open 1 June to 30 September, Mondays, Wednesday-Saturday, 1000 to 1200 and 1400 to 1900; Sundays and public holidays, 1400 to 1900; otherwise, 1400 to 1800. Closed Tuesdays; 1 January, 25 December. 12F. ☎ 47 50 97 52.

MONTOIRE-SUR-LE-LOIR

St Giles' Chapel – Apply to M. Chéreau in the antique shop, Rue St-Oustrille.

Castle – Not open to the public at present.

MONTPOUPON

Outbuildings – Guided tour (30 min) July and August, 1000 to 1900; 15-30 June and September, 1000 to 1200 and 1400 to 1900; 1 April to 14 June and October, weekends and public holidays only. 20F. ☎ 47 94 30 77.

MONTRÉSOR

Château – Park and ramparts: open 1 April to 31 October, 1000 to 1200 and 1400 to 1800.
Château interior: guided tour (30 min). 29F. ☎ 47 92 60 04.

MONTREUIL-BELLAY
☐ Rue du Marché, 49260 ☎ 41 52 32 39

Château – Guided tour (45 min) 1 April to 1 November, 1000 to 1200 and 1400 to
1800. Closed Tuesdays. 32F. ☎ 41 52 33 06.

Maison Dovalle – Open 1 July to 10 September, 1400 to 1800, otherwise by
appointment only. Closed Tuesdays. ☎ 41 52 48 46.

Excursions

La Salle Water-Mill (Moulin de la Salle) – Guided tour 1 May to 15 September, Sundays
and public holidays, 1500 to 1800. 20F. ☎ 41 52 30 62.

Asnières Abbey – Guided tour (30 min) July and August, daily except Tuesday 0930 to
1200 and 1400 to 1800. 6F

MONTRICHARD
☐ 1 Rue du Pont, 41400 ☎ 54 32 05 10

Wine Cellars – Guided tour (45min) Palm Sunday to 11 November, 0900 (1030
Sundays and public holidays) to 1200 and 1400 to 1900; otherwise, Monday-Saturday
only, 0930 to 1100 and 1430 to 1630. ☎ 54 32 07 04.

Keep – Open Easter holidays and 15 June to 31 August, daily; Palm Sunday to 15 June
and September, weekends and public holidays only, 0930 to 1200 and 1430 to 1800.
8F, ☎ 54 32 05 10.

Excursion

Thésée: Archæological Museum – Guided tour (45min) 15 June to 15 September, daily,
1000 to 1200 and 1400 to 1800; Easter to 14 June, weekends and public holidays only,
1400 to 1700, 10F. ☎ 54 71 40 20.

MONTSOREAU

Castle – Guided tour (1 hour) 1000 to 1200 and 1400 to 1800. Closed 1 January,
1, 11 November, 25 December and Tuesdays from mid-December to late February.
21F. ☎ 41 51 70 25.

La Herpinière Windmill – Guided tour (1 hour 15min) all year, 1 May to 30 September, 1000 to 1300 and 1500 to 2000; 1 October to 30 April, 1400 to 1800. 18F.
☎ 41 51 75 22.

N

NOYANT-LA-GRAVOYÈRE

Blue Mine – Open 1 March to 15 November, 1000 to 1800; daily May to September;
closed Tuesdays in March, April, October and November. Funicular operates every
15 minutes (last descent at 1700). Temperature 13°C-55°. Warm clothes and walking
shoes recommended. 65F (children 45F). ☎ 41 61 55 60. Trains leave from the Leisure
Park (see below).

St-Blaise Leisure Park – Open 1 April to 1 November. ☎ 41 61 75 39.

O

ORLÉANS
☐ Place d'Arc, 45000 ☎ 38 53 05 95

Guided tour of the city: apply to the Tourist Information Centre.

St Cross Cathedral Crypt and Treasury – Guided tour (45min) 15 June to
15 September, daily except Fridays, 1500 to 1900. 9F. ☎ 38 66 64 17 (M. Grandet).

Fine Arts Museum – Open daily except Tuesday, 1000 to 1200 and 1400 to 1800.
Closed 1 January, 1, 8 May, 1 November, 25 December. 14F; no charge Sunday
mornings and Wednesdays. ☎ 38 53 39 22.

Historical Museum – Same times as Fine Arts Museum. 8F; no charge Sunday
mornings and Wednesdays. ☎ 38 53 39 22.

Charles Péguy Centre – Open Monday-Friday, afternoons only. Closed public
holidays and August. ☎ 38 53 20 23.

Joan of Arc House – Open 2 May to 31 October, 1000 to 1200 and 1400 to 1800;
otherwise, 1400 to 1800. Closed Mondays, 1 January, 29 April, 25 December. 9F.
☎ 38 42 25 45.

Joan of Arc Centre – Open 0900 to 1200 and 1400 to 1800 (1600 Fridays). Closed
weekends 1 January, 8 May, 14 July and 25 December. ☎ 38 42 22 69.

Hôtel Toutin: Courtyard – Open daily except Sundays, Mondays, public holidays and
August 1000 to 1230 and 1400 to 1830.

Natural History Museum – Reorganisation in progress. ☎ 38 54 61 05 or 38 42 25 58.

La Source Floral Park – Open 1 April to 11 November, 0900 to 1800; otherwise, 1400
to 1700. 18F. ☎ 38 63 33 17.

P

Le PERCHE-GOUËT

Semur-en-Vallon: Tourist Railway – Train in operation: 1 July to 31 August, Saturdays, 1600 to 1800; Sundays and public holidays, 1430 to 1830; 1 May to 30 June and September, Sundays and public holidays, 1430 to 1830 (Monday-Saturday by prior arrangement). 10F. ☎ 43 71 30 36 (at mealtimes).

Montmirail: Castle – Guided tour (45min) 1 July to 5 September, daily except Tuesdays, 1400 to 1830; 1 March to late June and 6 September to 31 October, Sundays, and public holidays, 1400 to 1830. 25F. ☎ 43 93 72 71.

PITHIVIERS
🏛 Mail Ouest Gare Routière, 45300 ☎ 38 30 50 02

Guided tour of the town: apply to Tourist Information Centre.

Transport Museum – Open 1 May to 11 October, Sundays and public holidays only, 1430 to 1800. 28F (includes museum and train ride). Further details and steam railway reservations: ☎ 38 30 50 02.

Municipal Museum – Open daily except Tuesdays and public holidays, 1000 to 1200 and 1400 to 1800 (1700 Saturdays). 2F. ☎ 38 30 10 72.

Le PLESSIS-BOURRÉ

Château – Guided tour (1 hour) 15 February to 30 November daily except Wednesdays and Thursday mornings, 1000 to 1200 and 1400 to 1830 (1700 in winter); July and August 1000 to 1830. The double drawbridge is raised on the last Sunday of the month or by prior arrangement. The attics, which are not easily accessible, are only open on the last Sunday of the month or by prior arrangement. The cellars are only open in summer. 32F. ☎ 41 32 06 01.

Excursion

La Hamonnière Manor – Guided tour (20 min) 14 July to 31 August, 1400 to 1800. 10F.

Le PLESSIS-MACÉ

Château – Guided tour (1 hour) 1 June to late September, 1000 to 1200 and 1400 to 1830; May, 1330 to 1800; March, April and October, 1330 to 1730. Closed November to February and Tuesdays; except in July and August. 21F. ☎ 41 32 67 93.

PONCÉ-SUR-LE-LOIR

Craft Centre – **Workshops:** open Monday-Saturday, 0900 to 1200 and 1400 to 1800. **Shop and exhibition** only (plus audio-visual show): open Sundays and public holidays, 1400 to 1830. ☎ 43 44 45 31.

Château – Open 1 April to 30 September, 1000 to 1200 and 1400 to 1800. Closed Sunday and public holidays mornings. 20F. ☎ 43 44 45 39.

PONTLEVOY

Abbey – Guided tour (1 hour 15min) July and August 0930 to 1900, 1 April to 30 June and 1 September to 3 November, 1000 to 1200 and 1430 to 1830. Closed Mondays except July and August. 20F; ticket also valid for the **Road Transport Museum** and **Municipal Museum.** ☎ 54 32 60 80.

LA POSSONIERE

Manor House – Guided tour (45min) July and August, weekends and public holidays at 1500 and 1700. 20F.

POUANCÉ

Castle – Guided tour (1 hour) daily except Sunday mornings, 0900 to 1200 and 1400 to 1900. Closed 1 January, 1 November and 24 December. 12F. ☎ 41 92 45 02.

Excursion

La Motte-Glain Château – Guided tour (40 min) 15 June to 15 September, daily except Tuesday, 1430 to 1830. 25F. ☎ 40 55 52 01.

R

RICHELIEU

Richelieu Museum – Open daily except Tuesdays, 1000 to 1200 and 1400 to 1800 (1600 1 September to 30 June). Closed September to June, weekends. 7F. ☎ 47 58 10 13.

Park – Open 15 June to 15 September, 1000 to 1830.

Excursions

Steam Railway – Train operates weekends from late May to early September. Departures at 1515, 1615 and 1715. 50F (ticket also valid for Locomotive Museum). Information Richelieu Station. ☎ 47 58 12 97.

La Roche-du-Maine Château – Guided tour (1 hour) 15 June to 15 September, daily at 1500, 1600 and 1700; 1 April to 14 June and 16 September to 31 October. Sundays only. 25F. ☎ 49 22 84 09.

Bois-Aubry Abbey – Open daily 1000 to 1800.

Le RIVAU

Castle – Guided tour (45 min) Palm Sunday to 1 November, 1000 to 1200 and 1400 to 1900. 30F. ☎ 47 95 77 13.

La ROCHE-RACAN

Château – Guided tour (45 min) 5 August to 15 September, 1000 to 1200 and 1500 to 1700. 15F.

ROMORANTIN-LANTHENAY
🛈 Place de la Paix, 41200 ☎ 54 76 43 89

Guided tour of the town: apply to the Tourist Information Centre.

Archæological Museum (Maison du Carroir d'Orée) – Open July and August, Mondays to Saturdays, 0830 to 1200; afternoons by prior arrangement only. Guided tour (30 min) available. 8F. ☎ 54 76 22 06.

Sologne Museum – Open 1000 to 1200 and 1400 to 1800. Closed Tuesdays, Sunday mornings, 1 January, 1 May and 25 December. 8F. ☎ 54 76 07 06.

Motor Racing Museum – Open 15 March to 11 November, 1000 to 1200 and 1400 to 1800. Closed Tuesdays, Sunday mornings and 1 May. 8F. ☎ 54 76 07 06.

S

SABLÉ-SUR-SARTHE

River Cruises – Boats for hire ; see the table on p 216.

SACHÉ

Château – Guided tour (30min) July and August, 0930 to 1830; otherwise, 0900 to 1200 and 1400 to 1800 (1700 out of season). Closed Wednesdays out of season and December. 20F. ☎ 47 26 86 50.

ST-AIGNAN
🛈 Mairie, 41110 ☎ 54 75 22 85

St Aignan's Church – Audio-guided tour except Sunday mornings.

Château – Access to courtyard only. Apply to custodian.

Provost's House – Open only for exhibitions Easter to September. Apply to the Town Hall. ☎ 54 75 04 58.

Excursions

Beauval Zoological Park – Open daily, 0900 to dusk. 32F. ☎ 54 75 05 56.

Chémery Château – Restoration in progress. Open daily, 1000 to dusk. 20F. ☎ 54 71 82 77.

ST-BENOÎT-SUR-LOIRE

Basilica – Guided tour Easter to late October, for times see notice at entrance. No tour during Holy Week. Information ☎ 38 35 72 43.

Services – Gregorian chant; discreet attendance requested. Community mass Monday-Saturday, 1200; Sundays and feast days, 1130. Vespers, daily, 1820.

ST-FLORENT-LE-VIEIL

Local History Museum – Open 1 July to 15 September, daily, 1430 to 1830; Easter to 30 June, weekends and public holidays, 1430 to 1830; 16 September to late October, Sundays only, 1430 to 1830. 13F. ☎ 41 72 75 41 and 41 72 50 20.

Les Coteaux Abbey Farm – Open 1 June to 15 September, 1430 to 1900; April and May, weekends only, 1430 to 1900; 16 September to 1 November, Sundays only, 1430 to 1800. 25F. ☎ 41 72 52 37.

STE-CATHERINE-DE-FIERBOIS

Boucicault Almonry – Closed for restoration. Information ☎ 47 65 65 36 (Museum) or 47 65 43 46 (Town Hall).

SARTHE VALLEY

Malicorne-sur-Sarthe: Pottery – Guided tour (1 hour 15min) Easter to 30 September, 0900 to 1200 and 1400 to 1700. Closed Sunday mornings, Mondays, Whit Sunday and the third Sunday in September. 15F. ☎ 43 94 81 18.

SAUMUR

🖻 Place de la Bilange, B.P. 241, 49400 ☎ 41 51 03 06

Guided tour of the town: apply to the Tourist Information Centre.

Château – Museum of Decorative Arts – guided tour (1 hour 15min) – and **Equine Museum,** open 15 June to 15 September, 0900 to 1900; 1 April to 14 June and 16 to 30 September, 0900 to 1200 and 1400 to 1800; 1 October to 31 March (except Tuesdays), 1000 to 1200 and 1400 to 1700. Evening visits July and Augusts, 1900 to 2200. Closed 1 January and 25 December. 28F. ☎ 41 51 30 46.

Toy and Figurine Museum, open 1 July to 31 August, 1100 to 1800; 1 April to 30 June and in September, 1030 to 1200 and 1430 to 1800. 10F. ☎ 41 67 39 23.

Cavalry School Museum – Open Tuesdays, Wednesdays, Thurdays and Sundays, 0900 to 1200 and 1400 to 1700; Saturdays, 1400 to 1700. Closed 1 January and 25 December. ☎ 41 51 05 43 ext 306 and 448.

Tank Museum – Open 0900 to 1200 and 1400 to 1800. 20F. ☎ 41 67 20 96.

National Equitation Centre – Guided tour (1 hour 30min), including Black Squad training in dressage arena, late March to late September, mornings, 0930-1030; 30F; afternoons, tour (1 hour) of the centre, 1430-1600; 20F.
Closed Monday mornings, Saturday afternoons, Sundays and from early October to late March. Displays of horsemanship by the Black Squad several times a year in dressage arena. Repeat performances of Airs above the ground and Dressage with commentary. For details: ☎ 41 50 21 35 ext 381.

Mushroom Museum – Open 1 March to 15 November, daily, 1000 to 1900. Guided tour (45min) available. 28F. ☎ 41 50 31 55.

Excursions: Bagneux

Engine Museum – Open 1 June to 5 September, daily except Thursdays, 1430 to 1830; 19 April to 31 May and 6 September to 4 October, weekends, 1430 to 1800. 20F. ☎ 41 50 26 10.

Dolmen – Open 16 March to 30 September, 0900 to 1900; otherwise, 0900 to 1800. 6F. ☎ 41 50 23 02.

St-Cyr-en-Bourg: Wine-Makers' Cellar – Guided tour (45min) 1 May to 30 September at 1030, 1430 and 1730. 6F. ☎ 41 83 43 28.

SAVONNIÈRES

Petrifying Caves – Guided tour (1 hour) 1 April to 30 September, 0900 to 1900; 5 February to 31 March and 1 October to 15 December, 0900 to 1200 and 1400 to 1800. Closed Thursdays out of season. 21F. ☎ 47 50 00 09.

SEGRÉ

Excursions

La Lorie Château – Guided tour (30min) 1 July to 15 September, daily except Tuesday, 1500 to 1800. 20F. ☎ 41 92 10 04.

Raguin Château – Guided tour (30min) 1 July to 1 September, 1400 to 1800. 25F. ☎ 41 61 40 20.

SELLES-SUR-CHER

Castle – Guided tour (45min) and *tableaux vivants* with costumed actors, summer holidays, 1000 to 1900; late March to early November, 1000 to 1200 and 1400 to 1800. 25F or 30F depending on the time of year. ☎ 54 97 63 98.

Cher Valley Museum – Open Whitsun to mid-September, daily except Mondays, 1430 to 1830. 15F. ☎ 54 97 40 19.

Excursion

Meusnes: Gunflint Museum – Open 0900 to 1300. Closed Sundays, Mondays and public holidays. 5F. ☎ 54 71 00 23.

SERRANT

Château – Guided tour (1 hour) 28 March to 1 November, 0900 to 1130 and 1400 to 1730.
Closed Tuesdays except in July and August. 32F. ☎ 41 39 13 01.

SOLESMES

Abbey services – Daily: Gregorian chant at 0945, Sext at 1300, Nones at 1350, Vespers at 1700 and Compline at 2030.

The SOLOGNE

Train Rides – All details on dates and times of operations, charges etc from Compagnie du Blanc Argent, Romorantin-Lanthenay Station. ☎ 54 76 06 51 and 54 76 02 72.

Gy-en-Sologne: Sologne Cottage (Locature de la Straize) – Guided tour (1 hour) 20 March to 1 September, daily except Tuesdays, 1000 to 1100 and 1500 to 1730; 2 September to 15 November, 1000 to 1100 and 1500 to 1700 (1600 15 October to 15 November). 14F. ☎ 54 83 82 89.

SULLY-SUR-LOIRE

Guided tour of the town: apply to the Tourist Information Centre, Place Général-de-Gaulle. ☎ 38 36 23 70.

Castle – Guided tour (45 min) 1 May to 30 September, 0900 to 1145 and 1400 to 1745; 1 March to 30 April and 1 October to 30 November, 1000 to 1145 and 1400 to 1645 (1745 in April and October). 12F. ☎ 38 36 36 86.

T

TALCY

Castle – Open 1 April to 30 September, 0930 to 1100 and 1400 to 1800 (all day weekends July and August, Easter Sunday and Monday and Whit Sunday and Monday); otherwise, 1000 to 1115 and 1400 to 1630. Guided tour (30 min) available. Closed Tuesdays out of season, 1 January, 1 May, 1, 11 November, 25 December. 20F. ☎ 54 81 03 01.

TOURS
🖪 9 Rue Buffon, 37000. ☎ 47 31 48 05

Coach tour of the city, apply to the Tourist Information Centre. Guided tour of foot, apply to Direction Départementale du Tourisme, 9 Rue du Buffon. ☎ 47 31 47 97.

Tristan's House: Courtyard – Open to visitors during school hours Mondays to Fridays except public holidays.

Gemmail Museum – Open daily except Mondays, 30 May to 15 October, 1000 to 1200 and 1400 to 1830. 25F. ☎ 47 61 01 19.

Museum of St Martin – Open mid-March to mid-November, daily except Mondays and Tuesdays, 0930 to 1245 and 1400 to 1800. 15F. ☎ 47 64 48 87 and 47 05 68 73.

Hôtel Gouin – Open 15 May to 15 September, 1000 to 1900; 15 March to 14 May, 1000 to 1230 and 1400 to 1830; 1 February to 14 March and 1 October to 30 November, 1030 to 1230 and 1400 to 1730. Closed Fridays in winter. 17F. ☎ 47 66 22 32.

The Psalette – Guided tour (30 min), daily, 0900 to 1200 and 1400 to 1800 (1700 1 October to 31 May). Closed 1 January, 1 May, 1 and 11 November and 25 December. No admission during services. 20F.

Contemporary Arts Centre – Open Wednesdays to Sundays, 1500 to 1900. Closed 24 and 25 December. ☎ 47 66 50 00.

Fines Arts Musuem – Open daily except Tuesday, 0900 to 1245 and 1400 to 1800. Closed 1 January, 1 May, 14 July, 1, 11 November, 25 December. 30F. ☎ 47 05 68 73.

Historical Museum – Open 16 June to 15 September, 0900 to 1830; 16 March to 15 June and 16 September to 15 November, 0900 to 1130 and 1400 to 1830; otherwise, 1400 to 1730. 29F. ☎ 47 61 02 95.

Aquarium – Open 1 July to 31 August, 0930 to 1900; 1 April to 30 June and 1 September to 15 November, 0930 to 1200 and 1400 to 1800; otherwise, 1400 to 1800. 22F. ☎ 47 64 29 52.

Tours History Workshop – Open 15 April to 15 October, daily except Tuesdays, 1400 to 1800; otherwise by prior arrangement. ☎ 47 66 72 37.

Touraine Wine Museum – Open daily except Tuesday, 0900 to 1200 and 1400 to 1800 (1700 1 October to 31 March). Guided tour (45 min) available on prior application in writing to the Director of Trade Guild Museum. Closed 1 January, 1 May, 14 July, 1, 11 November, 25 December. Ticket sales cease 30 min before closing time. 10F. ☎ 47 61 07 93.

Trade Guild Museum – Open 16 June to 15 September, 0900 to 1830; otherwise, 0900 to 1200 and 1400 to 1800 (1700 16 September to 31 March). Ticket sales cease 30 min before closing time. Closed Tuesdays in winter; 1 January, 1 May, 14 July, 1 and 11 November and 25 December. 20F. ☎ 47 61 07 93.

St Cosmas' Priory – Open July and August, 0900 to 1800; otherwise, 0900 to 1200 and 1400 to 1800 (1700 early February to mid-March and 1 October to 30 November). Closed Wednesdays out of season. 20F. ☎ 47 37 32 70.

Plessis-lès-Tours Château – Guided tour (45 min) 1000 to 1200 and 1400 to 1800 (1700 1 October to 31 March). Closed Tuesdays; January, 1 May, 14 July, 1, 11 November, 25 December. 10F. ☎ 47 37 22 80.

Excursion

Meslay Tithe Barn – Open Easter to 1 November, weekends and public holidays, 1500 to 1830. 15F. ☎ 47 29 19 29.

TROO

Petrifying Cave – Open 1 April to 30 September, daily, 0900 to 1900 5F. ☎ 54 72 52 04.

This guide, which is revised regularly ,
is based on tourist information provided at the time of going to press.
Changes are however inevitable owing to improved facilities and fluctuations in
the cost of living.

U - V - Y

USSÉ

Château – Guided tour (45min) Easter to 30 September, 0900 to 1200 and 1400 to 1900 (all day 14 July to late August); 15 March to Easter, 0900 to 1200 and 1400 to 1800; 1 October to 11 November, 1000 to 1200 and 1400 to 1730. 49F. ☎ 47 95 54 05.

VALENCAY

Château – Guided tour (45min) of the apartments 15 June to 15 September, 0900 to 1815 (time of last tour); 16 March to 14 June and 16 September to 14 November, 0900 to 1115 (time of last morning tour) and 1400 to 1815 or earlier according to the closing of the Park (see below). Dining room and kitchens, afternoons only. Closed 15 November to 15 March. 30F; ticket also valid for the Park and Car Museum; 7F supplement for dining room and kitchens. ☎ 54 00 10 66.

Park – Open 16 March to 14 November, 0900 to dusk; closed 1 January, 25 December. 7F.

Car Museum – Open 0900 to 1200 and 1400 to 1900. 30F; ticket also valid for the château and park.

Excursion

Luçay-le-Mâle: Gunflint Museum – Open all year, afternoons. ☎ 54 40 43 97.

VENDÔME

🏠 Hôtel du Bellay, Parc Ronsard, 41100 ☎ 54 77 05 07

Guided tour of the town: apply to the Tourist Information Centre.

Boat trips on the Loir – Departures from the landing stage at the "Vieux Moulin" restaurant, 21-23 Rue du Change, afternoons in July and August. Trip lasts approx. 30min. 15F.

Holy Trinity Abbey Chapter House – Apply to museum (see below).

Museum – Open daily except Tuesday, 1000 to 1200 and 1400 to 1800. Closed 1 January, 1 May, 25 December. 12F. ☎ 54 77 26 13.

Castle – Open 1 April to 31 May, 0900 to 1900; 1 June to 15 October, 0900 to 2000; 15 October to 31 March, 0900 to 1800. Guided tour available, apply to the Tourist Information Centre (see above).

VILLANDRY

Gardens – Open 1 June to 15 September, 0830 to 2000; 1 April to 31 May and 16-30 September, 0900 to 1930; otherwise, 0900 to dusk. 23F (20F 1 December to 28 February). ☎ 47 50 02 09.

Château – Open 16 April to 15 September, 0900 to 1830; mid-March to 15 April and 16 September to 11 November, 0900 to 1700. Guided tour available (45min). 12F.

VILLESAVIN

Château – Guided tour (45min) 1 May to 30 September, 1000 to 1900; 1 March to 30 April, 1000 to 1200 and 1400 to 1900; 1 October to 20 December, 1400 to 1700. 20F; only 10F. ☎ 54 46 42 88.

YÈVRE-LE-CHÂTEL

Fortress – Guided tour (45min) 1 May to 31 October, daily except Tuesday, 1400 to 1800. 7F. ☎ 38 34 22 69.

INDEX

Tours Indre-et-Loire......... Towns, sights and tourist regions followed by the name of the *département*.

Amboise Conspiracy......... People, historical events, artistic styles and local terms mentioned in the guide.

A

Abbo	175
Abd el-Kader	46
Aigre (Valley)	102
Alain-Fournier	14, 30
Alcuin	20, 29, 192
Alexandrine	83
Alluyes Eure-et-Loir	74
Amboise Indre-et-Loire	44, 219
Amboise Conspiracy	45
Ancenis Loire-Atlantique	137
Angers Maine-et-Loire	48
Angers, David of	31, 52, 178
Angevin Corniche Road	136
Angevin style	37
Anjou	218, 219
Anjou, House of	48, 49
Anne of Brittany	68, 120
Antin, Duke of	66
Arbrissel, Robert d'	111
Areines Loir-et-Cher	56
Argent-sur-Sauldre Cher	56
Arville Loir-et-Cher	56
Asnières (Former Abbey)	156
Asnières-sur-Vègre Sarthe	57
Aubigné, Françoise d'	140
Aubigné Maine-et-Loire	122
Aubigny-sur-Nère Cher	57
Audoux, Marguerite	58
Auvers-le-Hamon Sarthe	174
Avon-les-Roches Indre-et-Loire	146
Azay-le-Rideau (Château)	59, 219
Azay-sur-Indre Indre-et-Loire	127

B

Babou Family	153
Bagneux Maine-et-Loire	184
Baïf Jean Antoine de	30
Baillou Loir-et-Cher	152
Balesmes Indre-et-Loire	105
La Balue, Cardinal	126, 200
Balzac, Honoré de	30, 174, 203, 208
Bastarnay, Imbert de	155
Baudri de Bourgueil	29
Baugé Maine-et-Loire	60
Baugeois, The	61
La Baume le Blanc, Louise de	87
Bazin, Hervé	30
Bazin, René	30
La Bazoche-Gouet Eure-et-Loir	167
Bazouges-sur-le-Loir Sarthe	63

Beauce	15
Beaufort-en-Vallée Maine-et-Loire	63
Beaugency Loiret	63
Beaujeu, Anne de	115
Beaulieu-lès-Loches Indre-et-Loire	65
Beaulieu-sur-Layon Maine-et-Loire	123
Beaumarchais	30
Beaune-la-Rolande Loiret	65
Beaune-Semblançay, Jacques de	157, 199
Beaupréau Maine-et-Loire	148
Beauregard (Château)	65
Beauval (Zoological Park)	175
Becket, Thomas	145, 166
Becquerel, Henri	104
Béhuard Maine-et-Loire	65
Bellay, Joachim du	30, 124
Bellegarde Loiret	66
Benjamin, René	30
Béranger	30
Bercé (Forest)	67
Berengaria, Queen of Navarre	139, 142, 145
Bergson, Henri	30
Bernanos, Georges	30
Berthelot, Gilles	59
Béthune, Philippe de	186
Birds, Anjou	150
Birds, Loire	159
Blancafort Cher	67
Bléré Indre-et-Loire	93
Blois Loir-et-Cher	68, 219
Blou Maine-et-Loire	63
Bluebeard	119
Blues, The	148
Bohier, Thomas	91
Les Bois (Lake)	137
Bois-Aubry (Abbey)	172
Boiscommun Loiret	66
Le Bois-Montbourcher (Château)	150
Bois de Nottonville (Abbey)	86
La Boissière Maine-et-Loire	74
Bollée, Amédée	140
Bonaventure (Manor)	128
Bonchamps	23, 147, 178
Bonneval Eure-et-Loir	74
Bouër Sarthe	166
Boumois (Château)	74
Bourdichon, Jean	31
Bourdin, Michel	31
Le Bourg-d'Iré Maine-et-Loire	185
La Bourgonnière (Chapel)	75
Bourgueil Indre-et-Loire	75
Bournan Indre-et-Loire	180
Bourré, Jean	168
Bourré Loir-et-Cher	157
Bracieux Loir-et-Cher	189

Brain-sur-Allonnes
Maine-et-Loire.................................. 14, 76
Branicki, Xavier................................... 155
Breil Maine-et-Loire........................... 76
Brétignolles (Château)..................... 99
Bretonneau, Pierre............................ 31
Briçonnet, Catherine........................ 91
Bridoré Indre-et-Loire....................... 126
Brissac (Château)............................. 77
Broc Maine-et-Loire........................... 138
Broglie, Princesse de....................... 90
Brou Eure-et-Loir............................... 77
La Bruère-sur-Loir Sarthe................ 130
Bueil Family...................................... 78, 201
Bueil, Honorat de.......................... 78, 172
Bueil-en-Touraine Indre-et-Loire..... 78

C

Cabernet de Saumur........................ 135
Calder, Alexander............................. 174
Calvin, Jean................................. 22, 164
Candes-St-Martin Indre-et-Loire..... 78
Capets, The........................ 21, 49, 193
Carême, Marie-Antoine.................. 202
Carnutes, The............................. 20, 160
Cathelineau................................. 23, 147
Catherine de' Medici. 28, 29, 70, 89, 91
Cavalry Museum................................ 184
La Celle-Guenand Indre-et-Loire..... 117
Cenomanni.. 20
Cerdon Loiret..................................... 56
Ceton (Church).................................. 108
Chabris Indre..................................... 187
Chalonnes-sur-Loire Maine-et-Loire 136
Chambiers (Forest).......................... 106
Chambord, Count of................. 80, 186
Chambord (Château)......... 79, 218, 219
Champagne....................................... 14
Champeigne...................................... 15
Champigny wine.............................. 135
Champigny-sur-Veude
Indre-et-Loire................................. 82
Champtoceaux Maine-et-Loire........ 137
Champtocé-sur-Loire
Maine-et-Loire............................... 119
Chandelais (Forest)........................... 62
Chanteloup (Pagoda)........................ 82
Chanzy, General.............................. 24
La Chapelle-du-Chêne Sarthe.......... 174
Charlemagne........................... 114, 192
Charles V, The Emperor................. 79
Charles VI... 139
Charles VII.................. 21, 28, 96, 161
Charles VIII........................ 21, 44, 120
Charles of Anjou............................. 49
Charles of Orléans..................... 29, 68
Charles, Jacques........................ 31, 64
Charles Martel........................... 20, 179
Charlotte de Savoie................... 28, 101
La Chartre-sur-le-Loir Sarthe.......... 129
Château : see proper name
Château-du-Loir Sarthe.................... 130
Châteaudun Eure-et-Loir.................. 83
Château-Gontier Mayenne 86, 218, 219
Château-la-Vallière Indre-et-Loire... 87
Châteauneuf-sur-Loire Loiret.... 88, 218
Château-Renault Indre-et-Loire....... 89
Le Châtellier (Château).................... 105
Châtillon-sur-Cher Loir-et-Cher....... 186
Chaumont-sur-Loire Loir-et-Cher ... 89
Chaumont-sur-Tharonne
Loir-et-Cher.................................... 189

Chemazé Mayenne............................ 87
Chémery (Château)........................... 175
Chemillé Maine-et-Loire.................... 148
Chênehutte-les-Tuffeaux
Maine-et-Loire............................... 135
Chenillé-Changé Maine-et-Loire..... 150
Chenonceau (Château)............. 91, 219
Cher (Valley)...................................... 93
Cherré (Archaeological site)..... 14, 130
Cheverny (Château)................... 94, 219
Chigné Maine-et-Loire...................... 138
Children's Crusade.......................... 102
Chinon Indre-et-Loire................. 95, 218
Chinon (Forest).................................. 95
Chinon (Nuclear Power Station) 100
Choiseul.. 82
Cholet Maine-et-Loire....................... 100
Chouans, The............................. 23, 148
Chouzé-sur-Loire Indre-et-Loire...... 76
Christopher, Saint........................... 45
Cinq-Mars, Marquis of.............. 69, 101
Cinq-Mars-la-Pile Indre-et-Loire...... 101
Le Ciran (Domain).............................. 109
Claude of France....................... 29, 68
Cléry-St-André Loiret.............. 101, 218
Clos (Stand of trees)......................... 67
Le Clos-Lucé (Manor)....................... 46
Clouet, François.............................. 31
Clouet, Jean.................................... 31
Clovis.. 192
Cloyes-sur-le-Loir Eure-et-Loir........ 102
Colombe, Michel............................. 31
Combreux Loiret 88
Conie Eure-et-Loir............................. 128
Connerré Sarthe................................ 146
Corbineau, Jacques........................ 77
Cormery Indre-et-Loire...................... 102
La Corroirie (Chapel)........................ 123
Cortona, Domenico da................... 31
Cossé, Charles de........................... 77
Coteaux du Layon............................. 122
Cottereau, Jean.............................. 23
Coudray-Montbault (Château)........ 101
Coudray-Montpensier (Château) ... 99
Coudre (Fontaine de la)................... 67
Coulangé Indre-et-Loire 118
Coulée de Serrant........................... 136
Courier, Paul-Louis................ 30, 80, 93
Courgenard Sarthe 166
Courtangis (Château)........................ 166
Courtanvaux (Château).................... 103
Courteline, Georges........................ 30
Courtineau (Road)............................. 147
Couture-sur-Loir Loir-et-Cher.......... 129
Craon Mayenne................................. 103
Cravant (Vieux Bourg de)
Indre-et-Loire................................. 98
Crissay-sur-Manse Indre-et-Loire ... 146
Cross of Anjou...................... 60, 61, 74
Cross of Lorraine............................. 61
Crotti, Jean...................................... 40
Crouzilles Indre-et-Loire................... 99
Cunault Maine-et-Loire..................... 104
Cuon Maine-et-Loire......................... 62

D

Daillon Family.................................. 138
Dampierre-en-Burly
Maine-et-Loire............................... 104
Dangeau Eure-et-Loir 104
Daon Mayenne................................... 150
David d'Angers.................... 31, 52, 178

Delorme, Amédée.............................. 154
Dénezé-sous-Doué
　　Maine-et-Loire.............................. 106
Deodatus, St 133
Descartes Indre-et-Loire.................. 105
Descartes, René 30, 105
Desportes, François 116
La Devinière 99
Diane de Poitiers.................... 29, 89, 91
Dodun.. 83
Dolet, Étienne................................... 29
Doué-la-Fontaine
　　Maine-et-Loire...................... 105, 218
Dovalle, Charles............................... 156
Dried Apples............................. 133, 135
Du Bellay, Joachim.................... 30, 124
Dumas, Alexandre............................ 158
Dunois............................... 83, 160
Dupetit-Thouars, Aristide................. 75
Dupin, Madame 92
Duplessis-Mornay 182
Durtal Maine-et-Loire 106

E

Eleanor of Aquitaine.......... 63, 111, 112
Epau (Abbey) 145
Equitation Centre.............................. 184
Escoublère (Manor) 150
Esves-le-Moutier Indre-et-Loire 180
Étampes, Duchess of........................ 29
Les Étilleux Eure-et-Loir 166

F

Faience Factory................................. 116
Faluns Sea 14
Fay-aux-Loges Loiret 88
Faye-la-Vineuse Indre-et-Loire 107
Fercé Sarthe 181
Ferrière-Larcon Indre-et-Loire 105
La Ferté, Maréchal de....................... 109
La Ferté-Bernard Sarthe................... 107
La Ferté-St-Aubin Loiret 109
La Ferté-Villeneuil Eure-et-Loir....... 102
Fillé Sarthe 180
La Flèche Sarthe 109
Floral Park of La Source 165
Fontaine-Guérin Maine-et-Loire...... 62
Fontaines-en-Solognes
　　Loir-et-Cher.................................. 189
Fontevraud (Abbey) 111
Fontevraud-l'Abbaye
　　Maine-et-Loire.............................. 111
La Fosse (Hamlet) 106
Fougères-sur-Bièvre
　　(Château)...................................... 113
Fouquet, Jean.................... 31, 125, 193
Fra Giocondo.................................... 31
France, Anatole................................. 30
François I............ 21, 28, 44, 68, 79, 173
Frazé Eure-et-Loir............................ 113
Fréteval Loir-et-Cher........................ 128
Fronde, The................................ 22, 115
Le Fuilet Maine-et-Loire 149
Fulk, the Good.................................. 48
Fulk Nerra............................ 20, 48, 68
Fulk V.. 48

G

Gabarre... 131
Gallerande (Château)........................ 130
Gamay.. 137
Gargantua.. 95
Garnier, Robert.................................. 107
Gaston of Orléans....................... 68, 80
Gâtine.. 14, 15
Gaucourt.. 160
Gauzlin 175
Gemmail...................................... 40, 195
Genevoix, Maurice..................... 30, 189
Genillé Indre-et-Loire 119
Gennes Maine-et-Loire..................... 114
Genneteil Maine-et-Loire 138
Germigny-des-Prés Loiret 114, 218
Gien Loiret....................................... 115
Gilles de Rais........................... 119, 125
Gizeux Indre-et-Loire 116
La Goubaudière (Rural Museum) .. 100
Goum Museum.................................. 158
La Grande Mademoiselle............... 80
Le Grand-Pressigny
　　Indre-et-Loire 117
Gregory of Tours....................... 29, 192
Gresset, Jean-Baptiste.................... 109
Grez-Neuville Maine-et-Loire 150
Grignon Loiret................................... 137
Grillemont (Château) 180
Le Gué-du-Loir Loir-et-Cher 128
Gué-Péan (Château) 117
Guise, Henri de............................ 68, 70
Gunflint Museum 187, 203
Gy-en-Sologne Loir-et-Cher............ 189

H

La Haie-Longue Maine-et-Loire 136
La Hamonnière (Manor)
　　Maine-et-Loire 168
Happy Valley (Lake) 88
Haute-Guerche (Château)............... 123
Henri II 91, 92
Henri III.. 68
Henri IV 109
Henri V 80
Henry II of England 49, 96, 112
Hermitière (Springs)......................... 67
Herpinière (Windmill) 158
Hitler... 24
Hoche, General................................. 23
Houdin, Robert.................................. 71
Hubert, Saint..................................... 45
Hunting Museum.............................. 116

I

L'Ile-Bouchard Indre-et-Loire 117
Illiers-Combray Eure-et-Loir 118
Indre (Valley)............................ 60, 127
Indrois (Valley).................................. 118
Ingrandes Maine-et-Loire................. 119
L'Isle-Briand
　　(National Stud of) 123
L'Isle-Verte 129
Ivanoff, Vassil................................... 56

J

Jacob, Max 30, 176
La Jaille-Yvon
   Maine-et-Loire 150
Jarzé Maine-et-Loire 119
Jeanne de France 157
Joan of Arc 21, 96, 161, 164, 190
John Lackland 96
Juigné-sur-Sarthe Sarthe 181
Juste Family 31

L

La Baume la Blanc,
   Louise de 87
Langeais Indre-et-Loire 120
Lanthenay (Church) 189
La Renaudie 45
Lassay-sur-Croisne
   Loir-et-Cher 121
Le Lathan (Château) 76
La Vallière, Duchesse de 87
Lavardin Loir-et-Cher 121
Law, John 154, 202
Layon (Valley) 122
League, The 22, 49, 68, 77
Léandre, Charles 156
Lerné Indre-et-Loire 99
Lesbahy, Philippa 59
Leszczynski, Stanislas 80
Leugny (Château) 93
Leygue, Louis 205
Le Liget (Charterhouse) 123
Ligueil Indre-et-Loire 180
Linières-Bouton Maine-et-Loire 158
Le Lion d'Angers
   Maine-et-Loire 123, 219
Liré Maine-et-Loire 124
Loches Indre-et-Loire 124
Loir (Valley) 127
Loire (Valley) 131
Loire Museum 84, 141
Loiret (Spring) 165
Longueville, Duchess of 156
La Lorie (Château) 185
Lorris, Guillaume de 29, 137
Lorris Loiret 137
Loudon (Woods) 146
Louis VII 63
Louis IX, Saint 20, 68
Louis XI 28, 101, 124, 193, 200
Louis XII 21, 69, 157
Louis XIII 80
Louis XIV 80
Louis of Orléans 68
Louise de Lorraine 92
Louise de Savoie 29, 44
Louise de la Vallière 87
Louvois, Marquis de 103
Luçay-le-Mâle Indre 14, 203
Luché-Pringé Sarthe 130
Le Lude Sarthe 138, 219
Lully 80
Lunay Loir-et-Cher 129
Lurçat, Jean 40, 54
Luther, Martin 22
Lutz-en-Dunois
   Eure-et-Loir 86
Luynes Indre-et-Loire 120

M

Madeleine (Dolmen) 114
Maeterlinck, Maurice 30
Maine, The 15
Maintenon, Marquise de 140
Malicorne-sur-Sarthe Sarthe 181
Le Mans Sarthe 139, 218
Manse (Valley) 146
Marboué Eure-et-Loir 128
Marcel, Alexandre 149
Marçon Sarthe 130
Marguerite de Valois 29
Marie de' Medici 68
Marmoutier (Abbey) 134
La Maroutière (Château) 87
Martigné-Briand
   Maine-et-Loire 122
Martin, Saint 192
Les Mauges 147
Maulévrier Maine-et-Loire 149, 218
Maulévrier (Forest) 149
Maves 73
Mayenne (Valley) 149
Mazangé Loir-et-Cher 129
Mazzoni, Guido 31
Ménars (Château) 151
La Ménitré Maine-et-Loire 218
Mercier, General 86
Mercogliano, Pacello de 38
Meslay (Tithe Barn) 200, 218
Mettray (Dolmen) 200
Meung, Jean de 29, 151
Meung-sur-Loire Loiret 151
Meusnes Loir-et-Cher 187
Michel, Jean 29
Les Minières (Zoo) 105
Minitel 214
Miré Maine-et-Loire 151
Moléans Eure-et-Loir 128
Molière 80
Molineuf Loir-et-Cher 219
Mondoubleau Loir-et-Cher 152
Montbazon Indre-et-Loire 200
Montesquiou, Countess of 103
Montfort-le-Gesnois Sarthe 146
Montgeoffroy (Château) 152
Montigny-le-Gannelon
   Eure-et-Loir 153
Montjean-sur-Loire
   Maine-et-Loire 136
Montlouis-sur-Loire Indre-et-Loire . 153
Montmirail Sarthe 166
Montmorency-Laval, François de .. 109
Montoire-sur-le-Loir
   Loir-et-Cher 24, 154
Montplacé (Chapel) 119
Montpoupon (Château) 155
Montrésor Indre-et-Loire 155
Montreuil-Bellay
   Maine-et-Loire 155
Montrichard Loir-et-Cher 157
Montsoreau Maine-et-Loire 158
Mortiercrolles (Château) 103
Mosnier, Jean 31, 94, 95
La Motte-Glain (Château) 170
Mouliherne Maine-et-Loire 158
Moulin (Château) 121
Moulin, Philippe du 121
Moulins, The Master of 31
Mulsans Loir-et-Cher 159
Muscadet 137
Mushroom Museum 184
Musset, Alfred de 128, 191

239

N

Nanteuil (Church) 157
Négron Indre-et-Loire 134
Néricault-Destouches 30
Nerra, Fulk 48
Neuvy Loir-et-Cher 189
Neuvy-le-Roi Indre-et-Loire 179
Nini 90
Notre-Dame-de-Lorette
   (Chapel) 147
Notre-Dame-de-Montplacé
   (Chapel) 119
Notre-Dame-des-Ardilliers
   (Church) 184
Nouans-les-Fontaines
   Indre-et-Loire 118
Nourray Loir-et-Cher 206
Noyant-la-Gravoyère
   Maine-et-Loire 159
Noyen-sur-Sarthe Sarthe 181
Nyoiseau Maine-et-Loire 186

O

Odo 175
Olivet Loiret 165
Onzain Loir-et-Cher 11
Orléans Loiret 160, 218
Orléans Canal, Loire Reach 88
Orléans Canal, Seine Reach 137
Orléans Family 68
Orléans-la-Source Loiret 160
Oudon Loire-Atlantique 137
Oudry, Jean-Baptiste 116

P

Paladines, Aurelle de 24
Paola, Francis of 29, 200
Papin, Denis 31, 72
Parçay-sur-Vienne Indre-et-Loire 99
Parcé-sur-Sarthe Sarthe 181
Passavant-sur-Layon
   Maine-et-Loire 122
Pays Fort 14
Péguy, Charles 30, 164
Pelouze, Madame 92
Le Perche-Gouët 165
Philippe I 63
Pierre Couverte (Dolmen)
   Maine-et-Loire 61
Pierre Frite (Menhir) 170
Pignerolle (Château) 55
Pirmil Sarthe 181
Pithiviers Loiret 167
Plantagenets, The 20, 49, 111, 112, 139, 143
Plantagenet, Geoffroy 49, 139
Plantagenet Style 37
Péiades, The 30, 124, 170
Plessis-Bourré (Château) 167
Plessis-lès-Tours (Château) 200
Le Plessis-Macé (Château) 168
Pompadour, Marquise de 151
Poncé-sur-le-Loir Sarthe 169
Pont-de-Ruan Indre-et-Loire 60
Pontigné Maine-et-Loire 62
Pontlevoy Loir-et-Cher 169
Les Ponts-de-Cé Maine-et-Loire 55
Portsmouth, Duchess of 58

La Possonnière (Manor) 170
Pouancé Maine-et-Loire 170
Poulain, Auguste 169
Le Prieuré Maine-et-Loire 114
Pringé Sarthe 130
Proust, Marcel 30, 118
Puits (Lake) 56
Le Puy-Notre-Dame
   Maine-et-Loire 170

Q - R

Quarts de chaume 136
Rabelais, François 29, 95, 99
Rablay-sur-Layon Maine-et-Loire ... 123
Racan, Marquis de 30, 172
Radegund, Saint 98
Raguin (Château) 186
Rais, Gilles de 119, 125
Les Réaux (Château) 76
Reignac Indre-et-Loire 127
Renazé Mayenne 103
René, Good King 49, 60
Restigné Indre-et-Loire 76
Rhodon Loir-et-Cher 206
Ribou (Leisure Park) 100
Richard the Lionheart 97, 112, 124
Richelieu 68
Richelieu 171
Rivau (Château) 172
Robbia, Girolamo della 31
Robbia, Luca della 202
Robertet, Florimond 73
Robert Tatin (Museum) 103
Rochambeau Loir-et-Cher 128
Rochechouart-Mortemart,
   Gabrielle de 111
La Roche-Clermault (Château) 100
Rochecorbon Indre-et-Loire 134
Rochefort-sur-Loire
   Maine-et-Loire 136
Rochemenier (Village) 106
La Roche-Racan (Château) 172
Les Roches-l'Évêque Loir-et-Cher .. 129
Roche-Tranchelion
   (Collegiate Church) 146
Rohan-Guéménée, Pierre de .. 170, 206
Roman de la Rose 29, 137, 151
Romance of the Rose 29, 137, 151
Romilly-sur-Aigre Eure-et-Loir 102
Romorantin-Lanthenay
   Loir-et-Cher 173
Ronsart, Pierre de 30, 129 170, 191, 199
Les Rosiers Maine-et-Loire 114
Rotrou (Mill) 130
Rougemont (Farm) 166
Roujoux (Leisure Park) 113
Rousseau, Jean-Jacques 92
Le Royer de la Dauversière,
   Jérôme 109
Ruggieri 89

S

Sablé-sur-Sarthe Sarthe 174
Les Sacavins 48, 156
Saché Indre-et-Loire 174
St-Agil (Château) 152
St-Aignan Loir-et-Cher 174
St-Barthélemy-d'Anjou
   Maine-et-Loire 55

St-Benoît-sur-Loire Loiret   175, 218, 219
St-Brisson-sur-Loire Loiret 116
St-Calais Sarthe 177
St-Christophe Eure-et-Loir.............. 128
St-Christophe-sur-le-Nais
    Indre-et-Loire 179
St-Claude Loir-et-Cher 128
St-Cosmas (Priory) 199
St-Cyr-en-Bourg Maine-et-Loire 185
St-Denis-d'Anjou Mayenne............. 174
St Deodatus 133
St-Dyé-sur-Loire Loir-et-Cher 133
St-Épain Indre-et-Loire 147
St-Étienne-de-Chigny
    Indre-et-Loire 178
St-Florent-le-Vieil
    Maine-et-Loire...................... 148, 178
St-Georges-sur-Loire
    Maine-et-Loire 178
St-Hilaire-St-Florent
    Maine-et-Loire 184
St-Jean (Chapel) 123
St-Jean-Froidmentel Loir-et-Cher .. 128
St-Lambert-du-Lattay
    Maine-et-Loire 123
St-Laurent-de-la-Plaine
    Maine-et-Loire 149
St-Laurent-des-Eaux
    (Nuclear Power Station).............. 133
St-Laurent-en-Gâtines
    Indre-et-Loire 89
St-Lazare (Chapel) 175
St-Martin-le-Beau Indre-et-Loire 93
St-Maur-de-Glanfeuil (Abbey) 136
St-Ouen (Château) 87
St-Paterne-Racan Indre-et-Loire 179
St-Quentin-sur-Indrois
    Indre-et-Loire 119
St-Ulphace Sarthe 166
St-Viâtre Loir-et-Cher 179
Ste-Catherine-de-Fierbois
    Indre-et-Loire 179
Ste-Maure (Plateau)........................ 180
Ste-Maure-de-Touraine
    Indre-et-Loire 180
Salbris Loir-et-Cher.......................... 189
Salisbury, Earl of............................. 160
La Salle (Water-Mill)........................ 156
Sancerre 41, 42
Sapines 131
Sargé-sur-Braye Loir-et-Cher 152
Sarthe (Valley) 180
Saumur 41, 182
Saumur Maine-et-Loire............ 182, 218
Saumurois, The................................ 15
Le Saut-aux-Loups
    (mushroom galleries) 135
Sautret (Château)............................ 150
Savennières Maine-et-Loire 136
Savonnières Indre-et-Loire 185
Saxe, Maurice de............................. 80
Say, Mlle.. 90
Scarron, Paul........................... 140, 143
Segré Maine-et-Loire 185
Selles-St-Denis Loir-et-Cher 189
Selles-sur-Cher Loir-et-Cher 186
Semur-en-Vallon Sarthe 166
Serrant (Château)............................ 187
Seuilly-Coteaux Indre-et-Loire 99
Sforza, Ludovico.............................. 126
Silk 193
Slate Museum 55, 159
Sleeping Beauty............................... 201
Solesmes Sarthe.............................. 187
Sologne, The................................... 188
Son et Lumière Shows..................... 219

Sorel, Agnès 29, 124
Sorinière (Chapel) 149
Souday Loir-et-Cher......................... 152
La Source (Floral Park) 165
Spay Sarthe 146
Staël, Madame de............................ 90
Stofflet... 23, 147
Stuarts, The 57
Stuart, Mary 29
Sue, Eugene 64
Suèvres Loir-et-Cher........................ 190
Sully, Duc de.................................... 190
Sully-sur-Loire Loiret............... 190, 218
La Suze-sur-Sarthe Sarthe 180

T

Talcy Loir-et-Cher............................. 191
Talleyrand-Périgord, Charles-
    Maurice de 202
Tatin, Robert.................................... 103
Tavant (Church)............................... 99
Templars, The 56
Le Temple Loir-et-Cher 152
Le Tertre Rouge (Zoo) 110
Theodulf, Bishop of
    Orléans........................... 20, 114, 175
Thésée Loir-et-Cher 157
Thiron Eure-et-Loir........................... 166
Le Thoureil Maine-et-Loire 136
Torfou Maine-et-Loire....................... 148
Toues.. 131
Tours Indre-et-Loire 192, 218
Trélazé Maine-et-Loire...................... 55
Trèves-Cunault Maine-et-Loire 136
Troglodyte Houses..................... 15, 106
Troglo' Tap 135
Troo Loir-et-Cher.............................. 200
Troussay (Château)......................... 95
Trousseau, Armand.......................... 31
Tufa.. 14

U - V

Ussé (Château)................................ 201
Unexplodables, The 131
Vaas Sarthe...................................... 130
Valençay Indre 202, 219
Val Joyeux (Lake)............................. 88
Valois, Marguerite de....................... 29
Valois, The....................................... 28
Varenne.. 14
Varennes Indre-et-Loire.................... 76
Varennes-Bourreau (Chapel).......... 174
Vaujours (Château) 88
Vaux (Château) 151
Velpeau, Alfred................................. 31
Vendée War, The.............. 23, 147, 178
Vendôme Loir-et-Cher....................... 203
Vendôme, César de.......................... 203
Vénevelles (Manor)......................... 130
Verdelles (Château) 57
Le Verdon (Lake) 101
Véretz Indre-et-Loire 93
Le Verger (Château)........................ 206
Vernantes Maine-et-Loire 116
Vernoil Maine-et-Loire...................... 116
Vernou-sur-Brenne Indre-et-Loire... 208
Le Véron.. 134

La Verrerie (Château) 58
Vibraye Sarthe 166
Le Vieil-Baugé Maine-et-Loire 62
Vieilles-Maisons Loiret 137
Vienne (Valley) 98
Vieux-Bourg d'Artins Loir-et-Cher .. 129
Vieux-Bourg de Cravant
   Indre-et-Loire 98
Vigny, Alfred de 30, 124
Vikings, The 48
Villaines-les-Rochers
   Indre-et-Loire 60
Villandry (Château) 207
Villedieu-le-Château Loir-et-Cher ... 129
Villeherviers Loir-et-Cher 189
Villemardy Loir-et-Cher 206
Villeneuve-la-Barre
   Maine-et-Loire 122
Villesavin (Château) 207
Villiers-sur-Loir Loir-et-Cher 128
Villon, François 29, 151

Vinci, Leonardo da 31, 45, 46
Visconti, Valentine 68, 83
Voguë, Melchior de 58
Volney, Comte de 103
Voltaire 190
Vouvray 41, 42, 208
Vouvray Indre-et-Loire 208

W - Y - Z

Whites, The 147
Wine Museum 96, 123
Wright, Wilbur 140
Yèvre-le-Châtel Loiret 208
Yèvres Eure-et-Loir 78
Yolanda of Aragon 60
Yron (Chapel) 102
Zola, Émile 83, 102

Chanteloup Pagoda

ACKNOWLEDGEMENTS OF PHOTOGRAPHS AND DRAWINGS

p 13 S. Chirol, Paris
p 15 M. Guillard/SCOPE, Paris
p 16 J. D. Sudres/SCOPE, Paris
p 20, 29 Archives Snark/EDIMEDIA, Paris
p 22 EXPLORER, Paris
p 25 H. Boulé, Rennes
p 27 EDIMEDIA, Paris
p 28 (top and bottom of page) PIX, Paris
p 29 Archives Snark/EDIMEDIA, Paris
p 31 Biblioteca Réale di Torino, EXPLORER, Paris
p 32 After photo C. Mesnage/MICHELIN, Paris
p 39 Pélissier/VLOO, Paris
p 40 Musée Lurçat, Angers © A.D.A.G.P. 1987
p 43 G. Sioen/CEDRI, Paris
p 45 M. Desjardins/TOP, Paris
p 47 J. L. Charmet/EXPLORER, Paris
p 50 (top of page) S. Chirol, Paris
p 50 (bottom of page) H. Champollion OUEST-FRANCE
p 55 Musée Européen de la Communication, Angers
p 57 After photo C. Breteau/Ed Delmas
p 59 A. Gaël, Paris
p 62 After photo J. P. Guyonneau/Comité du Tourisme de l'Anjou, Angers
p 69 After photo Cie Aérienne Française
p 75 After photo Karquel
p 77 H. Boulé, Rennes
p 79 S. Chirol, Paris
p 90 After photo H. Boulé, Rennes
p 91 Mary Evans Picture Library/EXPLORER, Paris
p 94 H. Boulé, Rennes
p 95 C. Rives/CEDRI, Paris

p 104 Cauchetier/PIX, Paris
p 105 J. Weyland, St-Maur-des-Fossés
p 112 M. Guillard/SCOPE, Paris
p 114 M. Guillard/SCOPE, Paris
p 118 M. Guillard/SCOPE, Paris
p 120 PIX/Paris
p 124 S. CHIROL, Paris
p 131 PIX, Paris
p 139 J. P. Langeland/DIAF, Paris
p 140 Kid Aco/Automobile Club de l'Ouest
p 147 Lauros/GIRAUDON
p 156 C. Delu/EXPLORER, Paris
p 158 G. Sioen/CEDRI, Paris
p 159 Y. Monet, Vauchrétien
p 161 Bibliothèque Nationale, Paris/ARTHEPHOT, Paris
p 167 H. Boulé, Rennes
p 168 After photo Chrétien, Angers
p 176 After photo S. Chirol, Paris
p 182 After photo Association © « Les Amis du Cadre Noir », Saumur
p 188 J. P. Varin and J. P. Ferrero (bottom of page)/JACANA, Paris
p 192 F. Joly/Bibliothèque Municipale de Tours
p 196 B. Regent/DIAF, Paris
p 202 PIX/Paris
p 205 R. Mazin/TOP, Paris
p 209 S. Chirol, Paris
p 215 Bouin/Comité du Tourisme de l'Anjou, Angers
p 217 R. Mazin/TOP, Paris
p 235 F. Jalain/EXPLORER, Paris
p 242 After photo Yvonne Sauvageot

MANUFACTURE FRANÇAISE DES PNEUMATIQUES MICHELIN

Société en commandite par actions au capital de 2 000 000 000 de francs

Place des Carmes-Déchaux - 63 Clermont-Ferrand (France)
R.C.S. Clermont-Fd B 855 200 507

© **Michelin et Cie, Propriétaire-Éditeurs 1993**
Dépôt légal 4e trim. 93 - ISBN 2-06-132 203-4 - ISSN 0763-1383

Printed in the EC 10.93.40
Photocomposition : M.C.P., Fleury-les-Aubrais
Impression et Brochage : KAPP LAHURE JOMBARD, Éveux

TRAVELLING COMPANIONS
Michelin tourist Guides and detailed Maps are designed to be used together.